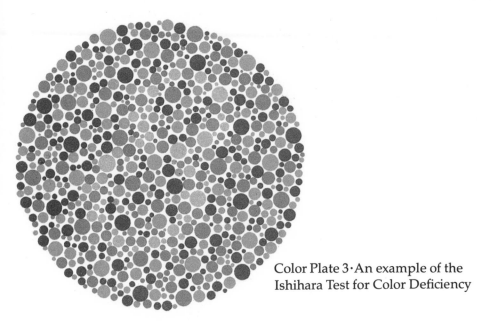

Color Plate 3·An example of the
Ishihara Test for Color Deficiency

Color Plate 4·Atmospheric perspective

PERCEPTION

Margaret W. Matlin

State University of New York at Geneseo

Allyn and Bacon, Inc.
Boston   London   Sydney   Toronto

Library of Congress Cataloging in Publication Data

Matlin, Margaret W.
   Perception.

   Bibliography: p.351
   Includes index.
   1. Perception. I. Title.
BF311.M4263   1983   152.1   82-16327
ISBN 0-205-07849-4

Printed in the United States of America

10 9 8 7 6 5 4 3 2   86 85 84

Art editor: Elaine Ober

Series editor: Bill Barke

Credits

Figure 1-1, p. 3—Photo by Arnold H. Matlin, M.D. Figure 2-6, p. 21—Dowling, J. E., & Boycott, B.B. Organization of the primate retina: Electron microscopy. *Proceedings of the Royal Society* (London), Series B, 1966, *166*, 80–11. Copyright 1966 by the Royal Society; reprinted by permission. Demonstration 3-8, p. 56—Photos by Ron Pretzer. Figures 4-4 and 4-5, pp. 65, 68—Lindsay, P.H., & Norman, D.A. *Human information processing* (Second Edition). New York: Academic Press, 1977, Figure 3-21, p. 112. Copyright 1977 by Academic Press; reprinted by permission. Figures 4-6 and 4-7, pp. 73, 75—DeValois, R.L., & DeValois, K.K. Neural coding of color. In E.C. Carterette & M.P. Friedman (Eds.), *Handbook of Perception*, Volume V. New York: Academic Press, 1975, Figures 1 and 5. Copyright 1975 by Academic Press; reprinted by permission. Figure 4-8, p. 80—Riley, Bridget. *Current.* 1964. Synthetic polymer paint on composition board, 58⅜'' x 58⅞''. Collection, The Museum of Modern Art, New York. Philip Johnson Fund. Figure 5-3, p. 88—McClelland, J.L. Perception and masking of wholes and parts. *Journal of Experimental Psychology: Human Perception and Performance*, 1978, *4*, 210–223, Figure 4. Copyright 1978 by the American Psychological Association; reprinted by permission. Figure 5-7, p. 94—Jackson, William H. *Eroded Sandstones, Monument Park, Colorado.* Collection, George Eastman House. Reprinted by permission. Figure 5-8, p. 95—Wood, Grant. *American Gothic.* 1930. Collection, Art Institute of Chicago. Figure 5-10, p. 99—Coalition for a New Foreign and Military Policy. *Building national security: Disarmament action guide,* pamphlet cover. Demonstration 5-6, p. 103—Eleanor J. Gibson, *Principles of Perceptual Learning and Development,* 1969, p. 88. Reprinted by permission of Prentice-Hall, Inc., Englewood Cliffs, New Jersey. Figure 5-13, p. 107—Palmer, S.E. Visual perception and world knowledge: Notes on a model of sensory-cognitive interaction. In D.A. Norman & D.E. Rumelhart (Eds.), *Explorations in cognition.* San Francisco: Freeman, 1975. Figure 11.6, p. 296, Copyright 1975 by W. H. Freeman; reprinted by permission. Figure 5-14, p. 108—Palmer, S.E. The effects of contextual scenes on the identification of objects. *Memory and Cognition, for Arnie*

Contents

Preface xi

Acknowledgments xiii

chapter 1
INTRODUCTION 1
Outline 1
Preview of the Book 2
How to Use This Book 5
A Brief History of the Study of Perception 6
Overview of Psychophysics 9
Review 11
New Terms 12

chapter 2
THE VISUAL SYSTEM 13
Outline 13
Preview 14
The Visual Stimulus 15
The Anatomy of the Eye 16
The Pathway from the Eye to the Brain 23
Common Disorders in the Visual System 30
Review 33
New Terms 33

chapter 3
BASIC VISUAL FUNCTIONS 34
Outline 34
Preview 35
Acuity 36
Adaptation 43
Eye Movements 47
Accommodation 54
Review 58
New Terms 59

chapter 4
COLOR 60

Outline   60
Preview   61
The Nature of Color   62
Color Vision Deficiencies   69
Color Vision Theory   72
Issues in Color Perception   76
Review   81
New Terms   82

chapter 5
SHAPE   83
Outline   83
Preview   84
Contour   84
Perceptual Organization   91
Pattern Recognition   101
Review   112
New Terms   112

chapter 6
DISTANCE AND MOTION   113
Outline   113
Preview   114
Distance Perception   115
Motion Perception   131
Review   142
New Terms   143

chapter 7
CONSTANCY AND ILLUSIONS   144
Outline   144
Preview   145
Constancy   146
Illusions   158
Review   169
New Terms   170

chapter 8
  HEARING   171
Outline   171
Preview   172
Sensory Aspects of Hearing   173
Perceptual Qualities of Sound   181
Complex Auditory Perception   186
Applications of Hearing Research   192
Review   197
New Terms   197

chapter 9
  TOUCH AND THE OTHER SKIN SENSES   199
Outline   199
Preview   200
Background on the Skin Senses   201
Touch   204
Temperature   211
Pain   214
Review   222
New Terms   222

chapter 10
  SMELL   224
Outline   224
Preview   225
Sensory Aspects of Smell   226
Olfactory Processes   231
Applications of Research on Smell   238
Review   242
New Terms   243

chapter 11
  TASTE   244
Outline   244
Preview   245

Sensory Aspects of Taste   247
Taste Processes   252
Applications of Taste Research   259
Review   263
New Terms   263

chapter 12
ATTENTION   264

Outline   264
Preview   265
Selective Attention   266
Theories of Attention   271
Search   274
Viewing Pictures   281
Review   285
New Terms   285

chapter 13
MOTIVATION AND PERCEPTION   286

Outline   286
Preview   287
The Effect of Motivation on Perception   288
The Effect of Perception on Motivation   300
Review   306
New Terms   307

chapter 14
THE DEVELOPMENT OF PERCEPTION   308

Outline   308
Preview   309
Infancy   310
Childhood   321
Late Adulthood and Old Age   325
Review   331
New Terms   331

chapter 15
    PSYCHOPHYSICS   332
Outline   332
Preview   333
Measuring Responses to Low-Intensity Stimuli   333
Measuring Responses to High-Intensity Stimuli   344
Review   350
New Terms   350

Bibliography   351
Author Index   367
Subject Index   375

Preface

The purpose of this textbook is to provide an overview of perception. I have written it for students who have no other specialized background in physiology, mathematics, or experimental psychology. It is intended for use in courses in perception or sensation and perception. *Perception* is primarily a textbook for undergraduates, although beginning graduate students who want an overview of the subject may also find it useful.

I have tried to achieve a comprehensive coverage of topics, including information on nonvisual perception in addition to the standard topics on vision. Within each topic, length limitations prohibited me from reviewing the literature extensively. Instead, I was selective by providing a basic introduction to each area, supplemented by discussions of the recent research.

Perception is organized in terms of an introductory chapter and three major parts. The first part includes six chapters on vision. The second part covers nonvisual perception: hearing, the skin senses, smell, and taste. The remaining part examines additional topics in perception, including attention, motivation and perception, and the development of perception. The final chapter on psychophysics can be used either for reference, or as a standard chapter.

Perception is a fascinating topic, yet there is often a gap between the richness of our perceptual experiences and the pallid, academic discussion of these experiences in most perception texts. Furthermore, students often regard the material in perception courses as difficult. To overcome these problems, I've tried to write a textbook that is interesting and student-oriented. Here are some of the features I've included:

1. The writing style is clear and straightforward.

2. There are numerous examples of how perception operates in everyday experience.

3. Throughout the text there are applications of perception in areas such as education, art, traffic, safety, and advertising.

4. The text includes many small-scale demonstrations that students can try by themselves, using minimal equipment and time.

5. New terms are introduced in **boldface print,** with their definitions in the same sentence.

6. Phonetic pronunications are supplied for new terms that are difficult to pronounce.

7. I often supply mnemonic devices, or memory aids, particularly when they would be useful for memorizing lists of items.

8. Each chapter begins with an outline and a preview.

9. There is a summary at the end of each of the major sections in the chapter, rather than a long summary at the end of the entire chapter.

10. Each chapter ends with review questions and a list of new terms.

Students can consult the section in Chapter 1 entitled *How to use this book* for details on how to employ these learning aids most effectively. I hope that people who read this book will acquire an appreciation and a fascination for the richness of their perceptual worlds.

Acknowledgments

Numerous people deserve credit for their contributions to this book. The people with whom I've worked at Allyn and Bacon have been superb. Bill Barke, Psychology Editor, was the prime mover in this project. It was he who suggested that I write the book, and he enthusiastically guided its writing and preparation. Elaine Ober directed the editing of the book. I appreciated her intelligent comments and careful attention to detail throughout the editorial process. I would also like to thank Jeff Johnston, Barbara Willette, Donna Hession, Scientific Illustrators, Heidi Shahbaz, and Nancy Murphy for their contributions during all phases of the book's preparation.

I would like to acknowledge several professors who inspired my interest in perception. These include Leonard Horowitz, Douglas Lawrence, and Eleanor Maccoby of Stanford University, and Daniel Weintraub, Richard Pew, Irving Pollack, and W. P. Tanner at University of Michigan.

Other people helped in diverse ways. Tony Del Bove did a spectacular job in locating and duplicating references, proofreading the manuscript, checking citations, and preparing the name index. Ron Pretzer supplied most of the photographs for the book . . . he paled only slightly at requests to photograph egg cartons, stale waffles, and old shoes. Jean Amidon typed the manuscript; her intelligence, accuracy, and speed are much appreciated. Mary Lou Perry and Connie Ellis kept other aspects of my life running smoothly, allowing me more time to work on the project. Deborah Trinka and Dawn Ellis also helped in the final compilation of material.

Several students in my courses provided examples that I used in the book. I would like to thank Bruce Edington, Jeanette Gray, Laura Hasby, and Deborah Swallow for allowing me to use their material.

Many people supplied useful information that was incorporated into the book. Melvyn Yessenow shared his expertise with me on many occasions, particularly in the area of sensation. I would also like to thank Nila Aguilar-Markulis, Lucie Arbuthnot, A. K. Das, Kathleen Mary Huebner, Daniel Levin, Ray Mayo, Lanna Ruddy, Rosemary Teres, and David Van Dyke.

In addition, I wish to thank the reviewers who provided useful suggestions for improving both factual and stylistic aspects of the manuscript. Lester Lefton (University of South Carolina) read the entire manuscript and revised sections. My appreciation also goes to Douglas Bloomquist (Framingham State College), Tom Bourbon (Steven F. Austin State University), and William Tedford (Southern Methodist University).

I am also grateful to the State University of New York for granting me a sabbatical leave, during which a substantial portion of this book was written.

Finally, I want to thank my husband, Arnie, and my children, Beth and Sally, for their advice, encouragement, optimism, and appreciation, as well as their help on several photographs.

chapter 1

INTRODUCTION

Outline   Preview of the Book

How to Use This Book

A Brief History of the Study of Perception

The Empiricist Approach

The Gestalt Approach

The Gibsonian Approach

The Information-Processing Approach

Overview of Psychophysics

Measuring Responses to Low-Intensity Stimuli

Measuring Responses to High-Intensity Stimuli

This very moment, you are busy perceiving. Your eyes are moving along this page at a steady pace, identifying letters at a speed so fast that it seems to defy explanation. You glance away from this book and perceive a world that is rich with color, depth, and motion. Actually, from the moment you woke up you have been continuously perceiving. You heard the alarm clock, you touched, you smelled, and you tasted. **Perception** is the study of the way you gather and interpret information about the world around you. In fact, everything you know about the world is based upon perceptual information.

We are so accustomed to seeing, hearing, touching, smelling, and tasting that we tend to take perception for granted. We simply open our eyes and see people and trees and giraffes. We open our mouths, insert a morsel of food, and taste chocolate mousse or green beans or curried goat. However, perception is really a puzzle that has mystified philosophers and psychologists for centuries. Basically, it is difficult to explain how the qualities of objects out there in the world can be recreated inside our own heads.

Consider an example. Look at Figure 1-1, a picture of my daughter in mime makeup. This picture contains neatly organized segments—a leotard, an eyebrow, an earring. Each of these structured segments is broken up by our receptor system and nervous system into a series of impulses. As Gregory (1974) notes,

> All of the rich information about perceptual structure which we take for granted has somehow dissolved into a series of yes or no electrical blips moving along some tiny, poorly insulated fibers [p. 76].

Nonetheless, our nervous system manages to reconstruct the real world of leotards, eyebrows, and earrings from this series of electrical blips. Our perceptions are neatly organized, and our perceptions are a reasonably accurate mirror of the real world.

Preview of the Book

Our task in this book is to examine how we take in information about the outside world and how the world appears to us. In general, we will not emphasize the anatomy and physiology of the sensory systems. Instead, we will concentrate on the way that information from the sensory systems is interpreted to form our perceptions. Let's preview the variety of perceptual experiences that we will consider in the 15 chapters of this book. First of all, Chapter 1 outlines the scope of the book, offers hints on how to use this book, summarizes the history of the study of perception, and introduces the topic of psychophysics.

Chapter 2 gives an overview of the visual system. We need to know what the visual equipment looks like before we can proceed to other topics. We will look at the anatomy of the eye, and we will discuss how visual information travels to the brain. Some of the topics that we will consider in this chapter may answer questions that you have had about the visual system. For example, why can you see clearly the objects that you are looking at, whereas the objects that appear "in the corner of your eye" look fuzzy? What causes certain diseases of the eye such as conjunctivitis, cataracts, and glaucoma, and how are these conditions treated?

Chapter 3 considers several basic tasks that our visual system can perform. We will discuss our ability to see fine detail, the change in sensitivity that occurs when we are exposed to dark and light, eye movement, and focusing. Some issues we will raise include the following: What does 20/20 vision mean? If you are driving at night and you look at the headlights of the oncoming car, why do you have trouble seeing afterwards? Why are eye movements important in driving, and how does alcohol consumption influence these eye movements?

Chapter 4 examines color perception, including a discussion of color vision deficiencies and theories about how we perceive color. We will also discuss how we can perceive colors that are not present in the stimulus. Some of the questions we will answer include: Why do we get green if we mix yellow and blue paints but

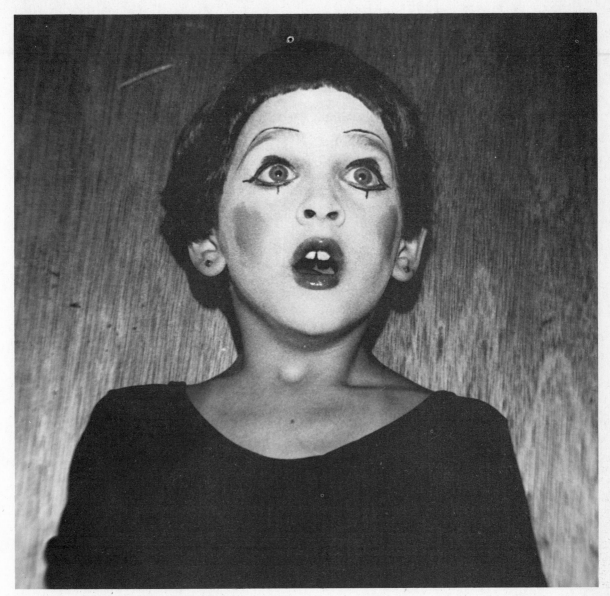

Figure 1-1   Organization in perception.

get white if we mix yellow and blue lights? Why are men more likely to be "color-blind" than women, and why is the term "color-blind" incorrect? If you are stranded on a desert island, why should you wear red or green, rather than yellow or blue?

In Chapter 5, we will look at shape. Shapes have contours, or sudden changes in brightness. Our perception of shape also shows impressive organization; an eyebrow seems to have a shape that sets it apart from the surrounding forehead. We also recognize patterns; we identify a curved line as an eyebrow and not a shoelace. Here are two of the issues we will discuss: How do advertisements and paintings make effective use of similar shapes? How accurate is our memory for pictures?

Chapter 6 is concerned with distance and

motion. Our visual world is neither flat nor stationary. Somehow, we manage to perceive objects as being three-dimensional, even though our eyes appear to represent only two dimensions. We also perceive a wide variety of movements, even when the objects are not moving. Three of the questions we will answer in this chapter are: Why is your depth perception poor if you only use one eye? How can a two-dimensional painting convey the impression of three dimensions? Why does the world seem to spin in the opposite direction after you get off the SuperSpin carnival ride?

Chapter 7 examines two areas that are closely related to each other, constancy and illusion. In constancy, objects seem to stay the same, despite changes in the way we view the object; our perceptions match reality quite nicely. In illusions, such as the one in Figure 1-2, our perceptions do not match reality. For example, the two central circles are really equal in size, though the one on the right looks smaller. Here are some issues we will consider in Chapter 7: Why does your friend Maria seem to stay the same size as she walks away from you, even though the image registered in your eye clearly shrinks. Why does a marshmallow look white in the moonlight, even though it is reflecting less light than a piece of coal in the sunlight? How did an illusion cause a plane crash that left four people dead and 49 injured?

As you have seen, Chapters 2 through 7 are concerned with vision. The next four chapters discuss the nonvisual perceptual systems.

Chapter 8 examines hearing. After discussing sound waves and the auditory system, we consider four qualities of sound: pitch, loudness, timbre, and localization. Three additional topics are speech perception, noise pollution, and hearing impairments. Some issues we will address include: How does the ear manage to record the pitch of a train squeaking to a halt, Pavarotti singing an aria, and your grandfather snoring? Why do some tone combinations sound pleasant, whereas others are unbearable? Why are hearing aids more useful for some kinds of deafness than for other kinds?

Chapter 9 examines the major senses that are related to our skin. Objects and people in the world touch us, and we touch them back. We also perceive warm and cold temperatures, as well as pain. Here are some topics we will cover: Why were you aware of your watch pressing against your skin when you put it on this morning, though you hadn't noticed it again until I mentioned it? Why do you sometimes have difficulty deciding whether water is warm or cold? Why do we have to feel pain in order to survive?

Chapter 10 deals with smell. It is difficult to describe and classify various smells, so it is hard to examine this perceptual system. We will discuss our sensitivity to smells, how smells become less noticeable as we are exposed to them, and our recognition for smells. Several applications of research on smell will also be considered, including perfume manufacturing and the importance of smell in communication. Three issues we will examine are: Why does food taste so bland when you have a cold? Why don't you smell the perfume or shaving lotion you put on this morning, though a friend who just joined you for lunch notices it immediately? Why do certain odors seem familiar from your childhood?

Chapter 11, on taste, is closely related to the chapter on smell. Tastes, fortunately, are easier to categorize than smells, and this chapter begins with a discussion of taste categories. Then we examine taste receptors and the taste system. Other topics include sensitivity to taste, how tastes become less noticeable as we are exposed to them, and applications of taste research in food tasting and beverage tasting. Some questions we will answer include: What characteristics of food do we notice, in addition to its taste and its odor? Why was the information incorrect that your junior-high science teacher gave you about the regions of the

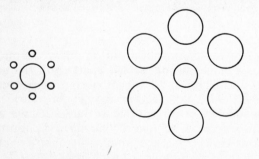

Figure 1-2   An example of an illusion.

tongue? Why does water taste vaguely sweet after your morning grapefruit?

The last chapters of the book cover four additional topics in perception. The emphasis in these chapters is on vision and hearing, primarily because the other perceptual systems have not been as completely investigated.

Chapter 12 discusses attention. An important area of attention is selective attention, which occurs when we receive several messages at once and pay attention to only one message. Two related areas are the search for specific objects and viewing pictures. Some issues we will raise include: Why can't you pay attention to three simultaneous conversations at a party? Can you search just as fast for three objects as you can for one? What part of a picture do people look at the longest?

Chapter 13 examines the relationship between motivation and perception. Our needs and desires can influence the way we perceive things, so that motivation influences perception. Also, the perceptual qualities of objects influence how much we like something, so that perception influences motivation. Some questions we will consider are: If the projectionist in the movie theater briefly flashes the message "DRINK COKE," will you immediately march out to the refreshment stand? Why does a $10 bill seem to weigh more than a $1 bill? What is the most popular color?

Chapter 14 is concerned with the development of perception. You will learn that our perceptual skills are reasonably well developed in infancy. However, these skills become more sophisticated during childhood. Elderly people sometimes have impaired vision or hearing, but the other perceptual processes seem to be relatively unaffected by the aging process. Three of the questions we will discuss are: How do we know that babies divide colors into the same categories as adults? Why do young children reverse their letters so often? Are elderly people more sensitive to pain, in contrast to young adults?

Chapter 15 discusses psychophysics, which is the study of the relationship between physical stimuli and our psychological reactions to those stimuli. Two of the questions we will consider are: How are decision-making strategies responsible for your saying, "I hear the train!" when it hasn't even left the previous station? Why can you notice a five-pound weight loss more readily in a friend who weighs 100 pounds than in a friend who weighs 200 pounds?

How To Use This Book

A number of different features in this book have been included to help you understand, learn, and remember the material. This section tells you how to use these features most effectively.

Each chapter begins with an outline. Inspect the outline before you read a new chapter, paying particular attention to the structure of the topic. Notice, for example, that there are four major sections in Chapter 2 (The Visual System): (1) The Visual Stimulus, (2) The Anatomy of the Eye, (3) The Pathway from the Eye to the Brain, and (4) Common Disorders in the Visual System.

Each of the remaining chapters in this book includes a chapter preview, a brief summary of the material to be covered. This preview supplements the outline and explains important terms that might be unfamiliar in the outline.

This textbook stresses applications. One kind of application you will read about is the application of perception research to professions such as medicine, education, and consumer psychology. This feature has been included because concrete material is typically more memorable than abstract material. A second kind of application occurs throughout the text when I ask you to recall examples of various phenomena from your own experience. Psychologists concerned with human memory have demonstrated that we recall material better if we ask ourselves whether the material applies to ourselves. Therefore take advantage of your past experience! The third kind of application this book stresses is the informal experiments labeled "Demonstrations." I intentionally designed each demonstration so that it requires only a short time commitment and no specialized equipment. You can perform most of these demonstrations by yourself. These demonstrations should also help to make the material more concrete and help you relate it to your own experiences.

New terms are introduced in boldface print (for example, **superior colliculus**), and the definition appears in the same sentence. In many cases I will include a phonetic pronunciation for a new term, so that you don't have to guess whether you are dealing with a superior "kole-*lick*-you-luss" or a superior "kole-like-*you*-loos."

This textbook also includes some **mnemonic** (pronounced "nee-*mon*-nick") **devices**, which are aids designed to help you remember material. Sometimes I will encourage you to form a mental picture. Other times I will discuss how the structure of a topic can help you remember the material. There are also some cases in which I make a sentence or word out of the first letters of words that must be remembered together. For example, *Fred Rolls Jelly Beans Slowly* may help you remember the five characteristics of one common kind of eye movement, and SIP may help you remember the sclera, iris, and pupil in the eye. It should be stressed, however, that an even more effective way to use mnemonics is to make up your own device, particularly if my suggestion does not strike you as memorable.

If you glance through the last part of Chapter 1 and the remaining chapters in this book, you will notice that there is a summary at the end of each of the major sections in a chapter, rather than at the end of the entire chapter. For instance, Chapter 2 has four section summaries. I chose to include frequent, small summaries rather than a single lengthy summary for two reasons: (1) you can review the material more often, and (2) you can master small segments before you move on to unfamiliar material. You can take advantage of this feature by testing yourself when you reach the end of a section. Then read the summary and notice which items you forgot. Test yourself once more, and recheck your accuracy. You may wish to read only one section at a time, rather than the whole chapter. When you begin a study session in the middle of a chapter, reread the previous section summaries before reading the new material.

Each chapter ends with review questions and a list of new terms. The review questions may ask you to apply your knowledge to a practical problem or to integrate material from several parts of the chapter. The new terms are listed in their order of occurrence in the chapter. Test yourself to see whether you can give a definition for each new term. If you are not confident about your answer, you can find the definition by checking the subject index at the end of the book and noting the page number on which the term is defined.

A Brief History of the Study of Perception

We need to outline briefly some of the major approaches that have developed in the history of perception. The purpose of this section is to provide you with a background for several theoretical topics that we will discuss more completely in other chapters.

A thorough history of perception would probably begin by tracing theories of perception that Greek philosophers proposed more than 2000 years ago. Other sources can be consulted for details on the early history of perception (for example, Boring, 1942; Wertheimer, 1974). We will restrict our survey to the more recent past and examine four approaches to perception: empiricist, Gestalt, Gibsonian, and information-processing. Much of our discussion is based on a chapter by Hochberg (1979).

The Empiricist Approach

In the early 1700s, George Berkeley struggled with a very basic problem: How can we perceive objects in the world as having depth, if our eyes register only height and width? We will consider this important question again in Chapter 6 when we discuss the perception of distance and depth. Berkeley (1709/1957) was influential in developing an approach to perception called empiricism. **Empiricism** (pronounced "em-*pirr*-uh-sizz-um") is an approach that states that all information is derived from sensory perceptions and experiences. Thus we do not know how to perceive depth when we are born; instead, we must acquire this perceptual ability by learning.

In 1866, Helmholtz extended the empiricist approach to account for size constancy, a topic we will cover in more detail in Chapter 7. As we discussed at the beginning of this present chapter, objects seem to stay the same size as they move away from us. Helmholtz proposed that we figure out how big something is by combining two sources of information: (1) how big the image of the object is on our retina and (2) how far away the object appears to be. Thus perception involves both information from our senses and the interpretation of that sensory information. In the empiricist tradition, Helmholtz argued that our previous experiences are responsible for our ability to maintain size constancy.

The empiricist explanations for distance perception and size constancy are still popular today, as we will see in later chapters. However, other approaches have placed less emphasis on the role of learning in perception.

The Gestalt Approach

A number of German Gestalt psychologists in the first part of this century objected to the empiricist approach to perception. In particular, these Gestalt psychologists believed that the empiricists had not paid enough attention to the relationship among the various parts of a stimulus. The word **Gestalt** (pronounced "geh-*shtahlt*") means "configuration" in German. The **Gestalt approach** emphasized that we perceive objects as well-organized wholes, rather than as separated, isolated parts. Thus the shape that we see is more than the sum of its individual elements. For example, the square that you see in Figure 1-3 is more than the simple combination of four separate lines; it is a well-organized configuration.

The Gestalt approach developed many principles to account for the organization of shapes. Whereas the empiricists emphasized that all of our perceptions are based on learning and experience, Gestalt theorists stressed that the perception of shape was inborn. These in-

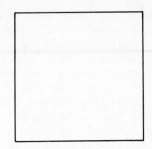

Figure 1-3 A well-organized configuration, in which the whole is more than the sum of its isolated parts.

born tendencies served as the basis for learning and experience, which Gestalt theorists de-emphasized in contrast to the empiricists. In Chapter 5 we will see that the Gestalt principles are still considered to be an important part of shape perception.

The Gibsonian Approach

James J. Gibson, who was a psychologist at Cornell University, offered an approach to perception that was different from either the empiricist or the Gestalt approach. The **Gibsonian approach** (pronounced "Gibb-*sone*-ee-un") emphasized that stimuli in our environment are rich with information. Psychologists interested in perception should therefore explore the objects that we see, the sounds that we hear, and so on, in order to determine which features are directly responsible for our perceptions.

We will consider the Gibsonian approach to perception in some detail in Chapters 6 and 7. Gibson argued that depth perception, size constancy, and other perceptual phenomena could be explained in terms of certain features of the stimuli themselves. For example, once we know what the surface texture of an object looks like, we know roughly how far away this object is.

Gibson emphasized that perception is direct. We can perceive how far away an object is, for example, on the basis of information from the stimulus itself. As a consequence, we do not need to calculate its distance on the basis of what we have learned in our past experience. Other books can be consulted for more details on Gibson's theories, both in their early version (for example, J. J. Gibson, 1950) and their re-vised version (for example, J. J. Gibson, 1979). A chapter by Mace (1977) provides an excellent overview of Gibson's theory, and the title of that chapter provides a capsule summary of the Gibsonian approach: "James J. Gibson's strategy for perceiving: Ask not what's inside your head, but what your head's inside of." Thus Gibson believed that when we can ade-quately describe the features of our environ-ment, we do not need to devise fancy theories to explain psychological processes underlying perception.

The Information-Processing Approach

Information processing was developed by people who were interested in computers and communication science. In the **infor-mation-processing approach,** information is handled by a series of stages. One stage per-forms its specified operations, and then the information passes on to the next stage for another kind of processing. Psychologists who favor the information-processing approach create models that outline the series of stages. For example, one very influential model pro-posed that information from our sensory re-ceptors passes first into a very brief sensory storage, then to short-term memory, and then to long-term memory (Atkinson & Shiffrin, 1968).

Information-processing models typically stress that humans have limited capacities. Thus we cannot perceive too many items at one time. If we are paying close attention to one message, we must ignore another message. We will discuss the limited capacity of human in-formation processing in detail in Chapter 12 (Attention).

The information-processing approach points out that there is a continuity in the way we handle information. Earlier psychologists often made distinctions among several areas of experimental psychology. For example, "sen-sation" referred to the immediate contact be-tween stimuli and the sensory receptors. The term "perception" referred to adding meaning and interpretation to these basic sensations. Thus these psychologists believed that sensa-tions were pure and were not influenced by

previous learning and experience. Perceptions, they believed, were very different from sensa-tions because they were influenced by learn-ing and experience. Information-processing psychologists, however, stress that sensation, perception, and higher mental processes —such as memory—must all be treated within a single system (Haber, 1974). Thus we may use strategies that involve memory when we per-ceive. Information-processing psychologists urge us not to divide sensation, perception, memory, and other processes into isolated compartments. Instead, we must realize that each process depends upon other processes.

In this section we have provided capsule summaries of four approaches to perception: empiricist, Gestalt, Gibsonian, and infor-mation-processing. You may have noticed, incidentally, that we did not discuss one approach that has been particularly important in other areas of experimental psychology, be-haviorism. **Behaviorism** stresses the objective description of the *behavior* of an organism. Thus behaviorists are uncomfortable with the area of perception, which deals with how the world *appears* to people, rather than how people be-have. As Hochberg (1979) describes, perception research declined to a bare trickle when be-haviorism was dominant in the United States in the 1930s and 1940s. In recent years, how-ever, interest in perception has been renewed, partly because of psychologists' enthusiasm for the Gibsonian and information-processing approaches.

Summary: A Brief History of Perception

- Empiricism, which was primarily devel-oped by Berkeley and Helmholtz, proposes that all information is derived from sensory perceptions and experience.
- Empiricists believe that perception involves sensory information and the interpretation of sensory information.
- The Gestalt approach emphasizes that we perceive objects as well-organized wholes, instead of separated parts.
- The Gestalt approach proposes that shape perception is inborn and that learning is re-latively unimportant.

- The Gibsonian approach stresses that stimuli in our environment are rich with information.
- The Gibsonian approach argues that perception is direct; we do not need to perform calculations and interpretations in order to perceive.

- The information-processing approach maintains that information is handled by a series of stages.
- The information-processing approach stresses that sensation, perception, and other higher mental processes are interconnected rather than isolated from each other.

Overview of Psychophysics

The previous section gave you a brief background in the history of approaches to perception. Before reading the other chapters in this book you also need a brief background in measuring perception.

How do we measure how the world appears? After all, perception is a very private activity. If you watch a friend who is busy perceiving, you won't notice anything dramatic. The area of psychophysics is concerned with measuring the perception of stimuli. Specifically, **psychophysics** is the study of the relationship between physical stimuli and the psychological reaction to those stimuli. Chapter 15 contains more information about psychophysical techniques for those who wish more extensive coverage. However, this overview of psychophysics provides a brief background in psychophysics, which is necessary preparation for Chapters 2–14.

Basically, the questions that psychophysicists ask can be divided into two categories: (1) How do people respond to low-intensity stimuli? and (2) How do people respond to relatively high-intensity stimuli? Let's consider these issues separately.

Measuring Responses to Low-Intensity Stimuli

The night is foggy and you are driving home. You look ahead and wonder whether you see—or detect—the faint light of an oncoming car. In **detection** studies, the experimenter presents a range of low-intensity stimuli and notices whether people report them or not. From the reports, the experimenter calculates a detection threshold. A **detection threshold** is the smallest amount of energy necessary for the

stimulus to be reported 50% (one half) of the time.

One way to envision a threshold—actually an *incorrect* way—is to think of a threshold as an abrupt change. Thus a person might say, "I *can't* see it" whenever the stimulus intensity is 1, 2, 3, or 4. However, at a stimulus intensity of 5 and above, the person consistently says, "I *can* see it." Figure 1-4 illustrates the proposed relationship between stimulus intensity and the observer's responses. In reality, however, we rarely find abrupt changes from "I can't see it" to "I can see it." Figure 1-5 shows the relationship between stimulus intensity and the observer's response that is typically obtained. Notice that the observer shows a gradual increase in the proportion of "I can see it" responses. In real life, then, our perceptual systems show a gradual transition as stimulus intensity increases in the region of the threshold.

Let's discuss the relationship between threshold and sensitivity, because people often find this relationship confusing. When you

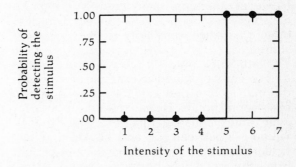

Figure 1-4   Incorrect conception of a threshold, showing abrupt change.

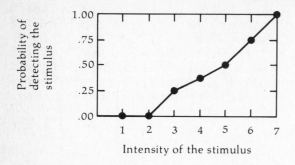

Figure 1-5   The results of a typical threshold study, showing gradual change.

have a low threshold for a stimulus, that means that only a low intensity of that stimulus is required in order for you to say, "I perceive it." In other words, you are very sensitive to that stimulus. Thus the *lower* the threshold, the *higher* the sensitivity. Conversely, the *higher* the threshold, the *lower* the sensitivity. For example, when you have been out in the bright sunshine and first enter a dark room, you have a high threshold for perceiving a dim light; your sensitivity is low. After you have been in the dark room for 20 minutes, however, you have a low threshold for perceiving a dim light; your sensitivity is high.

Chapter 15 describes and illustrates three methods of determining detection thresholds. These techniques were devised more than 100 years ago, and so they are called "classical psychophysical methods." The classical psychophysical methods are still extremely useful in many situations, particularly when they are used with highly trained observers. However, there are many cases in which an observer's responses are determined by factors other than their sensitivity to the presented stimuli.

A student in one of my classes (Bruce Edington) recently provided an example of some additional factors that can determine how an observer responds. He had recently applied for a job, and the manager had told Bruce that he would call between 3:30 and 4:00 on that particular afternoon. Within that half-hour period, Bruce thought that he heard the phone ring two or three times. In other words, the response "I can hear it" was much more likely than it would

have been in other circumstances. The "I can hear it" response was more frequent for two reasons: (1) the high probability that the phone would actually ring during that period and (2) the important benefits of answering the phone if it did actually ring as opposed to the substantial harm in not answering the phone if it did ring. In other words, the probability of saying "I detect a stimulus" is influenced by people's decision-making strategies.

Decision-making strategies are an important part of the Theory of Signal Detection. The **Theory of Signal Detection** (TSD) states that the likelihood of saying "I detect a stimulus" depends upon two factors, a sensitivity measure and the observer's criterion. The **sensitivity measure** is determined by two factors: (1) the intensity of the stimulus and (2) the sensitivity of the observer. The loudness of a telephone's ring and the sensitivity of your hearing, for example, would determine a sensitivity measure. The symbol d' (pronounced "dee prime") is used to represent sensitivity. The **criterion** reflects our decision-making strategies; it measures our willingness to say, "I detect the stimulus" when we are uncertain about whether it really occurred. The criterion depends upon several factors, including (1) the probability that the stimulus will occur and (2) the **payoff**, or the rewards and punishments associated with a particular response. The symbol β (pronounced "*bay*-tuh") is a letter from the Greek alphabet that is used to represent the criterion.

Let's see how each of these factors was relevant in the case of the student listening for the phone to ring. The sensitivity measure, d', reflects the intensity of the ring and the sensitivity of the listener. This measure would be high if the phone had been adjusted so that the ring was loud and if the listener has unimpaired hearing; d' would be low with a low-intensity ring and a hearing-impaired listener. The criterion, β, reflects the probability that a phone call would occur and the payoff associated with answering the phone. In the example we have been discussing, the student would be very willing to say, "I detect the stimulus." In contrast, most of us would be less likely to say, "I detect the stimulus" if the stimulus is improbable (perhaps because it is 3 A.M.) or if the payoff favors our not answering the phone (perhaps because the only people who call are salespeople and those who have dialed the wrong number).

The Theory of Signal Detection is quite elaborate. Chapter 15 provides more information on the Theory of Signal Detection, and additional details are available elsewhere (for example, Egan, 1975; Gescheider, 1976; Green & Swets, 1966).

Measuring Responses to High-Intensity Stimuli

In everyday life, high-intensity stimuli are perhaps even more important to us than low-intensity stimuli. We need to decide, for example, which basket of fruit feels heavier, which alarm clock is noisier, and which flashlight is brighter. Notice that in all these cases the intensity of each stimulus is high enough that the stimulus can easily be detected. When psychophysicists study high-intensity stimuli, they generally focus on two issues: (1) How different in intensity do two stimuli need to be in order for an observer to notice the difference? and (2) What is the relationship between the physical intensity of the stimulus and the psychological reaction of the observer?

The first issue involves discrimination. In **discrimination** studies we examine whether people can tell the difference between two stimuli and we determine the smallest amount of change in a stimulus that a person is capable of perceiving. Observers compare two stimuli and decide whether one stimulus is the same as the other stimulus or whether it is greater than or less than the other stimulus. As Chapter 15 describes, each of the three classical psychophysics methods can be used to study discrimination, as well as detection.

The second issue involves the correspondence between a change in the stimulus "out there" in the world and the change in our psychological reaction "in here" in our perceptual systems. Specifically, as a stimulus becomes increasingly larger in magnitude, do our psychological reactions increase to the same extent? For example, if we double the number of candles in a room, does it seem twice as bright? Chapter 15 considers several approaches to this issue.

Summary: Overview of Psychophysics

- Psychophysics is the study of the relationship between physical stimuli and the psychological reaction to those stimuli.
- Psychophysics can be divided into two parts: (a) reactions to low-intensity stimuli and (b) reactions to high-intensity stimuli.
- A detection threshold is the smallest amount of energy necessary for the stimulus to be reported 50% of the time.
- A detection threshold is not an abrupt change from nondetection to detection; instead, the transition is a gradual one.
- A low threshold means high sensitivity; a high threshold means low sensitivity.
- Observer's responses can be determined by factors other than sensitivity; the Theory of Signal Detection argues that responses depend upon a sensitivity measure and a criterion.
- Sensitivity, d', depends upon two factors: (a) the intensity of the stimulus and (b) the sensitivity of the observer.
- The criterion, β, depends upon several factors, including (a) the probability that the stimulus will occur and (b) the payoff.
- In discrimination studies we examine whether observers can tell the difference between two stimuli.
- Another issue associated with high-intensity stimuli, in addition to discrimination, is the relationship between the magnitude of the physical stimulus and the magnitude of the psychological response.

Review

1. What is perception, and what is the particularly puzzling aspect of perception? Describe this puzzle with respect to your perception of a letter of the alphabet on this page.

2. Imagine yourself eating a piece of pizza. Review the section of the chapter called "Preview of the Book" and illustrate how some aspect of the very mundane act of eating a piece of

pizza can be related to each one of the chapters of this book.

3. Describe, in one or two sentences, each of the four major approaches to perception. Explain briefly how each of these approaches would account for your perception of the picture in Figure 1-1.

4. What is behaviorism, and why hasn't this approach been an important influence in the history of the study of perception?

5. What is a detection threshold? Suppose that you read that people have a low threshold for a particular odor that smells like rotten eggs. Does that mean that they are sensitive or insensitive to that odor? Suppose that you read that

certain members of the population have a low sensitivity for detecting the bitter flavor in caffeine. Does that mean that these people have a low or high threshold for that substance?

6. Think of an example from the last few days in which your response "I perceive the stimulus" was influenced by the probability that the stimulus would occur. Now think of another example in which your response was influenced by the payoff associated with saying "I perceive the stimulus."

7. What is the difference between detection and discrimination? Give an example of each related to the following perceptual systems: (a) touch, (b) odor, (c) taste.

New Terms

perception	information-processing approach	sensitivity measure
mnemonic devices	behaviorism	d'
empiricism	psychophysics	criterion
Gestalt	detection	β
Gestalt approach	detection threshold	payoff
Gibsonian approach	Theory of Signal Detection (TSD)	discrimination

chapter 2

THE VISUAL SYSTEM

Outline   The Visual Stimulus
           The Anatomy of the Eye
               External Eye Structures
               Internal Eye Structures
           The Pathway from the Eye to the Brain
               The Optic Chiasm
               The Superior Colliculus
               The Lateral Geniculate Nucleus
               The Visual Cortex
           Common Disorders in the Visual System

Preview

This chapter is divided into four parts: (1) the Visual Stimulus, (2) The Anatomy of the Eye, (3) The Pathway from the Eye to the Brain, and (4) Common Disorders in the Visual System.

The first section of this chapter is concerned with the nature of light, or the visual stimulus. Light can be represented by wavelengths. The distance between the peaks of the waves is related to hue, and the height of the waves is related to brightness.

The section on the anatomy of the eye includes some visible parts of the eye, such as the sclera, the iris, and the pupil, as well as the transparent covering, the cornea. Important structures behind the cornea are the lens and the retina. We will discuss the retina in some detail, because this is the part of the eye that absorbs the light rays. We will pay particular attention to the two kinds of receptor cells, the rods and the cones.

In the third section we will move along the visual pathway from the eye to the brain. Parts of the optic nerves cross over to the other side of the head, an arrangement that is useful in order for our two eyes to work together. The nerve fibers then proceed on to the superior colliculus and the lateral geniculate nucleus. Finally, other nerve fibers proceed from the lateral geniculate nucleus to the visual cortex. The cells in the visual cortex are sensitive to features of stimuli such as orientation, length, and movement.

In the last section of this chapter we will talk about common eye problems. These include disorders of various parts of the eye, the eye muscles, the visual pathway, and the visual cortex. Some of these problems can be corrected by surgery, some improve spontaneously, and some lead to permanent blindness. This section should be particularly useful to students interested in applied areas of psychology.

The human eye is an incredible organ. It is about the size of a jumbo olive, and yet it can perform impressive tasks. It can handle information about both colored and uncolored objects that are near or far away. Furthermore, it can work when the lighting is dim or glaring. Our major task in this chapter is to examine the structure of the eye, as well as the later stages in the processing of visual information.

Before considering the eye itself, however, we must talk about the properties of the visual stimulus. Specifically, let's talk about the na-

ture of light. An understanding of the visual stimulus and the basic visual equipment is necessary before we can examine other aspects of visual perception.

You will find that this chapter contains many new terms. You will probably manage best if you read this chapter slowly, pausing and reviewing sections frequently. Some memory aids have been included to help you remember the new terms, and you may want to invent others.

The Visual Stimulus

Before we discuss the structure and functions of the eye, we need to examine the nature of the visual stimulus. In particular, what are the properties of light?

Light is one kind of electromagnetic energy. According to one viewpoint, light is made up of waves. We can describe light in terms of its **wavelength**, which is the distance the light travels during one cycle, that is, the distance between two peaks as illustrated in Figure 2-1. Thus the light wave in Figure 2-1a has a longer wavelength than the light wave in Figure 2-1b.

Wavelength is typically measured in nanometers. (An earlier equivalent measure was called millimicrons.) A **nanometer** (pronounced "*naa*-noe-*mee*-tur"), which is abbreviated nm, is equal to one billionth of a meter. The shortest wavelengths that we can see are represented by the color violet, which has a wavelength of about 400 nm. The longest wavelengths that we can see are represented by red, which has a wavelength of about 700 nm. Color Plate 1, inside the front cover of this book,

shows the spectrum between red and violet. You can remember the colors of the spectrum, from longest to shortest, by remembering an imaginary name, ROY G. BIV, for the colors Red, Orange, Yellow, Green, Blue, Indigo, and Violet. (You're right—indigo is a color name you usually don't find outside a paint store; it is a deep violet-blue.)

We call wavelengths between 400 and 700 nm **light.** The receptors in our eyes are sensitive to these wavelengths. However, the entire spectrum of electromagnetic energy is much broader. When you consider the whole spectrum, you will find that we can only see a tiny part of it. There are extremely short waves such as gamma rays, X-rays, and the ultraviolet rays that give you a suntan. X-rays, for example, are about 5 nm in length. All of these are too short to be visible to our human eyes.

On the other hand, there are waves that are too long to be visible to human eyes. These include infrared rays, microwaves, TV waves, and radio waves. Radio waves, for example, are about 1 kilometer or .6 mile in length. If this length is converted to nanometers, a radio wave is one trillion nanometers long!

We have talked about the length of light waves. As we will discuss in the chapter on color vision (Chapter 4), the length of light waves is related to the **hue** of a visual stimulus. Light waves have two other characteristics, purity and amplitude. Purity, or the mixture of different wavelengths contained in the light, is related to the perceived saturation of a visual stimulus. Finally, **amplitude**, or the height of the light wave, is related to the brightness of a visual stimulus. Figure 2-2 shows how light waves can differ in the height of their peaks. Notice that Figure 2-2a has greater amplitude than Figure 2-2b, because its peaks are higher. We perceive light waves that have greater amplitude as being brighter.

You may have noticed that we mentioned three *pairs* of attributes: (1) wavelength and hue, (2) purity and saturation, and (3) amplitude and brightness. The first member of each pair describes a characteristic of the physical stimulus, whereas the second member describes what we perceive, a psychological reaction. For example, large-amplitude

a. Example of long wavelength

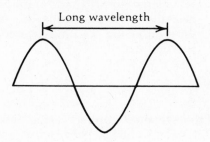

b. Example of short wavelength

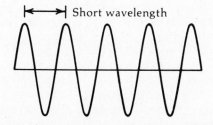

Figure 2-1　Examples of light waves.

a. Example of a bright-looking light, with light
    waves of greater amplitude

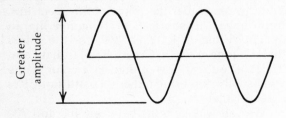

b. Example of a dim-looking light, with light
    waves of smaller amplitude

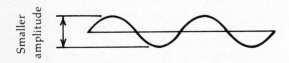

Figure 2-2   Examples of light waves varying in
amplitude.

wavelengths in a physical stimulus will usually
be perceived by humans to be bright. Thus we
should say "a light that *looks* bright" rather than
"a bright light," because brightness describes
our perceptions rather than the physical
stimulus.

We said that wavelength is typically measured in nanometers. There are numerous
ways to measure the amplitude of light, summarized by Walsh (1958). A frequent measure
used in psychology journals is **candelas per
meter square**, or **cd/m²**, a measure based on
how much light is reflected from the surface of
the stimulus. To give you a feeling for this
measure, the light reflected from the page you
are reading now is approximately 32 cd/m².
However, under the best conditions, you can
detect a light that is only .000003 cd/m².

Review the characteristics of the visual
stimulus by trying Demonstration 2-1.

Summary: The Visual Stimulus

- Light is made up of waves, which can vary
  in length and height.
- Short wavelengths are perceived as violet,
  and long wavelengths are perceived as red.
- In addition to these visible wavelengths,
  there are waves that are too short or too
  long to be visible to the human eye.
- Light waves that have greater amplitude
  are generally perceived as being brighter or
  lighter.
- Wavelength, purity, and amplitude
  describe physical stimuli, whereas hue,
  saturation, and brightness describe our
  perceptions.

The Anatomy of the Eye

Our discussion of the eye covers (1) the external eye structures and (2) the internal eye
structures.

External Eye Structures

Look at your eye in the mirror. Three parts are
very noticeable: the sclera, the iris, and the
pupil. Figure 2-3 shows these three parts. (It
may help you to remember the word SIP to
represent the order of the three parts as you
move inward toward the pupil.)

The **sclera** (pronounced "*skleh*-rah") is the
shiny white part, made of relatively thick membrane. The sclera serves to maintain the shape

of the eye and to protect it from injury (Riggs,
1971). The floating eyeballs you see in horror
movies are accurate in one respect: The sclera
does continue around on the back of the eye!

The **iris** is a ring of muscles having a color
that may range from light blue to dark brown.
We tend to attach great importance to eye color,
writing songs, stories, and poetry in which eye
color is stressed. It certainly sounds unroman-
tic, then, to describe the iris simply as a ring of
muscle!

The iris has two kinds of muscles, one to
make the iris **constrict** or close (making the
pupil smaller) and one to make it **dilate** or open
(making the pupil larger). When the lights are

Demonstration 2-1

The Visual Stimulus

Turn to Color Plate 1. Select ten colored objects near you, and find their approximate location on the figure. Make sure you include both short wavelengths (which look violet and blue) and long wavelengths (which look red and orange). Note also which objects look bright and which look dim.

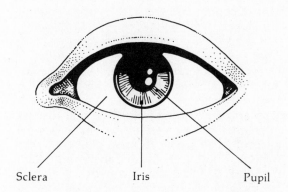

Sclera   Iris   Pupil

Figure 2-3   Three noticeable parts of the eye.

bright, the iris closes up; when the lights are dim, it opens. Try Demonstration 2-2 to illustrate this process. The size of the iris also changes as you become interested in something, as we will see in Chapter 14.

The **pupil** is simply the opening in the center of the iris. In humans this opening is round. The next time you look at a cat, however, notice that its pupils are not round. In fact, they become thin vertical slits when the lights are bright.

Why does the pupil look black? Why can't you look into the pupil and see the eye's internal structure? There are two reasons. First of all, most of the light that enters the eye is absorbed by **pigments,** or coloring material, inside the eye. However, a small amount of the light is reflected directly out of the pupil. You might think that doesn't make sense because the pupil doesn't look at all lighted; it looks pure black. The second reason why the pupil looks black is that you ordinarily cannot see the small amount of reflected light from someone's eye. If you stand directly in front of someone, you will be blocking the source of light right in front of that person's pupil. On the other hand, if you stand

to the side, you will not block the light source. Unfortunately, however, the light will be reflected from the person's eye to a point straight ahead. You will not see this reflection, since you are standing at the side.

Ophthalmologists (pronounced "off-thal-*moll*-uh-jists"), who are doctors specializing in eye diseases, and other physicians use a special tool called an **ophthalmoscope** (pronounced "off-*thal*-muh-skope") in order to look inside the eye. The ophthalmoscope is equipped with a special mirror and lens so that the light from a person's eye *can* be reflected back to the observer. Instead of the black pupil we ordinarily see, the physician can see structures inside the eye.

As you look in the mirror at your own eye, there is one structure on the outside that you cannot ordinarily see, because it is transparent. This is the **cornea** (pronounced "*kore*-nee-uh"), a clear membrane just in front of the iris, which joins with the sclera and bulges out slightly. The cornea is illustrated in Figure 2-4. You may have noticed a cornea if you ever looked sideways at someone wearing "hard" contact

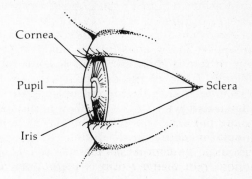

Cornea

Pupil

Iris

Sclera

Figure 2-4   The cornea, as seen from the side.

Demonstration 2-2

Iris and Pupil Size

Go into a dark room or closet that has a door that can be opened to let in a little light. Bring with you a mirror and a flashlight. Open the door just enough so that your left eye (next to the door) can see your right eye (away from the door) in the mirror. Notice the size of your pupil. It should be relatively large, because the iris is open. Now quickly turn on the flashlight so that it beams directly upon your right eye. Watch how rapidly the pupil shrinks in size, because the iris is closing up. Turn off the flashlight and watch the pupil dilate.

lenses. If you look carefully, you will notice that the contact lens seems to be floating some distance away from the iris. Actually, it really is resting on the cornea. The cornea is important because it bends the light rays as they enter the eye.

If you look once more in the mirror, you will see the **conjunctiva** (pronounced "con-junk-*tie*-vah") which is the pink-colored mucous membrane that lines the eyelid and attaches the eye to the eyelid. Many people buy contact lenses for the first time and secretly worry that a lens might slip around to the back of the eye. Never fear—the conjunctiva prevents this from happening! The conjunctiva also covers the muscles that allow our eyes to move. You typically are not aware of these muscles, except when you strain them. However, we will see in the next chapter that eye movements are critically important in human vision.

Before we move on, let's review some terms. Visible parts of the eye include the sclera, the iris, and the pupil. The cornea is in front of the iris, and the conjunctiva is the pink part under your eyelids.

Internal Eye Structures

Now let's look at some internal structures that are illustrated in Figure 2-5. Notice that the lens is located behind the pupil and the iris. The **lens** is important because its shape changes in order to bring objects into focus. We will discuss this process in detail in the next chapter, but you can achieve a basic appreciation for the lens by trying Demonstration 2-3.

We noted earlier that the cornea bends the

light rays as they enter the eye. The lens completes the job. Since the lens can change its shape, it can focus the light rays from both nearby and faraway objects. (We will discuss the details of this process in the next chapter.) As a result, you see clear, crisp objects, rather than blurs. The lens is almost transparent, but it is slightly yellow in color. It consists of a series of layers, a bit like the layers of an onion.

Now notice the ciliary muscles in Figure 2-5. These **ciliary muscles** (pronounced "*sill*-ee-air-ee") are attached to the lens, and they control the shape of the lens. For example, when you are looking at a nearby object, the ciliary muscles contract.

Notice that the lens divides the eye into two compartments. Both of these compartments are filled with special material. The small area at the front of the eye is filled with a fluid that

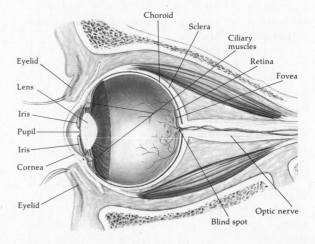

Figure 2-5   Inside the human eye.

Demonstration 2-3

The Lens

Look at this sentence and focus so that you can read it clearly. Your lens is now almost round. Now look up from your book and focus upon a faraway object. Your lens quickly changes its shape when you change your focus. Now it is the long, thin shape that is shown in Figure 2-5.

---

resembles water, and it provides nutrients for the cornea. The large area behind the lens has a jellylike fluid that helps to maintain the shape of the eyeball. If you press gently on an eyelid covering the sclera, you will notice that your eyeball can be slightly depressed, but you clearly cannot collapse it. The fluids keep it rather round.

Now look at the choroid, located just inside the sclera. The **choroid** (pronounced *"kore*-oid") does two things: (1) It absorbs extra light that is scattered in the eye, and (2) it contains many small arteries and veins, which provide nutrients for the eye. It is dark brown in color. Some animals do not have a choroid layer. For example, cats have a different kind of layer that resembles a mirror. You have probably noticed that cats' eyes glow in the dark if you shine a light at them. Their special layer provides them excellent eyesight at night. A cat can see and catch a mouse while you are still fumbling for the light switch!

The Retina

The **retina** (pronounced *"reh*-tih-nah") absorbs light rays and changes them into information that can be transmitted by the **neurons** (pronounced *"new*-rons"), or nerve cells. Notice that the retina is located at the back of the eyeball and covers a large part of the inner surface. This extremely important part of the eye is about as thick as a page in this book! It contains light receptors called rods and cones and different kinds of nerve cells, as you will see shortly.

Look carefully at one area on the retina. The **fovea** (pronounced *"foe*-vee-ah") is an area, smaller than the period at the end of this sentence, in which vision is the sharpest. In fact, as you are reading this paragraph, your eyes are jumping along the page in order to register new words on your fovea. If you look at one word on this page, you will notice that other words more than three centimeters away look somewhat

---

Demonstration 2-4

The Blind Spot

Close your left eye and use your right eye to look at the X. Gradually move this page toward your eye and then away from it, keeping the distance in the range of 10 to 40 centimeters. At some point, you will reach a distance at which the spot seems to disappear. At this distance the spot is falling upon the blind spot. In the blind spot, the nerve fibers gather together and leave the eye. There are no light receptors at this point, so there is no way to register the spot on the retina here. In Chapter 3 we will discuss how our visual system compensates for the blind spot.

X   ●

---

blurry—in order to read them, you must move your fovea to those words. We will be discussing eye movements during reading in the next chapter.

Now notice the area of the retina labelled the "blind spot." At the **blind spot** the optic nerve leaves the eye. There are no light receptors in the blind spot, so you cannot see anything that reaches this part of the retina. Try Demonstration 2-4 to illustrate the blind spot.

Since the retina is extremely important in vision, we need to consider the kinds of cells in the retina in some detail. Figure 2-6 shows the six kinds of cells. Cones and rods are the two kinds of light receptors. We will discuss these two kinds of cells in more detail later. For now, though, you should know that **cones** are used for color vision under well-lit conditions. **Rods**, on the other hand, are used for black-and-white vision under poorly lit conditions. You can remember these two names by imagining an ice-cream *cone* with many colorful scoops of ice cream on a bright, sunny day and a black-and-white *rod* sitting in a dark corner.

The rods and cones receive the light, so they begin the visual process. The bipolar cells are next in the chain. The **bipolar cells** (pronounced "*buy*-pole-ur") receive information from the rods and cones and pass it on to the next level in the chain, the ganglion cells. The **ganglion cells** (pronounced "*gang*-glee-un") take the information from the bipolar cells and bring it to the optic nerve. (Perhaps you can remember this sequence by the mnemonic "*Cones* and *rods* are good *buys* for *gangs*.")

Some recent studies have shown that there are actually three kinds of ganglion cells (Blakemore, 1975). If you are already dazed with an early case of "jargon shock" from too many new terms, you can relax temporarily—they are called **W, X, and Y ganglion cells.** These three kinds of cells differ from each other in several respects: (1) size, (2) location on the retina, (3) the kind of moving stimuli to which they are sensitive, and (4) the speed with which they send signals. Descriptions of the three cell types can be found in the chapter by Blakemore. Nevertheless, it is important to know why psychologists were excited to find out that there were different kinds of ganglion cells. Previously, people thought

that the brain was responsible for all of the processing of information about an object's shape and movement. However, since there are three different kinds of ganglion cells, it now appears that some information is sorted at the retinal level. Thus many aspects of an object may be recorded in the cells before the information leaves the paper-thin sheet at the back of your eyeball!

The chain of cells—from cones and rods to bipolar cells and then to the ganglion cells—carries information vertically from the eye to the brain. However, information also travels horizontally across the retina, through horizontal cells and amacrine cells. These cells allow for communication among cells that are next to each other. **Horizontal cells** allow the light receptors—the rods and cones—to communicate with each other. Notice how a horizontal cell can link together many different receptors. **Amacrine cells** (pronounced "*am*-ah-krihn") allow the ganglion cells to communicate with each other. Later in the book we will see why these kinds of communications with other cells are important. Specifically, you will learn that when one light receptor is stimulated, the activity of the nearby light receptors can be inhibited. This kind of inhibition would be impossible if there were no horizontal cells and amacrine cells to connect cells with their "neighbors."

Look at Figure 2-6 and notice something strange about the location of the light receptors. If the light is coming in from the front of the eye (at the bottom of the figure), why are the light receptors at the back of the eye, near the choroid and the sclera? In fact, the light has to travel through a small jungle of ganglion cells, bipolar cells, amacrine cells, and horizontal cells in order to reach the light receptors. First of all, this kind of inside-out arrangement is necessary because the light receptors need to be next to the blood vessels in the choroid in order to obtain oxygen. Second, this arrangement is not as bad as it looks because this jungle of cells is rather transparent—certainly more transparent than blood vessels would be if they were on the inside. In short, this inside-out arrangement really works better than an arrangement in which light receptors would be closer to the light.

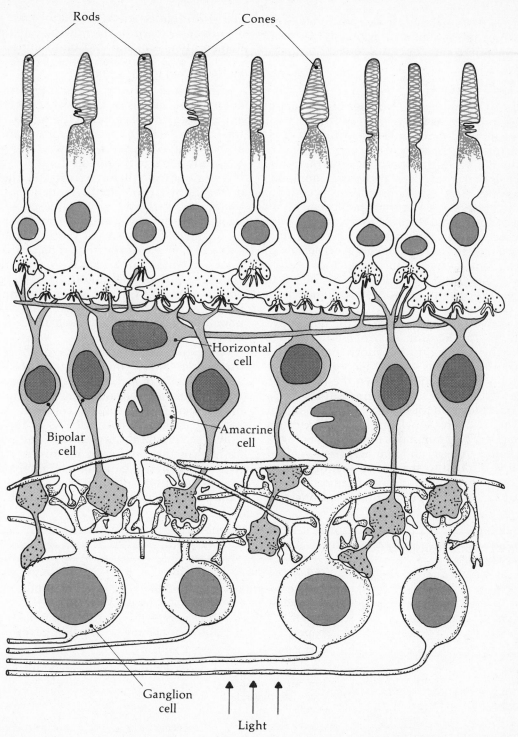

Figure 2-6 A diagram of the kinds of cells in the retina (adapted from Dowling & Boycott, 1966).

Now that you have a basic knowledge of the cells and the retina, you are ready for more information about cones and rods.

Details about Cones and Rods

Table 2-1 summarizes a number of facts about cones and rods. As we have already mentioned, cones are used for color vision in well-lit environments, whereas rods are used for black-and-white vision in poorly lit environments. Animals that are awake at night have more rods than cones. Bats, for example, have no cones at all (Riggs, 1971), a fact that should make you very curious about the light receptors in Count Dracula's retinas. Animals that are awake during the day, in contrast, have a good supply of cones. Some of these animals, such as lizards, snakes, birds, and squirrels, have no rods at all (Riggs, 1971). Humans, fortunately, have both rods and cones.

In Table 2-1, notice that specific ranges are listed for the lighting environments. Cones work when the lighting is more than about 3 cd/m², whereas rods work when the lighting is less than about 3 cd/m². When the lighting is about 3 cd/m², we can imagine situations in which it is too dim for the cones and too bright for the rods to work at their maximum efficiency. This ambiguous time of day occurs a little before sunset, and you may have noticed that it is difficult to see well at this time.

Cones and rods also differ from each other in terms of their shape and number. Cones are fat, with pointed ends, a little like the classic ice-cream cone. Rods, like the objects they are named after, are thin and blunt-ended. Each eye has "only" 7 million cones, whereas each eye has 125 million rods.

Cones and rods are concentrated in different parts of the retina. Cones are concentrated at the fovea, in the center of the retina. In contrast, rods are found nearly everywhere *except* at the fovea. As Figure 2-7 shows, their highest concentration is in the region about one-third of the way out from the fovea toward either edge of the retina. (You might remember this by imagining that you see an ice-cream cone straight in front of you and rods on either side.)

Let's combine some of the information in Table 2-1. If we know that rods are used in poorly lit conditions and that there are no rods at the fovea, then vision should be very poor for objects registered on the fovea at nighttime. Try Demonstration 2-5 to illustrate that vision is poor for objects registered on the fovea at nighttime.

In Figure 2-6 you may have noticed that there were many more receptor cells than ganglion cells. In fact, there are only about one million ganglion cells on the entire retina. That means that many receptor cells will have to "share" each ganglion cell. As it turns out, however, the sharing is unequal—the cones get more than their share. In the fovea, which is rich with cones, a ganglion cell might receive information from only one, two, or three cones. Toward the edge of the retina, which is rich

Table 2.1 A comparison of cones and rods.

CHARACTERISTICS	CONES	RODS
Kind of vision:	color	black and white
Lighting conditions required for best functioning:	well-lit (more than 3 cd/m²)	dimly lit (less than 3 cd/m²)
Shape:	fat, pointed	thin, blunt
Number:	7 million	125 million
Distribution:	in the fovea	not in the fovea
Number of receptors for each ganglion cell:	few	many
Acuity:	excellent in cone region	poor in rod region

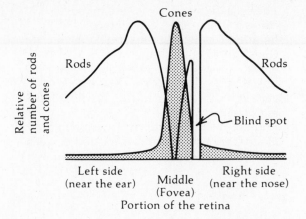

Left side (near the ear)   Middle (Fovea)   Right side (near the nose)

Portion of the retina

Figure 2-7   The distribution of rods and cones in the retina of the left eye. Cones are concentrated in the fovea, and rods in the area outside the fovea. Notice that there are no rods or cones in the blind spot.

with rods, a ganglion cell might receive information from as many as 100 rods.

The number of receptor cells for each ganglion cell is related to the next entry in the table, acuity. **Acuity** is a major topic in the next chapter; it refers to the precision with which we can see fine details.

Why should acuity be greater in the cone region? When you want to see fine details in a picture, for example, you would like each tiny receptor on the retina to keep its information

separate from the information that neighboring receptors have. If you pooled all the information together, however, the acuity would be reduced. Suppose, for example, that a design consisting of very narrow black-and-white stripes is falling upon an area in which 100 receptor cells share a single ganglion cell. All of the information about black and white would be combined at the ganglion, making a blurry gray instead. If each receptor cell had its own ganglion cell, however, the black-and-white pattern would be preserved. Thus acuity is greater in the cone region because cones have a lower receptor-to-ganglion cell ratio than rods do.

It makes sense that acuity would be greater in the cone region because you know already that acuity is best in the fovea area. The fovea, after all, is the area in which vision is the sharpest.

Rods and cones are necessary to the visual process because they take the light rays and change them into a form that can be sent along the nerves. The chemical processes that are responsible for these changes are very complex. If you want to learn more about them, consult a physiological psychology textbook such as *Physiology of Behavior* (N. R. Carlson, 1980).

Summary: The Anatomy of the Eye

• Three visible parts of the eye are the sclera, the iris, and the pupil.

Demonstration 2-5

Nighttime Vision and the Fovea

Choose a clear night and find a place where there are no bright lights nearby. Look up at the stars and notice an unusual phenomenon. You may see a very dim star slightly off to the right or the left of the point at which you are gazing. If you shift your focus to gaze at this star, however, the star seems to disappear! Rest assured that this is not a new Unidentified Flying Object that can disappear whenever humans look directly at it. Here is the explanation: In a dimly lit situation, rods operate but cones do not. Therefore if an object is registered on the areas of your retina that are filled with rods, you can see it. In other words, you can see objects best on the areas a bit outside the fovea. However, if an image of an object falls on the area of your retina that is filled with cones, you cannot see it. Consequently, an image that falls on the fovea will not be seen.

- The cornea, a clear membrane in front of the iris, bends the light rays.
- The conjunctiva is the pink-colored membrane that lines the eyelid and attaches the eye to the eyelid.
- The shape of the lens changes in order to bring objects into focus. The shape of the lens is controlled by the ciliary muscles.
- The choroid absorbs extra light and contains arteries and veins.
- The retina absorbs light rays and changes them into information that can be transmitted into activity in the neurons. The fovea is the area in which vision is sharpest. The blind spot is the area in which there are no light receptors.

- The cells in the retina are the rods and cones, bipolar cells, ganglion cells, horizontal cells, and amacrine cells.
- Cones allow color vision in well-lit environments. They are located in the fovea, and very few cones share each ganglion cell. As a result, acuity in the cone region is excellent.
- Rods allow black-and-white vision in dimly lit environments. They are located in areas of the retina outside the fovea, and many rods share each ganglion cell. As a result, acuity in the rod region is poor.

The Pathway from the Eye to the Brain

Look again at Figure 2-6 and notice at the bottom of the figure how the ends from the ganglion cells are gathered together. The **optic nerve** is this bundle of ends from ganglion cells. This nerve is almost as big around as your little finger. Figure 2-8 shows the optic nerve and other structures in the pathway to the brain.

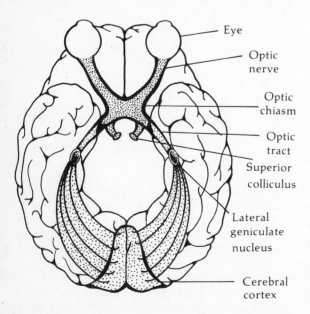

Figure 2-8 The visual pathway, from the eye to the brain.

Eye

Optic nerve

Optic chiasm

Optic tract

Superior colliculus

Lateral geniculate nucleus

Cerebral cortex

The Optic Chiasm

Now look at Figure 2-9 to see the best illustration of the optic chiasm. We need to examine this part of the visual pathway in some detail. The **optic chiasm** (pronounced "*kie*-as-em," the first syllable rhyming with "eye") is the area in which the two optic nerves come together and portions of each nerve cross over. The word "optic," as you may know, means "having to do with the eye." "Chiasm" is based on the Greek letter χ, which you may know from either fraternities and sororities or the χ^2 statistics test. Notice that the Greek letter χ resembles the crossover in the optic chiasm.

The same ganglion cell endings continue on the other side of the optic chiasm; they do not transfer information to new cells. However, they do such a neat job of splitting and regrouping that professional square dancers should be envious! Figure 2-9 shows this process in more detail. Since this is quite complicated, it will help if you trace along on the diagram as you read this section. Let's begin at the retina on the right-hand side. Trace the path of the optic nerve to the optic chiasm and notice how the paths separate at the optic chiasm. Half of the fibers cross over, but half remain on the same side. The same pattern is true for the retina on the left-hand side. Notice that this complex crossing produces an interesting effect. Everything that is registered on the right side of each

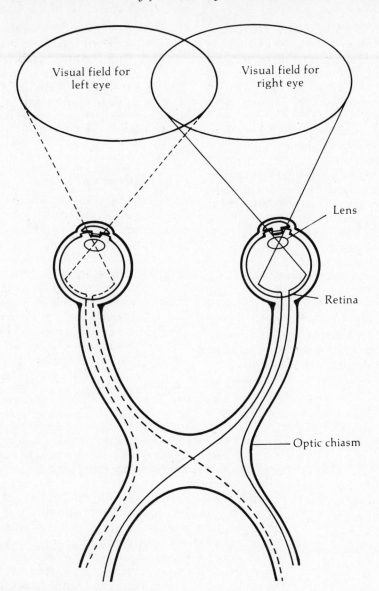

Figure 2-9   A schematic diagram showing how
stimuli from one side of the visual field are
registered on the opposite side of the retina and end
up on the opposite side of the head.

retina ends up on the right side of the head,
after crossing the optic chiasm. (Convince
yourself of this by tracing with your finger.)
Similarly, everything that is registered on the
left side of each retina ends up on the left side of
the head.

However, there is one other crossing that
occurs even before objects are registered on the

retina. The lens in the eye reverses the image.
As you look out at the world, something on the
left-hand side **(left visual field)** is registered on
the *right*-hand side of your retina. In contrast,
something on the right-hand side **(right visual
field)** is registered on the *left*-hand side of your
retina. Once again, trace with your fingers to
show where objects in the world are recorded

on your retina and where these fibers end up. You will see that things on the left-hand side of your visual world end up on the right-hand side of your head, whereas things on the right-hand side of your visual world end up on the left. Trying Demonstration 2-6 may help you understand this process.

Why does this complex crossing pattern exist? In many other species there is a complete crossover. Everything from the right retina crosses to the left, and everything from the left retina crosses to the right. However, humans and some other species have **binocular vision**—their two eyes work together and have overlapping fields of view (Abramov & Gordon, 1973). We need some way of coordinating what our two eyes see. Look straight ahead now and notice some object out to the left. This object is being registered on both the right and left retinas. However, information from both of these sources will end up on the right side of your head, where the information can be combined. As we will see in later chapters, humans use information from their binocular vision in order to know how far they are from a particular object.

Notice in Figure 2-8 that the bundle of fibers is called the **optic tract** after they cross the optic chiasm. Thus the order of the structures is optic nerve, optic chiasm, optic tract. (You may want to make up some mnemonic for the letters N, C, T.) The optic tract travels to two areas. Some of the fibers go to the superior colliculus, but most go to the lateral geniculate nucleus.

The Superior Colliculus

The superior colliculus would make an interesting name for a new rock group, but so far nobody has rushed to claim it. The **superior colliculus** (pronounced "kole-*lick*-you-luss") is a part of the brain that is important for locating objects. There are two of these structures, one for each optic tract; the plural is "superior colliculi" (the last syllable rhymes with "eye").

In birds and some other vertebrates, most of the optic tract fibers proceed to a structure similar to the superior colliculus (Abramov & Gordon, 1973). Moving targets, such as bugs, are important to these animals, so you can understand why the superior colliculus is so critical.

Demonstration 2 - 6

Understanding the Crossovers at the Lens and at the Optic Chiasm

The purpose of this demonstration is to make certain that you have mastered the complex crossovers in the visual system. It often helps if you relate something abstract to your own body and experiences.

First of all, notice some prominent object out at the *left* side of your visual field—something that both eyes can see. This object will be registered on the *right* side of your retinas. Point to the right side of both your left and right eyes. Now trace across the top of your head how the information about this object travels to your cerebral cortex. (For a reference point, the optic chiasm is located several centimeters above the point where your tongue is attached in your mouth.) That is, from the right side of the retina of your right eye, trace a path to the optic chiasm and then to the right side of the back of your head. From the right side of the retina of your left eye, similarly trace a path to the optic chiasm and then to the right side of the back of your head. Notice, then, that objects on the left of the visual field end up on the right side.

Now repeat this exercise with some object on the right side of your visual field, using Figure 2-9 as your guide. Notice that objects on the right side of the visual field end up on the left side.

For humans, however, the lateral geniculate nucleus is generally more important.

The Lateral Geniculate Nucleus

Jargon shock may reach an advanced state as you read the name of this section. The name "lateral geniculate nucleus" (pronounced "jen-*ick*-you-late") can be analyzed to make it look more friendly. "Lateral" means "on the side," and you will notice that there is one structure on each side of the brain. "Geniculate" means "bent like a knee," and this description is accurate. "Nucleus" means "little nut." So a lateral geniculate nucleus is like a little nut that is bent like a knee, located on the side of the brain!

The **lateral geniculate nucleus** (abbreviated LGN) is a part of the thalamus where some of the ganglion cells that began in the retina finally stop, transferring their information on to new neurons. Incidentally, this means that ganglion cells are fairly long in comparison to most other cells in the human body.

In humans the lateral geniculate nucleus has six different layers of cells. The current opinion is that each layer receives information from only one eye. Thus the coordination of information from the two eyes (that is so necessary for binocular vision) must occur at a higher level. Notice that the pathway from the lateral geniculate nucleus to the visual cortex is straightfor-

ward. Fortunately for people who are trying to remember the various complex pathways, there are no more crossovers!

The Visual Cortex

The **visual cortex** is the part of the **cerebral cortex** (pronounced "suh-*ree*-brul")—or outer part of the brain—that is concerned with vision. Notice in Figure 2-10 that the visual cortex is located in the rear part of the brain. The neurons that began in the LGN have branchlike endings that meet neurons in the visual cortex and transfer information to these new cells. These new visual cortex cells receive their information from several LGN cells.

Most important, the visual cortex cells receive information from both eyes. Remember that when we discussed the LGN, we said that information from the two eyes is probably kept separate in the LGN. In humans the visual cortex is probably the first level at which input from both eyes reaches the individual nerve cells (Abramov & Gordon, 1973). You will recall that humans have binocular vision, and so it is necessary to combine the information that our two eyes record. This combination seems to take place at the cortex level.

The visual cortex is just one part of the cerebral cortex. The cerebral cortex is absolutely vital for human functions, so let's consider this structure more carefully. In animals other than mammals the cerebral cortex is either extremely tiny or nonexistent. In some primates, such as monkeys and chimpanzees, the cerebral cortex is quite important, but in humans it is even more essential. As Hubel and Wiesel (1979) remark, a human "without a cortex is almost a vegetable, speechless, sightless, senseless" [p. 150].

In the entire cerebral cortex there are about 10 billion neurons. The cortex is only about two millimeters thick. In other words, the cover on your textbook is thicker than the covering on your brain! This covering is elaborately folded; if we could spread it out, the total area of the human cortex would be about 1400 square centimeters, which is about the size of the screen on a 21" television. As Hubel and Wiesel note, the folding probably occurs because this extensive structure has to be packed into a box that is

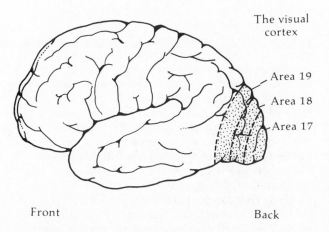

The visual cortex

Area 19

Area 18

Area 17

Front   Back

Figure 2-10   The visual cortex.

the size of a skull. We will consider other areas of the cerebral cortex when we consider the other sensory systems later in this book, but for now let's return to the visual cortex.

Notice that the visual cortex has three different sections. These are called **Areas 17, 18, and 19** in a numbering system that is used to describe parts of the brain. Area 17 is the "lowest level" in the visual cortex; the neurons from the LGN go directly to Area 17. Areas 18 and 19, in contrast, handle the "higher-level" kinds of visual processing. There is evidence that the neurons in Area 17 transfer information to cells in Area 18, which in turn transfer information to cells in Area 19.

The Spatial Arrangement in the Visual Cortex

There are many complexities in the visual system, and there are probably many times when the facts about vision do not match your common sense. You are in for a pleasant surprise regarding the spatial arrangement in the visual cortex. Now if I asked you to guess how the cells in Area 17 were arranged, you might guess that they correspond to the areas of the retina. That is, two neighboring areas of the retina would feed information into two areas of the cortex that are also next to each other. This arrangement is, in fact, the case! There is a **retinotopic** arrangement on the cortex, so that nerve cells that receive information from neighboring areas of the retina lie near each other in the visual cortex.

We could make a map showing how each point on the retina is represented on the visual cortex. When you look at a road map, you see that Michigan is closer to Ohio than it is to California, and this map corresponds to geographic reality. Similarly, when you look at a picture of the Mona Lisa, this visual cortex map would represent her left eye as being closer to her right eye than it is to her mouth. Thus this visual cortex map corresponds to the patterns that are registered on your retina.

Do not take this retinotopic arrangement too literally, however. When you look at a picture of the Mona Lisa, there is *not* a perfect representation of her (complete with smile) in your visual cortex. Many factors make the representation less than perfect. For example, about half of the neurons in the visual cortex receive in-

formation from the fovea, that very small central part of the retina. Thus the part of a picture that is registered on the fovea will be represented by more than its normal share of space in the visual cortex.

Still, the correspondence between the pattern on the retina and the pattern on the visual cortex is rather remarkable. Dobelle, Mladejovsky, and Girvin (1974) conducted a study in which electrodes arranged in a particular shape were placed over a person's visual cortex. The person reported "seeing" the geometric shape that corresponded to the pattern of electrode stimulation. It would be wonderful if this kind of system could be used to restore sight to people whose blindness is peripheral—and whose visual cortexes could work correctly if they received appropriate stimuli. Unfortunately, however, tissues are damaged when the electrical stimulation is used on a long-term basis. Therefore simple, direct stimulation of the cortex is not a good solution.

Neurons in the Visual Cortex

Recent research has uncovered information about the neurons in the visual cortex. Specifically, researchers have explored how these cells are able to extract information about the shapes of objects. As in many new fields, the experts often disagree; the controversy is summarized by N. L. Carlson (1980). Despite some other competing viewpoints, most people support the findings of Hubel and Wiesel.

David Hubel (pronounced "*Hew*-bell") and Torsten Wiesel (pronounced "*Wee*-zell") presented the first reports of their research in the late 1950s and early 1960s. A more recent, very readable report of their studies appeared in *Scientific American* (Hubel & Wiesel, 1979). In their experiments, visual shapes and patterns are presented to a cat. Meanwhile, they record the activity of a single neuron. This is accomplished by sinking an electrode into the cortex. The electrode is connected by long wires to a computer, which records electrical activity. The patterns that are presented vary in size, shape, color, and movement. Numerous stimuli are presented until the researchers are satisfied that they have found the best stimulus for the cell that is being tested—that is, the stimulus that produces the most activity. Then they move on to another cell.

As you can imagine, the procedure is very time-consuming and requires extremely precise techniques. However, it provides useful information about the organization of the receptive field. The **receptive field** is the area on the retina that produces a change in the activity of the visual system when it is stimulated by a light of a certain quality and intensity.

Hubel and Wiesel used this procedure to record the activity of neurons in the lateral geniculate nucleus, in the ganglion cells of the retina, and in the visual cortex. We will concentrate on their findings for neurons in the visual cortex. The most striking early finding was that the visual cortex had neurons that were sensitive to lines and angles (Hubel & Wiesel, 1959). For example, one neuron might show a sudden burst of activity when a horizontal line is presented. Another neuron might respond only when a vertical line is presented. These findings were particularly exciting to psychologists because they suggested a way in which the visual system could analyze the parts of a pattern.

Hubel and Wiesel (1965) isolated three different kinds of neurons: simple, complex, and hypercomplex. These authors should be praised for their pleasantly straightforward terms! The only unfamiliar term—hypercomplex—loses its mystery once you know that "hyper" means "extra," as in the term "hyperactive." Let's look at these three types of neurons.

1. The **simple cell** is found in Area 17 (the most basic area in the visual cortex), and it responds when lines are presented. These cells are fairly "choosey." Like a picky eater who responds only to vanilla ice cream, but not chocolate, and certainly not raisin-rum, the simple cell responds only when the conditions are just right. The light must fall in a particular part of the visual world. Diffuse illumination of that area will not work, though the cell might give a sputter of activity to small spots of light. They respond *enthusiastically* only to lines that have the correct orientation. As we discussed earlier, the most effective orientation depends upon which cell you are examining. However, these cells are so picky that a change of about

15° may cause the cell to stop responding. (In other words, a cell that would respond to the small (hour) hand of a clock that reads 1:00 would stop responding if that hand advanced to the position it holds at 1:30!)

2. The **complex cell** is found in Areas 17 and 18, and it responds to *moving* stimuli. Thus a moving bar of light might produce a response. Like the simple cells, the complex cells prefer lines, rather than single spots of light. However, unlike the simple cells, they are not so picky about the precise orientation of the lines. There is some evidence that simple cells pass on their information to the complex cells, and the complex cells abstract this information. However, the relationship among the different kinds of visual cortex cells is still unclear.

3. The **hypercomplex cell** is found in Areas 18 and 19, but not in Area 17; this cell responds to lines presented at certain orientations and lines that move in certain directions, as well as lines that have an appropriate size and shape. For example, a hypercomplex cell might respond vigorously only when a right angle containing lines of certain sizes moves diagonally upward and toward the left. This cell might not respond at all if the same stimulus is moved in the opposite direction, downward and toward the right.

The discovery of these three kinds of cells in the visual cortex was very exciting for psychologists interested in perception. After all, Hubel and Wiesel's research suggested that we have cells in our visual cortex that are specially equipped to detect features such as line size and angle. If this is the case, then our visual system probably makes use of these cells when we perform complicated visual tasks such as reading. In Chapter 5, on shape perception, we will see that one theory of how we recognize letters involves detecting the differences between letters on the basis of their features. This theory is consistent with the information about simple cells, complex cells, and hypercomplex cells.

Summary: The Pathway from the Eye to the Brain

- The bundle of ends from ganglion cells is called the optic nerve.

- Half of the fibers in each optic nerve cross over at the optic chiasm. As a result, everything that is registered on the right-hand side of both retinas ends up on the right-hand side of the head, and everything registered on the left-hand side ends up on the left.
- After crossing the optic chiasm, the bundle of fibers is called the optic tract.
- The optic tract travels to the superior colliculus and the lateral geniculate nucleus.
- The superior colliculus is a part of the brain that is important for locating objects.
- The lateral geniculate nucleus is the place where some of the ganglion cells stop and transfer their information to new neurons.
- The visual cortex is the portion of the outer part of the brain that is concerned with vision. The cortex combines information from both eyes and is responsible for higher levels of visual processing.
- The visual cortex is divided into three different sections, known as Areas 17, 18, and 19.
- There is a retinotopic arrangement on the cortex; nerve cells that receive information from neighboring areas of the retina lie near each other in the visual cortex.
- According to Hubel and Wiesel, there are three different kinds of neurons—simple, complex, and hypercomplex, each of which is located in a different area of the cortex and is responsive to a different aspect of visual stimuli.

Common Disorders in the Visual System

The branch of medicine that is concerned with visual problems is called **ophthalmology** (pronounced "off-thal-*moll*-uh-jee"). A brief discussion of ophthalmology should be worthwhile, because you probably know people who have had eye problems. Furthermore, if you choose a career in education, industrial psychology, or counseling, you will be working with people with visual problems. Naturally, we will not cover this area in detail. If you want more information, I recommend a readable basic textbook in the area, *General Ophthalmology* (Vaughan & Asbury, 1977).

In the next chapter we will talk about the disorders that you know best, nearsightedness and farsightedness, when we consider the focusing of the eye; in Chapter 4 we will discuss color deficiencies. In this chapter we will look at some other common problems, beginning with those in the eye.

Let's begin with the cornea, that transparent layer at the front of the eye. Even though it is almost invisible, the cornea is a strong barrier against disease germs (Vaughan & Asbury, 1977). If the cornea is somehow injured, however, disease germs can enter easily. Without proper treatment the cornea could be destroyed within 24 hours. As a result, corneal problems are considered to be very serious. One of the most common corneal problems is the presence of a foreign body in the cornea. As you probably know, a **foreign body** does *not* mean a recent immigrant to the United States—it is some object that does not belong there. In the case of the cornea, for example, it might be a small chip of metal from an industrial accident. Obviously, anyone with a corneal foreign body should be taken immediately to an ophthalmologist. A foreign body can also scratch the cornea, producing a painful **corneal abrasion**, which also requires medical attention.

You will recall that the iris is the colored area just underneath the cornea. **Iritis** (pronounced "eye-*rye*-tis"), or inflammation of the iris, is reasonably common in young and middle-aged people (Vaughan & Asbury, 1977). Its cause is usually unknown, and it typically affects only one eye. A person with iritis complains of pain and blurred vision, and feels more comfortable without bright lights. The part of the sclera that circles the iris is generally red. If iritis is not treated, parts of the iris may become attached to the lens, causing the opening of the pupil to be fixed in size.

Conjunctivitis (pronounced "con-junk-ti-*vie*-tis") is an inflammation of the conjunctiva, the pink membranes that line your eyelids and attach to the eye. Sometimes known as "pink-eye," it is the most common eye disease in the Western Hemisphere (Vaughan & Asbury, 1977). When you think about it, the conjunctiva is exposed to numerous organisms, irritants, and dangerous materials. This membrane is attacked by smog, smoke, dust, bacteria, viruses, and substances to which you might be allergic. Fortunately, your tears usually help you resist these attacks; they dilute the offending substances and wash them away. Conjunctivitis occurs when the tears have failed! The major symptoms of conjunctivitis are the bright red color of the conjunctiva and an itchy sensation. The treatment for conjunctivitis depends upon the cause of the disease. For example, soothing eyedrops may be used for some kinds of conjunctivitis, whereas antibiotics may be used when the conjunctivitis has been caused by bacteria.

The muscles that move the eyeballs are located behind the conjunctiva. Normally, the muscles move the two eyes so that an image falls upon the same part of both retinas. **Strabismus** (pronounced "struh-*biz*-muss"), sometimes called "cross-eye," occurs when the muscles for the two eyes do not work together. As a result, if the image falls upon the fovea in one eye, it falls upon a different region in the other eye. Strabismus occurs in about 3% of all children (Vaughan & Asbury, 1977), and you have probably seen many people whose eyes do not move together.

Strabismus must be corrected for three reasons: (1) to allow good vision in each eye, (2) to allow binocular vision, and (3) to improve appearance. Ideally, therapy should be started before six months of age. Otherwise, the child will favor the stronger eye and ignore the image in the weaker eye. If this happens, the child will not be able to see with the other eye, a condition known as **amblyopia** (pronounced "am-blih-*owe*-pih-ah"), or "lazy eye."

If the strabismus is noticed early enough, the condition can be corrected by putting a patch over the good eye. "The sooner, the better" is the rule here. If the eye is patched at one year of age, the treatment may take only a week. If the child is six years old, however, it may take a year to make the acuity equal for the two eyes. After the acuity has been restored to the weaker eye, a surgeon can correct the unbalanced muscles.

You will remember that the lens of the eye is usually almost transparent. **Cataracts** result when injury or disease causes a clouding of the lens. If the lens is too cloudy, light cannot pass through it, and blindness will occur. The most common form of the disease is the kind found in elderly people (Van Heyningen, 1975). There is no way to prevent cataracts, unfortunately, and there is no cure. There is a partial remedy, however. The lens of the eye can be surgically removed, and special thick eyeglasses can be worn instead. Since more than a million people develop cataracts each year, this operation is quite common. In fact, cataract removal is the sixth most common surgical operation in the United States (Van Heyningen, 1975).

We will discuss only two of the diseases that can occur in the retina: detached retina and blindness caused by diabetes. Look again at Figure 2-5, the view inside the human eye, to see how the retina can sometimes become detached. Notice that the retina lies just inside the choroid layer. The retina is only loosely attached to the choroid layer, and fluid from the eye can separate the two layers if there is a hole in the retina. A person who has retinal detachment may complain of a sudden loss of vision or perceive lightning flashes. The treatment involves surgically attaching the retina back in its place. The surgery is often effective if it is performed soon after the condition is noticed (Vaughan & Asbury, 1977).

You may know a diabetic person who has become blind. Diabetes has in fact become a leading cause of blindness in the Western world (Vaughan & Asbury, 1977). Blindness is more likely for people who have had diabetes for a long time and for those whose diabetes has been poorly controlled. Blindness occurs because the blood vessels that supply the retina become thicker. Fluid leaks out of the blood vessels, often causing a deposit of substances on the retina and a fluid-filled retina. As a result, the light on the retina is scattered. Sometimes, the vision can improve spontaneously, and surgery can often be helpful. Unfortunately, however, the disease usually becomes worse, leading to complete blindness.

Recall that we discussed the liquids inside the eyeball, which maintain the eye's characteristic shape. In **glaucoma** (pronounced "glaw-*koe*-mah"), however, there is too much of the fluid inside the eye, causing too much pressure. If the pressure is great enough for a long period of time, there is extensive damage to the eye. The optic nerve and the ganglion cells in the retina deteriorate, and the iris and the ciliary muscles are damaged. The lens may become cloudy, resulting in cataracts. Vaughan and Asbury estimate that about 2% of people over age 40 have glaucoma and that about 50,000 people in the United States are blind as a result of glaucoma. Because glaucoma is relatively common, a test for this disease is usually included in eye examinations for older people. Most often, the test involves measuring the eye pressure with an electronic device. If glaucoma is detected, special drugs can be prescribed to reduce the pressure. If the disease is treated in time, the outlook is usually good.

The visual pathway from the eye to the brain is also susceptible to a variety of diseases. For example, some diseases attack the coating on the optic nerve. Multiple sclerosis, a disorder of the nervous system, is one such disease. A common symptom is a blind area in some part of the visual field. Tumors near the optic chiasm can also affect vision. Physicians can often detect the exact anatomical location of a tumor because a mass in a given location will have a predictable effect on the visual fields. In other words, if the patient cannot see anything in a particular region of the visual fields, the physician can use this information to figure out the problem area in the visual pathway.

The visual cortex can be damaged in accidents or in war. For example, a bullet may enter through the back of the head, causing damage to the visual cortex. As a consequence, the person will be blind in a particular part of the visual field. This blind area is called a **scotoma** (pronounced "skuh-*toe*-muh"), and the plural is **scotomata** (pronounced "skuh-*toe*-muh-tuh"). You will recall that there is a correspondence between the pattern on the retina and the pattern on the visual cortex. Some of the information about this correspondence has been gathered from patients who have scotomata. The researcher notes the damaged area of the visual cortex and the area of the visual field containing the scotoma.

Migraine headaches affect the blood flow to the visual cortex. Therefore one common symptom of migraines is visual disturbances. In many cases the disturbance may be simple blurring of vision. Other times, people suffering from migraines report abnormal sensations such as pinwheels or lightning flashes. Some people report even more complex visual phenomena. Objects may appear to shrink or grow in size, for instance. There is an interesting suggestion for the amazing size changes that Alice experiences in *Alice in Wonderland* (Lippman, 1952; Van Dyke, 1980). Lewis Carroll, the author, suffered from migraines, and the shrinking and growing may simply reflect his own visual experiences!

Summary: Common Disorders in the Visual System

- Ophthalmology is the branch of medicine that is concerned with visual problems.
- The cornea can be damaged by a foreign body, allowing disease germs to enter.
- Iritis is an inflammation of the iris. If untreated, parts of the iris may become attached to the lens.
- Conjunctivitis, a very common disorder, is an inflammation of the conjunctiva.
- Strabismus occurs when the muscles for the two eyes do not work together. If uncorrected, this may lead to amblyopia, or suppression of the image in the weaker eye.
- Cataracts involve a clouding of the lens and are often found in elderly people. They can be partially treated by removing the lens and by using thick eyeglasses.
- Two diseases of the retina are detached retina and blindness caused by diabetes.
- In glaucoma there is too much fluid inside the eye. The extra pressure causes deterioration of the optic nerve and other damage.
- The visual pathway from the eye to the brain can be damaged by multiple sclerosis and tumors.
- The visual cortex can be damaged in accidents or in war. Migraine headaches may affect the blood flow to the visual cortex, leading to visual disturbances.

Review

1. What does the length of light waves determine? What perceptual reactions often correspond to the shortest wavelengths and the longest wavelengths? What does the amplitude of light waves determine? What perceptual reactions often correspond to the wavelengths with the greatest and the smallest amplitude?

2. We can see a wide range of colors, but there are many wavelengths that we cannot see. Discuss this statement.

3. Review the location and the function of the following terms: sclera, iris, pupil, cornea, and conjunctiva. Point out what kinds of diseases can influence the iris, the cornea, and the conjunctiva.

4. What does the lens of the eye do, and what are cataracts? As you have read, the partial remedy for cataracts involves removing the lens and substituting a pair of glasses. Why are glasses an unsatisfactory substitute for the original lenses?

5. What is the fovea, and where is it located?

How is the distribution of rods and cones relevant to a discussion of the fovea?

6. Contrast rods and cones as to each of the following characteristics: (a) lighting conditions in which the receptor functions best, (b) kind of vision, (c) number, and (d) acuity in the rod region versus the cone region.

7. Why could the crossover at the optic chiasm be referred to as an incomplete crossover? What is the purpose of this complex crossing pattern?

8. Where do the fibers in the optic tract travel to, and what is the function of these two areas?

9. Why is the arrangement of the cortex called retinotopic? Describe one area of research that contributed to our knowledge of the retinotopic organization of the cortex.

10. What three kinds of neurons did Hubel and Wiesel isolate in the visual cortex, and why was their discovery important?

New Terms

wavelength
nanometer
light
hue
amplitude
candelas per meter square (cd/m²)
sclera
iris
constrict
dilate
pupil
pigments
ophthalmologists
ophthalmoscope
cornea
conjunctiva
lens
ciliary muscles
choroid

retina
neurons
fovea
blind spot
cones
rods
bipolar cells
ganglion cells
W, X, and Y ganglion cells
horizontal cells
amacrine cells
acuity
optic nerve
optic chiasm
left visual field
right visual field
binocular vision
optic tract
superior colliculus

lateral geniculate nucleus (LGN)
visual cortex
cerebral cortex
Areas 17, 18, and 19
retinotopic
receptive field
simple cell
complex cell
hypercomplex cell
ophthalmology
foreign body
corneal abrasion
iritis
conjunctivitis
strabismus
amblyopia
cataracts
glaucoma
scotoma (scotomata)

chapter 3

BASIC VISUAL FUNCTIONS

Outline **Acuity**
  Types of Acuity
  Factors Influencing Acuity
  Applications of Acuity

 Adaptation
  Dark Adaptation
  Light Adaptation
  Applications of Adaptation

 Eye Movements
  Version Movements
  Vergence Movements

 Accommodation
  Normal Focusing
  Focusing Problems

Preview

In the four sections of this chapter we will look at four kinds of basic visual functions: (1) Acuity, (2) Adaptation, (3) Eye Movements, and (4) Accommodation.

In the first section we will examine several different ways of measuring acuity, or the ability to see fine details. Since this is such an important topic in vision, we will also explore some factors that influence acuity; some factors are characteristics of the eye, and other factors are characteristics of the stimulus. We will also note several applications of acuity.

Adaptation involves the change in sensitivity as you are exposed to darkness (dark adaptation) or light (light adaptation). During dark adaptation, sensitivity increases gradually until dark adaptation is complete after about 30 minutes. During light adaptation the eye becomes less sensitive to a light stimulus. This process is much faster and takes about one minute.

Eye movements can be divided into two basic groups, depending upon whether the eyes keep the same angle between the lines of sight during eye movement (version movements) or whether the angle changes (vergence movements). Version movements include saccadic movement (rapid movements of the eye from one fixation point to the next), pursuit movements (eye movements made in tracking a moving object), and miniature eye movements. Vergence movements are necessary so that both eyes can focus upon the same target. For example, you use vergence movements if you have been looking at an object in the distance and then move your eyes closer together to look at a nearby object, perhaps the textbook in front of you.

Accommodation involves a change in the shape of the lens, which is necessary in order to keep an image in focus on the retina. In this section we will also discuss focusing abnormalities: nearsightedness, farsightedness, and astigmatism.

In the last chapter you learned about the anatomy of the visual system; we concentrated on the physical characteristics. In this chapter you will learn about the basic visual functions; we will concentrate on what the eye can do.

It seems that we often do not appreciate these basic functions sufficiently. They are so basic that we take them for granted. However, imagine how inadequate we would be without them. Without acuity, for example, we could not read, watch movies, or look at a painting. Clearly, we would be limited without this ability to see details. Without adaptation we would be unable to function in both sunlight and moonlight. Eye movement is also essential; without it we could change our fixation points only by moving our heads. If you doubt the importance of eye movements, try walking to class without moving your eyes, or try reading the next sentence without eye movement. Finally, without accommodation we could see things clearly only if they were a certain, fixed distance from us. How would you operate if you could see clearly only those objects that are two feet away from you, for example, everything closer or farther away being a big blur?

So let's look at our visual system's basic talents: We can make discriminations in space, we can see in various lighting conditions, we can move our eyes, and we can focus.

Acuity

Visual acuity is the ability to see fine details in a scene. With good acuity we can discriminate two dots placed close to each other as being two separate objects, rather than one blurred object. Good acuity allows us to notice, for example, that a friend has chicken pox —rather than a mild sunburn—before the friend gets too close. It also permits us to read a road sign announcing the name of the next exit in enough time to move into the right-hand lane.

Acuity is concerned with discriminations made between stimuli in space. For example, an acuity task might involve judgments about whether a white area separates two black areas. We will see that there are several different methods of measuring acuity. However, all of them involve a description of the amount of space occupied by the target, called visual angle. **Visual angle** means the size of the angle formed by extending two lines from your eye to the outside edges of the target. (Consult Demonstration 3-1 as we discuss this term.)

The visual angle is measured in terms of degrees, minutes, and seconds. There are 360 degrees (symbolized °) in a circle, but since your eyes cannot see in back of your head, or even straight above your head, the visual angles we would be concerned with would always be much smaller than 360 degrees. Just as an hour of time is divided into minutes and seconds, a degree in space is divided into minutes and seconds. Each degree has 60 minutes, and each minute has 60 seconds.

As you can see, the size of the visual angle depends upon the size of the target and the

---

Demonstration 3-1

Visual Angle

Hold this book up in front of you, with your elbows bent at 90° angles; or if you have a ruler, measure 35 cm away from your eyes. Look at the 1.2-cm circle below. This circle occupies a *visual angle* of about 2°. The diagram beneath illustrates this relationship schematically.

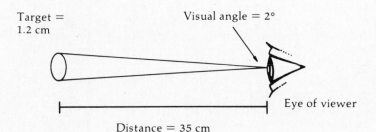

Target = 1.2 cm

Visual angle = 2°

Eye of viewer

Distance = 35 cm

distance of the target from the eye. In Demonstration 3-1, you are looking at a circle that is 1.2 cm across. Larger circles would occupy larger visual angles. The size of the visual angle also depends upon the distance of the target from the eye. As you move the circle away from you, it occupies an increasingly smaller visual angle. Draw a diagram to convince yourself that a circle that is 2.4 cm across, viewed from a distance of 70 cm, would occupy the same visual angle as a circle 1.2 cm across, viewed from a distance of 35 cm.

In this section on acuity we need to consider several issues. First of all, what kinds of acuity are there, and how are these different kinds measured? Second, what factors influence acuity? Finally, what are some of the applications of acuity?

Types of Acuity

There are four basic types of acuity tasks, illustrated in Demonstration 3-2. Recognition is the most common kind, but other measures are also used. Most acuity tasks involve determining some kind of threshold, a procedure we mentioned in Chapter 1 that is described in more detail in Chapter 15.

Recognition

Recognition, which requires observers to identify a figure, is probably one measure you know well. The Snellen eye chart, devised by Snellen in 1862, is a standard screening test in many doctors' offices. As Figure 3-1 will remind you, the eye chart has rows of letters that range in size from large to small. The task of the observer is to say the names of the letters in each row. The tester notes the row with the smallest letters that the observer can name correctly.

Acuity on the Snellen chart is often measured by comparing your performance with the performance of a normal observer. You stand 20 feet (6.1 meters) away from the chart. If you can read the letters that a person with normal sight can read at 20 feet, then you have 20/20 vision. If your acuity is poor, however, you would have to stand closer in order to read the letters. If you stood 10 feet (3.0 meters) from the chart, then you would have 10/20 vision, which is usually called 20/40 vision. (The figure is doubled, since numbers below 20 are not typically used.) That means that you could see at 20 feet what a person with normal sight could see at 40 feet. In some states, a person with 20/400 vision is declared "legally blind" (Riggs, 1971). This person would need to stand 1 foot from the

---

Demonstration 3-2

Four Kinds of Acuity Tasks

Try each of these kinds of acuity tasks. Stand across the room from your book (after reading the instructions) and see whether you can recognize, detect, resolve, and localize.

A. Recognition tasks.
   N   What letter is this?

B. Detection tasks.
   | Can you see this line?
   · Can you see this dot?

C. Resolution tasks.
   ·· Is this one dot or two?
   ▓ Is this a grating of black and white bars, or is it a uniform gray patch?

D. Localization task.
   | Is the upper line to the right or the left of the lower
   | line?

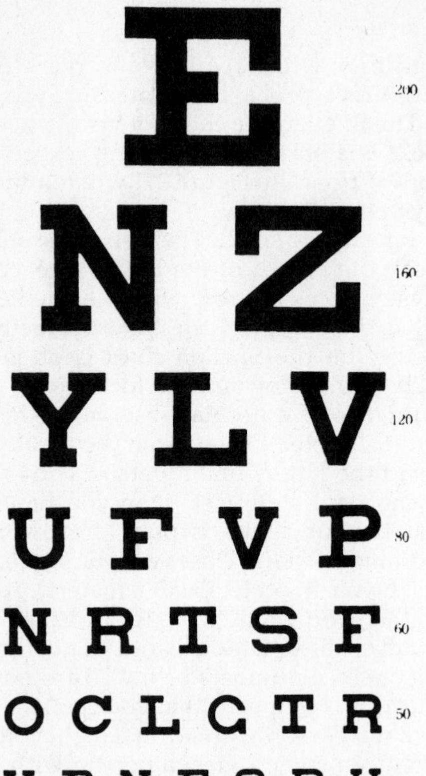

E 200

N Z 160

Y L V 120

U F V P 80

N R T S F 60

O C L C T R 50

U P N E S R H 40

T O R E C H B P 30

F N E C H B S C R 25

T V H P R U C F N C 20

P T N U E H V C B O S 15

Figure 3-1   The Snellen chart. Note that the size on this chart is reduced. On the full-sized chart, someone with 20/20 vision would be able to recognize the letters on the next-to-last line at a distance of 20 feet.

chart to read the letters that a person with normal vision could read at 20 feet.

Let's relate this method of reporting acuity to the visual angle method we used earlier. If you have 20/20 vision, you can make discriminations in letter widths that occupy one minute (1') of an arc when you are standing 20 feet from the letters. If you have 20/40 vision, you can

recognize letters that occupy two minutes (2') of an arc, at a distance of 20 feet.

The Snellen eye chart has some problems, though. Some letters, like Y and V, are easily confused with each other. Other letters, like T, are easy to recognize. In most cases there are too many different letter features that can help the observer arrive at the correct response. Consider the big E at the top of the chart, for instance. The straight horizontal line on the top tells us that the letter cannot be a C, D, G, H, and so on. The straight vertical line on the left tells us that the letter cannot be an A, C, G, J, and so on. The Snellen chart has another disadvantage that a student pointed out to me. Young children, anxious to avoid having to wear glasses, may memorize the eye chart! Because of these drawbacks the Snellen chart has often been replaced by other acuity measures. In its defense, however, the Snellen chart has practical significance. In real life we need to recognize letters at a distance, and the Snellen chart does measure letter recognition.

Other Acuity Measures

We have discussed the recognition measure of acuity in some detail, because it is the most common. However, we must also consider three other acuity tasks that assess other aspects of visual precision. **Detection** tasks require the observer to judge whether a target is present or absent. Riggs (1971) notes that observers can detect a dark line that is 1/2 second wide (0.5'' arc) when the line is shown against a light background. He speculates that observers may be so extraordinarily good at detection partly because of cortical cells that favor straight-line orientations. (Recall our discussion of orientation preferences in the visual cortex, covered in Chapter 2.)

Resolution tasks require the observer to discriminate a separation between the parts of a target. Demonstration 3-2 shows a grating pattern that is used in resolution tasks, with black and white bars of equal width. If you hold the book close to your eyes, you can see distinct black lines. However, if you prop the book up and walk across the room, this grating will probably look like a uniform gray patch. Under the best conditions, human eyes can **resolve**

(detect a separation in) a pattern in which the line widths are about 35 seconds wide (Shlaer, 1937). Notice, therefore, that this width is about 70 times as great as for the detection of a single line. Acuity for resolution is therefore much lower than acuity for detection.

Riggs (1971) adds that the grating pattern is often used to test optical performance of instruments such as cameras and telescopes. Notice why resolution is an appropriate acuity measure for a telescope, for example. Astronomers need equipment that will not only detect the presence of a distant star but will also tell them whether that spot is one star or two stars that are close together, with just a narrow dark space in between.

Localization tasks require the observer to tell whether an upper vertical line (see Demonstration 3-2) is to the right or the left of the lower line. Thus it measures relative position. Naturally, if the upper line is placed a great distance from the lower line, the task is an easy one. However, when the two lines are close together, the task is difficult. At some point, the observer will no longer be able to report reliably on the position of the upper line. Riggs (1971) notes that the size of this barely discriminable offset is about 2 seconds wide, a distance that is four times as great as for the detection of a single line.

Incidentally, in everyday life we often perform tasks that require localization. For example, to open child-proof aspirin bottles, the points of two arrows must be matched up exactly. Also, when you open up a combination lock, you must carefully line up the notch above the dial with the appropriate notch on the dial. Can you think of other examples of localization?

Factors Influencing Acuity

Since acuity is such an important topic in vision, researchers have conducted numerous experiments on factors influencing acuity. We can divide these factors into two basic categories, those dealing with characteristics of the eye and those dealing with characteristics of the stimulus.

Characteristics of the Eye

The focus of the eye is one obvious factor influencing acuity. Some people have spectacular acuity, perhaps as good as 20/10. In contrast, other people have poor acuity; remember that people with vision worse than 20/400 may be classified as legally blind. We will consider eyesight problems and their correction in the section on accommodation in this chapter.

Try Demonstration 3-3 to illustrate another important influence on acuity, which is position on the retina. We discussed this issue briefly in Chapter 2; now let's consider the details. You can see letters in Demonstration 3-3 clearly only when they are registered on the fovea. The fovea is the central 1 to 2 degrees of the eye, which is not very large. In fact, if you are holding your book about 45 cm away from you—a normal reading distance—only about eight letters of the text will fall on the fovea. Just a short distance from the center, acuity drops off rapidly. Look at Figure 3-2, which illustrates the relative acuity at various points on the retina. Notice that 10° away from the center, the relative visual acuity is only about 20% of the acuity found at the fovea. Notice the relative acuity for different parts of your eye as you look at this sentence in your book. The letters you are looking at right now are clear and sharp, but on either side the letters are quite blurry. Later in the chapter we will discuss this phenomenon in more detail in a section called "Saccadic Movement and Reading."

Think about how you may have noticed the relationship between acuity and retinal position in your past experiences. A friend may have accused you of snubbing her, but in fact, she may have been in your **peripheral vision** (that is, the image was registered on the side of the retina rather than at the fovea). To use our terms for acuity tasks, you may have detected the presence of someone but failed to recognize that person. You may have been astounded by the performance of a close-up magician because everything happening in the area registered on your fovea looked honest and legal, and you did not see the cards being exchanged in your peripheral vision. You may have had a near accident while driving because you did not

---

Demonstration 3-3

Retinal Location and Acuity

Place this book flat on your desk and move your head away until it is about 13 cm away from the book. Cover your left eye with your left hand. Look directly at the cross on the right-hand side of the figure, just above the 0° mark. Keep your eye on this fixation point. Notice that you can see the letter at 0° quite clearly, and the letter at 5° is also fairly clear. However, the letters at 10°, 20°, and 30° are fuzzy. You will probably be unable to read the letters at 50°.

D	P	N	A	B	Q	W
+	+	+	+	+	+	+
50°	40°	30°	20°	10°	5°	0°

---

notice the car to your left as you entered the left-hand lane.

Notice that Figure 3-2 includes the blind spot, which we discussed in Chapter 2. Hochberg (1978a) comments on why we are unaware of the blind spot in everyday visual activities. Usually, if we miss something with one eye, we pick it up with the other. Second, we have a tendency to spontaneously complete objects that are interrupted by the blind spot; we will

return to this issue in the chapter on shape perception. Third, and perhaps most important, the blind spot is in an area far from the fovea. If we really want to see something, we look at it with our sensitive foveas, rather than keeping the object in our peripheral vision. Our relative acuity would only be about 15% in this region even if there were no blind spot there.

Try to remember the explanation for the tremendous increase in acuity at the fovea. Look back at Figure 2-7, which shows the distribution of cones across the retina. Clearly, this figure is similar to Figure 3-2. In the fovea, where cones are abundant, acuity is excellent. In the periphery, where cones are "few and far between," acuity is very poor.

Other characteristics of the eye do not seem to have much influence on acuity. For example, the size of the pupil is not very important when we consider the normal range of pupil diameters. Riggs (1971) summarizes studies in which the size of the pupil was varied. Artificial pupils were placed in front of the eye to create pupil diameters smaller than 2 mm. Special drugs that dilate the pupil (you may have been given these drops in the ophthalmologist's office when your eyes were to be checked) were used to create extra large pupils. The results of these studies showed that acuity was not influenced by pupil diameter for the range of 2.5 to 5 mm, which is the range of diameters found in normal visual activities. Narrowing the pupil diameter to smaller than 1 mm did reduce acuity. For

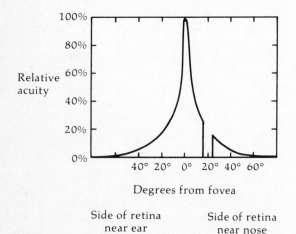

Figure 3-2 Relative visual acuity, as a function of position on the retina. Note that the acuity at the center of the fovea is set at 100%; observe how the relative acuity declines on either side of the fovea.

everyday visual activities we can conclude that pupil diameter is irrelevant.

Characteristics of the Stimulus

If you have ever struggled to read a map in the car at night, you know one stimulus characteristic that influences acuity: **luminance**, or the amount of light reflected by a surface. That map would be perfectly legible in the daytime, but you are not going to find the street you are pursuing if you have to rely on occasional light from dim street lamps. Riggs (1971) notes that in starlight (luminance of about .0003 candelas per meter square, or cd/m²) we can see the white pages of a book, but not the writing on them. In moonlight (luminance of about .03 cd/m²) we can notice that there are separate letters but cannot read the text. (In other words, if you are planning to read poetry by moonlight, bring a flashlight.) We need a luminance of about 30 cd/m² before we feel comfortable about reading, and acuity increases rapidly until it begins to level off at about 3000 cd/m². Figure 3-3 illustrates the relationship between luminance and acuity.

Notice that Figure 3-3 actually consists of two curves. With low levels of luminance, only the rods are called into action. Acuity is poor at these low levels because rods are not located in the fovea where vision is best. As you know, they are concentrated in the outer portion of the retina.

Notice the second curve now, the one that operates at higher levels of luminance. This curve represents vision with cones. In this

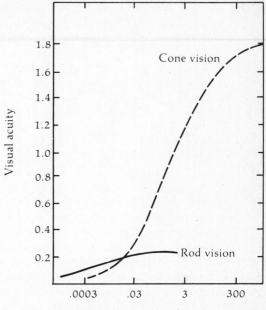

Figure 3-3   Visual acuity, as a function of luminance.

brighter region the fovea can now be used. The higher acuity in the foveal region is responsible for the dramatic improvement in acuity as the luminance increases. Now try Demonstration 3-4 to illustrate the relationship between luminance and acuity for yourself.

The orientation of the stimulus can also influence acuity. Westheimer (1972) sum-

---

Demonstration 3-4

The Relationship Between Luminance and Acuity

Try to identify five different levels of luminance that you encounter in a typical day. For example, they might be: (1) outside in the intense sunlight at noon; (2) your room in the late afternoon, with all lights turned on; (3) your room at night, with one medium light turned on; (4) your room at night with just one small light turned on, far away from you; and (5) your room at night with no lights on, but some light coming in the window. In each of these conditions, turn to the Snellen Eye Chart in Figure 3-1, prop the book up, and move about three meters away. Try to see which is the smallest print for which you can successfully identify all the letters accurately. Does your acuity decrease as the luminance decreases?

marizes some studies that show that gratings like the one in Demonstration 3-2 are seen more clearly if the lines are either horizontal or vertical. If the gratings are diagonal, acuity is lower.

Let's summarize what we have discussed about factors influencing acuity. Characteristics of the eye that influence acuity include: (1) focus of the eye (to be discussed in a later section) and (2) position on the retina, but *not* size of the pupil. Characteristics of the stimulus that influence acuity include: (1) luminance and (2) orientation of the stimulus.

Applications of Acuity

One important application of acuity is in the area of consumer psychology. Have you ever squinted at the list of ingredients and additives on a carton of cereal? Poulton (1969) took lists of ingredients from the containers of 60 different foods and reproduced these lists using different sizes of type. Figure 3-4 shows an example of the largest and the smallest prints he used. There were two levels of illumination in the experiment, corresponding to the level of brightness typically found in supermarkets and the considerably lower level of brightness typically found in home pantries. Women were instructed to look through the lists for certain key words. The women found the words about twice as fast when the large print, rather than the small print, was used. They were also faster with the bright, supermarket-style lights than with the dim, pantry-style lights. As we noted earlier, lighting is an important determinant of acuity because cones work best at high luminance levels.

The study of visual acuity has many applications, for example in the area of driving. Forbes (1972) has summarized many studies on the visibility of highway signs. A rule of thumb derived from these studies is that a person with 20/20 vision can read familiar signs with letters 10 cm high at a distance of 80 meters. For un-

familiar signs you would need to be about 67 meters away. However, most states require only 20/40 vision. A driver with 20/40 vision would therefore be only 40 meters away when those 10 cm letters are visible.

In many cases, however, time is a limiting factor in looking at a sign. Forbes notes that drivers on a highway often have time for only one short glance, lasting about one second. With such a short glance, a driver would need to be 10 to 15% closer in order to read the sign. A driver with 20/20 vision, for example, might need to be 70 meters—rather than 80—from a sign with 10-cm letters in order to read it. Also, only three to four familiar words can be recognized with a short glance. If you have ever been driving and glanced up at a sign that said something like "Kensington Expressway, left lane; Scajaquada Expressway, right lane," you have realized the limits of acuity under time pressure!

On the New York State Thruway, most of the road signs are white letters on a green background—something I had not given much thought to until I began to write this chapter. Forbes cites data to demonstrate that with white letters on a green background, you can read a sign at a distance about 30% farther away than with black letters on a white background. Thus we have seen in this section that highway designers need to consider the acuity of drivers, time limitations, word familiarity, and color contrast when they are making decisions about highway signs.

Summary: Acuity

- Visual acuity is the precision with which we can see fine details; it is the ability to discriminate objects in space.
- A recognition acuity task asks observers to identify a target; an example is the Snellen chart.
- A detection task asks observers to judge whether a target is present or absent.
- A resolution task asks observers whether there is a separation between parts of a target.
- A localization task asks observers to judge the relative position of two lines, for exam-

pyridoxine hydrochloride

pyridoxine hydrochloride

Figure 3-4   The print sizes used by Poulton.

ple, whether an upper line is to the right or the left of a lower line.
- Characteristics of the eye that influence acuity are focus and position on the retina. Pupil size does not have much influence on acuity.
- Characteristics of the stimulus that influence acuity are lighting and the orientation of the stimulus.
- Acuity has applications in the size of printing on packages and on road signs.

Adaptation

You have probably had an experience like this: You go to a movie theater in the middle of the afternoon. Outside, the sun is shining. You walk inside, and you seem to be temporarily blind, particularly if the movie has already started. You try to locate an empty seat, groping at what you hope are the backs of chairs rather than people's arms. Eventually, you might sit down on someone's hat or, even worse, on *someone.* (My grandfather, thinking fast when a woman sat on his lap in a dark theater, identified her nationality as "Laplander.") You have not yet dark adapted.

Now the movie is over, and you emerge from the dark theater into the intense sunlight. The strain on your eyes is painful, and you squint or cover your eyes. You may bump into someone by mistake or wander close to an oncoming car. You have not yet light adapted.

These processes of dark adaptation and light adaptation are also relevant at night. You turn off the light and stumble off to bed. As you lie there, forms that you didn't notice before become slowly visible (dark adaptation). If you get up in the middle of the night and turn on the light to find something, you have to wait a few seconds before you can make out any shapes whatsoever (light adaptation). Try noticing other examples of dark adaptation and light adaptation during the next few weeks.

Adaptation is the adjustment of the eye to a particular light intensity. **Dark adaptation** is the increase in sensitivity that occurs as the eyes stay in the dark and changes take place in our receptors. On the other hand, **light adaptation** is the change in sensitivity that occurs as the eyes are suddenly exposed to light and changes take place in our receptors. (Notice that you can remember which adaptation is which by observing whether the present lighting conditions

are dark or light.) Let's look at the processes of dark adaptation and light adaptation in more detail.

Dark Adaptation

Many laboratory studies have been performed on dark adaptation. Typically, studies on dark adaptation represent the performance of a single subject. Thus the curve shown in Figure 3-5 illustrates how one person's right eye adapted to light. In these studies, the subject is first exposed to an intense light for several minutes. Then the light is turned off, and the threshold for a small spot of light is measured. That is, the experimenter shows a low-intensity light and slowly makes it increasingly more intense. The experimenter records the intensity at which the subject reports seeing the light. We call this point the subject's threshold. The experimenter repeats the procedure, each time allowing a different amount of time in the dark before measuring the threshold. Try Demonstration 3-5 to illustrate dark adaptation for yourself.

In Figure 3-5, look at the portion of the curve a few minutes after the light has been turned off. The light must be relatively intense in order for it to be detected. After about 30 minutes, however, dark adaptation is nearly complete, and the sensitivity is high. In other words, the threshold is low (that is, a low-intensity light can be detected). In fact, the eye is now about 100,000 times as sensitive as it was in the light. A **dark adaptation curve**, such as the one in Figure 3-5, shows the relationship between time in the dark and the **threshold**, or the intensity of light that can barely be detected.

Notice the kink in the curve that occurs after

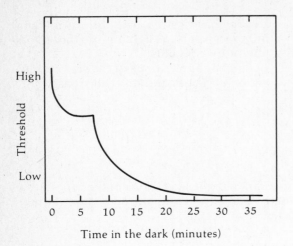

Figure 3-5   Dark adaptation, as a function of time in the dark. Note that a lower threshold means that the eye is *more* sensitive.

about five or ten minutes in the dark. This kink occurs consistently with many different observers who are being tested in many different conditions—it is not just an accident. Curves like this make researchers suspicious that two factors, rather than just one, must be involved in the dark adaptation process. In fact, one part of the curve represents the activity of cones, and the other part represents the activity of rods.

Figure 3-5 was obtained by shining the light on an area of the retina that contained both cones and rods. What would happen if only cones or only rods were involved? If we could shine the light only on the fovea, where there are cones but no rods, we might find a dark adaptation curve like that in Figure 3-6a. Notice that there is a quick drop in the threshold during the first few minutes. However, the sensitivity levels off at this point, and the threshold remains relatively high.

On the other hand, notice what would happen if we could shine the light only on the periphery, where there are many rods but few cones. The dark adaptation curve for rods, as in Figure 3-6b, is quite different in shape. The threshold is immeasurably high for five to ten minutes. Then the threshold decreases suddenly and later levels out. Dark adaptation is essentially complete after 30 minutes, although

some slight decrease in threshold may be noticed as much as several hours later.

In short, the threshold stays quite high for the first few minutes of dark adaptation; only cones are active then. After several minutes, however, the threshold drops abruptly and then levels out; only rods are active then. Remember that rods are used in noncolored or **achromatic** vision, rather than color vision. You may have heard the saying, "In the night, all cats are gray." A marmalade-colored cat indeed looks orange in daylight, when cones can be used. At night, after dark adaptation has taken place and the rods are functional, that cat can only look gray.

Why does the eye become more sensitive to light, as time passes in darkness during dark adaptation? The complete answer to this question is not known. Let's consider several factors. First of all, as you move from an intense light into darkness, your pupil dilates, or widens. When the pupil of the human eye is fully dilated, it lets in about 16 to 17 times as much light as when the pupil is small. The human eye can increase its sensitivity somewhat, then, by letting in more light. (For comparison's sake, you should notice the much more dramatic pupil size changes in a cat. In intense light the cat's pupils are tiny slits; at night the cat's pupils are huge.) Pupil size changes can increase the eye's sensitivity to light in a limited way. However, the dark-adapted eye is about 30,000 times more sensitive than the light-adapted eye. Pupil dilation is thus only a very small part of the story.

A second factor that permits the eyes to be more sensitive in the dark is that dark-adapted eyes have a higher concentration of rhodopsin. **Rhodopsin** (pronounced "rode-*dop*-sin") is a chemical used in vision that is found in the tips of the rods. Rhodopsin is extremely sensitive to light. When light reaches the rods, it changes the rhodopsin into other chemicals. Thus intense lights reduce the supply of rhodopsin. When the lights are turned off, the level of rhodopsin rises again. The greater levels of rhodopsin available to eyes in darkness is another part of the story, but this explanation still is insufficient. For example, threshold changes are found less than one second after a light has been turned off, and the level of

Demonstration 3-5

Dark Adaptation

Find a flashlight that is opaque on all sides except where the beam of light shines through. Take about 15 index cards and the flashlight, and go into a very dark room where you can stay for 15 to 20 minutes. Place all of the index cards over the beam of light. Remove the cards one at a time until you can barely see the light. Calculate the number of cards remaining on the flashlight. After a few minutes the light will look brighter to you. Add a card and see whether you can still see the light. If not, wait another minute and try again. Keep repeating the process for 15 more minutes. Notice that as time in the dark increases, you can detect an increasingly dim light.

rhodopsin could not change quickly enough to be responsible for the change in threshold (Riggs, 1971).

It is the third—and perhaps most important—factor that is the least understood. Researchers believe that neural processes at a higher level than the receptor cells must have a role in dark adaptation. Dark adaptation is too spectacular a phenomenon to be accounted for by mere pupil dilation and changes in rhodopsin level. However, the details of these neural activities have not yet been established.

Light Adaptation

In dark adaptation, as we have seen, eyes become more sensitive as they remain in the dark. In light adaptation, however, eyes become less sensitive as they are exposed to light. The surrounding illumination is intense, and we do not need to be sensitive to dim lights.

In a light adaptation study, the observer is first completely dark-adapted. Then the experimenter turns on the lights. A typical illumination might be the illumination found in a well-

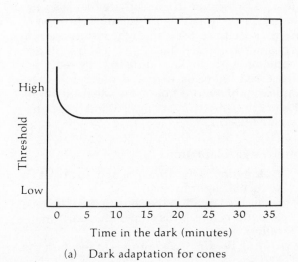

(a)   Dark adaptation for cones

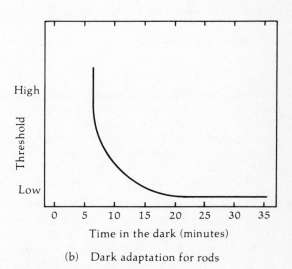

(b)   Dark adaptation for rods

Figure 3-6   Dark adaptation for (a) an area in the fovea having only cones and (b) an area in the periphery having only rods.

lit room. Now the experimenter measures the threshold for a small spot of light. As in dark adaptation, a very low-intensity light is presented at first, and the intensity is increased until the subject reports seeing the light. The whole procedure is repeated many times in order to determine thresholds with different lengths of exposure to light.

During light adaptation the pupils quickly become smaller. As a result, less light enters the eyes. Shortly after the light is presented, the rods stop functioning. After all, the light changes the rhodopsin, so the critical chemical for rod vision cannot be used. Instead, the cones start to function. The chemical used in cone vision is changed by the light at first, but then more of this chemical is manufactured.

We said that light adaptation makes us less sensitive to light. However, at the levels of illumination that we use during the daytime, we do not need to be very light sensitive. Instead, it is more important to have acuity, and the cones that are active in light-adapted eyes allow us to have impressive acuity.

Studies typically show that light adaptation is almost complete after about one minute. Thus light adaptation is a faster process than dark adaptation, which takes about 30 minutes. This observation probably fits with your experiences. You light adapt after coming from a dark theater into the intense sunlight faster than you dark adapt after coming from sunlight into the dark.

Applications of Adaptation

An understanding of dark adaptation and light adaptation has probably alerted you to some applications in your day-to-day life. Also, think how these applications might be extended to animals as well as humans. For example, a student of mine wrote that she learned about adaptation in horses when taking horseback riding lessons:

> One does not enter a dark, heavily wooded area at a gallop when leaving a bright sunshiny field. The horse loses its sense of orientation for a minute or so. . . . Clearly one application of this is that if one is riding in the company of 50 or so other riders and

their horses, one should not enter the woods at fast speed nor should one ride too close to other horses—proper spacing may help prevent accidents [Gray, 1979].

In the section on acuity we discussed the visibility of highway signs. Naturally, at night a well-lit sign would be seen better than an unlit or poorly lit sign. However, now that you know about dark adaptation, consider the disadvantages of a sign that is too intensely lit. If you are driving at night and your eyes are fairly well dark-adapted, the intense light from a sign would require you to begin dark adaptation all over again (Forbes, 1972). Your sensitivity to other stimuli would be lowered.

In connection with night driving, you can probably guess why drivers are urged to use their dim lights, rather than their bright lights, when another car approaches. Drivers also find that they can retain their dark adaptation better by looking over to the right-hand side of their lane, avoiding looking into the headlights of the oncoming car.

Dark adaptation also has applications to certain professions. Soldiers who must be on patrol at night may occasionally need to consult a map. If they turn on a flashlight, even for a few seconds, they will lose a large portion of their dark adaptation and must wait about 20 to 30 minutes to recover the sensitivity that is so essential for night patrol. Fortunately, however, the rods that are used in night vision are not very sensitive to red light. As a result, military people on night lookout duty may be required to use red lights or wear red goggles if they require light before going on watch at night (Riggs, 1971). Astronomers also find these precautions useful.

Summary: Adaptation

- Adaptation is the adjustment of the eye to a particular light intensity.
- In dark adaptation the sensitivity of the eye to light increases, as shown in a dark adaptation curve.
- During the first five minutes in the dark the sensitivity of the cones increases, but then their sensitivity remains constant.
- The rods are insensitive to light for the first

ten minutes in the dark. Then their sensitivity increases and levels off about 30 minutes after the lights have been turned out.
- Dark adaptation is caused by pupil dilation, the higher concentration of rhodopsin in dark-adapted eyes, and neural processes.
- In light adaptation the eyes become less sensitive to light.

- Light adaptation is complete after about one minute.
- During light adaptation the pupils become smaller, the light bleaches the rhodopsin, and the cones start functioning.
- Adaptation has implications and applications in the management of animals, in driving, and in night patrol work.

Eye Movements

Think about the number of different reasons you may have for moving your eyes. You watch a kite as it trembles and jerks on its way to a crash landing. You trace the smooth course of a robin as it approaches its nest. You move your eyes in small jumps along the page as you read this paragraph. You move your eyes inward to focus upon a fly landing on your nose.

To appreciate eye movements more thoroughly, imagine how your life would be limited if your eyes were "glued" in a stable position in your head. Imagine that you could change the direction of your gaze only by moving your entire head. This kind of system would be extremely awkward, inefficient, and time-consuming in a task such as reading. Fortunately, however, our eyes are attached to muscles that can move our eyes independent of head movement.

Some animals cannot move their eyes. Humans and other mammals, however, have a distinct advantage. They can move their two eyes together to look in the same direction. This kind of **binocular vision** (that is, vision in which the two eyes are used at the same time) is used by all mammals. However, humans generally make more use of eye movements than other mammals.

The human perceptual system is very reliant on eye movement. Cumming (1978) points out that this reliance on eye movement has both benefits and costs. The benefits include being able to watch an object that is moving and being able to move the eye so that the most sensitive part of the eye can fixate on an object. On the other hand, there are costs that are associated with eye movement. After all, when you move your eyes, there are sudden, drastic changes in

the retinal image. However, you have stability in your vision; you do *not* see a jumpy sequence of pictures with blurs in between. Our visual system has to build in special features in order to keep our perceptual world looking stable. Thus we benefit from being able to move our eyes, but the "cost" of this ability is a more complex visual system.

Eye movements can be classified into two basic groups, according to whether the angle between the lines of sight for the two eyes remains constant or changes as the eyes move. Before we discuss the classifications, take a moment to appreciate this distinction. First, look up at a boundary between a distant wall and a ceiling. Let your eyes trace along this line, and notice how your eyes move as a pair in the same direction. If you were to draw a line from each eye to the spot upon which it was focusing, the angle between the two lines would remain the same as you moved your eyes. **Version movement** is the term used for eye movement in which the angle between the lines of sight remains constant and the eyes move in the same direction.

In contrast, gaze at some distant spot and then turn your eyes inward to look at the tip of your nose. The angle between the lines of sight changes drastically as you perform this eye movement. There is a narrow angle when looking at the distant spot and a wide angle when looking at your nose. **Vergence movement** is the term used for eye movement in which the angle between the lines of sight changes, and the eyes move toward each other or away from each other. You can remember which term is which because *vergence* sounds more like *changes*.

Version Movements

There are several different kinds of version movements, which depend upon the nature of the task that must be performed. We will consider three important kinds of version movements, saccades, pursuit, and miniature eye movements. A mnemonic for these three kinds of version movements can be: "According to my *version* of the story, *S*am *P*unched *M*ike."

Saccadic Movements

As your eyes glance over this sentence, become aware of the way they are moving. Do they move smoothly and uniformly across the page, or do they make a series of "jumps"? Actually, the series of jumps accurately describes eye movement in reading. **Saccadic movement** (pronounced "suh-*kaad*-dick") is the term used to refer to these very rapid movements of the eye from one fixation point to the next. These movements are necessary to bring the fovea of the eye (the area with the highest acuity) into position over the letters or words that you want to look at (E. J. Gibson & Levin, 1975). During the **saccade** (pronounced "suh-*kaad*") the eye moves from one location to the next. During the **fixation pause**—the pause between saccades—you read the letters or words.

Characteristics of Saccadic Movements. Let's look at some important characteristics of saccadic movement. First of all, it occurs frequently. In fact, Bahill and Stark (1979) suggest that saccades are the most frequent kind of eye movement. Cumming (1978) notes that we make several billion saccadic movements in our lifetimes. Second, saccades are rapid. They are faster, for example, than the relatively leisurely eye movements used in pursuing the flight of a bird or in the vergence movement that we will discuss shortly. Third, saccades are jerky, rather than smooth; your eyes jump in a saccade, though they glide in pursuit.

Thus saccades are frequent, rapid, and jerky; these are characteristics that seem obvious. A fourth characteristic is not as obvious: Saccadic movement is ballistic. **Ballistic movements** are movements that have predetermined destinations. The path of a rocket, for example, is partially ballistic because the direction and the distance of its flight have been determined before the flight begins. Similarly, when the eyes take off on a saccadic jump, the brain has already programmed which direction they will move in and how far they will go. The eyes will reach their destination, even if some new information is added between the time of the programming and the time of the jump.

This programming of the ballistic movement has been described by Ditchburn (1973). Several studies have been conducted in which observers are asked to look at a target, which is moved abruptly to a new location and then moved just as abruptly back to the original location. Now a fixation pause lasts 200 milliseconds (1/5 second). What happens if the target is moved and returned in less than 200 milliseconds, say 150 milliseconds?

Notice that it would be most efficient if the eye could remain in the same position, because the target returns before the saccadic movement to the next location begins. Nonetheless, the eye has already been programmed to move, and so it must obey the command, even though this command is no longer relevant. In a way, it is like the foolish, wasted arm movements we make in trying to swat a speedy mosquito. We see the mosquito land, we aim (that is, we program the ballistic movement of our hand), and we swat—even if the mosquito has departed 1/10 of a second before the hand arrives.

The fifth characteristic of saccadic eye movements is that vision is suppressed before and during a saccade (Bahill & Stark, 1979). You can demonstrate this suppression by switching your gaze back and forth between two objects, perhaps two words on the opposite sides of your textbook. The image on your retina clearly moves, yet the book is not seen in swirling motion. It is not known just how much suppression occurs during saccadic movement. We are not completely blind while the eye is jumping. However, sensitivity is reduced enough that the blur of images across the retina does not bother or distract us (Volkmann, Schick, & Riggs, 1968).

There are probably two mechanisms for suppressing vision during the saccade: (1) the brain itself suppresses vision during movement, and (2) the extremely high speed of saccades means that the retinal excitation at any given moment on a particular point on the retina is very weak—it simply takes time to see (Alpern, 1971). As you read the next few sentences, try to become aware that as your eye jumps forward to a new fixation point, the words you pass do not swim by. In fact, you probably cannot notice any blur during saccadic movement.

To review, saccadic eye movements are frequent, rapid, jerky, and ballistic; vision is suppressed during these movements. These five characteristics, beginning with the letters F R J B S, can be remembered by the sentence *"Fred Rolls Jelly Beans Slowly."*

Saccadic Movement and Reading. How do good readers differ from poor readers? Figure 3-7 illustrates how the eye movements of two readers might differ. Notice how the good reader makes larger jumps, typically involving several words. Poor readers have another disadvantage, because they make more regression movements. **Regression movements**, as the name implies, are the eye's backward movements to parts of the text that have already been read. For example, after you read the end of the last sentence, you may have returned to the beginning of the sentence to read the phrase "regression movements" once again. Now that you are aware of these eye movements, notice your own reading pattern. You might notice, for instance, that you make more regression movements when you are reading a textbook than when you are reading the Sunday comics.

In addition to shorter jumps and more regression movements, the poor reader also spends longer on each fixation pause. A good reader might pause for 1/5 second on a fixation pause, whereas a poor reader might pause for as long as 1/2 second.

Lefton (1978) examined the eye movement patterns of fifth grade children with reading disabilities. In this study, reading disabled children were defined as those with normal intelligence and no sensory defects, whose reading scores were at least 1 1/2 grade levels below average. The children were instructed to match a particular letter sequence with one of four alternatives. They were allowed to take as long as they wished on each trial. Try Demonstration 3-6, which is a modification of Lefton's study. The results showed that the reading disabled children required a large number of fixations to perform the task. In fact, they even required more fixations than normal *third* graders.

We have seen that poor readers differ from normal readers in their eye movement patterns. It is important to note, however, that abnormal eye movement patterns are probably the *result* rather than the *cause* of poor reading. Poor readers are not very systematic, and they are impulsive. Also, they may have difficulty understanding the material. As a result, their eye movement patterns are abnormal. If we tried to cure poor readers by encouraging different eye movements, we probably would not improve their reading substantially. As Lefton argues, it

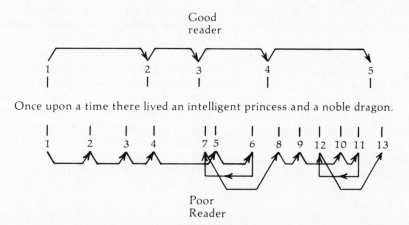

Figure 3-7 Fixation pauses for a good reader and a poor reader.

Demonstration 3 - 6

Assessing Eye Movement Patterns

For each of the three items below, match the first sequence of letters with one of the four sequences that follows. As you perform this task, notice the number of fixations you make.

1.	EFLTH	LFTEH	EFTLH	EFLTH	EFLHT
2.	OCSQG	OCSGQ	OSCQG	OCSGQ	OCSQG
3.	PBRTD	PRBDT	PBRTD	PBTRD	PBRDT

would be wiser to try to improve reading by training poor readers to gather information systematically and to control their impulses.

E. J. Gibson and Levin (1975) summarize some of the techniques for measuring eye movements during reading. Early methods included a system of mirrors arranged so that the experimenter could see the reader's eyes and count the number of saccades.

Rayner and McConkie (1977) describe a new method for studying eye movement in reading. This method involves tracking readers' eyes by computer and changing the text display as the readers progress through the text. Let's look at this procedure in more detail. A piece of equipment called an **Eye Movement Monitor** detects eye position by measuring how much light is reflected from certain parts of the eye's surface. The Eye Movement Monitor is attached to a computer that is programmed to check the position of the eye 60 times per second. The computer analyzes the information on the position of the eye and can produce a particular image on the screen, depending upon the results of the computer's analysis. Thus researchers can control what readers see in a way that was not previously possible.

Using this new method, Rayner and McConkie learned something about the **perceptual span**, the region seen during the fixation pause. Specifically, the perceptual span is slightly lopsided for English-speaking readers. We can identify letters further to the right than to the left.

College students are often intrigued by the idea of speed-reading—wouldn't it be wonderful to read a chapter for your history of psychology class in 20 minutes and have perfect recall? Speed-readers claim speeds of 500 words per minute, in contrast to the normal rate of 200.

Rayner (1978) examined eye movements in speed-reading, and his results may discourage you. He points out that the studies done in this area often record eye movements during speed-reading but seldom test comprehension adequately.

Rayner summarizes the results of several studies that tested comprehension. Some of these studies demonstrated that speed-readers can move their eyes down the middle of the page, skipping several lines during each saccade. However, recall of the material was confused and incorrect. In another study, some graduates of a speed-reading course were able to move their eyes down the center of the page, as the course had encouraged them to do, but these people scored less than 50% correct on a true-false test! To discourage you even further from enrolling in a speed-reading course, consider Rayner's observation that most speed-readers slow down to a normal reading speed when they have been told that a comprehension test will be given.

Saccadic Movement and Driving. Saccadic eye movements are extremely important in driving. Imagine how hazardous it would be to drive if your eyes were in a fixed position, looking straight ahead. As we saw in the section on acuity, vision outside of the foveal area of the retina is quite poor. Blurry peripheral vision would make driving unsafe. Fortunately, saccadic eye movements allow us to fixate our foveas on objects we must see, such as a child about to dash into the street, a brick on the side of the road, or a car passing us on the left. Rockwell (1972) wrote in a book on highway traffic safety:

Research indicates that extra-foveal vision plays a large part in driving. Indeed it may well be said that driving is largely a dynamic peripheral vision task . . . visual acuity may be less important in driving than the detection of movement by peripheral visual processes [pp. 154–155].

Thus if you detect something "suspicious" in your peripheral vision, a saccadic movement immediately moves the fovea to that object. As you might imagine, a beginning driver must learn how to make the best use of saccadic movements. Rockwell notes that beginning drivers use a frantic searching pattern with their eye movements, focusing upon irrelevant cues such as lamp poles and guardrails. They spend most of their time looking to see if they are in the correct lane. In contrast, experienced drivers use their *peripheral* vision to determine that they are in the correct lane, and so almost all of their foveal attention is concentrated on directional cues in the distance.

Belt (1969) has found that alcohol changes eye movement patterns for drivers. With blood alcohol levels of 0.08% (equivalent to three 1-oz. drinks for a 120-pound person or five 1-oz. drinks for a 200-pound person), drivers almost doubled the amount of time they spent looking straight ahead of them. For example, one driver with this level of alcohol made *no* fixations on passing cars. It may be that drivers try to restore some kind of control to the chaos they are experiencing when they are drunk. They restore control, perhaps, by narrowing the area of the world they will look at, looking only straight ahead rather than to the sides. Since attention to objects in the peripheral vision is so essential to safe driving, this loss of eye movements to peripheral areas is certainly one cause of increased accidents for drunken drivers.

We have been discussing how important eye movement is in driving; here is some further proof. Burg (1971) wanted to determine what factors were most closely related to the number of traffic accidents and traffic citations for automobile drivers. He obtained information on about 18,000 California drivers and compared it with their driving records. As you can imagine, factors like age, sex, and mileage driven were closely related to accidents and citations.

However, we are primarily interested in the visual factors related to driving. The visual test that was most closely related to the number of traffic accidents and traffic citations was one called **dynamic visual acuity.** (In this term, "dynamic" means "in motion.") This test measured the ability to perceive details of an object when there was relative motion between the observer and the object. It was tested with a special slide projector that rotated a picture from side to side.

Static visual acuity, or the ability of the observer to perceive details of an object that is standing still, was weakly related to driving records, but not nearly as strongly as was dynamic visual acuity. Chances are good that you were tested for your driver's license on one of the recognition acuity tests we discussed in the first section of the chapter. This test measured your static visual acuity. However, your Department of Motor Vehicles would have been wiser to measure your dynamic visual acuity, because that measure is a better predictor of traffic safety.

Finally, you may wonder what happens to your eye movements when you increase your driving speeds. Surprisingly, McDowell and Rockwell (1978) found that the fixation pauses became *longer* at higher speeds. The authors believe that the explanation for this finding is that when we travel at higher speeds, we must make finer discriminations. These finer discriminations demand more time than the easy discriminations.

Pursuit Movements

You watch a bird fly through the sky, a baseball being hit out of the ball park, a child riding by on a bicycle. In these cases you are using **pursuit movements**, the kind of eye movements required to track something moving against a stationary background. These movements are necessary in order to keep a stable picture of the moving objects on the retina. After all, it is much easier to identify an object if you can keep the picture of it in the same location on the retina than if the picture of the object moves across the retina.

Pursuit movements have several important characteristics. First of all, they are relatively slow. Second, they are quite smooth, rather than jerky. Third, they attempt to match the speed of a target. Roll a pencil across your desk and notice these three characteristics as you visually pursue the target.

During some kinds of eye movements your acuity is reduced. Keep your eyes in a fixed position, for example, and move your head quite rapidly. Notice how you see a big blur in front of you. Is there loss of acuity during pursuit movements? As you track the bird, does the background become a blur? The answer to this question depends upon the intensity of the background. Mackworth and Kaplan (1962) found that when a stationary background pattern was very intense, subjects could see the background quite clearly. However, with a dim background pattern, acuity was reduced. The acuity reduction was particularly great with high target speeds. Thus if you are bird-watching on a bright day, you can see the background trees as you track a bird in flight. However, in evening bird-watching, your acuity would be reduced for those background trees as your eyes skim by them. This loss of acuity would be especially noticeable if you were tracking a fast-moving bird.

Miniature Eye Movements

Miniature eye movements are the unavoidable small movements that our eyes make when we try to hold them still in order to fixate on something. We cannot consciously control these movements; they occur spontaneously. Try as hard as you can to look at the period at the end of this sentence. Notice how difficult this is! Sometimes your eye makes slow, miniature drifts away from the target. After it has drifted about 10 to 20 cones in distance, the muscles give a tiny jerk to bring it back. The pattern of this alternation is a little like the pattern you might use if you were fishing in a slow-moving stream; you let the line drift slowly, gently down the stream and then swiftly jerk it back to the target.

Your eye also makes miniature trembling motions, which you may have noticed as you were trying to keep your eye on the period. This movement is small in distance—perhaps equivalent to 1 to 2 cones—but it is continuous. It seems that our eye "equipment" does not maintain the eye in an exact position for a long period of time.

Figure 3-8 illustrates these tiny eye movements. Notice that the direction, curvature, and length of these movements are random.

Fine eye movements, strange as it may seem, serve to improve vision rather than to reduce it. Procedures have been developed that stabilize the image that is projected onto the retina; these procedures are called **stabilized retinal image techniques**. One method that sounds particularly uncomfortable involves placing a contact lens on the cornea. This lens supports a small column, to which is attached a tiny projector. The projector presents a particular image back to the retina. If the eye moves, the contact lens and the projector move as well. Thus the projector continues to present the same stabilized image to the retina. This system effectively eliminates the variety of images that would be seen with normal eye movements.

What happens once the image has been stabilized? Gradually, the borders of the target fade, and the entire object disappears! There is a temporary blindness (Alpern, 1971). Apparently, the retina requires a modest variety in its input in order for shape perception to be maintained. (In the chapter on shape perception we will consider this issue again.)

Vergence Movements

So far, we have been considering *version movements*, the four different kinds of eye movements that keep the same angle between the lines of sight during eye movement. In contrast, recall that *vergence movement* involves eye movement in which the angle between the lines of sight changes.

More specifically, the eyes **converge**, or move together, in order to look at nearby objects. The eyes **diverge**, or move apart, in order to look at distant objects. (**Convergence** and **divergence** are the nouns corresponding to those verbs; they refer to the act of moving together or moving apart. Notice that you can remember the general term **vergence** because it is a part of those two words.)

The purpose of vergence movements is to allow both eyes to focus upon the same target. Try Demonstration 3-7 in order to show how you would have double vision if you avoid vergence movements.

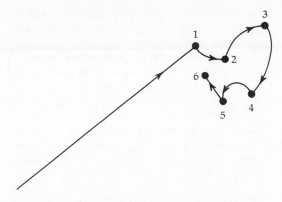

Figure 3-8 An example of miniature eye movements. The numbered dots show the order of eye movement. The time interval between dots is about 1/5 second. The distance traveled between dots 1 and 2 is about 4 cones.

fields, so it is not necessary for the eyes to work together.

Vergence movements take longer than many other eye movements, lasting about one second. They take about the same amount of time as pursuit movements. Demonstrate the speed of vergence movements to yourself by changing your fixation point from a nearby object to a distant object.

In Chapter 6 we will talk about vergence movements in connection with distance perception. As it turns out, we may use degree of convergence as one cue to how far away an object is. If our eyes have moved apart from each other, we know we are looking at a distant object. If our eyes have moved together, we know we are looking at something close.

Alpern (1971) points out that in higher primates, such as humans, the eyes are located at the front of the head. As a result, the visual fields of the two eyes overlap—the eyes share most of the same territory. We have binocular vision. As we saw in Demonstration 3-7, when both eyes can look at the same object, vergence movements are a necessity. In lower animals, however, the eyes are frequently on the sides of the head. Think about a goldfish, for example, a relatively flat fish with one eye on each side. These two eyes have very different visual

Summary: Eye Movements

- Version movements of the eyes occur when the angle between the lines of sight remains constant; they include saccadic movements, pursuit movements, and miniature eye movements.
- Saccadic movements are the rapid movements of the eye from one fixation point to the next. They are frequent, rapid, jerky, and ballistic. Vision is suppressed before and during a saccade.

Demonstration 3-7

Convergence

Hold your left finger as far as possible away from your body, and fixate both your right and your left eye upon the finger. Now slowly bring the finger in toward your left eye, but do not use convergence. That is, keep fixating upon your finger with your left eye, but keep your right eye in the same position it held when you first began fixating. (In other words, it will be looking generally straight ahead and should resist the temptation to turn inward.) As you move your finger inward, stop about 10 cm from your left eye. Notice that you will have double vision. Each eye will receive a different picture of your finger. Incidentally, you may find it extremely difficult to *avoid* convergence! We make vergence movements so automatically that it is difficult to work without them.

- Poor readers differ from good readers in eye fixation patterns. However, abnormal fixation patterns seem to be a result, not a cause, of reading problems.
- The perceptual span, the region seen during the fixation pause in reading, is lopsided; it extends further on the right than on the left.
- During driving, saccadic movements are used to scan details in the periphery. People who have good dynamic visual acuity are less likely to have traffic accidents and traffic citations.

- Pursuit movements are used to track a moving target; these movements are slow and smooth.
- Miniature eye movements are very fine eye movements that we make when we fixate upon something. Without these movements the borders of figures would slowly fade.
- Vergence movements occur when the angle between the lines of sight changes. The eyes converge to look at nearby objects and diverge to look at distant objects.

Accommodation

Accommodation is a change in the shape of the lens that is necessary to keep an image in proper focus on the retina. Suppose that the lens of the eye were rigid and could not change its shape. Suppose also that the lens were designed so that objects at a distance could be seen clearly. A problem would arise if you wanted to look at a nearby object. The light rays from that object would be focused on a point *behind* the retina, rather than on the retina itself. The image of the object would be blurred. Fortunately, however, the lens is flexible, and its shape changes so that the light rays change their angle as they pass through the lens. As a result, the light rays end up on the retina, and the image of the object is sharp.

Normal Focusing

Imagine that you are looking at a white circle on a dark background. If that circle is far away, the light rays going from the circle to the eye are parallel to each other—that is, they are the same distance apart. However, if the circle is close, the light rays are not parallel; instead, they diverge as they approach the eye. (The physics explanation underlying this phenomenon is beyond the scope of this book.)

Look at Figure 3-9. Let's first consider two situations in which the circle is far away and the light rays are parallel to each other. If the light rays enter a thick lens, the thick lens bends them too much, and they would gather to-

gether in focus at a point in front of the retina. If the light rays enter a thin lens, however, they are bent just the right amount so that they gather together in focus right at the retina.

Now consider two situations in which the circle is near, and the light rays are not parallel. If the light rays enter a thick lens, the thick lens bends them substantially, enough so that they gather together in focus at the retina. If the light rays enter a thin lens, however, the thin lens does not bend them enough, and they gather together in focus at a point behind the retina. Now try Demonstration 3-8, which illustrates accommodation.

Accommodation is performed by the **ciliary muscle**, a tiny muscle attached to the lens, which you were introduced to in Chapter 2. When this muscle contracts, the lens becomes thicker, and you can see things that are nearby. When this muscle relaxes, the lens becomes thinner, and you can see things that are far away.

Notice that accommodation involves a muscle that is inside the eye. All of the eye movements we talked about in the previous section involved muscles outside of the eye.

Accommodation takes about .40 second. In the section on vergence we noted that convergence or divergence took approximately one second. Thus the focusing performed by the muscles inside the eye is faster than the vergence performed by the muscles outside the eye, even though both operations are used in shifting fixation from far objects to near ones.

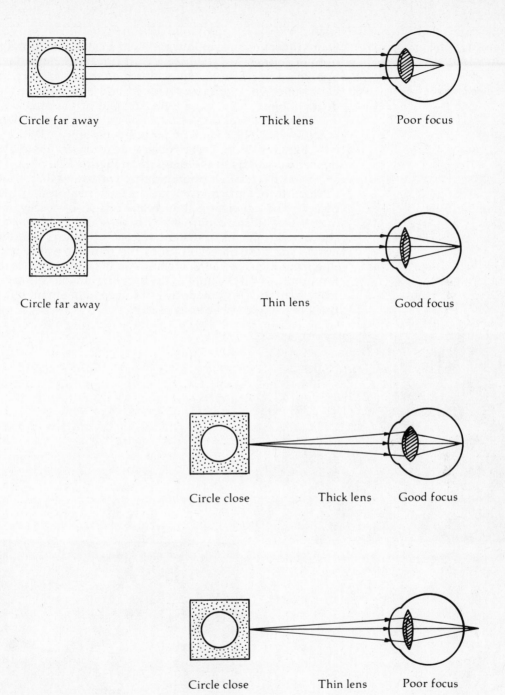

Figure 3-9 Focused and unfocused images. If a circle is far away, a thick lens brings the light rays into focus in front of the retina; a thin lens focuses them on the retina. If a circle is close, a thick lens brings the light rays into focus on the retina; a thin lens focuses them behind the retina.

Demonstration 3 - 8

Accommodation

Stand in front of a window and hold a finger about 20 cm in front of your eyes. Focus upon your finger, forcing your lens to become thick. Notice how blurry all the objects are in the view out of your window. With a thick lens, light rays from distant objects focus on a point in front of the retina.

Now focus upon a distant object, forcing your lens to become thin. Now your finger will look blurry. With a thin lens, light rays from nearby objects focus on a point in back of the retina, just as in the diagram in Figure 3-9.

If you have taken photographs, you know that it can be difficult to obtain clear images of both nearby and distant objects. The top picture shows clear images of nearby objects (but blurry distant objects), whereas the bottom picture shows clear images of distant objects (but blurry nearby objects). The next time you go to the movies, watch for this phenomenon. The camera focuses on the woman's face in the foreground, and the man in the background looks fuzzy. The focus may shift to provide a clear image of the man, but then the woman's face becomes blurry.

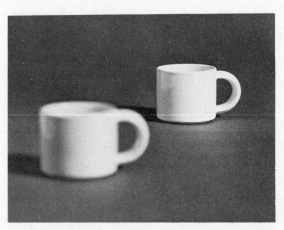

Focusing Problems

A normal eye can bring into focus a point that is very far away. It does not do as well with close objects, but nearby objects can be kept in focus until they are just a few centimeters away from the eye. (Incidentally, figure out for yourself how close to your eye you can bring your finger and still keep it in focus.)

Remember that the cornea bends light. However, the lens makes other adjustments by bending the light even more. Unfortunately, the shapes of many people's eyeballs and lenses do not allow them to bring an image into clear focus on the retina. Vision for objects at certain distances is therefore blurred. People who are **myopic,** or **nearsighted,** can see objects that are nearby but cannot see objects clearly that are far away. They cannot focus on a point that is very far away; in fact, they may not be able to see clearly any object that is farther than a meter away. (If you are like me, for

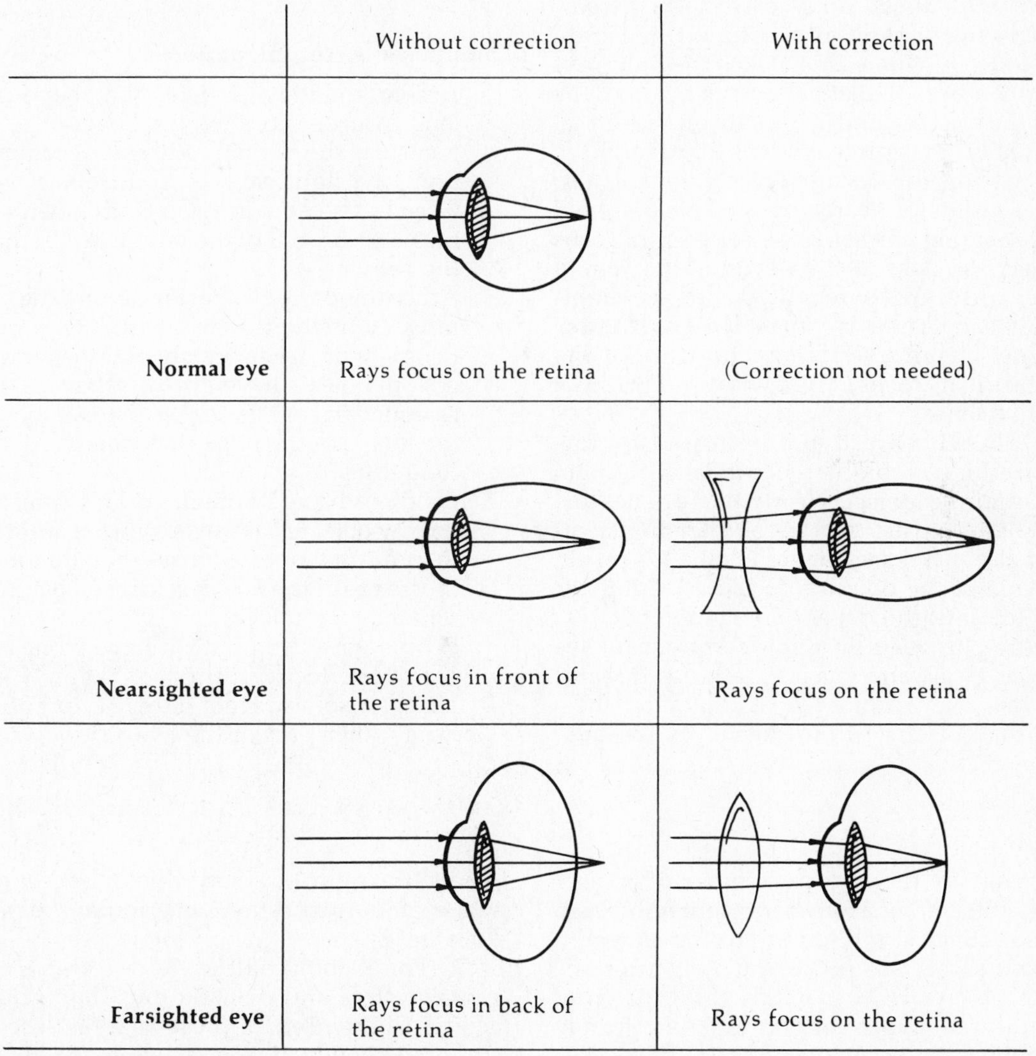

	Without correction	With correction
Normal eye	Rays focus on the retina	(Correction not needed)
Nearsighted eye	Rays focus in front of the retina	Rays focus on the retina
Farsighted eye	Rays focus in back of the retina	Rays focus on the retina

Figure 3-10   Normal, nearsighted, and farsighted eyes.

example, you have to wear corrective lenses to look at your weight on the scale, or else perform gymnastics to get your eyes within 20 cm of the dial!) Nearsighted people have eyeballs that are longer than normal, or else their lenses are too thick. Figure 3-10 shows the situation in which the eye is too long. Notice that without correction, the image of objects is focused in front of the retina for nearsighted people. Remember, then, that *nearsighted* (myopic) people can see things *nearby*, and images are focused in *front* of the retina.

Nearsightedness can be corrected by wearing corrective lenses, as illustrated in Figure 3-10. Notice how this lens makes the light rays diverge more, so that after passing through the lens of the eye they end up exactly on the retina. Incidentally, the corrective lens is intended to correct vision for distant objects, but it also changes vision for nearby objects. Nearsighted people wearing corrective lenses cannot focus on objects as close to their eyes as they could without corrective lenses. If you are nearsighted and wear glasses or contact lenses, see how close you can bring your finger to your eye and still keep it in focus, both with and without corrective lenses.

People who are **hypermetropic**, or **farsighted**, can see objects that are far away, but they cannot see objects clearly that are nearby. They have eyeballs that are shorter than normal, or else their lenses are too thin. As a result, the image of the object is focused behind the retina for farsighted people. Remember that *farsighted* (hypermetropic) people can see things *far* away, and images are focused *behind* the retina. They cannot read a book if it is held the normal distance from their eyes, because

the print is blurry. With an appropriate corrective lens the light rays converge more. After the light rays pass through the lens, they end up on the retina.

People who have **astigmatism** have a cornea that is not perfectly round. Some of the areas of the cornea have more curvature than other parts. As a result, if the eye is focused for some parts of the cornea, it is out of focus for other parts of the cornea. These people need corrective lenses that have more curvature in some areas than in other areas.

Summary: Accommodation

• Accommodation changes the shape of the lens in order to keep an image in proper focus on the retina. Without accommodation, the light rays from an object would often be focused on a point either behind the retina or in front of the retina, rather than on the retina.

• Accommodation is performed by the ciliary muscles inside the eye.

• People who are nearsighted and cannot see distant objects have eyeballs that are longer than normal or else lenses that are too thick; the image of the object is focused in front of the retina.

• People who are farsighted and cannot see nearby objects have eyeballs that are shorter than normal or else lenses that are too thin; the image of the object is focused behind the retina.

• People with astigmatism have corneas that are not perfectly round, so that an object in focus for some part of the eye is out of focus for another part of the eye.

Review

1. What are the four basic types of acuity? Identify the kind of acuity represented by each of these activities: (a) You are trying to read a sign across the ball park, and you can't see whether it says HOT or HUT. (b) A patch of gray in a newspaper cartoon looks uniformly gray, but it is really composed of tiny black dots on a white surface. (c) The dial on your scale is clearly to the left of the 130-pound line, rather

than to the right. (d) One radiologist sees a tiny white spot on an X-ray, but another radiologist does not see it.

2. Think about all the characteristics of the visual system and of a stimulus that influence acuity. Combining all these factors, describe a situation in which acuity would be the best possible. Then describe a situation in which acuity would be the worst possible.

3. We discussed vision and driving in three places in this chapter. Summarize the information about this topic with respect to acuity, adaptation, and eye movements.

4. Explain why dark adaptation curves make us suspicious that two different factors must be responsible for dark adaptation.

5. Give an example of occasions on which you have been aware of dark adaptation and light adaptation. How long should each of these processes take?

6. Identify the kind of eye movement represented in each of these situations: (a) You watch a bird flying toward you from the side. (*Hint:* There are two kinds of eye movements here.) (b) You are staring into someone's pupils, but your eyes move slightly. (c) You are examining a painting in art class.

7. The child next door has reading problems, and the parents are interested in an expensive program designed to train eye movement patterns. What would you advise?

8. For each of the following, supply an example that occurred today and identify whether the movement is slow or fast, smooth or jerky: pursuit movements, miniature eye movements, vergence movements, and saccadic movements.

9. Describe the normal focusing process involved in accommodation and then summarize how this focusing is abnormal in nearsightedness, farsightedness, and astigmatism.

10. Contrast the focusing performed by the muscles during accommodation with the other eye movements we have mentioned in this chapter. Be sure to mention location of the muscle and speed of the activity.

New Terms

visual acuity
visual angle
recognition
detection
resolution
resolve
localization
peripheral vision
luminance
adaptation
dark adaptation
light adaptation
dark adaptation curve
threshold
achromatic

rhodopsin
binocular vision
version movement
vergence movement
saccadic movement
saccade
fixation pause
ballistic movements
regression movements
Eye Movement Monitor
perceptual span
dynamic visual acuity
static visual acuity
pursuit movements

miniature eye movements
stabilized retinal image techniques
converge
diverge
convergence
divergence
accommodation
ciliary muscle
myopic
nearsighted
hypermetropic
farsighted
astigmatism

chapter 4

COLOR

Outline

The Nature of Color
The Color Solid
Color Mixing

Color Vision Deficiencies
Kinds of Color Deficiencies
Origins of Color Deficiencies
Diagnosis of Color Deficiencies

Color Vision Theory
The Receptor Level
Post-Receptor Levels
What Does the Theory Explain?

Issues in Color Perception
Color Phenomena
Factors Affecting Color Vision

Preview

Our examination of color perception begins with a discussion of the nature of color. First, we will see how color depends upon hue, saturation, and brightness. Then we will discuss two methods of mixing colors. The additive method is relevant when we add together different colored lights. The subtractive method, which is quite different, is relevant when we add paints together.

Our next topic is color deficiencies, often mistakenly called color blindness. Most people have normal color vision; they are called normal trichromats. However, a significant number of people have relatively minor deficiencies, and they combine colors differently. A smaller percentage of people are called dichromats, and they have a much more limited range of colors. A very small percentage of color-deficient people are called monochromats, and they are the only ones who are truly "color-blind." We will also discuss the origins and the diagnosis of color deficiencies.

Color vision theory, as it is currently stated, proposes two stages in the processing of color information. In the first stage, three kinds of color receptors, or cones, absorb wavelengths from somewhat different parts of the spectrum. In the second stage these color receptors pass the information on to ganglion cells. These ganglion cells operate according to opponent processes; they are excited by some wavelengths and inhibited by others. Color vision theory accounts for many of the characteristics of color perception.

In the final section of the chapter we will look at three color phenomena. These phenomena illustrate how color perception is influenced by other stimuli seen either at the same time or beforehand; sometimes we even see colors that are not present in the stimulus. We will also examine some factors, such as stimulus size, that affect color vision.

Imagine yourself eating dinner tonight and looking down at a blue lamb chop, red corn-on-the-cob, white tomatoes, and green milk. In all probability, the only way you could finish the meal would be with your eyes closed! Color is so important that violations of our color expectations overwhelm us.

We know that food color is important to Americans. Health advocates warn us about the coloring agents that we add to make our hotdogs redder, our eggnogs yellower, and our beans greener. Think about the importance of color in other areas, such as interior decoration and fashion design. I recall being unable to find a blouse to match a skirt I owned; as the sales-person told me, the skirt was "last year's blue, rather than this year's blue."

Think about the importance of color throughout your own life. Color was probably prominent in your childhood as well. Preschool children in my neighborhood, for example, had two standard questions upon meeting a new child: "What's your name?" and "What's your favorite color?" Color was so central in our lives that it superceded information about age, siblings, and residence!

Color has enormous social significance. Actors and actresses rise to stardom on the basis of the color of the irises of their eyes. Hair color is even more important. Skin color, of course, is most important. People have been enslaved, deprived, and killed because of the color of their skin.

The use of color is also important in many areas of applied psychology. An educational psychologist might color code certain letter combinations to help children with reading difficulties. A human engineer may try to identify an appropriate red and green for traffic lights that would be visible to drivers with color deficiencies. An industrial psychologist should know that color aids search, as Poulton (1979) has noted. As you will see in Chapter 12, a search is quicker and more likely to be successful if you know the color of the object you are looking for. For example, charts in doctors' offices are often color-coded according to the letters of the patient's last name in order to aid search and prevent errors when the charts are refiled.

Color is enormously important in consumer psychology. Eastman Kodak Company spends a large amount of money to make certain that the quality of "Kodak yellow" is controlled

within very well-defined limits (Boynton, 1971). A color advertisement, rather than a black-and-white one, might be adopted because of its attention-attracting power (Loudon & Della Bitta, 1979). Package color is also important (Judd & Wyszecki, 1975). Kupchella (1976) describes a study in which people were given the same detergent in three differently colored boxes. They thought that the detergent in the yellow-orange box was too strong, whereas the detergent in the blue box was too weak. The box that was blue with yellow-orange splashes was judged best!

In this chapter we will consider four aspects of color: the nature of color, color theories, color defects, and issues in color perception. Color will also figure prominently in Chapter 13 (Motivation and Perception). We will talk about emotional and esthetic aspects of color in that chapter. If you are interested in other aspects of color, such as color matching and color discrimination, recent books by Boynton (1979) and Hurvich (1981) will be helpful.

The Nature of Color

Color, as we typically use the term, has several components. There are three terms used to describe our perceptions: hue, saturation, and brightness. Each of these qualities is generally determined by a physical component of light, as we discussed in Chapter 2. A color's hue is determined by wavelength, a color's saturation by purity, and a color's brightness by the intensity of the light. Let us first examine **hue**.

As we discussed in Chapter 2, the longest wavelengths that we can see are represented by red, which has a wavelength of close to 700 nanometers (nm). In contrast, the shortest wavelengths that we can see are represented by violet, which has a wavelength of about 400 nm.

The history of research on color vision might have been quite different if there had not been a plague in London in the summer of 1666. Isaac Newton escaped this plague by moving to Cambridge that summer, according to Wasserman (1978), and his major publications on the nature of light were based on his research

there. Newton closed himself in a room that was entirely dark except for a beam of sunlight passing through a small hole in a shutter. Then he took a prism and held it up to the beam of light. The prism refracted, or bent, the white light from the sun into the rainbowlike spectrum you see in Color Plate 1, with colors ranging from red to violet. Thus Newton discovered that white light really consists of a combination of different colored lights.

The Color Solid

One common way to organize colors is in terms of a **color wheel**, a circle with all the different wavelengths arranged around the edge. Figure 4-1 illustrates a color wheel. This figure has several important aspects. First of all, hues that seem similar are arranged near one another. Yellow is near red, and it is also near green. However, red and green, which seem quite different, are separated from each other on the color wheel.

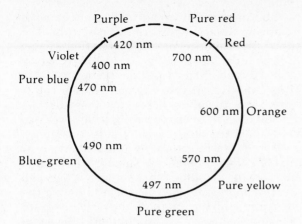

Figure 4-1   The color wheel.

Next notice that there is a dotted line at the top of the color wheel. This part of the circle represents hues that cannot be described in terms of a single wavelength. Instead, these hues are produced by combining other hues. Purple is a combination of blue and red. Similarly, a red that people describe as "pure red" requires a little touch of blue, or it will look slightly yellowish.

Notice also that some colors are not located on the circle. Brown and pink aren't there, let alone the more exotic metallic colors such as silver and gold. In fact, you see on the wheel only a small proportion of the crayons you can buy in the extra-fancy, super-duper collection. Where is burnt sienna or carnation pink or periwinkle or mauve? The outside of the color wheel represents only the **monochromatic** colors—those that could be produced by a single wavelength—plus the true red and purple that are necessary to complete the circle.

We can change the color wheel so that the purity of the color can also be represented. The physical **purity** of a stimulus is determined by the amount of white light that is added to the monochromatic light. Colors that are very high in purity and have no white light added are arranged around the edge of the circle. As we move toward the middle of the circle, we see the colors that are very low in purity and have increasing amounts of light mixtures added. The very center of the circle represents white or gray, an evenly balanced mixture of light waves, with no single wavelength dominant.

Figure 4-2 shows an example. Notice that as we move inward from blue to white, we move from a true, deep blue to more "washed out" shades of blue, such as sky blue and baby blue. As we have discussed, it is customary to refer to the physical characteristic as "purity." The *apparent* purity of a color, however, is called **saturation**; purity is a term from physics, and saturation describes a psychological reaction. Thus we say that baby blue looks highly unsaturated to us, because we are discussing our psychological reaction.

Now that we have added saturation to hue, we can describe a large number of colors. However, one aspect of color is still missing: brightness. Remember from Chapter 2 that light waves can vary in their height as well as in their length. Intense or high-amplitude lights have high peaks on their waves, as Figure 2-2 showed; these lights are perceived as being brighter and whiter. Lights with low peaks, in contrast, are perceived as being darker. Thus **brightness** is the apparent intensity of a color; brightness describes our psychological reaction to the physical characteristic, intensity.

It is customary to represent brightness by adding a third dimension to the color wheel. This is illustrated in Figure 4-3, which is a picture of a color solid. A **color solid** represents the hue, saturation, and brightness of all colors. Notice that the color solid looks like two cones

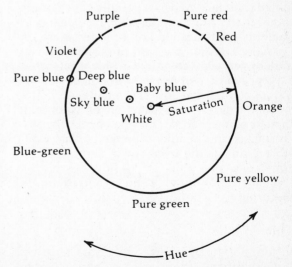

Figure 4-2   A color wheel, with saturation added.

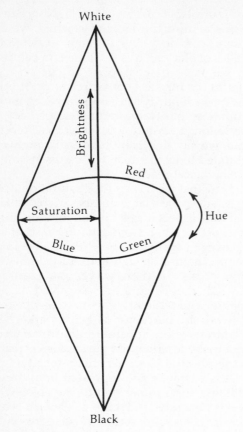

Figure 4-3   The color solid.

joined together. Why is it pointed at both ends, rather than being cylinder-shaped? Some combinations of saturation and brightness are impossible. For example, you cannot have a very dark or very light color that is highly saturated. Look at a dark color near you. It cannot look like a pure color; it has low saturation.

Many different versions of the color solid have been created, for use by both psychologists and people in applied areas. Color Plate 2, inside the front cover, shows one example of a color solid. Notice how the colors in this illustration differ in hue, saturation, and brightness.

Color Mixing

What happens when we mix colors together? As it happens, there are two very different ways to mix colors. The **additive mixture** method means that we add together beams of light from different parts of the spectrum. The **subtractive mixture** method means that we mix dyes or pigments together, or we place two or more colored filters together (Wright, 1972). Thus, additive mixtures involve mixing colors from separate light sources, whereas subtractive mixtures involve only a single light source. We will discuss these two methods separately.

It is interesting to note, incidentally, how mixing colors differs from mixing stimuli that are relevant for some other senses. When you mix red and blue, by either the additive or the subtractive mixture method, the result is a color of uniform shade. You cannot detect the separate parts that constitute the mixture. Contrast this situation with the combining of two fairly different sounds, say a C and an A on the piano. Here, you can definitely separate the two notes when they are played together. Frequently, too, we can detect the separate parts when we taste something. A chocolate mint mousse has two distinct, separable flavors of chocolate and mint.

Additive Mixtures

Let's consider the color wheel once more. Look at Figure 4-2 and choose two colors that are exactly opposite each other on the wheel. In other words, a line connecting your chosen colors must pass through the center of the wheel. If we mixed equal amounts of lights of these two colors, the result would be a white or a gray, that is, a color with low saturation. **Complementary hues** are hues that are opposite each other on a color wheel and whose additive mixture makes white or gray. Figure 4-4 shows how an additive mixture would work if you mixed lights of the two complementary hues blue and yellow.

If mixing equal amounts of complementary hues produces gray or white, what do you produce when you mix unequal amounts of other colors? In general, you will produce a color that is in between the two colors and is low in saturation. Here is how you can predict the results: (1) Locate the two colors on the color circle and connect them with a line: (2) Place a dot along the line to represent the relative amount of each light in the combination. (3) Draw a second line from the center of the circle so that it

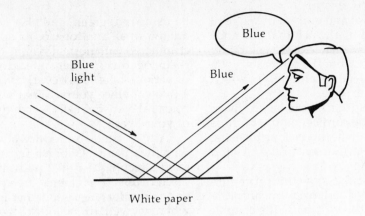

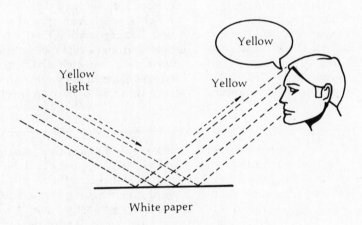

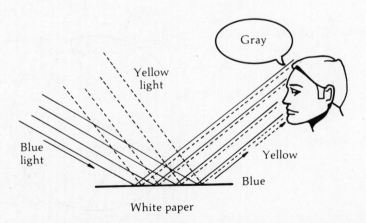

Figure 4-4   Additive mixtures, using two colored lights.

passes through the dot and ends at the edge of the circle. (4) The point at which that line ends on the circle tells you the name of the color, and the distance of the dot from the center tells you its saturation. Try Demonstration 4-1, which illustrates additive mixtures.

The colors of the spectrum can be produced by mixing together the correct amount of three colored lights. Most often, this is done by using the colors red (650 nm), green (530 nm), and blue (460 nm).

Wright (1972) describes how this procedure works, including how you have to cheat a little to create a true blue-green. Later in the chapter we will see the significance of being able to create all colors from three basic colors. This system allowed researchers to speculate that there are three types of color receptors.

In our everyday lives we do not mix beams of lights of different colors. Another way to produce additive mixtures is to place small patches of color next to one another. Color television produces its range of colors, for example,

by using red, green, and blue dots. These dots are too small and too closely spaced to be discriminated with normal vision. Your eyes blend them together in what appear to be solid colors of various hues. However, try Demonstration 4-2 to convince yourself that when you watch color TV, you are really watching spots in front of your eyes!

Artists can also produce additive mixtures with their paints. Georges Seurat, for example, used a technique called **pointillism**, in which discrete dots of pigments are applied to a canvas; these dots blend together into solid colors when viewed from a distance. People who weave or do needlework are also aware of additive mixtures. Wasserman describes, for example, how 19th century tapestry weavers tried to predict how a given thread would look on a given background. Observers looking at a tapestry from a distance would see a single color rather than two distinct colors. Additive mixtures are also relevant in theatrical lighting. A technician who plans to spotlight an actor by

---

Demonstration 4 - 1

Predicting Additive Mixtures

What happens if we make an additive mixture of equal amounts of green and violet? We must place the dot halfway between green and violet. Notice that the result is a blue color, tending slightly toward green, with intermediate saturation. Try an additive mixture that is mostly violet, with just a little green. To do this, we must place the dot nearer to the violet side. Notice that we get a blue color. Similarly, try a mixture of mostly orange, with just a little green, and notice that the result is yellow.

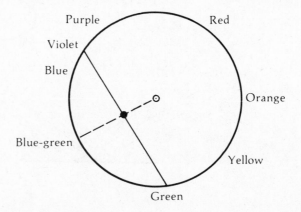

Demonstration 4-2

Additive Mixtures and Color Television

The screen of a color television is like a miniature patchwork quilt, consisting of many tiny dots. Typically, it has about one million dots of three types. When irradiated from behind the screen by a special beam, one type glows blue, another glows green, and another glows red (Boynton, 1979).

How can a patch on the screen look yellow? Take a magnifying glass and notice that a yellow patch is really tiny green and red dots. The dots are too small to be seen with the unaided eye when you sit at a normal distance from the television, but they are combined by additive mixture. With the magnifying glass, notice other blends of colored dots. See whether you can predict what they would look like from the normal viewing distance.

---

using blue and yellow lights may end up with a white light!

Notice, also, how you make additive mixtures in everyday life. You look at an autumn hillside from a distance, and it looks brown, rather than patched with separate spots of gold, red, green, and brown.

Subtractive Mixtures

Subtractive mixtures, as we said before, involve mixing dyes together or placing colored filters together. They are called *subtractive* because when a beam of white light passes through dyes or filters, parts of the spectrum are absorbed or subtracted. As Figure 4-5 shows, blue paint absorbs the yellow, orange, and red (the long wavelengths) from the white light. Only the violet, blue, and green pass on to your eyes. However, yellow paint absorbs violet and blue (the short wavelengths). Consequently, when you mix blue and yellow together, the only color that is *not* absorbed is green (a medium wavelength), and so you report seeing green.

Remember that we are dealing with subtractive mixtures whenever we mix dyes or pigments together. Thus artists work with subtractive mixtures when they mix pigments together on a palette or when they put one color on top of another on the canvas. If you are repainting a room, you will also need to worry about subtractive mixtures, because a yellow painted over a blue may turn out to be a sickly green. Anyone who works with colored filters would also be concerned about subtractive mixtures.

For example, a window display that uses various colors of cellophane might unintentionally reveal a new color if two colors overlap.

You may recall that when we mix blue and yellow together in an additive mixture, we produce a gray or a white. However, when we mix blue and yellow together in a subtractive mixture, we produce a green. Thus the two mixture techniques produce different results. Try Demonstration 4-3 to illustrate the two techniques.

How can we predict what kinds of colors will result from the subtractive mixture technique? Unfortunately, there is no simple diagram such as the color wheel to help us. It is difficult to predict exactly what wavelengths will be absorbed by a particular pigment, and the pattern of absorption may be very complex. For example, the light green color you see on a cabbage absorbs the short and medium-long wavelengths, but reflects the medium and very long wavelengths (Clulow, 1972). If we do not know exactly what wavelengths will be absorbed by the individual pigments, we cannot predict the results of the combination of pigments.

Summary: The Nature of Color

- Color has enormous importance in everyday interactions, and it is also relevant for many areas in applied psychology.
- Hue corresponds to the length of light waves, and it can be represented by points

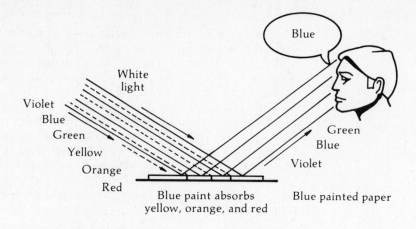

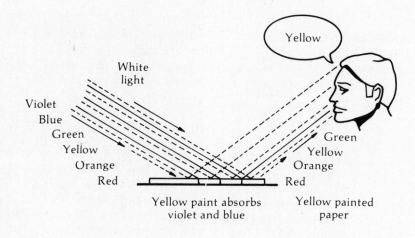

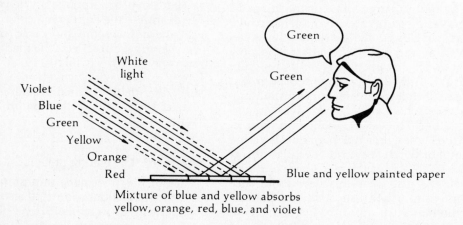

Figure 4-5 Subtractive mixtures, using two colored paints.

Demonstration 4-3

The Two Mixture Techniques

First, try making an additive mixture. Take small pieces of blue and yellow paper. Cut the blue paper into narrow strips, and then cut these strips into tiny squares. Arrange the squares in random order on part of the yellow paper, so that they cover about half of the surface. Tape the squares in place, and then tape the yellow paper on a wall at the end of a long hallway. Walk backwards down the hallway, looking at that paper, until you can no longer see the individual squares. The combination of yellow and blue should look gray.

To make a subtractive mixture, color a piece of white paper with yellow paint or crayon. Then color over this with blue paint or crayon. The combination should look green.

---

along the edge of a color wheel. The color wheel also shows colors that are not part of the spectrum, such as purple and true red.

- On a color wheel the saturation of a color is represented by the distance from the center of the circle.
- A color solid represents brightness along the vertical dimension. Hue and saturation are represented by the two horizontal dimensions.
- The additive mixture method means that we add together beams of different colored light. We can predict the color of the resulting mixture by using a color wheel. Additive mixtures can also be accomplished by color television and an artistic technique called pointillism.
- The subtractive mixture method means that we mix dyes together or place colored filters together. Parts of the spectrum are subtracted or absorbed by the filters. It is difficult to predict the color of the resulting mixture because the patterns of absorption may be very complex.

Color Vision Deficiencies

Some people cannot tell the difference between two colors that differ in hue. We often refer to those people as being "color-blind," but that term is much too strong. As you will see, only a very few people are totally unable to discriminate colors. We will use the term "color vision deficiencies" instead. People with **color vision deficiencies** have difficulty discriminating different colors.

About 8% of males of European descent have some form of color vision deficiency, in contrast to about 0.4% of females (Jaeger, 1972). In other words, if you have 1000 males and 1000 females in a room, approximately 80 males and 4 females will have some trouble discriminating colors.

We need to discuss color vision deficiencies for two reasons. First, it is a fairly common problem. You may be color deficient yourself, and you probably have several friends who are color deficient. Second, color deficiencies have important implications for color theories, a topic we will examine in the next section. In this section we will consider the kinds of color deficiencies, the origins of the deficiencies, and their diagnosis.

Kinds of Color Deficiencies

The kinds of color vision are listed in Table 4-1. If you have normal color vision, you are a normal trichromat. A **normal trichromat** (pronounced "*try*-crow-mat") requires three primary colors, such as red, blue, and green, in order to match all the other colors. The word trichromat consists of two parts: "tri," which

Table 4-1   The kinds of color vision, normal and deficient.

CLASSIFICATION	DESCRIPTION
normal trichromat	normal color vision
anomalous trichromat	weak color vision
dichromat	
protanope	insensitive to red
deuteranope	insensitive to green
tritanope	insensitive to blue
monochromat	no color vision

means "three," and "chroma," which means "color"; so the choice of the term makes sense.

In contrast to normal trichromats, anomalous trichromats have a mild color deficiency. The word "anomalous" (pronounced "uh-*nohm*-uh-luss") means abnormal. An **anomalous trichromat** is similar to a normal trichromat in requiring three colors to produce all other colors, but this person will use different proportions of the three colors than the normal person would use. Most often, anomalous trichromats require more red or green in a mixture than would a person with normal color vision. Anomalous trichromats cannot distinguish nearly as many hues in the spectrum as the normal trichromat can, and they are confused by browns and dark greens (Rushton, 1975).

A **dichromat** (pronounced "*die*-crow-mat") is a person who requires only two primary colors in order to match his or her perception of all other colors. Note that the choice of the term makes sense because "di" means "two." The dichromat can see colors, but the range of colors is narrow compared to normal color vision.

The dichromats fall into three groups. **Protanopes** (pronounced "*proe*-tuh-nopes") are insensitive to deep red colors. You can remember this by the memory trick, "*Pro*tein in a raw steak is *R*ed." **Deuteranopes** (pronounced "*doo*-tur-uh-nopes") are insensitive to green. (*D*euteranopes have trouble in *D*ecember, with all the green Christmas trees.) Both protanopes and deuteranopes confuse red and green with each other; these colors appear to be yellow. Protanopes and deuteranopes occur fairly often in a population of color-deficient people. The third kind of dichromat is much more rare. **Tritanopes** (pronounced "*try*-tuh-nopes")

have trouble with blue shades. (Think of a blue tricycle.)

How can we tell what the world looks like to a dichromat? Some evidence comes from a study by Graham and Hsia (1958). They located a woman who, amazingly enough, had normal vision in her right eye but was a deuteranope in her left eye. These researchers presented different hues to each eye and asked the woman to match colors. For example, they might show a red to her color-defective eye and ask her to adjust the color presented to the normal eye until it seemed to be the same hue. They found that her color-deficient eye saw all the colors between green and violet as being blue and all of the colors between green and red as being yellow.

We have discussed trichromats, who make matches based on three colors, and dichromats, who make matches based on two colors. Who's left? The monochromats. A **monochromat** (pronounced "*mah*-noe-crow-mat") requires only one color in order to match his or her perception of all other colors. Thus every hue looks the same to this person. Monochromats are the only people who are truly "color-blind." Fortunately, this disorder is relatively rare, with an incidence of only about one person in a million. The world of a monochromat is similar to your world when the lights are out—everything is simply a different shade of gray.

Origins of Color Deficiencies

Some color deficiencies are hereditary, whereas some are acquired. Let's discuss the most common hereditary deficiencies, which are found among the protanopes, the deuteranopes, and the anomalous trichromats.

(If you are suffering from jargon shock, take a moment to review the various names.)

These types of deficiencies are transmitted by a recessive X-linked mode of inheritance (Jaeger, 1972). The gene for this type of deficiency is located on the X chromosome. Since females have an XX combination of chromosomes, both of the X chromosomes must be affected in order for females to be color deficient. If only one X chromosome is affected, a woman's color vision will be normal, but she will be a carrier for color deficiency; her son might be color deficient. Females are not likely to be color deficient because it is unlikely for both X chromosomes to be affected.

On the other hand, males have an XY combination of chromosomes. If his one X chromosome is affected, a man will be color deficient. Unlike females, males have no other X chromosome to protect them. Details on the heredity patterns of these X-linked recessive deficiencies can be found in a chapter by Boynton (1979). The chapter also describes the genetics of other, less common kinds of color deficiencies.

Color deficiencies can be acquired from illness or aging, as well as being inherited. In a chapter on acquired color vision defects, Grützner (1972) notes that people are not generally aware of the frequency of these defects. The acquired color vision defects are rarely as clear-cut as the inherited ones, which may be why they are less emphasized.

A common cause of acquired color deficiencies is diabetes. Diabetics may have difficulty making color discriminations between blues and yellows, according to Grützner. Furthermore, a study by Lakowski, Aspinall, and Kinnear (1972) tested diabetics between the ages of 10 and 70. For all age ranges, diabetics made more errors in color matching than controls did.

Diagnosis of Color Deficiencies

Many different ways of diagnosing color deficiency have been developed. The most common is the **Ishihara Test**, in which the observer tries to detect a number hidden in a pattern of different colored circles (Davidoff, 1975). Demonstration 4-4 shows one example of the Ishihara Test. A person with normal color vision will see this number as 8. However, a person who has trouble distinguishing reds and greens may read the number as 3. There are also other tests that allow more precise measurement (Boynton, 1979). One kind of other test measures, for example, the amount of red and green required to match another color, and it identifies protanopes and deuteranopes.

Summary: Color Vision Deficiencies

- Normal trichromats have normal color vision, whereas anomalous trichromats use different proportions of the three primary colors to produce all other colors.
- A dichromat requires only two primary colors in order to produce all other colors. The most common kinds of dichromats are protanopes, who are insensitive to deep reds, and deuteranopes, who are insensitive to greens. Tritanopes, the third kind of dichromats, are insensitive to blues.
- A monochromat requires only one primary color to produce all other colors; these people are truly color-blind.
- Many common color deficiencies are transmitted by a recessive X-linked mode of inheritance.
- Color deficiencies can also be acquired from aging and from illness, such as diabetes.
- A common test of color deficiency is the Ishihara Test, in which people must distinguish the colors of circles in order to detect a specified numeral.

Demonstration 4 - 4

Color Deficiency

Turn to Color Plate 3, inside the front cover, and look at it under lighting conditions that are a little less bright than you would use for normal reading. What number do you see?

Color Vision Theory

You are probably accustomed to theoretical arguments in other areas of psychology. Arguments are alive and well in perception, too. For example, in Chapter 6 (Distance and Motion) you will see that there is a heated debate between those who think that the stimuli reaching the eye are rich with distance information and those who think that these stimuli are impoverished. If I had written this textbook in the 1970s, I would have described an equally fierce argument between the supporters of two different theories of color vision. In one corner we would have had the Trichromatic Theory people, and in the other corner we would have had the Opponent-Processes people.

Happily enough, however, the argument has been satisfactorily resolved. Both theories are correct, but the two theories apply to different zones of the visual processing system. Trichromatic theory operates at the receptor level and applies to the cones, whereas opponent-process theory operates at the level beyond the receptors. Perhaps the best short description of current color vision theory has been supplied by DeValois and DeValois (1975):

> Color vision requires, then, a limited
> number of receptors of different spectral
> sensitivity, plus a neural system that
> compares the output of different receptor
> types [p. 119].

In this section we will first consider how color is coded by the receptors. Then we will see how this information from the receptors is interpreted by the neural system. Finally, we will see how this theory of color vision accounts for some color vision facts that we have discussed in the first half of the chapter.

The Receptor Level

The **trichromatic theory** (pronounced "try-crow-*mat*-ick") of color vision argues that there are three different kinds of color receptors, each sensitive to light from a different part of the spectrum. Many people (for example, Rushton, 1975) believe that the trichromatic theory was first proposed in 1802 by an English physician named Thomas Young, who also achieved fame by translating the Rosetta Stone. In his history of color vision, Wasserman (1978) dis-

agrees and claims that Young was simply being arbitrary when he chose three colors. Wasserman gives the credit instead to Sir Isaac Newton and James Clerk Maxwell. We will leave this argument to psychology historians and simply note that an early form of trichromatic theory was thriving by the middle of the 19th century.

In any event, a major figure in the development of trichromatic theory was Hermann von Helmholtz, a German anatomist, physiologist, and physician, whose name appears frequently throughout this book. His careful research, together with theoretical refinements by Maxwell, explained how three primary colors could be combined to match the other colors of the spectrum (Wasserman, 1978).

About 100 years later, researchers began to produce physiological evidence in support of three different kinds of color receptors. You will recall that we discussed in Chapter 2 the two kinds of receptors that are found in the retina. Rods are used for black-and-white vision in poorly lit environments. Cones are used for color vision in well-lit environments. Whereas there is only one kind of rod, the evidence is now clear that there are three kinds of cones.

Rushton (1958, 1975) performed a landmark experiment in which he concluded that there were at least two different kinds of cones. In this study he projected a beam of light into the eyes of human observers. Now when a light is shined on a cat's eye at night, the light that is reflected back is greenish; the light corresponding to other wavelengths has been absorbed. Similarly, Rushton measured absorption patterns for human eyes by comparing the composition of ingoing and returning light. He found two kinds of color receptors by this process. One kind absorbed mostly long wavelengths, and the other absorbed mostly medium wavelengths. However, he did not find any kind of receptor that absorbed mostly short wavelengths, possibly because his technique was unsuitable for detecting this kind.

Marks, Dobelle, and MacNichol (1964) used extremely delicate physiological techniques in order to measure the responses of cones from dissected human retinas. Their conclusion tells the story:

Thus the commonly held belief, for which there has previously been no direct and unequivocal evidence, that color vision is mediated by several kinds of receptors (possibly three), each containing photopigments absorbing in different regions of the spectrum, is confirmed [p. 1181].

One kind of receptor absorbed the most light in the short wavelength range, another absorbed most in the medium range, and the third absorbed most in the long range.

DeValois and DeValois (1975) took the results of Marks and his colleagues and combined them with other, later studies in order to construct a diagram. Figure 4-6, an adaptation of their diagram, shows the absorption curves for the three cone pigments. Incidentally, some books call the short wavelength curve ''blue,'' the medium curve ''green,'' and the long curve

''red,'' but this is misleading. As you can see, the medium and the long curves both absorb primarily in the yellow region. Notice, also, that the three curves overlap considerably. In other words, the curves do not differ very much in their **spectral sensitivity**, or region of the spectrum in which they absorb light. Finally, notice that the long and medium curves absorb some amount from nearly the entire spectrum, and the short curve absorbs from almost half of the spectrum.

We have seen that there are three kinds of color receptors. Recall from Chapter 3 that the rods contain a special chemical that changes into other chemicals when light reaches the rods. Similarly, each of the three kinds of cones contains its own kind of chemical, each of which is most sensitive to a different wavelength. Thus the chemical in one kind of cone is most sensitive to the short wavelengths, the chemical in a second kind of cone is most sensitive to the medium wavelengths, and the chemical in a third kind of cone is most sensitive to the longest wavelengths.

The color system must be more complex than this, however. As DeValois and DeValois point out, with three color receptors we could only discriminate three colors from each other. In reality, we can discriminate hundreds, and the system is so highly developed that we can even discriminate a 5-nm wavelength difference between, say, 590 nm and 595 nm. There must be another mechanism that detects and magnifies the differences in spectral sensitivity. To discuss this mechanism, we must leave the receptor level of the color-processing system and proceed to levels beyond the receptors.

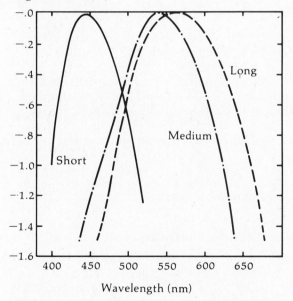

Relative sensitivity
(logarithmic scale)

Figure 4-6 Absorption curves for the three cone pigments. Each curve is plotted so that its maximum sensitivity is set at −.0, and other sensitivities are plotted relative to that maximum sensitivity, using a logarithmic scale. For example, the short cone pigment curve has a maximum sensitivity at 450 nm; at a wavelength of 400 nm its sensitivity is 1/10 of the maximum (because the logarithm is −1.0).

Post-Receptor Levels

In this section we will see how the visual system uses opponent processes in order to handle information about color. In its most general form, the **opponent-process theory** specifies that there are cells that respond to stimulation by an increase in activity when one color is present and by a decrease in activity when another color is present. For example, the activity rate might increase for a given cell when green colors are present and decrease when red colors are present.

Ewald Hering, a German physician, developed the earlier work on the opponent-process theme into a formal theory. His work on the subject was published between 1878 and 1920. Hering incorrectly proposed that these opponent processes occurred at the receptor level, rather than higher levels in the nervous system. Thus the *original* version of opponent-process theory was incompatible with trichromatic theory.

Hering suggested that there were six psychologically primary colors, which are assigned by pairs to three kinds of receptors. There is a white-black receptor that responds positively when white light is shown and negatively when no light is shown. There is a red-green receptor that responds positively to red and negatively to green. Finally, there is a yellow-blue receptor that responds positively to yellow and negatively to blue.

Hering's theory did not receive a wide following until Hurvich and Jameson (1957) wrote an article called "An Opponent-Process Theory of Color Vision." The purpose of their psychophysical studies was to determine the amount of light of one color that was necessary to cancel all perception of the opponent color. For example, they showed a red light and measured the amount of green light that had to be added in order for observers to report that the light no longer looked red. (Remember from our discussion of additive color mixing that the right amounts of red and green will make a neutral color, one that is neither red nor green, because red and green are complementary colors.) This procedure was repeated with different shades of red and with various shades of green, yellow, and blue. One very important contribution from this research, according to Wasserman, was the development of a technique that allows us to directly measure opponent response functions.

DeValois and DeValois (1975) show how the information from the three kinds of cones, at the receptor level, could be passed on to ganglion cells. It is important to emphasize how their treatment of opponent processes differs from Hering's. DeValois and DeValois propose that opponent processes operate at the ganglion cells and beyond, rather than at the receptor level, as Hering had originally proposed. De-Valois and DeValois suggest that there are six kinds of higher-level cells, as illustrated in Figure 4-7. For example, the first kind of cell, labeled + B − Y, is excited by blue wavelengths and inhibited by yellow wavelengths. At the top of the diagram are the three kinds of cones. As you will recall, one responds to short wavelengths, one to medium, and one to long.

When light of a particular wavelength reaches a cone, the cone passes on the information to at least two of the six kinds of higher-level cells. Notice that the short wavelength cones pass on information to only two kinds of higher-level cells, whereas the long wavelength cones pass on information to all six kinds of cells.

Notice that the + Wh − Bl cell receives only excitation. The + Bl − Wh cell receives only inhibition. However, the other two sets of cells work in an interesting opposing, or mirror-image, fashion. The +B −Y cells are stimulated by short wavelengths and inhibited by long; the reverse is true for the +Y −B cells. The same opposing operation holds true for the +G −R and +R −G system. Each of these four kinds of cells can therefore compare the excitation from one kind of cone with the inhibition from another kind of cone.

This information about the relative excitation and inhibition is coded in the ganglion cell. Then it is passed on to the lateral geniculate nucleus, and eventually to the cortex. Unfortunately, little is known about how the cortex handles the information (DeValois & DeValois, 1975). It is estimated, however, that about half of the cells in the cortex respond to specific colors (Boynton, 1979).

What Does the Theory Explain?

So far we have seen that there are three kinds of cones that differ in their spectral sensitivity. We have also seen that higher-order nerve cells make use of the output from these three kinds of cones. Now we need to see why this two-level theory of color vision is appealing. Specifically, we need to see why it accounts for many features of color vision. Let us consider several points briefly.

First of all, the colors in the color solid can be accounted for by this theory (DeValois & De-

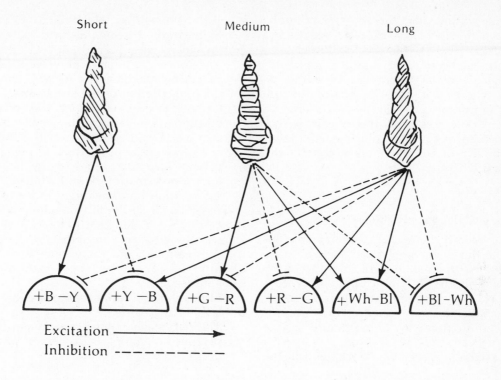

Short   Medium   Long

Excitation ⟶
Inhibition - - - - - - ⟶

Figure 4-7 A model of how three cone types send information to higher-level cells.

Valois, 1975). Hue would be determined by the relative activity among the opponent cell types red-green and yellow-blue. The brightness could be determined by the activity rates of the white-black cells. The saturation could be determined by which kinds of cells are most active. Thus if the red-green and yellow-blue cells are more active, the color would be saturated. If the white-black cells are more active, the color would be unsaturated.

Second, this theory predicts the color names that will be used for various portions of the spectrum. Werner and Wooten (1979) asked people to describe the amount of red, green, blue, and yellow that was present in monochromatic lights, and their responses agreed quite well with the predictions based on Hurvich and Jameson's model. Furthermore, as we will discuss in detail in Chapter 14, Bornstein, Kessen, and Weiskopf (1976) found that four-month-old infants tended to use four categories for stimuli: blue, green, yellow, and red. Notice that these are the same four color categories that are proposed by opponent-process theory.

The opponent processes part of the theory also explains why some colors cannot coexist. Specifically, a color cannot coexist with its complementary color. Try to visualize a greenish-red, for example. Now try a bluish-yellow. It can't be done! You can see a color, or its opponent, but not both. (On the other hand, you can combine colors that are not opponent. Greenish-blue, greenish-yellow, reddish-blue, and reddish-yellow are all possibilities.) According to the opponent-process idea, we cannot see, for example, red and green at the same time because the red-green cells must respond only to red (by becoming less active) or only to green (by becoming more active). The red-green cells cannot respond to both colors at the same time.

The theory that we have discussed also fits the data on color deficiencies. In general, people who cannot see red also have difficulty with green. Furthermore, people who cannot see blue also have difficulty with yellow. Thus if there is difficulty with one color, there is also difficulty with the opponent color. Color perception for other colors, however, may not be harmed. Thus a person who cannot see red and green usually *can* see blue and yellow.

We have been discussing a color vision theory that consists of three kinds of color receptors. These color receptors pass on their information to other cells that work in terms of opponent processes. This theory can explain the appearance of colors, color names, the incompatibility of complementary colors, and color deficiencies.

Summary: Color Vision Theory

- Until recently, there was a disagreement between those who supported a trichromatic theory, with three kinds of color receptors, and supporters of the opponent-process theory. Now it is generally agreed that trichromatic theory applies at the receptor level and opponent-process theory applies at levels beyond the receptor.
- Trichromatic theory was developed in the mid–19th century; Helmholtz was a major figure in the theory's history.
- Physiological evidence supports the existence of three kinds of color receptors, each absorbing wavelengths from a somewhat different portion of the spectrum.
- Opponent-process theory was originally developed by Hering at the end of the 19th century. According to current theory, green and red work in opposition, as do blue and yellow. Two other kinds of cells handle information about black and white.
- Information from the three kinds of cones is passed on to six kinds of ganglion cells, such as a $+B -Y$ cell that is excited by short wavelengths and inhibited by long. The cells can compare the excitation from one kind of cone with the inhibition from another kind.
- Little is known about color processing at the level of the cortex.
- The two-stage theory can explain the appearance of colors, color names, and color deficiencies.

Issues in Color Perception

We have two issues to discuss in this last section of the chapter. First of all, we will look at several color phenomena; for example, humans can see particular colors even in the absence of appropriately colored stimuli! Second, we will examine some factors that influence color vision, such as the size of the stimulus and the region of the retina that is stimulated.

Color Phenomena

Throughout this book we will examine situations in which reality and perception differ. In Chapter 6, for example, you will read about stationary objects that seem to move. In Chapter 7 you will learn about many illusions—the true size of an object is sometimes quite different from its perceived size. In this part of the chapter we will talk about color phenomena. We sometimes think we see color when the stimulus is truly neutral in hue, and we sometimes think we see a color that is different from the color that is actually shown.

Simultaneous Color Contrast

Try Demonstration 4-5, which shows simultaneous color contrast. "Simultaneous" means "at the same time," so **simultaneous color contrast** means that the appearance of a color can be changed because of another color that is present at the same time. Notice in Demonstration 4-5 that the neutral color gray appears to be slightly yellow when a blue background is present. However, it appears to be slightly blue when a yellow background is present. Thus "The color seen in a region of space is determined not only by the characteristics of the stimuli in that region, but also by those simultaneously present in surrounding regions" (DeValois & DeValois, 1975, p. 156).

How can we predict which hue a neutral color will adopt? Recall our discussion of complementary hues from the first part of this chapter. Complementary hues are opposite each other on the color wheel—blue and yellow are complementary, for example. As it turns out,

Demonstration 4-5

Simultaneous Color Contrast

For this demonstration you will need blue, yellow, and gray paper. Cut a large ring from the gray paper. Place the blue and yellow papers next to each other and place the ring so that it overlaps both other colors, as illustrated below. Look at the color of the gray paper against the blue background and contrast it with the color against the yellow background.

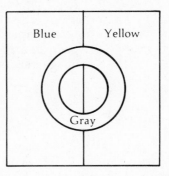

the neutral color tends to adopt a hue that is the complementary to the surrounding hue. Thus gray will look slightly blue when its background is yellow.

Simultaneous color contrast was first reported by Chevreul in the 1800s. Chevreul was in charge of dyes at the world-famous Gobelins tapestry works in France, and he became interested in special color effects when people began to complain that certain blacks in tapestries lacked depth and strength. Chevreul observed, in fact, that perception is greatly influenced by the surrounding colors (Birren, 1976). Ironically, however, psychologists have not developed an explanation for simultaneous color contrast, even though it was documented more than a century ago. DeValois and DeValois reject several plausible explanations and suggest that color contrast must somehow be produced at the level of the cortex. Unfortunately, the mechanisms for this contrast have not yet been discovered.

Successive Color Contrast

Demonstration 4-6 is an illustration of successive color contrast. **Successive color contrast** means that the appearance of a color can be changed because of another color that is pre-

sented beforehand. For example, in Demonstration 4-6, part of the white paper seems to be somewhat yellow because you looked at a blue figure earlier. Thus staring at a figure of a particular hue produces the complementary hue when you change your focus. **Negative afterimage** is a term that is often used as a substitute for successive color contrast, but negative afterimages also include black-and-white afterimages. The term makes sense because it is an *image* that appears *after*wards, and it is the opposite, or the *negative,* of the original image. In special cases these afterimages may persist for hours and even days (Stromeyer, 1978).

DeValois and DeValois note that the afterimage can produce interesting effects when the second color has a hue that is not neutral. For example, think for a moment what color would result if the first figure is red and the second color is yellow. The red figure produces an afterimage that is green. When the green afterimage is combined with a yellow background, the result should be yellowish-green.

Subjective Colors

Subjective colors are color impressions that result from black-and-white stimuli. Try Dem-

Demonstration 4-6

Successive Color Contrast

For this demonstration you will need blue, yellow, red, green, and white pieces of paper. Cut circles from each of the colored papers and arrange them on one piece of white paper, as shown below. Mark a dot in the middle of the sheet. Take a second sheet of white paper and keep it handy. Now stare at the dot in the center of the sheet with the colored circles for two to three minutes. (It will get boring, but don't stop too soon!) Then quickly transfer your focus to the plain sheet of white paper. The complement of each color should now appear, and the afterimage will look somewhat like a mirror-image version of the original.

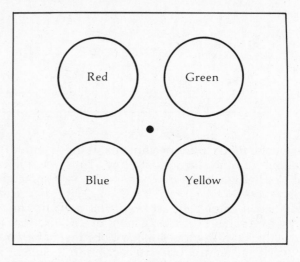

onstration 4-7 to see how colors can appear from uncolored figures. This pattern is often known as Benham's top, in honor of its 19th century inventor. Notice that the colors are pastel, rather than highly saturated colors. The mechanisms for subjective colors are not well understood. Festinger, Allyn, and White (1971) review many possible explanations and present data to support an explanation that involves a kind of Morse Code for color. Thus black-and-white flashes of certain intensities and durations may be a signal for particular colors.

Op Art is an artistic movement that developed in the 1960s in the United States and Europe. Op Art tried to produce a strictly optical art, and so it emphasized perceptual experiences. Many Op Art pictures have thin black lines in geometric designs that tend to vibrate and produce visions of pastel (Birren, 1976).

Figure 4-8 shows one such example. In some lights, the wavy regions in the middle may look quite yellow! I have an inexpensive East Indian rug that has elaborate black-and-white patterns. From a distance, parts look distinctively yellow, and I must keep reminding myself that the color is purely subjective.

Factors Affecting Color Vision

Let's briefly consider several factors that influence color vision. First of all, the region of the retina that is stimulated has an important effect on the perception of color. As you may recall from Chapter 2, cones are concentrated primarily in the central part of the retina, called the fovea. As Jameson (1972) points out, most of the theorizing about color vision is therefore restricted to a 2° portion of the retina! Stimuli

Demonstration 4 - 7

Subjective Colors

Make a good photocopy of the design below. Cut it out and glue it to a piece of cardboard. Punch a hole in the center at the X spot, and place it on the end of a pencil or ball-point pen. Hold the pencil with one hand, and spin the edge of the circle with the other. When the speed is just right—neither too fast nor too slow—you should see pastel colors. If the top is turning clockwise, the bands should look somewhat blue (outside band), green, yellow, and red (inside band). If the top is turning counterclockwise, the bands should seem to be in the reverse order: red, yellow, green, and blue.

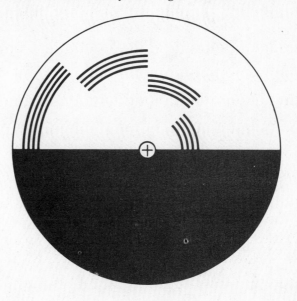

that are registered in the peripheral areas just outside the fovea may look somewhat different in color (Moreland, 1972). However, stimuli that appear in the far periphery will not reach the cones and will look uncolored (Boynton, 1971).

Surprisingly, the size of the stimulus also affects color perception. Try Demonstration 4-8 to see how yellow and blue stimuli look colorless when they are very small. Red and green stimuli can still be seen at this distance, although they will also look colorless if you back up further. This demonstration shows that we are all somewhat color-deficient if the stimuli are small enough.

Wasserman (1978) remarks that it is ironic that many rubber lifeboats are yellow. Lifeboats should be designed so that they can be readily seen by airplanes flying overhead. These airplanes will be flying high enough that the lifeboat will be registered on only a small portion of the searchers' retinas. The lifeboat may therefore look colorless. Red or green would be better lifeboat colors, though green would be ruled out because the sea is sometimes green. If you are planning a cruise, check to make sure that your ship has red or fluorescent orange lifeboats!

Exposure time is another variable that influences color vision. With very long viewing time the eye adapts to the color, and it may look very different. On the other hand, stimuli also look different if they are presented for very brief exposure periods, one twentieth of a second or less. In particular, small, dim stimuli may look white.

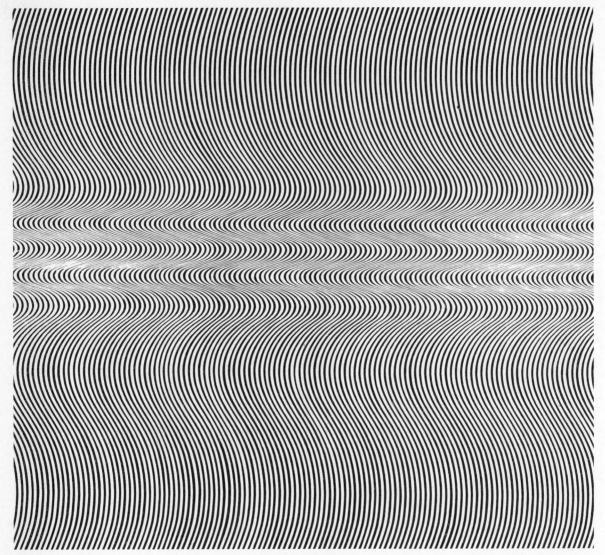

Figure 4-8   An example of Op Art: *Current,* by Bridget Riley.

Demonstration 4 - 8

Stimulus Size and Color Vision

For this demonstration you will need a piece of gray paper and small pieces of yellow, blue, green, and red paper. Cut a shape about 1 cm in size from each of the colored papers and tape them onto the piece of gray paper. Tape the paper to a wall at the end of a hall. Walk backwards until you reach a distance at which you can still see the shapes of the cutouts. However, the yellow and blue shapes should look colorless. If you back up still further, the green and red should also look colorless.

Summary: Issues in Color Perception

- In simultaneous color contrast, the appearance of a color is changed because of another color present at the same time. For example, gray looks slightly blue against a yellow background.
- In successive color contrast, the appearance of a color is changed because of another color presented beforehand. For example, white looks slightly blue if you looked at yellow beforehand.
- Subjective colors are pastel colors resulting from black-and-white stimuli.
- Color vision is influenced by the area of the retina stimulated, the size of the stimulus, and the amount of time that it is exposed.

Review

1. Go to a supermarket with the diagram of a color solid. Locate each of the following on the diagram, paying attention to hue, saturation, and brightness: (a) the colors of laundry detergent packages, (b) wrapping paper with the specification "masculine," (c) baby cards for girls, (d) baby cards for boys. Do these four categories occupy different portions of the color solid?

2. Each of the following is an example of color mixture; specify whether it represents an additive mixture or a subtractive mixture: (a) you wind strands of purple and blue yarn together to knit a sweater; (b) you paint a layer of green over a blue car fender; (c) you mix red food coloring into yellow egg yolks; (d) you cover one flashlight with green cellophane and cover another flashlight with red cellophane and then shine both of them on a white paper.

3. Predict the color of the mixtures in as many of the combinations as possible in Question 2. Why can't you make predictions for subtractive mixtures?

4. What is a normal trichromat, and how does this person's color vision differ from that of an anomalous trichromat?

5. Name the three kinds of dichromats, and point out some everyday kinds of color discriminations that they would find difficult.

6. Ask 20 males and 20 females whether they have color deficiencies. Why are you likely to find more color-deficient males than females in your sample?

7. Summarize the trichromatic theory, as developed by Helmholtz, and the original form of the opponent-process theory, as developed by Hering. Why were the two incompatible, and what modification in the opponent-process theory made the two compatible?

8. Think about the two-stage theory of color vision. Suppose you shine a monochromatic light having a wavelength of 460 nm in someone's eye. What kinds of cones will respond? Which kind of ganglion cells will be excited? Which will be inhibited? Which will not be affected? How about a monochromatic light with a wavelength of 650 nm?

9. What are complementary hues? What happens when you make an additive mixture of complementary hues? Why does this make sense, now that you know about opponent-process theory?

10. Suppose that someone who didn't know much about color vision asked you each of the following questions about things he or she had noticed. What explanation would you give? (a) Why does a blue bird look gray when it's far away? (b) Why does a white blouse look a little green when worn with a red vest? (c) Why does the world look slightly yellow after one takes off blue-tinted dark glasses? (d) Why does a red stop sign look uncolored if you look at it out of the side of your eye, so that you can just barely see it?

New Terms

color	complementary hues	Ishihara Test
hue	pointillism	trichromatic theory
color wheel	color vision deficiencies	spectral sensitivity
monochromatic	normal trichromat	opponent-process theory
purity	anomalous trichromat	simultaneous color contrast
saturation	dichromat	successive color contrast
brightness	protanopes	negative afterimage
color solid	deuteranopes	subjective colors
additive mixture	tritanopes	Op Art
subtractive mixture	monochromat	

chapter 5

SHAPE

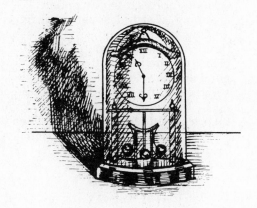

Outline   Contour
        Aspects of Contour
        Masking
        Subjective Contour
      Perceptual Organization
        The Laws of Grouping
        The Figure-Ground Relationship
        The Law of Prägnanz
        Problems with Gestalt Approaches
      Pattern Recognition
        Theories of Pattern Recognition
        The Influence of Context on Pattern Recognition
        Picture Recognition

Preview

In this chapter we will explore how our visual world is organized into shapes and patterns, rather than random specks and patches. In particular, we will examine three aspects of shape perception: (1) contour, (2) perceptual organization, and (3) pattern recognition.

Contours or borders are the locations in our visual world in which there is a sudden change in brightness. Visual and motor disturbances occur when we are deprived of contours, and physiological factors cause an exaggeration of contours. In this section we will also discuss how one figure can mask the contour of another figure and how we can sometimes see contours even when they are not physically present.

In the section on perceptual organization we will discuss the Gestalt approach to perception. We will look at several laws of grouping, which describe what figures will be perceived as belonging together, and several characteristics that differentiate a figure from its background. We will also examine another Gestalt principle, the idea that people tend to perceive figures that are good and simple, rather than complex. Finally, we will consider some criticisms of the Gestalt approach.

In the section on pattern recognition we will look at two theories of pattern recognition. Then we will see how context can influence pattern recognition. Finally, we will examine research on picture recognition.

Let's briefly review what we have learned so far about the visual system's many talents. In Chapter 3 we saw that the visual system can discriminate between two objects that are separated in space. The visual system also adapts to impressive ranges of dark and light, and it shows a variety of movements particularly tailored to our visual demands. Furthermore, it can focus so that we can see either distant or nearby objects. In Chapter 4 we saw how information about color is coded and processed.

Impressive as these talents may be, they only encompass a fraction of the visual system's abilities. Look up from your book and glance around. Is your visual world a mass of random patches of light and dark, colored and uncolored fragments? In fact, your world is not chaotic, because it is filled with objects having distinct shapes. Let's see, first of all, why contours are essential in perception of shape.

Contour

A **shape** is an area that is set off from the rest of what you see because it has a contour. A **contour** is a location at which there is a sudden change in brightness. For example, draw an outline of a circle on a white piece of paper with a black marker. There will be a contour on the

outside of the circle, between the white paper and the black line. There will be another contour on the inside of the circle, as well. In each case there is a sudden change in brightness. We need these contours in order to perceive shapes. However, if the brightness changes gradually over a region we are examining, then there is no distinct contour, and we do not perceive definite shapes.

Aspects of Contour

In our everyday experience, contours are everywhere. Look around you for a moment and notice the many regions in which there is a sudden change in brightness. For example, as I sit here typing, there are numerous contours formed by the letters on the sheet of paper, and the white paper forms a contour against the blue typewriter, which forms a contour against the black rubber mat, which forms a contour against the brown desk, which forms a contour against the blue rug.

The Ganzfeld

A visual field that has no contours is called a **Ganzfeld** (pronounced "*gahntz*-feldt"), which is the German word for "whole field" or "blank field." I recall learning in my undergraduate perception course that we could make a Ganzfeld by cutting a ping-pong ball in half and taping one half over each eye. I didn't happen to have a ping-pong ball in my room, and I suspect you don't either. However, Coren, Porac, and Ward (1979) have offered a creative alternative—two white plastic spoons. Place the bowl of one spoon over each eye while looking at a source of light. You will see uniform light, without contours. Continue in this position for several minutes (having explained beforehand to your roommate not to be concerned about your performance). Notice what happens. You will soon feel that you are blind—your eyes are open, yet you can only see gray. In order to see, you need to have contours. You can restore your vision by restoring a contour, for example by lifting your knee up so that it casts a shadow over your visual field.

In the laboratory, Ganzfelds are created with equipment more elaborate than plastic spoons or ping-pong balls. Avant (1965) describes, for example, a Ganzfeld created by filling a glass cylinder with a fogging solution, through which the observer looks at a uniform white field. Observers in laboratory studies report that they experience a "sea of light" or a fog or a cloud. Some observers search hurriedly

for something to focus upon, in order to orient themselves. They may become aware of the blood vessels in their retina. In extreme cases they may report hallucinations. Other observers mention that they have a complete disappearance of vision for periods of time after being in the Ganzfeld for 10 to 20 minutes. Observers may also report that they are uncertain whether or not their eyes are open.

The Ganzfeld experience may also influence other systems (Avant, 1965). After 20 minutes of the homogeneous stimulation of a Ganzfeld, some observers felt extremely fatigued and reported that their bodies felt light. Motor coordination, balance, and time judgments were also abnormal, and the observers complained of dizziness.

Contour is such a basic part of form perception that we tend to take it for granted. However, in the absence of contour—such as in the Ganzfeld—vision is wildly distorted, and this distortion creates motor system disturbances. Contour perception is therefore an extremely important aspect of vision.

Contrast and Mach Bands

Visual processes have a special feature that makes it even more likely for us to see contours. This feature is called **border contrast**, referring to the fact that the contrast that occurs at a contour seems to be much stronger than it really is. Try Demonstration 5-1 in order to see an example of border contrast.

Did you pick some area in the gray stripe that was third from the right? In fact, however, all parts of each gray stripe are uniform throughout. You can prove this to yourself by taking white pieces of paper and placing them on each side of a stripe, isolating the stripe from the surrounding stripes. All of a sudden, the light border on the left of the stripe and the dark border on the right of the stripe disappear.

These bands that seem to appear at the contours are called **Mach bands** (pronounced "Mahck"). They are named after Ernst Mach, an Austrian who described them in 1865. Mach bands are one example of border contrast, because the contrast that already exists is exaggerated still further (Ratliff, 1965).

Figure 5-1a represents the true intensity of

Demonstration 5 - 1

Mach Bands

Look at the figure below, focusing on the region just to the right of the arrow. Find another shade of gray in a different stripe that seems to match that shade as closely as possible.

↑

---

the stripes at each position. Note that each step is flat, representing a uniform intensity at every point within each stripe. However, the brightness of an area depends not only on its intensity; it also depends upon the intensity of the surrounding areas.

Mach bands can be explained by the principle of **lateral inhibition**: whenever a light reaches one point on the retina, the neural activity for nearby points is inhibited. The more intense the light, the greater the inhibition. As Figure 5-1b illustrates, this will cause a dark appearance on the right-hand side of each stripe and a light appearance on the left-hand side of a stripe. By lateral inhibition, therefore, the contours are exaggerated and even easier to notice than they would normally be.

Masking

Suppose that someone presented, very briefly, a black square, as in Figure 5-2a. Then that square disappeared and was quickly replaced by the square-outline shape in Figure 5-2b, the shape being carefully constructed so that the square fit neatly inside its inner boundary. What would you see? Under appropriate conditions, you might not perceive the square that was initially presented.

Forward and Backward Masking

Werner (1935) was the first to demonstrate the failure to perceive a shape, a phenomenon that has important implications for the perception of contours. Werner found that if he presented the black square very briefly, then a gray interval for about .15 second, then the square-outline shape, subjects failed to see the first square. Werner had discovered **backward masking**, the tendency for a second figure to mask a first figure. Notice that the masking works backward, the second figure wiping out an earlier figure.

Werner suggested that backward masking occurred because the contour in the first figure did not have time to form before it was wiped out by the second figure. However, if he presented the first figure and then presented the gray interval for a relatively long time— perhaps one second—then backward masking did not occur. One second is enough time for the contour to form for the first figure, so the second square-outline figure cannot prevent contour formation. Both figures were therefore perceived.

Werner did not find **forward masking**, which is the tendency for a first figure to mask a second figure. When he presented the square-

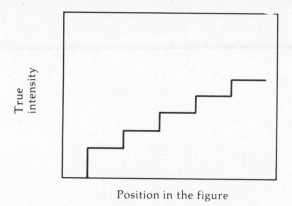

a. The actual intensity of light at each point

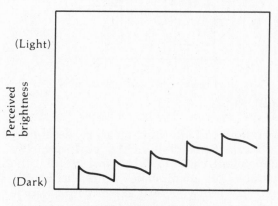

b. The perceived intensity of light at each point

Figure 5-1 An explanation for Mach bands.

outline shape (Figure 5-2b) and then the black square (Figure 5-2a), subjects perceived both figures. Werner proposed that when the square-outline pattern is presented first, its double contour was too strong to be erased. In general, it is more difficult to demonstrate forward masking than backward masking.

Werner demonstrated masking by using a figure with an inner contour matching the outer contour of the first figure. Kahneman (1968) summarizes other kinds of masking effects. For example, backward masking can occur when the first stimulus is a flash of light and the second stimulus is a larger, overlapping flash. The mask can also be a uniformly lit field or a

random pattern, presented at the same time as the test figure. The important thing is that when another stimulus interferes with the formation of a contour, the shape will not be seen.

Are some masks more effective than other masks? McClelland (1978) found that masks do differ in their effectiveness, depending upon the nature of the target. Figure 5-3 illustrates the kind of stimuli that were used in McClelland's experiment. The target stimuli (that is, the stimuli that the subject was supposed to detect) were either straight-line segments, as in Figure 5-3a, or three-dimensional objects that contained the straight-line segments, as in Figure 5-3b. Furthermore, the masks were designs of either flat-line arrangements, as in Figure 5-3c, or three-dimensional objects, as in Figure 5-3d.

Which kind of mask permits more accurate identification of the target, the flat-line mask or the three-dimensional objects mask? Actually, the answer to this question depends on the kind of target we are discussing. When the *object* is the target, the type of mask has one kind of effect: people perform better when the mask consists of flat lines. However, when the *single line* is the target, the type of mask has a different kind of effect: people perform better when the mask consists of three-dimensional objects. One kind of relationship holds true for object targets, but exactly the opposite relationship holds true for flat-line targets.

Thus McClelland's study shows that different masks can conceal different targets. A mask with three-dimensional objects is very effective in disrupting the perception of a target that is an object, whereas a mask with flat lines is very effective in disrupting the perception of a target that is a line.

Hochberg (1971a) points out that studies of

a.   b.

Figure 5-2 Shapes used in masking studies.

a. A straight-line-segment target   b. A three-dimensional-object target

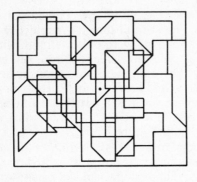

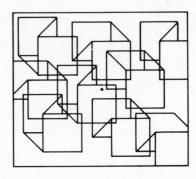

c.   A flat-line mask   d. A three-dimensional-objects mask

Figure 5-3   The targets and masks used in McClelland's experiment.

masking must be concerned with *criterion*. As you may recall from Chapter 1, subjects are sometimes anxious to report that they have perceived something, and they will say that they have seen it, even if it did not occur. Other times, subjects will not report something unless they are absolutely convinced it occurred. Subjects therefore differ in the kind of criterion they use in reporting.

The criterion is relevant in studies of masking because subjects see a figure for a very brief period—they do not have a second chance. It is possible for answers to be biased, therefore, by subjects' motivations. For example, subjects who are anxious to impress the experimenter with their keen detecting abilities might say, "Yes, I saw the square" even if no square had been presented. Hochberg discusses possible methods of handling the criterion problem. For example, subjects may be required to choose which one of several letters has been used as the test stimulus. A forced-choice method removes the criterion problem.

We have focused briefly upon criterion because it is important to consider the dependent variable in perception experiments. As you may have learned in other courses, the **dependent variable** is a measure describing the subject's behavior. In contrast, the **independent variable** is the variable that the experimenters manipulate. Thus the dependent variable in a masking experiment might be the probability of a subject's reporting a square, and the independent variable might be the amount of time lapse between the presentation of the first and second figure. Kahneman (1968) has observed,

> Whether we like it or not . . . the content of the subject's criterion determines his performance, and should, therefore, be described with the same care that is customarily devoted to specifying the stimulus. It is common practice in visual science to devote pages of text to the independent variable and to dismiss the dependent variable in a sentence [p. 414].

We have examined some of the conditions in which masking operates. At this point you may be wondering, "*Why* does it operate?" Breitmeyer (1980) proposes some answers in an article appropriately titled, "Unmasking Visual Masking: A Look at the 'Why' Behind the Veil of the 'How.' " He notes that the human eye has a foveal region that has high visual acuity. However, the fovea can take in only a very small portion of the visual field. This causes a problem because we often want to look at things that are widely separated in space or things that move. For example, in the section on eye movement in Chapter 3 we discussed saccadic movements—those small jumps that serve to bring the next area of text into contact with the fovea. Suppose that the eye pauses for a fixation on an area of text, then moves on to a second and a third area, pausing for a fixation each time. Suppose, also, that the pattern perceived during the first and second pauses happens to persist into the third pause. We would end up with an alphabet soup like the one in Figure 5-4, with the new letter strings superimposed on the old ones.

Breitmeyer proposes that saccades have a second purpose, in addition to changing the fixation point. They also inhibit any activity that remains from a preceding fixation interval. Thus as the eye jumps forward, the material from the preceding fixation is masked so that the next view is a clear one. As a result, we can clearly read the sentence at the bottom of Figure 5-4. Thus masking allows our eyes to wander freely without producing a big blur of superimposed images.

Metacontrast

In masking, the first and second figures are presented to the same area of the retina. In **metacontrast**, masking occurs when the first and second figures are presented to *different* areas of the retina. In a metacontrast study, one figure is presented on one area of the retina, then a second figure is presented on a nearby area of the retina, and the subject fails to see the first figure. Notice how impressive this phenomenon is—contour formation is inhibited even though the mask does not cover the same area as the first stimulus!

In an attempt to unravel the mystery, Lefton (1973) examined the dozens of studies performed on metacontrast. He discusses several theories that might explain metacontrast, most of which involve lateral inhibition. (Remember lateral inhibition from our discussion of Mach bands? It occurs when neural activity in one region inhibits neural activity in nearby re-

You can read this sentence clearly.

a. If material from every fixation pause were retained during the later fixation pauses, a sentence might look like this at the third fixation pause.

You can read this sentence clearly.

b. Fortunately, masking prevents the persistence of earlier material, and so we see a sentence that looks like this.

Figure 5-4   Fixation pauses and masking.

gions.) Unfortunately, however, the studies on metacontrast use many different methods, and they frequently produce conflicting results. Lefton concludes, "Not until some of the basic contradictions in the literature are resolved, however, will an integrated theory of metacontrast be available" (p. 169).

The research on forward masking, backward masking, and metacontrast demonstrates the importance of time factors in perception. In Chapter 4 we saw that a color could influence the perception of another color presented immediately afterwards. Here, we have seen that contour perception can be influenced by other shapes presented immediately beforehand or immediately afterwards—even when those shapes are presented to another area of the retina. Thus shape perception does not occur instantaneously. Instead, shape perception requires a certain amount of time. If other shapes are presented within too short a time period, we may not perceive a shape's contour.

Subjective Contour

Sometimes we can see a shape against a background, even when there is no concrete contour between the shape and the background. Try Demonstration 5-2. Do you see a white triangle against a background of three circles and an outline triangle? Probably, each of the sides of the white triangle appears to be a straight line, even though the true contour is only about one centimeter long at each corner of

Demonstration 5 - 2   Describe, as accurately as you can, the figure that you see in
                           the picture below.

Subjective Contours

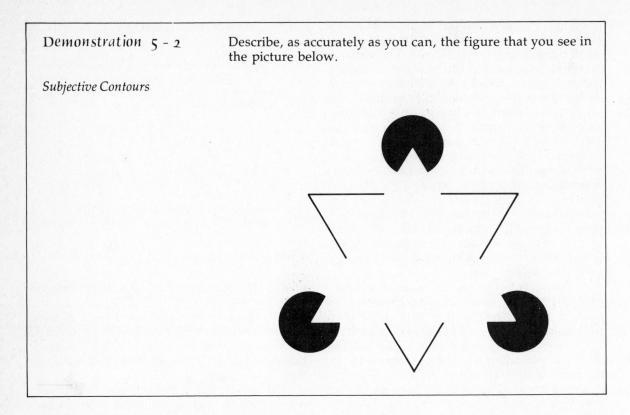

the figure. In **subjective contour figures** we see contours even though they are not physically present.

Kanizsa (1976) discusses these subjective contours, and he notes that the figure bounded by the subjective contour appears to be in front of the other figures. Furthermore, the figure bounded by the subjective contour seems to be lighter than the background, even though the intensity registered on the retina is identical.

Why do we see subjective contours? Coren (1972) argues that we create subjective contours because we see simple, familiar figures in preference to meaningless, disorganized parts. Notice that in Demonstration 5-2 we *could* see three circles with wedges sliced out, alternating with three V-shaped lines. However, this interpretation of the picture is complicated and bulky. Instead, we use depth cues (described in detail in Chapter 6) to sort out the picture, placing a simple white triangle in front of the background. This figure "explains" why there are peculiar gaps in the three squares—the triangle

is merely hiding portions of them. In summary, our ability to perceive shapes is aided by our ability to perceive subjective contours. A stimulus is interpreted as a collection of familiar shapes, rather than a chaotic combination of elements.

Summary: Contour

- Our visual worlds are not filled with randomly arranged stimuli, since objects have distinct shapes.
- Shapes are defined by their contours, or locations at which there is a sudden change in brightness.
- A Ganzfeld, or blank field, is created when there is no contour; the Ganzfeld produces strange disturbances in vision and in the motor system.
- Lateral inhibition exaggerates the contrast at the borders in a figure.
- In backward masking, a second figure

masks a first figure, if the interval between the two presentations is short enough.

- Different masks are effective in concealing different kinds of targets.
- The results of masking studies may depend upon the criteria that subjects adopt.
- Visual masking is essential in reading, or else we might see a big blur of superim-

posed images when we move our eyes.

- In metacontrast, masking occurs when the two figures are presented to different areas of the retina.
- In subjective contour figures we see contours even though they are not physically present.

Perceptual Organization

In Chapter 1 we discussed the Gestalt psychology approach to perception. As you may recall, the **Gestalt approach** emphasizes that we perceive objects as well-organized "wholes," rather than separated, isolated parts. We don't see little specks in disarray as we open our eyes to look at the world. Instead, we see large regions with definite shapes and patterns. The "whole" that we see is larger than the sum of its parts; shape is more than a gathering of specks.

Gestalt psychologists investigated three areas that we must consider here: the laws of grouping, figure-ground relationship, and "goodness" of figures. We will see that many of their ideas are still considered central to an understanding of perception, though the theories do have certain limitations.

The Laws of Grouping

Figure 5-5 illustrates some of the **laws of grouping**, which describe why certain elements seem to go together. Take a minute to look at each of the laws and try to find something around you that demonstrates each one, in addition to the examples I have provided. These five laws (*Nearness, Similarity, Continuation, Closure,* and *Fate*) can be remembered by this memory trick: "*Nancy Sings Continuously, Captivating Frank.*"

Notice, incidentally, that it is possible to see each of the designs another way, if you make a great effort. For example, you can force yourself, in the design of crosses and circles, to see seven columns. Nonetheless, an arrangement of rows is the pattern that emerges spontaneously.

Sometimes we can have a contest between

two of the laws to see which is "stronger." For example, try opposing the law of nearness and the law of similarity. Make a row of crosses and circles fairly close to each other. Underneath, at a distance greater than the distance between the crosses and circles, make another identical row of crosses and circles. Continue this process until you have six rows. Do you see rows or columns? You may be able to create a design in which no design is the clear-cut winner. The grouping will be unstable, and it will shift from one moment to the next. In contrast, try *combining* the laws of nearness and similarity. The grouping will be nearly permanent, and it will be extremely difficult to disrupt.

Max Wertheimer (1923/1958), an important Gestalt psychologist, was the first to describe these laws of grouping. Although the grouping laws may be most obvious for visual perception (and that is why they are discussed in this chapter), Wertheimer noted that the laws of grouping occur with the other senses as well. For example, tap on the desk three times, pause, and tap again three times. The taps organize into groups on the basis of nearness. Now alternate soft and loud tapping; the loud taps will group together, and the soft taps will group together. Or suppose you are listening to a duet in which the singers at one point hit the same note and cross over; the law of good continuation may operate. Can you think of examples from nonvisual systems of the laws of closure and common fate?

Try to notice the laws of grouping and how they may be used commercially. For example, try to identify the laws of grouping shown in the giftwrapping paper in Figure 5-6. Start to notice wallpapers, fabrics, and package designs.

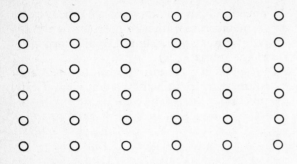

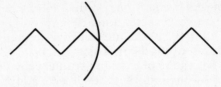

a. **The law of nearness.** You will see this arrangement as a set of columns—not a set of rows. Items are grouped together that are near each other. Now notice the typing in this book. You see rows of letters, rather than columns, because a letter is closer to the letters to the right and left than it is to the letters above and below.

c.**The law of good continuation.** You will see a zigzag line with a curved line running through it, so that each line continues in the same direction it was going prior to intersection. Notice that you do not see that figure as being composed of these two elements:

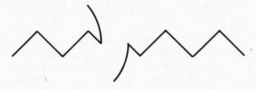

Look out the window at the branches of a tree, and focus on two branches that form a cross. You clearly perceive two straight lines, rather than two right angles touching each other.

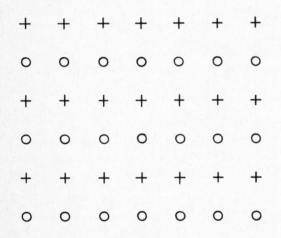

b. **The law of similarity.** You will see this arrangement as a set of rows, rather than columns. Items are grouped together that are similar to each other. Now look at this sentence that has a phrase in **boldface type.** Notice how those two words in heavier print cling together in a group, whereas the words in regular, lighter print form their own separate groups.

d. **The law of closure.** You will see a circle here, even though it is not perfectly closed. A complete figure is simply more tempting than a curved line! Now close this book and put your finger across one edge, focusing on the shape of the outline of your book. You will see a rectangle rather than a bent line with four angles.

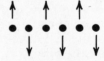

e. **The law of common fate.** If dots 1, 3, and 5 suddenly move up and dots 2, 4, and 6—at the same time—suddenly move down, the dots moving in the same direction will be perceived as belonging together. The next time you look at automobile traffic on a moderately busy street, notice how clearly the cars moving one direction form one group and the cars moving in the opposite direction form another group.

Figure 5-5   The laws of grouping.

Figure 5-6 The laws of grouping in giftwrapping paper.

Photography is one area in which professionals have written about the laws of grouping. If you are interested in photography, you will find the book *Perception and Photography*, by Richard Zakia (1975), to be extremely interesting. Zakia points out how the laws of nearness and similarity are especially effective in encouraging viewers to form groups from the elements in a photograph. Examine Figure 5-7, for example. Notice that the similarity in shape of these three sandstone monuments forces you to view them as a group. However, the farthest two monuments group together as a pair because of their similarity in size and shape and because they are near to each other.

Advertisers also make use of the laws of grouping, according to Zakia. For example, an ad for an air conditioner may show the rounded form of a curled-up, sleeping cat next to the rounded form of the grid on an air conditioner. The viewer would tend to group the cat and the air conditioner because of the law of similarity. This grouping in turn encourages the association between the legendary quietness of the sleeping cat and the implied quietness of this particular air conditioner. Similarly, Loudon and Della Bitta (1979) note that advertisers show mentholated cigarettes in beautiful green, springlike settings to suggest freshness.

Zakia also urges us to look for Gestalt principles in other art forms, such as paintings. Look closely at a painting you have surely seen before, Grant Wood's *American Gothic* (Figure 5-8). In particular, pay attention to the law of similarity. Notice how the three-prong design in the shape of the pitchfork is repeated elsewhere in the picture. It is most obvious in the pattern in the bib of the man's overalls. You can also see it in the cactus on the porch. Less obvious, but still noticeable, is the trident shape of each of the two faces, with the lower portion of the faces echoing the outer portion of the fork and the long nose and lines above the mouth echoing the inner portion. The three prongs are repeated in the man's shirt and the windows, and the curvature of the fork is repeated in the collars and the apron border. This classic picture of rural Americans brought an uproar from Midwestern viewers when it was first shown at the Art Institute of Chicago in 1930. The pitchfork, after all, is symbolic of the devil, and symbols of the devil were not welcome in a portrait of upstanding citizens.

Ideally, you will now be inspecting photos and paintings for evidence of Gestalt principles. Look to other art forms as well. Do the dancers in a ballet, for example, illustrate the law of common fate, as some move forward and some move backwards? Notice, also, how breaking a Gestalt law of grouping can be particularly effective. Recently, I saw Marcel Marceau, the pantomime artist, perform a sketch of David and Goliath. There was a small screen on stage, behind which "David" would disappear and emerge as "Goliath" on the other side. Now we are accustomed to seeing things disappear on one side of a screen and appear on the other side, but the law of good continuation demands that the nature of the thing remain the same. However, David on the left-hand side of the screen was tiny, nimble, and dancing, but the Goliath who emerged from the right-hand side of the screen was huge, muscular, and angry. The audience was clearly impressed and surprised by the transformation that violated the law of good continuation.

The Figure-Ground Relationship

In the previous section we saw that perceivers group parts of a design together according to

Figure 5-7   A photograph illustrating the Gestalt laws of similarity and nearness: *Eroded Sandstones, Monument Park, Colorado,* by William H. Jackson.

certain rules. Organization is not random; there are patterns in what we perceive. Another important way in which parts of a design are organized is with respect to figure and ground. When two areas share a common boundary, the **figure** is the distinct shape with clearly defined edges. The **ground** is what is left over, forming the background. Look, for example, at a book (the figure) lying on a desk (the ground). The figure-ground relationship was one of the most

Figure 5-8 A painting illustrating the Gestalt law of similarity: *American Gothic*, by Grant Wood.

important contributions of Gestalt psychologists.

Properties of Figure and Ground

Edgar Rubin (1915/1958), a Danish psychologist, was one of the first to try to clarify what constitutes the figure, as opposed to the ground. Here are the conclusions he reached:

1. The figure has a definite shape, whereas the ground appears to have no shape. The figure is a "thing," whereas the ground is only a substance.

2. The ground seems to continue behind the figure. For example, try Demonstration 5-3.

3. The figure seems closer to us, with a clear location in space. In contrast, the ground is farther away, and there is no clear location in space; it is simply somewhere in the background. Try Demonstration 5-4 to illustrate this idea.

4. The figure is more dominant and more impressive than the ground; it is also remembered better and associated with a greater number of shapes. As Rubin states, the figure seems to dominate consciousness. If you were describing what you see in Demonstration 5-4, for example, you might say something like, "a black blob on a white piece of paper." The ground, on the other hand, seems to become part of the general environment.

5. In addition to the four characteristics of figure that Rubin outlined, Coren (1969) has provided experimental evidence for a fifth characteristic: the figure looks *brighter* than the ground. Coren showed subjects a picture that looked like a gray rabbit against a dark background or else—when turned

---

Demonstration 5 - 3

The Ground Continuing Behind the Figure

Which is figure and which is ground in this picture? Probably, the cross with the radial marks looks like the figure, and the concentric circles look like the ground, continuing behind the figure. With some effort you can force the radially marked cross to become the ground and the concentrically marked cross to become the figure. However, this is difficult because the radial marks do not seem to continue behind the new figure.

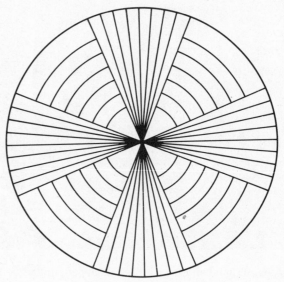

Demonstration 5 - 4

The Figure Appearing Closer than the Ground

Take a plain piece of rectangular white paper and a small figure cut from a piece of black paper. Look at the white paper for a moment. Now place the black figure quickly in the middle of the white paper. Suddenly, the white surface seems to recede. This illustrates how the ground seems to be farther away, with no clear location in space.

In addition, notice whether Rubin's other points regarding figure-ground hold true in this case.

---

upside-down—two dark faces against a gray background. The subjects were asked to judge the brightness of a particular patch of gray, which was part of the figure in one condition (when it was the belly of the rabbit) and part of the ground in the other condition (when it was part of the gray background). They judged the brightness by selecting a shade of gray from comparison samples.

Coren's results showed that subjects chose much brighter shades when the patch they were judging was perceived to be a part of the figure than when it was perceived to be a part of the ground. That patch of gray in the picture looked light gray when it seemed to be a figure, but darker gray when it seemed to be a ground.

In summary, figures have definite shapes, whereas the ground continues behind the figure. Figures also seem closer, more dominant, and brighter. These five characteristics (*S*hape, *C*ontinuation, *C*loser, *D*ominant, *B*righter) can be remembered by the memory sentence, "*Some Cows Can Donate Butter.*"

Ambiguous Figure-Ground Relationships

As you stare at some figures against certain backgrounds, you may notice that an interesting reversal begins to occur. In Demonstration 5-3, for example, you probably began by seeing the radially marked cross as the figure. Perhaps, though, after a few seconds of looking at the figure, the concentrically marked cross popped out at you, forcing the radial markings into the background.

Ambiguous figure-ground relationships are situations in which the figure and the ground reverse from time to time, the figure becoming the ground and then becoming the figure again. These reversals often appear

spontaneously, though you can also force the reversals to occur if you concentrate upon seeing a prominent shape to the ground. Figure 5-9 shows the vase-faces problem, one of the most famous examples of the ambiguous figure-ground relationship. One of my students, on viewing this illustration, reported that her brain seemed to be having a "tug-of-war" as she looked at it—a nice analogy! You can see either a white vase or two outlined faces. However, you cannot see both vase and faces at the same time.

Incidentally, the interest in ambiguous figures is not limited to European cultures. Carpenter (1980) describes how ambiguous figures (or, as he calls them, "visual puns") have been widely appreciated by people in other cultures, such as Eskimos, Melanesians, and Aztecs.

You may have seen some of the pictures of the Dutch artist, M. C. Escher, who enjoyed

Figure 5-9   The vase-faces problem.

playing perceptual tricks on his viewers. In one picture, for example, light-colored horsemen and dark-colored horsemen take turns becoming figure and ground. You might wish to look at some of his pictures in a book, *The Graphic Work of M. C. Escher* (Escher, 1971).

Ambiguous figure-ground relationships can be used effectively to convey a message. Figure 5-10 shows the cover of a disarmament booklet produced by a peace group, Coalition for a New Foreign and Military Policy. Notice how the weapons can be converted into peace doves.

In everyday life we do not see many examples of ambiguous figure-ground relationships, except in the symbolic sense. For example, a verse that has been written in many high-school yearbooks runs:

As you go through life, my son
Whatever be your goal
Keep your eye upon the doughnut
And not upon the hole.

Similarly, we are told to regard a cup as being half-full, rather than half-empty.

Although this is a chapter about vision, you might take a moment to think about ambiguous figure-ground relationships in the other sensory modes. As you taste a Chinese dish, for instance, you might notice how you can force the flavor of the garlic to become the figure, rather than the ground, and then you might concentrate upon the fresh ginger, causing it to become the figure. In listening to music, too, you can alternate between the singer and an accompanying instrument, reversing which is figure and which is ground.

In the section on Gestalt laws of grouping, we discussed how the laws could help our appreciation of art forms. Notice how figure-ground relationships are also important in art. For example, the ground in Figure 5-7 can be forced to become the figure. The background shapes formed by the spaces between the three monuments are quite interesting, particularly because the two shapes are similar to each other. Furthermore, the shadows cast by the trees on the monuments are very intriguing. On the nearest monument, for example, the sunlit patch can be the figure, or the dark shadow can be the figure. Zakia (1975) points out how photographers make use of

figure-ground relationships, which they would be more likely to call positive-negative space. For example, a scene in which figure and ground would be unambiguous in real life because of context, depth, and color cues can be rendered ambiguous in a photograph.

Similarly, look at a painting and force the background to become figure. Interesting shapes and textures appear, and you may find unusual details that you would have ignored if you had only looked at the figure. According to Gestalt principles, the figure is more thing-like and more impressive, so we must make a strong effort in order to overcome the tendency to ignore the background.

The Law of Prägnanz

The **Law of Prägnanz** (pronounced "*prayg-nahntz*") is a term used by Gestalt psychologists to refer to the tendency to perceive figures as good, regular, and simple. Thus in the subjective contour example in Demonstration 5-2, the best and simplest perception of the figure involved the creation of a triangle. The laws of grouping and figure-ground relationship operate to make us see good, simple figures. Unfortunately, the Law of Prägnanz is rather vague. After all, how can we measure "goodness" or derive some index of "figure simplicity"?

Hochberg and McAlister (1953) wrote an article called, "A Quantitative Approach to Figural 'Goodness'," in which they address the issue. Try a simplified version of their study in Demonstration 5-5. In their experiment, Hochberg and McAlister asked subjects to indicate their perceptions at random intervals during the 100-second viewing period. Their results showed that Figures *b* and *d* were almost always seen as three-dimensional. In two dimensions these figures were just too complex. Figure *b*, for example, has 16 line segments and 25 angles. This figure is not good and it is not simple, and so the three-dimensional cube—a good, simple figure—will be perceived instead. Figure *a* is considerably simpler as a two-dimensional figure, in comparison to Figure *b*, so the two-dimensional figure can compete with the three-dimensional figure in perception. Figure *a* was seen as two-dimensional

Figure 5-10   Ambiguous figure-ground relationships on the cover of a disarmament booklet.

Demonstration 5 - 5

Figural Goodness

Find a friend who will act as the subject. You will need a watch with a second hand. Cover up the last three figures, so that only the first one is exposed. Ask the subject to look at Figure *a*. Every ten seconds, give a signal to indicate that the subject should report whether the figure looks two-dimensional or three-dimensional. (Probably, the response "two" or "three" would be easiest.) Continue for 100 seconds, until you have 10 reports on the figure. Then repeat the procedure with each of the other figures.

Record the percentage of the time that the subject reports seeing a two-dimensional figure. Is the percentage about zero for Figures *b* and *d*, and about 50% for Figures *a* and *c*?

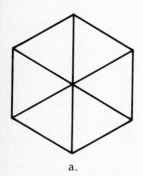

a.

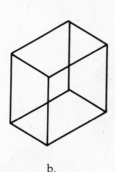

b.

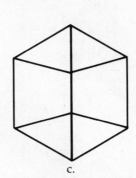

c.

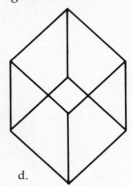

d.

60% of the time in the Hochberg and McAlister study.

In a later study, Hochberg and Brooks (1960) made a further step toward measuring simplicity in an objective fashion. They derived a scale of complexity for two-dimensional figures, based on the number of angles, the number of continuous lines, and the number of different angles. Subjects in this study saw a variety of figures and reported, as in the earlier experiment, whether they saw two or three dimensions. As the complexity score for the two-dimensional version increased, subjects reported seeing the three-dimensional figure much more frequently. In summary, geometric properties of a design can be used to predict what we see. If the figure is simple in its two-dimensional form (as in Figures *a* and *c*), then we will often see the figure as a two-dimensional arrangement. On the other hand, if the figure is complex in its two-dimensional form and simple in its three-dimensional form (as in Figures *b* and *d*), then the figure will usually be seen as three-dimensional.

Problems with Gestalt Approaches

Although Gestalt principles are still considered to be very important in the study of form perception, the Gestalt approach has several problems that we must consider here.

1. Gestalt theorists proposed a neurological explanation for their principles. Research has not supported this explanation, and so the original neurological aspects of the theory have been abandoned.

2. The laws are really descriptions of perceptions, rather than explanations. We know *what* kind of organization occurs, but not *why* it occurs.

3. Forms in the real world are not as ambiguous as Gestalt theorists may have suggested. Rock (1975), for example, discusses figure-ground relationships. In most real-life situations there are numerous cues to depth that tell us that the figure is in front of the ground. It would be extremely difficult for the background to organize itself spontaneously

into a figure. The depth cues are simply so overwhelming that they prohibit the background from coming forward as the figure. Try demonstrating this to yourself by looking at a friend standing in front of a wall. It is extremely difficult to make the friend retreat into the background.

4. Most shapes that we see are perceived to be whole units already. A face, for example, seems to form a whole unit rather than a series of distinct parts. In order to use Gestalt principles to describe perception of the face, we would need to break the face into distinct parts and then demonstrate that Gestalt principles could be used to recombine the parts into a whole. This certainly doesn't sound like an efficient explanation!

5. Gestalt theorists argued that properties of the stimulus were responsible for the groupings. More recent studies have demonstrated that we are likely to make groupings based on our *interpretations* of those properties, rather than on the simple properties themselves. For example, Rock and Brosgole (1964) found that similarity judgments were influenced by size constancy information. (Recall from Chapter 1 that size constancy means that an object seems to stay the same size even when its distance from us changes.) Thus groupings may depend upon other factors in addition to the "raw" stimulus information. Gestalt forces are therefore not as primitive and basic as the Gestalt theorists believed.

6. Similarly, hints can have an enormous influence on figure-ground perception. For example, Kennedy (1974) suggests that you think of the figure in Demonstration 5-3 as a beach ball, rather than a cross. Probably you have no difficulty doing this. If hints can influence perception so strongly, argues Kennedy, then figure-ground perception cannot be very basic and primitive.

In summary, Gestalt principles of organization are useful. They describe a limited range of phenomena that help us understand certain perceptual findings; however, they are not thorough, complete descriptions of all perceptual phenomena. In general, the criticisms of the Gestalt approach focus upon the lack of explanations for the principles and on the fact that most stimuli are already organized.

Summary: Perceptual Organization

- The Gestalt approach emphasizes that we see objects as well-organized "wholes," rather than separate parts.
- The laws of grouping include the laws of nearness, similarity, good continuation, closure, and common fate. These laws have been applied in decoration, photography, advertising, and painting.
- The figure is a distinct shape with clearly defined edges, in contrast to the ground, or background.
- The figure has a definite shape, whereas the ground continues behind the figure. The figure seems closer, more dominant, and brighter.
- In ambiguous figure-ground relationships, the figure and the ground reverse from time to time.
- The Law of Prägnanz refers to the tendency to perceive figures as good, regular, and simple. People tend to see figures as three-dimensional if this interpretation is simpler than the two-dimensional interpretation.
- Although Gestalt principles of organization are useful, their usefulness is limited by the lack of explanations for their effects and by the organization inherent in many stimuli.

Pattern Recognition

In the previous two sections we have seen that contours are important in shape perception and that organizational processes influence the shapes we see. In this section we will discuss how we recognize certain patterns. Think about this for a moment. You see a picture in a year-book, and you recognize that it is the person who sits next to you in biology. You look at each of the letters on this page, and you can identify them. A dog runs up to you and you know that it is Spot, the next-door neighbor's dog. As Juola (1979) writes, "pattern recognition is essential to almost all our waking activities. In fact, every living thing must recognize patterns when it interacts meaningfully with its world'' (p. 493). **Pattern recognition** occurs when we identify a complex arrangement of sensory stimuli.

In this section of the chapter we will consider three issues. First of all, we will look at two of the most important theories of pattern recognition. Then we will see how context influences pattern recognition. Finally, we will discuss picture recognition.

Theories of Pattern Recognition

How do we manage to identify patterns? Several theories of pattern recognition have been developed, but two theories have received the most attention: distinctive features theory and prototype-matching theory. Both theories are supported by experimental evidence, and we cannot yet conclude which one is "best."

Distinctive Features Theory

One of the most widely accepted approaches to the recognition of patterns was developed by Eleanor Gibson of Cornell University in order to explain how we identify letters (E. J. Gibson & Levin, 1975). She argues that we can tell the difference between letters because of distinctive features. **Distinctive features** are characteristics of letters, such as straight versus curved lines. Thus the letter H has many straight lines, whereas the letter O has no straight lines.

Each letter has a pattern of distinctive features that is unique to that letter. Some pairs of letters, such as G and W, are quite different from each other; they do not share any distinctive features. Other pairs of letters, such as P and R, are quite similar; they differ on only one distinctive feature, a diagonal line on the R. Distinctive features remain constant, whether the letter is typed or printed.

E. J. Gibson (1969) developed a chart that shows contrasting distinctive features for the 26 letters of the alphabet. Try Demonstration 5-6, which introduces you to Gibson's distinctive features. This list of features, which Gibson notes is probably not complete (E. J. Gibson & Levin, 1975), evaluates each letter with regard to each kind of feature.

Which kinds of distinctive features are most important? In other words, which characteristics do we rely on the most when we are trying to identify a letter? E. J. Gibson, Schapiro, and Yonas (1968) asked college students to make rapid judgments about pairs of letters. A projector showed two letters at the same time on a screen. If subjects thought that the letters were the same, they pressed one button. If they thought they were different, they pressed a different button. The experimenters measured the **latency**, or the time taken to respond, as an index of similarity. If the latency was short, as it might be for G and W, then the two letters were considered to be very different from each other. If the latency was long, as it might be for P and R, then the letters were considered to be similar to each other.

Gibson and her coauthors found that the first distinction that people make is between letters that have only straight components (such as M, N, and W) and letters that have curved components (such as C, G, P, and R). Furthermore, another important distinction is between round letters (such as C and G) and letters with an intersection in the middle (such as P and R).

Dunn-Rankin (1978) points out how children are typically left on their own to learn how to recognize letters. A teacher or a parent may reinforce the correct response, but the child must use trial and error in order to learn the particular features that are critical in identifying each letter. Thus different children develop different strategies for letter recognition. As you can imagine, some strategies are more effective than others. Dunn-Rankin illustrates an example of an inefficient strategy. Imagine that a young child sees the letter B on a white card but the remains of a squashed spider also decorate that card. The child might assume that one of the distinctive features of the letter B is a strange black blur near the letter. This strategy would be inefficient because few other B's are likely to have that particular visual cue associated with them.

One attractive aspect of the distinctive features theory is that it is consistent with some physiological evidence. Remember that in Chapter 2 we discussed the different kinds of neurons in the visual cortex? Some of these neurons, we noted, responded enthusiastically

Demonstration 5-6

Distinctive Features

Below is a table of distinctive features, as proposed by Gibson. Pay attention to just the top three kinds of features: Straight, Curve, and Intersection. Notice, for example, how *A* and *B* share only one feature in these categories: Intersection. Now look to see how similar *M* and *N* are. Do *O* and *E* have any features in common? Notice that *B* and *P* are identical with respect to these three categories, though they differ on other characteristics.

Features	A	E	F	H	I	L	T	K	M	N	V	W	X	Y	Z	B	C	D	G	J	O	P	R	Q	S	U
Straight																										
horizontal	+	+	+	+		+	+								+				+							
vertical		+	+	+	+	+	+	+	+	+					+	+		+				+	+			
diagonal /	+							+	+		+	+	+	+	+											
diagonal \	+							+	+	+	+	+	+	+	+								+	+		
Curve																										
closed																+		+			+	+	+	+		
open V																				+						+
open H																	+		+						+	
Intersection	+	+	+	+			+	+					+			+						+	+	+		
Redundancy																										
cyclic change		+							+		+					+									+	
symmetry	+	+		+	+		+	+	+		+	+	+	+		+	+	+			+					+
Discontinuity																										
vertical	+		+	+	+		+	+	+	+				+								+	+			
horizontal		+	+			+	+								+											

only to lines that had particular orientations. Thus the visual system is already appropriately "wired" to notice the kinds of differences that distinguish one letter from another.

Although the distinctive features theory has gathered strong support, the theory does have some conceptual difficulties. Naus and Shillman (1976) point out one problem. It is often difficult to identify distinctive features. Consider, for instance, the two triangles . · . and △ . Now you identified the three dots as being a triangle, even though this stimulus lacked two characteristics that we might consider to be distinctive features of triangles: three straight-lined sides and three angles. Thus very different physical stimuli often seem similar, even though they seem to differ in terms of important distinctive features. The prototype-matching theory may offer a more satisfactory answer to this particular problem.

Prototype-Matching Theory

An alternative approach to pattern recognition is called prototype matching. According to the **prototype-matching theory**, we store abstract, idealized patterns in memory. When we see a particular object, we compare it with a **prototype**, or an ideal figure. If it matches, we recognize the pattern. If it does not match, we compare it with other prototypes until we find a match. For example, you have probably developed a prototype for your college president. This prototype represents a person of a certain height and body build and certain facial features. This prototype does not need to specify a particular facial expression or a particular kind of clothing—after all, a prototype is abstract. When you see the president, recognition occurs because the person in front of you matches the prototype.

How does prototype-matching theory differ from distinctive features theory? Probably the most important difference is that prototype-matching theory emphasizes the importance of the entire shape of the stimulus. In contrast, distinctive features theory proposes that pattern recognition takes place by detecting specific important parts of the stimulus (Naus & Shillman, 1976).

Notice that the prototype-matching view is quite flexible. The prototype is a general pattern, not a specific one with every feature well-defined. After all, we can recognize a letter even when it is quite distorted. Consider the letter M, for example. Look at all the assorted M's in Figure 5-11. You recognize those letters to be M's even though they are all quite different from each other. You can also recognize an *M* in various orientations like *M* and *M* and in various sizes like M and M.

In contrast to the prototype-matching view, let us consider a similar but less flexible view,

template matching. According to the **template-matching theory**, we have many templates or *specific patterns* stored in memory. When we see a letter, for example, we see whether it matches one of the templates. If it matches, we recognize the letter. If it does not fit the template, we search for another template. In a way, the template is like a lock and a letter is like a key. As you know, a key may be only a tiny bit different from the appropriate shape, and yet it is different enough that it will not open the lock.

Now the idea of each pattern fitting into an appropriate template sounds interesting, but it has a clear drawback: We would need literally millions of templates in order to be able to recognize all the variations of all the letters and shapes. The system would have to be overwhelmingly bulky in order to store all the templates. Furthermore, it would be overwhelmingly time-consuming. In order to recognize a letter we would have to try the letter out with numerous templates. How could you ever read at an average rate of perhaps 200 words per minute if you had to struggle with dozens of templates for each letter?

Because of the inefficiency of the template theory, we must abandon that view for the more flexible prototype matching. Remember that the prototype-matching theory says the patterns stored in memory are abstract, idealized, and not rigidly specific in their shape.

Let's look at some studies on prototype recognition. Posner, Goldsmith, and Welton (1967), for example, examined prototype recognition for letters and figures. They created a prototype of a letter or a figure by placing nine dots in an arrangement on a sheet of graph paper that was 50 squares high and 50 squares wide. Then the original prototype was systematically distorted by moving each of the dots into neighboring squares on the graph paper. Notice in Figure 5-12 that Figure 5-12b is quite close to the original letter *M*; but as you proceed through the series, the forms become increasingly distorted until in Figure 5-12f the pattern of dots looks quite random. In addition to the letter *M*, subjects also saw the letter *F*, triangles, diamonds, and random dots.

During the experiment, the subjects saw

Figure 5-11   Variations of the letter M.

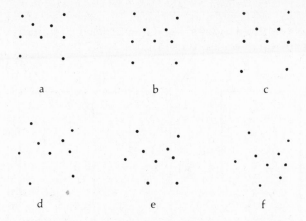

a   b   c

d   e   f

Figure 5-12 Stimuli similar to those used by Posner et al.

slides of the patterns, one at a time, and pressed a button in order to indicate whether the pattern was a triangle, a diamond, an *M*, an *F*, or random. The number of errors made before subjects mastered the task was about 20 times as great for patterns such as Figure 5-12f as for patterns such as Figure 5-12b. Thus recognition is easier when a pattern looks about the same as the prototype, but recognition errors are increasingly likely as the pattern deviates from the prototype.

No doubt your elementary school teachers urged you to improve your handwriting. They probably marked over your wobbly letters with their own firm red pencils. The problem was that your letters deviated too much from the prototype! We often hear about the dangers of bad handwriting. Furthermore, in an article entitled "Doctors' Scrawl," the *New York Times* (1980) described a program that was aimed at teaching doctors in the Kaiser program in California how to write more legibly.

A study by Franks and Bransford (1971) provides further information on recognition of prototypes, using geometric forms rather than dot patterns. Base designs, like those in Figures *a*, *b*, and *c* of Demonstration 5-7, were constructed by arranging four figures on a card. Subjects in this study were told to look at each figure and then to draw it; they were not told to remember the figures. Try Demonstration 5-7 now before we proceed further.

After a delay, subjects were shown more figures, some of which were the base designs that had already been presented and some of which were transformations of these base designs. The subjects marked "Yes" or "No" on an answer sheet to indicate whether they had seen each design before. The results showed that people were much more likely to recognize a design if it was not much different from the original (like Figure *g*). Transformations that were greatly different from the original (like Figure *h*) were seldom recognized. Thus this study reinforces the findings of Posner and his colleagues. Shapes are more likely to be identified and recognized if they are similar to prototypes.

The Influence of Context on Pattern Recognition

In the section on contours at the beginning of the chapter we concentrated on features of the stimulus and their influence on shape perception. For example, we saw how lateral inhibition of neuronal activity produced exaggerated contrast between two surfaces in a contour. The approach to perception that emphasizes the importance of the stimulus is called **data-driven processing.** Data-driven processing depends upon the arrival of data from the sensory receptors. The data arrive, and the arrival sets into motion the process of recognizing various shapes.

Conceptually Driven Processing

Conceptually driven processing is a different approach to perception; it emphasizes the importance of the observers' concepts in shaping perception. In conceptually driven processing, observers have expectations and concepts about how the world is organized. They believe that certain objects are likely to be found in certain situations. These expectations and concepts set into motion the process of recognizing various shapes.

Data-driven processing can be called **"bottom-up" processing**. We recognize simple, low-level features, and the combination of these simple features allows us to recognize more complex, whole patterns. Conceptually driven processing, on the other hand, can be called **"top-down" processing**. We begin by

Demonstration 5 - 7

Study each of these three figures, spending just five seconds on each figure. Then cover up these figures.

Prototype Recognition

a.

b.

c.

Now do something else for five minutes. Then look at each of the figures below and mark on a sheet of paper which ones you have seen before.

d.

e.

f.

g.

h.

i.

Which ones looked familiar? Figures *d* and *i* were in fact the same as the original, and *g* was a minor transformation of *b*, with the right-hand two figures switched. Figures *e* and *f* involved more major transformations. Figure *h* involved the greatest transformations, and you probably judged that figure to be unfamiliar.

recognizing a whole pattern, which may be very complex, and the recognition of the whole allows us to identify the simpler elements that are present in the whole.

Let's be more concrete. You are walking to class, and you recognize your professor for your course in perception. How did you manage to do that? If you used data-driven processing, recognition depended upon information about contours that was received from the sensory receptors. Information was collected about the contour of the nose, the contrast between the eyebrow and the surrounding skin, and numerous other minute features. These data about the parts allowed you to recognize the whole.

If you used conceptually driven processing to recognize your professor, recognition was prompted by your knowledge of the situation. In the past, you had seen your professor emerge from an office, turn right, and walk down the hall toward the classroom at 9:55 on a Tuesday. Context, expectancies knowledge, and memory—concepts that you have as an observer—"drive" the recognition process.

Palmer (1975a) has pointed out a problem with accepting *only* the data-driven ("bottom-up") or *only* the conceptually driven ("top-down") approach, but not both:

> which happens first: interpreting the whole or interpreting the parts? How can someone recognize a face until he has first recognized the eyes, nose, mouth and ears? Then again, how can someone recognize the eyes, nose, mouth, and ears until he knows that they are part of a face? This is often called the parsing paradox. It concerns the difficulties encountered with either a pure "bottom-up" (part-to-whole) or a pure "top-down" (whole-to-part) strategy in interpretive processing [p. 295].

Thus we have a puzzle in shape perception: We cannot recognize the parts without the context of the whole, yet we cannot recognize the whole without the information about the parts. How can we solve the parsing paradox? Palmer proposes that perception usually proceeds in both bottom-up and top-down directions at the same time. Both processes must occur simul-

taneously in order to guarantee quick and accurate recognition of shapes.

Palmer provides a useful example of the interactions of the two processing strategies. Look at each of the line fragments in Figure 5-13b. Each squiggle, by itself, is meaningless and unrecognizable. However, when each squiggle is placed within the context of a face, as in Figure 5-13a, the irregular bump is suddenly, unmistakably, a nose. In context, then, primitive, unrealistic lines can be recognized as features. In fact, convince yourself of this by drawing a variety of lines to represent a mouth. Almost any segment of a reasonable length could pass for a mouth in the context of a face. You may have already discovered this if you are an enthusiastic pumpkin carver at Halloween. A mouth can be a circle, a jagged line, a series of

a.　in context

face

b.　out of context

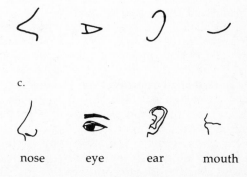

c.

nose　　eye　　ear　　mouth

Figure 5-13　Features in context and out of context.

curves, or a single curve. Similarly, a pumpkin eye can be a triangle, a crescent moon, or a perfect oval. In context, shapes can be recognized that would be meaningless out of context.

How can we recognize features out of context? If we add internal structure for each of the features, adding realistic details, then the angular bump is clearly a nose, as in Figure 5-13c.

In summary, we can recognize the pattern in Figure 5-13a because of both "bottom-up" and "top-down" processing. We recognize the face as a whole because we recognize the parts, but we could not recognize the parts without the context of the whole.

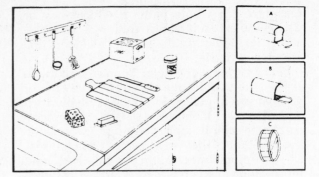

Figure 5-14 The context scene and target objects used in Palmer's experiment.

Research on Conceptually Driven Processing

We have discussed conceptually driven processing and looked at an example of how the context of a face might influence recognition of facial features. Let's now look at some research that demonstrates the importance of context.

One experiment by Palmer (1975b) explored the influence of "world knowledge" on recognition. You know that you are likely to find bread in a kitchen, a mailbox in a front yard, and a drum in a band. If you know what kind of a scene you are examining, you can rely upon important information about the kinds of objects you are likely to find in that scene. Similarly, if you are looking at a scene we could call "Psychology Building on a Tuesday Morning," you know that you are more likely to find your perception professor there than, say, Ronald Reagan or William Shakespeare.

Palmer showed his subjects scenes such as the one on the left in Figure 5-14. Then he very briefly showed them figures such as Figures 5-14a, 5-14b, and 5-14c. In some cases the figure was appropriate for the scene (such as the bread in Figure 5-14a). In other cases the figure was inappropriate for the scene, but its shape was similar to that of an appropriate figure (such as the mailbox in Figure 5-14b). In still other cases the figure was inappropriate, and the shape was different from the appropriate figure (such as the drum in Figure 5-14c). In a final condition, subjects did not see any contextual scene; they were asked to identify the figure without any context. In each of the conditions, subjects were asked to name the object and to rate their confidence that their identification had been correct.

When the figure was appropriate for the scene, such as a loaf of bread in a kitchen, the subjects were 84% accurate in their identification. They were substantially less accurate when they had no contextual scene. However, they were even less accurate when the figure was inappropriate for the scene, such as the mailbox or the drum in the kitchen.

Think about how you may have noticed the effect of appropriate context in your past experience. A friend whom you would recognize readily in an appropriate setting, such as a college classroom, is suddenly unrecognizable in your hometown supermarket or a New York City art gallery.

Mandler and Johnson (1976) wrote an article called "Some of the Thousand Words a Picture Is Worth," in which they compared pictures of objects in real-world scenes with unorganized arrangements of the same objects. Subjects in this study saw scenes that were organized according to a realistic orientation in space (for example, people and school-related objects in a classroom) or disorganized and unrealistic (for example, people and school-related objects in random order on a page). Then they were shown additional scenes, which were either identical to the original scenes or else scenes that had been changed in some way. One kind of change was a rearrangement, with two objects of about the same shape interchanged. Another kind of change was a deletion, with an entire object left out of a picture. Subjects were asked to respond "same" or "different" to each of the test pictures.

Demonstration 5-8

Which of the following pictures and illustrations appeared earlier in this textbook, and which are new? The answers appear in the text.

Recognition Accuracy

a.

b.

c.

d.

e.

f.

Mandler and Johnson's results showed some findings that we would expect but other findings that are surprising. Subjects were more likely to notice a rearrangement when the pictures were organized. However, they were more likely to notice a deletion when the pictures were disorganized. It seems that organization sometimes imposes an orderliness upon a picture, so that deviations from this orderliness "stick out like a sore thumb." Other times the organization is actually a disadvantage; the relationship among the items is so important that the absence of a single item will not be detected.

The context and organization of things we see therefore influence our recognition. Sometimes the context is helpful and improves our accuracy; it may help you, for example, in identifying your professor on the way to the classroom. Sometimes the context may mislead you, however. You have probably had the unfortunate experience of thinking a stranger was a friend because you met that stranger in a context appropriate for your friend. The context was so compelling that you made a mistake in pattern recognition.

Picture Recognition

Picture recognition is the subject of several books (for example, Hagen, 1980; Kennedy, 1974) and many articles. In this discussion of picture recognition we will see that people are highly accurate in identifying which pictures are familiar and that the recognition of photographs is probably not a learned skill. We will discuss another aspect of pictures—perceiving depth and three-dimensionality in pictures—in Chapter 6. Chapter 6 will also include a brief discussion of the perception of motion in static pictures.

Recognition Accuracy

Try Demonstration 5-8 to see how accurate you are in identifying which pictures you have seen in the early chapters of this book. One of the most impressive human abilities is our skill in picture recognition. For example, Shepard (1967) selected 612 pictures of familiar objects from magazines. They included pictures of objects such as a typewriter, a wallet, and a

flashlight. People viewed all 612 individual pictures by projecting them at their own rate on a screen. A recognition test followed, in which 68 of the pictures were paired, one at a time, with a new picture. People were instructed to indicate which member of each pair they had previously seen. When they were tested immediately after the original viewing, their accuracy was 96.7%. When they were tested two hours later on a different set of old and new pairs, their accuracy was an incredible 99.7%! Even four months later, their recall was still impressive. Did you recognize Figures *a*, *c*, and *f* as familiar, whereas *b*, *d*, and *e* had never appeared before?

This study inspired other researchers to test the limits of human picture recognition. Standing (1973) found similar recognition rates with 10,000 pictures. Furthermore, Standing, Conezio, and Haber (1970) found that people were 63% accurate a *year* after viewing 2560 pictures! In general, however, lower recognition rates are found in studies that have used a measure of recognition that is more stringent than the forced-choice method. (The **forced-choice method** asks the subject to select between two stimuli; in this case they must select which picture they have seen previously.) Thus your accuracy on Demonstration 5-8 would have been even higher if you had been asked to select which members of several picture pairs were familiar.

Is Picture Recognition Learned?

How do we know how to interpret and recognize objects in photographs? We take this skill for granted (of course that picture on the second page of the scrapbook is Aunt Gertrude!). But is this skill inborn, or must we learn how to interpret it? Hagen (1974) examines the evidence on this issue, most of it indicating that we do not need special training in order to understand photographs.

Hochberg and Brooks (1962), being truly dedicated researchers in perception, raised their child until the age of 19 months without any exposure to experiences in which pictured objects were named. In addition, the child had extremely restricted exposure to pictures. However, at 19 months the child could identify line drawings and photographs of objects.

Davenport and Rogers (1971) had even better control in depriving their subjects of exposure to pictures—their subjects were two chimpanzees and an orangutan. These animals had been trained to match an object they were looking at and a second object that they only touched. Then the animals were required to match a *photograph* of an object with a second object that was touched but not seen. With color photographs the animals were impressively accurate, about 90%. With black-and-white photographs they were somewhat less accurate, about 80%, but still far better than chance.

Other researchers have gathered data using a cross-cultural approach, testing groups of people who are unfamiliar with photographs. Segall, Campbell, and Herskovits (1966) note:

> To those of us accustomed to the idiom of the realism of the photographic lens, the degree of conventionalization that inheres in even the clearest, most accurate photograph is something of a shock. For, in truth, even the clearest photograph is a convention; a translation of a three-dimensional subject into two dimensions, with color transmuted into shades of black and white. In the instance to which I refer, a Bush Negro woman turned a photograph of her own son this way and that, in attempting to make sense out of the shadings of grays on the piece of paper she held. It was only when the details of the photograph were pointed out to her that she was able to perceive the subject [p. 32].

This observation indicates that we must *learn* to translate, for example, the two dimensions of the photo into the three dimensions of real life. However, Hagen (1974) reports other studies in which rural African people were quite accurate in recognizing objects in photographs.

Considering all the studies done with children, chimpanzees, and people unfamiliar with photographs, it seems that in many circumstances, learning is not required to interpret the shapes represented in photographs.

Summary: Pattern Recognition

- Pattern recognition refers to the identification of a complex arrangement of sensory stimuli.
- The distinctive features theory of pattern recognition proposes that we can distinguish among stimuli because of distinctive features. This theory has been particularly useful in research on letter recognition.
- The prototype-matching theory of pattern recognition proposes that we compare an object with an ideal figure or prototype to see if it matches. Patterns that are similar to prototypes are easier to recognize.
- The template-matching view, in which an object is compared to a specific pattern or template, is too inefficient, and it is no longer widely accepted.
- According to the data-driven ("bottom-up") view of processing, the data from our sensory receptors begin the process of pattern recognition.
- According to the conceptually driven ("top-down") view of processing, expectations, context, and concepts shape our perceptions.
- Data-driven and conceptually driven processing probably occur simultaneously, guaranteeing rapid recognition of shapes.
- Research has supported the importance of context in determining pattern recognition. Context can be helpful, but it can also be misleading.
- People are impressively accurate in identifying which pictures they have seen before, even a year after the original exposure.
- Studies done with children, chimpanzees, and people unfamiliar with photographs indicate that learning is not necessary to interpret shapes in photographs.

Review

1. Why is contour important, and what physiological factors are responsible for emphasizing contour?

2. Imagine that you are driving, using saccadic eye movements continuously. How would masking be important in that activity? Which would be most important: forward masking, backward masking, or metacontrast?

3. Draw an example of a figure with a subjective contour. What is one explanation for the subjective contour in your drawing?

4. The laws of grouping apply in architecture, a topic discussed by Prak (1977). Examine the architecture and organizational structure of your college buildings and try to find examples of as many of these laws as possible.

5. Select a magazine advertisement that illustrates a particular product against a background. Point out how the five properties of figure and ground are demonstrated in this advertisement.

6. Look at a painting and discuss how the Law of Prägnanz operates (or does not operate) in this painting.

7. Summarize the criticisms of the Gestalt approaches to perceptual organization.

8. Imagine that you are teaching kindergarten. What aspects of the section on picture recognition would be relevant when your students look at picture books?

9. As you are driving along, you see a hand-lettered sign that says, "EGGS FOR SALE." Describe how the following theories account for your recognition of the letters in that sign: template-matching theory, distinctive features theory, prototype-matching theory.

10. Relate the two dominant theories of pattern recognition to data-driven processing and conceptually driven processing. Which theory is closer to the data-driven approach, and which is closer to the conceptually driven approach?

New Terms

shape
contour
Ganzfeld
border contrast
Mach bands
lateral inhibition
backward masking
forward masking
dependent variable
independent variable
metacontrast
subjective contour figures

Gestalt approach
laws of grouping
law of nearness
law of similarity
law of good continuation
law of closure
law of common fate
figure
ground
ambiguous figure-ground
    relationships
Law of Prägnanz

pattern recognition
distinctive features
latency
prototype-matching theory
prototype
template-matching theory
data-driven processing
conceptually driven processing
"bottom-up" processing
"top-down" processing
forced-choice method

chapter 6

DISTANCE AND MOTION

Outline   Distance Perception
              Factors Influencing Distance Perception
              Theories of Distance Perception
              Distance in Paintings and Movies
           Motion Perception
              Real Movement
              Apparent Movement

Preview

In this chapter we will progress beyond flat, stationary objects as we consider objects that have depth and movement.

In the section on distance perception we will consider 12 factors that may influence distance judgments. Eight of these factors can be seen with just one eye and do not involve movement. Two factors can be seen with one eye and do involve movement. The last two factors are binocular and require the use of both eyes. We will also consider two important theories of distance perception. Finally, we will see how paintings and movies make use of distance information.

Our visual systems encounter constant motion; seldom do we have a stationary retinal image in everyday life. In the section on motion perception we will discuss velocity thresholds and see that the eye can detect movement, even when that movement is very slow. We will also see that observers can quickly identify the actions of a person by watching the movement of lights attached to the person's joints. Some aspects of people's perceptions of their own motions will also be considered. We will next discuss some explanations for motion perception. Finally, we will examine five kinds of apparent movement, situations in which people perceive that an object moves, even though it is really stationary.

In Chapter 5 we considered the perception of shape. In general, we looked at objects that were two-dimensional or flat—simple figures whose shapes could be represented on a piece of paper. Furthermore, we only examined objects that stayed in the same place and did not move, and we only considered situations in which you—the observer—did not move.

However, your visual world is astoundingly more complex than that. Aside from reading, very little of your visual activity is confined to flat shapes. You reach out in space toward a coffee cup and rotate the handle so that it is closer to you. You look out the window at a friend walking toward you. You eye a chocolate brownie, which clearly has depth as well as height and width.

Also, think about the importance of motion in vision. You move around in the world, and your vistas change dramatically. This change is most spectacular when you are driving in scenic, mountainous country when each turn in the road presents a new view. On a more modest scale, look around you now; with a simple turn of your head, new objects pop into view. Furthermore, objects move in front of your eyes even when your own eyes are in a stable position. Look at an area with many people, such as a cafeteria, and notice the swirl of activity and motion as people move in different directions and at different speeds. There are also times in which something that is truly stable appears to move. Your visual world is in constant motion!

Let's move beyond flat, stable shapes, then, as we consider distance and motion. We will discuss these two topics separately. However, the separation is somewhat artificial, because you will see that motion information helps us judge distance, and distance information is also related to the perception of motion.

Distance Perception

There are three kinds of situations in which distance perception is important. First of all, there is **egocentric distance,** which refers to the distance of an object from you, the observer. (You can remember the word egocentric because it literally means "self-centered.") When you estimate how far you are from the finish line in a race, you are judging egocentric distance. Second, there is **relative distance,** or how far two objects are from each other. When you decide that the library looks farther away than the gym, you are judging relative distance. Finally, there is **depth perception,** in which you perceive objects as three-dimensional; objects have depth or thickness in addition to height and width. Thus some parts of an object look farther away than other parts. You use depth perception as you notice the three-dimensional qualities of your desk lamp and this book. Distance is involved in all three kinds of situations, and psychologists do not emphasize the differences among these situations when they theorize about distance.

Distance perception was one of the first topics to be studied by people interested in perception. Artists in the Renaissance period faced a very practical problem: How could they portray three-dimensional depths and distances on a two-dimensional canvas? Later, in the 17th century, philosophers wondered how humans come to know about the world: How do we know that the world is three-dimensional if the eye appears to represent only two dimensions?

We will return to the ideas of philosophers and painters later in this section when we examine theories of distance perception and applications of distance perception. However, we will begin our discussion of distance perception by examining the factors that help us judge distance.

Factors Influencing Distance Perception

Before we look at factors influencing distance perception that psychologists have examined, it is worthwhile to see how many you can identify on your own. Select two objects you can see from where you are sitting. List some reasons why you know one object is nearer to you than the other.

We will discuss 12 different factors in this section. We will divide them into three groups: (1) monocular factors (no movement), (2) monocular factors (movement), and (3) binocular factors.

Monocular Factors (No Movement)

Eight of the factors that influence distance perception are **monocular**—that is, they can be seen with one eye—and require no movement of the head or the object. These factors are accommodation, size, linear perspective, texture gradient, atmospheric perspective, shading, interposition, and height. (You may find it helpful to remember all eight by making up a sentence with the first letters of these eight factors, A S L T A S I H, such as: *A*lice *S*lyly *L*aughed, *T*aking *A*ll *S*uckers *I*n *H*ere.) It should be mentioned, incidentally, that this list is not exhaustive; Hochberg (1971b) discusses other factors.

1. **Accommodation,** as you recall from earlier chapters in this book, is the change in the shape of the lens in your eye as you focus on objects at different distances. When you look at distant objects, the lens is relatively thin. When you look at nearby objects, the lens is relatively thick. Eye muscles that control lens shape therefore respond differently to objects at different distances. However, do we pay attention to the information that these muscles provide and use this information to make distance estimates? As Hochberg (1971b) concludes, "Seventy years of research . . . leave us with the conclusion that accommodation is, at best, a pretty weak cue to distance even at short distances" [p. 479].

Accommodation involves information provided by muscles. The remaining seven monocular, nonmovement cues have been called pictorial cues. **Pictorial cues** are cues that artists can use to represent distance in a picture. A **cue** is a factor that lets you make a decision automatically and spontaneously. Notice that we do not use the phrase "pictorial *clues*," because clues are factors that provide information but require a great amount of thought. (Sherlock Holmes discovered clues—not cues—and then he sat down with his pipe and thought before reaching a decision.) When you see a pictorial cue, you automatically make a distance judgment.

2. **Size cues** is a term that refers to the influence of an object's size upon distance estimates. If two similar objects are presented together, the object that occupies more space on the retina is judged to be closer. In a classic experiment, Ittelson and Kilpatrick (1951) asked people to judge which of two balloons was closer. The two balloons were actually the same distance away, and their size could be controlled by inflating them with bellows. Furthermore, the room was dark, so other distance cues were missing. People reported that the larger balloon appeared to be closer. As a balloon was inflated, it seemed to zoom forward in space. As the air was let out, it seemed to zoom backward. Thus **relative size**—an object's size relative to other objects—can be a helpful cue in telling us which of two objects is closer.

The **familiar size** of an object can also be a helpful cue, because some objects are normally found in standardized sizes. For example, you know how big this textbook is. If it occupies a very tiny space on your retina, you judge it to be far away from you. Of course, someone might be able to fool you by showing you a giant-sized version of this book in a room with no other distance cues. You would probably estimate that it is closer to you than it truly is.

People who have participated in perception experiments have seen a wide variety of objects of abnormal sizes, all designed to test the effectiveness of size cues. For example, Epstein and Franklin (1965) showed photographs of three coins, a dime that was the size of a quarter, a normal-sized quarter, and a fifty-cent piece the size of a quarter. Subjects judged the dime, which was bigger than normal, as being closer than the quarter. In contrast, the fifty-cent piece, which was smaller than normal, was judged as being farther away.

Familiar size is an interesting topic to psychologists because some people believe that past experience is necessary for the perception of distance. Other people argue quite strongly that experience is irrelevant. If familiarity, or previous experience with an object, is an important distance cue, then the "past experience" position would be supported. Gogel (1976) has

found that people's verbal reports about distances do depend upon familiar size. However, when other, more subtle methods are used to obtain distance judgments from people, familiar size is not as important. In summary, familiar size is a helpful cue, but other cues are more helpful. This might strike you as strange, because most people without a background in perception think that size cues are the major factor in distance estimates. In fact, other factors that *seem* much more subtle and unimportant—such as motion parallax—are really more helpful.

3. **Linear perspective** means that parallel lines appear to meet in the distance. Look at Figure 6-1 for an example of linear perspective on the underside of a highway bridge. The true width of the bridge is constant, yet it occupies an increasingly smaller part of the retina as we look toward the horizon. The linear perspective cue is very important in distance judgments, yet little experimental work has been done in this area (Richards, 1975). However, as we will see later in the chapter, artists have made extensive use of this distance cue.

4. **Texture gradient** refers to the fact that the texture of surfaces becomes denser as the distance increases. Texture gradients can be illustrated in a picture, but, in contrast to linear perspective, this cue has not been appreciated until recently (J. J. Gibson, 1979). You can also see examples of texture gradients in the picture in Figure 6-1.

Try Demonstration 6-1 to make you more aware of texture gradients in your visual world. The units that make up the texture are the same size throughout the scene, yet they look closer together in the distance than in the foreground. Notice how texture gradient is similar to linear perspective because distant objects look closer together in both cases.

James J. Gibson (1950) was among the first psychologists to emphasize texture gradients. In a way, the texture gradients provide a kind of scale by which we can measure objects. Thus a nearby object that hides three texture units is the same size as a distant object that also hides three texture units—whether the texture units are floor tiles, strands of rug yarn, or pebbles.

Newman and his colleagues have also dem-

Figure 6-1 An example of linear perspective.

onstrated the importance of texture gradients. For example, Newman (1970) had subjects peek with one eye through a small hole in a viewing box. They saw two surfaces at an angle, a standard textured surface and a surface that was artificially constructed so that the texture changed rapidly from coarse to fine. When they were asked which of the two surfaces was longer, they chose the one with the rapidly changing texture. In other words, people used texture gradient as a cue to decide the distance of the far end of a surface. Newman, Whinham,

and MacRae (1973) found that surface structure influenced judgments for six kinds of surfaces found in natural environments. This was true for three kinds of irregular textured surfaces (pebbles, concrete aggregate, and grass) as well as for three kinds of regular textured surfaces (paving stones, brick walls, and tiles).

5. **Atmospheric perspective** refers to the fact that distant objects often look blurry and bluish, in contrast to nearby objects. This is because the air between you and the distant

---

Demonstration 6 - 1	Select three places where the floor or the ground is covered with a textured surface. For example, you might choose a lawn, a room with a rug, a driveway, or a tiled floor. Look at the surface that lies immediately in front of you and note how the texture elements have distinct separations between them. Now look out toward the horizon and note how densely packed the texture elements are.
Texture Gradients	

object may not be perfectly clear. As a result, light reflected from the object will be changed somewhat. The farther away the object, the greater the change. Color Plate 4 inside the front cover is an illustration of the atmospheric perspective in New York state. Note that the distant hills are softly blurred and bluish in color. Close your eyes and try to visualize a mountain—chances are that it will be blue! Notice that realistic-looking paintings of mountains are also blue.

We use atmospheric perspective as an informal scale to judge the distance of faraway places. Furthermore, we acquire a scale that is appropriate to the region in which we live. Easterners who live in humid areas and city-dwellers who live in smoggy atmospheres develop a scale that does not work in the Rockies, for example. A mountain that looks blurry and blue enough to be 10 kilometers away by their scale might really be 25 kilometers away!

6. **Shading** is a cue provided by the pattern of light and shadows. Look at any object on your desk and notice how the lighting is definitely *not* uniform and even across the entire surface. Shading gives us information about parts of an object that stick out or cave inward and about parts that are flat or curved. Shading gives the impression of solidity.

Normally, we are accustomed to overhead lighting. Except for the floor lights in movie theaters and discos, have you ever seen lighting from below? As a result, we often assume that there is overhead lighting in ambiguous pictures (Richards, 1975). Sometimes this assumption is incorrect. Look at Demonstration 6-2, which illustrates the importance of shading in depth perception. Notice that the inside of an egg carton looks more like the outside when the picture is turned upside-down.

Shading can also tell us which objects are in front of other objects. An object that is nearest to the light source casts a shadow on objects that are farther away. Look, for example, at the shadow that your textbook casts on the desk, because your textbook is closer to the light than your desk is. Look around the room for other examples of distance cues arising from shadow-casting.

7. **Interposition** means that one object overlaps or partly covers another object. When in-

terposition occurs, we judge the partly covered object to be farther away than the object that is completely visible. For example, your textbook looks closer to you than the desk that it partly covers.

In some respects the interposition cue resembles the shading cue. In shading, the shadow from the object nearer to the light source covers other objects. In interposition the object nearer to the viewer covers other objects.

8. **Height cues** or elevation cues refer to the fact that objects near the horizon appear to be farther away from us. Look at Figure 6-2, for example. Triangle *a* seems to be closer to us than Triangle *b*, because Triangle *b* is closer to the horizon. Similarly, Cloud *a* seems to be closer to us than Cloud *b*, because Cloud *b* is closer to the horizon. This means that there is reversal in the height cue at the horizon. Below the horizon (on the ground), things at the bottom of our view are close. Above the horizon (in the air), things at the top of our view are close. Look out a nearby window to demonstrate the usefulness of height cues.

Before we move on to other kinds of cues, let's review once more the monocular/no movement factors that influence distance perception. Remember that memory trick: *Alice Slyly Laughed, Taking All Suckers In Here.* The eight cues are accommodation, size, linear perspective, texture gradient, atmospheric perspective, shading, interposition, and height. Accommodation is different from the other factors because it is a muscular cue, whereas the other seven are pictorial cues. Size, linear perspective, and texture gradient are somewhat related to each other because faraway objects are smaller (size), faraway objects represent a fixed distance with a smaller space on the retina (linear perspective), and faraway surfaces have smaller distances between the texture elements (texture gradient). Atmospheric perspective and shading are both factors that involve lighting. Interposition and height both involve the placement of objects in the visual field.

Monocular Factors (Movement)

All the depth perception factors that we have discussed so far involve rigid head positions

Demonstration 6 - 2

Shading Cues

Look at this picture and decide which surface is closer to you, the observer. Now turn the picture upside-down and decide which surface now appears closer to you.

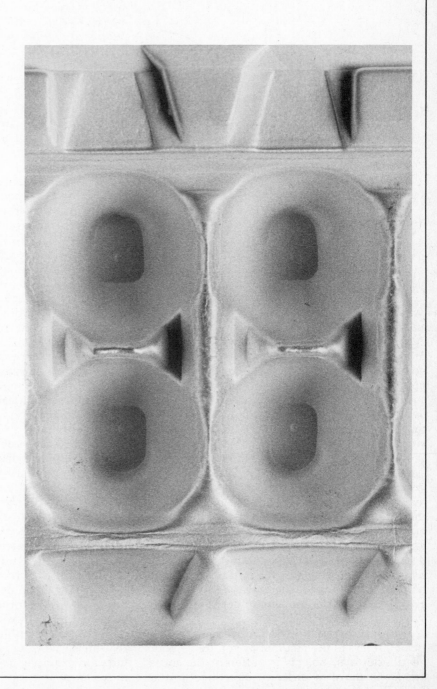

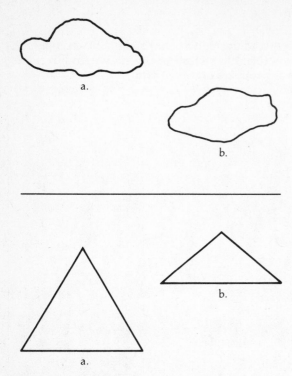

Figure 6-2   Height cues.

different speeds. The word **parallax** means a change in position, and so motion parallax is a change in the position of an object that is caused by motion.

Motion parallax is an excellent source of space information (Johansson, 1974). For example, Wallach and O'Leary (1979) found that people could discriminate distances when their only available cue was parallax caused by moving their heads. However, you may never have noticed how much information these head movements provide. Go to a window and focus upon a part of the window frame. Hold your hand in front of your eyes. Now move your head to the left and notice that your hand seems to move in the opposite direction, to the right. In contrast, objects that you can see out the window, which are further away than the window frame upon which you are focusing, appear to move to the left. Thus they seem to move in the same direction as your head.

Notice that the direction in which objects appear to move is related to the fixation point, the part of the scene that is registered on your fovea. Objects that are closer to you than the fixation point seem to move in a direction that is the opposite to your own movement. In contrast, objects that are farther away than the fixation point seem to move in a direction that is the same as your own movement. My daughter remarked when she was four years old and riding with me at night, "Mommy, the moon is following us!" Indeed, the distant moon does seem to move in the same direction as your own movement.

The next time you ride in a car or bus, fixate on a point in the distance and notice how the speed of motion also depends upon distance. Posts on a highway that are relatively close to you seem to whiz past, whereas a billboard that is farther back—just in front of your fixation point—seems to move more slowly.

I mentioned earlier that these monocular factors that involve movement cannot be represented in a picture. As Pirenne (1975) has noted, spectators tend to move about in front of a painting. When they move, the various objects in the picture do *not* move in different directions at different speeds, as the objects in a real-life scene would do. As you walk past a still life, for example, the bowl of fruit does not move to the left and the distant curtains do not

and stable objects. In reality, most of our visual experience involves moving objects or moving retinas, as we turn our heads and move our bodies past objects. In fact, as Braunstein (1976) points out, motion is an extremely important source of information about distance and depth. There are two kinds of distance factors that involve motion: motion parallax and the kinetic depth effect.

You may not have been aware of these factors previously, because they do not seem as important to nonpsychologists as do some of the factors we have just discussed. Perhaps they are relatively unknown because they cannot be represented in a picture, and the only formal training most of us receive regarding depth perception is likely to be elementary school art. You probably learned how to draw railroad tracks and to shade trees, but did you ever hear about the movement depth cues that cannot be drawn?

Motion parallax (pronounced "*pair*-uh-lacks") refers to the fact that as you move your head sideways, objects at different distances appear to move in different directions and at move to the right. Because a picture cannot represent motion parallax, no artist can make a picture look perfectly three-dimensional to a roving spectator.

James J. Gibson (1966) proposed that motion parallax is part of a more general motion pattern, which he calls motion perspective. **Motion perspective** refers to the continuous change in the way objects look as we move about in the world. As you directly approach a point straight ahead of you, objects on all sides of you seem to move away from that point. For example, as you walk between the rows of

books in the library, staring straight ahead, you should have the sense of motion perspective illustrated in Figure 6-3.

The second monocular/movement factor is the kinetic depth effect. The **kinetic depth effect** involves the motion of objects, rather than observers; a figure that looks flat when it is stable appears to have depth once it moves. Try Demonstration 6-3 to illustrate the kinetic depth effect with a rotating figure. The kinetic depth effect was first demonstrated with the shadows of rotating objects and has been explored in many other studies, according to

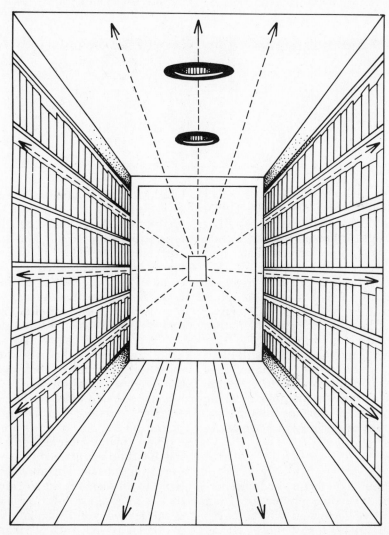

Figure 6-3 Motion perspective.

Demonstration 6 - 3

The Kinetic Depth Effect

Take a pipe cleaner or a paper clip and bend it into a clearly three-dimensional figure. Find a piece of paper and a lamp. Place the figure between the lamp and the paper and notice that the figure, as seen through the paper, looks flat and two-dimensional. Now rotate the figure and notice how it suddenly appears to have a third dimension.

Braunstein (1976). In one well-known set of experiments, Wallach and O'Connell (1953) found that solid blocks, wire figures, straight rods, and other figures looked flat when they were stationary and three-dimensional when they rotated.

Notice that most other depth cues are missing in Demonstration 6-3. For example, cues such as interposition, shading, and texture gradient do not appear on the paper. Nonetheless, once the figure moves, you notice that some parts move faster than other parts, and they also move in different directions. This kind of movement compels you to conclude that the object casting the shadow must be three-dimensional. Once the movement stops, however, the object can be interpreted as two-dimensional.

Binocular Factors

We first talked about eight factors in depth perception that did not involve movement. Then we talked about two factors in which movement was central. For all ten of these factors, however, one eye is sufficient. A person who is

blind in one eye, who has lost one contact lens, or who wears a patch over one eye to look distinguished—all these people perceive these ten depth factors to the same extent as a person with binocular vision. However, there are two binocular factors that contribute to depth perception: convergence and binocular parallax. Like the motion-related factors we discussed in the previous section, neither of these two factors can be represented in a single picture.

Convergence, as you may recall from Chapter 3, means that the eyes **converge** or move together, in order to look at nearby objects. Demonstrate convergence for yourself by looking at a distant object on the horizon and then shifting your focus to the tip of your finger, placed on the end of your nose.

Now if you had to design a visual system so that it would extract as much information about depth as possible from visual experiences, wouldn't it seem like a good idea to make use of this convergence information? Perhaps, for example, we could calculate the distance of a particular object once we knew the distance between the eyes and the angle formed at the intersection of the two lines of sight—a wide angle for nearby objects and a narrow angle for distant objects. High school students calculate distances like these when they study trigonometry. Does your visual system calculate objects' distances in a similar fashion, though more automatically?

Actually, the answer to this question is not yet clear. There is evidence that some observers can use the information from convergence some of the time (Hochberg, 1971b). However, this information is useful only for judging the distance of nearby objects. This makes sense because the degree of convergence does not change much as you change your fixation from an object 10 kilometers away to one 9 kilometers away. In contrast, the degree of convergence does change quite impressively when you change your fixation from an object 10 meters away to one 10 centimeters away. In summary, convergence may sometimes act as a depth cue, particularly when other, more helpful cues are absent.

Binocular parallax is the second depth factor that makes use of information from both eyes. You know that "binocular" means "two eyes" and that "parallax" means "a change in position." Thus **binocular parallax** means a change in the position of an object as a result of having two eyes, or two points of view. When we examined motion parallax, you saw that the relative positions of objects shifted as you moved your head from one position to another. Similarly, the relative positions of objects shift as you look through your right eye and then through your left eye. After all, your two eyes are about 7 cm apart from each other!

Show yourself how binocular parallax works by holding your left thumb about 15 cm from your eyes and your right thumb as far away as possible. Keeping your head still, close your left eye and open your right eye. Now close your right eye and open your left eye. Does your left thumb appear to jump back and forth in front of your right thumb? Incidentally, another term often used instead of binocular parallax is **retinal disparity.**

DeValois and DeValois (1980) note that the recent literature on depth perception has been dominated by studies on binocular parallax. This may seem strange, considering that binocular vision constitutes only a small part of

the information upon which depth perception is based. DeValois and DeValois propose that the reason that binocular parallax is such a popular research topic is that there are possible physiological explanations for how this factor contributes to depth perception. These authors review the conflicting studies and explanations. They also discuss the possibility that there are cells in Area 17 of the visual cortex that are selective for binocular parallax.

You know that the right eye and the left eye have slightly different views of the world. So what? Why is this relevant for depth perception? Perhaps the best way to illustrate how this works is to show you a stereoscopic picture. We said earlier that binocular parallax cannot be represented in a single picture. A **stereoscopic picture,** however, consists of two pictures, one for the right eye and one for the left eye. Notice how the two pictures in Demonstration 6-4 are slightly different from each other. When each eye looks at the appropriate view and you manage to fuse the two images, you should have a sensation that one rectangle floats in front of the other.

Ross (1976) describes the invention of the stereoscope by Charles Wheatstone in 1838. A **stereoscope** is a piece of equipment that presents two photographs of a scene taken from slightly different viewpoints—viewpoints that were separated to the same extent as human eyes are separated. One photograph is seen by the right eye, and the other photograph by the left eye. When the two pictures are seen at the same time, they combine to make a three-dimensional scene. Stereoscopes became very popular in the 19th century, and you may have seen one in a museum. Perhaps you had a modern version of the stereoscope, called a "Viewmaster," when you were younger. If you can convince a child to lend you one, you will be impressed at the three-dimensional qualities of cartoons and landscapes.

There have been two other popular ways of producing three-dimensional views by recreating binocular parallax. People born before 1950 probably remember the fad of 3-D comic books. They used the **anaglyph** technique (pronounced "*ann*-uh-gliff"), in which two overlapping pictures are printed, using different colored inks, such as red and green. The pictures show slightly different views of the

Demonstration 6 - 4

A Stereoscopic Picture

Take a piece of blank cardboard that is about 20 cm wide and line it up along the dotted line in the figure below. Rest your nose on the cardboard edge that is the closest to you. Each eye should stare at just the one figure on the appropriate side of the cardboard. Try to fuse the two separate images into a single, unified image. You may find it helpful to try converging your eyes by looking slightly cross-eyed. When you achieve a single image, it should look three-dimensional.

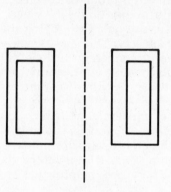

same scene. Then one eye looks through a red filter, so that only the green print is visible, and the other eye looks through a green filter, so that only the red print is visible. Thus an anaglyph selectively presents the two views to the two eyes and produces three-dimensionality. Several books have interesting examples of anaglyphs (for example, Frisby, 1980).

The third way of recreating binocular parallax involves placing a thin piece of clear plastic, with special ridges on its surface, on top of a picture containing two sets of images. The right eye looks through the ridges in one direction to see one set of images, and the left eye looks through in the other direction at another set of images. A three-dimensional effect is produced by the fusion of the two sets of images. You may have seen this technique used on the covers of children's books and in advertisements. The three-dimensional quality of the picture is quite startling, and you may be tempted to peel away the plastic to see the images underneath!

You may recall our discussion in Chapter 2 of **amblyopia,** which occurs when vision is suppressed in one eye because the two eyes do not work together. If amblyopia is not corrected, binocular vision will not develop prop-

erly. Both eyes need to be strong in order to create binocular parallax.

Ophthalmologists have a piece of equipment called an **amblyoscope** that is specially designed to test the degree to which people can fuse images presented to the two eyes (Vaughan & Asbury, 1977). For example, the amblyoscope might show a picture of a bird to one eye and a picture of a cage to the other. A person with good binocular vision will fuse these two images into a single picture of a bird in a cage. Using different equipment, Richards (1977) has reported that many people in a normal population are partially blind to these binocular depth cues.

How important is binocular parallax in depth perception? Opinions vary on this issue. Many researchers have demonstrated that binocular parallax is a very powerful cue. For example, Ritter (1977) found that people could use binocular parallax to judge the thickness of geometric figures at distances, and their judgments were quite accurate. Graham (1965) showed that binocular disparity operates over a range of approximately 500 yards, which is an impressive distance.

Other researchers acknowledge the importance of binocular parallax but stress that other depth factors are more important. Johansson (1974), for example, writes that binocular parallax ought to be included among the factors influencing space perception,

> because it forms a very important complement to monocular motion parallax. However, we must also recognize that it is an important complement but not the primary source for depth perception, contrary to the classical assumption. Happily enough for one-eyed people, motion parallax is a more basic source of space information, in the sense that monocular space perception presents good and in most cases efficient information about the environment [p. 137].

In summary, binocular parallax is important, but depth perception can be achieved with monocular vision. Psychologists disagree, however, about whether monocular depth perception is just barely adequate or whether it is quite satisfactory.

Theories of Distance Perception

We have listed 12 different distance factors. However, many psychologists interested in distance perception stress some of these factors and reject others. Their selection of factors depends upon their theoretical orientation, as you will see. This section of the chapter provides a brief summary of the two major theoretical orientations toward distance perception, the empiricist position and the Gibsonian position. A third theoretical orientation, a Gestalt approach, is less popular today than the other two, but if you are intrigued, you can find a summary of this approach in a chapter by Hochberg (1978b).

The Empiricist Position

As discussed in Chapter 1, **empiricism** (pronounced "em-*pirr*-uh-sizz-um") is a philosophical approach that states that all information is derived from sensory perceptions and experiences. We are not born knowing how to perceive distance, for example; we must acquire this skill by learning. The empiricist position was outlined by George Berkeley in 1709 in an essay titled *An Essay Towards a New Theory of*

Vision. Basically, the problem that Berkeley tackled was this: The stimulus that is registered in the eye has only two dimensions, height and width. Nonetheless, we also see depth or distance. How can we judge how far away an object is if "We cannot sense distance in and of itself . . ." (Berkeley, 1709/1957, p. 13)? We do have retinal *size* information—the amount of space an object occupies on the retina—but there is no equivalent way in which distance is registered on the retina. Still, we do perceive depth, so where does this perception come from?

Berkeley proposed that we can perceive distance by learning and experience. Specifically, we learn to associate various cues for distance with kinesthetic information about distance. **Kinesthetic information** (pronounced "kinness-*thet*-ick") is nonvisual information that includes all the muscular cues we receive as we interact with objects. For example, we might feel a certain amount of muscle strain in our eyes as we look at an object 10 cm from our eyes. We receive muscular cues as we reach out for an object a certain distance from our bodies or as we walk toward a distant object. Thus we know about distance indirectly because we link up kinesthetic information with various kinds of visual distance cues (the pictorial distance cues, for example). Notice that kinesthetic information is primary in Berkeley's theory, and vision is secondary.

As you might imagine, accommodation and convergence are important distance cues if kinesthetic information is basic to distance perception. The pictorial cues, such as interposition and linear perspective, are important learned cues. Familiar size, as we suggested earlier, is particularly relevant for the empiricist approach because of the importance of learning and experience.

Empiricism was developed further by later theorists. Helmholtz, a 19th century physiologist, applied the empiricist position to the issue of constancy, as we will see in Chapter 7. More recently, Brunswik proposed that observers add the necessary mental structure in order to judge distance. For example, you perceive an object to be far away because of the converging lines in linear perspective. Depth cues act as symbols, and each depth cue is effective because it has been associated previously with other depth cues and with the kind of kinesthetic information we just discussed. Sometimes the mental structure will be incorrect, and you will make errors. However, you will be right more often than you are wrong (Hochberg, 1978b).

Hochberg (1978b) added further to the depth perception theories developed by the empiricists and by Brunswik. However, his theory stresses the active role of the perceiver in interpreting the visual world. Hochberg argues that we constantly interact with objects around us. As a consequence, we develop certain expectations about objects. When we encounter a new scene, we perceive what we expect to perceive. That is, we construct the most reasonable interpretation of the evidence before us, and this interpretation is what we actually see.

In summary, the empiricist position emphasizes that the visual stimulus that reaches the retina is impoverished and inadequate. Other kinds of cues must be added for accurate distance perception.

The Gibsonian Position

James J. Gibson proposes that the visual stimulus that reaches the retina is really quite rich and full of information. He argues, in fact, that there is enough information in the stimulus to allow for correct perception. Visual information does not need to be supplemented by nonvisual information.

Gibson argues that most of the traditional cues—such as linear perspective, size, overlap, and atmospheric perspective—are not relevant for depth perception in real-world scenes (J. J. Gibson, 1979). He arrived at this conclusion after inspecting research on student pilots. Tests that were based on the cues for depth did not predict the success or failure of the student pilots. Therefore Gibson suspected that the traditional list of cues for depth was not adequate.

Gibson's early writing emphasized the importance of texture gradients as a source of information about distance (J. J. Gibson, 1950). As we discussed earlier, texture gradients provide a scale whereby we can measure objects' distances from us.

Gibson's emphasis on texture gradients is part of his more general ground theory. Accord-

ing to **ground theory,** distance perception depends upon information provided by surfaces in the environment. The ground, floors, and building walls are all examples of the surfaces that provide information. In the real world these surfaces help us know the distance of objects. As you look out your window, the objects that you see do not float in air. Instead, the ground serves as their background, and so distance can be seen directly (J. J. Gibson, 1979).

Gibson's early theories stressed the importance of texture gradients. His later work (for example, J. J. Gibson, 1966) pointed out the importance of motion perspective, or the change in the way things look as we move through space. As we will note in the next section on motion perception, observers and objects are continually moving. This movement provides rich information about objects' depth and distance.

Perhaps the best summary of Gibson's theory is provided by Hochberg (1974) in a book of essays written in honor of Gibson:

> His proposal is that many or most of the properties of the perceived world are evoked directly by the variables of stimulation that the sensory system receives from the normal ecology, and are not the end-products of associative processes in which kinesthetic and other imagery comes to enrich two-dimensional and meaningless visual sensations with tri-dimensional depth and object meaning [p. 17].

We have discussed the empiricist position on depth perception, which stresses how we enrich the visual stimulus with associations and expectations, and the Gibsonian position, which stresses that the visual stimulus contains a wealth of information. It seems likely, in reality, that the two positions can be reconciled. Indeed, the objects that we see probably do contain a large amount of information about depth—more information than the empiricists had originally envisioned. However, humans are active perceivers who use their past associations and expectations to further enrich the visual stimulus. Depth perception therefore involves both a visually rich environment and an active, thinking perceiver.

Distance in Paintings and Movies

The representation of distance in paintings is a topic that has been widely discussed, and our survey here will be relatively brief. However, if the topic interests you, examine chapters and books that have been written by Arnheim (1974), Hagen (1980), and Pirenne (1975). Distance in movies has received much less coverage, but a chapter by Hochberg and Brooks (1978) has some discussion of this topic.

Paintings

As we noted earlier in the chapter, artists in the Renaissance period studied depth cues in order to help them portray distance on a flat canvas. For example, Leonardo da Vinci, who lived from 1452 to 1519, was aware of practically all of the distance and depth cues available to the painter (Hochberg, 1971b). Some artists, like Leonardo, use these cues extensively in their paintings. Other artists, however, have ignored them—either intentionally or unintentionally.

Paintings cannot take advantage of several potential distance cues. Accommodation, the two monocular/movement factors (motion parallax and the kinetic depth effect), and the two binocular factors (convergence and binocular parallax) simply cannot be represented in a flat picture that does not move.

Thus we are left with "only" seven ways to represent distance in a painting. Let's look at several paintings to see which cues they use and which they ignore. The picture of the woman in Figure 6-4, for example, makes use of size (the distant people are small), linear perspective (the lines on the distant building converge), shading (there is depth information in the woman's dress), interposition (her left arm covers part of the window and part of her body), and height (the distant couple is higher on the page than the woman is). The full-sized picture may also show texture gradient and atmospheric perspective, but they are not obvious in this reproduction.

Other painters are not concerned about the representation of distance. Grandma Moses, for example, "never studied art" (Kallir, 1946, p. 141). Notice how few distance cues there are in her picture *Christmas at Home*, rep-

resented in Figure 6-5. The following cues are not shown: size (notice that the people in the background are the same size as the people in the foreground), linear perspective (notice that the ceiling and window lines do not show convergence), atmospheric perspective (although in most landscape paintings, Grandma Moses does paint distant hills blue), and shading (there are no shadows and light patches on the bodies to convey depth, and no one casts a shadow). Interposition and height are represented, however, and there is some use of texture gradient.

Other painters often deliberately try to break the "rules" of pictorial cues in order to present a dreamlike, irrational image. For example, a surrealistic painter may violate the interposition cue. Thus a painting may show a faraway tree, which is close to the horizon, blocking a nearby horse.

Movies

Movies can show some depth cues that cannot be included in stationary paintings, but some depth cues are still missing. Movies offer no advantage over stationary paintings if we consider the eight kinds of monocular factors that require no movement. They cannot represent accommodation, because you do not change your lens shape when you change your focus from mountains in the background to a cowboy in the foreground. Size, linear perspective, texture gradient, atmospheric perspective, shading, interposition, and height can all be shown, however.

Some directors may exploit these monocular/no movement factors for special effects. For example, a friend of mine who teaches film studies described how most of the directors who made films starring Marilyn Monroe used the shading cue. Now suppose that you had been one of these directors, and you wanted to emphasize the size of Marilyn Monroe's bustline when you were photographing her from the front. In other words, you wanted to convey the impression of differences in depth for various parts of her body. How would you do it? The directors solved the problem by using overhead lighting, which created large shadows. If you like to watch 1950s movies, watch for this special lighting in all Marilyn

Figure 6-4   *Mlle. du Val d'Ognes,* by Constance Marie Charpentier.

Figure 6-5 *Christmas at Home* (1946), by Grandma Moses.

Monroe films except "Gentlemen Prefer Blondes," in which standard lighting was used.

Movies also offer no advantage over paintings when we consider the binocular factors. After all, your eyes converge upon the movie screen, and they converge equally for all objects. Furthermore, except for the old 3-D movies, the same image is available for both the right and the left eye.

Movies do offer an advantage, however, when we consider the two monocular factors that involve movement. The camera can duplicate your head movements to create motion parallax. This is accomplished by a **tracking shot,** which is a special film technique in which the camera moves along a track at right angles to the direction of the camera (Hochberg & Brooks, 1978). Figure 6-6 illustrates three rep-

resentative shots from a series of frames that could be taken as the camera moves sideways. If the camera is focused on the man, the child in front of him moves to the left as the camera moves to the right. On the other hand, the picture on the wall moves to the right as the camera moves to the right.

The kinetic depth effect can also be illustrated in movies. The kinetic depth effect is most impressive when an object or a person looks two-dimensional, and then movement reveals the third dimension. In movies the picture seldom looks two-dimensional. Occasionally, however, you may see a shadow or a figure in an unlit corner that looks flat until it moves or rotates. Watch for this effect especially in horror or mystery movies!

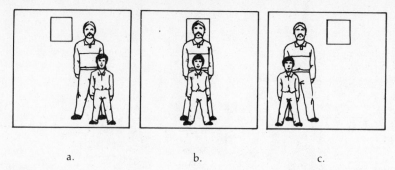

a.   b.   c.

Figure 6-6   An example of a tracking shot.

Summary: Distance Perception

- Distance perception is relevant for most of our visual activity.
- Of the factors influencing distance perception, there are eight monocular factors that require no movement.
  a. Accommodation, or a change in lens shape, is probably not an important factor.
  b. Size (either relative size or familiar size) has been shown to be important in laboratory studies of distance perception.
  c. Linear perspective, which means that parallel lines seem to meet in the distance, is an important pictorial cue.
  d. Texture gradient, or the increase in surface density at greater distances, was emphasized by Gibson; its importance has been experimentally demonstrated.
  e. Atmospheric perspective means that distant objects often look blurry and blue-colored.
  f. Shading conveys depth information because the lighting is not uniform across a surface and because objects near a light source cast shadows on objects that are farther away.
  g. Interposition means that we judge a partly covered object to be farther away than the object that covers it.
  h. Height cues tell us that objects near the horizon are farther away.
- There are two monocular factors that involve movement.
  a. Motion parallax means that as you move your head sideways, objects at different distances seem to move in different directions.
  b. In the kinetic depth effect an object seems to have depth when it rotates.
- Two binocular factors have been proposed.
  a. Convergence, in which the eyes move together in order to look at nearby objects, can sometimes be a helpful depth cue.
  b. Binocular parallax, in which the two eyes present two slightly different points of view, is important but not essential for depth perception.

- The empiricist position on depth perception states that we perceive distance by associating various cues for distance with kinesthetic information; the visual stimulus itself is inadequate. Modern variations of empiricism stress the importance of our expectations in determining what we perceive.
- Gibson's theory on depth perception argues that the visual stimulus is full of information; texture gradients and motion perspective are particularly important.
- Paintings can illustrate seven of the monocular/no movement factors: size, linear perspective, texture gradient, atmospheric perspective, shading, interposition, and height cues. However, painters can ignore these factors, either unintentionally or for special effects.
- Movies can illustrate the seven monocular/no movement factors that can be shown in paintings, as well as motion parallax and the kinetic depth effect.

Motion Perception

We have often used the term "retinal image" in our discussion of vision. However, many psychologists (for example, Johansson, von Hofsten, & Jansson, 1980) believe that "flow" is a better term. They believe that the kind of static perception implied by the term "retinal image" is artificial—it is interesting to study in the laboratory, but it does not describe perception in the real world.

James J. Gibson (1950) describes the constant motion that our visual systems encounter. Normal human beings are continually active. Our heads never remain in a fixed position for any length of time except when they are artificially restrained. We may be walking, driving, or riding, or we may change our posture while we are sitting. All of these movements change the position of our eyes in space.

Think also about the movement of other people and objects in your world. As you are sitting here reading your perception book, there probably is not much movement except for your own eyes. After all, you probably chose a place to study in which there was little activity. However, think of the constant activity that you find in other situations. In the classroom the professor may walk around the room, people wiggle, and your pen moves across the notebook. In social situations we watch people approach us, move their mouths and bodies, and depart. Most entertainment involves motion—television, movies, sports, games, dancing, and so on. Try to notice the richness of movements in your visual world, and notice how rarely you experience a frozen visual image!

There is also evidence that motion perception is an extremely basic aspect of vision. As Sekuler (1975) notes, "During evolution, motion perception was probably shaped by selective pressures that were stronger and more direct than those shaping other aspects of vision" (p. 387). Even in your relatively civilized life you have probably found that it is more important to respond quickly to a moving object than to recognize precisely what has moved. For example, if an object is being thrown toward your head, you detect the motion and you duck your head. You probably don't stop to contemplate whether the object is a brick, a book, or a box. Sekuler suggests that our visual systems contain nerve mechanisms that are specialized for the analysis of motion because of this selective evolutionary pressure to detect motion.

Motion perception is so basic that it can be found in organisms that lack other visual skills. For example, babies can follow a moving object with their eyes as soon as they are born (Barten, Birns, & Ronch, 1971). Sekuler also remarks that sensitivity to the direction of visual motion is present in newborn mammals, though other visual functions require environmental stimulation to develop. Furthermore, he notes that when brain injuries in human adults cause the temporary loss of all visual functions, the first function to recover is often movement perception.

If you were asked to design a human visual system, how would you account for motion perception? One answer you might suggest is that we notice motion whenever the image of an object moves around on the retina. This answer is appealing, but it is incorrect. After all, the images of the words on this page are sliding all over your retina as you read, and yet the page does not seem to wiggle. In this case, images move, yet we do not perceive motion. Furthermore, as your eyes follow the flight of a bird in smooth pursuit movement, the image of the bird remains on approximately the same part of your retina. In this case, images do not move, yet we perceive motion. Finally, we can sometimes see motion when the eye and the retinal image are both absolutely stationary; we will discuss this apparent movement at the end of the chapter. We must conclude that motion perception involves more than the movement of images on the retina. We will explore various mechanisms throughout this section on motion perception, as we examine both real movement and apparent movement.

Real Movement

This part of the chapter is concerned with real movement, which involves either movement of the observer or movement of the objects and people that are being watched by the observer. We first need to discuss the limits of human skill in judging movement, that is, the thresholds for motion perception. Our next topic will be biological movement, or the detection of special movement patterns produced by moving humans. Then we will discuss movement of the observer, paying particular attention to people's estimates of their own velocities. Finally, we will examine some of the explanations for motion perception.

Thresholds for Motion Perception

How good is the human eye in detecting motion? You cannot watch grass grow, or hour hands on clocks move, or bread rising. These movements are all too slow; the eye is impressive, but it isn't *that* good!

The **velocity threshold** is the minimum velocity that can be detected. It is usually expressed in terms of minutes/second, or the number of minutes of angular velocity that an object moves in one second of time. Hochberg (1971b) reviewed a number of threshold studies. In general, when only the moving object is presented, the human eye has a velocity threshold of about 10 to 20 minutes of angular velocity per second. In case you have trouble remembering the discussion of visual angles from Chapter 3,

If your head is 30 cm away from this book, you would notice motion if the bug in Figure 6-0-a slowly crawled from point 1 to point 2 during a 60-second interval.

1   2

a.

With a stationary background, you would notice motion if the bug in Figure 6-0-b slowly crawled from point 1 to point 2 during a 60-second interval.

b.

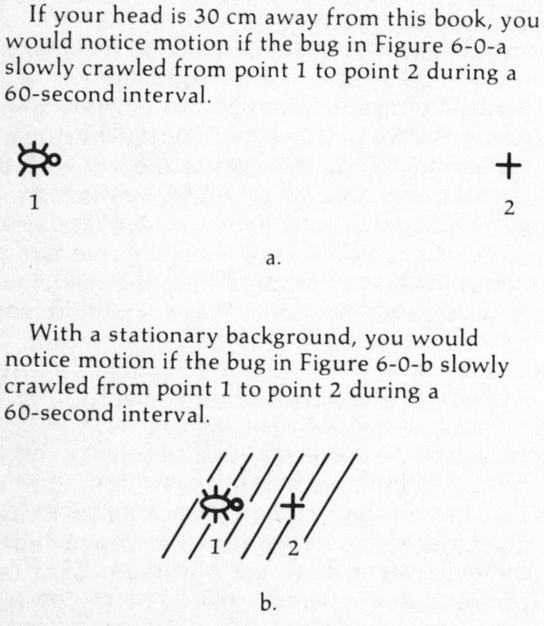

Figure 6-7   Velocity thresholds.

let's translate those numbers into a concrete example in Figure 6-7a.

You are even better when a stationary background is provided for the moving object. When some parts of the visual field stay still, your velocity threshold for a moving object is about 1 to 2 minutes/second. Notice how impressive this is by looking at Figure 6-7b. Do you remember playing games when you were younger that involved trying to move toward a goal without the leader noticing? Now you know why the leader could spot your movement so readily. You might have escaped detection without the stationary background in which you were being watched.

Psychologists have tried to identify other factors that influence the velocity threshold, in addition to the presence of a stationary background. The luminance of a target, for example, is *not* a very important factor. In fact, at moderate-to-high levels of luminance the target luminance has no influence on the threshold (Henderson, 1971). Thus the movement of a very bright moving object is no easier to detect than the movement of a medium-bright moving object.

Other researchers have tried to determine whether the region of the retina influences the velocity threshold. You may recall that the region of the retina has an important influence on acuity. Acuity is much greater at the fovea, or center of the retina, than at the periphery. Similarly, velocity thresholds are much lower at the fovea. In other words, less motion is necessary at the fovea in order to be detected.

On the other hand, there is evidence that the peripheral regions of the retina are quite good in their detection of *rapid* motion. Try Demonstration 6-5 to demonstrate this for yourself.

Sekuler (1975) reviews some studies on vision in the peripheral regions of the retina and reports that acuity for a slowly moving target is somewhat better than for a stationary target. This is just the opposite of the relationship for the fovea, where stationary targets can be seen more clearly than moving targets.

Notice how often you pay attention to things that move in your peripheral vision. For example, when you are driving, you can see a car approaching you on the left or a pedestrian moving on your right. Notice, also, how you

Demonstration 6 - 5

Motion Detection in the Periphery of the Retina

Stare at a point straight ahead of you. Hold the forefinger of your right hand directly in front of your eyes. Move it slowly toward your right, keeping the height at eye level, until you can no longer see it. Keep it stationary and make sure that you cannot see it at this location. Then wiggle your finger rapidly. It is likely that you *will* see it when it is moving.

use your peripheral vision for moving objects in social situations and in sports.

Biological Motion

So far, we have discussed the motions of rather simple objects, such as spots of light. However, most of the motion patterns that we watch in everyday life are much more complex than that. For example, consider the movement of humans. How does your friend's body move as she walks toward you? You perceive that she is moving toward you, but you also perceive more subtle kinds of movements as she alternately moves her legs, swings her arms, tilts her head, and moves her facial features into a smile.

In this section we will discuss **biological motion,** or the pattern of movement of living organisms. We will examine how observers can guess what people are doing and who they are from very subtle motion cues. We will see, too, that people are very sensitive to facial movements that reveal emotions.

The first research on biological motion perception was conducted by Johansson (1973, 1975), a Swedish psychologist. Johansson attached small flashlight bulbs to the main joints of a male co-worker. Thus the man wore bright spots on his shoulders, elbows, wrists, hips, knees, and ankles. Johansson made a movie of this man as he moved around in a darkened room; Figure 6-8 shows a lighted man and the light tracks he made as he walked.

Now Figure 6-8 looks like meaningless streaks, because it is a record of continuous movement. However, the movie showed isolated dots moving in patterns that observers could easily interpret. Johansson (1975) reports that during the opening scene, when the man is sitting motionless in a chair, the observers were puzzled because they saw only a random set of lights. This pattern might have looked like a constellation of stars, but it had no meaning as

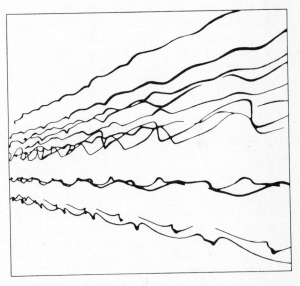

Figure 6-8 A projection of motion tracks made by lights fastened on the head and joints of a man walking in darkness.

long as the form was motionless. However, as soon as the man stood up and started to move, the observers instantly perceived that the lights were attached to a human being, who was invisible except for the lights. The observers could easily tell the difference between walking and jogging movements. Furthermore, they could recognize subtle peculiarities in the man's movement. For example, when he pretended to limp, they could detect it. Remember that observers can detect all this information from very few cues—just 12 tiny lights!

In another study, Johansson (1975) placed 12 lights on each of two dancers and filmed them performing a lively folk dance. Observers who watched the film immediately recognized that the 24 swirling dots of light represented a dancing couple! We do not need extra cues such as the contours of body parts or the continuous lines of the body in order to recognize complex movement. Mere spots, representing the body's joints, are sufficient.

In other work that Johansson (1975) summarizes, researchers found that one tenth of a second was enough time to allow an observer to identify a familiar biological movement, such as walking. One tenth of a second is equivalent to two frames in a motion picture! Johansson concludes that the visual system must have fixed pathways from the retina to the cortex, so that we do not have to decipher and sort out the movements each time we see a new pattern. Instead, we can recognize movements quickly, even before these movements reach consciousness.

Other researchers have discovered that observers can even identify the gender of the person wearing the spots of light! Barclay, Cutting, and Kozlowski (1978) selected females and males who were about the same height and weight. These researchers fastened strips of reflectant tape around the wrists, arms, ankles, and legs of the "walkers" and attached additional strips at their waists and shoulders. The lighting was arranged so that only the tape showed, and Barclay and her colleagues took movies of each walker in motion.

The movies of the walkers were then shown to a group of viewers. Viewers who saw each person for only 4.4 seconds were able to guess whether the walker was a male or a female! Barclay and her colleagues also demonstrated that viewers identified genders accurately even when the movie image was so out of focus that all the lights blurred together.

If people can judge the motions of the body from a few lights, can they also judge facial emotion from such subtle cues? Think about a friend's face as it changes from a neutral expression into a smile. We tend to think that facial features on a motionless face are important cues to a person's feelings. For example, you judge that your friend is happy if the outer corners of the mouth are raised. Indeed, static facial features do allow the recognition of emotion.

However, Bassili (1978) has argued that the motion of the face provides enough information for the recognition of emotion. Bassili adapted Johansson's techniques for use with the human face. He covered actors' faces with black makeup and scattered about 100 tiny white spots on each completely black face. Then he instructed each actor to portray six different emotions: happiness, sadness, fear, surprise , anger, and disgust. As in Johansson's studies, the camera recorded only the movement of the white spots.

Observers watched the movies and tried to judge which emotion was being portrayed. They were much more accurate than chance in their guesses. Recognition was highest for the expression of surprise and lowest for the expression of fear. Bassili describes the facial movement involved in the expression of surprise:

> a sudden expansion of the lower part of the face (caused by the dropping of the jaw), along with an expansion in the lower area of the eyes (caused by the raising of the eyebrows) and a corresponding compression of the forehead [p. 378].

Thus we watch the changes that occur as parts of the face move into new positions. This movement information lets us identify an emotion.

You may be familiar with the research in the area of nonverbal communication of "body language" (for example, LaFrance & Mayo, 1978). Many of the studies in this area have focused upon static body position. In the future we may see an increased emphasis on the information available in the motion of the body and the face.

Movement of the Observer

In the previous two sections we talked about the movement of objects (both inanimate objects and people) and the impressive ability of the human visual system to detect movement. In this section we will examine situations in which the observer, rather than an object, is moving.

First of all, we should note that it is sometimes difficult to decide what is moving, the observer or the object. Have you ever been in a car stopped in traffic and sensed that you were moving, only to find that other cars were moving and you were stationary? This happened to me recently, and I tried to step on the brakes even more firmly. Suddenly, I realized that the car to my left had been inching up, but I hadn't moved a bit! You may have had a similar experience in a train, especially if you were expecting your own train to move soon. The perception that you are moving when you are really stationary is sometimes called the **self-motion illusion** (Dichgans & Brandt, 1978).

Some of the most interesting research on observers' movements has examined people's perceptions of their movement speeds, particularly when they are driving. Think about how you estimate your car's speed when you drive. If you are an experienced driver, you can probably guess your driving speed fairly accurately. Still, you might glance down at the speedometer and discover that you were traveling at a different speed than you estimated. For example, if you are on a long, open section of a good highway, you might find that your speed is way above the speed limit.

Schmidt and Tiffin (1969) noted that drivers who have been driving at a constant speed for a long time often report that this speed seems much slower than it did at the beginning. Consequently, speeds slower than this level seem to be extremely slow. Schmidt and Tiffin tested these observations by asking drivers to try to maintain specified speeds. At the beginning of the study they were asked to bring the car to a speed of 40 miles per hour. They were quite accurate—the average speed they were really traveling when they thought that they were driving at 40 miles per hour was 41.4 miles per hour. Then they were instructed to accelerate to a speed of 70 miles per hour, hold that speed for 5 seconds, and then bring the car to an estimated speed of 40 miles per hour. In this condition their true speed was 44.5 miles per hour. In another condition they drove at 70 miles per hour for 20 miles before bringing the car to an estimated speed of 40 miles per hour. In fact, their true speed in this condition was 50.5 miles per hour.

With the lower speed limits that are enforced today, you cannot try to replicate Schmidt and Tiffin's experiment exactly. However, notice what happens if you have been traveling at 55 miles per hour and you enter an area where the speed limit is 35. You might find that you slow down to only 45! Motion speed estimates are clearly influenced by our previous driving experiences.

Explanations for Motion Perception

Many different explanations have been proposed for motion perception. Some explanations focus on the neurons that register motion. Other explanations stress that the feedback from the body allows us to identify whether objects are moving or we are moving. Additional explanations emphasize the visual information provided by the stimulus. Let us consider these three kinds of explanations.

1. *Motion-Detecting Neurons.* Think back to Chapter 2 when we discussed the neurons in the visual cortex. Do you remember the simple cell, the complex cell, and the hypercomplex cell, which are located in the visual cortex? The complex cells respond to moving stimuli. For example, if a bar of light moves across the field, the complex cells will fire. Thus we know that there is a biological mechanism for detecting motion. This biological mechanism is discussed by Sekuler, Pantle, and Levinson (1978).

However, the explanation for motion perception must be more complex. As we mentioned earlier, we must be able to explain why we perceive motion when we watch a bird in flight—even though the image stays on the same part of the retina. We must also be able to explain why we do not perceive motion when we move our eyes across a page—even though the image moves on the retina. Thus we must consider some other mechanisms.

2. *Corollary Discharge Theory.* Some explanations emphasize the importance of feedback from the body in the perception of motion. One of these explanations is called corollary discharge theory. (The word "corollary," pronounced "*core*-uh-lehr-ee," means "related".) According to **corollary discharge theory,** voluntary movements of the eye muscles or the body muscles produce neural signals or corollary discharges. These neural signals cancel out or modify the perception of motion (Richards, 1975).

Let's consider an example. Suppose that you are looking at a picture, and you decide to move your eyes to the right. Your brain sends a signal to your eye muscles that commands them to move to the right. Your eyes move to the right, and the image of the picture moves across your retina. At this point it might be possible to perceive motion. However, when your eyes move, they also produce those special signals called corollary discharges. These corollary discharges arrive in the brain and cancel out the perception of motion. Consequently, the picture looks stable, rather than moving.

You have probably had experiences that are similar to the corollary discharge mechanism. For example, you put your dark glasses on, and a smaller amount of light reaches your eyes. You could conclude that the world is coming to an end and that the sudden darkness is just the first sign. You could conclude that you are going blind. However, there is feedback from your hands' motions that tells you that you put on your glasses, and there is feedback from the sensation of the glasses resting on your nose and ears. This feedback allows you to correct for the impression of darkness. In effect, the feedback tells your brain to cancel the impression of darkness. Similarly, when you move, the feedback from the body and eye muscles tells your brain to cancel the impression of movement.

Put your finger up to your lower eyelid and press gently. Notice what happens when your eye is moved passively, by your hand, rather than voluntarily, through the brain's normal commands to the eye muscles. As Gregory (1978) concludes, stability does not hold for passive eye movements. Have you ever fainted and had the sensation that the world was tilting up toward you as you fell? This sensation occurs because you did not command your eyes to move, and yet images are flying across your retina as you fall. Because corollary discharges were not produced, there was no feedback to indicate "cancel that sensation of movement."

Incidentally, I should mention that corollary discharge theory is just one of the explanations that uses the concept of feedback in explaining motion perception. Other explanations are discussed by Richards (1975) and Gregory (1978).

3. *Information in the Stimulus.* Gibson and others have argued that the stimulus is rich with information about movement. We will examine six sources of information. For example,

we can tell whether we are moving or whether an object is moving by noticing whether or not the object's background moves. Look at Figure 6-9 as you read the next section. In Figure 6-9a, notice that the child is always in front of the same background, the poster. Because the child does not move in relation to the poster, you conclude that the child is stationary and you—the observer—are moving. In Figure 6-9b, the child is moving in relation to the background. In the first picture, he is in front of the poster, then he moves in front of the blackboard, and then he moves in front of the globe. You therefore conclude that he is moving and you are stationary.

Furthermore, moving objects show a systematic covering and uncovering of the background. Pick up your textbook and move it from right to left in front of your eyes. It systematically covers up the background on the left; this process is called **occlusion** (pronounced "uh-*clue*-zyun"). At the same time it systematically uncovers the background on the right; this process is called **disocclusion** (pronounced "dis-uh-*clue*-zyun"). Occlusion and disocclusion tell us the direction of movement of objects (J. J. Gibson, 1979).

Objects that move toward us also show a systematic occlusion and disocclusion pattern. Pick up your textbook again and move it toward you so that it is about to hit your face. Notice how the occlusion occurs to the same extent on both the right and the left side of the book. When the occlusion is equal, we perceive that an object is coming directly toward us. Other times the occlusion is not equal—for instance, when you move your book toward your left ear. In this case the left side of the background becomes occluded at the same time as the right side becomes disoccluded. You perceive that the object will miss you. If the occlusion is extremely unequal, then the object will miss you by a large distance.

The next time you are playing a game such as volleyball, notice how this occlusion/disocclusion process works. You hold your hands in front of your face and move your body so that the occlusion pattern is equal on the right and the left. The ball appears to be coming directly at you! On the other hand, if someone is throwing a snowball at you, you move your head so that the occlusion patterns are unequal, and the

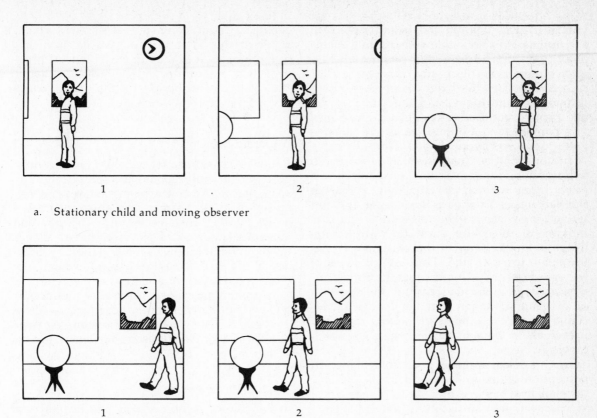

a.   Stationary child and moving observer

b.   Moving child and stationary observer

Figure 6-9   Information about motion that is available in the stimulus.

snowball will miss you. Notice, then, that you—the perceiver—can control what you perceive by adjustments of your body.

The size of the image also increases as you approach objects and they approach you, as Regan, Beverley, and Cynader (1979) have described. Notice that image size is a monocular cue. Regan proposes that the strength of monocular cues such as image size explains how some pilots and ballplayers can continue to perform effectively after they have lost their vision in one eye. Their professions depend upon successful motion perception, yet they have enough information about motion from monocular cues. Have you ever noticed how motion is shown in cartoons? Someone falls off the cliff, and the features on the ground below expand suddenly until we see the final "splat!" from a side view. Thus cartoonists successfully exploit the image size cue for motion.

We discussed two other aspects of motion in the section on distance perception, and both of them are relevant when observers are moving. Remember that motion parallax occurs when you move your head, and objects at different distances from your head appear to move in different directions. Goodson, Snider, and Swearingen (1980) have demonstrated that motion parallax is a very important cue to motion. Motion perspective, which we discussed earlier, is a more general term that includes motion parallax; motion perspective means that objects continuously change the way they look as you move about in the world. As you drive down a road, images of objects flow across your retina at different rates. If you look straight ahead, for example, nearby objects on either side of you flow by quickly. Objects that are farther away flow slowly. Parts of the world expand and contract as you move around. The next time you are in a car, look straight ahead at a point on the horizon and notice how everything seems to expand outward from that point.

We have been discussing monocular cues so far. Corollary discharge theory can apply to one eye, and background information, the occlusion/disocclusion process, image size, motion parallax, and motion perspective can also work with one-eyed vision. Regan and his coauthors point out that binocular cues are also helpful in motion perception. As a ball moves toward you, for example, the image moves at the same speed on both your right and left retinas. However, if the left retinal image is moving more slowly than the right retinal image, then you perceive that the ball will pass toward your right side. Thus comparisons of the speeds of the left and the right retinal images gives you information about the direction of movement. Regan and his coauthors describe several experiments that confirmed the usefulness of binocular cues when we watch moving objects.

In this discussion of explanations of motion perception we have discussed many possible mechanisms. First we discussed a physiological mechanism, motion-detecting neurons. Then we talked about how feedback from muscles could cancel the sensation of movement when your eyes move across a scene. Finally, we talked about six aspects of the stimulus that provide information about motion: the background, the occlusion/disocclusion process, image size, motion parallax, motion perspective, and binocular cues. (If you haven't devised your own memory trick for these stimulus aspects, beginning with B O I M M B, try this: *B*ad *O*liver *I*s *M*aking *M*onstrous *B*lobs.)

As you might expect, people disagree about which of these mechanisms are most important. Sekuler (1975), for example, argues that the physical aspects of the stimulus cannot explain motion perception: "We cannot reduce motion perception to obvious aspects of the stimulus. We must consider the contribution of our sensory apparatus" (p. 390). On the other hand, it is clear that aspects of the stimulus are sometimes sufficient to give the experience of motion, even when there are no muscular cues. For instance, have you ever seen a movie in Cinerama or on a very large screen? I recall

seeing a Cinerama movie that was shot from a roller-coaster. The audience gasped collectively at the sensation of motion we all felt. At present, then, we cannot draw conclusions about the relative contributions of the many factors involved in motion perception.

Apparent Movement

In our discussion so far we have stressed how observers and objects move continuously. For some reason, however, perception researchers are often more interested in apparent movement than in real movement. In **apparent movement,** observers perceive that an object moves, even though it is really stationary. Incidentally, **illusory movement** is a phrase that is often substituted for apparent movement.

Apparent movement is not very common in our everyday experiences, yet it occurs often enough to justify a brief discussion. We will discuss five kinds of illusory movement in this section.

Movement in Pictures

In the comics section of your newspaper you have probably seen illustrations of static figures that show motion. However, as Friedman and Stevenson (1980) note, researchers have generally ignored the topic of movement in pictures. Of course, movement occurring over time cannot really be captured in a static representation. We cannot really be fooled by pictorial movement, as we might be fooled by pictorial depth. Still, a picture can often convey some sense of movement, as in Figure 6-10.

If you are interested in art, read Friedman and Stevenson's article on the perception of movement in pictures. They examined paintings from many cultures and many historical periods in order to look for consistencies and differences in the depiction of movement. They found, for example, that Greek vase paintings were particularly likely to show movement.

Photographs can also convey motion. If you enjoy photography, you should look at Zakia and Todd's (1969) book called *101 Experiments in Photography.* One section tells how to adjust the shutter speed of your camera to give the impression of movement.

Figure 6-10 Apparent movement in a static picture.

Autokinesis

Autokinesis (pronounced "ah-toe-kih-*nee-*siss") occurs when a stationary object, with no clear background, appears to move. Try Demonstration 6-6 to see if you can experience autokinesis. Hochberg (1971b) notes that the autokinesis effect was first reported by astronomers who found that the stars they watched through telescopes seemed to drift. Incidentally, Sharma and Moskowitz (1972) reported that the autokinesis effect increased after their observers had smoked marihuana.

One explanation for autokinesis is that it is caused by the spontaneous tiny movements of the eyes. Do you remember the miniature eye movements that we discussed in Chapter 3 —particularly the miniature drifts that the eyes make when you try to fixate on something? Now if your eyes drift, without your voluntarily controlling them, there will be no corollary discharges to cancel out the perception of movement. As a result, you will see movement.

Other evidence for the eye-movement explanation of autokinesis comes from a study by Pola and Matin (1977). These researchers placed a contact lens on the eye and recorded eye movements. They found that there was a systematic relationship between the direction of the target's apparent movement and the eye movements that they recorded.

Would you believe that personality psychologists have also been interested in autokinesis? Rechtschaffen and Mednick (1955) presented a pinpoint of light and told observers that the moving light would write words. In fact, the light was really stationary. The observers were encouraged to guess whenever they could not make out every letter of a word. All of the observers reported words being written by the point of light—an average of 15 words per person. Some of the observers reported an astonishing number of words. One person reported that the light "wrote":

When men are tired and depraved, they become mean and callous individuals. When men learn to master their souls, the world will be a more humane and tolerant place in which to live. Men should learn to control themselves [p. 346].

The autokinesis effect seems to be an interesting projective technique in which people

Demonstration 6-6 *Autokinetic Movement*	Find a flashlight that has opaque sides, so that light shines out only through the front. Take a piece of opaque cardboard and poke a tiny hole in it with a pin. Attach it to the flashlight so that the only visible light shines through the pinhole. Find a totally dark room and turn on the flashlight. Place it about 2 meters from you so that you can clearly see the tiny spot of light. Fixate steadily on the light for about 2 minutes. The light may appear to move slightly.

respond to relatively unstructured and ambiguous stimuli. It's like a combination of a Rorschach inkblot test and a Ouija board!

Induced Movement

Induced movement occurs when a visual frame of reference moves in one direction and produces the illusion that a stationary target is moving in the opposite direction. The next time the moon is bright and there are some clouds in the sky, see whether you notice any induced movement. The moon is essentially stationary, yet the clouds are moving in front of it. Consequently, the moon may appear to move in a direction opposite to the clouds' motion.

Many astronomers believe that induced movement, perhaps in combination with autokinesis, is responsible for the majority of Unidentified Flying Object reports! People look up at a star against the background of moving clouds, and it appears to drift noticeably.

Induced movement is a popular topic in laboratory research. Gogel (1978) summarizes some of the situations in which induced movement can be produced. For example, if a stationary dot is shown in the middle of a square frame that moves from side to side, the dot seems to move in the direction that is opposite to the frame's movement. If a dot is moving up and down, while the frame moves from side to side, the dot appears to move along a diagonal course.

Some variables influence the magnitude of the induced movement effect. Gogel and Tietz (1976) found, for example, that the effect was reduced when the surrounding frame and the target object seemed to be different distances away from the observer.

The surrounding frame that induces movement in the target object does not need to be very elaborate. Day (1978) showed, for example, that one other spot of light is sufficient to produce the induced movement effect. When the background is dark and one of two spots of light moves slowly, observers report movement. Sometimes they report that the moving spot appears to move, and sometimes they report that the stationary target appears to move. Thus induced movement occurs when one object moves *relative* to another and there are no background cues to tell which object is stable. As a result, an object that is truly stationary may appear to move.

Stroboscopic Movement

Stroboscopic movement (pronounced "stroe-buh-*skope*-ick") is the illusion of movement produced by a rapid pattern of stimulation of different parts of the retina. In a typical demonstration of stroboscopic movement a light flashes on briefly at location 1. About a tenth of a second later, another light flashes on briefly at location 2. Observers usually report that the

Figure 6-11 Stroboscopic movement from frames of movie film.

light seemed to move from location 1 to location 2. If the time interval between the two flashes is much shorter or much longer, then the illusion of movement is lost.

Motion pictures use stroboscopic movement in order to give the impression of movement (Anstis, 1978). Movie film is like a series of snapshots pasted together, as in Figure 6-11. Have you ever wondered how a series of isolated snapshots can give the impression of movement? Observers perceive movement because the movie projector exposes each frame in the series very quickly, so that there is stroboscopic movement of the dog's paw in Figure 6-11 from position 1 to position 2. You perceive movement from one place to the next, rather than a succession of static views (Hochberg & Brooks, 1978).

Naturally, the projector speed must be just right. If the speed is too fast, you may perceive a blur. If it is too slow, you will see the separate frames of the movie, and there will be a flicker. You can demonstrate the importance of projector speed if you have a movie viewer, an inexpensive piece of equipment that home-movie-makers use to review their movies. You control the speed of the movie by hand, and the impression of movement is achieved by finding the ideal speed, intermediate between the blurs and the flickers. Also, some children's books are available that show cartoon characters in a sequence of frames in the upper corner. If you thumb through the pages at just the right speed, you might see a mouse performing a juggling act!

Movement Aftereffects

Movement aftereffects occur when you have been looking at a continuous movement and

---

Demonstration 6 - 7

Movement Aftereffects

Make a photocopy of the spiral shape. Glue it onto firm cardboard and cut out the spiral. Poke a hole in the center and place the figure on a phonograph turntable. Turn on the phonograph at a speed of 33⅓. Stand directly over the rotating figure and fixate on it for 1 to 2 minutes. Then turn off the phonograph and hold the turntable stationary. The spiral should seem to be moving in a direction opposite to its previous motion, even though nothing is really moving.

then look at another surface; that surface will seem to move in the opposite direction. You might try to demonstrate movement aftereffects if you can visit a waterfall. Stare for several minutes at the waterfall, and then turn your gaze toward the nearby bank. The rocks and plants will seem to move upward! Try Demonstration 6-7 to see another example of movement aftereffects.

An early explanation of movement aftereffects involved eye movements. This explanation has been replaced by other mechanisms, such as fatigue (Favreau & Corballis, 1976). Sekuler (1975) discusses how movement aftereffects could be due to depressed responding from the motion-sensitive cells after they have been stimulated for a long time.

In this section we have examined the five kinds of apparent movement: picture movement, autokinesis, induced movement, stroboscopic movement, and aftereffects. (The initials P A I S A can be remembered by the sentence, *"Poor Arthur Is Swatting Ant-eaters."*) In all of these cases the object is stationary, and the observer is also stationary. Nonetheless, movement is perceived. In apparent movement effects, our perceptions do not match the true qualities of objects. We will see other examples of the differences between our perceptions and reality in the next chapter on Constancy and Illusions.

Summary: Motion Perception

- Motion perception is an important, basic aspect of vision.

- Velocity thresholds depend upon whether there is a stationary background for the moving object.
- In the peripheral area of the retina, acuity for a slowly moving target is better than acuity for a stationary target.
- Observers can quickly identify the actions and gender of a person by watching the movement of lights attached to the person's main joints. They can also judge emotions on the basis of facial motion.
- When observers have been traveling at high speeds, slower speeds seem very slow.
- Two explanations for motion perception involve motion-detecting neurons in the visual cortex and corollary discharge theory, a theory in which voluntary movements of the muscles produce feedback that cancels the impression of movement.
- A third explanation for motion perception involves information available from the stimulus: background information, the occlusion/disocclusion process, image size, motion parallax, motion perspective, and binocular cues.
- Five kinds of apparent movement are (a) movement illustrated in pictures; (b) autokinesis, or apparent movement of a stationary object that has no clear background; (c) induced movement, or apparent movement of a stationary object when the frame of reference moves; (d) stroboscopic movement, or apparent movement from consecutive stimulation of two areas of the retina; and (e) movement aftereffects, or apparent movement of a surface following inspection of another moving surface.

Review

1. Draw a picture that shows at least one example of each of the seven kinds of monocular factors without movement that can be represented in a picture. Label each factor.

2. List the five distance factors that cannot be represented in a picture and describe why a picture will not work for them.

3. Binocular parallax was described in more detail than the other distance factors. Describe binocular parallax, distinguish it from motion parallax, and discuss its importance (both applied and theoretical).

4. Summarize the empiricist position and Gibson's theory with regard to distance perception. Some research has shown that vision is dominant over kinesthetic information—that is, vision is primary and kinesthetic information is secondary. Which theory does this research support?

5. Watch the Saturday morning cartoons

and notice which of the 12 distance factors are represented. Then watch an action show on TV or go to a movie and see which additional factors are represented.

6. William Shakespeare wrote, "Things in motion sooner catch the eye than what stirs not." How is this relevant to your peripheral vision? Describe other evidence that motion perception is a very basic aspect of vision.

7. Imagine that an industrial employee has been instructed to report whether a dial on a piece of equipment moves the slightest amount. Describe how luminance and background might be important and mention why apparent movement might be a problem.

8. Summarize the studies on biological motion and speculate why the perception of biological motion occurs so quickly.

9. You are playing basketball. Describe how each of the five aspects of the stimulus that provide information about motion might help

in your perception of motion as the ball comes flying toward your head. You twirl around at one point, and the world seems to remain stable. How might corollary discharge theory account for the stability despite the motion of images across your retina?

10. Name the kind of apparent movement that is represented in each of these situations: (a) A billboard has a line of light bulbs that light up and dim in rapid succession. The light appears to travel across the billboard. (b) On a dark night you see a single light that is on in a neighbor's house, and the neighbor is on vacation. Suddenly the light moves, and you suspect a burglar. (c) You are on a "fun ride" at a carnival, spinning about rapidly. As soon as you stop, the world seems to be moving in a different direction. (d) On a dark night you watch a plane fly over a radio tower. For a brief moment the plane seems to be stationary, and the tower light seems to move.

New Terms

egocentric distance	height cues	kinesthetic information
relative distance	motion parallax	ground theory
depth perception	parallax	tracking shot
monocular	motion perspective	velocity threshold
accommodation	kinetic depth effect	biological motion
pictorial cues	convergence	self-motion illusion
cue	converge	corollary discharge theory
size cues	binocular parallax	occlusion
relative size	retinal disparity	disocclusion
familiar size	stereoscopic picture	apparent movement
linear perspective	stereoscope	illusory movement
texture gradient	anaglyph	autokinesis
atmospheric perspective	amblyopia	induced movement
shading	amblyoscope	stroboscopic movement
interposition	empiricism	movement aftereffects

chapter 7

CONSTANCY AND ILLUSIONS

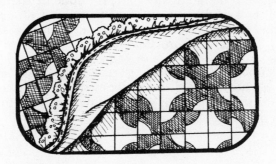

Outline Constancy
  Size Constancy
  Shape Constancy
  Brightness Constancy
  Other Constancies
Illusions
  Size Illusions
  Direction and Shape Illusions

Preview

In this chapter we will investigate two areas in which our perceptions do not correspond to the patterns that are registered on our retinas. These two areas are constancy and illusions.

We will first consider constancy, or the tendency for the properties of objects to seem constant and stable, in spite of the circumstances in which we view them. We will see that objects seem to stay the same size, even though we view them from different distances. Also, objects seem to stay the same shape, even though we view them from different orientations. Furthermore, objects seem to stay the same brightness, even though we view them in different illuminations. Finally, we will briefly consider several other constancies: color constancy, motion constancy, constancy under bending, position constancy, and existence constancy.

The second section is concerned with illusions, or perceptions that are incorrect. Though psychologists disagree about whether illusions are important in our daily lives, the volume of research on illusions has nonetheless been impressive. In this section we will discuss size illusions and direction and shape illusions. Several different theories for the illusions have been proposed. It seems that each illusion requires more than one theory in order to explain the effects.

Do our perceptions match the patterns that are registered on our retinas? In many cases they do. However, when we examine the areas of constancy and illusions, we find that we often "see more than meets the eye."

In the section on constancy you will learn that objects seem to stay the same to viewers, even though the representations of those objects on the retina change enormously. For example, a little boy who is 1 meter tall produces an image on the retina that is fairly large if he is standing in front of you shouting, "Trick-or-Treat!" As that same child walks away down the street, the image on your retina shrinks. However, you perceive the child as staying the same height. The perceived sizes do not correspond to the retinal sizes. In the case of constancy, the perceived size corresponds to the object's true size—the child *seems* to stay the same size, and in fact (fortunately) the child's true size does stay the same.

In the section on illusion you will see that two objects may seem to be quite different to viewers, even though the representations of those objects on the retina are just the same.

One line may look much longer than another in the Müller-Lyer illusion (see Figure 7-7). Nevertheless, the actual lines are exactly the same length, and their retinal images are also identical. In the case of illusions the perceived size does not correspond to the object's true size.

We need to have some vocabulary to refer to the objects "out there" and the objects as they are registered on the retina. The term **distal stimulus** refers to the objects "out there" in the world, such as a phonograph record. A distal stimulus has no contact with a sense organ, such as the retina. The term **proximal stimulus** refers to the representation of objects in contact with a sense organ. Thus the size, shape, and brightness represented by the phonograph record on your retina are examples of proximal stimuli. Incidentally, you can remember which term is which by thinking of distal as "in the distance." Table 7-1 outlines the size relationships for both constancy and illusions.

Don't get the wrong impression from the names "constancy" and "illusions." It is tempting to think that constancy is a normal process,

Table 7-1 Constancy and illusion.		OBJECT'S TRUE SIZES (DISTAL STIMULI)	RETINAL SIZES (PROXIMAL STIMULI)	PERCEIVED SIZES
CONSTANCY (e.g., two identical objects at different distances from viewer)		same	different	same
ILLUSIONS (e.g., two identical objects with different surrounding lines)		same	same	different

whereas illusions are abnormal. However, illusions are universal—they occur for everyone—and they are predictable; we can tell in advance what kind of distortion people will perceive. As Coren and Girgus (1978) have argued, illusions are not special or rare cases of deviant perception. Instead, they are part of normal perception, and in fact they may be an inevitable product of normal perception. Thus any discussion of perceptual processes must include information about illusions.

Constancy

As you move around in the world, you change your distance from objects, approaching them and then moving away. An image of these objects is registered on your retina. However, that image will vary from time to time—it may be large or small, round or elliptical, bright or dark. Nonetheless, properties of objects seem to stay the same, or constant, even though we view them in different conditions.

Consider a phonograph record, for example. If you hold it very close to your eyes, it takes up nearly the whole view, and the image on your retina is large. If you stand across the room, however, the image on your retina may be as small as a period on this page. The shape of the image can also change, from round to elliptical to a straight line. The brightness of the record also changes, because it reflects much more light to your retina if you are looking at it in bright sunlight than if you are in a candlelit room. Still, a record is a record. The visual qualities of the record seem to stay the same. The phenomenon that is operating is **constancy,** which is the tendency for qualities of objects to seem to stay the same, despite changes in the way we view the objects.

Consider another example, Demonstration 7-1. How many right angles did you count? When I first saw this demonstration, I systematically began counting four angles for each of the three sides I could see. However, there really are no right angles in this diagram! Because of constancy, we believe that this diagram represents a cube, placed at an angle. We count the number of right angles that would appear in a cube, ignoring the figure that is really in front of us.

One reason that constancy is an interesting phenomenon is that the distal stimulus is often quite different in size, shape, and brightness from the proximal stimulus. For instance, the round shape of a phonograph may be represented by an ellipse on your retina. Nonetheless, we tend to perceive the *true* shape, rather than the shape on the retina. This section of the chapter will discuss how we are able to perceive "more than meets the eye." We will consider size, shape, and brightness constancy in some

---

Demonstration 7 - 1   Count the number of right angles in the figure below.

*An Example of Shape
Constancy*

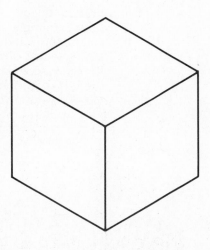

---

detail. There are also several other constancies that we will discuss briefly, because they demonstrate how general the constancy phenomenon is.

Size Constancy

Size constancy means that an object seems to stay the same size despite changes in its distance. Notice, then, that the proximal size of an object can shrink and expand, yet the distal size of the object seems to stay the same. Try Demonstration 7-2 to help you notice how the visual angle and retinal size change as an object moves away from your eye. **Visual angle,** a term used in Chapter 3, means the size of the arc formed on the retina by an object. **Retinal size** refers to the amount of space the object occupies on the retina. Visual angle and retinal size are closely related terms.

Think about how size constancy operates in the real world. As your professor steps forward to make a particularly important point, he or she does not expand magically before your eyes. As a car drives away from you, you don't believe that it is shrinking to matchbox size. As a dog plays "fetch the stick" with you, it does

not expand and contract. The next time you get up from reading this book, notice how objects seem to stay the same size as you move away from them.

You might argue that you have size constancy because you know how big your professor, a car, and Rover are. Yes, familiarity may help to preserve size constancy (Leibowitz, 1971), but size constancy operates for unfamiliar objects as well. If you cut a nonsense shape out of white paper and changed your distance from that shape, it also would seem to stay the same size.

Distance Cues and Size Constancy

In everyday life you have many distance cues to tell you how far away an object is. You could combine knowledge about an object's distance and knowledge about its retinal size to determine how big an object "really" is.

Look at Figure 7-1. The picture on the left shows a cake and a pie that you would judge to be about the same size. The retinal size of the cake is certainly smaller, but distance cues (linear perspective and distance from the horizon, as discussed in the last chapter) tell you

Demonstration 7 - 2

Size Constancy

Take your pen and hold it about 3 cm in front of your eyes. Notice the size of the visual angle that it occupies, and think about how big the retinal size must be for a pen held this close. Now move the pen out to 30 cm. Notice how the visual angle is much smaller; the retinal size is also much smaller. Now prop up the pen and walk across the room. The visual angle is now extremely small, and the retinal size is also extremely small. Think about how the pen looked to you. Did it seem to shrink to doll-sized proportions as you walked away from it? In fact, it seemed to stay a constant size, despite the fact that the retinal size was much, much smaller when the pen was viewed from across the room.

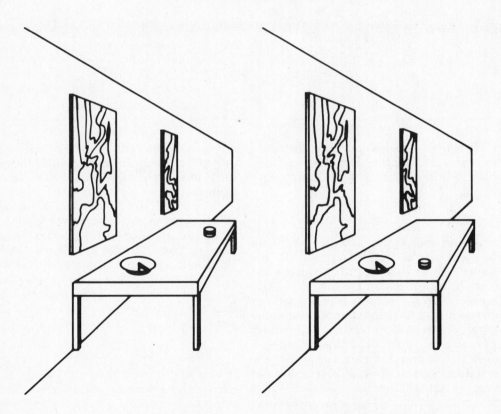

a. In this picture, both desserts have a size appropriate for their distance from the viewer.

b. The same scene, except that the cake has been moved forward. Because it retains the same retinal size, it now looks small.

Figure 7-1   Distance cues.

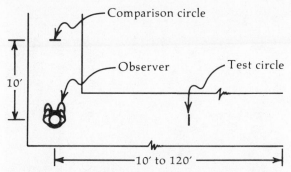

Figure 7-2 The setup for the Holway and Boring experiment (looking down).

that it is also farther away. In the picture on the right, the distant cake has been moved forward, so that it is the same distance from the viewer as the pie. However, its retinal size has remained the same. We defied the relationship between distance cues and retinal size, and size constancy disappeared. We now have a puny little cupcake!

A classic experiment demonstrated the importance of distance cues in size constancy (Holway & Boring, 1941). As Figure 7-2 shows, subjects were seated so that they could look down either of two darkened hallways. Down the right-hand hallway, a standard stimulus could be placed at any distance from 10 feet to 120 feet. The standard stimulus was a circle whose size was systematically varied to produce a visual angle of 1°. (Consequently, the circle was much bigger at the 120-foot distance than at the 10-foot distance.) Down the left-hand hallway, 10 feet away, there was a comparison circle, which the subjects were instructed to adjust until it matched the size of a particular test stimulus.

There were four experimental conditions in this study:

1. Normal, binocular viewing, with all distance cues present.

2. Monocular viewing, with all other distance cues present.

3. Monocular viewing through a peephole, which removed the distance cue of motion parallax (the head-movement cue).

4. Monocular viewing through a peephole,

with drapes along the hallway, which removed almost all distance cues.

Notice, then, that the number of distance cues available to subjects differed in the four conditions.

Figure 7-3 shows the subjects' performance in the four conditions. First, look at the two dotted lines, which are placed on the figure as guidelines. One dotted line represents how subjects would perform if they had perfect size constancy and the object seemed to stay exactly the same size, no matter how far it was from the viewer. The other dotted line represents how subjects would perform if they had absolutely no size constancy—if they considered only the retinal size but not the distance of the object in judging its true size.

Now notice how subjects in the four conditions performed. In the normal viewing condition (1), subjects showed a little **overconstancy;** they overcorrected for distance and actually gave overly large estimates for distant objects. In the monocular condition (2), subjects showed almost perfect size constancy. In the monocular/peephole condition (3) and in the monocular/peephole/drapes condition (4), subjects showed **underconstancy;** they gave estimates that were too small for distant objects. Without distance cues, people do not show much size constancy.

Photographs and paintings can look quite startling if they remove distance cues. Figure 7-4 shows my daughter Beth waving. There are few distance cues in this picture, and so you

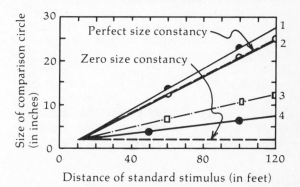

Figure 7-3 Performance on the Holway and Boring experiment.

Figure 7-4   Without many distance cues, a hand thrust forward toward the viewer looks abnormally large.

do not correct the size of her hand for its distance from you. It looks enormous!

Similarly, it is often difficult to judge the distance of objects in the sky, because there are so few distance cues. Maybe you once were flying a kite high in the sky and lost all sense of size constancy as you gazed at that pinpoint of white against the blue sky. That old familiar cry, "It's a bird! It's a plane! It's Superman!" reflects (as you can now explain to attentive audiences) the loss of size constancy with reduced distance cues. Notice from Figure 7-3, incidentally, that people are particularly poor at preserving size constancy, without the benefit of distance cues, when objects are far away. When Superman is miles away, we should be particularly unlikely to use size constancy.

Explanations for Size Constancy

Even though more research has been conducted on size constancy than on the other con-

stancies (Leibowitz, 1971), psychologists disagree about what factors are responsible. Several factors have been proposed, and it seems likely that each of them may be involved in some aspect of size constancy. We mentioned already that familiarity may be helpful. If you know how big a book is, you can guess its size even when the distance varies. As Leibowitz (1971) points out, this mechanism is a learned one; young children misidentify a man in the distance as a boy and a distant large animal as a dog.

The size-distance invariance hypothesis is an explanation that applies to both familiar and unfamiliar objects. According to the **size-distance invariance hypothesis,** a viewer calculates objective size by combining an object's retinal size and its distance. Specifically, if two objects have the same retinal size, then the object that looks like it is farther from you will be perceived to be larger. This classic theory was originally proposed by Helmholtz (1866), who was an empiricist in the tradition of Berkeley; we discussed Berkeley's and Helmholtz's theories of distance perception in Chapter 6. Do not take this principle too literally, however! You don't take out a pocket calculator to figure the objective size. In fact, you probably are only rarely aware of this process. Even animals seem to be guided by this principle (Gogel, 1977), so it cannot involve elaborate conscious calculations. However, many psychologists (for example, Rock, 1977) believe that people make unconscious judgments on the basis of this relationship between size and distance.

Some researchers have tried to figure out exactly what distance cues people take into account in the size-distance invariance hypothesis. Leibowitz, Shiina, and Hennessy (1972), for example, have discovered that the distance cues of accommodation and convergence led to size constancy for objects that were closer to the eye than 1 meter. Other researchers have found that the size-distance invariance hypothesis is not perfectly reliable. For example, Vogel and Teghtsoonian (1972) found that judged size was related to distance in different ways in three different conditions that they tested. Thus the relationship between size and distance was variable, rather than invariant.

Another explanation for size constancy concerns the relative sizes of objects being judged (Rock & Ebenholtz, 1959). According to this **relative-size explanation,** people notice the size of an object, compared to other objects. For example, look at your pen on the desk. Now get up and walk across the room. The image of the pen grows smaller, but the image of the desk also grows smaller. In fact, the ratio of the retinal sizes remains constant. The retinal size for the pen may be 1/10 as long as the retinal size for the desk, whether you are 1 meter or 10 meters away. Thus objects seem to stay the same size as we move away from them because they keep their same size relative to other objects near them. Notice that in this theory the viewer does not need to take distance into account. All the information necessary for constancy is present in the relationship among the stimuli.

There is one other explanation that is concerned with the relationship among stimuli. According to Gibson's **texture explanation** (J. J.

Gibson, 1959), people notice how big an object is in comparison to the texture of the surrounding area. (You will recall from Chapter 6 how Gibson emphasized texture in distance perception; texture is equally important in Gibson's theory of size constancy.) Try Demonstration 7-3 to illustrate this to yourself. The Rock and Ebenholtz explanation and the Gibson explanation are similar in that they maintain that all the information necessary for size constancy is present in the proximal stimulus. The two explanations differ in terms of what they consider to be helpful information. Rock and Ebenholtz propose other stimuli, and Gibson proposes surrounding texture.

Although the answer is not yet certain, all the factors we have discussed may contribute in some way to size constancy. In other words, objects seem to stay the same size because of familiarity, the size-distance invariance hypothesis, the relative size of other objects, and the texture of the surrounding areas. (A sentence you might use to remember F S R T is "*F*rank *S*amples *R*aspberry *T*arts.")

Shape Constancy

Shape constancy means that an object seems to stay the same shape despite changes in its orientation. The proximal shape of an object is the same as the distal shape *only* if the object is exactly perpendicular to your line of view. In all other cases, the proximal shape is distorted.

Notice what happens to the proximal shape of a familiar object, such as an index card, as you change its orientation. In fact, when an index card is viewed at an angle, the proximal shape is a trapezoid, rather than a rectangle.

Get up from your chair and walk around the room. Look at a particular object, such as a window, and view it from different angles. Notice that the shape registered on your retina is a trapezoid from every orientation except when you are facing it directly. Observe how the rim of a cup usually forms an ellipse, rather than a perfectly round circle. Nevertheless, the window seems to stay rectangular and the rim of a cup seems to stay circular. Objects do not grow distorted and then normal-shaped again as we change our orientation to them.

Notice also how shape constancy is related

Demonstration 7-3

The Influence of Surrounding Texture on Size Constancy

Select a long, flat area that has noticeable texture patterns, such as a tile floor, a sidewalk, or a rug with a regular geometric pattern. Take two same-sized sheets of paper and place them about 1 m and 5 m away from you. Notice how the paper covers the same number of texture units in both cases. For example, it may cover 1¼ tiles; this coverage is the same whether the paper is near or far from you.

---

to size constancy. Stand next to one side of the window and notice the proximal shape of the window frame. As we said before, it is a trapezoid. Notice that one of the most striking aspects is that the side nearest to you has a bigger retinal size than the farther side. As in the case of size constancy, objects that are closer to you have a bigger retinal size.

Shape Constancy in the Laboratory and in Real Life

In many laboratory studies, subjects have shown underconstancy. In other words, when they are asked to judge the true shape of a circle that they are viewing at a slant, they do not believe that it is a perfect, round circle. Instead, they respond that it is somewhat elliptical, as in Figure 7-5. Thus their response is a compromise

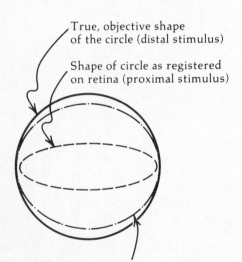

True, objective shape of the circle (distal stimulus)

Shape of circle as registered on retina (proximal stimulus)

Subjects' "compromise" response

Figure 7-5   When subjects view a circle from a slant, their response is a compromise between the distal stimulus and the proximal stimulus.

between the true shape of the circle (the distal stimulus) and the image registered on their retina (the proximal stimulus).

Why don't subjects in the laboratory demonstrate more shape constancy? V. R. Carlson (1977) proposes that one problem may be that subjects do not understand the instructions. If I show you a slanted circle and ask you to judge what you see, you may not know whether I want you to respond in terms of what is registered on your retina or what you think the shape really is. Also, you might think that the answer "a circle" would be too simple-minded! Carlson cites studies that demonstrate that people have excellent shape constancy if the instructions are precise, specifying that subjects must respond in terms of the true, objective shape of the figure.

Another reason that subjects in the laboratory do not demonstrate more shape constancy is that the laboratory conditions have been too deprived. Lappin and Preble (1975) argue that laboratory studies on shape constancy typically show circles, rectangles, and simple geometric forms in plain, uncluttered backgrounds with most of the potential depth cues missing. You may recall from the section on size constancy that people show much less constancy when depth cues are missing. Consequently, those laboratory studies probably underestimate subjects' true ability for shape constancy. Lappin and Preble believe that it would be more useful to study shape constancy in more complex environments—ones that have more ecological validity. (**Ecological validity** means that the results we obtain in the laboratory also hold true in "real life.") Laboratory environments are unnatural, without all the useful clutter that real-life environments have. Thus it may be difficult to generalize from the laboratory environment to the real world.

Lappin and Preble made up photographic slides of complex and meaningful scenes, such as a messy office desk. Included in the scene was an octagon (eight-sided figure), which was placed in the picture at a specified angle. Lappin and Preble found that people were quite accurate in guessing the true shape of the octagon. Thus when people have the cues available to them that they would have in real life, they show excellent shape constancy.

Explanations for Shape Constancy

In the section on size constancy we discussed possible explanations for constancy in some detail. Fortunately, some of the same ideas can be modified slightly to explain shape constancy. Familiarity, for example, has a role in shape constancy. Since you know that a phonograph record is round, you know that the true shape of the record is round, even when it is seen at a slant.

The size-distance invariance hypothesis, used for size constancy, can be translated into the shape-slant invariance hypothesis. (Notice that distance, the potential distorter for size, is translated into slant, which is the potential distorter for shape.) According to the **shape-slant invariance hypothesis,** a viewer calculates objective shape by combining information about an object's retinal shape and its slant. This explanation may not work too well for shape constancy, however, because Lappin and Preble found that people had trouble judging objects' retinal shape. (For the record, remember that Lappin and Preble found that people were excellent at judging objects' *true* shape.) If they cannot judge the objects' retinal shape very accurately, then their calculation of objective shape will be inaccurate.

Remember that James J. Gibson believes that people take texture into account in order to maintain size constancy. Gibson (1950) has proposed a similar explanation for shape con-

---

Demonstration 7 - 4

The Relationship Between Slant and Compression of Texture Units

Look at the two pieces of waffle in the picture below. You are looking straight at one of the pieces, but the other one is viewed at a slant. Which one is at the slant? Is *a* or *b* farther away from you? (Notice that both of them are cut into unfamiliar shapes, so you cannot use a familiar rectangular or oval shape as a cue for slant.)

a.

b.

stancy. When an object with a clear texture is slanted, the texture units that are farther away from the viewer are compressed together. Try Demonstration 7-4 to help you understand the relationship between slant and compression of texture units.

Brightness Constancy

Brightness constancy means that an object seems to stay the same brightness despite changes in the amount of light falling on it. For example, the white paper on this page looks equally bright, whether you are reading indoors or outdoors. Similarly, the black letters on this page look equally dark, whether you are reading indoors or outdoors. The amount of light reflected from the page and the letters is vastly different in the two cases, with perhaps 100 times as much light reflected when you are outdoors on a sunny day (Hurvich & Jameson, 1966). Try Demonstration 7-5 to show you how objects appear to be equally bright under different illuminations.

The Nature of Brightness Constancy

Let us examine brightness constancy in more detail. Keep in mind as you read this section that there is a difference between the physical characteristics of objects and our psychological reactions to these objects. We describe objects in terms of the intensity of amplitude of light waves. In contrast, we describe our psychological reactions in terms of **brightness.** Thus an intense light *generally* looks bright to us. However, the phenomenon of brightness constancy demonstrates that perceived brightness also depends upon other factors.

Here is another way to look at brightness constancy. The amount of light falling on an object changes from one situation to the next, for example, as you move a book from indoors to outdoors. However, an object always reflects the same *proportion* of that light. Figure 7-6 illustrates how a constant proportion of light can be reflected in different lighting situations. The black record may reflect only 10% of the light falling on it, whereas the white label may reflect 90% of the light falling on it. The term **albedo** (pronounced "al-*bee*-doe" with a short *a* to rhyme with "pal") refers to the proportion of light reflected by an object. For example, the printing on this page might have an albedo of 3%. Albedo is a property of an object that stays

---

Demonstration 7 - 5

Brightness Constancy

Take a piece of cardboard or some other thin object that light will not shine through. Place one edge of the cardboard upright on the dotted line. Orient your book near a desk lamp so that the lamp is in the direction indicated. Place your head so that your nose touches the top edge of the cardboard. Your left eye should see the one gray patch, and your right eye should see the four comparison patches. Which of the four patches most closely matches the true shade of gray that your left eye is looking at? Now remove the cardboard so that both sides have the same illumination, and see whether you choose the same match.

←————Lamp

                    1   2   3   4

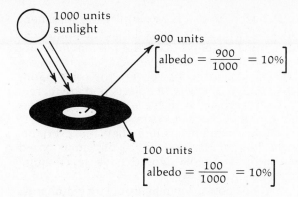

1000 units
sunlight

900 units

$$\left[\text{albedo} = \frac{900}{1000} = 10\%\right]$$

100 units

$$\left[\text{albedo} = \frac{100}{1000} = 10\%\right]$$

Figure 7-6   Albedo. 1000 units of sunlight strikes a black record and its white label. The record reflects only 100 units; its albedo is therefore 10%. The label reflects 900 units; its albedo is therefore 90%.

the same even when the amount of light falling on the object changes.

Strangely, a black object can sometimes reflect more light than a white object. For example, suppose you are looking at a black record on a sunny day, when the illumination is 1000 units (in some unspecified light measurement system). If the record has an albedo of 10%, it will reflect 10% of the 1000 units, or 100 units. In contrast, suppose you are looking at the white label indoors, where the illumination is 10 units. If the label has an albedo of 90%, it will reflect 90% of 10 units or 9 units. Your eye receives 100 units from the black record outdoors and 9 units from the white label indoors. However, you would certainly say that the white label *looks* brighter. We do not make brightness judgments on the basis of the amount of light that is reflected into our eyes. The proximal stimulus is not what we "see," even though it is registered on our retinas. Instead, we see the properties of objects. Ordinarily, what we see resembles the distal stimulus and is related to qualities of that stimulus such as its albedo.

Explanations for Brightness Constancy

There are two basic theories of brightness constancy. According to the explanation based on Helmholtz's (1866) theory, we take illumination into account when we judge brightness. This "taking into account" explanation should sound familiar, because it is like the theory that people take distance into account when judging size, and slant into account when judging shape. What kinds of cues do people use in judging illumination? One kind of cue is the position of the object in relation to the light. In Demonstration 7-5 you knew that the left-hand side was near a light and the right-hand side was hidden from the light. Shadows provide further cues; we know that an object in a shadow receives less illumination. On the other hand, bright spots on metal or other shiny objects tell us that an object is in a bright light.

Notice that Helmholtz's theory involves a large amount of mental activity. The information is not directly available in the stimulus. Instead, we judge brightness by first figuring out the illumination. Then we assess how much light an object is reflecting onto our retina and take illumination into account to calculate brightness. One reason that Helmholtz's explanation is not widely accepted is that people are not very accurate in judging how much light an object reflects onto their retinas (Beck, 1974). (Remember that this was also a weakness with the similar shape constancy explanation; people are not very accurate in judging slant.) Without that information they could not calculate brightness very accurately.

The second explanation for brightness constancy is called contrast theory. According to **contrast theory,** the important factor that determines how bright an object looks is how bright that object looks in comparison to other objects in the scene. Thus the label on the record looks bright because it is surrounded by a dark region. The label looks relatively brighter, whether the record is seen in sunlight or in a dark room.

Gelb (1929) performed the classic experiment to demonstrate that judgments of brightness depend upon the brightness of nearby objects. To perform this study, he created an unusual situation. Subjects sat in a dark room and looked at a circle, which was made of black velvet. From a hidden projector, Gelb projected a bright beam of light that fell precisely upon the black velvet circle. The subjects reported that they saw a white circle. After all, the illuminated black circle was lighter than the surrounding darkness. In contrast, the circle looked light. Then Gelb placed a little slip of white paper in front of the circle, so that the light was shining on it. Presto! Subjects suddenly reported that the circle was black. The circle may have been light in comparison to the dark background, but next to a white slip of paper, it was dark!

When I first heard of this study, I suspected that Gelb probably could not have fooled his subjects for long. Now that they knew that the circle was truly black, they would certainly remain convinced that it was black, wouldn't they? However, Gelb found that when he removed the slip of paper, people again reported seeing a white circle. In social psychology we are accustomed to thinking that we cannot fool a person twice—once someone is aware of a deception, he or she will not fall for the same trick again. However, in Gelb's experiment the contrast between the dark background and the relatively light circle was so convincing that subjects were willing to ignore what they knew and report only what they saw.

According to the contrast theory of brightness constancy, observers pay attention to the relative intensity of the stimuli, rather than the absolute intensity. An object may be objectively dark, but it will appear bright as long as it is brighter than other objects. Brightness constancy occurs because the relative intensity of an object remains the same when illumination varies. Your white sweater therefore looks bright in the moonlight because it is the brightest object in sight. Your dark shoes look dark in the noonday sun because they are the darkest objects in sight.

Notice that contrast theory, unlike Helmholtz's theory, allows the viewer to gather all the necessary information from the world "out there." In this respect, contrast theory is similar to some of the theories we discussed in connection with the other constancies. For example, remember Rock and Ebenholtz's (1959) theory that size constancy is caused by noticing how big an object is in comparison to other objects. In both of these theories the relationship among the stimuli provides enough information for us to maintain constancy.

Although contrast theory is quite popular, some studies have shown that this explanation

may be too simple. For example, an experiment by Gilchrist (1977) showed that the brightness judgments depend upon the relative intensity of objects that are perceived to be the same distance from the viewer. On the other hand, the relative intensity of objects that are merely next to each other in the retinal image is less important. Thus viewers must make depth perception judgments before they make brightness judgments, and any explanation based on contrast theory would have to be quite complicated.

At this point, you may throw up your hands in despair! *Neither* theory seems to explain brightness constancy! The answer probably is that neither theory *alone* is a sufficient explanation, but some combination of them may work. Brightness constancy probably depends to some extent upon contrast as determined by the stimulus itself, but there is probably also some contribution from more complex mental processes.

Other Constancies

Most of the research on the constancies has been conducted on size, shape, and brightness constancies. However, constancy invades almost every area of perception, and there are other constancies that we should consider briefly.

Think about color constancy, for example. Because of **color constancy,** we tend to see the hue of an object as staying the same despite changes in the color of the light falling on it. For example, a rose still looks red, even when you have a green light bulb in your lamp. However, color constancy is not like the other constancies we have considered; the color may not remain very constant. Fabric buyers are told to take the bolt of material outside if they want to see the colors under natural light rather than under the fluorescent lights found in the stores, which throw a blue color on objects. Makeup mirrors are available with special lighting arrangements that duplicate the lighting conditions of natural sunlight, fluorescent light, and dimly lit rooms. Presumably an eye shadow that is attractive by candlelight might look quite different in a fluorescent-lit office.

Motion constancy means that an object seems to maintain the same speed despite changes in its distance from us. However, motion constancy occasionally breaks down. For me, this is most striking when I am waiting for a subway. The tiny dot of light seems to approach so slowly when the train is far away, but it races toward me over those last 50 meters!

Constancy under bending means that an object is not greatly changed by bending it or distorting it. Johansson, whose work on motion perception we discussed in the last chapter, has commented on this constancy:

> In current texts on space perception the term object constancy implicitly denotes perception of *rigid* objects. In everyday perception of our environment, however, we are adequately dealing also with perceptual objects that are constant in far more limited meaning. As an example of such an object which has permanent shape without being rigid in the ordinary meaning we can think of the pages of this book. A sheet of paper is flexible and bendable but cannot expand or contract [Johansson, 1977, pp. 391–392].

Think of other objects that retain constancy under bending: a leaf, a piece of fabric, a pancake, the bristles of a paintbrush.

Position constancy means that an object seems to stay in the same place, despite the body's movement relative to that object. For example, I can get up from my desk and walk off to the right-hand side. The image of my typewriter was formerly in the center of my retina and is now on the left of my retina. Nonetheless, my typewriter does not appear to jump across the room to the left.

Existence constancy may be the most general constancy of all. **Existence constancy,** or object permanence, means that objects still seem to exist, even if they are no longer in our vision. For example, if you cover your pen with your hand, you know that the object is still in existence, even if it is no longer registered on your retina. You may have learned about this constancy if you had a course in human development, because Piaget (1954) and his followers have studied it extensively. However, it is usually considered to be a part of cognition, rather than perception, because it relies more heavily on knowledge than on visual information. (Incidentally, if you are as frustrat-

ed by lost objects as I am, you might use my remedy: Temporarily stop believing in object permanence!)

We have been considering only the visual constancies. There are constancies for the other senses as well, although information on them is certainly scarce. For example, consider what we could call taste constancy. The taste of lemon juice seems to retain its tartness, whether you are eating Mom's lemon meringue pie or a French restaurant's garlicky veal in lemon sauce. Constancy also operates in hearing. You might be startled to hear a tune on a music box that you originally heard played by a huge symphony orchestra. Nonetheless, you recognize it! The tune remains constant despite changes in its loudness, tone, and pitch. In the chapter on smell we will discuss how the intensity of an odor remains the same, despite the volume of air you inhale. Can you think of a constancy for touch?

We have looked at a large number of constancies in this chapter. Constancies simplify our perceptual world enormously, yet we often fail to appreciate them. Take just a moment to fantasize what a nightmare life would be without all of these constancies! Think about the chaos you would live in if everything grew and shrank, became regular in shape and then irregular, and grew light and dark as you moved about in the world. Without constancy, objects could change their colors from one moment to the next, and we would have to devise another color name system. Objects would seem to change their speed as they approached and passed us. They would change the moment we bent them. They would move every time we moved. And, as a final insult, they would disappear as soon as we stopped looking at them.

Summary: Constancy

- In constancy, objects seem to stay the same, though the representations on the retina change. In illusions, objects look quite different, though the representations on the retina stay the same.
- Size constancy means that an object seems to stay the same size despite changes in its distance.
- In experiments in which distance cues are

removed, people do not show much size constancy.

- Four explanations for size constancy are familiar size, the size-distance invariance hypothesis, the relative size explanation, and Gibson's theory about the texture of the surrounding area.
- Shape constancy means that an object seems to stay the same shape despite changes in its orientation.
- In the laboratory, people do not show much shape constancy, probably because they may not understand the instructions and because the laboratory conditions are deprived of cues.

- Two explanations for shape constancy are the shape-slant invariance hypothesis and Gibson's theory that people use information about the compression of texture units.
- Brightness constancy means that an object seems to stay the same brightness despite changes in illumination.
- Two explanations for brightness constancy are (1) Helmholtz's theory that we take illumination into account when we judge brightness and (2) contrast theory.
- Other constancies include color constancy, motion constancy, constancy under bending, position constancy, and existence constancy.

Illusions

An **illusion** is a perception that is incorrect. In an illusion, what we see does not correspond to the true qualities of an object. In the Müller-Lyer illusion in Figure 7-7, for example, the line on the bottom looks longer than the line on the top. However, take out a ruler to measure the "true qualities" of the lines. You will discover that the two lines are exactly equal in length.

Actually, there are two kinds of illusions or incorrect perceptions: those due to physical processes and those due to psychological processes. Illusions due to physical processes include mirages and distortions caused by water. **Mirages,** according to Fraser and Mach (1976), are caused by the optical properties of the atmosphere. In one famous example of a mirage, explorers at the North Pole thought that they saw beautiful scenery in front of them, including hills, valleys, and snow-capped peaks. They then tramped 30 miles over arctic ice to discover that the scene had been a mirage. You may have seen a more modest mirage, such as a pond of water on a hot highway. Also, you have probably noticed distortions caused by water. For example, a stick dipped partway into water looks like it bends at the point where it enters the water. In all of these cases a physical condition such as water or water vapor distorts an image. The image recorded on the retina, however, corresponds to our perception. Thus the psychological processes are accurate. In this

chapter we will be concerned only with illusions due to psychological processes. With this kind of illusion the image recorded on the retina does not correspond to our perception.

Psychologists disagree about whether or not illusions are important. James J. Gibson (1950) believes that we are seldom misled by illusions in our everyday lives. On the other hand, Coren and Girgus (1978) write in their book, *Seeing Is Deceiving: The Psychology of Visual Illusions,* "illusory phenomena are extremely prevalent in the world outside the laboratory" (p. 24). This section should encourage you to look for applications of illusions and to agree with Coren and Girgus. One aspect of illusions is certain, however: People like to study illusions! Gillam (1980) notes that more than 200 illusions have been discovered, and Coren and Girgus report that more than 1000 articles have been written on illusions. Impressively, however, most of the common illusions date back to Helmholtz (Robinson, 1972).

Despite the extensive research on illusions, psychologists are still struggling to find a good way to classify the illusions. Coren and Girgus find this disturbing because most sciences develop a classification system and then add new items to the system with new research. An advantage of this kind of system is that researchers can notice where there are gaps in the classification system and can then do research to fill the gaps. Unfortunately, illusions are

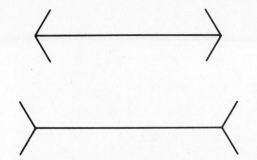

Figure 7-7 The Müller-Lyer illusion.

more difficult to classify than flowers or the chemical elements. Two reasons for this difficulty are that people vary somewhat in their responses to illusions and that any distortion may involve several explanations, rather than just one.

Coren, Girgus, Erlichman, and Hakstean (1976) tackled the problem of developing a classification system by asking 221 observers to make judgments about 45 different illusions. An analysis of the data showed that people divide illusions into two basic categories: illusions involving size and illusions involving shape and directions. Let's consider several illusions in each of these two categories.

Size Illusions

The category of size illusions can conveniently be divided into two further subcategories, illusions in which the length of a line is misjudged and illusions in which the area of an object is misjudged.

Illusions Involving Line Length

Figure 7-7 shows you one of the most famous illusions, the Müller-Lyer (pronounced "*mew*-lur-*lie*-ur"), which was first demonstrated in the late 1800s. In the **Müller-Lyer illusion** the two lines are actually the same length. Nonetheless, the line on the bottom with the wings pointing outward looks about 25% longer than the line with the wings pointing inward.

Coren and Girgus estimate that more work has been done on the Müller-Lyer figure than on all other illusions combined. As you would

expect, psychologists have tried many variations of the figure, including those in Figure 7-8. Impressively, the illusion remains strong in all these variations. Specific characteristics of the standard Müller-Lyer illusion have also been studied. For example, the illusion is most effective if the wings of the arrows are bent close to the line and if the wing length is about 25% as long as the line (Coren & Girgus, 1978).

Try to see if you can find examples of the Müller-Lyer illusion. As I was preparing this chapter, I noticed that my feet looked smaller than usual in a new pair of shoes. After looking more closely, I noticed that it was a variation on the Müller-Lyer illusion! Look at Figure 7-9 and notice how the upper toe and the lower heel are shaped like inward-turning arrow wings. Clearly, clothing manufacturers should become acquainted with the illusions!

Another line length illusion is the **Sander parallelogram,** which is presented in two versions in Figure 7-10. My students are usually convinced that I have drawn this one incorrectly until they measure it with a ruler.

A third line-length illusion is the **horizontal-vertical illusion,** as illustrated in Demonstration 7-6. This illusion is effective for two reasons. First of all, vertical lines look

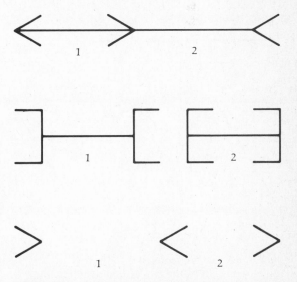

Figure 7-8 Variations of the Müller-Lyer illusion; in each case, segment 1 is equal in length to segment 2.

Figure 7-9   An example of the Müller-Lyer illusion.

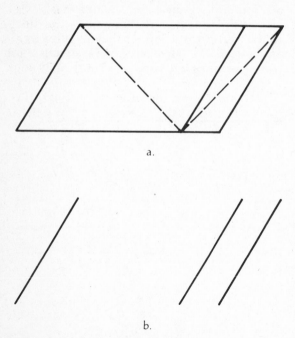

a.

b.

Figure 7-10   Two versions of the Sander parallelogram. In A, the two dotted diagonal lines are equal in length; in B, two diagonal lines that you can imagine in the same location as in A are also equal to each other in length.

longer than horizontal lines. Second, when one line is interrupted by another line, we judge the interrupted line as being shorter. To make a "pure" horizontal-vertical illusion, therefore, neither line should be interrupted. If you try drawing an *L* so that the two lines are equal in length, you will find that you will be more accurate than you were in Demonstration 7-6.

Think about applications of the horizontal-vertical illusion. I once looked at my sleeping daughter and speculated that she had shrunk. Then I recalled that the horizontal-vertical illusion guaranteed that she would look smaller when horizontal than in the upright orientation in which I view her more often. Similarly, if you want to photograph a fish you have just caught, by all means hold it vertically!

Coren and Girgus point out other natural occurrences of the horizontal-vertical illusion. People overestimate the height of vertical objects such as parking meters, lamp posts, and buildings, often by as much as 25%. A tree looks shorter when it has been cut down than it did when it was standing. One of the most famous architectural examples of this illusion is the Gateway Arch in St. Louis (Figure 7-11). Only by measuring can you convince yourself

Demonstration 7 - 6

Extend the vertical line upward until it seems equal in length to the horizontal line. Then measure the two lines and check your accuracy.

The Horizontal-Vertical Illusion

Figure 7-11   The Gateway Arch in St. Louis, Missouri—an example of the horizontal-vertical illusion.

that the height and the width are equal. In reality, both height and width are 630 feet.

The **Ponzo illusion** is shown in Figure 7-12. Notice how the figure on the top creates the impression of linear perspective, even though it is drawn with only a few lines. On the bottom, there are additional distance cues to convince you that the distant bar must be larger because it has the same retinal size as the closer figure. We can call the figure on the top an illusion. The figure on the bottom, however, shows the appropriate use of size constancy. As you can see, the boundary between "inaccurate" perception in illusions and "accurate" perception in size constancy is extremely thin! Suppose the observer interprets certain cues in a line drawing to be depth cues, although no instructions specified to do so. In this case, judging two equal figures to be unequal in objective length is called an illusion. When there are more depth cues present, judging two equal figures to be unequal in objective length is called size constancy. Yes, it *does* sound arbitrary!

One explanation for the Ponzo illusion, which we will consider in more detail later in the chapter, has been called the misapplied constancy theory. According to this hypothesis, people have had experience with con-

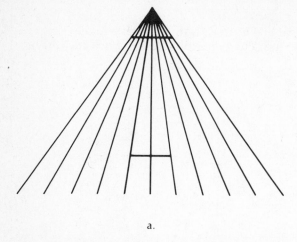

a.

b.

Figure 7-12   The Ponzo illusion. The two horizontal lines are actually the same length in a; the two bars are the same length in b.

verging lines in the past, and they inappropriately use this experience in making judgments about the Ponzo illusion. According to this view, then, *experience* is a crucial factor, and people who have had less experience should be less deceived by the illusion.

Leibowitz (1971) discusses two groups of

people who lack experience with linear perspective, young children and people living in areas with few perspective cues. Leibowitz summarizes studies that demonstrate that the Ponzo illusion has no effect for children five years of age and younger. The magnitude of the illusion then increases dramatically; it is as effective for 10- to 15-year-olds as it is for adults.

Leibowitz summarizes his research with people living on the island of Guam, where there are no railroads and where the perspective cues are far less prevalent than in the United States. Leibowitz compared English-speaking undergraduates at the University of Guam with undergraduates at the Pennsylvania State University. Both groups of subjects judged the illusions as drawn with straight lines. They also judged the illusions in photographs, one with texture depth cues and one with perspective depth cues plus texture depth cues. For the Guam students, adding the depth cues of texture and perspective did not increase the magnitude of the illusion. For the Pennsylvania students, adding these cues increased the magnitude of the illusion by about 200%. Experience with depth cues therefore makes it more likely for people to use these cues in judging some illusions. Ironically, the more knowledge and experience we acquire, the less accurately we perform on some illusions!

Explanations for the Line-Length Illusions.   As you may recall, over 1000 articles have been written about more than 200 illusions; most were written on the line-length illusions. You can probably guess that we will not have one simple explanation for all of them! However, let's take a brief look at several of the most widely accepted current theories.

We have already touched upon one of the most popular theories, the theory of misapplied constancy. According to the **theory of misapplied constancy,** observers interpret certain cues in the illusion as being cues for maintaining size constancy. Therefore they make length judgments on the basis of size constancy, and a line that looks farther away will be judged as being longer (Day, 1972). This theory fits the Ponzo illusion quite nicely—the upper line in the Ponzo illusion does look farther away and therefore larger.

Other illusions require more elaborate variations of the misapplied constancy theory. For example, the Müller-Lyer illusion might be due to our experience with similar-looking figures in architecture. In Figure 7-13, notice how the corner on the top looks like the "wings-inward" version of the Müller-Lyer and the corner on the bottom looks like the "wings-outward" version. Gregory (1973) has suggested that when we look at the Müller-Lyer illusion, we are reminded of our experiences with corners. Therefore we recall that the vertical line is farther from us in the "wings-outward" version. We misapply size constancy and conclude that the line is longer in the "wings-outward" version. Ward, Porac, Coren, and Girgus (1977) found evidence that observers did tend to see many—but not all—of the illusions as having depth. Thus the misapplied constancy theory may explain some illusions (such as the Ponzo illusion in Figure 7-12), but it cannot handle others (such as the horizontal-vertical illusion).

The **eye-movement theory,** an alternative explanation, states that illusions can be explained by the effort involved in moving the eyes across each design. For example, the eyes might have to work harder on the "wings-outward" version of the Müller-Lyer illusion, and therefore it looks longer. This eye-movement explanation has some evidence against it, but it might contribute to several of the illusions.

The **incorrect comparison theory** states that observers base their judgments on comparisons of the incorrect parts of the figures. This explanation works particularly well for the Müller-Lyer illusion. Observers may be unable to separate the lines from the wings in the diagram, and so they compare the distances between the ends of the wings. Experimental evidence supports this theory. For example, Coren and Girgus (1972) asked observers to judge Müller-Lyer illusions in which the wings were a different color from the lines, so that the wings would not be likely to enter into the comparison. The magnitude of the illusion was greatly reduced.

None of these three theories—misapplied constancy, eye movement, or incorrect comparison—can handle all of the line-length il-

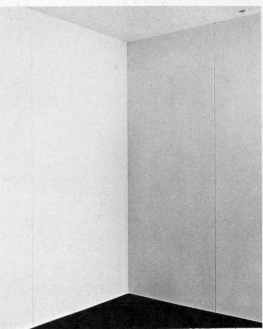

Figure 7-13   The Müller-Lyer illusion in corners; architectural examples of the "wings-inward" and "wings-outward" versions of the Müller-Lyer illusion.

lusions by itself. Each illusion probably depends upon at least one of these explanations, as well as other factors that no one has yet developed. It would make life simpler if we could all believe in just one explanation, but the one-explanation approach to illusions is, in fact, another illusion!

Illusions Involving Area

The four illusions we have considered so far —the Müller-Lyer illusion, the Sander parallelogram, the horizontal-vertical illusion, and the Ponzo illusion—are primarily concerned with line length. Other illusions are concerned with area, rather than length alone. Several miscellaneous area illusions are shown in Figure 7-14.

The most famous area illusion, however, is one you can demonstrate to yourself on a clear

night under a full moon. Early in the evening when the moon is on the horizon, go to a place where objects—such as trees or buildings—can be seen on one or both sides of the moon. Notice the size of the moon and notice how close it looks to you. Later that same evening when the moon is approaching its zenith (or overhead position in the sky), look up at the moon and again notice its size and closeness.

In the **moon illusion** the moon looks larger when it appears on the horizon than when it is seen overhead. Observers may judge the moon to be more than twice as large in the horizon location. Incidentally, there is also a sun illusion, in which the sun looks larger on the horizon. However, do not try to demonstrate this illusion; you might damage your eyes.

The moon illusion is not a mirage; it cannot be explained by atmospheric conditions, for example. Photographs taken of the horizon moon and the zenith moon show that the moon occupies the same visual angle in both cases. (The visual angle may strike you as surprisingly small—it is about 0.5°. If you hold a nickel at arm's length, that nickel will form an image on your retina that is comparable to either the horizon moon or the zenith moon.) Other experiments have ruled out differences in color and brightness as possible explanations for the moon illusion (Kaufman & Rock, 1962).

We know, then, that the moon occupies the same space on the retina in both positions. What psychological processes can explain the distortion? Basically, two different explanations have been proposed, and both may contribute to the moon illusion.

The most widely accepted theory at present is called the apparent-distance theory. One form of this theory was proposed in the 11th century (Ross & Ross, 1976), but the modern version was developed by Kaufman and Rock (1962). This theory is related to the size-distance invariance hypothesis, which we discussed in the size constancy section of this chapter. Recall that this hypothesis states that if two objects have the same retinal size, then an object that seems to be farther from you will be perceived to be larger. (That is why, for example, the top line in the Ponzo illusion in Figure 7-12 looks larger.)

Kaufman and Rock's **apparent-distance**

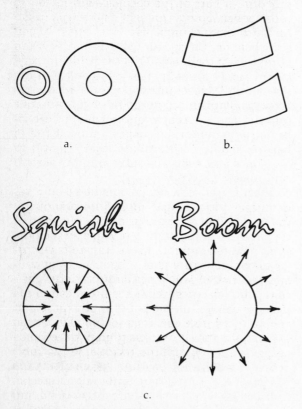

Figure 7-14   Miscellaneous area illusions; in each case the two figures are equal in area.

theory argued that the moon seems to be farther from the viewer when it is on the horizon than when it is at the zenith. This point needs further explanation. In Kaufman and Rock's research, observers were asked to report whether an imaginary point at the horizon seemed nearer or farther away than a similar point at the zenith. Almost all of the observers said that the point seemed farther away when it was at the horizon. To the observers, the sky looked somewhat flattened, almost Frisbee-shaped! Figure 7-15 illustrates how the sky seemed to them.

Now let's relate this sky-shape finding to the size-distance invariance hypothesis. The explanation is difficult, so use Figure 7-15 as you are reading this paragraph. The moon keeps the same retinal size, whether it is at the horizon or the zenith. According to the size-distance invariance hypothesis, then, people should think that the moon is larger when they believe that it is farther from them, given a constant retinal size. If they believe that the sky is Frisbee-shaped, then the moon is larger when it is on the horizon, because the horizon is farther from them. In contrast, when the moon is at the zenith, they believe that the moon is relatively close to them (after all, the sky above is closer). If the moon is close to them and the retinal size is still the same, then it looks

small. Remember: At the horizon, distance seems large, so perceived size is large; at the zenith, distance seems small, so perceived size is small.

The apparent-distance theory is complicated enough already, but you may have thought of another problem. The *moon* seems closer, rather than farther away, when it is on the horizon, even though the *surface* to which the moon is attached may seem farther away. Yes, this is puzzling, but perceptions are occasionally contradictory. For example, you may have been at a party or some event where you have two contradictory time perceptions: "It seems I just got here five minutes ago" and "It seems that this party has been going on forever." Our estimates of time passage depend upon the method of estimating it. Similarly, our estimates of distance depend upon whether we are making a judgment of the closeness of the moon or a judgment of the closeness of the surface upon which the moon "hangs," in order to judge its size.

Kaufman and Rock conducted an extensive series of experiments in order to rule out other theories of the moon illusion and to test the apparent-distance theory. One theory they ruled out was that the moon illusion occurred because observers had to raise their eyes to look at the zenith moon, and objects somehow looked smaller when eyes were raised (Holway & Boring, 1940). In their controlled tests, the eye-elevation hypothesis did not hold true. They did find, though, that the presence of terrain cues next to the horizon were necessary for the moon illusion to occur. All the hills, trees, and buildings that clutter the horizon are necessary if the moon is to look larger on the horizon.

The other major theory of the moon illusion is similar to one of the other theories of size constancy. Recall the theory that proposed that size constancy is produced by the observer's noticing an object's size relative to other objects around it. Restle (1970) proposed a **relative-size explanation;** people judge the size of the moon relative to other objects around it. When the moon is overhead, it must be judged relative to a huge, uncluttered dome of sky. Compared to that vast sky, the moon looks small. When the moon is on the horizon, it is judged relative to

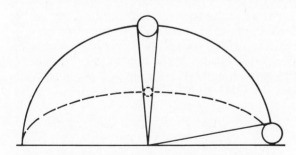

Figure 7-15 The effect of the apparent distance of the moon on judgments of moon size. The solid curve represents the true path of the moon in the sky, and the dashed curve represents the apparent path of the moon against the flattened sky. The solid circle represents the true size of the moon at the horizon and at the zenith, and the dashed circle represents the apparent size of the moon at the zenith. (At the horizon, the apparent size is the same as the true size.)

other objects that have tiny retinal sizes. Looking at the horizon moon in the city, for example, we see objects such as windows, ledges, cars, and signs. Compared to the small retinal sizes of these objects, the moon looks huge.

It seems likely that both the apparent-distance and the relative-size theories may work for the moon illusion. It is such a strong illusion that it might require cues from both apparent distance and relative size in order to produce the illusion. In fact, there may even be other cues, as yet undiscovered, to help the moon look larger at the horizon.

Direction and Shape Illusions

One of the most familiar of the direction and shape illusions is the Poggendorf illusion (see Demonstration 7-7). In the **Poggendorf illusion** a line disappears at an angle behind a solid figure. It appears on the other side of the solid figure at a position that seems wrong. In the classic version of the Poggendorf illusion, the "solid figure" is simply two lines. However, the Poggendorf illusion can be produced by placing almost anything in front of a thin line. A map of the state of New York and your own textbook both work well.

Coren and Girgus (1978) point out that the

Poggendorf illusion has many important applications in everyday life. A surgeon may use a probe to try to remove a bullet. In an X-ray the probe, a bone, and the bullet might be arranged as in Figure 7-16. Although it looks as though the probe is lined up so that it will touch the bullet, the Poggendorf illusion is at work—it will miss it completely. Architects also need to be concerned with this illusion. A line hidden behind a column will look displaced when it emerges on the other side.

The final example of Coren and Girgus's book is particularly chilling. In 1965, two airplanes were preparing for landing in the New York City area. A cloud formation was between them, and because of the Poggendorf illusion, they seemed to be headed for each other. Quickly, the two pilots changed their paths to correct for what they thought was an error. With the revised routes, the two planes collided. Four people died and 49 were injured, and only an illusion was to blame.

Gillam (1980) uses a variation of the misapplied constancy theory to explain the Poggendorf illusion. She argues that an observer sees the display as a solid figure facing forward, with the line receding in space. For example, in Demonstration 7-7a, the lower left end of the line might be nearer to you than the upper right

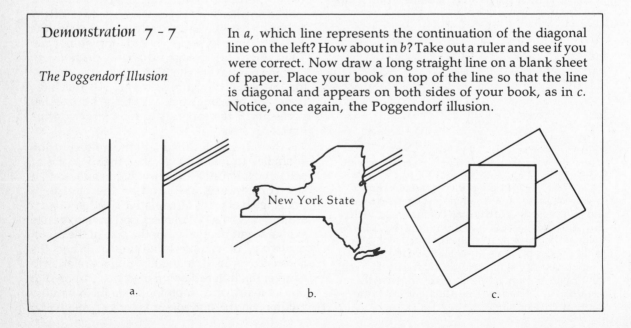

Demonstration 7 - 7

The Poggendorf Illusion

In *a*, which line represents the continuation of the diagonal line on the left? How about in *b*? Take out a ruler and see if you were correct. Now draw a long straight line on a blank sheet of paper. Place your book on top of the line so that the line is diagonal and appears on both sides of your book, as in *c*. Notice, once again, the Poggendorf illusion.

New York State

a.   b.   c.

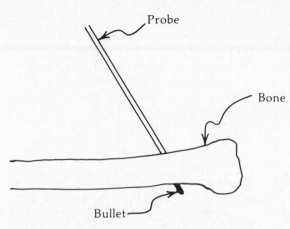

Figure 7-16 An example of the Poggendorf illusion.

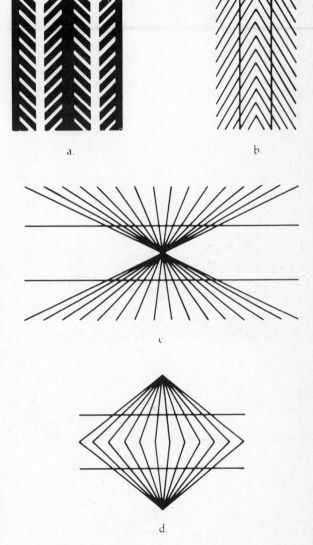

Figure 7-17 Several illusions of direction and shape.

end. If the line really were receding in space, then it should emerge from the other side of the solid figure at a place several millimeters lower than it does. On the other hand, Coren and Girgus (1978) argue that much of the Poggendorf illusion can be traced to anatomical and physiological factors, such as blur and lateral inhibition. (Remember that lateral inhibition means that stimulation of one point of the retina leads to inhibition at other points on the retina.) As we have mentioned with other illusions, more than one explanation may be necessary to produce the effect.

Let's look at a variety of other illusions of direction and shape. First notice the illusion in Figure 7-17a. In this illusion the lines are really parallel, yet they look as though they are a bit tilted. Notice that this illusion really represents many tiny Poggendorf illusions, all combined. Look carefully at the next sports jacket you see that is made out of herringbone tweed, and see if you notice this illusion. Notice the other bent-looking lines in Figure 7-17. You may need a ruler to convince yourself that they are straight!

Several effective illusions can be constructed out of lines that look as though they are made of twisted cords (see Demonstration 7-8). Several decorative trims are available that are in fact made out of twisted cords. If you are sewing an outfit and are placing the trim on checkered gingham, be prepared for the consequences!

In other illusions the surrounding lines distort the shape of an object. Notice how the square in Figure 7-18a looks like it is a parallelogram. Notice, also, that this particular figure is a variation on the Ponzo illusion. In Figure 7-18b the wood grain of the frame is very noticeable. As a result, the frame looks like it is badly warped. Any woodworker should beware of highly visible wood grains unless he or she wants chair and table legs to look crooked and tables to look lopsided!

Demonstration 7 - 8

Twisted Cord Illusions

In *a*, convince yourself that the letters are oriented straight up and down. Either measure the distance of the top and bottom of a letter from one of the sides, or notice that the top and bottom of each letter are located along the same column of dark diamonds in the checked pattern. In *b*, place your finger at any point along the "spiral" and trace around, trying to get to the center of the design. In fact, you will return to the starting place because the pattern is a series of concentric circles.

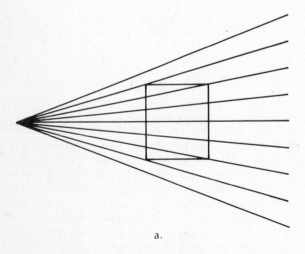

a.

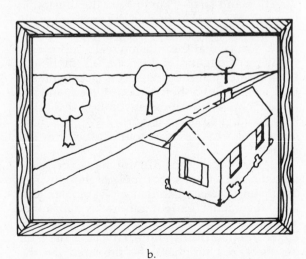

b.

Figure 7-18   Two illusions of shape.

In this section on illusions we have seen that illusions can cause distortions in line length, area, direction, and shape. In many cases they seem to be governed by the same rules that govern the constancies. Furthermore, they have practical importance in many applied areas. We discussed the use of illusions in some applied areas, but if you are interested in illusions in painting, read two books called *Illusion in Nature and Art* (Gregory & Gombrich, 1973) and *Illusion in Art* (Mastai, 1975).

Summary: Illusions

- An illusion is a perception that is incorrect.
- Theorists disagree about whether illusions are important or not.
- Line-length illusions include the Müller-Lyer illusion, the Sander parallelogram, the horizontal-vertical illusion, and the Ponzo illusion.
- Explanations for the line-length illusions include the theory of misapplied constancy, the eye-movement theory, and the incorrect comparison theory. Each illusion probably depends upon at least one of these explanations.
- The most famous of the many illusions involving area is the moon illusion, whereby the moon looks larger at the horizon than it does at the zenith.
- Explanations for the moon illusion include the apparent distance theory and the relative-size explanation.
- Direction and shape illusions, such as the Poggendorf illusion, can have important applications in daily life.

Review

1. Suppose that you have two lines that are identical in length. You place one 1 m from yourself and the other 5 m from yourself. Compare the retinal sizes and the perceived sizes of the two objects. Now you place them both 1 m from yourself. You decorate one with wings pointing inward and one with wings pointing outward. Again compare the retinal sizes and the perceived sizes. Which situation is constancy and which is illusion?

2. In the discussion of size constancy we saw that the removal of distance cues leads to a reduction in size constancy. Explain why each of these theories would account for that effect: (a) the size-distance invariance hypothesis; (b) the relative size explanation; and (c) Gibson's texture explanation.

3. In a study by MacDonald and Hoffman (1973), road pavement messages were written either in normally proportioned letters or in tall letters (so that when a driver viewed them from the typical slant from the automobile, the retinal images were normally proportioned). From what you know about constancy, which kind of letter would you guess was recognized more accurately? What kind of constancy is this?

4. You wear a black-and-white checked shirt and come out of a dark movie theater into the bright sunlight. How would Helmholtz's theory and contrast theory account for the brightness constancy you experience when you look at your shirt. Discuss albedo somewhere in your explanation.

5. Think about an experience you have had in the last 24 hours to illustrate each of the following: motion constancy, position constancy, color constancy, existence constancy, and constancy under bending.

6. Show why the empiricist explanations for the three major constancies—size constancy, shape constancy, and brightness constancy—are similar to one another.

7. J. J. Gibson (1950) argues that humans and animals react to the spatial environment with enormous accuracy and precision and that our visual worlds agree very closely with the environment. How does this correspond with his views on the importance of illusions?

8. Explain the Müller-Lyer illusion in terms of each of the following theories: (a) misapplied constancy, (b) movement, and (c) incorrect comparison.

9. Draw a variation of each of the following illusions: the Ponzo, the horizontal-vertical, the Sander, and the Poggendorf.

10. Your ten-year-old nephew comes to

visit, and he asks the question you dread: Why is the moon so big early in the night? Give a simple, clear summary of each of the two dominant theories about the moon illusion.

New Terms

distal stimulus
proximal stimulus
constancy
size constancy
visual angle
retinal size
overconstancy
underconstancy
size-distance invariance
   hypothesis
relative-size explanation
texture explanation
shape constancy

ecological validity
shape-slant invariance hypothesis
brightness constancy
brightness
albedo
contrast theory
color constancy
motion constancy
constancy under bending
position constancy
existence constancy
illusion
mirages

Müller-Lyer illusion
Sander parallelogram
horizontal-vertical illusion
Ponzo illusion
theory of misapplied constancy
eye-movement theory
incorrect comparison theory
moon illusion
apparent-distance theory
relative-size explanation
Poggendorf illusion

chapter 8

HEARING

Outline

Sensory Aspects of Hearing
The Auditory Stimulus
The Auditory System

Perceptual Qualities of Sound
Pitch
Loudness
Timbre
Localization

Complex Auditory Perception
The Perception of Tone Combinations
Speech Perception

Applications of Hearing Research
Noise Pollution
Hearing Impairments

Preview

Hearing is an extremely important perceptual system, and its role in communication is vital. Our examination of hearing consists of four parts: (1) sensory aspects of hearing, (2) perceptual qualities of sound, (3) complex auditory perception, and (4) applications of hearing research.

The sounds that we hear can be described in terms of sound waves that vary in their frequency and amplitude. The first section of the chapter also examines the parts of the auditory system, including the three sections of the ear and the pathway from the ear to the brain. We also consider two different theories about how frequency is registered in the auditory system and how these theories can be reconciled.

In the second section of the chapter we look at psychological qualities that are related to the physical features of sound. Although there are complications, pitch is roughly correlated with frequency, and loudness is roughly correlated with amplitude. Timbre, or a tone's quality, is what distinguishes the tone of an oboe from the tone of a clarinet; timbre depends largely on the complexity of sound waves. A final topic in this section is localization; we are more accurate in judging the direction of a sound than its distance from us.

The section on complex auditory perception begins with a discussion of the combination of two tones. Depending upon the physical characteristics of the tones, the combination may be heard either as a single tone or as two tones that are either pleasant or unpleasant in combination; one tone may also mask the other tone. In this section we also talk about speech perception. In particular, we discuss how speech sounds can be classified and why a thorough explanation of speech perception must involve more than a simple analysis of speech sounds.

Throughout the chapter, we consider the study of music as an application of hearing research. In the last section we look at applications in two other areas, noise pollution and hearing impairment. The discussion of noise pollution includes how your threshold can shift after you hear a loud noise, how noise pollution influences behavior, and how noise pollution can be reduced. The discussion of hearing impairments focuses on two kinds of deafness, conduction deafness and nerve deafness.

Take a moment to appreciate the variety of sounds that you can hear right now. You may hear voices and music, rattles, thuds, whines, buzzes, squeaks, and roars. Some sounds are loud, and some are soft. Some are high, some low. Sounds also vary in their quality and their location.

Think about the variety of ways in which hearing provides us with information about the world. Hearing can inform us of danger—we hear a barking dog, a car horn, and a shout of "Fire!" It is also important in human communication; hearing is central in social interactions and in transmitting knowledge. In addition, it is a major source of entertainment in music, movies, and plays.

We will begin this chapter by examining sensory aspects of hearing, and then we will discuss various perceptual qualities of stimuli. Next we will turn to more complex tasks, such as the perception of speech. Our final topic is the application of hearing research in the study of noise pollution and hearing impairments.

Sensory Aspects of Hearing

In Chapter 2 you learned about the visual stimulus, light, and the structure of the visual system. In this section we need to examine the equivalent topics for hearing. We will begin with an overview of the nature of the auditory stimulus, and then we will look at the structure of the auditory system. Both of these topics will be covered only briefly; more details can be found in books by Green (1976) and Durrant and Lovrinic (1977).

The Auditory Stimulus

The auditory stimuli that we hear are caused by tiny disturbances in air pressure. Something vibrates, and the vibration causes molecules of air to change their positions. For example, if you knock on your desk, the vibration from the knock will bump into air molecules that are right next to the desk. These air molecules will bump into nearby air molecules and then bounce back. Those nearby air molecules, in turn, will bump into their neighbors, setting up a chain reaction. Eventually, some air molecules will reach your eardrum, and the air pressure disturbances will cause your eardrum to move.

Let's examine vibrations more closely. You may have seen a tuning fork in a science laboratory, a music class, or a doctor's office. A **tuning fork** is a two-pronged instrument that creates a particular tone when it is struck; one is illustrated in Figure 8-1a. Each of the prongs vibrates by moving up and down in a very regular fashion. This particular, regular kind of vibration is called sine-wave motion; it is illustrated in Figure 8-1b.

Most vibrating objects produce more complex vibration patterns, but let's deal now with the simplest case. Notice how Figure 8-1b corresponds to the movement of one of the prongs of the tuning fork. (For the purpose of illustration, the movement is exaggerated in Figure 8-1b.) First, the prong moves upward (at time 2), then it moves back to its original position (at time 3), then it moves downward (at time 4), then back to its original position (time 5); then the cycle repeats itself.

The vibrations of the tuning fork cause the nearby air molecules to vibrate in the same kind of sine-wave fashion. Furthermore, the surrounding air pressure varies from one moment to the next as air molecules cluster together (high pressure) and then bounce away from each other (low pressure); air pressure also varies in a sine-wave fashion. Thus after you have knocked on your desk or sounded a tuning fork, the air pressure near your eardrum will show a cyclic pattern of change. This rapid increase and decrease in pressure will cause your eardrum to move back and forth, also in a sine-wave fashion. These successive pressure changes are called **sounds.**

Thus you hear a sound because of tiny disturbances in air pressure. This seems incredible. How can the movement of invisible air molecules possibly be strong enough to cause your eardrum to move? The truth is that they only need to displace your eardrum by a minute amount—about .000000001 cm (Green, 1976). Try to imagine this distance; it is one billionth of a centimeter! (Incidentally, we should note that sound can travel through other substances,

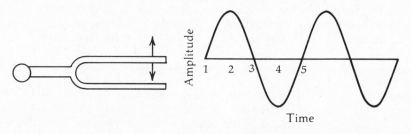

a.　Tuning fork　　　　b.　Vibration pattern made by a prong of the tuning fork

Figure 8-1　A tuning fork and the sine-wave vibration pattern made by one prong.

such as water, but we will primarily be concerned with sound moving through air.)

Sound waves can be described in terms of their frequency and their amplitude. Try Demonstration 8-1 to illustrate these two qualities.

Frequency

Let's first discuss frequency. **Frequency** is the number of cycles that a sound wave completes in one second. For example, middle C on the piano has a frequency of 262 cycles per second, or 262 Hz. (The abbreviation **Hz,** pronounced "hurts," is derived from the name of Heinrich Hertz, a German physicist.) Thus the prongs of a tuning fork that has been constructed to create a sound at 262 Hz will vibrate back and forth 262 times each second. In general, frequency corresponds to the psychological experience of pitch. Thus middle C on the piano, with a frequency of 262 Hz, sounds higher in pitch than the lowest note on the piano, which has a frequency of about 27 Hz.

What range of frequencies can humans hear? Young adults can typically hear tones with frequencies as low as 20 Hz and as high as 20,000 Hz. Older adults, as we will see in Chapter 14, may have difficulty hearing tones as high as 20,000 Hz. However, most of our auditory experience involves only a small fraction of the range between 20 Hz and 20,000 Hz. For example, singers at a concert are unlikely to sing below 75 Hz or above 1000 Hz.

Let us examine detection and discrimination for tones of various frequencies. Humans are more sensitive in detecting tones in the 3000-Hz range than they are in detecting higher or lower tones (Sivian & White, 1933). Intriguingly, agonized human screams may reach as high as 3000 Hz. If the Blob from Outer Space ever attacks, give a high-frequency scream! The frequency of a tone influences discrimination as

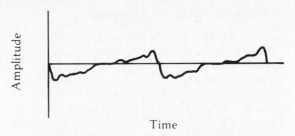

Figure 8-2   An example of a complex tone.

well as detection. We notice changes in frequency more for low-frequency tones than for high-frequency tones. A 60-Hz tone can be discriminated from a 62-Hz tone, but a 3000-Hz tone cannot be discriminated from a 3002-Hz tone. High-frequency tones in the range of 3000 Hz require a tone that differs by at least 16 Hz (for example, 3016) in order to be perceived as different.

So far our discussion of frequency has only included pure tones. A tuning fork produces a **pure tone,** a tone that can be represented by a simple sine wave. Most of the sounds we hear in our everyday lives—including tones on musical instruments and speech sounds—are **complex tones,** tones that cannot be represented by one simple sine wave. For example, look at the complex tone illustrated in Figure 8-2, which represents the combination of several different tones.

A complex sound wave may be broken into a series of components. The component that has the lowest frequency is called the **fundamental frequency,** so 100 Hz is the fundamental frequency in a complex tone representing 100 Hz, 200 Hz, and 300 Hz. The other components of a complex tone are called **harmonics;** harmonics have higher frequencies than the fundamental. In this example, 200 Hz and 300 Hz are harmonics.

Demonstration 8-1

The Frequency and Amplitude of Sound Waves

Place a rubber band over an open box. By plucking the rubber band gently or vigorously, you can vary the amplitude or height of the sound waves associated with the sound of the rubber band. By pulling the rubber band tightly on the side of the box, you can vary the frequency of the sound waves associated with the sound of the rubber band.

Musical instruments have harmonics or **overtones** that are multiples of the fundamental frequency. For example, if you play the A above middle C on the piano, the fundamental tone of 440 Hz is produced. In addition, however, the overtones of 880 Hz (2 × 440) and 1320 Hz (3 × 440), as well as higher-frequency overtones, are produced. The fundamental frequency contributes the greatest amplitude to the tone, but the harmonics also contribute substantially. We will discuss complex tones again in connection with timbre.

Amplitude

So far, we have just described the frequency of sound waves. Now let's describe their **amplitude,** or the change in pressure created by the sound waves. In general, amplitude corresponds to the psychological experience of loudness. That is, a high-amplitude sound wave moves your eardrum more than a low-amplitude sound wave, and the sound seems louder to you.

We described the frequency of sound waves in very direct, obvious units, in terms of the number of cycles per second. Unfortunately, the units used to describe amplitude are more indirect and difficult to understand. The reason for this is that the range of amplitudes that we can hear is impressively extreme. The most intense sound that we can tolerate is about 1,000,000,000,000 more intense than the weakest sound we can detect (Lindsay & Norman, 1977). Thus it would be inconvenient to use a direct, unconverted scale that would involve measurements such as 875,934,771. Instead, we use decibels as units of intensity measurement.

Decibels (pronounced "*dess*-uh-bells") measure the amount of pressure created by a stimulus such as a sound wave, relative to a specified reference point. Generally, the reference point that industry uses is the pressure of the weakest sound that a human can hear. Thus if you read that the amplitude of a particular sound is 20 decibels (abbreviated **dB**), you know that this amplitude is based on a comparison with a barely detectable sound.

In order to avoid the inconvenience of a direct scale, decibels are expressed in terms of a logarithmic scale. The important aspect of logarithms that you need to know here is that logarithmic transformations shrink down the large numbers but change the small numbers much less drastically. Thus the amplitude of heavy auto traffic could be given as 10,000,000,000 (in comparison with a barely detectable sound). However, the logarithmic scale shrinks this large number down to 100 dB, a manageable number. The amplitude of a soft whisper, which could be given as 100, is converted to 20 dB—a much less drastic change.

Table 8-1 shows some representative decibel levels for sounds that humans can hear. Note that decibels are standardized so that 0 dB represents the weakest sound you can hear. Incidentally, our discussion of decibel measurement here is greatly simplified. More details on the mathematics and physics of the decibel measurement system—as well as a discussion of another component of sound waves

Table 8-1 Some typical amplitudes of various noises, measured by the decibel scale.	LEVEL	dB	EXAMPLE
		160	loudest rock band on record
	intolerable	140	very painful
		120	very loud thunder
	very noisy	100	heavy automobile traffic
	loud	80	loud music from radio
	moderate	60	average conversation
	faint	40	quiet neighborhood
	very faint	20	soft whisper
		0	softest detectable noise

called phase—are available elsewhere (B. C. J. Moore, 1977; Green, 1976; Leshowitz, 1978). Also, an article by L. E. Marks (1979) outlines a theory about how the intensity of sounds is processed in a hierarchy of stages, from the sensory level to the more central, cognitive level.

The Auditory System

We have been discussing sound pressure changes. Once these sound pressure changes have been transmitted to a human observer, then certain changes must occur in the auditory system in order to transform the physical energy into a kind of energy that can be transmitted by neurons. We need to examine what happens to sound when it reaches the ear and how the various parts of the ear contribute to the transformation process.

There are three anatomical regions in the ear. Their names, fortunately, are refreshingly straightforward: the outer ear, the middle ear, and the inner ear. We will discuss each of these regions separately. Then we will discuss how frequency is registered in the inner ear. Finally, we will briefly consider the pathway from the ear to the brain.

The Outer Ear

The most obvious part of the outer ear is what people ordinarily refer to as "the ear." The technical name for this flap of tissue is the **pinna.** In humans the pinnae protect the inner parts of the ear. Other animals—such as dogs and horses—have more useful pinnae; their ears can be moved around to help localize sounds. Even your Uncle Fred, who can move his ears entertainingly at family reunions, cannot move his pinnae enough to help his localization ability.

Figure 8-3 shows other structures in the outer ear. Notice the tube, called the **external auditory canal**, that runs inward from the pinna. The external auditory canal is about an inch long. It helps to protect the eardrum and to concentrate the sound so that it can move the

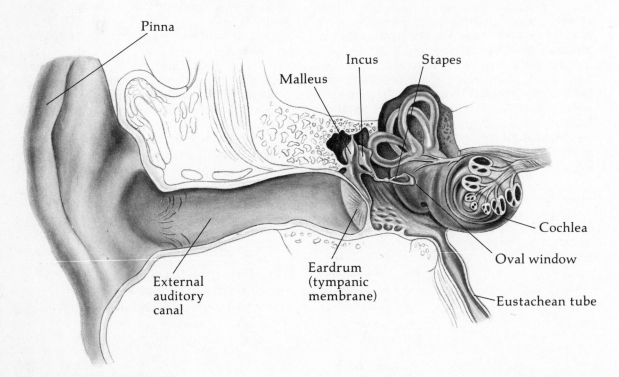

Figure 8-3   Anatomy of the ear.

eardrum more forcefully. Finally, there is the **eardrum,** or **tympanic membrane,** the thin piece of membrane that vibrates in response to sound waves. Thus the outer ear has three parts: the *Pinna,* the *External* auditory canal, and the *Tympanic* membrane. (Remember the mnemonic, PET.)

The Middle Ear

Just behind the eardrum are three bones in the middle ear. These bones are named in Latin according to their shapes: the **malleus** (or hammer), the **incus** (or anvil), and the **stapes,** pronounced *"stay*-peas" (or stirrup). The function of these three bones is to vibrate in rhythm with the eardrum and to transmit these vibrations to the inner ear. This set of three bones increases the pressure substantially on the inner ear, so they are not merely decorative structures. These bones also have tiny muscles attached to them that contract in response to a loud sound; this reflex may sometimes protect the cochlea from damage. (Incidentally, one way to remember the three bones in order is to notice that as you move from the *M*alleus to the *I*ncus to the *S*tapes, you *M*ove *I*n*S*ide the ear. Also, a blacksmith might use a hammer and anvil to make a stirrup.)

Notice, also, the **eustachian tubes** (pronounced "you-*stay*-she-un"), which connect the ears to the throat. We will have more to say about these tubes in the section on hearing problems.

The Inner Ear

Notice that the stapes rests on the side of the **cochlea** (pronounced *"cock*-lee-ah"), a fluid-filled structure that is curled up like a miniature snail shell. The anatomy of the cochlea is very complex; you can find more information by consulting Green (1976). However, if we were to look at a cross section through one segment of the coil, we would see something like Figure 8-4. The most critical part of Figure 8-4 is the **organ of Corti** (pronounced *"court*-eye"), which contains the receptors that change the pressure energy from a sound wave into the kind of electrical and chemical energy that can be carried through the higher pathways in the auditory system.

The organ of Corti has three important parts: (1) the **basilar membrane,** which is on the base of the organ of Corti; (2) the **tectorial membrane,** which rests at the top of the organ of Corti; and (3) the **hair cells,** which are the actual receptors for hearing. (Remember, the *b*asilar is the *b*ottom; the *t*ectorial is the *t*op.) When the stapes move, the fluid in the cochlea causes these tiny hair cells to rub against the tectorial membrane and bend. When these hair cells bend, electrical activity is produced in the **auditory nerve,** which has endings in the basilar membrane. In a later section we will consider how the auditory nerve transmits electrical impulses to the brain. We will also see how the destruction of hair cells causes one kind of deafness. Incidentally, more information on cochlear physiology can be obtained from a recent review by Dallos (1981).

Notice how each part of the auditory system plays a role in the hearing process. The pinna protects the important, delicate inner parts of the ear. The external auditory canal also protects the eardrum; in addition, it concentrates the sound. The eardrum vibrates when the sound waves strike it. The three bones in the middle ear vibrate when the eardrum vibrates, and their design allows them to increase the pressure on the inner ear or cochlea. When those bones vibrate, the hair cells in the organ of Corti—a part of the cochlea—are forced to bend. This bending action produces electrical activity.

The Registration of Frequency in the Inner Ear

We have examined how sound is transmitted into the inner ear. One of the major mysteries of the auditory system concerns how the inner ear registers frequency. When middle C is played on the piano, you hear a different pitch than if, say, the note A is played. How can the bumping of air molecules, the movement of fluid in the cochlea, and the bending of hair cells in the organ of Corti possibly account for the subtle kinds of distinctions we can make with respect to sound?

There are many theories that attempt to explain how the ear codes frequency information. Among the most popular are the place theory and the frequency theory.

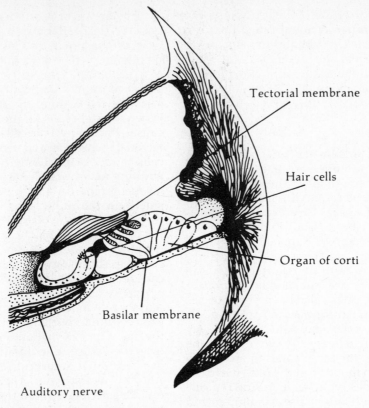

Tectorial membrane

Hair cells

Organ of corti

Basilar membrane

Auditory nerve

Figure 8-4   Cross-section of the cochlea, showing the organ of Corti.

The **place theory** proposes that each frequency of vibration causes a particular place on the basilar membrane to vibrate. This theory was originally suggested by Helmholtz, the 19th century scientist whose work we considered in other chapters. More recently, von Békésy (pronounced "fohn *Beh*-keh-shee") conducted research that won him the Nobel prize. Von Békésy (e.g., 1960) demonstrated that different locations on the basilar membrane are indeed sensitive to different frequencies of vibration. He determined that locations in the base of the basilar membrane (the part nearest the stapes in the coil) are sensitive to high frequencies. In contrast, locations near the end of the basilar membrane (nearest the inside of the coil) are sensitive to lower frequencies. However, no location on the basilar membrane is sensitive to very low frequencies. Thus this theory has difficulty explaining how we perceive very low notes.

Now let us consider the other major theory, frequency theory. According to **frequency theory,** the whole basilar membrane vibrates; this vibration almost matches the vibration patterns of the sound waves that are transmitted to the basilar membrane. Frequency theory can be traced back to the 19th century, but Wever (1970) has been the primary advocate of this theory in recent years. Frequency theory also suggests that the frequency of impulses that travel along the auditory nerve carries information about a tone's frequency. Thus an 800-Hz tone would produce about twice as many electrical responses in the auditory nerve as a 400-Hz tone.

Frequency theory can explain a number of puzzling hearing phenomena but in its simplest form it does have a serious drawback. Each neuron can handle "only" about 1000 impulses every second. How is it possible for us to discriminate between frequencies as fast as 20,000 cycles if our neurons cannot even respond at 1/20th of that rate?

Wever (1970) proposed a **volley principle,** whereby clusters of neurons share in producing the required firing rate. Consider an analogy. Suppose that for some obscure reason, you wanted to produce one scream each second for a period of about a minute. This task would be impossible for you alone, but with the appropriate community spirit you and four friends could organize your screams so that you would take turns. As a consequence, each of you would have to produce only one scream every 5 seconds—a manageable task. The net result, however, would be the required one scream per second. Similarly, a 4000-Hz tone could be registered if each of five neurons fires 800 times each second—again, a manageable task. However, even with the addition of the volley principle, frequency theory has difficulty explaining how tones with frequencies greater than 4000 Hz can be registered.

Which theory is correct, place theory or frequency theory? You may recall that in Chapter 4 we concluded our discussion of the battle between opponent-process theories and trichromatic theories by saying that both theories could live happily with each other. The same conclusion is relevant to our discussion of frequency registration. Specifically, place theory handles the high frequencies well, but it has difficulties with very low frequencies. On the other hand, frequency theory handles the low frequencies well, but it has difficulties with very high frequencies; even groups of neurons would be unable to fire fast enough to handle the very high frequencies. In the middle range that we use for most of our daily activities, however, both theories may apply. If sound wave frequencies are registered in terms of both place and neuron-firing frequency, we have an explanation for why humans' auditory skills can be quite remarkable.

The Pathway from the Ear to the Brain

Let us briefly consider how information is transmitted from the cochlea to the brain. As we saw earlier, the hair cells located in the organ of Corti pass information along to the auditory nerve. The auditory nerve travels to the **cochlear nucleus,** which is located at the bottom of the back part of the brain. Most of the auditory nerve cells transmit their information to other cells in the cochlear nucleus.

You may recall that the visual system has a complex mechanism for insuring that information from each eye is distributed to each of the two sides of the brain. Similarly, in the auditory system, each of the two cochlear nuclei sends its information on to two structures located on different sides of the brain. Figure 8-5 is a schematic diagram of this division. The name of these two structures sounds like the name of the leader of a mystical vegetarian cult—the superior olive. The **superior olive** can compare the information that it receives from the two ears. We will discuss the significance of this comparison process in the section on localization.

Each superior olive sends its information on to an **inferior colliculus,** which is located just below (or inferior to) the superior colliculus that we discussed in connection with the visual system; here, it is possible that information in the auditory system is compared with the nearby information in the visual system. From the inferior colliculus, information passes on to the **medial geniculate nucleus** (remember the lateral geniculate nucleus in the visual system?). From there it passes to the **auditory cortex,** which is located in a deep groove on the side of the brain. The inaccessible location of the auditory cortex makes it quite difficult to study. A short section written by Yost and Nielsen (1977) provides a readable overview of research on frequency maps of the cortex and electrical activity in response to auditory stimuli.

Let's briefly review the pathway from the cochlea to the auditory cortex. The *A*uditory nerve travels to the *C*ochlear nucleus; then the information travels to the *S*uperior olive, then the *I*nferior colliculus, then the *M*edial geniculate nucleus, and finally the *A*uditory cortex. (One mnemonic for ACSIMA is *A*lways *C*arry *S*nakes *I*n *M*inor *A*ccidents.)

Summary: Sensory Aspects of Hearing

- Hearing can inform us of danger, and it is central in human communications.
- Sound waves, which ultimately cause the eardrum to vibrate, can be described in terms of their frequency and their amplitude.

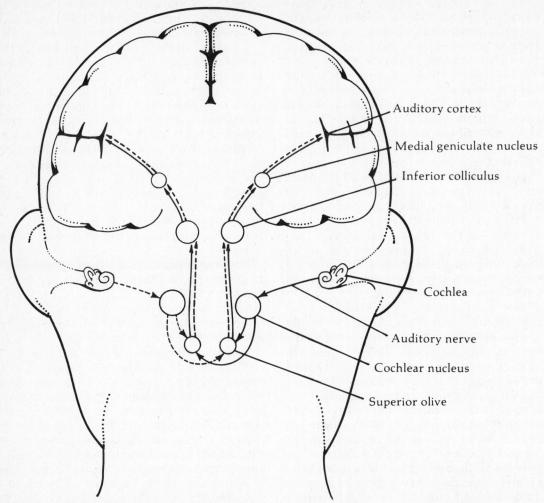

Figure 8-5 The pathway from the ear to the brain (schematic representation). Only the structures on the right side of the head have been labeled; notice that there are corresponding structures on the left side of the head.

- Frequency is the number of cycles that a sound wave can complete in one second, abbreviated Hz; frequency is an important determinant of pitch.
- We hear tones with frequencies between 20 and 20,000 Hz.
- We detect tones best in the 3000-Hz range, but we discriminate tones best in the low-frequency range.
- Complex tones cannot be represented by a simple sine wave; a complex tone has a fundamental frequency (or lowest frequency) plus harmonics (or overtones) that are multiples of the fundamental frequency.
- Amplitude is the change in pressure created by the sound waves, measured in decibels; amplitude is an important determinant of loudness.
- The outer ear consists of the pinna, the external auditory canal, and the tympanic membrane.
- The middle ear contains three bones—the malleus, the incus, and the stapes—and the eustachian tube.
- The inner ear contains the cochlea, the most important part of which is the organ of Corti; the organ of Corti has three major parts: the basilar membrane, the tectorial membrane, and the hair cells.
- There are two major theories explaining

how the ear registers frequency information: (a) the place theory proposes that each sound wave frequency causes a particular place on the basilar membrane to vibrate; (b) the frequency theory proposes that sound wave frequency is translated into the frequency of impulses along the auditory nerve.

• Place theory may explain how we hear high frequencies; frequency theory may explain how we hear low frequencies; and both theories may hold for our hearing of intermediate frequencies.

• The auditory nerve travels to the cochlear nucleus. The auditory pathway continues to the superior olive, then to the inferior colliculus, then to the medial geniculate nucleus, and finally to the auditory cortex.

Perceptual Qualities of Sound

Listen to a sound right now and think about the perceptual qualities that you notice. You notice whether it is high or low (pitch) and whether it is loud or soft (loudness). You also notice its sound quality (timbre); for example, the tone of a flute is different from the tone of a clarinet. In addition, you notice where the sound seems to be coming from. All of these qualities are subjective or psychological qualities of sound, as opposed to the physical qualities such as frequency and amplitude that we discussed in the last section.

Pitch

As we said in our discussion of frequency, high-frequency tones are generally associated with high pitch, whereas low-frequency tones are generally associated with low pitch. In other words, there is a correlation between frequency and pitch. However, the correlation is far from perfect. For example, pitch perception can depend upon the amplitude of the sound. In experiments using pure tones, the pitch of low notes seems to be lower when the amplitude of the tone is increased. In contrast, the pitch of high notes seems to be higher when the amplitude is increased. However, the pitch of complex tones is relatively unchanged by amplitude.

Another reason that pitch is not perfectly correlated with frequency involves the case of the missing fundamental. Admittedly, this term sounds like the latest in a series of teenage mystery stories. However, the **case of the missing fundamental** refers to the fact that listeners report the pitch of certain complex stimuli as being the pitch of a fundamental that

was never even presented. You will recall that the fundamental frequency is the lowest frequency in a complex tone. Suppose that an experimenter presents a complex tone that contains 700-Hz, 800-Hz, 900-Hz, and 1000-Hz tones. In other words, this complex tone is missing the 100-Hz fundamental for which these four tones represent harmonics. Even so, listeners report that they hear a 100-Hz tone associated with this complex stimulus (Fletcher, 1934). Thus a further reason that pitch is not perfectly correlated with frequency is that we can sometimes hear a pitch appropriate to a frequency that is missing from a complex tone.

Yet another reason that the correlation between frequency and pitch is not perfect is that characteristics of the observer can influence pitch. Thurlow (1971) discusses the influence of arousal on pitch perception. If you are sleepy, for example, a tone will sound lower in pitch than it would if you were alert.

We talked about the units of measurement used to scale the physical attribute, frequency. How is the psychological quality of pitch measured? Musicians use the term "octave" in connection with pitch. An **octave** is represented by the distance between two notes that have the same name. Thus there is an octave between one C and the next higher or next lower C on the piano.

In describing pure tones, psychologists often use the mel scale, which was suggested by S. S. Stevens, Volkman, and Newman (1937). The **mel scale** is a scale of pitch obtained by the magnitude estimation technique. In the mel scale, a 1000-Hz pure tone is arbitrarily assigned a pitch of 1000 mels. Then listeners are asked to adjust a comparison tone until it seems to be half as high as this 1000-Hz tone; this tone is assigned a value of 500 mels. Other points in the scale are filled in by asking listeners to locate comparison tones that represent other fractions and multiples of the standard 1000-Hz tone.

Loudness

As we noted earlier, loudness is roughly determined by a tone's amplitude. However, as in the case of pitch and frequency, we find that the correlation between loudness and amplitude is not perfect. For example, loudness perception depends upon the duration of the tone. It also depends upon the frequency of a tone (just as pitch perception depends upon the amplitude of a tone). For example, a 1000-Hz tone at an amplitude of 30 dB seems just as loud as a 300-Hz tone at an amplitude of 40 dB.

In general, tones around 3000 Hz seem louder even though they are physically equivalent to higher- and lower-frequency tones presented at the same amplitude. Thus tones around the level of 3000 Hz have lower detection thresholds (as we saw in the discussion of frequency in the previous section), and they also seem to be louder when they are presented at above-threshold levels.

Loudness depends not only upon duration and frequency, but also upon other physical qualities such as background sounds. In addition, loudness depends upon the perceiver. As Scharf (1978) notes, the loudness of a sound depends upon whether we pay attention to a sound or merely hear it and whether our ears are "fresh" or recently exposed to sound. Try

Demonstration 8-2 to illustrate the influence of previous sounds upon loudness perception.

How is the psychological quality of loudness measured? Musicians scale loudness in terms of an eight-level marking system that ranges from *ppp* for the very softest sound through *fff* for the very loudest sound. Psychologists measure loudness in a number of different ways. One of the most widely used systems is the sone scale (S. S. Stevens, 1955). The **sone scale** is a scale of loudness obtained by the magnitude estimation technique. (Recall that the mel scale is a scale of *pitch* obtained by the same kind of magnitude estimation technique.) In the sone scale, a 1000-Hz pure tone at 40 dB is arbitrarily assigned a loudness of 1 sone. Listeners judge the loudness of other tones in relationship to this standard tone. Thus a tone that appears to be twice as loud would be judged as 2 sones, and a tone that appears to be half as loud would be judged as .5 sone.

In general, Stevens found that the amplitude of a tone had to be increased by 10 dB in order for listeners to judge a tone as being twice as loud. Thus a 50-dB tone appeared to be twice as loud as a 40-dB tone; the 50-dB tone would therefore be 2 sones. A good feature of the sone scale is that the measures correspond to our everyday perceptions of sound in a more meaningful fashion than the decibel system. For example, suppose that you are working in a quiet office where the noise level is measured at 40 dB or 1 sone. The company may wish to introduce a new kind of equipment that will raise the noise level to 50 dB. This 10-dB increase would not strike most people as a substantial increase, and they would not be alarmed at the prospect

---

Demonstration 8-2

The Influence of Previous Noises on Loudness

Find a watch that makes a ticking noise and place it in a location so that you can clearly hear it; the ticking should definitely be above threshold. Then turn on a record player or a radio so that it is loud but not painfully loud; leave it on for 10 minutes, and then turn it completely off. Return to the location from which you originally heard the ticking watch. Judge its loudness relative to your original judgment. We will talk more about the influence of previous noises on hearing in the section on noise pollution.

of such a change. However, you now know that this increase represents an increase from 1 sone to 2 sones; the new noise level would really sound *twice* as loud.

Incidentally, despite its advantages, the sone scale has been criticized because people's judgments are heavily influenced by the order in which stimuli are presented and other biasing factors (B. C. J. Moore, 1977). Jesteadt, Luce, and Green (1977) discuss other aspects of sequential effects in loudness judgments.

Timbre

Pitch and loudness are familiar concepts to you. Timbre is also a familiar concept, although the term itself may be new. **Timbre** (pronounced "*tam*-burr") is a tone's sound quality. Thus two sounds may have the same pitch and the same loudness, and yet they differ in quality. A piece of chalk squeaking across a blackboard seems different from the sound produced by a valuable violin, and they both seem different from the voice of a soprano. Furthermore, your voice seems different from the voice of someone else, even though the pitch and loudness may be identical.

If pitch is related to frequency and loudness is related to amplitude, what physical feature of sound is timbre related to? The psychological quality, timbre, corresponds to complexity. Complex tones, remember, cannot be represented by a simple sine wave; instead, they must be represented by complex wave forms. The specific nature of the complexity is related to the tone quality, or timbre. Figure 8-6 illustrates the sound waves that are associated with several different kinds of complex tones.

Complex sound waves, such as those in Figure 8-6, can be analyzed into their components by a process called Fourier analysis. **Fourier analysis** (pronounced "Four-ee-*ay*") is based on the theory that any repeating kind of wave form can be represented as the combination of several simple sine waves, each wave having its own frequency and amplitude. The specifics of Fourier analysis are beyond the scope of this book; it is discussed in detail elsewhere (e.g., Weisstein, 1980; Yost & Nielsen, 1977). Impressively, our human ears can perform a rough Fourier analysis for complex tones. Thus our ears can isolate several of the

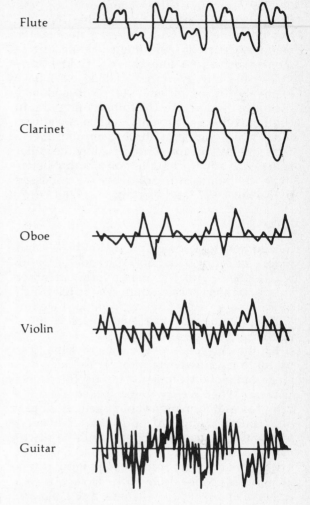

Figure 8-6 The sound waves of several kinds of complex tones produced by musical instruments.

simple sine waves when we hear a complex tone.

The timbre of musical instruments is related to the overtones that we discussed earlier. For example, suppose that you play the A above middle C on several different musical instruments. The fundamental note of 440 Hz will be produced in each case, and so the pitch will be identical for all instruments. However, one instrument may emphasize the overtone of 880 Hz, and this overtone may have a greater amplitude than other overtones. In contrast, a different instrument may emphasize the overtone of 1320 Hz.

Our ears can analyze complex tones and detect which overtones are emphasized. We can therefore distinguish among the sounds made by different instruments. Some instruments, such as the flute, have very few overtones, and any overtones that do exist have relatively low amplitude. As a consequence, the tones produced by the flute sound pure. In contrast, other instruments, such as the guitar, have many high-amplitude overtones. As a consequence, the tones produced by the guitar sound rich and thick. Other factors that determine the timbre of instruments are discussed by Backus (1977) and Nordmark (1978).

Localization

In addition to a tone's pitch, loudness, and timbre we can also identify with some accuracy where the sound is coming from; in other words, we show **localization.** We can tell which direction a sound is coming from, and we can also tell (with less impressive accuracy, however) the distance of the source.

In the chapters on vision we saw that it is useful to have two eyes in order to judge distance and motion. Similarly, it is useful to have two ears when we try to localize sounds. We can process information about pitch, loudness, and timbre using only one ear. However, **binaural** (pronounced "bin-*awe*-rull") or two-ear cues are essential for accurate localization. That is, we are more accurate in judging where a sound is coming from if we have two ears rather than a single ear (Durlach & Colburn, 1978).

Let us consider separately the perception of direction and the perception of distance. More information on localization can be found in the work of B. C. J. Moore (1977) and Yost and Nielsen (1977). In addition, Thurlow (1971) dis-

cusses how echoes are useful for some animals, such as bats and porpoises, and for blind people in determining the location of objects.

Direction

As we mentioned, people are more accurate in judging direction than in judging distance. Try Demonstration 8-3 to illustrate this point. Some kinds of direction judgments are easier than others. For example, it is easy to tell whether a sound is coming from your right or your left side. However, it is more difficult to tell whether a sound is coming from directly in front of you or directly in back of you. Why should this be true? In order to answer this question, we will need to look at the cues we use for judging direction. Two cues are most important, time difference and intensity difference.

Look at Figure 8-7, which illustrates how sound reaches the two ears at different times. Notice that the sound will reach the left ear before it reaches the right ear. We can make use of this information about differences in time of arrival, even though the differences may be very small. Even differences smaller than one millisecond (1/1000 of a second) can provide useful information about the direction of a sound source. However, sounds directly in front of you would reach your two ears at the same time. Similarly, a sound directly behind you would reach your right ear and your left ear simultaneously.

Not only does the sound in Figure 8-7 reach your two ears at different times; the sound also reaches your two ears at different intensities. For example, your left ear is closer than the right ear to the sound source in Figure 8-7, and so the sound is slightly more intense. More important, however, is the fact that your head

---

Demonstration 8 - 3

Judging the Direction and Distance of a Sound

Try this demonstration outside with a friend. Close your eyes. Your friend should move around to a new location and then call to you. Try to judge the direction by pointing and the distance by estimating the number of feet or meters from you. Repeat this demonstration several times, your friend varying his or her voice amplitude each time. Compare the accuracy of your direction and distance estimates.

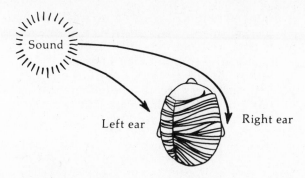

Figure 8-7 Diagram of sound traveling toward the left and right ears.

produces a **sound shadow,** or a barrier that reduces the sound intensity. We are accustomed to a reduction in intensity when something large—say, a bedroom door—separates us from a sound source. Have you ever thought that your head blocks some of the sound coming from sources on the opposite side? The shadowing effect is particularly strong for high-frequency sound waves, which have difficulty bending around the head. With tones having frequencies of 5000 Hz, for example, there may be a 20-dB difference in the intensity of sound reaching the two ears (Thurlow 1971). Notice, however, that sounds directly in front of you and directly in back of you do not produce differences in intensity for your two ears.

In summary, we judge the direction of a sound source on the basis of time differences and intensity differences. The ear that receives the sound first and loudest is the closest to the sound source. As we noted in our discussion of the auditory pathway, the superior olive compares information that it receives from the two ears; time of arrival and intensity are two attributes that it can compare.

Distance

Although our ability to make distance judgments is relatively poor, compared to direction judgments, we still use this ability in everyday life. In the dark you can tell roughly how far you are from the annoying tick of the alarm clock or the more pleasant sound of the stereo. The two most important cues in distance judgments are intensity and reverberation.

Remember that in our discussion of visual distance, size was an important cue. In general, objects look smaller when they are farther away. Similarly, in audition, sound sources generally seem less intense when they are far away. A faint cry of "Help!" would usually come from a person far away from your ears, whereas "ear-splitting" shrieks come from nearby. However, intensity is not a very trustworthy cue. For example, a stereo blaring down the hall may sound just as loud as a stereo playing softly next door. Nonetheless, intensity may be useful for familiar sounds that have a constant intensity. For example, you can tell that your phone—rather than the next-door neighbor's—is ringing, on the basis of intensity information.

Another cue to the distance of sound sources is **reverberations,** or reflected sounds. The natural world contains many objects that reflect sounds. Look around yourself now; if you drop a pencil on your desk, the sound will reach you directly, but it will also reach you after the sound waves bounce off your book, the walls, and your lamp. The farther you are from a sound source, the greater the amount of reverberated sound relative to the amount of direct sound. If you put your ear close to the desk, most of the sound reaching your ear will come directly from the point where the pencil hits the desk. However, if you throw your pencil across the room, most of the sound will be reflected, rather than direct. In summary, our somewhat limited ability to judge distances comes primarily from intensity cues and the ratio between direct sound and reverberated sound. Other aspects of auditory distance perception are discussed by Coleman (1963).

Summary: Perceptual Qualities of Sound

- Pitch depends mainly on frequency, but it also depends upon (a) amplitude, (b) missing fundamentals, and (c) the arousal of the perceiver.
- Pitch can be measured by octaves and by the mel scale.
- Loudness depends mainly on amplitude, but it also depends upon (a) duration, (b) frequency, (c) other physical qualities, and (d) characteristics of the perceiver.

- Loudness can be measured by an eight-level musical system and by the sone scale.
- Timbre, a tone's sound quality, corresponds to complexity, or combinations of sound waves.
- The ears perform a rough Fourier analysis on complex tones, isolating several simple sine waves from a complex tone.
- The nature of the overtones is one deter-

minant of the timbre of musical instruments.
- People are quite accurate in judging the direction of a sound; time difference and intensity difference are the most useful cues.
- People are less accurate in judging the distance of a sound; intensity and reverberations are the most useful cues.

Complex Auditory Perception

So far, we have talked about the perception of a single tone. Sometimes these tones were simple, such as those produced by a tuning fork; sometimes they were complex, such as those produced by a guitar. Still, we only considered single tones in isolation. In this section we discuss the complex perceptions that occur when we combine two or more tones. First we will examine the perception of tone combinations, and then we will look at that familiar but complicated process called speech perception.

The Perception of Tone Combinations

In Chapter 4 we considered the perception of color mixtures. What happens when we combine a red light and a yellow light? We get an orange light, rather than the separate components of red and yellow. What happens when we combine two tones? The answer depends on the similarity of the two tones.

When two tones are sounded that are very similar in frequency, we do not hear two distinct components. Instead, we hear a single strange tone whose quality depends upon the difference in frequency between the two notes. There seem to be three distinct kinds of combination tones:

1. When the tones differ by less than 6 Hz (for example, 400 Hz and 404 Hz), we hear a single tone that surges up and down in loudness.

2. When the tones differ by 6 Hz to 24 Hz, we hear a single tone that appears to be a series of distinct impulses; the number of impulses per second equals the difference in frequency. Thus a 400-Hz tone and a 412-Hz tone would produce 12 impulses per second.

3. When the tones differ by 25 Hz to about

10% of the frequency, we hear an unpleasant roughness rather than distinct impulses. For example, a 400-Hz tone would produce roughness with any tone between 425 Hz and 440 Hz (Nordmark, 1978).

The changes in loudness found in the first and second categories—either the tone that surges up and down or the distinct impulses—are called **beats.**

What happens when we combine two tones that differ substantially? When two tones differ in frequency by more than 10%, we can hear two distinct tones. (Plomp (1976) discusses the combination of tones in more detail.) A **consonance** is a combination of two or more tones, played at the same time, that is judged to be pleasant. In general, tone combinations are consonant if the ratios of the frequencies of the two tones are simple fractions. For example, if you strike the A above middle C (440 Hz) and the A one octave higher (880 Hz), the combination is very pleasant. Notice that the ratio of their frequencies is 2/1, a simple fraction. Other frequency ratios such as 3/2 and 4/3 also sound consonant.

In contrast, a **dissonance** is a combination of two or more tones, played at the same time, that is judged to be unpleasant. In general, when the ratio of two tones is not a simple fraction, the combination sounds dissonant. Consonance and dissonance are the result of matches and mismatches among the notes' overtones. More information about consonance and dissonance can be found in a chapter by Risset (1978).

The perception of consonance and dissonance also depends upon individual differences and cultural background. For example, an American who hears East Indian music for the first time may judge the combination of notes to be dissonant and unpleasant. There are many musical intervals in Indian music that do not correspond to simple ratios. However, the combinations do not sound unpleasant to Indians; instead, the music sounds rich and extremely varied in mood (B. C. J. Moore, 1977). Similarly, cultural preferences change as a function of time. The music of Stravinsky was condemned as unpleasant dissonance 60 years ago, yet it sounds pleasant to most of us today.

Remember that we discussed visual masking in Chapter 5. In some conditions the presence of one visual stimulus prevents the perception of another visual stimulus. The same phenomenon occurs in audition; in some tone combinations one tone masks another tone. If one sound is intense and another is very weak, it seems obvious that the loud sound will mask the softer sound. However, auditory masking phenomena are really quite complex, as discussed in reviews by Patterson and Green (1978) and Zwislocki (1978). Masking is not simply a matter of relative intensity. In fact, masking depends almost as much on the frequencies of the tones as it does on the intensities of the tones. In general, a tone masks tones higher in frequency than itself to a greater extent than it masks tones lower in frequency than itself.

One of the most effective masking noises is **white noise,** which is a mixture of a wide range of frequencies. (Remember that white light represents a mixture of many different wavelengths of light.) You often hear white noise when an FM radio is tuned in between stations; the radio produces a static that has no particular pitch.

Speech Perception

We use our ears to hear the barks of angry dogs, the car horns of irate motorists, and the cries of hungry babies—as well as the sweeter sounds of a symphony orchestra. However, the single most important function of hearing for humans is to perceive speech. We hear speech constantly, and we process speech very quickly, so we take speech perception for granted. Nonetheless, speech perception is a complex process that is not completely understood. Let us first look at the speech stimulus, the "data" upon which our speech perception is based. Then we will see why a purely data-driven approach to speech perception is inadequate. Finally, we will discuss a theory of speech perception that has been advanced by Cole and Jakimik (1980). Speech perception will be reconsidered in Chapter 12 when we examine attention. Also, cognitive aspects of speech perception are discussed in other textbooks (for example, Dodd & White, 1980; Matlin, 1983).

The Speech Stimulus

The basic unit of speech is the **phoneme.** A phoneme is the smallest unit that makes an important difference between speech sounds. Thus /h/ and /r/ are both phonemes in the English language because it makes a difference whether you say you want to wear a *hat* or want to wear a *rat*. (Notice, incidentally, that a phoneme is written with slashes on either side.)

There are two basic ways to classify speech sounds. One method focuses upon the way the sounds are produced by varying the position of the lips and tongue, the nature of the airflow, and the vibration of the vocal cords. Table 8-2

Table 8-2 Producing vowel sounds.	PART OF TONGUE USED	HEIGHT OF RAISED PORTION OF TONGUE		
		HIGH	MEDIUM	LOW
	front	tr*ee* h*i*d	l*a*te l*e*t	f*a*5
	middle	carr*y*	sof*a*	n*u*t
	back	r*oo*t n*u*t	c*oa*t s*ough*t	t*o*p

Note: This table shows how 13 vowel sounds are produced. For example, notice that when the front part of your tongue is raised high in your mouth, you can produce either the ee *sound in* tree *or the* i *sound in* hid.

shows how vowels are produced, and Table 8-3 shows how most of the consonants are produced.

Classifications such as those in Tables 8-2 and 8-3 may remind you of the distinctive features of written symbols that we discussed in Chapter 5. Just as a written D and F differ with respect to curved versus straight components and the presence or absence of an intersection in the middle, a spoken D and F differ in the placement of the tongue and lips, the restriction of the airflow, and the vibration of the vocal cords. These systematic differences have encouraged some psychologists to propose that we use distinctive features in speech perception and that we have feature detectors for speech that operate like feature detectors in vision (e.g., Eimas & Corbit, 1973). (However, other researchers, such as Remez (1979) and Bryant (1978) argue against feature detectors.)

Whereas this first classification method emphasizes how the sounds are produced, the second classification method emphasizes the nature of the sounds themselves. In this method, speech is represented in a **sound spectrogram** or **speech spectrogram,** a diagram that shows the frequency components of speech. A sample sound spectrogram appears in Figure 8-8. The speaker is saying the word ''dough.'' Notice that Figure 8-8 shows horizontal bands of concentrated sound called **formants.** In this figure a first formant is located at about 500 Hz, and a second formant is initially located at

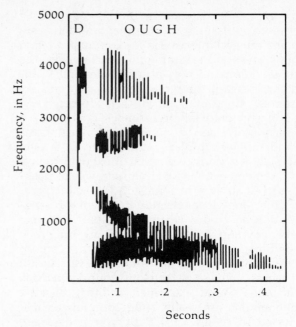

Figure 8-8   A speech spectrogram of the word ''dough.''

about 1500 Hz. You can also see a third formant at about 2500 Hz and a fourth formant at about 3800 Hz.

Problems with a Data-Driven Approach to Speech Perception

Remember from Chapter 5 that a data-driven approach to perception emphasizes the impor-

Table 8-3   Producing some of the consonant sounds.

	PLACE OF ARTICULATION			
	TWO LIPS	LIP + TEETH	TONGUE + TEETH	TONGUE TO RIDGE BEHIND TEETH
complete closure	pin bin			toe doe
narrowing at point of articulation		fit vigor	thick this	save zebra
mouth closed; nasal cavity opened	mouth			nice

Note: This table shows how 12 of the 24 consonant sounds are produced. For example, notice that when you completely close two lips to make a sound, you can produce either the p *sound in* pin *or the* b *sound in* bin.

tance of the stimulus. Data in the form of speech sounds arrive. We use either feature detectors or some kind of formant information to analyze the speech and identify the phonemes and the words that were spoken. This sounds like a reasonable approach to speech perception except for some important complications. There are three major problems with the data-driven approach: the absence of word boundaries, the variability of a phoneme's sound, and the influence of context.

If you have ever heard people speaking a foreign language, you have probably noticed that the words seem to flow on in a stream. There seem to be no boundaries dividing words into the neat little bundles of letters we see on the printed page. Usually, however, we are able to perceive the divisions among words in our own language, even when the speech stimulus lacks any pauses.

Bond and Garnes (1980) have cataloged several kinds of "slips of the ear," or cases in which we misperceive speech. One common kind of misperception involves word boundary errors, which take three forms. Sometimes the word boundary is deleted; "Get a pill out" was heard as "Get a pillow." Sometimes the boundary is shifted; "There's some iced tea made" was heard as "There's a nice teammate." Sometimes a word boundary is inserted; "Oh, he's Snoopy in disguise" was heard as "Oh, he's Snoopy in the skies."

My favorite example of a boundary error (of the boundary shift variety) was mentioned by Safire (1979). A grandmother, who was more familiar with intestinal disorders than with psychedelic experiences, heard the line "the girl with kaleidoscope eyes" in the Beatles' song "Lucy in the Sky with Diamonds." She perceived the line as "the girl with colitis goes by."

It is amazing that we do not make more mistakes in the perception of word boundaries. Cole and Jakimik (1980) estimate that a physical event, such as a pause, marks a word boundary less than 40% of the time. Thus fluent speech is often ambiguous, and there is not enough information in the data alone to produce accurate speech perception.

You may be aware of the word boundary problem from your own slips of the ear. However, a second and more subtle difficulty with a data-driven approach to speech perception is the variability of a phoneme's sound. Tables 8-2 and 8-3 imply that a phoneme always has a consistent pronunciation. For example, you might conclude that an /s/ always requires the same placement of tongue and lips, restriction of airflow, and vibration of vocal cords, no matter what word it is used in. However, notice the shape of your mouth for the /s/ sound when you say the words *seat* and *sorry*. The corners of your mouth are stretched far from each other in *seat*, but they are close together in *sorry*. Your mouth anticipates the letters that follow the /s/ sound. Thus a single phoneme has varying sounds as a result of the context of other sounds in the word. Nonetheless, we hear the sounds as being similar even though they are physically different. Once again, our perceptions differ from the simple information in the data.

The third difficulty with a data-driven approach to speech perception is that words themselves are often ambiguous when context is missing; once context is supplied, ambiguity decreases. In Chapter 5 we discussed the influence of context on visual pattern recognition. We noted, for example, that people recognize a loaf of bread more quickly within the context of a kitchen scene than when the context is absent. The perception of isolated words in audition is probably even more difficult than

---

Demonstration 8-4

The Perception of Sentences in Unusual Sequences

Read each of the following sentences to several friends. Try to read them without major variation in pitch or volume that would convey distinctive boundaries or emphasis. Write down what each friend thought she or he heard.

in mud eels are   in clay none are

in pine tar is   in oak none is

the perception of isolated shapes in vision because our conversational speech is so sloppy. Pollack and Pickett (1964) recorded the conversation of subjects who were waiting for an experiment to begin. Later, the subjects were asked to identify isolated words from their own conversations. When the surrounding context words were eliminated, people identified fewer than half of the words correctly.

Try Demonstration 8-4, a variation of a study summarized by Cole and Jakimik (1980). In a nonsense sequence such as the sentence about eels, listeners are deprived of context, and their ability to identify the individual words is poor.

Suppose that you heard a word fragment *-eel*, which was preceded by a cough. If that fragment appeared in a sentence, you would use the context of the sentence to identify the fragment. Warren and Warren (1970) played four sentences to their listeners.

1. *It was found that the ∗eel was on the axle.*
2. *It was found that the ∗eel was on the shoe.*
3. *It was found that the ∗ eel was on the orange.*
4. *It was found that the ∗eel was on the table.*

(The asterisk symbol, ∗, represents a loud cough that replaced a speech sound.)

Using tape recorders, Warren and Warren produced four sentences that were identical to one another except for a different word spliced on at the end of each sentence. Thus all of the above sentences were exactly equivalent through the final *the*.

What did the listeners report hearing? Warren and Warren found that the interpretation of the ambiguous word ∗eel depended upon which final word they had heard. Listeners reported hearing *wheel* in the first sentence, *heel* in the second sentence, *peel* in the third, and *meal* in the fourth. Context clearly influenced speech perception.

Notice, though, that context does not always increase the accuracy of identifying the physical stimulus; people did not report hearing "cough-eel." In fact, Warren and Warren argue that their study represented an auditory illusion. Just as the arrows surrounding the lines in the Müller-Lyer illusion influence visual perception, the words surround-

ing a speech segment can influence auditory perception.

Warren and Warren (1970) provided additional evidence about the importance of context. They recorded the sentence, "The state governors met with their respective legislatures convening in the capital city." Then they carefully cut one phoneme out of the recorded sentence, specifically, the first /s/ in *legislatures.* A coughing sound was inserted to fill the gap. When listeners heard this revised sentence, they experienced a compelling auditory illusion. They reported that the /s/ sound was just as clear as were any of the phonemes that were actually present.

The listeners were then told that one sound was missing, and they should select the missing sound. Even with these instructions, the listeners were unable to locate the missing sound. They reported that the cough seemed to coexist with the other speech sounds, rather than replace any of them. Furthermore, the illusion was also obtained when either a buzz or a tone replaced the missing phoneme. Finally, the illusion even worked if the entire segment *gis* in *Legislatures* was replaced by an irrelevant noise.

In real life, speakers presumably do not try to deceive us by inserting inappropriate coughs, buzzes, or tones. However, the clatter of dishes may mask a dinner speaker, and our use of context helps us identify what was spoken. Context also helps us identify what speakers would have said if their pronunciation had been meticulous. Thus you can hear a friend say, "Whadja wanna do thuh seevning" and identify the intended message, "What do you want to do this evening." Once again, our perceptions are different from the speech stimulus.

In summary, then, a purely data-driven approach has difficulty explaining why we perceive word boundaries when none exist, how we perceive phonemes in spite of their variability, and how context influences perception. An adequate theory of how we perceive speech must address these issues.

Theories of Speech Perception

Several different theories of speech perception have been proposed. For example, Halle and Stevens (1964) suggested a theory called **analysis-by-synthesis,** which states that the auditory system makes up hypotheses about various possibilities for the speech stimulus. We then compare the speech stimulus with each of the hypothesized messages. The closest match wins, and that is what we hear.

Ronald Cole and his colleagues have developed an alternative approach to speech perception. First of all, Cole and Scott (1974) argued that phoneme variability is not a major problem. Specifically, all consonant phonemes possess some features that do not vary, called **invariant features.** For instance, the letters *s* always has a hissing sound, even though the shape of the lips varies when we pronounce the *s* in *seat* and *sorry.* Furthermore, the letter *s* has a higher pitch than the letter *z.* The invariant features allow us either to identify the phoneme or else to narrow down the possibilities to two or three phonemes.

Cole and Jakimik (1980) propose a model of speech perception that addresses the other two problems with a data-driven approach, word boundaries and context. The first assumption of their model emphasizes that words are recognized through the interaction of data from the speech stimulus and our previous knowledge:

> fluent speech is an ambiguous stimulus. A given stretch of speech can often be parsed into words in more than one way, and because of phonological variation, the acoustic information that accompanies an intended word may be insufficient, by itself, to uniquely specify its identity. The first assumption of the model, that words are recognized through the interaction of sound and knowledge, is an attempt to come to grips with the fact that words are often recognized from partial acoustic information. The assumption is that words are constrained both by their acoustic structure and the context in which they occur, and that listeners use both sources of information to recognize words from fluent speech [p. 139].

Cole and Jakimik's theory contains three other assumptions. The second assumption is that we process speech sequentially, or word by word. The recognition of one word accomplishes two purposes: (1) it locates the beginning of the next word in the sequence, and (2) it provides constraints that limit the number of possibilities that would be appropriate for the correct grammar and meaning of the sentence. For example, consider the phrase *green grass.* Once you recognize the word *green,* you realize that a boundary must follow (unless you are talking about obscure topics like greengage plums or British greengrocers). Furthermore, the word *green* constrains the grammatical forms of the word that follows; it will probably be a noun, though it might be another adjective. The word *green* also constrains the meaning of the word that follows; unless you are hearing something like Dr. Seuss's *Green Eggs and Ham,* the word will be something that customarily has a green color. Thus Cole and Jakimik's second assumption addresses both the word boundary problem and the influence of context.

Cole and Jakimik propose two additional assumptions: We identify words from their beginning sounds, rather than their middle sounds or their final sounds; and we recognize a word when our analysis of its acoustic structure narrows down the possibilities to only a single candidate. In summary, their theory proposes that "Word recognition is conceptually guided, but data *driven*" (p. 150). As we saw in the discussion of visual pattern recognition in Chapter 5, an adequate explanation of speech perception must involve both data-driven processing and conceptually driven processing.

Summary: Complex Auditory Perception

- When two tones are combined, the resulting sound depends upon the difference in frequency between the two tones: (a) if they are very similar, we hear a single tone that surges in intensity or produces beats; (b) if they are somewhat different from each other, we hear an unpleasant roughness; (c) if they differ still further, we hear two distinct tones.
- The combination of two distinct tones can sound consonant if the ratios of the frequencies of the two tones form a simple fraction; otherwise, the combination sounds dissonant.

- One tone can mask another in a tone combination, depending upon the relative amplitude and frequency of the two tones.
- Speech sounds can be classified either in terms of how the sounds are produced or in terms of the nature of the sounds themselves (via a sound spectrogram).
- A data-driven approach to speech perception is inadequate because of three factors: (a) the absence of word boundaries in speech, (b) the variability of a phoneme's sound, and (c) the influence of context.
- One theory of speech perception, analysis-by-synthesis, states that we make up hypotheses about the speech stimulus and compare speech with these hypotheses.
- Cole and his colleagues propose that words are recognized through the interaction of sound and knowledge and that we process speech word-by-word.

Applications of Hearing Research

One application of hearing research is in the perception of music. We have discussed music at several points in the chapter, for example, in connection with timbre and tone combinations. Other aspects of music that might interest you are discussed elsewhere. For example, Roederer (1975) considers the psychophysics of music in detail. D. Deutsch (1978) examines memory for music as well as musical figure-ground relationships that resemble the visual figure-ground relationships we observed in Chapter 5. Backus (1977) and Risset (1978) discuss how instruments make music. Finally, B. C. J. Moore (1977) examines concert hall acoustics and acoustical considerations in choosing a hi-fi.

Other important applications of hearing research include work in two areas, noise pollution and hearing impairment. As we will see, the two areas are related; noise pollution frequently leads to hearing impairment.

Noise Pollution

Try Demonstration 8-5 to assess the noise pollution you customarily experience. **Noise** is any irrelevant or excessive sound. As you have probably noticed, people differ with respect to what they classify as noise. A sound that is irrelevant and excessive to you may be sweet music to your roommate.

In recent years, psychologists, engineers, and audiologists have become increasingly concerned about noise pollution at home, at entertainment places, and at work. For example, people whose homes are near airports may experience a 120-dB sound every time a nearby jet takes off or lands (Ludel, 1978). Rock groups can sometimes produce 110- to 120-dB music, nonstop, for several hours. At work, a jackhammer produces sounds of 120 dB. In some cases, noises at work have produced deafness. Weavers in a mill were exposed to a sound level of about 100 dB for an 8-hour day, a level so intolerable that they were partially deaf—even on weekends—after several years of employment (Taylor, Pearson, Mair, & Burns, 1965). Let us examine three topics: (1) the study of noise pollution, (2) the effects of noise pollution, and (3) reducing noise pollution.

The Study of Noise Pollution

For ethical reasons, psychologists cannot study noise pollution by presenting very loud noises to humans. A common approach is therefore to

---

Demonstration 8-5

Noise Pollution Journal

For the next three days, keep an informal journal of the number of instances of noise pollution that you encounter. Some examples might be a motorcycle starting underneath your window, a fire engine, the honking horns of a wedding motorcade, students laughing loudly outside your classroom, and work noises at a construction site.

present loud, but safe, tones to humans for short periods of time and to observe the changes in hearing ability that result.

In order to discuss these changes in hearing ability we need to examine the differences among three terms: masking, auditory adaptation, and auditory fatigue. Masking, a term discussed in the previous section, occurs when you cannot hear one tone because another tone is presented *simultaneously*. In contrast, auditory adaptation and auditory fatigue concern the inability to hear a tone because of *previous* tone stimulation. Specifically, **auditory adaptation** occurs when one tone is presented continuously and the perceived loudness of that tone decreases as time passes. However, a large number of studies summarized by Scharf (1978) have shown that there is little, if any, decline in the loudness of sounds that last as long as 30 minutes.

Whereas auditory adaptation involves the continuous presentation of a single tone, **auditory fatigue** occurs when a loud tone is presented and then turned off, causing a change in threshold for *other* tones. For example, when people are exposed to a white noise having an intensity of 120 dB for 5 minutes, their threshold for a 4000-Hz test tone that is presented 2 minutes later shifts by 40 dB (Miller, 1978). Before exposure to the loud noise they could have barely heard the tone if it were presented at 0 dB; after the loud noise the tone would have to be presented at 40 dB (the loudness of a quiet neighborhood) in order to be heard at all. Keep this in mind if you are planning on hearing a 120-dB band this weekend!

Auditory fatigue can lead to two kinds of changes in hearing threshold. **Temporary threshold shift** is a temporary increase in a hearing threshold as a result of exposure to noise. "Temporary" generally means that the increase in threshold disappears within about 16 hours (Green, 1976). In the laboratory, temporary threshold shifts in humans are studied because of the insight they might provide regarding permanent threshold shifts. As you might guess, a **permanent threshold shift** is a permanent increase in a hearing threshold as a result of exposure to noise. Sometimes a permanent threshold shift is produced by a single loud noise, such as an extremely loud

firecracker explosion. More often, however, permanent threshold shifts are the result of repeated exposures to noise on a daily basis, as in the case of the weavers mentioned earlier. Details on both kinds of threshold shifts can be found in the work of Green (1976) and Miller (1978).

Since auditory adaptation is difficult to obtain, why should temporary and permanent threshold shifts occur? That is, if a sound cannot reduce its own loudness during continuous stimulation, why should a sound that has been turned off still reduce the loudness of another sound presented several minutes later? Scharf (1978) presents two explanations for this apparent paradox. First of all, in auditory fatigue the initial sound reduces the loudness of only those later sounds that have relatively low amplitude. Second, auditory fatigue has its primary influence on tones near threshold, rather than louder tones. Thus it is difficult to obtain auditory adaptation because the later segment of a sound is too loud and too much above threshold, relative to the level of the earlier segment of a sound.

The Effects of Noise Pollution

The most dramatic effect of noise pollution is hearing loss, an area we will discuss in the last section of the chapter. Other important effects of noise pollution are on: (1) physical health, (2) mental health, (3) task performance, and (4) social behavior.

In general, noise pollution has surprisingly little effect on physical health, aside from hearing loss itself. Loud noises seem to change blood pressure and other physiological measures temporarily, but at present there is no strong evidence for a relationship between noise and heart disease (Bell, Fisher, & Loomis, 1978).

Since loud noises have an influence on blood pressure and other measures associated with stress, we might expect noise pollution to be related to mental illness. In fact, industrial workers who are exposed to loud noises do report headaches, anxiety, sexual impotence, and other disorders (S. Cohen, Glass, & Phillips, 1977). Other studies suggest that people who live in noisy communities are admitted to psychiatric hospitals more frequently (Bell, Fisher, & Loomis, 1978). Obviously, noise pollution also influences mood.

Children who live in apartments near loud traffic noises perform more poorly in school than children who live in quieter apartments (S. Cohen, Glass, & Singer, 1973). However, loud noises do not always influence task performance. A review of the literature indicated that loud noises that are regular and predictable often have little influence on complex mental tasks (Glass & Singer, 1972). However, performance can be hindered when noise is unpredictable. Thus you may have trouble reading and remembering this paragraph if you are wondering whether the jackhammer at a nearby construction site will soon renew its racket.

Unpredictable noises can also influence persistence on later tasks. Glass, Singer, and Friedman (1969) manipulated the amount and kind of noise people heard. Some people heard no noise at all. Others heard either a soft noise (56 dB) or a loud noise (110 dB) that was either predictable or unpredictable. Then everyone worked on puzzles that were actually impossible to solve. Figure 8-9 shows the results. As you can see, people who had heard a loud, unpredictable noise showed only one quarter of

the persistence on a frustrating task that people showed who had heard no noise. Other information on noise and performance can be obtained from a book by Bell, Fisher, and Loomis (1978).

Bell and his colleagues also review the literature on the relationship between noise and social behavior. They conclude that people in noisy environments sit farther away from each other. Noise also increases aggression and decreases helping behavior.

In summary, noise pollution may not have a substantial effect on nonauditory aspects of physical health. However, it does adversely affect mental health, task performance, and behavior toward other people.

Reducing Noise Pollution

Current government regulations prohibit industries from exposing their workers to more than a 90-dB sound level for 8 hours a day. Even though this sound level may still produce some hearing loss (Miller, 1978), special interest groups continually pressure the government to reduce or eliminate these limits. Thus it seems likely that factory workers may still need to be concerned about the possibility of hearing loss.

One approach to the problem is to provide earplugs or earmuffs to workers who are exposed to loud noises. However, these devices must be carefully selected and used. People often complain that they are uncomfortable and interfere with work.

Fortunately, some efforts have been made to modify noise at its source. For example, the design of some jet airplanes has been changed to reduce their noise at takeoff and at landing. Furthermore, some companies have included sound absorbers, either on machines or in walls. However, these absorbers are much more effective for high-pitched sounds than for low rumbles. Ultimately, as Bershader (1981) says, "quiet is a commodity that costs money" (p. 74). Individuals and industries will have to decide how much must be paid to reduce the noise in our environment.

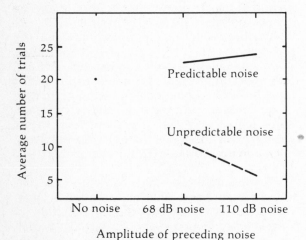

Figure 8-9 Average number of trials on an insoluble problem, as a function of noise amplitude and noise predictability (data from Glass, Singer, & Friedman, 1969).

Hearing Impairments

Several kinds of disorders can occur in the auditory system. For example, **tinnitus** is a high-pitched ringing in the ears that can be caused by taking large doses of aspirin and by a high fever or ear infection. Ear infections themselves are another common disorder, especially among young children. In an **ear infection** the eustachian tube (look back at Figure 8-3) becomes swollen, cutting off the middle ear from the respiratory tract. Bacteria may multiply in the middle ear, resulting in a painful earache and temporary hearing difficulties. As we grow older, we have difficulty hearing high-frequency sounds; we will discuss this difficulty in Chapter 14. Dirks (1978) discusses still other auditory problems.

The major kind of hearing impairment, however, is deafness. In the United States there are approximately 13 million hearing-impaired people, of whom 200,000 to 300,000 cannot be helped by a conventional hearing aid (B. C. J. Moore, 1977).

Deafness is usually assessed by **audiometry,** or the measurement of the sensitivity of audition. One technique is to present a series of pure tones, perhaps at frequencies of 250, 500, 1000, 2000, and 4000 Hz. The audiologist

measures the decibel difference between a person's threshold at each frequency and the average threshold of a normal population (Green, 1976). Other hearing tests measure the perception of speech sounds. Let us consider how three different hypothetical people might respond to a standard audiometry test. Figure 8-10 illustrates the hearing of a normal person and two hearing-impaired people. Notice that Person A shows a consistent loss of about 35 dB at all of the tested frequencies. In contrast, Person B shows no loss at the lower frequencies but substantial loss at the higher frequencies.

Person A and Person B are representative of two different kinds of hearing problems, known as conduction deafness and nerve deafness. **Conduction deafness** involves problems in conducting the sound stimulus; the problem occurs in either the external ear or the middle ear. Person A in Figure 8-10 shows conduction deafness and would be helped by a hearing aid, which would make sounds of all frequencies louder. This person can hear sounds conducted through the bone but cannot hear sound waves that travel through the air. (Try Demonstration

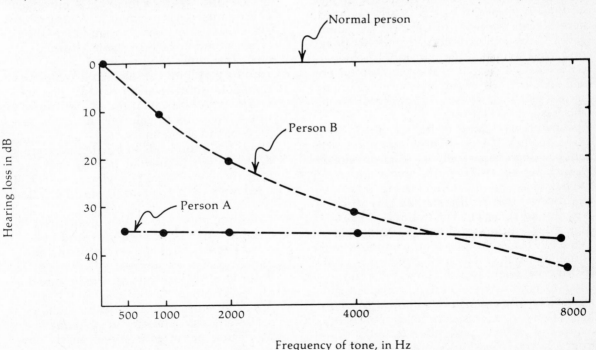

Figure 8-10   Hearing loss in two hearing-impaired people, in comparison with a normal person.

Demonstration 8-6

*Sound Waves Traveling
Through the Bone and
Through the Air*

Tape-record your own voice and play it back. This recording captures the sound waves from your voice that travel only through the air. Now talk in a normal voice; you hear both the sound waves that travel through the air and the sound waves that travel through the bony part of your skull. Finally, plug your ears so that no sound waves can travel through the air and pass into your external auditory canal; you hear only the sound waves that travel through the bony part of your skull.

8-6 to illustrate the two ways in which sound waves can travel.) A hearing aid would therefore be useful for people with moderate levels of conduction deafness. The hearing aid can channel airborne sound waves to the bony part of the skull below the ear, making it vibrate and stimulate the cochlea.

The other kind of deafness is called nerve deafness. Person B in Figure 8-10 has nerve deafness. In **nerve deafness** the problem occurs either in the cochlea or in the auditory nerve. For example, if the ear is exposed to extremely loud noises—the kind we discussed in the previous section—the hair cells in the organ of Corti may be destroyed. (Look back at Figure 8-4.) If all of the hair cells are damaged, there are no receptors to transmit the sound waves. Thus neither airborne sound nor bone-conducted sound can be transmitted; the person is deaf. A simple hearing aid would not help someone with complete nerve deafness, just as a pair of glasses would not help someone who has a detached retina.

What can be done to help a person with nerve deafness? A method of stimulating the auditory nerve electrically is being developed (B. C. J. Moore, 1977). Furthermore, if some of the hair cells are intact, the hearing aid can be modified so that it differentially amplifies the different frequencies. For example, Person B does not require amplification of the low-frequency tones but does require amplification of the high-frequency tones. However, people with nerve deafness also show a disorder related to loudness perception, called recruitment. **Recruitment** is a condition in which a deaf person perceives very loud sounds normally; this person's perception does not differ from a normal, hearing person's perception if we only consider loud sounds. However, very weak sounds are not heard at all.

Thus the design of a hearing aid for a nerve-deaf person has to take care of two problems: a differential sensitivity to the various pitches and a differential sensitivity to the various loudnesses. Green (1976) discusses the development of hearing aids in more detail, but he notes that research on hearing aids has probably not been as vigorous as it should be.

Summary: Applications of Hearing Research

- Noise pollution is an increasing problem in modern society.
- Auditory adaptation, or a decreased perceived loudness for a tone that is presented continuously, is minimal; in contrast, the auditory system does show auditory fatigue when a loud noise is presented, turned off, and other tones are presented.
- Auditory fatigue can lead to a temporary threshold shift or a permanent threshold shift; psychologists study temporary threshold shifts to gain insight about permanent threshold shifts.
- Noise pollution leads to hearing loss and a deterioration in mental health, task performance, and social behavior; however, it does not have a great influence on physical health.
- Noise pollution effects can be reduced by limiting workers' exposure to loud noises, providing earplugs and earmuffs, and modifying noise at its source.
- Three kinds of hearing impairments are tinnitus, ear infection, and deafness.
- A person with conduction deafness shows a consistent loss of hearing at all frequencies; the sound stimulus is not properly conducted, and this person can be helped by a hearing aid.
- A person with nerve deafness shows a hear-

ing loss at certain frequencies, though the person's hearing may be normal for other frequencies.

• A person with nerve deafness shows recruitment: very loud sounds are perceived normally, whereas very weak sounds are not heard at all.

• It is difficult to design a hearing aid for nerve-deaf people because of their differential sensitivity to various pitches and loudnesses.

Review

1. Describe as much as you can remember about the auditory stimulus. Then turn back to Chapters 2 and 4 to compare the auditory stimulus with the visual stimulus.

2. Summarize what you know about psychological reactions to tones of various frequencies, being sure to mention (a) the range of frequencies that humans can hear, (b) the tones they can most readily detect, (c) the tones they can most readily discriminate, and (d) the loudness of tones of various frequencies.

3. Listen to a selection of music. Identify variations in pitch, loudness, and timbre. Identify examples of consonance and dissonance. In each case, note the physical correlates of these features.

4. Discuss why pitch is not perfectly correlated with frequency and why loudness is not perfectly correlated with amplitude.

5. Draw a rough sketch of the auditory system, identifying the parts of the outer ear, middle ear, inner ear, and the pathway from the ear to the brain.

6. Discuss the two theories of how fre-

quency is registered in the inner ear, and point out how the two theories can be reconciled. Try to imagine the basilar membrane vibrating and the auditory nerve firing to register frequency.

7. Draw an illustration of the cues that help us judge the direction and distance of a sound source.

8. Discuss the two ways of classifying speech "data" and list three problems with a data-driven approach to speech perception. Then point out how the theory proposed by Cole and his colleagues addresses each of these problems.

9. Point out the differences among masking, auditory adaptation, auditory fatigue, temporary threshold shift, and permanent threshold shift. Which of these terms are relevant for the study of noise pollution?

10. Suppose that you have two friends who are deaf; one friend has conduction deafness and the other has nerve deafness. List various ways in which the perceptual experiences of these two friends would differ.

New Terms

tuning fork	decibels	cochlea
sounds	dB	organ of Corti
frequency	pinna	basilar membrane
Hz	external auditory canal	tectorial membrane
pure tone	eardrum	hair cells
complex tones	tympanic membrane	auditory nerve
fundamental frequency	malleus	place theory
harmonics	incus	frequency theory
overtones	stapes	volley principle
amplitude	eustachian tubes	cochlear nucleus

superior olive
inferior colliculus
medial geniculate nucleus
auditory cortex
case of the missing fundamental
octave
mel scale
sone scale
timbre
Fourier analysis
localization
binaural

sound shadow
reverberations
beats
consonance
dissonance
white noise
phoneme
sound spectrogram
speech spectrogram
formants
analysis-by-synthesis
invariant features

noise
auditory adaptation
auditory fatigue
temporary threshold shift
permanent threshold shift
tinnitus
ear infection
audiometry
conduction deafness
nerve deafness
recruitment

chapter 9

TOUCH AND THE OTHER SKIN SENSES

Outline   **Background on the Skin Senses**
The Skin's Structure
Theories About the Skin Senses
From the Skin to the Brain
Touch
Passive Touch
Active Touch
Temperature
Body Temperature Regulation
Warm and Cold Spots
Thresholds for Temperature
Adaptation to Temperature
Pain
Thresholds for Pain
Adaptation to Pain
Theories of Pain Perception
Pain Control

Preview

In this chapter we will discuss the major senses that are related to your skin. There are four sections here: background on the skin senses, touch, temperature, and pain.

The first section supplies some basic background on the skin senses. We will look at the anatomy of the skin and note that there are many different kinds of skin receptors. We will also discuss three theories about the skin senses. Finally, we will briefly consider the two systems that transmit information from the skin receptors to the brain.

The section on touch has two parts: passive touch, in which an object is placed on the skin of a passive person, and active touch, in which a person actively explores the environment by touching objects. In the part on passive touch we will examine touch thresholds, adaptation to touch, and the perception of vibrations, or repeated touches. In the part on active touch we will stress that touch can provide valuable information about objects in the world; we will also see that active touch provides blind people with alternatives to visual material.

In the section on temperature we will see that the body is well equipped to maintain its temperature at about 37°C. We will also examine temperature thresholds and adaptation to temperature changes. Adaptation explains why a swimming pool seems icy when you first jump in, yet the temperature is pleasant after just a few minutes.

Pain is unusual because it is more strongly linked with emotion than the other areas of perception. We will look at pain thresholds and pain tolerance, and then we will see that pain adaptation only occurs for mildly painful stimuli. We will also discuss three theories of pain perception, including the current favorite, gate-control theory. Our final topic is pain control. Pain can be reduced by giving medication and by giving an inactive substance that people think is a medication. Recently, Western physicians and researchers have been examining acupuncture and stimulation-produced analgesia, two methods in which pain is reduced by stimulating another area of the body. Psychologists have also developed several methods of controlling pain, such as hypnosis, behavior therapy, and modeling therapy.

Your skin represents the largest sensory system you own. In comparison, the size of the receptive surfaces for vision and hearing seem tiny. Contrast the size of your retina or your cochlea with the approximately 2 square meters of receptive surfaces on your skin!

Despite its impressive size, we often ignore the importance of the skin. Consider the protective value of the skin, for example. The skin senses inform you that you must go around large barricades, rather than through them, that a potentially suffocating object is covering your face, and that you should not try to fit through a narrow opening. The skin senses also protect you from extremely hot or extremely cold temperatures. Furthermore, the skin senses protect you from potential tissue damage when you feel a painful sensation.

Also consider the importance of the skin senses in social interactions. Touching is important to both infants and their parents in the development of infant-parent attachment. Furthermore, think about the variety of ways in which another adult might touch you: a pat on the head, a handshake, a hearty punch in the arm, or an arm around your waist. Each of these gestures implies a different kind of social message, and each of these messages is quite different from a hostile punch in the nose. Finally, the importance of touch in sexual interactions is obvious.

When you were in elementary school, you learned that there were five senses: vision, hearing, touch, smell, and taste. Aristotle used this classification system more than 2300 years ago, and it is probably still the most common system. Nonetheless, in the last century, various researchers have argued that there may be more than five senses. This expansion is typically accomplished by subdividing the "touch" category. For example, various people have claimed separate senses for pressure, warmth, cold, vibration, tickle, itch, muscular pressure, quick pain, and deep pain. We will use the chapter title, "Touch and the Other Skin Senses" to refer to all of these phenomena. We will treat all the skin senses together because they do belong in one cluster. As J. C. Stevens and Green (1978) remark, when we feel an object such as a tennis ball, an ice cube, or a piece of sandpaper, the experience seems unitary. We do *not* break down the experience into the various attributes such as temperature, roughness, size, and pressure.

Our discussion of the skin senses focuses upon touch, temperature, and pain. Another topic that is sometimes discussed in connection with the skin senses is **proprioception** (pronounced "proh-pree-oh-*sep*-shun"), the sense that provides information about the position of the limbs and the body parts relative to other body parts. Proprioception includes **kinesthesis** (pronounced "kin-ess-*thee*-siss" with the *th* similar to the *th* in *think*), which is the appreciation of movement in our muscles and joints, and **vestibular sensation** (pronounced "vess-*tih*-bue-lur"), which tells us whether our body is tilted, moving, slowing down, or speeding up. Thus, for example, kinesthesis is concerned with whether your wrist has been moved, whereas vestibular sensation is concerned with whether you feel upright or tilted. A chapter by Kenshalo (1978) gives further information on proprioception.

Background on the Skin Senses

Before we consider touch, temperature, and pain, we must discuss some background information on the skin senses. In particular, we must examine the skin's structure, theories about the skin senses, and how skin sense information is transmitted to the brain.

The Skin's Structure

In addition to its function in sensation, the skin has many other important duties. It holds our body fluids inside its remarkably elastic boundaries. It regulates our body temperature, with the aid of blood vessels and sweat glands. It protects us from the sun's radiation and from harmful microorganisms.

Figure 9-1 shows a diagram of **hairy skin**, the kind of skin that covers most of your body and contains either noticeable or almost invisible hairs. Another kind of skin, called **glabrous skin** (pronounced "*glay*-bruss"), is found on the soles of your feet, the palms of your hands, and on the smooth surfaces of your toes and fingers. Glabrous skin is similar to hairy skin, except that its epidermis is thicker and it has fewer receptors with free nerve endings.

Notice that the skin in Figure 9-1 can be divided into three layers. The **epidermis,** on the outside, has many layers of dead skin cells. The **dermis** is the layer that makes new cells. These new cells move to the surface and replace the epidermis cells as they are rubbed off. Underneath the dermis is the **subcutaneous tissue,** which contains connective tissue and fat globules. Also notice that the skin contains an impressive array of veins, arteries, sweat glands, hairs, and receptors.

Let's now concentrate on those receptors. Recall that visual receptors in the retina come in

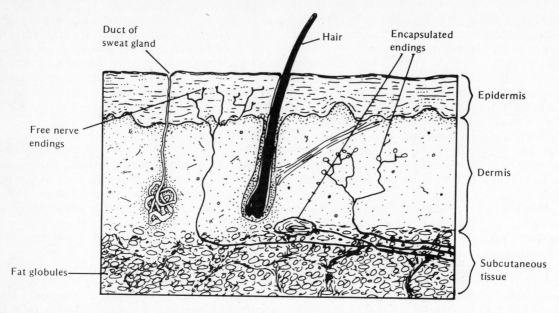

Figure 9-1   A cross section of a piece of hairy skin (schematic).

two styles, rod and cone, each with its own specialized function. In contrast, skin receptors come in an impressive variety of styles, each style bearing its own name. All skin receptors are the endings of neurons that carry information from the skin to the higher processing levels. Some skin receptors have **free nerve endings;** as Figure 9-1 shows, these receptors do not have any little bulbs or capsules on the end that is nearest the epidermis. In contrast, skin receptors with **encapsulated endings** have fancy little capsules on the end nearest the epidermis. These endings differ in their size, shape, and degree of organization. The names of some of these different kinds of skin receptors can be found elsewhere (Brown, 1975a; Kenshalo, 1971, 1978)

Wouldn't it be tidy if each kind of skin receptor performed a different function, with one kind responsible for touch, for instance, and another kind responsible for pain? Early researchers should be praised for the suffering they endured to try to locate a correspondence between the kind of receptor stimulated and the kind of sensation produced. For example, a researcher might take a sharp needle and poke around on his or her own skin until a tiny region of skin was found that was particularly

sensitive to the pain. Then this brave researcher snipped out that particular region of skin and used a microscope to determine what kind of receptor it was. The procedure was repeated to locate receptors that might be associated with either touch or temperature.

These researchers did demonstrate that certain tiny regions of the skin were responsive to one kind of sensation, for example, pain, rather than touch or temperature. However, they found no consistent pattern in the kind of receptors at each location. Eventually, these mutilated researchers conceded that although pain was typically associated with free nerve endings, the type of receptor was often unrelated to the type of sensation.

Theories About the Skin Senses

We need to discuss how the skin operates to provide us with information. There are three basic kinds of theories about the skin senses: specificity theory, pattern theory, and combined approach.

The specificity theory was responsible for the experiments we have just discussed about the relationship between skin receptors and sensation. Specificity theory was based upon the **doctrine of specific nerve energies,** an idea proposed by an early 19th century physiologist, Johannes Müller, that different sensory nerves have their own characteristic type of activity and therefore produce different sensations. A later researcher named von Frey extended the doctrine of specific nerve energies by suggesting that there was a particular type of receptor structure for touch, warmth, cold, and pain. Thus **specificity theory** states that each of the different kinds of receptors responds exclusively to only one kind of physical stimulus (for example, pain), and each kind of receptor is therefore responsible for only one kind of sensation. However, we have just seen that the research provided little support for this aspect of the theory.

A second theory, **pattern theory,** suggests that it is the pattern of nerve impulses that determines sensation. According to pattern theory, each kind of receptor responds to many different kinds of stimulation, but it responds more to some than to others. Thus a particular receptor might respond vigorously to a cold stimulus, less vigorously to a touch stimulus, even less to a pain stimulus, and very little to a hot stimulus. The brain can eventually interpret a code in terms of the relative strengths of the receptors' responses.

More recently, a theory has been proposed that combines both receptor specificity theory and pattern theory. Melzack and Wall (1962) incorporated some aspects of each theory into their proposal. They rejected the idea that each different receptor is specifically matched to a particular sensation. However, they accepted the idea that the receptors are different from one another. Specifically, each kind of receptor is specialized so that it can convert a particular kind of stimulus into a particular pattern of impulses. We feel pain if the impulses in one kind of nerve fibers are dominant. However, we feel other sensations such as warmth, cold, or pressure if the impulses in another kind of nerve fiber are dominant. Melzack and Wall developed their theory in more detail for painful stimuli, and we will discuss this issue further in the section on pain.

From the Skin to the Brain

In our examination of vision and hearing we discussed the pathways from the visual receptors and the auditory receptors to the brain. In each case the receptors occupied a relatively small, compact space. In contrast, the skin receptors are distributed over your entire body. The skin receptors in the part of your body below your neck transmit their information via the spinal cord. The precise pathways by which the information reaches the cortex are quite complicated; you can read more about them in the work of either N. R. Carlson (1980) or Brown (1975a).

However, it is important to know that there are two separate systems by which information travels from the skin receptors to the brain: the lemniscal system and the spinothalamic system. Researchers have tried to identify several factors that distinguish the two systems. For example, the **lemniscal system** (pronounced "lemm-*niss*-kull") has large nerve fibers, and it conveys information very quickly. In contrast, the **spinothalamic system** (pronounced "spy-know-thuh-*laa*-mick") has small nerve fibers, and it conveys information more slowly. (Remember: *S*pinothalamic is *S*mall and *S*low.)

A further distinction is that the "acuity" of the lemniscal system is much greater; the lemniscal system can transmit very precise information about the physical location of a stimulus, whereas the spinothalamic system does not code location so precisely.

Both the lemniscal and the spinothalamic systems eventually pass on their information to the **somatosensory cortex** (pronounced "soh-*mat*-oh-*senn*-seh-ree"). The somatosensory cortex is shown in Figure 9-2.

For many years, researchers have been trying to discover the relationship between points on the body and points on the cortex. Their efforts have not been very successful for the part of the cortex associated with the spinothalamic system, but some fairly precise mapping has been obtained for the lemniscal system. For example, Penfield and Rasmussen (1950) obtained information on patients whose skulls were opened up for tumor removal. Penfield and Rasmussen electrically stimulated various points on the somatosensory cortex. Then they asked the patients, who were alert because they only had local anesthetics, to identify the part of their body that tingled. Figure 9-3 shows the correspondence they

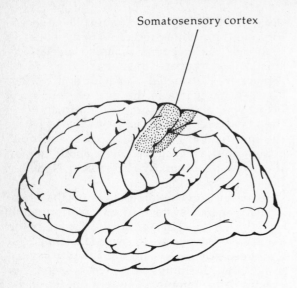

Somatosensory cortex

prioception, the sense that provides information about the position of the limbs and the body parts relative to other body parts; proprioception includes kinesthesis and vestibular sensation.

- Skin has three layers: the epidermis, the dermis, and subcutaneous tissue.
- There are many kinds of different skin receptors, which have either free nerve endings or encapsulated endings; however, there is little correspondence between the kind of receptor stimulated and the kind of sensation produced.
- Specificity theory is based on the doctrine of specific nerve energies; specificity theory states that each of the different kinds of receptors responds to only one kind of physical stimulus.
- Pattern theory proposes that the pattern of nerve impulses determines sensation.
- Melzack and Wall's (1962) theory combines specificity and pattern theory.
- There are two systems for conveying information from receptors to the brain: the lemniscal system and the spinothalamic system.
- The lemniscal system has large nerve fibers and conveys information quickly; it precisely codes the location of a stimulus.
- The spinothalamic system has small nerve fibers and conveys information slowly; it does not code the location of a stimulus precisely.
- Both the lemniscal system and the spinothalamic system pass their information to the somatosensory cortex; mapping studies have shown the correspondence between body parts and cortex region.

found. Notice that this distorted creature has its body parts scattered along the edge of the cortex in a pattern that bears little resemblance to your own body; its thumb is next to its eye. Furthermore, some large body parts, such as the leg, receive much less cortex space than some much smaller body parts, such as the lip. In the next section we will see that the amount of space occupied on the cortex is related to thresholds of the various body parts.

Summary: Background on the Skin Senses

- Skin is the largest sensory system; it has protective value and is important in social interactions.
- A topic related to the skin senses is pro-

Touch

Touch includes the sensations produced by deformation of the skin. Usually, **touch** refers to a single skin indentation, and **vibration** refers to repeated skin indentations (Kenshalo, 1978). Most researchers study **passive touch,** in which an object is placed on the skin of a passive person. However, we will also discuss **active touch,** in which the person actively seeks

interactions with the environment by exploring objects and touching them.

Passive Touch
Let's first examine thresholds and adaptation for the kind of isolated skin indentations we usually call touch. Then we will briefly discuss the perception of vibration.

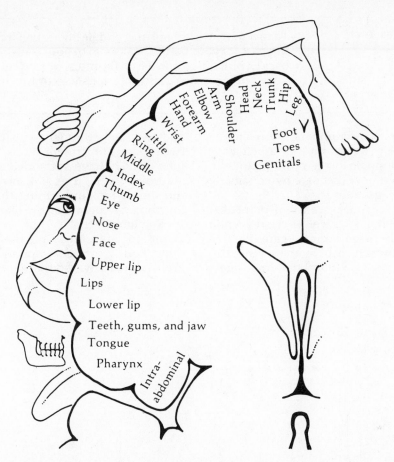

Figure 9-3 The correspondence between parts of the somatosensory cortex and body part (after Penfield and Rasmussen, 1950).

Thresholds for Touch

First, try Demonstration 9-1. As you can see, the various parts of your body have different detection thresholds. The rubber band was particularly noticeable when it touched your cheek, yet its effect on the sole of your foot was so minimal that you probably had to check visually to make certain that you were really touching it. A **detection threshold** is the boundary point at which something is reported half of the time. The most extensive research on thresholds was conducted by Weinstein (1968). Weinstein examined both men and women, touching them on 20 different body parts with a nylon hairlike strand, for which the force could be precisely measured.

Figure 9-4 shows the sensitivity for females, and Figure 9-5 shows the sensitivity for males. Notice that women are significantly more sensitive to touch than men are. Next, notice that the part of the body that is stimulated has a marked effect on sensitivity, for both men and women. For example, thresholds in the face region are much lower than thresholds for other parts of the body. A fly landing on your nose will be much more noticeable than a fly landing on your big toe!

We have been discussing detection thresholds. Another kind of threshold is called a **two-point discrimination threshold,** which measures the ability to notice that two different points on your skin are being touched, rather than a single point. Try Demonstration 9-2 to

> **Demonstration 9-1**
>
> *The Threshold for Touch of Various Body Parts*
>
> Take a narrow rubber band and lightly touch it to the following parts of your body: the bottom of your foot, your calf, your back, your nose, and your thumb. Notice that the parts of your body are not uniformly sensitive to touch.

illustrate two-point discrimination thresholds. Notice that when two toothpicks touch your calf, you feel one single touch, rather than two. However, on your nose there are two distinctly separate touch sensations.

Weinstein (1968) measured two-point discrimination thresholds, as well as the detection thresholds we discussed earlier. Again, the face was generally more sensitive than other regions. However, he also found that the fingers

and toes are extremely sensitive in detecting two separate touch sensations. Our fingers and toes, which have high detection thresholds according to Figures 9-4 and 9-5, have low thresholds for determining that a stimulus is touching two points rather than a single point.

Remember that certain body parts correspond to large areas on the cortex whereas other body parts correspond to small areas. Weinstein discovered that there was a relation-

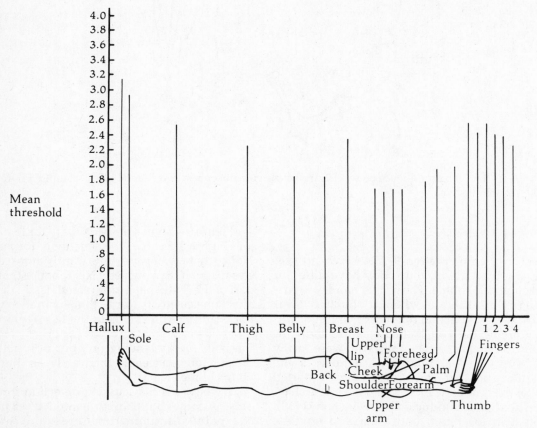

Figure 9-4   Detection thresholds for females. (After S. Weinstein, Intensive and extensive aspects of tactile sensitivity as a function of body part, sex, and laterality. In D. R. Kenshalo (Ed.), *The Skin Senses*, 1968. Courtesy of Charles C. Thomas, Publisher, Springfield, Illinois.)

ship between measures of cortex area and the size of the two-point thresholds. For example, a large space on the cortex is devoted to the lip, and the lip is very sensitive in the two-point discrimination thresholds. In contrast, relatively little space on the cortex is devoted to the leg, and our discrimination is also poor in this area. You may recall a similar relationship in Chapter 2. The largest space on the visual cortex is devoted to the fovea, which also happens to be the area in which discrimination is best. Thus there is a uniform pattern; when a large region of the cortex is devoted to information from a particular area of skin surface, we are usually able to make very precise discriminations when that area of skin is touched.

Other researchers have examined how peo-

ple scale above-threshold touch sensations. Information on intensity scaling can be found in chapters by Kenshalo (1978) and Verillo (1975).

Adaptation to Touch

As you will see throughout this book, the perceived intensity of a repeated stimulus often decreases over time. This process is called adaptation. Similarly, we show **touch adaptation;** we notice a touch at first, but the sensation gradually decreases. For example, this morning when you first put on your clothes, you might have noticed the feel of your waistband, your socks, and your watch. Very quickly, however, the sensations disappeared. You probably were not even aware of pressure

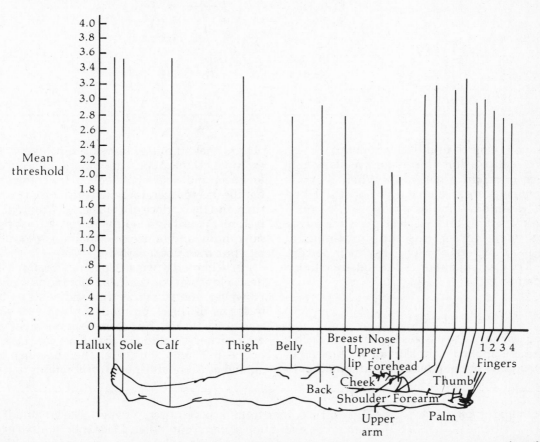

Figure 9-5 Detection thresholds for males. (After S. Weinstein, Intensive and extensive aspects of tactile sensitivity as a function of body part, sex, and laterality. In D. R. Kenshalo (Ed.), *The Skin Senses,* 1968. Courtesy of Charles C. Thomas, Publisher, Springfield, Illinois.)

Demonstration 9 - 2

Two-Point Discrimination Thresholds

Find two toothpicks and hold them so that their points can both touch your skin at the same time. Separate the toothpicks by about one centimeter. Touch your cheek with the toothpicks and describe the sensation. Now touch your calf with the toothpicks and notice whether the sensation is different. Move the toothpicks closer together and touch your cheek once more. How close can they be moved toward each other before you perceive only a single touch? Now move the toothpicks farther apart and touch your calf once more. How far apart can they be moved before you perceive two separate touches?

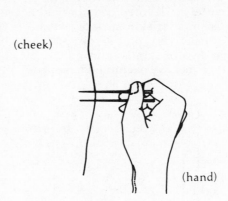

(cheek)

(hand)

from your clothes until I mentioned it.

We notice a stimulus as long as its weight moves our skin downward. When the skin movement stops, we no longer notice it. However, when the stimulus is removed, our skin moves upward, and we feel pressure sensations once more. Thus the movement of skin is an important aspect in touch perception. Try Demonstration 9-3 to illustrate touch adaptation.

The Perception of Vibration

So far, we have discussed situations in which a stimulus is applied to the skin for one time only. However, we frequently come into contact with

objects that stimulate our skin repeatedly. For example, think about the vibrations you can feel from the steering wheel on a car, the door handle of a refrigerator when the motor is whirring, and the surface of a musical instrument. In fact, rest your hand lightly on your throat right now, hum, and notice the vibrations produced by your own vocal cords.

In Chapter 8 we discussed vibrations we hear. Now we are discussing vibrations we feel. However, the vibrations can still be described in terms of their amplitude (in dB) and their frequency (in Hz). For example, remember that we can hear vibrations that have frequencies between 20 and 20,000 Hz. There is much less agreement about the range of vibrations that we

Demonstration 9 - 3

Touch Adaptation

Tear off a corner from a piece of scrap paper. The fragment should be about one square centimeter. Place it on your arm and notice how long it takes until you can no longer feel the paper.

feel. However, the range could be as wide as 10 to 10,000 Hz. In any event it is clear that the range for feeling vibrations is much more limited than the range for hearing vibrations.

In fact, our sense of touch is generally less sensitive than our sense of hearing. Whereas we notice displacements in our eardrum as small as .000000001 cm, we notice displacements in our skin "only" as small as .00001 cm (Verillo, 1975). However, .00001 cm is equal to 0.00004 inch, which is still *quite* remarkable.

Our hearing is most sensitive to vibrations of about 3000 Hz. As Figure 9-6 shows, however, our touch is most sensitive to vibrations in the range of 300 Hz.

Active Touch

So far, we have discussed situations in which a person sits patiently, waiting to be prodded and poked by stimuli in the environment. However, many of our touch experiences are much more active. Right now, your fingers may be twisting around a curl in your hair. You may also use active touch to figure out how to fasten a button at the back of your neck, to determine which apple is the ripest, and to see whether the shelf with the honey jar is still sticky.

The active aspects of touch have been particularly emphasized by James Gibson (1966), whose work is discussed frequently throughout the book. He emphasizes how we humans actively seek contact with things:

> The hand can grope, palpate, prod, press, rub, or heft, and many of the properties of an object can thus be detected in the absence of vision. The properties we call "tangible" are (1) geometrical variables like shape, dimensions and proportions, slopes and edges, or curves and protruberances; (2) surface variables like texture, or roughness-smoothness; and (3) material variables like heaviness or mass and rigidity-plasticity [p. 123].

We are accustomed to believing that vision is such an important sense that we ignore the capabilities of active touch. For example, Kruger (1970) has observed, "The fingers, as wielded by the hand, obtain information on the innards of objects, whereas the eye, remaining

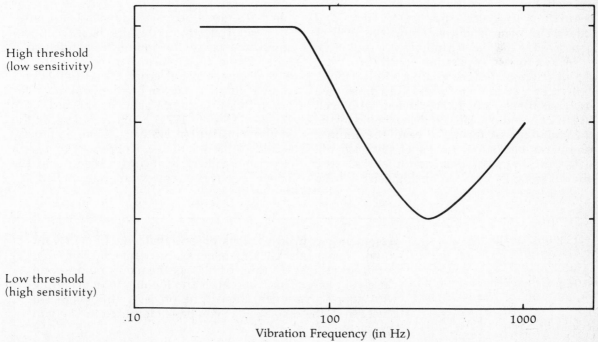

High threshold
(low sensitivity)

Low threshold
(high sensitivity)

.10   100   1000
Vibration Frequency (in Hz)

Figure 9-6   Thresholds for perceiving vibrations.

fixed on the outer surface of objects, plays a lesser role in developing the belief in the reality of the external world" (p. 337). If you were buying a new mattress for your bed, would you trust your visual sense or your tactile sense?

The perception of objects by touching them is called **haptic perception.** Haptic perception sometimes involves holding a hand against an object without any movement. More often, we seek additional information, and so we move our hands around, actively exploring an object's characteristics. Now try Demonstration 9-4 to illustrate the accuracy of your own haptic perception.

James Gibson (1962) demonstrated that our active, haptic perception of forms is much more accurate than our passive perception. He assembled six small metal cookie cutters that were shaped like a teardrop, a star, a triangle, and so forth. When the cookie cutter was pressed against the skin (passive perception), accuracy was only 29%. However, when people were encouraged to feel each cookie cutter (active perception), accuracy soared to 95%.

Active touch is also important in identifying the characteristics of surfaces. For example, if a surface is smooth and cool, you may judge it to be wet. You also notice whether a surface is regular or irregular, slippery or firm, and granular or plain. Think about the feel of velvet compared to the feel of sandpaper or motor oil.

An important application of active touch is the development of material for blind people. The most well-known system was developed by Louis Braille, a blind Frenchman who lived in the 19th century. He was discouraged by the difficult task of trying to read the limited number of books that were specially prepared with raised versions of standard letters. After all, our visual system can distinguish a P from

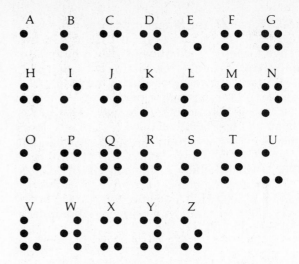

Figure 9-7   The braille alphabet.

an R, but the task is much more challenging for our tactile system.

Figure 9-7 illustrates the letters in the **braille** alphabet; notice that each letter consists of raised dots, which can be either large or small. Most braille readers can read about 100 words a minute, a speed that is impressive but considerably slower than the 200 words a minute that sighted people read in standard print.

Several electronic devices have been designed to increase the options for blind people. For example, the **Optacon** converts material on a printed page into electrical impulses that produce a vibration pattern on the tip of the index finger (Bliss, Katcher, Rogers, & Shepard, 1970; Bliss & Moore, 1974). Another device, the **vision substitution system** (White, Saunders, Scadden, Bach-y-Rita, & Collins, 1970), uses a television camera to record a scene, and the image is converted into vibrations applied to a

---

Demonstration 9 - 4

Haptic Perception

Assemble ten miscellaneous objects that you find in your room, such as a small paperclip, a large paperclip, a rubber band, a thumbtack, and so forth. Place them on your desk and close your eyes. Touch an object and identify it by exploring with your active touch. Repeat the process, removing each object from the display after you have identified it. Did you make any errors?

person's back. People can control the scanning pattern of the television camera and can thus appreciate complex arrangements of objects. According to reports, viewers do not require extensive practice with the system in order to perceive simple objects. With experience they can perceive more complex objects and appreciate depth information. Clearly, these electronic devices offer rich details about the visual world to those who are blind.

Summary: Touch

- Studies of touch thresholds show that thresholds are different for females and males and for various body parts.

- Two-point discrimination thresholds show no sex differences, but they are different for various body parts.
- We show touch adaptation, or a gradual decrease in touch sensation, as a result of prolonged stimulation.
- We feel vibrations over a narrower range of frequencies than the vibrations we hear.
- In active touch, people actively seek interactions by exploring objects and touching them.
- Haptic perception is the perception of objects by touching them.
- An application of active touch is material developed for blind people, such as braille, the Optacon, and the vision substitution system.

Temperature

In this section we will discuss the perception of warmth and cold. In particular, we will examine four topics: (1) body temperature regulation, (2) warm and cold spots, (3) temperature thresholds, and (4) adaptation.

Body Temperature Regulation

Think about how hot or cold you feel right now. Probably you feel reasonably comfortable. Your body has an impressive ability to regulate its own temperature and keep it at about 37°C (98.6°F). If you are in a snowstorm and your body temperature starts to drop, you shiver, a useful process for making more heat. Also, the blood vessels near the surface of the skin shrink in diameter so that less of the warmth from your blood will be lost on the surface. If you are playing a fierce tennis game in the hot August sun, you sweat, and that cools your skin. Also, the blood vessels expand in diameter, so that more of the blood's warmth can be disposed of. Poulton (1970) notes that we may lose consciousness if our body temperature falls below 33°C or rises above 41°C. Thus the skin's role in temperature regulation is not merely a pleasant luxury; it is absolutely necessary. Other aspects of temperature regulation in vertebrates are discussed by Heller, Crawshaw, and Hammel (1978).

Generally, we find that a surrounding

temperature of about 22°C (72°F) is most comfortable. Figure 9-8 shows ratings of discomfort associated with various temperatures.

Warm and Cold Spots

The section you are reading is labeled "temperature," and so it might be tempting to think that we have just one kind of temperature sense. However, we really have separate systems for a warmth sense and for a cold sense. Researchers concluded that there are two separate systems because they were able to identify separate warm and cold spots on the skin. For example, Dallenbach (1927) took a stimulus the size of a pinhead, cooled it, and touched it to various precise locations in a patch of skin that was 2 square centimeters in size. The same procedure was repeated for the same patch of skin using a heated stimulus. He found no correspondence between areas that responded to the cool stimulus and areas that responded to the warm stimulus. (Also, as you might have guessed from our earlier discussion, he found no correspondence between the type of sensation and the type of receptor underlying the skin at the stimulation point.) Thus we should not speak of a "temperature sense" as if it were a single sense; the warmth sense and the cold sense are really separate.

Has this ever happened to you? You put

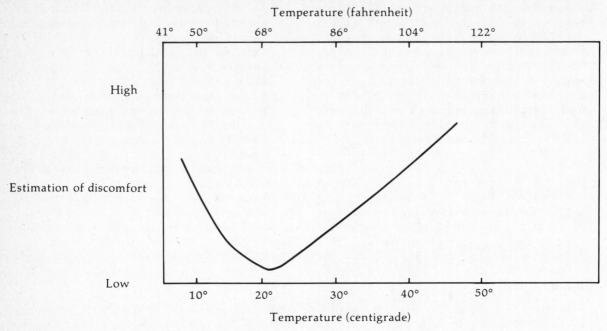

Figure 9-8   Amount of discomfort as a function of temperature.

your hand out to test the temperature of the shower water before entering. A few drops convince you that the water temperature is chillingly cold. However, a moment later, you realize that the water is really scaldingly hot. If so, you have experienced paradoxical cold. A paradox is a puzzle, and **paradoxical cold** occurs when a very hot stimulus produces the sensation of cold when it stimulates a cold spot. (Incidentally, people have searched for a corresponding ''paradoxical warmth'' for many years, but their search has been unsuccessful so far.) A possible explanation for paradoxical cold is that the cold spots appear to be active in temperature ranges between 45°C and 50°C, as well as in colder temperatures.

Thresholds for Temperature

Try Demonstration 9-5 to illustrate how temperature sensitivity varies greatly for different parts of your body. According to Stevens, Marks, and Simonson (1974), the forehead is particularly sensitive to heat. The chest, stomach, shoulder, and arm are less sensitive, and the calf of the leg is the least sensitive. Perhaps you have already noticed the differ-

ences in temperature sensitivity if you have ever sat at a campfire trying to warm your hands. Your forehead probably felt much hotter than your hands, even though it was farther away from the fire. Similar kinds of differences have been demonstrated for sensitivity to cold.

We can often detect very small changes in temperature, as minute as .003°C (Kenshalo, 1978). However, no single value can be supplied as the absolute threshold for warm and cold sensations because the threshold depends upon several factors. For example, the larger the portion of skin exposed to the warm or cold stimulus, the smaller the threshold; it makes sense that we can detect a tiny change more readily on an entire arm than on a pinpoint-sized dot of skin. Also, if the temperature changes quickly, we are more likely to notice it than if the change is gradual (Kenshalo, Holmes, & Wood, 1968). Kenshalo (1978) discusses other factors that influence threshold, such as current skin temperature, phase of the menstrual cycle in women, time of day, and stress.

Taus, Stevens, and Marks (1975) found that people are poor at localizing temperature sensations for above-threshold stimuli. They asked

---

Demonstration 9-5

The Threshold for Temperature of Various Body Parts

Find a metal fork or spoon. Touch the bottom of the handle to your forehead, chest, stomach, shoulder, arm, foot, and calf. Notice that the handle feels cold when you touch some parts of your body, but its temperature is not noticeable on other body parts. Now run hot water on the utensil handle, wipe it off quickly, and touch it to your forehead. Repeat the heating, drying, and touching process for your other body parts. Where is the heat most noticeable?

---

people to judge whether a stimulus was presented either below or above a particular reference point on their arm. Even with the warmest stimulus, accuracy ranged between 80% and 95%. In contrast, *touch* localization was 99% for a hair that was just barely perceptible. Thus we are better in identifying where something touched us than we are in identifying where something warmed us.

Adaptation to Temperature

When you first sit down in a hot bath, the temperature may seem unpleasantly hot. After a few minutes the temperature seems quite comfortable. However, if you slide down further into the water so that your back is now submerged, the temperature of the water surrounding your back is—once again—unpleasantly hot. The rest of your body had adapted to the hot temperature, but the newly immersed skin had not.

As you know, adaptation occurs when a stimulus is presented continuously, and the perceived intensity of the stimulus decreases over time. **Thermal adaptation** is therefore a decrease in the perceived intensity of a hot or cold temperature as time passes. Thermal adaptation is usually studied by placing warm or cold stimuli on the skin and asking the subject to report when the temperature sensation disappears. For example, Kenshalo (1971) reports that people seem to be able to adapt completely to temperatures on the skin in the range of about 29°C to 37°C (84°F to 99°F), starting from a normal skin temperature of approximately 33°C (92°F). Outside of this range, the temperature will seem persistently cold or warm, no matter how long the stimulus is left on the skin.

Thermal adaptation is related to the concept of **physiological zero.** Physiological zero is a temperature that seems neither warm nor cold to an observer. Usually, physiological zero is 33°C, but it actually varies for different parts of the body. Physiological zero is only 28°C for your earlobe, but it is 35°C for your cheek. Thus a 30°C stimulus would initially feel warm on your earlobe but cold on your cheek.

Try Demonstration 9-6 to illustrate an adaptation effect that John Locke discovered in the 17th century. Notice that your left hand, which has adapted to the hot water, feels cold in the neutral-temperature water. In contrast, your right hand, which has adapted to the cold water, feels warm in the same neutral-temperature water. Thus our skin is not an accurate thermometer; we perceive relative temperature, rather than absolute temperature. One particular temperature can feel either cold or hot, depending upon the temperature that we have become accustomed to.

Summary: Temperature

- The body has several mechanisms for regulating its temperature.
- A temperature of about 22°C is generally most comfortable to the majority of people.
- There are separate warmth and cold spots on the skin.
- Paradoxical cold occurs when a very hot stimulus produces the sensation of cold.
- Thresholds for temperature are influenced by factors such as body part, amount of skin exposed, and the speed of temperature change.
- Thermal adaptation is a decrease in the perceived intensity of a hot or cold temperature as a function of repeated exposure.
- Physiological zero is a temperature that seems neither warm nor cool to an observer.

Demonstration 9 - 6

Temperature Adaptation

Locate three bowls. Fill one with very hot tap water (but not so hot that it is painful). Fill the second bowl with very cold tap water. Fill the third with a mixture from the other two bowls. Arrange the three bowls as illustrated below. Place your left hand in the hot water and your right hand in the cold water. Leave your hands in these bowls for approximately three minutes and then quickly transfer both your hands to the middle (lukewarm) bowl. Notice the apparent temperature of each hand.

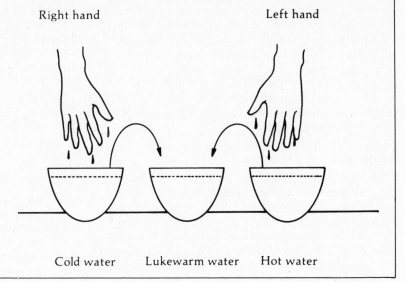

Right hand   Left hand

Cold water   Lukewarm water   Hot water

Pain

How would you define pain? If you are having trouble concocting an objective definition, join the crowd! Psychologists have always found it difficult to list the specific attributes of pain. We will use a definition provided by Carterette and Friedman (1978): **pain** "involves (a) the perception of actual or threatened tissue damage; and (b) the private experience of unpleasantness ('that which hurts')" (p. xiv). Notice, then, that pain has two important components, a sensory component and an emotional component. Pain is more strongly linked with emotion than are any of the other areas of perception. A visual perception, such as a beautiful sunset, seems to exist *out there* in the environment; we feel we can share those per-

ceptions readily with other people. In contrast, a perception of pain, such as a toothache, seems to exist *in here* within the confines of our own bodies; we feel that these perceptions are difficult to share with others (Verillo, 1975).

Early definitions of pain often stated that pain was the result of an overstimulation of either touch or temperature receptors. Thus if a cold receptor was mildly stimulated, we felt cold, but if it was stimulated too much, we felt pain. These early definitions are now acknowledged to be inadequate because pain is often unrelated to degree of stimulation. That is, pain often occurs with only a mild stimulation, and a strong stimulation often produces no pain.

You may wonder why pain is necessary.

Vision, hearing, and other perceptual activities all seem to have a purpose. However, when you have just scraped your knee, pain may seem entirely pointless. In many cases, though, pain has survival value; it serves to protect our bodies from further damage.

Sternbach (1978) describes the horrible things that can happen to people who have certain pain perception disorders and cannot feel pain. Initially, this might sound like an enviable condition. However, children who are born with pain insensitivity have picked away their nostrils and bitten off their tongues and fingers by mistake. Adults may suffer from a ruptured appendix, a fractured bone, or cancer, yet not detect the problem early enough to seek adequate treatment. In fact, one woman died because of damage done to her spine when she did not make the usual kinds of posture adjustments that we routinely make when our muscles and joints begin to ache (Sternbach, 1968). Another person felt only a mild headache when an axe was buried in his skull (Dearborn, 1932). Yes, pain is uncomfortable, but consider the dangers we would encounter without its warning capacity!

This section on pain has four parts. We will begin with discussions of pain thresholds and pain adaptation. Then we will consider theories about pain perception. Finally, we will examine several methods of relieving pain.

Thresholds for Pain

The **pain threshold** is the intensity of stimulation at which an observer says, "It's painful" half the time and "It's not painful" half the time. Notice, then, that the pain threshold differs from other kinds of thresholds, which involve responses such as "It's present" or "It's absent." Thus when we measure pain thresholds, we ask people to make a judgment about the *quality* of a stimulus. In contrast, when we measure a hearing threshold, for example, we ask people to make a judgment about whether a sound is present or absent (Sternbach, 1978).

Pain thresholds depend upon many different factors. You have already learned that touch sensitivity and temperature sensitivity depend upon the region of the body that is stimulated, so it will not surprise you that the different parts of your body also have different sensitivities to pain. The cornea, the back of the knee, and the neck region are particularly sensitive, whereas the sole of the foot, the tip of the nose, and the inside lining of the cheek are particularly *in*sensitive. You have probably already discovered that parts of the body differ in their sensitivity if you have ever compared the pain of a tiny paper cut under a fingernail with the pain of a large gash on the sole of your foot.

Pain tolerance is the maximum pain level at which people voluntarily accept pain. Ethical problems in research on pain tolerance are discussed elsewhere (e.g., American Psychological Association, 1973; Matlin, 1979).

Both pain threshold and pain tolerance show enormous variation from one individual to another. A particular stimulus may be perceived by one person as being below his or her pain threshold, whereas the same stimulus may be perceived as above another person's pain tolerance. Researchers have tried to identify personality characteristics that might be related to pain thresholds and pain tolerance. Some factors that have been studied are anxiety, extraversion, and depression (Liebeskind & Paul, 1977; Sternbach, 1978; Weisenberg, 1977).

Many researchers have wondered whether there are ethnic differences in pain tolerance. For example, an enormous study by Woodrow, Friedman, Siegelaub, and Collen (1972) tested 40,000 individuals as part of their routine physical examinations. They found that whites tolerated more pain than blacks, who tolerated more pain than Orientals. However, Weisenberg (1977) notes that the testers were probably white; black or Oriental testers might obtain different results. Another study examined various ethnic groups for their tolerance for pain and found the following ranking, from most tolerance to least: Protestants of British descent, Jews, Irish Catholics, and Italian Catholics (Sternbach & Tursky, 1965). In some cultures, people are taught to endure pain as long as they possibly can, whereas in other cultures, people are encouraged to avoid a painful situation when it becomes unpleasant.

Adaptation to Pain

Think about the last time you had a severe pain, such as a headache or a burn. If you took no medication, did the intensity of the pain seem to decrease over time? Most people report that the pain seems just as excruciating after half an hour as it did initially. In other words, pain adaptation does not seem to occur for intense pains.

However, adaptation does occur for mild pains. Try Demonstration 9-7 to illustrate how you can adapt to a mildly painful cold stimulus, particularly when only a small area of skin experiences pain. As Kenshalo (1971) points out, there is a physiological reason why we can adapt to painful cold stimuli; the chilling of nerve tissue blocks receptor activity and the conduction of impulses.

Adaptation also occurs for other mild pains, such as a pinprick and mildly painful hot stimuli. For example, we show adaptation for hot water temperatures up to about 46°C (115°F). However, we show little or no adaptation for hot water temperatures above 46°C (Hardy, Stolwijk, & Hoffman, 1968). Thus if your doctor advises you to soak a sprained ankle in water that is as hot as you can tolerate, keep the temperature at about 46°C.

Theories of Pain Perception

At the beginning of the chapter we discussed three theories about the skin senses: specificity theory, pattern theory, and a theory that combined specificity theory and pattern theory. Let us now see how each of the three theories accounts for pain perception.

The **specificity theory of pain perception** states that pain is produced by the stimulation of specific pain receptors, which transmit information directly to a pain center in the brain. Supporters of this theory believe that the specific pain receptors that are responsible for pain perception are the free nerve endings, which were illustrated in Figure 9-1. According to this specificity theory, there is a direct connection from the free nerve endings to the part of the brain where we feel pain. Thus when the receptors are stimulated, we must *always* feel pain, and we must *only* feel pain—rather than any other sensation.

There is a major difficulty with the specificity theory of pain perception, however; the specificity theory cannot account for the fact that many psychological variables influence the amount of pain that people report. For example, Beecher (1959) describes soldiers who have been seriously wounded in battle who are

> clear mentally, not in shock and with normal blood pressure, having had no narcotics for a period of four hours or more and some not at all, [yet they] state on direct questioning that they do not have wound pain great enough to require medication [p. 166].

Apparently, these soldiers are so relieved to have survived the ordeal that their perception of wound pain is drastically reduced.

Specificity theory also cannot account for **phantom limb pain,** which is perceived pain in an arm or a leg that has been amputated. How could someone feel pain in a missing arm, for example, when there are no longer any specific pain receptors in the skin to be stimulated? Clearly, then, there must be higher-level processes, in addition to pain receptors on the skin, that can either reduce or increase the perception of pain.

The **pattern theory of pain perception** states that pain is produced by particular patterns of stimulation; specifically, the stimulation of receptors must be added together, and the stimulation must reach a critical level in order for the pain to be perceived. Theorists who support the pattern theory have argued that there are no

---

Demonstration 9 - 7

Adaptation to Pain

Take a glass of cold water and add several ice cubes. Place your index finger in the water. Notice that you feel mild pain in your finger initially. Leave your finger in the water for several minutes. Do you still notice the pain?

specialized receptors that receive only pain information. However, the physiological evidence here supports the specificity theory—rather than the pattern theory—because the free nerve endings *do* seem to be responsible for pain perception (Verillo, 1975).

The most popular current theory of pain perception combines the specificity theory and the pattern theory, and it also emphasizes the importance of psychological factors in pain perception. Ronald Melzack and his colleagues have argued that specificity theory ignores psychological factors and pattern theory ignores physiological evidence (Melzack & Wall, 1965; Melzack & Casey, 1968; Melzack & Dennis, 1978). Their **gate-control theory** proposes that pain perception is a complex process in which the lemniscal system and the spinothalamic system interact together, and the brain also has an important influence on pain perception.

Remember that the lemniscal system has large nerve fibers that transmit information quickly, whereas the spinothalamic system has small nerve fibers that transmit information slowly. Melzack and his colleagues prefer the terms large fibers and small fibers; let's adopt this straightforward vocabulary.

The gate-control theory suggests that the large fibers and the small fibers both transmit information to a gate-control mechanism that is located in the spinal cord. Activity in the large fibers tends to close the gate, whereas activity in the small fibers tends to open the gate. The theory gets its name because the gate-control mechanism acts like a gate, regulating the flow of impulses from the receptors to the brain. The amount of pain we eventually feel is determined by whether the gate is open or shut. (There is some speculation that acupuncture —which we will discuss shortly—activates the large fibers, thereby closing the gate and preventing the perception of other pains.)

However, gate-control theory states that central, cognitive processes in the brain also influence pain perception. As Melzack and his colleagues have argued, pain perception is influenced not only by the information from the receptors, but also by psychological factors such as our state of mind and our past history. Gate-control theory proposes that the large fibers send direct information to the gate-control mechanism and that they also stimulate certain cognitive processes in the brain. The brain, in turn, sends information back down to the gate-control mechanism and can influence whether the gate is open or shut. In this fashion, factors such as attention, emotion, and memory can influence how much pain we feel.

Have you ever noticed that a painful stimulus often seems to produce two different kinds of pain? For example, if you scrape your knee, you may at first feel a sharp "bright" pain, followed by a different kind of pain that is more dull and nagging. This sharp pain followed by dull pain is known as **double pain.** Gate-control theory provides an appealing explanation for double pain. The painful stimulus activates both the large fibers and the small fibers. However, impulses travel faster through the large fibers; they are responsible for the initial, sharp pain. Impulses travel more slowly through the small fibers; they are responsible for the delayed, dull pain.

Let's now review gate-control theory by noting the differences between large fibers and small fibers. These differences are outlined in Table 9-1.

Gate-control theory is much more detailed than our brief overview suggests; more information can be obtained in the original description of the theory (Melzack & Wall, 1965) or in a more recent review (Melzack & Dennis, 1978). We also have not examined the criticism of gate-control theory, which focuses on the lack of evidence for a relationship between fiber size and pain inhibition (Weisenberg, 1977), Nonetheless, the gate-control theory of pain is

Table 9-1 The differences between large fibers and small fibers.

TYPE OF FIBER	SYSTEM	SPEED OF TRANSMISSION	ACTION ON GATE	NATURE OF PAIN
LARGE	lemniscal	fast	close	sharp
SMALL	spinothalamic	slow	open	dull

widely acknowledged to be the most influential and important theory of pain perception. Even if the specific details of the theory need to be modified, its emphasis on the importance of psychological variables represents a major breakthrough in our current ideas about pain.

Pain Control

Unlike the weather, people not only talk about pain, but they are doing something about it. Sometimes neurosurgeons cut the nerve pathways to relieve pain, but there are many less drastic methods that are effective. In this section we will discuss various other approaches to pain control. These approaches include medication, counterirritants, and approaches used by psychologists.

Medication

When you have a severe headache, you may take an aspirin. Aspirin is an **analgesic** medication (pronounced "aan-ull-*jee*-zick"), a drug specifically designed to relieve pain. Analgesics also include novocaine (which your dentist may inject before filling a cavity), codeine (which is stronger than aspirin), and morphine (which is even stronger than codeine and is highly likely to be addictive). Harmful side effects of these medications are discussed by Chapman (1978).

Psychological factors have an important impact on the effectiveness of analgesics. For example, analgesics can be ineffective if they are administered in a laboratory setting, rather than in a clinic setting such as a doctor's office.

Furthermore, pain can often be reduced by giving a patient a placebo. A **placebo** (pronounced "pluh-*see*-bow") is an inactive substance such as a sugar pill, which the patient believes to be a medication. If a doctor gives a patient a placebo and announces that it is a sugar pill, the pill will not have any pharmacological action. However, if the placebo is believed to be an analgesic, it may reduce pain significantly. Evans (1974) has noted that a placebo in a double-blind study is roughly half as effective as the drug itself. (In a **double-blind study,** neither the physician nor the patient knows whether a substance is a placebo or a real analgesic.) Thus physicians seem to communi-

cate to the patient some information about the expected strength of the medication. Other aspects of placebos are discussed by Beecher (1959).

Do placebos influence our sensitivity to pain or our willingness to report pain? In signal detection terms (recall the description of signal detection theory in Chapter 1), do placebos work because they change our d' values or our β values? In general, research has demonstrated that placebos influence β, our criterion for reporting pain, rather than d', the sensory detection of pain (Clark, 1969; Feather, Chapman, & Fisher, 1972). Thus if you swallow a sugar pill that you believe is an analgesic, you will still be able to detect a sensation, but you will be less likely to report the sensation as being painful. Incidentally, possible biochemical explanations for the placebo effect are discussed by Levine, Gordon, and Fields (1979).

Counterirritants

Maybe you have discovered that you can reduce the intensity of pain from a wound by scratching the surrounding skin. Several methods of pain control involve **counterirritants,** which stimulate or irritate one area in order to diminish the pain in another area.

One kind of counterirritant is the classical Chinese technique called acupuncture. **Acupuncture** (pronounced "ack-you-*punk*-ture") involves the insertion of thin needles into various locations on the body. In some cases the needles may be heated or twirled. Figure 9-9 shows a typical acupuncture diagram. Each of the locations is carefully charted, and stimulation of these locations relieves a particular symptom. Often, the stimulated point is far away from the painful area. For example, surgery for removal of the stomach is accomplished with four acupuncture needles in the pinna of each ear (Melzack, 1973).

Physicians in the United States have been reluctant to accept acupuncture as a method of controlling pain. In fact, most Americans were not interested in acupuncture until an American columnist, James Reston, had his appendix removed with the aid of acupuncture in an operation in China. Melzack (1973) reports that a large proportion of patients in China—perhaps as high as 90%—undergo surgery with the

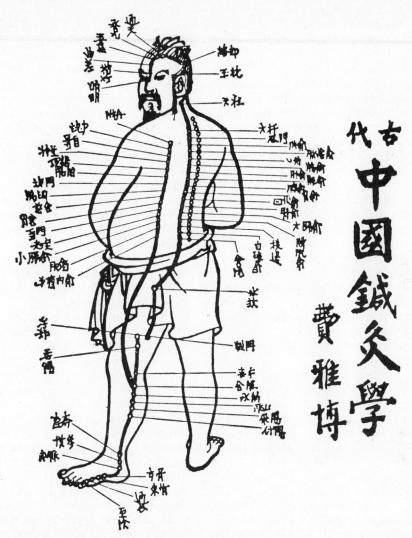

Figure 9-9 An acupuncture diagram (from Melzack, 1973).

acupuncture method. Patients who experience surgery with acupuncture are reported to be fully conscious during the operation. They chat pleasantly with the doctors, eat pieces of orange, and are keenly interested in the procedures of the operation. In China, acupuncture is part of an entire approach to medicine that involves rapport, explanations, and expectations (Liebeskind & Paul, 1977). Naturally, it is difficult to duplicate these conditions in Western medical practice.

It is possible that acupuncture, like placebos, influences our willingness to report pain, rather than our sensitivity to pain. Clark and Yang (1974), for example, used the signal detection method, and they demonstrated that acupuncture raised people's pain criterion but did not influence their sensitivity.

In contrast, Chapman, Wilson, and Gehrig (1976) demonstrated that acupuncture can also influence sensitivity. One group of subjects in their study received acupuncture; needles were inserted in the back of each hand between the bones of the first finger and the thumb, which is the acupuncture point for a particular kind of dental pain. Another group received "placebo acupuncture"; needles were inserted in the back of each hand between the bones of the fourth and fifth fingers. Then subjects in both groups received painful dental stimuli, and they were asked to rate the intensity of each painful stimulus. Chapman and his coauthors found that the placebo acupuncture influenced neither sensitivity nor criterion. However, the standard acupuncture treatment influenced *both* sensitivity and criterion. That is, acupuncture actually decreased sensitivity to pain, and it also changed the subjects' willingness to report pain.

Thus acupuncture seems to influence people's response to pain, and this may be a sufficient reason to encourage the use of acupuncture. However, researchers disagree about whether acupuncture decreases sensitivity to pain. The mechanisms of acupuncture are also unclear at this time, although we mentioned earlier that Melzack (1973) proposed that the gate-control mechanisms may be involved. Further discussion of acupuncture and its mechanisms can be found in the work of Bonica and Albe-Fessard (1976).

Recently, psychologists and others interested in pain control began exploring another kind of counterirritant method called stimulation-produced analgesia. **Stimulation-produced analgesia** involves the electrical stimulation of certain regions of the brain, which leads to analgesia, or a loss of sensitivity to pain. According to Cannon, Liebeskind, and Frenk (1978), stimulation-produced analgesia is as effective as high doses of morphine for suppressing pain in experimental animals. According to these authors, there is evidence that the mechanisms of stimulation-produced analgesia are similar to the mechanisms of opiate drugs such as morphine.

Procedures Used by Psychologists

So far, we have seen that pain can be controlled by swallowing analgesics and sugar pills and by being prodded with sharp needles and electrical shock. Now let us look at some procedures that psychologists use: hypnosis, behavior therapy, and modeling.

Hypnosis is a trancelike condition in which a person is susceptible to suggestions made by the hypnotist. It has been used to help people

suffering from chronic pain and to prevent pain in patients undergoing surgery. However, it can be used only with certain suggestible people, and it works consistently only in certain circumstances (Chapman, 1978). Thus hypnosis is not a cure-all.

Nonetheless, hypnosis can provide dramatic relief when the conditions are appropriate. For example, Hilgard (1978) cites the case of a man suffering from painful cancer of the throat. Under hypnosis he was told that he would feel a pleasant tingling sensation, similar to a weak electric current, whenever he started to feel pain in his throat. The patient successfully substituted the pleasant tingling for the pain. Hypnosis has also been used extensively to relieve pain during childbirth. In many ways its effects are similar to those of the **Lamaze method,** a technique of relieving pain in childbirth in which attention is concentrated on something other than the pain.

Hypnosis has also been effective in relieving anxiety and pain during dentistry. Migraine headaches also frequently respond to hypnotic treatment. Furthermore, hypnosis is currently the most effective way to relieve that mysterious ailment we discussed earlier, phantom limb pain. However, despite its documented success, hypnosis remains a puzzle. Chaves and Barber (1974) claim that hypnosis is effective because it heightens motivation, makes people more receptive to the physician's suggestions, and reduces fear and anxiety. Others have noted that the physiological indicators of pain remain, even when the hypnotized patients claim that they feel no pain. Hilgard (1973) believes that hypnosis is a different state of consciousness. Thus pain can reach one level of consciousness, but hypnotized people are able to prevent the pain from reaching the level of awareness that makes it distressing.

Behavior therapy is a systematic approach of modifying behavior by rewarding some behaviors and withholding reward for other behaviors. It has been extremely successful in helping people who have suffered from pain for many years. Fordyce (1978) discusses the learning processes that are related to pain. For example, for some people, pain may actually be reinforcing. A construction worker with a back sprain may prefer light-duty work; as a result, the pain persists long after the original sprain has healed. Thus Fordyce argues that people often complain about pain for reasons that may be totally unrelated to the original body damage.

Fordyce outlines the components of behavior therapy. (1) The therapist must specify what behaviors must be increased and what must be decreased. (2) A behavior increases when that behavior is systematically, promptly followed by effective positive reinforcement. (3) A behavior decreases when that behavior is no longer followed by the earlier positive reinforcers or when other incompatible behaviors replace the undesirable behavior. (4) Behavior change is permanent only when the new behavior, rather than the undesirable behavior, continues to be reinforced. Thus behavior therapy stresses the development of behavior appropriate for a healthy person as well as the reduction in inappropriate behaviors. Other behavioral therapies for pain, such as biofeedback, are discussed by Chapman (1978).

According to **modeling theory,** people can understand the consequences of a behavior by watching another person in a situation; they do not have to perform the behavior themselves. Thus children learn that the dental setting is painful by watching their parents' reactions. Parents who report being extremely anxious in a dentist's office tend to have children who are negative and uncooperative during dental examinations (Craig, 1978). Furthermore, children who frequently complain of stomachaches—yet who have no observable organic disease—tend to have a family history of stomachaches. Thus children learn to complain about pain by watching others.

Notice that modeling theory accounts for the ethnic differences in pain tolerance that we discussed earlier in this section. It also helps explain why acupuncture may be more effective in China than in the United States. Chinese patients have been exposed to others who have had successful acupuncture experiences. In fact, new patients are encouraged to talk to people who have previously experienced acupuncture (Craig, 1978).

Modeling therapy has been successfully used in dental care. For example, children saw a film in which a model was initially fearful but controlled his fear and received verbal praise and a toy at the end of a dental session. These children were much less anxious and disruptive during their own dental session than children who had not seen the film. Similarly, you may have heard about hospital programs in which children awaiting surgery see a movie about another child's experience in surgery. Experiments have confirmed the effectiveness of this kind of modeling program (Craig, 1978).

It is interesting to speculate why behavior therapy and modeling are effective in pain relief. Specifically, do these psychological procedures decrease sensitivity, or do they alter the criterion for reporting pain? It seems most likely that the pain still persists following therapy, but people are less likely to report the existence of pain.

Summary: Pain

- Pain involves the perception of tissue damage and the personal experience of unpleasantness.
- Pain often has survival value, protecting us from further damage.
- The pain threshold is the lowest intensity of stimulation at which we perceive pain.
- Pain tolerance is the maximum pain level at which people accept pain; there seem to be ethnic differences in pain tolerance.
- We adapt to mild pains but not to severe pains.
- The specificity theory of pain perception states that pain is transmitted directly from pain receptors to a pain center in the brain; this theory cannot account for the fact that psychological variables influence the amount of pain that people report.
- The pattern theory of pain perception states that pain is produced by a particular pattern of stimulation from the receptors; this theory cannot account for the physiological evidence that free nerve endings do seem to be responsible for pain perception.
- Melzack and his colleagues proposed a gate-control theory in which pain perception is hypothesized to be the result of the interaction of large fibers and small fibers, with the additional influence of central processes in the brain.
- Pain can be controlled by analgesics, such as aspirin and codeine; placebos may also relieve pain.

- Counterirritants, which diminish pain in one area by stimulating or irritating another area, include acupuncture and stimulation-produced analgesia.

- Three techniques that psychologists use in controlling pain are hypnosis, behavior therapy, and modeling.

Review

1. In this chapter we discussed thresholds and two-point discrimination thresholds for touch, thresholds for temperature, and thresholds for pain. We saw that each of these thresholds varied from one part of the body to another. Summarize the findings on these four kinds of thresholds and note the similarities and differences.

2. Adaptation was also a recurring theme in this chapter. Discuss adaptation to touch, temperature, and pain; think of an example of each of these kinds of adaptation from your own recent experience. Can you think of an occasion when adaptation did not occur?

3. What are the two basic kinds of skin that cover your body? Review the three layers of skin and the two kinds of skin receptors.

4. Imagine that you are blindfolded. Describe what you can learn about your immediate environment from passive touch and from active touch. Which kind of touch is more informative?

5. Refer to material in the chapter to explain each of the following observations about touch: (a) Something touches your leg, and you have no idea what shape it is; then it touches your face, and its shape now seems clear. (b) The fabric on a chair seems rough against your arms when you first sit down, but you do not notice it after 5 minutes. (c) You put your finger on a piccolo that is playing a very high note; you can hear it, but you cannot feel the vibrations.

6. Refer to material in the chapter to explain each of the following observations about temperature perception: (a) You stand too close to a kettle full of boiling spaghetti sauce, and a drop splatters on your wrist; surprisingly, it seems cold. (b) Maria has been sitting in front of the fire, and the kitchen seems cold to her; Pat has been outside in the snow, and the kitchen seems warm to him. (c) Your internal temperature remains at about 37°C, whether you spend your winter in an upstate New York blizzard or the Caribbean sunshine.

7. Knock your knuckles sharply against a wall or a desk, producing a mild pain. Explain the two systems by which that pain information travels from the skin receptors to the brain, and explain why you seem to feel two kinds of pain.

8. What is pain, why does it differ from other perceptual experiences, and why are its thresholds different? What function does pain serve?

9. Compare the skin senses with vision and hearing. Mention, for example, (a) the size of the receptive system, (b) the kind of receptors, (c) the ability to discriminate, (d) sensitivity, and (e) the nature of the stimuli.

10. Melzack and his colleagues emphasized that psychological processes influence pain perception; pain is more than the perception of impulses that flow from the receptors to the brain. Explain why each of the following topics documents the importance of central psychological processes in pain perception: (a) ethnic differences in pain tolerance; (b) phantom limb pain, (c) placebo action, (d) acupuncture, and (e) hypnosis.

New Terms

proprioception
kinesthesis
vestibular sensation
hairy skin

glabrous skin
epidermis
dermis
subcutaneous tissue

free nerve endings
encapsulated endings
doctrine of specific nerve energies
specificity theory

pattern theory

lemniscal system

spinothalamic system

somatosensory cortex

touch

vibration

passive touch

active touch

detection threshold

two-point discrimination
threshold

touch adaptation

haptic perception

braille

Optacon

vision substitution system

paradoxical cold

thermal adaptation

physiological zero

pain

pain threshold

pain tolerance

pain adaptation

specificity theory of pain
perception

phantom limb pain

pattern theory of pain perception

gate-control theory

double pain

analgesic

placebo

double-blind study

counterirritants

acupuncture

stimulation-produced analgesia

hypnosis

Lamaze method

behavior therapy

modeling theory

chapter 10

SMELL

Outline   Sensory Aspects of Smell
                The Stimulus
                The Olfactory System
           Olfactory Processes
                Thresholds for Smell
                Adaptation
                Recognizing Smells
           Applications of Research on Smell
                Perfume Manufacturing
                Odor Pollution Control
                Smell and Communication

Preview

As you will see in this chapter, the sense of smell is still rather mysterious, and there are many unanswered questions. Our examination of smell covers three topics: (1) sensory aspects of smell, (2) olfactory processes, and (3) applications of research on smell.

When we discuss the sensory aspects of smell, we will begin with the nature of the odor stimulus. We will consider what kinds of substances have noticeable odors and what kinds of systems have been devised to classify these odors. Then we will look at the olfactory system, beginning with the receptor cells and ending with the temporal lobe of the brain.

In the section on olfactory processes we will see that people can detect impressively tiny amounts of an odor, but they have trouble telling the difference between two concentrations. Also, humans adapt rapidly when they are continually exposed to a particular odor, and their sensitivity is greatly reduced. We will also find that people are normally poor at identifying smells, but with practice their accuracy is impressive. However, once they have smelled a particular odor, they are accurate in identifying it as familiar, even after a long delay.

The section on applications of research on smell covers the manufacturing of perfume and the control of odor pollution. It also considers chemical signals called pheromones, which play an important role in reproduction among lower animals and may also be important in human sexuality.

The sense of smell is both important and mysterious. We tend to ignore this sense because we seldom go out of our way to smell something. We seek out a movie to see, a concert to hear, a meal to eat, and a massage to feel. However, have you ever decided to entertain yourself with an evening of smells? ("Let's go down to the delicatessen and smell the cheeses!") Probably not.

Nevertheless, think how important smells are to you in your everyday behavior. You meet a new person and dislike him instantly because his after-shave lotion reminds you of someone you loathe. You smell a piece of fish and decide to throw it out because of the spoiled odor. You sniff out where the dead mouse must be hidden. You visit a friend's house, and one whiff immediately makes you think of your grandmother's attic, which you have not visited in 10 years. You decide to buy a particular car because it smells newer than another model.

Smell, also known as **olfaction** (pronounced "oll-*fack*-shun"), is particularly important in the way things taste. Usually, we say that something *tastes* good, when in fact we should be commenting on its smell. Try Demonstration 10-1 to illustrate the importance of smell in determining taste. Smell and taste are frequently discussed together, under the name **chemical senses,** because the receptor cells for smell and taste are sensitive to chemical stimulation.

Some people have claimed that smell is really a luxury for humans. They argue that losing the sense of smell would be no more disastrous than becoming color-blind. The role of smell in human behavior may be controversial, but everyone agrees that smell is critical for the survival of other animals. Smell is used to locate food and to identify the enemy. It is important also in sex discrimination, sexual behavior, and reproduction, which ensure the survival of the species (Schneider, 1974).

In spite of its importance, we do not know

Demonstration 10-1

The Importance of Smell for Taste Experiences

Take a piece of each of the following: apple, onion, and potato. Close your eyes, plug your nose, and take a bite out of each of them. Notice how the taste for all three of them is remarkably similar. They all have crisp textures, so that if you are deprived of odor cues, there are no important characteristics to distinguish among them.

---

much about smell. Gesteland (1978) writes that olfaction is the most mysterious of the senses. As we will discuss in this chapter, no one knows how to classify the different smells, no one can accurately predict a substance's smell on the basis of its chemical structure, and no one is certain what role smell plays in human sexual relations. Researchers have certainly made some valiant efforts to understand smell. Cain (1978a) points out that a bibliography on odors and smell included 3000 entries from the period of 320 B.C. to 1947. In more recent years there have been several hundred articles published annually. Cain remarks, however, that

many authors have published only one article on smell. It is possible that the sense of smell is so puzzling that researchers become discouraged after just one experiment!

This chapter is divided into three parts. The first part, on the sensory aspects of smell, examines the nature of the odorous stimulus and the olfactory apparatus. The second part of the chapter is called "Olfactory Processes"; it is concerned with thresholds, adaptation, and recognition of smell. The final part of the chapter discusses applications of research on smell, particularly in perfume manufacturing, pollution control, and communication.

Sensory Aspects of Smell

We need to begin our discussion of smell with an examination of sensory aspects of smell. In particular, what is the nature of the stimulus, and how can odors be classified? Furthermore, what is the basic "equipment" for smell? What do the sensory receptors look like, and how is information about smell transmitted to higher levels?

The Stimulus

Description

In order for substances to be smelled, they must be volatile. **Volatile** (pronounced "*voll*-uh-tull") means that something can evaporate, or change into a gas form. However, we cannot smell all the volatile substances. Water, for example, is volatile, because it can evaporate, and the vapor form of water bathes our nasal cavities every time we take a shower. However, pure steam has no odor. Thus volatility is necessary but not sufficient to permit smelling.

Another necessary but not sufficient characteristic of substances that can be smelled is that they must have a particular molecular weight. As you have learned in previous chapters, we can specify quite accurately the nature of stimuli that we see and hear. For example, the visible spectrum includes only the wavelengths from 400 nm to 700 nm. We can hear sounds only in the frequency range of 20 Hz to 20,000 Hz. In general, we can detect only the smells of substances that have molecular weights between 30 and 300. The **molecular weight** of a substance is the sum of the atomic weights of all the atoms in the molecule. For example, the molecular weight of the alcohol in a gin and tonic is 46. (The formula for ethyl alcohol is C_2H_5OH. Each of the two carbon atoms has an atomic weight of 12, each of the six hydrogen atoms has a weight of 1, and oxygen has a weight of 16; $24 + 6 + 16 = 46$.) Thus you can smell alcohol, but you cannot smell table sugar, ($C_{12}H_{22}O_{11}$), which has a molecular weight of 342. In summary, the substances that we smell must be volatile and must typically have molecular weights between 30 and 300. There are probably additional factors that have not yet been identified.

Classification

How can we classify the various smells? Colors, for example, can be classified on the basis of wavelength. Think for a moment how you might devise your own smell classification system. What characteristics and descriptions would you use? This issue of smell classifications has intrigued many people, probably beginning with Aristotle (Cain, 1978a). We will look at just two of the systems that have been proposed. Neither of them is perfectly satisfactory.

One commonly discussed system of classifications was proposed by Henning (1916). Figure 10-1 illustrates the prism-shaped

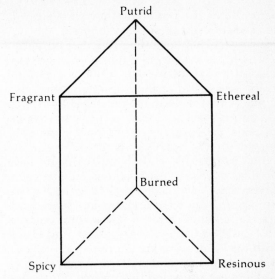

Figure 10-1   The smell prism devised by Henning.

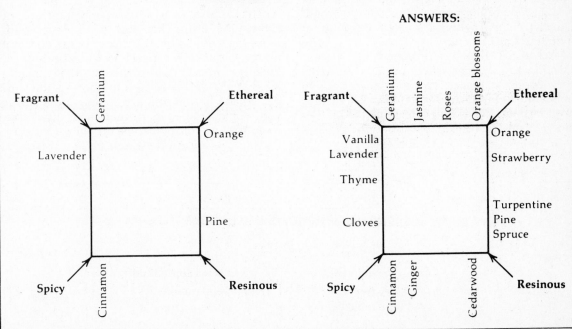

Demonstration 10-2

Filling in Some Odors on Henning's Prism

Cover the diagram on the right before you begin. Here is the front face of Henning's prism, taken from Figure 10–1. A few of the odors have been filled in to provide guidelines. From your knowledge of various odors, see how many of the following you can add: roses, orange blossoms, ginger, thyme, turpentine, jasmine, cloves, cedarwood, strawberry, spruce, and vanilla.

ANSWERS:

figure he devised to show how smells can be defined in terms of six basic odors.

Now try Demonstration 10-2. See how accurate you are in placing odors on the prism in relation to the square that contains the floral, fruity, spicy, and resinous odors. Notice, incidentally, that cooks in the Western hemisphere use only certain portions of this square. We use the side between floral and spicy, the spicy portion of the spicy-resinous side, and the fruity portion of the fruity-resinous side. Greeks, however, use resinous substances to flavor their wine called retsina (which tastes almost as if you were drinking a pine tree) and orange blossom water to flavor their pastries. East Indians flavor their desserts and drinks with rose water. We are depriving ourselves of some interesting sensory experiences!

Henning proposed that simple odors must be located on the surfaces of the prism. They could not be located somewhere inside the prism. Thus a simple odor could not be partly burned, partly spicy, and partly fruity because this combination of odors would be located inside the prism. However, a *complex* odor (such as burned apple-cinnamon pie) could be represented inside the prism. Cain (1978a) discusses some of the problems with Henning's model. For example, people differ enormously in their odor judgments. One person might show agreement with the system, but another might disagree strongly.

Amoore (1970) has proposed a different classification system in connection with his stereochemical theory of odor. According to the **stereochemical theory,** odorous molecules have definite shapes that determine the kind of odor we smell. For example, minty fragrances have molecules that are somewhat oval in shape. Fragrances that resemble mothballs are much rounder. He proposed that receptor sites are related to the shapes of molecules, the same way lock shapes are related to key shapes.

Amoore asked people to compare certain fragrances with five different standards. Fragrances that were judged to smell like the standards also resembled them in their chemical structure. Amoore suggested that there are several primary odors. Table 10-1 shows one version of the list of primaries, together with an example (Amoore, 1964).

Amoore's theory is controversial. As Beets says, "the question whether a relationship between molecular structure and odor exists is meaningless. The only legitimate question is whether it is simple enough to be detected" (1978, p. 246). Furthermore, Schiffman (1974) obtained judgments about various odors and found that judgments were often vastly different for two molecules of similar size and shape. Those of you interested in chemistry might want to look at the article by Beets (1978), in which he illustrates two complex molecules that have almost identical structures. However, one molecule smells strongly of sandalwood, and the other molecule is completely odorless. Thus any correspondence between the shape of a molecule and its smell is very complex.

In summary, a satisfactory method of classifying odors has not been developed. Henning's model of six primary odors does not match everyone's perceptual experiences. Furthermore, Amoore's theory—that molecular shape is closely related to odor—is too simple. Vision has its primary colors, and taste, as you will learn, has its primary sensations, but odors are too complex to be organized into any current classification system.

Table 10-1 Primary odors suggested by Amoore	ODOR	EXAMPLE
	camphoraceous	mothballs
	pungent	vinegar
	floral	roses
	ethereal	dry-cleaning fluid
	minty	peppermint stick
	musky	musk perfume
	putrid	rotten egg

The Olfactory System

Figure 10-2 shows an illustration of the anatomy of the **nasal** (or nose) area. First, look at the region called the **nasal cavity,** which is the hollow space behind each nostril. Air containing odors reaches the nasal cavity through two routes. Most obviously, we sniff and inhale to bring in the outside air. However, air can also come up from the back of the throat when we chew or drink. Trace the pathway from the mouth, up the throat, to the nasal cavity. Notice the importance of this throat passage the next time you are eating food with a strong odor. Plug your nostrils and notice its blandness. Suddenly release your fingers. A current of air will quickly flow from your mouth, carrying odor molecules with it, up the throat and into the nasal cavity. Instantly, you will experience a burst of flavor.

Notice that there are three bones neatly lined up in the nasal cavity, called the **turbinate bones.** (Think about how these bones would cause *turbulence* in the airstream, similar to rocks in a river.) Notice that they are positioned so that they force most of the air you breathe in to go down your throat. Thus only a little of the air will make its way up to the smell receptors at the top of the cavity.

As you can imagine, the hidden location of the smell receptors makes them difficult to study. (Incidentally, if the nasal cavity were a pinball machine, imagine how unlikely it would be for the ball to make it from the nostril up to the top! The ball would be much more likely to take one of the lower routes to the throat.) However, the air that does travel up to the top of the cavity has most of the dust cleaned away by the time it arrives.

At the top of the nasal cavity is the olfactory epithelium. The word "epithelium" (pronounced "epp-uh-*thee*-li-um") refers to skin. Therefore the **olfactory epithelium** is the kind of skin you smell with! The smell receptors are

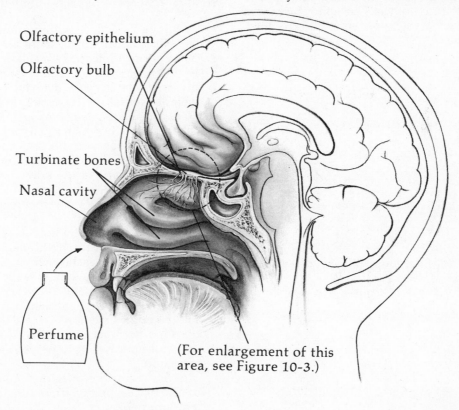

Olfactory epithelium

Olfactory bulb

Turbinate bones

Nasal cavity

Perfume

(For enlargement of this area, see Figure 10-3.)

Figure 10-2   The anatomy of the olfactory system.

contained in the olfactory epithelium. Just above the olfactory epithelium is the **olfactory bulb,** which performs the first processing on the signals from the smell receptors. Notice that I have drawn a dashed circle around this important area.

Figure 10-3 shows an enlargement of the area in the circle in Figure 10-2. Notice that there are tiny **cilia** (pronounced "*sill*-ee-uh"), or hairlike fringes. It is likely that the odor molecules make contact with these cilia (Brown, 1975b), so they are more important than they might look. Notice that the cilia are surrounded by **mucus,** the thick slimy secretion that you normally have in small quantities but you produce too abundantly when you have a cold.

The cilia are actually the tiny lower endings of the receptor cells. **Receptor cells** receive the information about smell and transmit it to higher levels. We humans have "only" about 5,000,000 receptor cells, in contrast to perhaps 100,000,000 receptor cells in some breeds of dogs. Notice that the upper ends of the receptor

cells meet up with new cells in the olfactory bulb. The olfactory bulb contains numerous fibers, which have many connections with each other (Gesteland, 1978). The nerve fibers travel from the olfactory bulb to many different places in the brain. One place these fibers travel to is a part of the cortex called the temporal lobe. The **temporal lobe** is located on the side of the cortex, near your temple. The exact pathways leading away from the olfactory bulb are not well understood at this time. You can read an article by Takagi (1978) for research on information processing in the nerve pathways.

To review briefly, the receptor cells have cilia that are surrounded by mucus. The receptor cells transmit information to nerves in the olfactory bulb. These nerves travel toward many locations in the brain, including the temporal lobe.

Summary: Sensory Aspects of Smell

- Although olfaction is important, particularly in lower animals, there are many aspects of this topic that are still mysterious.
- In order for substances to be smelled, they must be volatile and must have a molecular weight that falls within specified limits.
- Henning proposed a prism-shaped classification, in which smells are defined in terms of six basic odors.
- Amoore proposed a classification system in which the shape of the odor molecule determines the odor.
- Neither Henning's nor Amoore's system is perfectly satisfactory.
- The nasal cavity is the hollow space inside the nose, and the three turbinate bones are lined up in the nasal cavity.
- The olfactory epithelium is at the top of the nasal cavity, and the olfactory bulb lies above the olfactory epithelium.
- The receptor cells have cilia that are surrounded by mucus, and the receptor cells transmit information to nerves in the olfactory bulb.
- The nerves in the olfactory bulb travel to many places in the brain, including the temporal lobe.

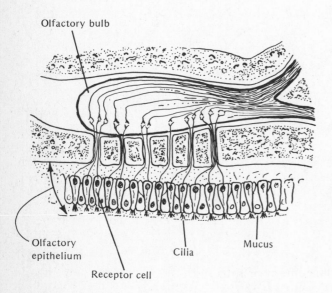

Figure 10-3   An enlargement of part of the olfactory system.

Olfactory Processes

In this section we will discuss three important aspects of smell. First of all, we will talk about thresholds for smell. Then we will examine adaptation and see how our sensitivity to various smells changes when we smell a particular odor for a long period of time. Finally, we will look at the ability to recognize smells.

Thresholds for Smell

As you may recall from the first chapter in this book, there are two kinds of thresholds. The **detection threshold** is a boundary point at which something is reported half of the time. In the case of smell, the detection threshold would be the concentration of a chemical for which a person says, "Yes, I smell it" half the time and "No, I don't smell it" half the time. For example, a person may be able to detect a chemical that has a concentration of 1.0 milligrams of the chemical per liter of air.

The **difference threshold,** or discrimination threshold, is the difference between two stimuli that a person can just barely tell apart. In the case of smell, the difference threshold would be the amount by which we would have to increase the concentration of a chemical in order for a person to tell us that the second concentration is stronger than the first. For example, a person may be able to tell the difference between a container of a substance that has a concentration of 1.0 milligrams per liter of air and a second container of the same substance that has a concentration of 1.2 milligrams per liter of air.

Both detection and difference thresholds are difficult to measure. Cain (1978a) discusses the various kinds of equipment that have been invented for presenting smells. Many have been based on the **olfactometer** (pronounced "ol-fack-*tom*-uh-ter"), or smell-measurer, that is shown in Figure 10-4. The bent ends of the tubes are inserted into the nostrils. The large tubes contain the odor stimulus that is being studied. Notice that a different odor could be presented to each nostril. The kind of equipment that is used has an enormous influence on the threshold (Cain, 1978b), so different researchers may report vastly different thresholds for the same chemical.

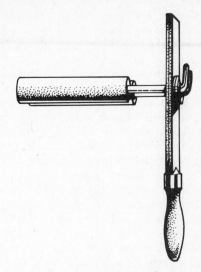

Figure 10-4   An early example of an olfactometer.

The situation is even more complicated because it is difficult to know just how much of a chemical substance actually reaches the smell receptors. Mozell (1971) points out that many molecules that enter the nose will be absorbed by the nose lining before they reach the receptors, and you already know that the turbinate bones effectively block many molecules from reaching the receptors. In fact, Mozell estimates that in a normal breath, approximately 2% of the odorous molecules entering the nose will reach the olfactory epithelium. (Remember that the olfactory epithelium is the layer of "smell skin" that contains the receptor cells.) The next time you smell a skunk, be thankful that only about 2% of those odor molecules are reaching your smell receptors!

Detection Thresholds

Humans are impressively sensitive to some odors. For example, one chemical that has a musky smell can be detected when less than .0000001 milligrams of the chemical is spread through one liter of air (Wenger, Jones, & Jones, 1956). A peanut weighs about one gram. Imagine dividing that peanut into ten billion parts, and taking one of those parts. That part still weighs more than the amount of the musky chemical that you can detect in a liter of air!

Naturally, we are not that sensitive to all smells. For example, we need at least 5 milligrams of ether per liter of air in order to detect that smell. We are also remarkably insensitive to the smell of some dangerous gases, such as carbon monoxide. Furthermore, humans are less sensitive to odors than are some animals. For example, dogs are about 100 times more sensitive than humans to some smells (Mozell, 1971). Therefore we use bloodhounds to track down villains, and we use pigs to sniff for gourmet truffles. In those situations, animal noses are superior to human noses.

There are many factors influencing thresholds. For one thing there are wide individual differences among people in their smell sensitivity. We are accustomed to the fact that people differ in their visual sensitivity. However, did you ever stop to think that people may differ in their sensitivity to odors? Try Demonstration 10-3 to illustrate some individual differences in smell sensitivity.

Cain (1978b) estimates that within any group of about 20 normal people, the threshold concentration typically varies over a range that is greater than 100 to 1. Thus the "best smeller" might detect .01 milligram of a substance per liter of air, and the "worst smeller" might require 1.0 milligrams per liter in order to detect it. Why do people differ so widely from one another? Cain suggests that people differ in the sizes of their nasal passages, and also in the wetness of these passages. Furthermore, there may be significant biological differences among individuals in their sensitivity to smells.

Did you notice any gender differences in Demonstration 10-3? Several studies have demonstrated that females are more sensitive to odors than males are. Koelega and Köster (1974), for example, obtained thresholds for many different chemicals. In most cases, females had lower thresholds. Furthermore, the gender differences were largest for odors that might be considered biologically meaningful. We will discuss this topic further in the last section of this chapter.

It is also possible that your sensitivity to smells is influenced by whether or not you are hungry. However, it is difficult to draw any firm conclusions about this research. Mozell (1971) has reviewed the research in this area and reports that people are sometimes more sensitive if they are hungry and sometimes more sensitive if they are full. It seems possible that people may differ in the extent to which hunger influences their threshold. Try to notice your own patterns. Can you smell donuts frying a block away when you are starved, yet find that you are insensitive to that smell after you have consumed a 12-inch pizza?

Let's review what you have learned about detection thresholds. Detection thresholds depend upon the equipment used to measure thresholds, the substance that is studied, and

---

Demonstration 10 -3

Individual Differences in Smell Sensitivity

For this demonstration you will need paper, tweezers, perfume or shaving lotion, and five containers. Cut a strip about 1 cm wide from the piece of paper. Cut this strip into pieces so that you have tiny pieces that are 1 cm, 2 cm, 3 cm, and 4 cm long. Take one container, fill it with water, and add one drop of perfume or shaving lotion. With the tweezers, dip each of the tiny pieces in the scented water, swirl it around, and place it in one of the four remaining containers. Place the containers in order, from strongest odor (longest piece of paper) to weakest odor (shortest piece). Ask four friends to sniff the containers, progressing from weakest to strongest, and identify which container contains the threshold concentration of the scent. See whether they differ substantially in their choices. (Incidentally, you may have to adjust the concentrations if your scent is too strong or too weak.) Save the containers so that you can use them again in Demonstration 10-5.

the species. There are enormous individual differences among people in their smell sensitivity. People differ in their response criteria, and there are also gender differences. Finally, hunger does not have a clear-cut influence on thresholds.

Difference Thresholds.   In the section on detection thresholds we saw that the nose can detect impressively tiny concentrations of certain substances. In contrast, our difference thresholds are probably not worth bragging about. For the vinegar smell of acetic acid, for example, the concentration of two samples must differ by about 26% in order to be detected (Mozell, 1971). For example, you should be able to tell the difference between 100 grams of vinegar and 126 grams of vinegar. This might sound reasonably sensitive until you compare the difference thresholds for smell with the difference thresholds for other senses. For example, when people are lifting weights, they can tell the difference between two weights if they differ by as little as 3% (Engen, 1971a). Thus you should be able to tell the difference when you lift a candy bar that weighs 100 grams and another candy bar that weighs 103 grams.

Some more recent evidence indicates that our difference thresholds may be somewhat better than researchers had previously believed. Cain (1977) used extremely refined procedures and found that the difference threshold was sometimes as small as 7%. Clearly, this is impressive. In fact, when humans can tell the difference between concentrations that differ by as little as 7%, they are rivaling the best performance of chromatographs, special equipment designed to measure gas concentrations. However, Cain obtained these outstanding discriminations from his subjects only by strictly controlling the odor stimuli. Thus the concentrations of the odors did not vary from moment to moment, as they had in previous studies.

Unfortunately, in real life, odor stimuli cannot be so carefully controlled. Our everyday difference thresholds are probably in the range of 20% to 30%.

When would difference thresholds be important in our everyday lives? When do people need to be able to notice the difference between two concentrations of odor? Sometimes, we use our olfactory skills to locate the source of an unpleasant smell. When you think about it, this unpleasant task resembles the children's game, "you're getting warmer." You wander around trying to locate the region in which the odor is stronger than it is elsewhere. To accomplish this, you must know whether a whiff is stronger or weaker than the previous whiff. Try Demonstration 10-4 to see how difference thresholds are important.

Furthermore, we talked about the importance of smell in eating, and you can probably think of occasions on which you can notice a difference in the strength of two odor samples. For example, there is an upstate New York specialty known as "Buffalo-style chicken wings." The pungent odor of vinegar is quite strong on the chicken wings that are cooked at the original restaurant that invented them. However, the concentration of vinegar on chicken wings prepared at another restaurant is noticeably lower. The difference between the two recipes clearly exceeds the difference threshold!

Do stronger sniffs make stronger smells? In other words, do people judge that a smell is stronger if they take a gigantic, deep breath, rather than a shallow, little sniff? A study by Teghtsoonian, Teghtsoonian, Berglund, and Berglund (1978) indicates that the answer is "no." They trained their subjects to breathe odors at two different "sniff vigors," one vigor being twice as strong as the other. Then the subjects sniffed various odors, using either strong or weak sniff vigor. Each time they made **magnitude estimations,** by supplying a

---

Demonstration 10 - 4

An Application of Difference Thresholds

Take a small piece of paper and dip it into a bottle of perfume or shaving lotion. Place it somewhere near the middle of your floor. Now close your eyes, get down on your hands and knees, and try to locate the piece of paper by noticing whether each whiff is stronger or weaker than the previous one.

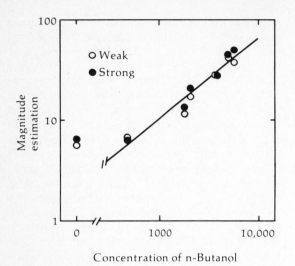

Figure 10-5   Magnitude estimation, as a function of odor concentration and sniff vigor.

number to correspond with the strength of the sensation.

Figure 10-5 shows the magnitude estimations for different concentrations of one of the odors. As you can see, people supply larger numbers for greater concentrations. Thus they can detect differences. What is more interesting, however, is that at each concentration, the estimates are almost identical for the weak and the strong sniff vigors. In fact, notice that the two dots are actually touching each other at six of the seven concentrations. Thus people supply equivalent judgments for a weak sniff and a sniff that is twice as strong, even though the stronger sniff presumably brings in twice as many molecules.

The authors propose that the results can be explained by what they call odor constancy. **Odor constancy** means that the perceived strength of an odor remains the same, despite variations in sniff vigor. Notice that odor constancy is therefore similar to the visual constancies. For example, remember size constancy, in which the size of an object remains the same, despite variations in distance. The authors suggest that information about the number of odor molecules is combined with information about sniff vigor. Thus the resulting perception of odor strength remains constant. Try Demonstration 10-5 to see if you can find evidence for odor constancy.

Adaptation

You have probably had this experience before. You walk into a room in which onions have been frying, and the odor is overpowering. If you stay in the room for several minutes, however, the smell seems fainter and fainter. After a while, you hardly notice any odor at all. You have experienced **adaptation,** which is the temporary loss of sensitivity as a result of continued stimulation (Beets, 1978). The power of adaptation is particularly impressive if you leave the room in which you have become adapted to an odor and then return to it. The odor is once again overwhelming. Try Demonstration 10-6 to illustrate the adaptation process.

Adaptation has both advantages and disadvantages in everyday life. If you are sitting in a room that is crowded with sweaty bodies, be thankful for adaptation! If you use well water that has a sulfurous bouquet, the smell will become less noticeable. Adaptation will also

---

Demonstration 10 - 5

Odor Constancy

Take the containers with the 2 cm, 3 cm, and 4 cm strips from Demonstration 10-3. Take a large sniff of the 2 cm container, so that you estimate that you are taking in about twice as much air as normal. Now take a normal sniff of each of the three containers. Try to identify which of the three has the same intensity as your first large sniff. If you have odor constancy, the 2 cm container should smell constant in its intensity, despite changes in sniff vigor. If you have no odor constancy, the 4 cm container may be your choice. If you have partial constancy, you may choose the 3 cm container.

Demonstration 10 - 6	Find a substance with a strong odor, such as an onion, nail polish remover, shaving lotion, or carbon paper. Place it near your nose as you read your book for the next 10 minutes. Notice how much fainter the odor seems after that time. Then remove the substance for the next 5 minutes, and then bring the substance back for a final whiff. At this point the odor should seem just about as strong as it did when you first smelled it.
Adaptation	

reduce the odor from a neighboring chemical plant. On the other hand, adaptation can also be undesirable. Perfumes seem to fade after a few minutes, and this property may be due to our noses as well as to the perfumes. A burning smell from an automobile may be unnoticeable after a short period of driving, when it really may be a warning sign for electrical problems. More dangerously, we may not notice a poisonous gas if we have adapted to the odor.

A knowledge of adaptation is also useful in planning a menu. You would not want to start out with a soup that smells strongly of garlic if you want people to notice the delicate hint of garlic in the chicken dish that follows. Speaking technically, adaptation leads to an increased threshold for a substance. That delicate hint of garlic would be below your guests' threshold, and they could not detect it.

Cain (1978b) points out that adaptation reduces our sensitivity to an odor, but it does not eliminate the sensitivity completely. We still smell *something*. On the average, the perceived magnitude of an odor decays at the rate of about 2.5% each second. After about a minute, adaptation is essentially complete. At this point, the perceived magnitude of an odor is about 30% of the initial magnitude. Thus the perceived magnitude certainly does not decrease to zero. Nonetheless, a 70% reduction is quite impressive.

What physiological explanations can account for this enormous reduction in sensitivity? The answer is not clear. One nice, intuitive answer might be that the receptors simply become tired after high levels of stimulation. Olfactory receptors probably play some part in adaptation, yet the greater part of adaption seems to occur at higher processing levels. It is likely that there are mechanisms for adaptation

located in the brain, but these have not yet been identified. Try repeating Demonstration 10-6, but plug your left nostril as completely as possible. After 2 minutes, quickly plug the right nostril and unplug the left nostril. You will find that the sensitivity in the left nostril is fairly low, even though the smell receptors in that nostril received only minimal stimulation when that nostril was plugged. Some mechanism must have "turned off" your sensitivity at a level more advanced than the receptors.

We have seen that adaptation is the temporary loss of sensitivity to an odor when that odor is presented for several minutes. However, sensitivity is often reduced, not only for that odor, but also for other related odors. This phenomenon is called cross-adaptation. **Cross-adaptation** means that exposure to one odor influences the threshold for other odors. Have you experienced cross-adaptation before? When someone has been frying onions, are you less sensitive to the odor of frying garlic? When you have been smelling one perfume at a cosmetics counter, do you then notice another perfume less? Does exposure to an acid in a chemistry lab reduce the odor of another acid?

A typical study concerning cross-adaptation was conducted by Engen (1963), who studied chemicals in the alcohol family. He first presented either an odorless liquid or an alcohol liquid. Then he presented a different alcohol liquid and measured people's thresholds. Engen found that the thresholds for these new alcohol liquids were much higher when the people had first smelled an alcohol liquid, rather than the odorless liquid. That is, exposure to one alcohol reduced their sensitivity to another alcohol.

Recall from the beginning of the chapter that many researchers have tried to devise some method of grouping similar odors together. Cross-adaptation should be a useful tool to identify odors that are similar to one another. After all, we can say that odors that show cross-adaptation to each other are similar. However, Beets (1978) reports that systematic, large-scale studies in this area are lacking. There are individual studies, however. For example, Engen found in his study that cross-adaptation was not related to the chemical structure of the alcohol liquids. Instead, it was related to their scaled psychological similarity.

Recognizing Smells

How good are humans at recognizing smells? The early studies in smell recognition were discouraging about our abilities. Sumner (1962), for example, presented various common odors to 200 people. Some odors, such as coffee, were identified correctly by most people. However, only 50% identified peppermint, and only 18% identified nutmeg. On the average, people correctly identified only 6 of the 12 odors. Try Demonstration 10-7 to see how well your friends perform.

However, as Moncrieff (1966) noted, practice can work wonders:

> A laboratory assistant with whom the author worked was so very poor at identifying smells when she started to work amongst them that some doubt was felt as to whether she could really smell at all. After a few months she was identifying smells exactly and instantaneously and affected to be frightfully bored at having to do such childishly simple work. With smells, practice makes perfect [p. 228].

Furthermore, James (1892) described an astounding blind deaf-mute who sorted laundry belonging to many people at an institution on the basis of the smell of the garments.

Desor and Beauchamp (1974) tested the effects of practice. First, they tested people who had no specific practice in identifying odors. Common, everyday odors, such as fried liver, popcorn, and motor oil, were presented to them. People were fairly accurate for smells such as coffee, paint, banana, and chocolate. However, fewer than 20% of them correctly identified smells such as cigar, cat feces, ham, and sawdust. Furthermore, people were less accurate on items that they rated as unfamiliar. It seemed that people made mistakes because they could not give the correct label, not because they confused the smells with other smells.

In the second part of Desor and Beauchamp's experiment, people were trained on 32 different odors. Each time they smelled a particular odor, the name was supplied if they did not spontaneously supply the correct name. They were trained extensively until they could identify all of the odors correctly on two successive trials. Five days later, they returned to the laboratory. Their performance was nearly perfect. Furthermore, these same people later learned to correctly identify 64 different odors. Thus when people have had practice, the recognition of smells is quite impressive.

The recognition of smells was further clarified by Cain (1979) in a study called "To know with the nose." His research led him to conclude that people have trouble identifying odors because of three factors. First of all, people have difficulty associating a particular odor

---

Demonstration 10 - 7

Recognizing Smells

For this demonstration you will need to locate about a dozen different odorous substances. Use your imagination to find them, but some suggestions would be the following: pencil shavings, a green leaf, mud, partly chewed gum, carbon paper, cinnamon, ground coffee, cheese, onion, and mustard. Take each of the substances and cover it with a sheet of paper. (If you can find opaque containers, they would be even better.) Invite several friends to see if they can identify the odors. See which odors are easiest and which are most difficult. Also notice whether your friends differ in their overall accuracy.

with its name. Second, it is often difficult to retrieve a name, even if the odor and the name have developed a strong association with each other. Probably some of your friends had this difficulty when they tried Demonstration 10-7, and you may well have had it too. You know you have smelled a particular odor hundreds of times before, but you simply cannot recall the name right now! The third factor that presents difficulty for the identification of odors is that odors may be confused with each other. This is typically true when pure laboratory chemicals are used, but it is not as important when everyday odors are presented.

There is one other odor that people can recognize very well: their own smell! Russell (1976) conducted an experiment with a setup that resembles those used in advertisements to demonstrate the superiority of some detergents. College students were asked not to wash themselves for 24 hours prior to the experiment, and then they wore a plain white T-shirt for the next 24 hours. The dirty T-shirts were then collected and placed in individual containers. Each person was presented with three containers. One held the person's own T-shirt, another held an unfamiliar female's T-shirt, and a third held an unfamiliar male's T-shirt. The results showed that 22 out of the 29 people correctly identified their own T-shirts! This accuracy was far more accurate than chance. Furthermore, in an additional test, 22 out of 29 correctly identified which of the two other T-shirts belonged to the male and which belonged to the female.

So far, we have discussed the ability to identify and name various odors. There is also another aspect to recognizing smells: How good are people at recognizing whether or not they have smelled a particular odor earlier in the session? Studies that examine this aspect of recognition do not require subjects to supply a label for the odor. For example, Engen, Kuisma, and Eimas (1973) presented one odor. Then, 3 to 30 seconds later, they presented a second odor. The subjects were required simply to say "yes" if the second odor was the same as the first, and "no" if it was not.

You are probably well aware that short-term memory for words decreases quickly as time passes. For example, you can hear someone's name and forget it 20 seconds later. However, Engen and his colleagues found that the ability

to recognize odors did not decrease as time passed. People were about 80% accurate if the second odor was presented 3 seconds after the first odor, and the accuracy remained at that level even if 30 seconds intervened between the two presentations. Even more impressive is Engen and Ross's (1973) finding that the percentage of smells recognized remained about the same *three months* after the original testing!

Summary: Olfactory Processes

- The detection threshold, which is the boundary point at which something is reported half of the time, and the difference threshold, which is the difference between two stimuli that can barely be discriminated, are difficult to measure for smell.
- Humans have extremely low detection thresholds for some substances.
- Factors influencing detection thresholds include kind of odor, type of equipment used for measurement, species, individual differences, criteria, and gender. Hunger does not have a clear-cut influence on thresholds.
- Difference thresholds are relatively large in everyday life; when measured with extremely refined procedures, however, the difference thresholds are smaller.
- Humans seem to show odor constancy; that is, the perceived strength of an odor remains the same, despite variations in sniff vigor.
- Adaptation is the temporary loss of sensitivity as the result of continued stimulation. Typically, there is a 70% reduction in sensitivity. The explanation for adaptation involves higher neural levels, in addition to the receptors.
- Cross-adaptation means that exposure to one odor influences the threshold for other, similar odors.
- Without practice, people are relatively poor at identifying odors. With practice, they do well.
- People have trouble identifying odors because of difficulty in associating an odor with a name, difficulty in retrieving a name, and confusion among odors.
- People recognize their own smells very ac-

curately, and they can distinguish male smells from female smells.

• People's ability to recognize whether or not they have smelled an odor remains at about the same level as time passes.

Applications of Research on Smell

There are three areas in which research in smell has particular importance: perfume manufacturing, pollution control, and communication among members of a species.

Perfume Manufacturing

Moskowitz (1978a) wrote a fascinating section on perfumery as part of a chapter in the *Handbook of Perception.* You should read those pages if you have more than a casual interest in perfumes.

There are a number of aspects involved in the development of a new fragrance, whether it is to be used as a perfume or as an additive to soaps, creams, or cosmetics. In the early stages the perfumer must consult the **fragrance library,** a room containing many small bottles of different fragrances at high concentrations. The library may have 30 to 50 chemicals that smell somewhat similar to each other but show subtle differences. Each of these fragrances is as chemically pure as possible. Furthermore, the contents of the bottles are replaced frequently, because many chemicals change their odors as they age. Natural fragrances, which constitute only about 5% of the fragrances used by perfumers, are particularly likely to change their odors as they age.

The perfumers gather together periodically to evaluate new chemicals that have recently been developed or synthesized. During these evaluation sessions a blotter is dipped into the chemical. The perfumers pay particular attention to three aspects of the fragrance. The **top note** is the first impact of the fragrance. Typically, the top note is light, perhaps involving a citrus smell like lemon or a green, leafy smell. If the chemical is pure, the top note is the only fragrance. However, if it is not pure, there will be a middle note and an end note. The **middle note** follows after the top note has disappeared; this is frequently a flower fragrance such as carnation or lilac. The **end note** is the fragrance that remains for a long period of time, after the top note and the middle note have evaporated. Thus the noticeable fragrance on the blotter changes substantially as time passes.

Perfume evaluators must have developed good memories, as you can imagine from the discussion in the last section. In fact, Jones (cited by Cain, 1979) tested two perfumers who could identify 100 and 200 different perfume fragrances. The perfumer must also be able to imagine how the particular fragrance would interact with other chemicals that might be added to create the perfume.

In the creation of a perfume the perfumers are inspired either by a natural product or by a synthetic product. They first make a basic mixture of four or five components. With the hundreds of fragrances in the fragrance library, literally a million different combinations would be possible. Thus perfumers must use educated guesses in order to find the right fragrances to combine. Once they find a mixture that brings out the smell to the best advantage, they experiment further to find an exact combination with the desired characteristics. The final result must have an appropriate top note, middle note, and end note.

If the product that is being developed is an expensive perfume, the process involves finding an appropriate name and selecting an appropriate container, both of which match the concept around which the perfume will be built. For example, a perfumer would not develop a romantic floral perfume, call it ''Isoeugenol,'' and package it in a modernistic bottle. Market researchers are responsible for the coordination of name, fragrance, and package.

Odor Pollution Control

Odor pollution means that unpleasant odors escape from a source and linger in the atmosphere (Moskowitz 1978a). Common sources of odor pollution include animal-rendering plants, paper mills, oil refineries, and numerous other industries (Cain, 1978b). I recall trying to fall asleep on summer nights in Staten Island with a perfumed handkerchief to mask the breezes from the New Jersey oil refineries. Now, in rural upstate New York, the warm spring winds sometimes carry fragrant odors from the dairy farm across the road. Think about some of the odor pollution you have experienced. Odor pollution can occur on a smaller scale within your home, as well as in a community.

Odor pollution is a serious problem, according to a summary provided by Moskowitz. Unpleasant odors can ruin a community's economic status and stifle its growth. Individual citizens suffer as well. They eat less and sleep less in a polluted environment. They also complain of headaches, nausea, and other discomforts.

How can psychologists study odor pollution? As you can imagine, it is not very easy to locate the offending odor, capture it, hustle it into the laboratory, and present it to the waiting subjects, using perhaps the method of constant stimuli. Some instruments have been devised for studying the odor on location. Lindvall and Svensson (cited by Moskowitz, 1978a), for example, use a bus with a special hood, and they drive to the location of an odor. At that location, observers match the odor in the air with other standard smells.

Odor pollution can also be studied by assessing citizens' attitudes. Moskowitz describes how surveys can be used to determine the severity of a pollution problem. For example, the survey might assess the kinds of actions that citizens have contemplated to protest the odor pollution, such as signing petitions and visiting officials. Some people assess citizens' attitudes by keeping a record of phone call complaints, but these records are less systematic than surveys.

How can odor pollution be controlled? Cain (1978b) discusses several kinds of procedures, such as burning the waste, adsorption with charcoal, and chemical conversion. Maugh (1975) also describes a new kind of chemical, called a malodor counteractant, that temporarily blocks the receptor site in the nose, so that the odor is less noticeable. However, this technique has not been fully developed.

One of the most common methods of trying to control odor pollution is odor mixture. In an **odor mixture,** two odors that do not cause a chemical reaction are presented at the same time. When you spray a room with an air freshener to get rid of the smell of boiled cabbage, you are actually making an odor mixture. Think about what happens when we make mixtures of visual or auditory stimuli. Remember, for example, that when we mix a yellow dye with a blue dye, we get a green dye—we can no longer sense the yellow and the blue components. When we mix several notes together in music, however, we usually *do* hear the individual components.

When we mix odors together, it is very difficult to predict just what the result will smell like. In some cases we find that the result is ideal for odor pollution control, because one smell masks another smell. In **masking,** one odor conceals an odor so completely that it cannot be detected. We hope that the air freshener will mask the cabbage odor, instead of the cabbage odor masking the air freshener!

More often, the two odors blend together. In a **blend**, the mixture resembles both of the components, and it is nearly impossible to separate the two parts. A blend of odors is therefore like the visual experience of a blend of colored dyes. On other occasions the two odors in some other mixtures can sometimes be perceived separately, like the mixture of notes in music. Finally, some mixtures of odors produce an interesting alternation of odors. You smell first one odor, and then the other. Try Demonstration 10-8 and see whether the mixtures produce masking, a blend, separate odors, or alternation.

So far, we have seen that the *quality* of the odor mixture is unpredictable. How about the *quantity,* or the intensity of the odor? When you add two odors together, how strong does the result smell? Cain and Drexler (1974) found that the mixture produced in their studies was always weaker than the sum of the odor intensities of the two components. The mixture was usually a compromise in intensity, so that it was in between the weaker and the stronger odor. Thus if you mix a strong air freshener odor with a weak cabbage odor, the intensity of the mixture should be intermediate.

We tend to think only of the negative side of unpleasant odors, and certainly most of the

---

Demonstration 10 - 8

Odor Mixtures

For this demonstration you will need to find some perfume or shaving lotion and, if possible, some air freshener. Then locate several odorous substances such as the ones used in Demonstration 10-7. Permeate the air with the perfume or shaving lotion and then stand different distances away from one of the odorous substances. Notice whether the distance influences how the mixture smells. Do you sometimes find a masking, sometimes a blend, and other times separate odors or alternation? Repeat this with other odorous substances. After the perfume or shaving lotion has faded, try the demonstration again with air freshener.

---

consequences of unpleasant odors are negative. However, there are some areas in which unpleasant odors are useful. For example, an unpleasant odor can be added to an odorless but poisonous gas so that gas leaks can easily be detected.

Smell and Communication

There is increasing evidence that smell has an important role in communication among the members of a species. Researchers are especially intrigued by substances called **pheromones** (pronounced "*fear*-uh-moans"), which act like chemical signals in communicating with other members of the same species. You will notice that the name "pheromones" looks like "hormones," which are chemicals used to send communications from one part of your body to another. Hormones are internal, though, and pheromones are external. These pheromones are excreted in the urine and by various sweat glands. The importance of pheromones to lower animals is well-established; the importance of pheromones to humans is still controversial.

Pheromones and Lower Animals

You are probably aware of the role of pheromones in the sexual behavior of lower animals, even if you have never seen the term "pheromones" before. For example, a female dog, horse, or cow releases pheromones when she is in heat. These odors attract the attentiveness and sexual interest of the male animals. Let's look at pheromones in two other species, the moth and the mouse.

The gypsy moth was originally brought to the United States in 1869 in order to produce silk; but unfortunately, some of the moths escaped. The caterpillar form of this moth eats about 0.1 square meter of leaf surface each day—that's an area larger than the front cover of this textbook. Since a female moth lays about 500 eggs each year, the invasion of gypsy moths can be devastating to any wooded area (Beroza & Knipling, 1972). Insecticides can be used, but they are expensive and dangerous to the environment.

Beroza and Knipling have explored the use of a sex attractant pheromone in controlling the population of gypsy moths. There is a chemical called disparlure that is highly specific to the gypsy moth. Beroza and Knipling describe how insect traps can be baited with this chemical. The chemical lures male gypsy moths inside, where they stick to the gummy surface. With the males cleverly trapped, they cannot breed with the females, and the population of moths declines. It sounds like science fiction, doesn't it? Nonetheless, Beroza and Knipling describe how an overall reduction in mating of about 98% should be achieved within one year of the trapping program.

We have seen that pheromones are important in attracting males during breeding. Pheromones have also been found to have an important role in pregnancy in some species. Research on mice has shown that if a strange male mouse is placed near the cage of a newly pregnant female, she is likely to abort the fetuses. Later in pregnancy, however, the odor of strange males has no effect (Parkes & Bruce, 1961).

Are There Pheromones in Humans?

If you have a lively imagination, you have probably been speculating whether there are pheromones as powerful for humans as for moths and mice. Researchers are in strong disagreement on this issue. Learned behavior is clearly extremely important in human sexual activity, but many researchers argue that pheromones operate in humans as well as in lower animals (e.g., Schneider, 1974). Cain (1978b) argues, for example, that if humans do not communicate via chemical secretions, then they are the exception to a very general rule. After all, other primates use odor secretions to mark their territories, assert their dominance, repel their rivals, and attract their mates. Cain speculates that humans' ability to describe their feelings verbally may have reduced the need to communicate with odors, but that odors may still be important.

As we discussed earlier in the chapter, males and females differ in their sensitivity to various odors. The sex differences are particularly striking for odors that have a sexual significance, such as steroid sex hormones. Some researchers have found that sex differences in detecting these sexually significant odors may not appear until adulthood. For example, Le Magnen (cited by Vierling & Rock, 1967) studied a chemical that smells very musky and is used as a fixative in perfumes. Sexually mature women perceived this odor very intensely. However, mature males, as well as immature females and immature males, barely noticed the odor. Furthermore, Vierling and Rock reported that women were more sensitive to the odor when they smelled it in the middle of their menstrual cycles, but the odor was very faint at the menstruation phase of their cycles. Thus it is clear that smell is related to sex, but these findings do not necessarily imply that smells influence our sexual functions and behavior.

One of the most striking demonstrations of the possibility of pheromone activity was demonstrated by a college student. Martha McClintock was a senior at Wellesley College when she examined the folk belief that if women live together, their menstrual cycles become similar (McClintock, 1971). She studied 135 women who lived in a dormitory and asked them to keep track of the dates on which their menstrual cycles began. She found at the beginning of the school year that close friends and roommates differed by 8 to 9 days in the date of the cycle onset. This difference decreased as the school year progressed. For example, by March their cycles began an average of 5 days apart. Some kind of chemical messages must be exchanged among women who see each other frequently, and these messages influence their menstrual cycles.

McClintock hinted that pheromones might be involved in the regulation of the menstrual cycle, but a study by Michael Russell and his colleagues (cited by Hassett, 1978) provided further evidence. In this study, a woman with regular menstrual cycles wore cotton pads under her arms every day. Then female volunteers rubbed these pads on their upper lips and left their faces unwashed for several hours. After 4 months of this treatment, the menstrual dates of the women were significantly closer to the menstrual date of the "donor" woman. Other women in a control group, who did not receive the odor treatment, did not show this change in their menstrual dates. We will be more confident about the role of odor in the regulation of menstrual periods when further studies have been conducted. Nonetheless, there are some intriguing early hints that people may communicate with one another through pheromones.

Hassett also summarizes the early stages of research that indicates that the frequency of human sexual intercourse may vary with the production of certain pheromones, but it is too early to draw conclusions about this topic. Incidentally, all of these studies on odor and sexuality suggest that when humans use deodorants in the underarm or genital regions, they may be upsetting some delicate pheromone communications (Comfort, 1971).

Summary: Applications of Research on Smell

- An important resource in the manufacturing of perfume is the fragrance library, which contains hundreds of chemicals that differ slightly from one another.
- Perfumes are evaluated in terms of their top note, middle note, and end note.

- Odor pollution has serious consequences for a community's status and for individuals' health.
- Odor pollution can be studied in the laboratory and on location. Surveys can assess the severity of a problem.
- One procedure for controlling odor pollution is odor mixture, in which one odor may mask another. However, it is difficult to predict what will happen in an odor mixture. Instead of masking, a mixture may produce a blend, separate odors, or alternation.
- The quantity of an odor mixture is less than the sum of the components, and the odor mixture generally has an intensity that is in between the weaker and the stronger odor.

- Pheromones are chemical signals that are important in communicating with others belonging to the same species. They are excreted in the urine and by the sweat glands.
- Pheromones can be used to trap male moths and control their population. The odor of strange males causes spontaneous abortion in a newly pregnant female mouse.
- There is a controversy about the importance of pheromones among humans.
- There are sex differences in sensitivity for sexually significant odors. These differences do not appear until sexual maturity.
- Pheromones released by underarm sweat glands may influence the onset of menstrual periods for a woman's close associates.

Review

1. Name five substances that have an odor and five that do not. What are two characteristics of odorous stimuli?

2. You smell an orange and a lemon, and they smell similar to each other. How would Henning's and Amoore's systems explain the similarities?

3. Move around the room until you locate something that has an odor. Trace the pathway that information about that odor will take from the moment it enters your nasal cavity.

4. In a laboratory at your college, a professor measures a student's threshold for a particular odor, and it is high. In a laboratory at another college, a different professor measures a different student's threshold for a second odor, and it is low. Identify five factors that might explain the different results.

5. What is odor constancy, and how might it be relevant in your everyday life?

6. What are adaptation and cross-adaptation, and how would they be important in pollution control?

7. Suppose that you have a friend who is teaching home economics in junior high school. What would you tell your friend about the recognition of odors that might be relevant in teaching cooking, and what suggestions would you make for improving recognition ability?

8. Point out the aspects of detection thresholds, difference thresholds, odor constancy, adaptation, cross-adaptation, and odor recognition that would be relevant for a perfumer.

9. Over vacation you cook a soup and serve it to company. Point out how each of the following might be important in the cooking or eating process: detection thresholds, difference thresholds, adaptation, cross-adaptation, odor recognition, and odor mixtures.

10. Summarize what you have learned about sex and smell, considering information about lower animals, about human sex differences, and about human sexuality.

New Terms

olfaction	cilia	cross-adaptation
chemical senses	mucus	fragrance library
volatile	receptor cells	top note
molecular weight	temporal lobe	middle note
stereochemical theory	detection threshold	end note
nasal	difference threshold	odor pollution
nasal cavity	olfactometer	odor mixture
turbinate bones	magnitude estimations	masking
olfactory epithelium	odor constancy	blend
olfactory bulb	adaptation	pheromones

chapter 11

TASTE

Outline   **Sensory Aspects of Taste**
The Stimulus
The Taste Receptors
The Relationship Between Taste and Tongue Regions
The Problem of Taste Coding
The Pathway from the Receptors to the Brain

Taste Processes
Thresholds
Adaptation
Cross-Adaptation and Cross-Enhancement

Applications of Taste Research
Food Tasting
Beverage Tasting

Preview

There are three sections in the chapter on taste: (1) sensory aspects of taste, (2) taste processes, and (3) applications of taste.

In the first section we emphasize that the term *taste* should really only be applied to the perceptions resulting from the stimulation of special receptors in the mouth, even though people typically use *taste* to include other perceptual experiences, such as smell and texture. Most psychologists agree that humans can taste four basic types: sweet, bitter, salty, and sour. In this section we will also discuss the anatomy of the taste system and the regions of the tongue and mouth that are sensitive to each of the four tastes.

In the section on taste processes we first consider three kinds of thresholds and the factors that can influence these thresholds, such as hunger, food color, and temperature. Then we discuss adaptation, a process in which your sensitivity to a taste decreases when you are continuously exposed to that taste. Exposure to a taste can also have an influence on your sensitivity to other substances. For example, after you drink lemon juice, plain water tastes sweet. We will also mention several taste modifiers, for example, a fruit that makes anything you eat later taste sweet.

Finally, we will consider applications of taste research. Food technologists working in taste-test laboratories use discrimination tests, affective tests, and descriptive tests to assess different foods. We will also talk about wine tasting and tea tasting in this section.

A cookbook describes a dish called *bisteeya*, which is

> the most sophisticated and elaborate Moroccan dish, a combination of incredibly tasty flavors representing the culmination of all the foreign influences that have found their synthesis in Moroccan culture. Bisteeya is a huge pie of the finest, thinnest, flakiest pastry in the world, filled with three layers—spicy pieces of pigeon or chicken, lemony eggs cooked in a savory onion sauce, and toasted and sweetened almonds—and then dusted on top with cinnamon and sugar [Wolfert, 1973, p. 2].

If you were to eat bisteeya, you would actually *taste* very little. **Taste** refers only to the perceptions that result from the contact of substances with the special receptors located in the mouth (Bartoshuk, 1971). When psychologists speak about taste, they mean only a very limited portion of the perceptions involved in the everyday usage of the word "taste"—only perceptions such as sweet and bitter.

Let us discuss the difference between taste and another characteristic that is often used to describe the taste experience, because the distinction is an important one. The word "flavor" is used to refer to the wide variety of perceptions we experience when we eat. **Flavor** includes smell, touch, pressure, pain, and so on, in addition to taste (McBurney, 1978). Thus the *taste* of bisteeya combines several taste qualities—the sour of the lemon, the sweet of the sugar, the bitter of the toasted almonds, and the salt of the chicken—though each of these qualities is quite mild.

However, the *flavor* of bisteeya includes additional richness and complexity. Among the smells are the buttery fragrance from the pastry, the strong overtones of onion and garlic, and the delicate hints of saffron and cinnamon. The flavor also involves the tactile qualities of food in the mouth, such as its temperature and its texture. The texture of bisteeya is richly varied, with the crisp flaky pastry, the hard nuggets of almonds, the chewy chicken, and the creamy eggs. (Although there are no painful qualities involved in the flavor of this dish, you are certainly familiar with this possibility if you have tasted the right dish of chili!)

James J. Gibson (1966) has described the variety of information that we can obtain about food, in addition to the information received about its taste and odor. For instance, we can register surface texture properties such as the slippery, rough, and smooth surfaces of butter, bread crust, and banana. When we chew, we can register a substance's consistency. We note the thickness of a substance—it may be thin broth or thick, rubbery gelatine. The consistency may also be elastic, soft, hard, or brittle. In addition, we can register the shape, size, weight, and granularity of a substance. Try Demonstration 11-1 to illustrate these characteristics. We will return to a discussion of these other dimensions of flavor at the end of the chapter, after we explore taste more thoroughly.

However, before we consider details on the

Demonstration 11 - 1

Texture Characteristics of Foods

Bring this textbook to your next meal, or else copy the list below. Judge everything you eat and drink by checking the appropriate choice in each category.

		Toast							
Surface texture	Slippery								
	Rough	✓							
	Smooth								
Substance thickness	Very thin								
	Thin	✓							
	Medium								
	Thick								
	Very thick								
Consistency	Elastic								
	Soft								
	Hard								
	Brittle	✓							

Foods and Beverages

taste system, think for a moment about how taste can be useful for both humans and animals. As Bartoshuk observes, some tastes seem to produce approach or avoidance in many different species. Things that taste sweet to humans are typically nutritious. Things that taste bitter to humans are often poisonous. Spoiled food can taste sour. Furthermore, Dethier (1977) suggests that sensitivity to salt may have evolved primarily to warn animals against too salty drinking water. Thus taste can be a helpful index that tells us whether to eat something or spit it out.

Let's now discuss sensory aspects of taste. After that, we will look at a number of different taste phenomena. In the last section of the chapter we will examine some applications of taste and flavor. One application, for example, is wine and tea tasting, which depend heavily upon visual qualities and smell as well as taste itself.

Sensory Aspects of Taste

In this section we will first discuss the stimulus for taste, paying particular attention to efforts to classify taste stimuli. Then we will examine the taste receptors. We will next investigate the relationship between taste and tongue regions and the problem of taste coding. Finally, we will briefly look at the pathway from the receptors to the brain.

The Stimulus

Nearly all substances that we taste are dissolved in saliva, which is a complicated kind of salt water. We typically cannot taste those substances that do not dissolve in saliva. When your tongue touches a clean drinking glass, there is no taste.

You may recall that an important issue in the last chapter concerned the classification of smell stimuli. Stimuli that we see can be described in terms of wavelength, and stimuli that we hear can be described in terms of frequency. However, as we discussed, the stimuli we smell seem to resist neat categories or measurement systems. Fortunately, the stimuli we taste are somewhat more cooperative than the smell stimuli. That is, there is some agreement about how taste stimuli can be classified. Although there is still some controversy, most psychologists maintain that we can taste four basic kinds of stimuli: sweet, bitter, salty, and sour.

The search for the basic categories for taste dates back into Greek history. For example, Aristotle proposed this list of basic categories: sweet, bitter, salty, sour, astringent, pungent, and harsh. Bartoshuk (1978) discusses the history of other kinds of classification systems. Hans Henning (1927) is generally credited with promoting the idea of four basic tastes. Remember that Henning proposed a six-sided prism to represent the six basic odors. Similarly, Henning proposed a **taste tetrahedron**, a four-sided figure with one of the basic tastes located at each of the four corners. Figure 11-1 illustrates Henning's taste tetrahedron.

Some recent researchers examined the issue of the number of basic categories by using a special statistical technique. This technique, called **multidimensional scaling**, involves asking people to judge the similarity of two tastes. The results of this analysis allow researchers to see whether there is any pattern in the way different substances taste. When Schiffman

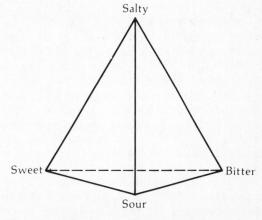

Figure 11-1 The taste tetrahedron proposed by Henning.

and Dackis (1975) performed this kind of analysis on reactions to the taste of vitamins and other nutrients, they found evidence for the traditional four tastes: sweet, bitter, salty, and sour. However, they also suggested that there were three other taste qualities that were not included in the basic four: alkaline, sulfurous, and fatty.

Other experts in taste perception disagree with the attempts to add additional tastes to the classic four. For example, McBurney and Gent (1979) state, "We argue that the four taste qualities together exhaust the qualities of taste experience" (p. 151). Some of the evidence that McBurney and Gent cite for their argument will be discussed later, such as the different taste that water has after adaptation to different substances, the influence of taste modifiers on taste perception, and the results of cross-adaptation studies. Elsewhere, McBurney (1978) has stressed that other suggested taste qualities, such as alkaline, are due to sensations from mechanisms other than the taste buds.

Although humans may have only four basic taste qualities, we should not assume that other animals are limited to four. Dethier (1978), for example, points out that insects seem to have taste systems that are quite different from human systems. The blowfly, for instance, has four kinds of taste receptors: sugar, water, and two different kinds of salt receptors.

Food substances are placed in the mouth and are broken down into constituent parts. It is the chemical properties of these parts that eventually allow us to taste the foods. How is the taste of a substance related to its chemical properties? We have some clues about the relationship, even though the issue is far from being completely understood (Beidler, 1978). Substances that produce a sour taste are all acids, such as vinegar and lemon juice. When saliva touches these acids, they release a special form of the hydrogen atom. A salty taste results from chemicals that belong to the salt category. Two examples are table salt, or sodium chloride, and salt substitute, or potassium chloride.

Sweet and bitter substances are more complicated than acids and salts (Beidler, 1978). Sweet substances are usually complex molecules that contain carbon atoms, such as sugar or saccharin. Sweet and bitter compounds are often closely related. For example, Beidler demonstrates that if NO_2 (nitrogen and oxygen) is added onto the sweet saccharin molecule, the result is a very bitter substance. Maybe you have tasted a drink that had so much saccharin that it was extremely bitter. If so, then you do not need chemical proof to convince you that sweet and bitter can be similar.

Remember that when you taste a food, it may contain several different tastes. The bisteeya mentioned at the beginning of the chapter has a mixture of sour, sweet, bitter, and salt. Similarly, we will see in the discussion of wine tasting later in the chapter that an ideal substance contains an appropriate balance of tastes. Specifically, wine tasters judge a wine in terms of the extent to which the sour, sweet, and bitter components are balanced, without a single taste's being dominant.

In this section we have seen that there is fair agreement regarding the existence of four basic tastes in humans. Furthermore, there is some relationship between the nature of these tastes and their chemical structure. Now let's examine the sensory system that processes information about taste.

The Taste Receptors

The basic receptor for taste stimuli is called the **taste bud**. Taste buds are visible only with a microscope. Located throughout the mouth, taste buds are also found inside your cheeks, on the roof of your mouth, and in your throat. However, most of the research and discussion focuses on the taste buds on the upper surface of the tongue.

The taste buds are located on little bumps on the tongue known as **papillae** (pronounced "paa-*pill*-ee"; one bump would be called a *papilla*). The papillae are small, but they are visible with the unaided eye, as Demonstration 11-2 shows. There are several different kinds of papillae, but the very tiny ones do not have any taste buds. Therefore we will only be concerned with the larger papillae that contain taste buds. Figure 11-2 shows an enlarged picture of a papilla. Note that the tiny taste buds are lined up in the pits on either side of the papilla. Thus the taste buds are *not* located on the actual tongue surface.

We can examine more closely the details of a single taste bud. Figure 11-3 shows an enlargement of one of the taste buds from Figure 11-2. Notice that it is rather pear-shaped. The taste bud contains several receptor cells that are arranged like the segments of an orange (Bartoshuk, 1971). The tips of the taste cells reach out into the opening. They can touch any taste molecules that are contained in the saliva that flows into the pit. The tips of the taste cells are called **microvilli** (pronounced "*my*-crow-*vil*-lie"), and the opening is called the **taste pore**.

Humans have about 10,000 taste buds (Bartoshuk, 1971). Other species differ widely; for example, chickens have only about 24 taste buds (Kare & Ficken, 1963), so a fine wine would be wasted on them. On the other hand, consider the catfish, which has more than 175,000 taste buds (Pfaffmann, 1978). Most of

these taste buds are found on the external body surface, so the catfish can "taste" the water it is swimming in without even opening its mouth.

As you are sitting here reading this book, your taste buds are dying away at a rapid rate. Beidler and Smallman (1965) demonstrated that the life span of the average cell in the taste bud is only about 10 days. Thus the cells in the taste bud that responded to the chocolate mousse you ate last night will be long gone by next month. Beidler and Smallman write such a depressing passage about the life of taste buds that you may be ready to go collecting door-to-door for the Taste Bud Relief Fund:

> the taste buds on the surface of the tongue are constantly assaulted by abrasion against the teeth and hard palate; by exposure to extremes of temperature; and by flooding the tongue with various solutions. This is particularly true in man who daily abrades his tongue by talking and chewing, and subjects the taste buds frequently to draughts of hot tobacco smoke, hot coffee or tea, ice-cold alcoholic drinks . . . [p. 263].

How do the taste buds renew themselves? It seems that the cells surrounding the taste bud move into the taste bud and migrate toward the center, replacing the dead cells (Beidler & Smallman, 1965).

The Relationship Between Taste and Tongue Regions

You can probably remember learning that different regions of the tongue are sensitive to different taste qualities. In fact, McBurney (1978) speculates that this concept is probably the most generally known fact about taste. Until recently, however, the only research evidence for this belief was the work of Hanig (1901).

A taste bud

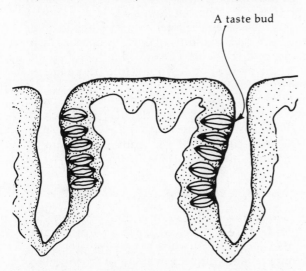

Figure 11-2 An enlargement of a papilla, containing many taste buds.

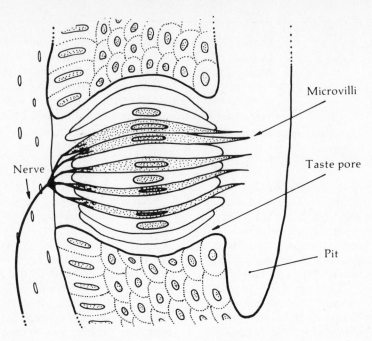

Figure 11-3   An enlargement of a taste bud.

In 1974, Collings conducted a careful study of the regions of the tongue and the **soft palate**, a region on the upper part of your mouth, just above the back of the tongue. Subjects in her study rinsed their mouths with distilled water and then extended their tongues. Collings dipped a tiny piece of filter paper into a solution and then placed it on the tongue or soft palate. There were four kinds of solutions: salty, sour, bitter, and sweet. The subjects then pointed to a card indicating the name of the taste quality—salty, sour, bitter, or sweet. They rinsed their mouths thoroughly and then tested another stimulus. By repeating this technique, Collings was able to determine thresholds for regions of the tongue and the palate.

She found that sour tastes were most noticeable on the sides on the tongue. Salty and sweet tastes were most noticeable on the front of the tongue. Bitter tastes turned out to be most noticeable on the soft palate. However, within the regions of the tongue alone, bitter tastes were most noticeable on the front of the tongue, *not* on the back of the tongue as is commonly believed. (Review this list for a minute and try to think of a system for memorizing it. Maybe you might remember sour lemons sitting on each side of your tongue, some bitter kind of medicine smeared on your soft palate, and a salt shaker and sugar bowl perched on the tip of your tongue.) Now try Demonstration 11-3 to see whether you find the same results.

How did the middle of your tongue react to the flavors in Demonstration 11-3? Actually, it should have been relatively insensitive to all of the flavors. The middle of the tongue lacks taste buds, and so it could be called a "blind spot." Like the blind spot on your retina, there are no receptors at this location.

Did the two sides of your tongue respond the same to the various flavors? Researchers have always assumed that the sides are similar, and Kroeze (1979) recently demonstrated their equivalence.

The Problem of Taste Coding

You may recall that color coding mechanisms include three kinds of color receptors and higher-level cells that use opponent processes. Unfortunately, our knowledge of taste coding is not nearly so detailed, and there are still many uncertainties.

Researchers in the area of taste once

Demonstration 1 1 - 3

Taste and Tongue Regions

For this demonstration you will need to assemble four kinds of substances: sour (vinegar or lemon), salty (salt), sweet (sugar), and bitter (unsweetened quinine water or unsweetened extra-strength coffee with caffeine). Dissolve the salt and the sugar in water (separately). Take a piece of absorbent white paper and cut it into 25 to 30 small squares. Divide the squares into four piles and place each pile in one of the substances.

It is best to use tweezers to place each square on your tongue; if you use your fingers, be careful to let drops of the solution drain off before proceeding. Place a drained square of one solution on each of these regions of the tongue and mark the location where the taste is most noticeable.

Region of the Tongue

	Front	Middle	Back	Left Side	Right Side	Palate
Sour						
Salty						
Sweet						
Bitter						

(Taste Quality)

searched for four different kinds of taste receptors, which might operate in the same way as the three kinds of color receptors. Some earlier researchers produced data that they felt could support the existence of four kinds of papillae, each sensitive to only one taste. However, more recent experiments contradicted those data; taste coding is not that simple.

Still, we know that there must be some relationship between the taste buds on the papillae and the code for taste. We need some explanation for the fact that there are regional differences on the tongue. There must be a reason, for example, why the taste buds at the tip of the tongue are particularly responsive to sweet stimuli. Currently, most researchers believe that each taste bud responds to at least one kind of taste. However, each taste bud responds *most vigorously* to only one taste. For example, Figure 11-4 shows the relative thresholds for a hypothetical taste bud that is particularly sensitive to a bitter taste. Notice that this taste bud (perhaps one located on your palate) is most sensitive to bitter tastes, least sensitive to sweet

tastes, and moderately sensitive to salty and sour tastes. Some other taste buds might have absolutely no sensitivity to a particular taste.

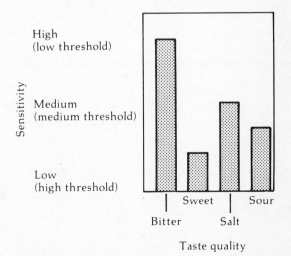

Figure 11-4 Sensitivities for a hypothetical taste bud that is sensitive to a bitter taste.

For example, a taste bud might be floating in vinegar and refuse to respond.

In summary, it seems that a taste bud does not restrict its responses to one single kind of stimulus. However, it probably responds *better* to one kind of stimulus than to any other kind. The higher levels of stimulus processing, beyond the receptor level, must somehow take into account the relative response rates in order to code tastes. However, the details of this process have not been established.

The Pathway from the Receptors to the Brain

When we discussed vision, we discussed in some detail the pathway from the receptors to the brain. Unfortunately, this kind of detail is simply impossible in a discussion of the pathway for taste. In fact, we know relatively little about what happens to information about taste once the information leaves the taste buds.

Figure 11-3 shows a nerve receiving information from the taste cell. The nerves in the mouth and the throat gather together into three separate bundles, one from the front of the tongue, one from the back of the tongue, and one from the throat. These three nerves travel from the mouth region to the base of the brain. From this location, information is transferred on to the cortex. Remember that the **cortex** is the outer part of the brain that is particularly important in human behavior. More details about recent research on the taste pathway to the brain are available in a review by Pfaffmann, Frank, and Norgren (1979). Further-

more, if you are interested in the neural mechanisms for the combination of information about smell and taste, read an article by Norgren (1977).

Summary: Sensory Aspects of Taste

- Taste refers only to perceptions resulting from substances in contact with special receptors in the mouth; flavor refers to the broader variety of perceptions associated with eating.
- Although there is some controversy, most psychologists believe that humans can taste four basic kinds of stimuli: sweet, bitter, salty, and sour.
- A sour taste is produced by acids, and a salty taste is produced by chemicals in the salt category; sweet and bitter tastes are more complicated and seem to be produced by chemically similar molecules.
- The taste receptors are called taste buds, which are located on some of the papillae of the tongue.
- Taste buds have a life span of about 10 days; they are constantly being replaced.
- Sour tastes are most noticeable on the sides of the tongue, bitter on the soft palate, and salty and sweet on the front of the tongue.
- Each taste bud responds to at least one kind of taste, but it responds most vigorously to only one taste.
- The nerves from the mouth and throat travel to the back of the brain and then on to the cortex.

Taste Processes

In this section we will first look at thresholds for taste and various factors that may have an influence on these thresholds. Then we will examine adaptation, which is the decrease in sensitivity that occurs when a stimulus is presented continuously. Finally, we will see how adaptation to one substance often influences the reaction to other substances.

Thresholds

A **detection threshold**, as we have discussed in

previous chapters, is the boundary point at which something is reported half of the time. For example, suppose that one gram of a particular substance is added to a liter of water, and you taste this solution. You might say "Yes, I taste it" half of the time and "No, I don't taste it" half of the time. We have already discussed one aspect of detection thresholds—the fact that detection thresholds vary across the different regions of the tongue. Thus a particular concentration of a solution may be just at your threshold on the side of your tongue, way above threshold on the tip of your tongue, and way below threshold in the middle of your tongue.

As you might expect, thresholds vary from one substance to another. Bitter quinine sulphate is very easy to detect in small quantities. In contrast, relatively large quantities of sweet glucose are necessary for detection. You can test your thresholds for table sugar by trying the demonstrations in Chapter 15.

McBurney (1978) notes that psychologists often make a distinction between the detection threshold and the recognition threshold. The detection threshold, as we said, is the boundary point or concentration of a solution at which something is reported half of the time. The **recognition threshold** is the concentration of a solution that can be recognized by quality. In other words, the recognition threshold specifies the amount of a substance that must be added to distilled water in order for tasters to recognize whether the taste is salty, bitter, sweet, or sour. As you can imagine, tasters require a relatively strong concentration of a substance in order to recognize that it is, for example, salty. Thus recognition thresholds are generally higher than detection thresholds.

As we have discussed before, the **difference threshold** is the difference between two stimuli that a person can just barely tell apart. Difference thresholds have not been thoroughly studied in the area of taste (McBurney, 1978). Psychologists have shown little interest in this area, perhaps because humans do not seem to make much use of intensity information when we taste.

The research that has been conducted, however, indicates that our difference thresholds are not very impressive. In general, the concentration of a substance must be increased by 15–25% in order for us to notice a difference in its taste. Thus if you have added five teaspoons of lemon juice to a sauce, you need to add about one more teaspoon in order to make it noticeably more sour. You may recall that our difference thresholds for smell are similarly unimpressive, about 20–30%.

In the remainder of this section on thresholds we will look at some factors that could influence thresholds: eating, smoking, color, temperature, and individual differences.

Do you think that your ability to taste might be influenced by whether you have just eaten a big meal? M. E. Moore, Linker, and Purcell (1965) studied taste sensitivity before and after eating, and they used a signal detection approach. (Remember that we discussed this method briefly in Chapter 1; there is a more complete discussion in Chapter 15.) People in this study were asked to taste a sugar solution in the morning and in the afternoon. Some people ate a noon meal in between the two sessions, and other people went without eating.

The researchers found that sensitivity was greater in the afternoon than in the morning. However, there was no difference in the sensitivity when the lunch and the no-lunch conditions were compared. Interestingly, though, the lunch and the no-lunch conditions did differ with respect to their criterion. People who had not eaten lunch showed a significantly greater bias toward reporting that they tasted sugar. In other words, the taste buds of hungry people are no more sensitive than the taste buds of well-fed people. However, hungry people are likely to say "I taste it" if they are uncertain whether a substance is present, whereas well-fed people are likely to say "I don't taste it" if they are uncertain. Their perceptual experiences are similar, but their reporting strategies differ.

It is commonly believed that smoking dulls the sense of taste. In fact, most researchers exclude smokers from their taste experiments. However, McBurney and Moskat (1975) noticed that previous research on the relationship between smoking and taste had been inconclusive. They conducted a total of four experiments in which they compared smokers and nonsmokers on their detection thresholds and their recognition thresholds. Their studies showed that there were no consistent differences between smokers and nonsmokers. For example, nonsmokers and heavy smokers— who smoked at least 15 cigarettes a day—were asked to judge whether a liquid was bitter, sour, salty, or sweet. The two groups did not differ significantly from each other on any of the four substances.

However, before you conclude that smokers experience the same *flavor* sensations as nonsmokers experience, remember that McBurney and Moskat studied only taste. Smokers and nonsmokers may indeed differ in their sensitivities to smells, textures, and other components of flavor. Furthermore, these researchers studied only college students. Older people who have been smoking for a longer period of time might be less sensitive to tastes.

The color of a substance can influence the accuracy of your taste discriminations. Maga (1974) examined how the four basic tastes can be influenced by adding food coloring. In general, taste thresholds were higher—and sensitivity was therefore lower—when color had been added. However, salty solutions were not influenced by color.

Perhaps you have noticed that temperature influences taste. A wine expert comments about the relationship between temperature and taste:

> while sugar can conceal and disguise certain faults in wine, its power to do so is limited. If you are evaluating a chilled white wine and the sugar is getting in the way of your taste, let the wine warm up to room temperature. The winemaker's errors will fairly leap out at you! [Kovi, 1980, p. 12]

Thus certain tastes that may be below threshold when you taste a chilled wine will be above threshold when the wine warms up.

Although most researchers agree that temperature does influence taste, they often disagree about the exact nature of this relationship. McBurney (1978) states that the majority of studies show that people are most sensitive to tastes when the substance is served at about room temperature or body temperature. Typical results are shown in Figure 11-5. Notice that sour substances are less affected by temperature than salty, sweet, or bitter substances. However, all of the curves show a maximum sensitivity (that is, a lowest threshold) at a point between 22° and 32° centigrade. Now try Demonstration 11-4 to see if you notice the same effect.

Think about the practical applications of the relationship between taste and temperature. Cookbooks frequently mention that the final seasoning of a dish must be performed when the food has reached the temperature at which it will be served. Suppose that you salted a soup when its temperature was about 25°C and then you heated it to 40°C. According to Figure 11-5, you would now be less sensitive to its saltiness—it might not taste salty enough. On the other hand, suppose that you were preparing a lemon pudding. If you adjusted the

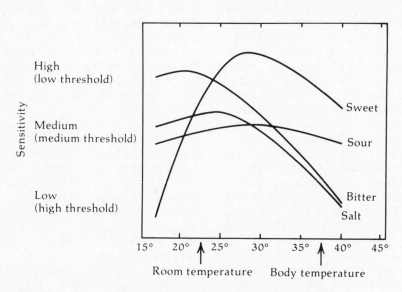

Figure 11-5   The relationship between temperature and taste.

Demonstration 11-4

Temperature and Taste

Take four small (4-ounce) glasses and place two pinches of sugar in each. Fill the first two with cold water from the tap. Stir until dissolved and add an ice cube to glass 1. Add lukewarm water to glass 3 and very hot water to glass 4. Now taste each of the four solutions. Do glass 2 and glass 3 contain the sweetest-tasting solutions?

---

amount of sugar and lemon so that it tasted just right when it was very hot, it would taste too sweet and too sour when it cooled down.

Several researchers have explored the area of individual differences in thresholds for certain substances. Remember that in the chapter on color vision we discussed the topic of color blindness (more properly called color deficiencies). Hall, Bartoshuk, Cain, and Stevens (1975) discussed a similar kind of phenomenon in taste, which they called taste blindness. There are certain substances that have a definite taste for many people, yet other people cannot taste them. These people who cannot taste a substance are called **nontasters** or **taste-blind**. One of the most commonly tested substances in taste blindness experiments is phenylthiocarbamide, abbreviated **PTC**. The ability to taste this bitter substance is genetically acquired, just like your eye color or your height.

Hall and her coauthors found that PTC-taste-blind people were not really taste-*blind*—they could taste PTC if the concentration was strong enough. However, they required concentrations about 300 times as strong as the concentrations that PTC-tasters required in order to taste the PTC. These researchers also found that PTC-taste-blind people were also much less sensitive to the bitter taste of caffeine than were PTC-tasters.

Adaptation

Remember that when a smell is presented continuously, your sensitivity to that smell decreases. **Adaptation**, or a decrease in sensitivity following the continuous presentation of a stimulus, also occurs for taste. In other words, when a specific substance is placed on your tongue, your threshold for that substance increases—you require a stronger concentration of the substance in order to taste it. The threshold reaches its maximum in about one minute. This relationship is illustrated in Figure 11-6. Notice that when the substance is re-

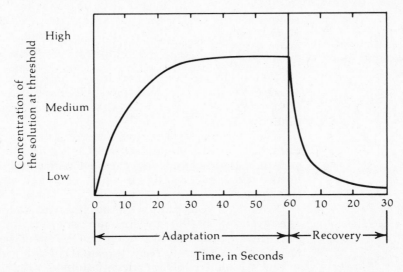

Figure 11-6   Adaptation to a specific taste.

moved, the threshold suddenly recovers to normal.

Try Demonstration 11-5 to see one example of the way adaptation works. When your tongue is adapted to the salt that is present in your own saliva, your threshold for salt is relatively high. However, when you rinse your mouth out with distilled water, your tongue becomes adapted to a salt-free environment. It is much more sensitive to salt, and so your threshold is relatively low.

Adaptation affects not only your thresholds; it also affects your judgments of intensity. When you make an **intensity judgment**, you taste a substance that is clearly above the threshold concentration, and you judge how strong it is. Lawless and Skinner (1979) asked people to make judgments about the sweet taste of sucrose. When the concentration of sucrose was strong, it took much more time for the intensity judgments to decrease. This makes sense, because these stronger solutions created higher peak intensities. Furthermore, the taste lasted longer when people sipped the solution than when the solution was poured on their tongues. The authors point out that when people sip a solution, they move their tongues. The tongue movement may prolong taste. Simi-

larly, you may have noticed that beverages taste different if they are sucked from a glass bottle than if they are sipped from a glass. It is possible that tongue movements may be responsible for delaying the adaption.

We may notice adaptation somewhat when we eat food in everyday life. However, adaptation is much more noticeable in the laboratory (Bartoshuk, 1971). In the laboratory the tongue is usually kept stable, and the taste stimulus is placed on a small area of the tongue. When you eat a salty cracker at lunch, however, your chewing movements and your tongue movements rotate the salty substance around so that it comes into contact with many different receptors. Thus a single receptor is unlikely to have prolonged, constant stimulation.

Cross-Adaptation and Cross-Enhancement

Cross-adaptation and cross-enhancement both refer to the effects that adaptation to one substance can have on the taste of another substance. **Cross-adaptation** means that adaptation to one substance *raises* the threshold for another substance; we will be less sensitive to the second substance. **Cross-enhancement**, which is just the opposite, means that adapta-

---

Demonstration 11 - 5

Adaptation to the Salt in Saliva

Take a quart jar, fill it with water, and add ½ teaspoon of salt. Stir the solution until the salt dissolves. Take four small glasses and fill the first glass with the solution. Fill the second glass ¾ full, the third glass ½ full, and the fourth ¼ full. Add water to these last three glasses until they are full, and mix the solutions thoroughly.

Take a sip of the solution in the fourth glass, swish it around in your mouth, and see whether you detect any trace of saltiness. If you do, mix up several glasses of increasingly diluted salty water.

If you do not taste saltiness in the fourth glass, test the third glass to see if you detect salt. Continue with the second and first glasses until you can just barely notice the salt. Record the number of the glass that contains a barely noticeable amount of salt.

Now rinse your mouth thoroughly with water. Use distilled water if possible, because tap water may be somewhat salty. Keep rinsing for about a minute. Repeat the threshold measurement process. Your threshold should now be lower, so that you detect lower concentrations of salt.

tion to one substance *lowers* the threshold for another substance; we will be more sensitive to the second substance. (You can remember which is which by remembering that adaptation is a decrease in sensitivity, whereas enhancement means an increase in sensitivity.)

Think of situations in which you have experienced cross-adaptation and cross-enhancement. For example, if you have been drinking tea with lemon, the vinegar marinade on the ribs will not taste so sour; you have experienced cross-adaptation. However, if you have been eating a sweet roll at breakfast, the orange juice tastes unpleasantly bitter; you have experienced cross-enhancement.

In general, cross-adaptation is specific to a particular taste quality (Bartoshuk, 1974). For example, if you are adapted to a sour taste, you will be less sensitive to other sour tastes. However, your sensitivity to salty, sweet, and bitter tastes will not be decreased, because these tastes represent different taste qualities. In fact, your sensitivity to these other substances may be increased, through cross-enhancement.

McBurney and Gent (1979) point out how the results on cross-adaptation support the theory that there are four basic taste qualities. Since there is little cross-adaptation that occurs across qualities, it seems likely that there must be separate receptor mechanisms for each of the taste qualities.

Kuznicki and McCutcheon (1979) have explored cross-enhancement, focusing on the influence of sweet tastes on later sour tastes. These authors asked subjects to stick out their tongues, and then a tiny drop of a substance was placed on an individual papilla that was sensitive to both sweet and sour. These careful techniques minimized the spread of the substance. First a drop of a sweet liquid was presented, followed 15 seconds later by a drop of a sour liquid. In the control condition a drop of water, rather than sweet liquid, was presented prior to the sour liquid. In each case, people used a magnitude estimation technique, supplying a number to indicate the intensity of the sour liquid. (The magnitude estimation technique is discussed in Chapter 15.) People judged the intensity of the sour solution to be greater when it had been preceded by a sweet taste than when it had been preceded by water.

Kuznicki and McCutcheon favor an explanation for cross-enhancement that involves chemical interactions that occur on the surface of the receptors.

Cross-adaptation and cross-enhancement are involved in several other taste processes. Two of these topics are the taste of water and taste modifiers.

Water Taste

What could be as tasteless as water? Actually, water can have a distinct taste when your tongue has been adapted to another taste; this phenomenon is called **water taste**. Try Demonstration 11-6 to show how water can acquire a specific taste that depends upon what you have previously eaten. In general, sour and bitter substances produce a sweet water taste, and sweet or salty substances produce a sour or bitter water taste. Incidentally, urea (a component of human urine) is one of the few substances that produce a salty water taste.

McBurney and Shick (1971) examined the water tastes of 26 different compounds. They wanted to determine whether there was some relationship between the taste of a compound and its water taste that was as clear-cut as the opponent-process relationship we saw for color vision in Chapter 4. Unfortunately, their data did not support an opponent-process view; many relationships were not complementary. However, this study provided interesting information about the *intensity* of the water taste. In general, the water taste was about one third as strong as the taste of the substance itself. For example, the intensity of a solution of salt water was judged to be about 32, and the intensity of the water tasted afterwards was judged to be about 12. Try to notice the nature and the intensity of various water tastes by drinking water with your meals. This amazing low-calorie beverage can assume many disguises!

Taste Modifiers

There are several special substances that change the flavor of other food by modifying the receptors on the tongue; these are called **taste modifiers**. The one that you are most likely to have tasted is monosodium glutamate, or MSG, which is frequently sold with spices in

---

Demonstration 11-6

Water Taste

There are three ways to produce a sweet water taste with an adaptation procedure. Try as many of these ways as possible.

1. Take a mouthful of diluted vinegar and swirl it around in your mouth for 30 to 40 seconds. Spit it out and then take a drink of plain water.

2. Repeat this procedure with strong coffee that contains caffeine (a teaspoon of instant coffee dissolved in a small amount of water works well).

3. Eat some artichokes (canned ones work well), making sure that they are thoroughly spread throughout your mouth. After swallowing them, sip some plain water.

There are two ways to produce a sour or bitter water taste.

1. Dissolve a teaspoon of salt in a small amount of water. Swirl it around in your mouth for 30 to 40 seconds, spit it out, and sip some plain water.

2. Repeat this procedure with sugar.

You may find it difficult to decide whether the water tastes produced by salt and sugar are sour or bitter, but the taste is definitely *not* salty, sweet, or neutral.

---

grocery stores under the trade name of Ac'cent. It is used extensively in Oriental cooking. Japanese researchers reported in the early part of this century that it was a component of seaweed. By itself, **MSG** has an unusual taste that seems to combine the four taste qualities; when added to other foods, however, the thresholds for sour and bitter tastes are reduced (Moskowitz, 1978b). In other words, if a Chinese hot-and-sour soup contains MSG, the chef will not need to add as much vinegar in order for the sour taste to be detected.

Another taste modifier is **gymnema sylvestre**, a climbing plant found in India and Africa. A British officer stationed in India first reported its effects in the Western literature after noticing that after chewing the leaves of the plant, he could not taste the sugar in his tea. Bartoshuk (1974) notes that after one tastes *gymnema sylvestre*, sugar crystals are indeed tasteless and feel like sand on the tongue.

A third substance, popularly called **miracle fruit**, changes the taste of sour substances. Africans have used miracle fruit to sweeten sour wines and beers (Bartoshuk, 1974). I once tasted miracle fruit, and the pure lemon juice I

drank afterwards tasted like the most delicious sweetened lemonade possible. The name "miracle fruit" is appropriate because a taste of this substance imparts a sweet taste to everything that is chewed for the next hour (G. J. Henning, Brouwer, Van der Wel, & Francke, 1969).

Bartoshuk (1974) has discussed some of the practical applications of these taste modifiers. Foods made from yeast and algae are extremely nutritious, but their taste is reported to be loathsome. Special diets that are designed for patients with particular diseases are similarly unappealing. In these cases it is often impossible or undesirable to use conventional flavorings. Thus it is possible that the taste of food can be controlled by temporarily altering the taste receptors. Furthermore, substances such as miracle fruit could be explored as alternatives to nonnutritive sweeteners such as cyclamates and saccharins, chemicals that may have undesirable side effects.

Summary: Taste Processes

- The detection threshold, which is the boundary point at which something is detected half of the time, depends upon the substance and the method of testing.

- The recognition threshold, which is the concentration of a solution that can be recognized by quality (e.g., salty), is generally higher than the detection threshold.
- People who have eaten a meal differ from people who have not eaten with respect to their criterion, but not in terms of their sensitivity to tastes.
- College-age smokers and nonsmokers do not differ in their taste detection thresholds or recognition thresholds.
- Color influences taste sensitivities for sweet, sour, and bitter substances.
- Temperature has complex influences on taste sensitivities.

- Some substances taste bitter to most people, yet have no taste for other people.
- Adaptation is a decrease in sensitivity when a stimulus is presented continuously; taste adaptation requires about one minute.
- Cross-adaptation occurs when adaptation to one substance raises the threshold of another substance; cross-enhancement occurs when adaptation to one substance lowers the threshold of another substance.
- Various substances can modify the taste of water.
- Three taste modifiers are MSG (which lowers the thresholds for sour and bitter tastes), *gymnema sylvestre* (which makes sugar tasteless), and miracle fruit (which makes sour substances taste sweet).

Applications of Taste Research

We have just seen that taste modifiers may have practical implications for food technology. In this section we will explore two other areas in which taste research has been applied to problems in the "real world." First, we will see how food technologists have developed systems of evaluating foods. Then we will look at beverage testing, examining wine tasting and tea tasting.

Food Tasting

As discussed at the beginning of the chapter, the phrase "food tasting" is really inaccurate, just as inaccurate as the phrase "wine tasting" that will be considered later in the chapter. In our culture we are accustomed to judging food in terms of its flavor, rather than its taste. As we said, flavor includes smell, touch, pressure, and pain, in addition to taste. In other cultures, visual and auditory components of food may be even more important than in the United States. For example, in Japanese cooking, the visual appearances of the food are particularly stressed (Steinberg, 1969). When Japanese food is served, colors, shapes, and textures are contrasted. Often the items on a plate are arranged in a special design. One dish, which is made for

the spring fish festival, consists of tuna, cucumber, radish, and lotus root—all arranged to suggest the flowers, rivers, trees, and mountains of Japan in springtime.

When you cook, you may consider how the dish will *look*, but have you ever considered how the dish will *sound*? Lang (1979) points out the auditory components of food in Chinese cooking:

Some foods are loved in China because they can be heard while you eat them, thus giving pleasure to another sense. (Eating crunchy jellyfish is a perfect example; in Western cuisine, celery perhaps comes close to it.) Chinese taste is much more complex than taste in the West; the cuisine includes texture foods which are frequently flavorless, and which must be combined with preparations having no other reason for existence than to lend flavor. The most perfect textural foods have no flavor, no fragrance, and, if possible, no color of their own. Shark's fin and bird's nest are perfect examples, of course, and other examples are fish maw, fish cheeks, and fish lips [p. 65].

At this point, you may be anxious to leave the exotic realms of Oriental food tasting and return to the more familiar limits of Western foods. The applied taste testing of foods is best described in a chapter written by Moskowitz (1978b) in the *Handbook of Perception*. Moskowitz describes the three principal classes of taste testing used today: discrimination tests, affective tests, and descriptive tests. He notes that more work has been done to develop testing procedures for the evaluation of food than for other applied research areas.

Discrimination tests involve determining whether two kinds of foods can be distinguished from one another. Discrimination tests are particularly useful when a product developer wants to substitute one kind of food for another. For example, would the consumer notice a flavor change if imitation vanilla were substituted for pure vanilla extract? Discrimination tests might be relevant if consumers have become accustomed to one product and the product developers want to introduce a variant product. After all, if the familiar product is quite different from the new product, consumers might believe that the new product has an off-flavor.

Discrimination tests are also used when a company wants to make certain that all the batches of a product are similar to each other. A company does not want one jar of applesauce to taste quite different from another jar. Typically, quality-control managers use panelists and discrimination tests to make sure that people cannot discriminate between the current batch being evaluated and a sample of the ideal product. For example, a panelist might sample two substances and report whether they taste similar or different.

Affective tests are used when the product developer wants to measure how much people like a new product. When a food is being developed, there is a long sequence of tests, from the tests in the laboratory to the taste testing in a supermarket, to trial testing in homes. Sometimes a simple "yes-no" affective scale is used. However, this scale produces less information than a scale with more categories, such as a commonly used nine-point scale.

Usually, panelists in the affective tests are provided with several varieties of a product, such as several different kinds of sausages. Sometimes the panelists also taste a reference sample, such as the best-selling product.

Descriptive tests require panelists to describe various qualities of a food product. Typically, the panelists have already been trained how to use a particular vocabulary, but they are also encouraged to develop their own additional terms. For example, panelists might describe the texture in terms of its hardness, brittleness, or chewiness. Several standardized sets of descriptive terms have been developed.

Moskowitz also describes the taste-test laboratories, which must be carefully constructed to control various factors. For example, the temperature of the room and of the food itself must be kept constant. Lighting is also important. Sometimes the testing booth is illuminated by a variety of different lights to simulate daylight, kitchen light, or supermarket lights. Other times the testing booth is illuminated with pure red lights, so that differences in surface colors are minimized. Under red lights, for example, pink, red, and brown meat would all look the same.

The taste-test laboratories must also be constructed so that odors other than those of the tested food are eliminated. As you can imagine, it would be difficult to try to judge chocolate pudding if smells of fresh paint, chlorine, or garlic were attacking your nostrils. Contact between the panelist and the experimenter must also be eliminated, so that the experimenter does not transmit any cues that could influence the panelist's judgments. Food can be passed through a small revolving door, for example. Finally, the time interval between tests must be regulated. With most foods a 30-second interval is sufficient, but spicy foods require a longer time lapse.

In summary, taste-test laboratories permit foods to be judged according to their similarity to other products, their pleasantness, and their descriptive characteristics. Ideally, testing conditions reduce the number of confounding variables that we encounter when we taste food in everyday life. As a consequence, when people taste food in a taste-test laboratory, the taste of the food is only minimally influenced by environmental factors, expectations, and other kinds of factors that have such a powerful impact on flavor in the real world.

Beverage Tasting

By now, you can probably guess that this section on beverage tasting involves much more than the stimulation of the taste buds. To show you how much we use our other senses to determine how something tastes, let's look more closely at wine tasting. If you have talked with a "wine pro," you know that other sensory qualities—in addition to taste—are involved in evaluating wines. As Meltzer (1980) describes wine tasting, the first step involves judging a wine's appearance. Thus a visual judgment comes first. The two important aspects of a wine's appearance are its clarity and color. Thus a wine should be clear and clean-looking. Any cloudiness or haze is a sign of a faulty fermentation process. H. Johnson (1971) describes 14 color terms that could be used to describe a wine's appearance, including brick-red, ruby, and *pelure d'oignon* (or onion skin). Our everyday color terms—such as red, pink, and yellow—seem dull by comparison!

The second step in wine tasting involves judging the odor of the wine. Meltzer notes that experienced tasters believe that the odor of the wine tells the taster practically everything about a wine's character. To smell a wine, the taster swirls it around in a glass to make the wine even more volatile. Then the taster takes a couple of deep sniffs. Some of the descriptive terms used to characterize a wine's odor include "foxy," "heady," "lively," "sappy," and "musty" (H. Johnson, 1971). Older wines are described in terms of their complex "bouquets."

Notice that wine tasters may generate a long list of adjectives before a single taste bud has been stimulated. The third step involves the actual tasting of the wine. The tasting confirms the impressions that have already been obtained by judging the wine's appearance and odor. Meltzer suggests that wine tasters should inhale a mouthful of air as they sip. They should next roll the wine around in their mouths. This step ensures that the wine comes into contact with all parts of the mouth and that the volatile odors reach the olfactory epithelium. Professional wine tasters spit out the wine, rather than swallowing it, because the back of the throat lacks a significant number of taste buds. Furthermore, a quantity of alcohol would reduce the accuracy of recall and perceptual judgments.

Wine tasters note three aspects of a wine's taste: sweetness, sourness, and bitterness. As Johnson remarks, all other words describing a wine's taste are actually derived from another sense. In a balanced wine the sweet, sour, and bitter tastes are in harmony with one another (Meltzer, 1980). For example, a wine that is too acid tastes tart, whereas a wine that has too little acidity tastes flat. Furthermore, a young red wine that has too much grape tannin will taste unpleasantly bitter.

The final step in wine tasting involves considering the wine's aftertaste. After the wine has been swallowed (or spit out), the wine taster determines how long the flavors remain. If the flavor is gone in less than six seconds, it is said to have a "short finish." A wine with a "good finish" has a crisp, lingering taste that remains more than six seconds. Furthermore, new flavors may appear after the wine is no longer in the mouth. The wine taster notes whether these flavors are pleasant or unpleasant. One important aspect of judging wines is determining whether the taste and the aftertaste meet the expectations that have been created by the initial judgments of the wine's odor.

We have seen that wine tasters consider visual and odor stimuli to be critical components in judging a wine. The actual taste of the wine is less important, as reflected by the short list of adjectives used to describe taste. Finally, judgments about aftertaste primarily concern the duration of the taste, rather than involving new categories of adjectives.

As you can see, wine tasting is a complicated process, one that involves much more than the taste buds. This process requires an evaluation of complex visual qualities. Wine tasting also relies strongly upon odor, and wine tasters take special precautions in order to enhance a wine's odor. Wine tasting also involves judgments about the relative contribution of the sweet, sour, and bitter tastes. Finally, it considers how the odor and taste components change with the passage of time.

Some human groups emphasize the importance of wine tasting. In some areas a whiskey taster would be held in higher esteem. Other beverages are awarded prestige in other cul-

Demonstration 11-7

Tea Tasting

This demonstration is an abridged version of the tea-tasting procedure used in tea research at the Tocklai Experimental Station, located in the Assam region of Northeast India (Das, 1981).

Select three different varieties or brands of tea. Place one teaspoon of each of the three kinds of dried tea leaves on a piece of white paper in front of you. Add another teaspoon of each kind of tea to three teapots or other containers. Heat fresh water to the boiling point and add one cup of water to each of the three containers. Allow the tea to brew for five minutes, and then pour each tea liquid into a separate cup. Place a sample of each of the three moist (infused) tea leaves on a plate. You are now ready to judge the dried leaves, the infused leaves, and the tea itself.

First, look at the dried leaves. Are the colors black, gray-black, or brown-black? A tea that is old will look spotted. Is each leaf well-rolled and tightly twisted, or is it open and flaky? Now smell the leaves. Place your nose near the leaves and breathe in. (In Assam a tea taster would bury his or her nose in the dry leaves in order to appreciate the full aroma.) The tea should not smell burnt or smoky. Finally, feel these leaves; they should not be spongy or damp.

Now judge the infused leaves. The perfect color for infused leaves is bright copper or red. Bright green, dull, or dark leaves indicate inferior teas or damage during processing. All leaves should be approximately the same size. Smell the infused leaves while they are still fairly hot. There should be a delicate aroma; fruity, burnt, smoky, and sour odors indicate faulty treatment during manufacturing.

Finally, judge the tea liquid. Suck in a quantity of liquid and air. According to A. K. Das, Tea Taster, the liquid should be tasted with as much noise as will ensure the sucking of the tea well up onto the palate. Roll the liquid on your palate and allow the air you sucked in to pass out slowly through your nose. (Notice that this process ensures that the aroma reaches your olfactory epithelium.) Observe whether the tea is brisk, as opposed to flat. For example, fresh spring water is brisk, whereas cold boiled water is flat. Now notice the color of the liquid. Is it pale and light or strongly colored? Allow the liquid to cool and notice whether there is a precipitate at the bottom of the cup. The presence or absence of a precipitate is not related to the quality of the tea. However, if a precipitate *is* formed, it should be bright, rather than dull or muddy.

As you can see, tea tasting—like wine tasting—involves far more than taste. Smell is critical in judging the dried leaf, the infused leaf, and the liquid. You also made visual judgments about the shape and size of the leaves, as well as many assessments of color. Finally, you touched the dried leaves. In fact, judgments about taste itself involve only a relatively small portion of the tea-tasting procedure.

tures. For example, in a region of India called Assam, the tea taster is highly revered. Demonstration 11-7 is a simplified version of some of the components of tea tasting in Assam.

Summary: Applications of Taste Research

- In other cultures, visual and auditory components of food may be even more important than in the United States.
- Discrimination tests involve determining whether two kinds of foods can be distinguished from one another; they are important for determining whether ingredients can be substituted and whether batches of a product are similar to each other.
- Affective tests measure food preferences; descriptive tests measure food qualities, such as hardness and chewiness.
- Taste-test laboratories must be carefully constructed to eliminate other variables.
- Beverage tasting involves judgments about the beverage's appearance, odor, and taste.

Review

1. Distinguish between *taste* and *flavor*. What are some representative terms that might be used to describe taste and flavor?

2. Describe the four basic taste qualities that humans perceive. Where is each of these qualities most noticeable in the mouth?

3. What is a possible mechanism whereby smoking could influence taste sensitivities, and what are the current findings about smoking and thresholds (at least for college-age subjects)?

4. A friend tells you that her high school biology teacher said that there were four different kinds of taste receptors, each sensitive to only one taste quality. How would you respond to this statement?

5. List three kinds of thresholds discussed in this chapter and provide information about taste in relation to these thresholds.

6. You have put too much sugar in a salad dressing. How would your dinner guests' ability to detect the sugar be influenced by each of these factors: (a) You serve the salad after the main course, rather than with the meal. (b) You add yellow food coloring to the dressing. (c) You chill the salad.

7. You have just had a cup of the cafeteria's coffee, and it tastes appallingly bitter. Your friend, however, doesn't notice any bitterness. What factor may be responsible for your different reactions?

8. Describe adaptation in the laboratory and contrast it with adaptation in everyday life.

9. Discuss the three kinds of taste modifiers and note whether each one causes cross-adaptation or cross-enhancement.

10. Imagine that you are a food technologist associated with a company that manufactures your favorite commercially prepared food. Discuss the discrimination tests, affective tests, and descriptive tests that might be used for this particular food and what kinds of questions could be addressed in these tests.

New Terms

taste	detection threshold	cross-enhancement
flavor	recognition threshold	water taste
taste tetrahedron	difference threshold	taste modifiers
multidimensional scaling	nontasters	MSG
taste bud	taste-blind	gymnema sylvestre
papillae	PTC	miracle fruit
microvilli	adaptation	discrimination tests
taste pore	intensity judgment	affective tests
soft palate	cross-adaptation	descriptive tests
cortex		

chapter 12

ATTENTION

Outline   **Selective Attention**
Features of the Unattended Message
Divided Attention
Reading and Attention

Theories of Attention
Bottleneck Theories
Data-Limited and Resource-Limited Processes

Search
The Nature of the Material
Practice
Application: Reading X-Rays

Viewing Pictures
Informativeness
Familiarity
Instructions

Preview

Attention is the focusing or concentration of mental activity. This chapter contains four sections: (1) selective attention, (2) theories of attention, (3) search, and (4) viewing pictures.

In selective attention you pay attention to one activity and therefore notice very little about other activities. For example, you may be so intent on watching a baseball game on television that you ignore the ringing telephone. People notice some features of the unattended message, but they ignore many other important features. It is often difficult to divide attention between two tasks, but practice can improve performance. We will also see in this section that attention is relevant in reading.

Many different theories of attention have been proposed in recent years. One theory, which has several variations, proposes that there is a bottleneck, or biologically based restriction on the amount of information to which we can attend. Another theory proposes instead that we have a limited amount of mental effort to devote to tasks.

Search involves looking for a specific target that is relatively hard to find. Many factors influence search speed, such as the similarity between the target and the background items. On some kinds of tasks, people who have practiced for a long time can search for ten targets as quickly as they can search for one target. An application of this area of research is a radiologist's search for abnormalities in an X-ray.

In viewing pictures we move our eyes so that the fovea registers the part of the picture that we want to examine. Picture viewing differs in several ways from reading, a topic we examined in earlier chapters. The pattern of picture viewing depends upon the informativeness of different parts of the picture, familiarity, and instructions.

Attention is a word with many, varied meanings. Let's consider some of these meanings by seeing the variety of ways in which attention can operate in a real-life setting. Imagine, for instance, that you are at a crowded party. One component of attention that is particularly noticeable in crowded settings is **selective attention**, in which a person receives several messages at once and tries to "pay attention" to only one of them. You experience selective attention when you are at a party and there are several simultaneous conversations. You ignore all of the other conversations, concentrating on only one.

When you first arrived at the party, you certainly engaged in another kind of attention activity, search. In search, a person hunts among a set of signals for one particular kind of signal. You probably searched the room for a familiar face or for one particular person you expected to meet at the party.

Perhaps you find yourself looking at a picture on the wall at some point during the party. When we view pictures, we reveal another aspect of attention, because we look at some parts of the picture more than others.

In this chapter we will discuss selective attention and theories of attention, as well as search and viewing pictures. There are several other aspects of attention that are beyond the scope of this chapter: vigilance, mental concentration, and activation. **Vigilance** refers to situations in which nothing much is happening, but a person pays attention in the hope of detecting something whenever it does happen. You are using vigilance when you wait for the red light to light up on the coffeepot, indicating that the coffee is ready. **Mental concentration** means that a person concentrates on a particular mental task and tries to exclude all other interfering stimuli. I hope you are using mental concentration as you read this sentence! **Activation** means that a person gets ready to deal with whatever happens next. When your fifth grade teacher told you to "pay attention," she or he was referring to the activation component of attention. Moray (1969) discusses these three kinds of attention in more detail.

Attention is the focusing or concentration of mental activity. Attention means that we perceive or notice certain stimuli but ignore others.

As we will see in this chapter, there is evidence that humans may have limited capacities for attention. That is, we cannot pay attention to everything at once. In this chapter we will see that attention can involve both the visual and auditory modes. The first section, on selective attention, concentrates primarily on the auditory mode and examines what happens when we hear more than one message at the same time. The sections on search and picture viewing concentrate on the visual mode and examine how we direct our visual attention when we hunt for specific targets or examine the parts of a picture.

Selective Attention

Selective attention is a phenomenon in which we concentrate our mental activity on one activity and notice very little about other activities. Selective attention has its advantages and disadvantages. An advantage is that we can concentrate on one kind of activity, without interference from other activities. Imagine how complicated life would be if you lacked this ability to focus and you were simultaneously aware of everything that was registered by your senses—all the sights, sounds, tactile sensations, odors, and tastes.

On the other hand, there are disadvantages. You may wish at times that you could study for an exam, eat pizza, carry on a conversation, and listen to music—all at the same time. Unfortunately, however, if you are studying for an exam, you may be able to eat pizza or listen to music, but you probably cannot carry on a conversation. Thus the selectivity of attention can be frustrating; attention to one activity means neglecting another activity. Incidentally, we discussed a similar situation in Chapter 5 when we examined ambiguous figure-ground relationships. Remember the impossibility of attending to both the vase and the faces simultaneously in Figure 5-9.

Selective attention is a topic that has intrigued researchers for the last 30 years. One of the most common issues in selective attention concerns the unattended stimulus. If two messages are presented and a person pays attention to only one of them, what features of the other message are noticed?

Features of the Unattended Message

Perhaps you have had this experience. You have been concentrating on the music from a radio while a friend has been talking to you. Suddenly, you realize that you haven't noticed much about the conversation. Your attention was focused on the music, and most of the features of the conversation were ignored.

One popular way to study selective attention is the shadowing technique. The **shadowing technique** requires a person to listen to a series of words and to repeat the words after the speaker. The name "shadow" is appropriate, because the listener must follow the speaker as closely as a shadow. The shadowing task is particularly difficult if the words are presented quickly; this task effectively captures the listener's attention. In many studies, one message is presented to one ear, and the listener must shadow that message while a second, different message is presented to the other ear. This kind of task, with two messages presented at the same time, is called **dichotic listening** (pronounced "die-*cot*-ick"). If the listener is struggling to shadow the first message, how much of the second message will he or she notice? The answer, as we will see, is "very little."

Cherry (1953) performed one of the classic

studies using the shadowing technique. Cherry recorded the same speaker reading two different messages. People wore earphones that presented a different message to each ear, and they were instructed to shadow one of the messages. Cherry found that people recalled very little of the unattended message. In fact, Cherry changed the message in the unattended ear to German words, and people reported that they assumed that the unattended message was in English. Their attention was so focused upon the material to be shadowed that they were even unaware of the switch to a different language!

In other studies, Cherry found that people were usually able to detect when the voice reading the unattended message was switched from a male to a female. However when the unattended message was played backwards (so that a message like *He goes home* became *moh zoge eeh*), only a few people noticed that there was anything unusual about the reversed speech. In summary, Cherry's study showed that the gender of the speaker (or more likely, the pitch of the speaker's voice) may be noticed in the unattended message, but people do not notice whether it is English, German, or gibberish.

One exception to the general rule about people noticing very little about the unattended message occurs when this message includes their own name. Moray (1959) asked people to shadow a passage of light fiction. The unattended ear sometimes received messages such as "All right, you may stop now" and sometimes received messages in which the listener's name appeared, for example, "John Smith, you may stop now." People were more likely to obey the instructions in the unattended ear if these were preceded by their own names. They rarely stopped for the "All right, you may stop now" instructions, but they stopped about a third of the time for the "John Smith, you may stop now" instructions.

In everyday situations you probably notice your own name even more often than one third of the time. You may be talking with one person, successfully ignoring the many other conversations within your hearing range. If your name is mentioned, however, you suddenly attend to that previously unattended conversation. In everyday situations we can probably switch more readily. After all, we are not shadowing the words of the person with whom we are conversing, and so it is easier to monitor other conversations.

So far, it seems that people notice very little about the message in the unattended ear. However, there is evidence that people can occasionally acquire some **semantic** information—that is, information about meaning—from the unattended message. Try Demonstration 12-1 to illustrate this point.

Did you switch your attention to the message you were supposed to ignore, in order to continue the meaningful sequence in the passage? Demonstration 12-1 is a visual variation on experiments in which subjects initially shadowed a meaningful passage (for example, Treisman, 1960). Suddenly, however, the message in that ear switched to a series of unrelated words. However, at that same time, the meaningful passage continued in the other ear. Some of the people began to shadow the message in the "wrong" ear. These people must have acquired some information about the meaning of the "wrong" message, or else they would not have known to switch their attention.

A study by Mackay (1973) further illustrates that people can acquire semantic information from the unattended message. As Figure 12-1

Demonstration 12-1

Acquiring Semantic Information from Unattended Messages

Read the following passage, paying attention only to the *italicized* words; ignore the words that appear in normal print.

Once upon a general *time there lived a* principle *most noble* system *and intelligent princess* processes *who longed* resource *to travel* performance *around the entire* experiment *world and* paper *to climb the highest* mountains *and to swim* data *the* widest oceans *interactions.*

"They threw stones toward
the bank yesterday."

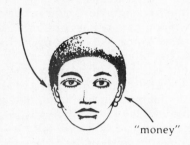

"money"

a. This subject chooses as an equivalent
   sentence, "They threw stones toward the
   savings and loan association yesterday."

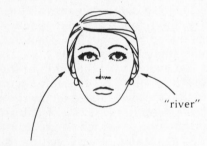

"river"

"They threw stones toward
the bank yesterday."

b. This subject chooses as an equivalent
   sentence, "They threw stones toward the
   side of the river yesterday."

Figure 12-1   Setup for the Mackay (1973) study.

illustrates, people listened to ambiguous sentences. For example, "They threw stones toward the bank yesterday" could refer either to a river bank or a bank where money is kept. During each ambiguous sentence the unattended ear received an important message. For the stone-throwing sentence, Mackay presented either the word "river" or the word "money" at the same time as the word "bank" entered the attended ear. People were then asked whether the sentence meant "They threw stones toward the side of the river yesterday" or "They threw stones toward the savings and loan association yesterday." They showed some tendency to

interpret the sentence so that it was consistent with the word presented in the "unattended" message.

Treisman, Squire, and Green (1974) emphasize that the effect of the unattended message was small in the Mackay study. In some conditions, for example, there was only a 4% shift in the interpretation of the attended sentence. These authors discuss other studies concerning the semantic processing of unattended messages. They conclude that it is difficult to find conclusive evidence for the notion that people understand the meaning of the unattended message. Klatzky (1980) speculates that people may analyze the message in the unattended ear if the shadowing task is not challenging enough. If they are not busy enough echoing the words in the attended ear, they can spare some attention for the unattended ear. Consequently, they may sometimes notice features of the unattended message that are relatively subtle, such as meaning.

In summary, we have seen that people do *not* notice the following characteristics of the unattended message: (1) whether it is in English or a foreign language and (2) whether it is normal English or the same sounds played backwards. However, they *do* notice, at least some of the time, (1) the gender of the speaker, (2) whether their own name is mentioned, and—if the task is not too challenging—(3) semantic characteristics of the message.

Divided Attention

So far, our discussion of attention has created a rather gloomy picture of human ability. When we pay attention to one event, we notice very little about another event. We have seen that when we pay very close attention to one conversation, we will not learn much about another conversation. In many cases, then, it is difficult to divide our attention so that two activities are performed accurately. Sometimes it is difficult to divide our attention because of physical limitations. For example, you cannot play the piano and eat a taco simultaneously with your right hand. It is even very difficult to play the piano with your right hand and hit a golf ball with your left hand.

Nonetheless, it is clear that you frequently divide your attention in everyday experiences.

Right now, for example, you may be listening to music as you read this sentence. You can walk and talk at the same time. In fact, several years ago a popular insult was that someone was so stupid that he or she couldn't walk and chew gum at the same time. Easy tasks can be done while walking, but more difficult tasks cannot. When you are walking with a friend, ask your friend to multiply 5 times 9. The friend will probably keep walking at the same rate. Then ask your friend to multiply 23 times 17 and watch the walking slow to a halt!

Let's first examine a study that demonstrates the difficulty of dividing attention between two activities; this study was conducted by Neisser and Becklen (1975). Neisser (pronounced "nicer") is one of the major figures in cognitive psychology. The subjects in this study watched a television screen that simultaneously showed two games. As Figure 12-2 shows, one game was a hand game that you probably played in elementary school. Subjects were told to press a switch with their right hands whenever one of the players successfully slapped the other's hands. The other game was a ball game, in which three men moved around and threw the ball to one another. Subjects were told to press a second switch with their left hands whenever the ball was bounced or thrown from one player to another.

Neisser and Becklen found that people had little difficulty following one game at a time, even though another game was superimposed. However, when they were required to monitor both games at the same time, their performance deteriorated drastically. In fact, when Neisser and Becklen recorded the number of times that subjects should have pressed the switch but failed to do so, this error rate was eight times as high when two games were monitored as when one game was monitored. Neisser and Becklen propose that it is difficult to follow two events at once for several reasons. Perhaps the most important reason is that event perception is so organized that when we follow one structured flow of information, we cannot follow a second, unrelated flow of information.

Can people learn to do two complicated activities at the same time? Spelke, Hirst, and Neisser (1976) trained two college students for an hour a day for a whole semester. These students read stories to themselves while the ex-

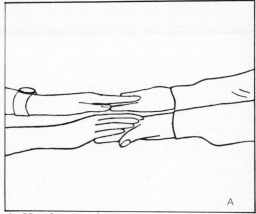

A. Hand game alone

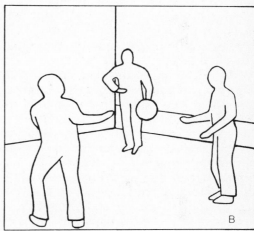

B. Ball game alone

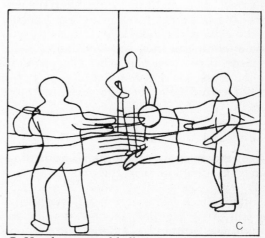

C. Hand game and ball game combined

Figure 12-2 Outline tracings of images in Neisser and Becklen's (1975) study.

perimenter dictated words to them to copy. At first, this task was very difficult. Imagine how slowly you would read this paragraph if you were simultaneously copying irrelevant words! However, after six weeks, reading speed and comprehension returned to normal. By the end of the semester the students were even able to categorize the dictated word (for example, write FURNITURE when they heard the word CHAIR) without any deterioration in their reading performance.

With practice, then, people can divide their attention with remarkable accuracy. Another study (Shaffer, 1975) showed similar results. In this study, a skilled typist was able to recite nursery rhymes while typing at a high speed from a visually presented text. Notice that with some kinds of tasks, well-practiced people seem to be able to pay attention to more than one task at a time.

At the beginning of the chapter you were asked to imagine yourself listening to a conversation at a crowded party. Let's see how the aspects of attention that we have discussed so far are relevant in that setting. We noted that you would probably pay attention to only one of the ongoing conversations, ignoring the surrounding chatter. You would notice very little about the other conversations, perhaps only the gender of the speaker and whether they mentioned your name. Perhaps you might try to divide your attention between two conversations. If so, you might find yourself in the embarrassing position of failing to respond to a question raised by people who thought you were attending to their conversation. A well-practiced party-goer might be able to follow two or more conversations successfully, but most of us find that our attention is much more limited.

Reading and Attention

One of the most important applications of research on attention is in the area of reading skills. The relationship between practice and attention, which we just discussed, is especially relevant. An influential paper on attention and reading was written by LaBerge and Samuels (1974). So far in this book we have discussed eye movements in reading (Chapter 3) and shape perception in reading (Chapter 5). LaBerge and Samuels emphasize another important component of reading: attention. These authors argue that reading is one of the most complex skills that adults have acquired. However, the fluent reader takes only a fraction of a second to read a word. LaBerge and Samuels point out that if each of the components involved in reading required attention, then performance of the complex reading skill would be impossible. After all, the capacity of attention would then be exceeded. However, if enough of the components can be processed automatically, then the burden on attention would be within the acceptable limits. Consequently, the skill can be performed successfully.

LaBerge and Samuels explore how processing becomes automatic for the components involved in reading. When an activity is **automatic**, that means that the activity can be completed while attention is directed toward another activity. For example, typing was probably an automatic process for the skilled typist in Shaffer's study. One of the activities involved in reading is the coding of features into letters, as we saw in Chapter 5. When children first learn to read, they must devote attention to this coding process. As they become more skilled, however, attention does not need to be activated. In other words, the features can be processed into a letter code automatically. For example, suppose that you look at the unfamiliar Greek letter γ. Your attention will be switched to the features. However, after that letter becomes familiar, the Greek letter γ can be seen as a unit, and it no longer requires attention for its separate features.

LaBerge and Samuels point out that it is a slow learning process for five-year-olds to achieve automatic recognition of the 26 letters of the alphabet. Each letter must be exposed frequently before recognition is automatic. At first, then, attention is focused upon coding features into letters. During this phase there is no attention available for other components of reading. After letter recognition becomes automatic, then attention is no longer necessary. Now attention can be directed toward other skills involved in reading, such as combining letters. (For a recent critique of LaBerge and

Samuels's model, consult an article by Paap and Ogden, 1981.)

Attention is also important in another component of reading: reading comprehension. In particular, researchers in educational psychology have wondered whether reading comprehension can be increased when questions are asked about the material. Wittrock and Lumsdaine (1977) review this literature. One common finding concerns **prequestions**, or questions that are asked before students read the material.

In general, students show increased learning and memory for the specific information addressed by the prequestions. However, they typically show reduced learning and memory for the rest of the information in the text. For example, suppose that I had inserted one prequestion at the beginning of this section of reading and attention, and suppose that this prequestion was "What is the influence of prequestions on learning and memory?" It is likely that you would remember this material on prequestions quite accurately. Unfortunately, however, you might be more likely to forget LaBerge and Samuels's work on automatic processes and attention, because no prequestion directed your attention to that work.

Wittrock and Lumsdaine conclude that prequestions work by focusing attention upon the material emphasized by the prequestions. As a result, students pay less attention to the rest of the material. This research demonstrates once more the potential limits of attention. Just as a listener ignores one message while shadowing another message, a reader ignores some material while concentrating on other material.

Summary: Selective Attention

- There are many different meanings of the word attention, but a general definition is that attention is the focusing or concentration of mental activity.
- In selective attention we concentrate our mental activity on one task and therefore notice little about other tasks.
- When people shadow one message, they do not notice whether the unattended message is in English or a foreign language or whether it is normal English or nonsense; however, they sometimes notice the gender of the speaker, whether their own name is mentioned, and some semantic features of the message.
- When attention is divided between two tasks, performance may suffer.
- With practice, people can divide attention with remarkable accuracy.
- As people practice reading, some of the components become automatic, and attention can be directed toward other aspects of reading.
- Prequestions, which are questions that are asked before students read the material, lead to increased recall for the specific information in the prequestions but reduced recall for other information.

Theories of Attention

We have seen that, in many cases, humans have limited capacities. Although we can sometimes combine tasks, it is obvious that we cannot pay attention to everything at once. Sights, sounds, pressures and pains, smells and tastes are flooding our senses, and yet we notice relatively little at any given moment. Somehow the information is lost. In order to explain these limitations, psychologists have devised a variety of theories of attention. We will consider two kinds of theories, bottleneck theories and Norman and Bobrow's (1975) model.

Bottleneck Theories

Several theories of attention involves a bottleneck. Think about what happens when you try to pour water from a bottle that has a narrow neck. Some of the water escapes through the opening immediately, but the rest of the water must "wait in line" in order to pass through the narrow opening. Some theorists have proposed that there is a similar bottleneck when humans process information. We cannot process all of the information at once because we have a biologically based bottleneck. Some information flows through the bottleneck, but other information is left behind. Bottles of water are ultimately emptied, but for human information processors, the information keeps on flowing. Consequently, the information that is left behind is forgotten before we can ever respond to it.

Bottleneck theories differ from one another in terms of the location of the bottleneck. Broadbent (1958), one of the earliest researchers in the field of attention, proposed that the bottleneck is located early in the processing of information, just after the information has been recorded by the sense organs. Figure 12-3 illustrates this early-bottleneck theory. Thus if a person hears the word "apple" in the attended ear, this word will pass through the bottleneck. The word "pencil," which was presented in the unattended ear, will be stopped at the bottleneck. This bottleneck occurs very early in the system, even before pattern recognition. However, there are problems with Broadbent's model. For example, it cannot account for people noticing their own name when it is spoken in the unattended ear.

Treisman (1964) presented a modification of Broadbent's early-bottleneck theory. According to her **attenuation model**, the message from the unattended ear is attenuated, or reduced, rather than being blocked completely. Still, enough of the message comes through for it to be partially analyzed. Consequently, some features of the unattended message will be noticed.

Other theorists propose that the bottleneck occurs much later in the processing of information. Deutsch and Deutsch (1963), for example, suggested that all of the information is fully processed, and the bottleneck occurs just before the person responds. As Figure 12-4 shows, pattern recognition occurs for all stimuli. The bottleneck in fact reflects the notion that our memory is limited. We choose to remember some things and to forget others. Consequently, we choose to report the message of the attended ear and to forget the message of the unattended ear.

In summary, the bottleneck theories of attention propose that there is a fixed limit on our ability to process stimuli. According to early-bottleneck theories, that fixed limit occurs prior to pattern recognition. According to late-bottleneck theories, that fixed limit occurs after pattern recognition but before the person responds.

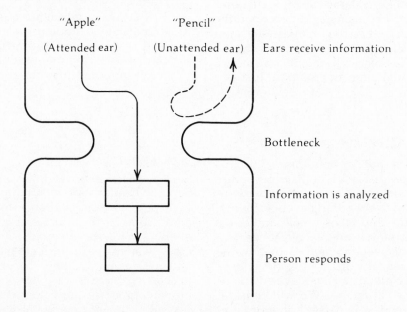

Figure 12-3   An example of an early-bottleneck model (schematic).

Data-Limited and Resource-Limited Processes

Norman and Bobrow (1975) have suggested a different approach to the limits of attention. According to their theory, there is no bottleneck to block information at a particular point in information processing. Instead, attention is limited because we have a limited amount of mental effort to spend on a task. Norman and Bobrow use the term **resources** to refer to such things as (1) the amount of effort involved in processing, (2) various kinds of memory, and (3) communication channels. They argue that resources are always limited. Several tasks may demand part of the same, limited resources. Consequently, the resources must be divided among the competing tasks. To some extent, then, performance depends upon the amount of resources that the task receives.

Norman and Bobrow describe a task as being a **resource-limited task** if performance on that task can be improved by providing it with more resources. In contrast, a **data-limited task** is one in which performance is not limited by the amount of available resources. Instead, performance is limited by the quality of the stimulus or by our limited memory capacities. Even if all the available resources are assigned to a data-limited task, performance would be poor. Try Demonstration 12-2 to clarify the difference between resource-limited tasks and data-limited tasks.

How does Norman and Bobrow's theory relate to the effects of practice on performance, which we discussed earlier in the chapter? Practice would probably have little or no effect on data-limited tasks. No matter how much you practice trying to hear a pin drop against a background of loud music, your performance would not improve much. However, practice *would* have an effect on resource-limited tasks. When people practice a particular task—for example, when the students learned to read passages and write words at the same time—performance becomes more automatic. The tasks require a smaller portion of the resources. Consequently, both tasks can be performed efficiently and accurately. If you practice enough, maybe you can manage to study, eat pizza, carry on a conversation, and listen to music!

Summary: Theories of Attention

• Some theories of attention propose a bottleneck, or biologically based restriction on the amount of information to which we can attend.

• Broadbent proposes an early bottleneck,

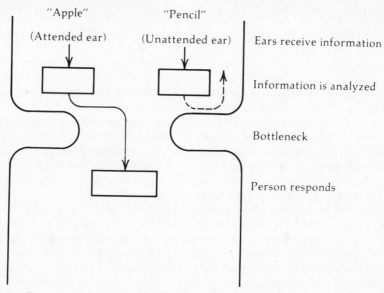

Figure 12-4   An example of a late-bottleneck model (schematic).

Demonstration 12-2

Resource-Limited Tasks and
Data-Limited Tasks

A.   First, try a resource-limited task. Try solving the follow-ing arithmetic problems while reciting "The Pledge of Al-legiance."

$$387 \qquad 486$$
$$\times 892 \qquad \times 295$$

Your performance on that arithmetic task could be improved by providing more resources to the task—by stopping the recitation.

B.   Now turn your radio up to full volume and place your ear as close to it as you can tolerate. Drop a paperclip or some other small object on the floor and see if you can hear when it reaches the floor. Notice that your performance on this hear-ing task could not be improved by paying closer attention to the task. Instead, performance is limited by the poor quality of the stimulus—the faint noise of the paperclip. This is a data-limited task.

immediately after the information has been recorded by the sense organs.

- Other variations of bottleneck models in-clude either a reduction—rather than a blocking—of the message from the unat-tended ear or a fixed limit later in the sys-tem, after pattern recognition.
- Norman and Bobrow suggest that there is no bottleneck at a specific point in informa-tion processing; instead, we have a limited amount of mental effort, or resources, to devote to tasks.

- According to Norman and Bobrow, a task is a resource-limited task if performance could be improved by providing it with more resources (for example, requiring less effort for other competing tasks); a task is a data-limited task if performance is limited by the quality of the stimulus or our limited memory capacities.
- According to Norman and Bobrow, practice helps resource-limited tasks but not data-limited tasks.

Search

So far, we have examined situations in which two or more simultaneous messages confront our auditory systems. In vision, too, we can pay attention to some material and ig-nore other material. However, our visual sys-tems have an additional feature that permits selectivity; we can move our eyes so that certain selected stimuli are registered on our sensitive fovea and other stimuli are ignored. Thus we move our eyes in search of the desired target, and we move our eyes across a picture so that some parts of the picture receive more fo-veal attention than other parts. In this section

and the next section we will explore visual attention.

Look back through the earlier pages of this chapter to find a reference to the study by Neis-ser and Becklen (1975). Now think about how you conducted that search. Did you reread the chapter, word for word, until you finally reached that study? It is more likely that your eyes skimmed the pages quickly. You probably ignored most of the other material in your single-minded search for Neisser and Becklen. In fact, Neisser (1964) demonstrated that ir-relevant words in a search are not examined closely enough to be recalled later. When his subjects were tested after searching through a list of words, they usually did not distinguish the words that had appeared on the list from the words that did not.

Think about the numerous occasions in everyday life in which you conduct searches. You arrive at a party and your eyes rapidly inspect the scene for a friend who said he would be there. You look at a menu, searching for the chicken enchilada you know you want. You look at a list on a bulletin board to find your own name and the grade you received in a course. You inspect another list to see if a course for next semester is still being offered.

We use the word "search" quite frequently in English. What does the word mean, and how are search tasks different from the other tasks related to visual attention? In **search**, people look for a specific target or targets that are relatively hard to find (Kahneman, 1973). Thus we could not say that you search a forest to locate all its trees, though you might search a haystack for a needle.

What region of the eye is used in conducting search tasks? Mackworth (1976) uses the phrase **useful field of view** to describe that area around the fixation point from which information can be processed. Information in regions outside of the useful field of view will not be stored in memory and will not be responded to during a given visual task.

Mackworth discovered that the size of this useful field of view is not constant. Instead, it is determined by the density of irrelevant items. If the irrelevant items are closely packed together, we scrutinize a very narrow region; if the irrelevant items are spread out, we scrutinize a wider region. Mackworth gives an example to make his findings more concrete. If you were looking for a needle in a haystack, your useful field of view would be very narrow—at any given moment you would examine only a tiny section. However, if you were looking for a needle on a billiard table, your useful field of view would be much wider—you could examine large sections without difficulty.

We saw that psychologists interested in auditory attention are primarily concerned with what people notice about the irrelevant message and whether they can combine two or more tasks. Psychologists interested in search are primarily concerned with the way in which performance is influenced by the nature of the material, that is, the characteristics of the relevant target and the irrelevant background. Practice, a topic we examined in connection with auditory attention, is another important topic in the investigation of search patterns.

The Nature of the Material

Try Demonstration 12-3, a variation of a classic study by Neisser (1964). First of all, did it seem to you as if you identified each letter to determine if it was an N? Neisser's subjects reported that the irrelevant letters often were only a blur or were simply not seen. Thus irrelevant stimuli are ignored in search tasks just as they are ignored in auditory attention tasks. The "blur" of irrelevant letters should have been especially true for you on list A, which contained letters with rounded shapes. Neisser found that search times were much faster for lists in which the irrelevant letters were very different in shape from the target. Thus similarity between the target and the background items is an important determinant of how quickly we can search.

Eriksen and Schultz (1979) examined some other physical characteristics that influence search speed. They found that a target could be located more easily if it had greater figure-ground contrast than the other items. It was also easier to locate if it was larger in size than the other items. Textbooks, such as the one you are now reading, take advantage of these two principles. Notice that new terms appear in boldfaced print, making them easier to find. Look back for the word "search" and notice how it is easy to locate. Then look for the word "forest," which is in regular print. It is relatively hard to find. Also, the headings in the chapters are larger than the other words. Thus you can readily find the section on SELECTIVE ATTENTION. Boldness of print and print size should help you learn material, and they should also be useful when you search for a specific topic.

Which is a better cue for visual search, shape or color? Rayner (1978) summarizes a number of studies that favor color as a cue. For example,

---

Demonstration 12-3

*Search Times as a Function of
Type of Irrelevant Letters*

A. Search the following strings of letters for the target letter
N. Measure the number of seconds that the task requires.

```
O S Q C O
Q S O C Q
S Q C S O
C Q S C O
S Q O Q C
O O S Q C
C S O C Q
Q S O N C
S Q Q S S
O C Q S Q
```

B. Search the following strings of letters for the target letter
N. Again measure the number of seconds that the task requires.

```
M W Z K W
W M K W M
K W Z W M
M Z K M W
Z K W M K
M W Z K W
K M K Z W
Z K W K Z
M Z N M Z
Z K W Z M
```

---

people searched for a target dial in an arrangement of 16 dials. Search speeds were faster if the dials differed in color than if they differed in shape. Rayner points out that these results make sense, given that visual acuity is relatively poor in our peripheral vision. Thus it is relatively difficult to identify a shape that is not registered on your fovea. However, peripheral vision can detect color somewhat more readily. We use the information from our peripheral vision to guide our next eye movements. If you are searching for a yellow target, a yellow blur in the periphery will alert your eye to move the fovea toward that area. If you are searching for a square, however, a square in the periphery may not be noticed. You may already have been aware of the importance of color in search. When you look for your car in a crowded parking lot, do you look for its color or its shape?

Egeth, Marcus, and Bevan (1972) note that another factor that determines search speed is the extent to which the targets form a natural set. Try Demonstration 12-4 to illustrate this point. Digits that are next to each other, such as 1, 2, and 3, form a natural set. They are easier to search for than members of an unnatural set, such as 1, 4, and 7. This study suggests a practical tip. If you must search for a large number of items, divide the targets into several natural sets rather than into arbitrary groups.

Try Demonstration 12-5 before you read the next sentence. These tasks both point out the importance of context in search. For example, Healy (1976) instructed subjects to circle instances of the letter *t* in a long passage. People were especially likely to overlook the *t*'s in the word *the*. Exercise A in Demonstration 12-5 has 36 *t*'s, of which 8 appear in the word *the*. Were most of your omissions on the word *the*? Healy suggests that high-frequency words such as *the* are searched in terms of units larger than individual letters.

Demonstration 12-4

*Searching for Natural Sets
and Unnatural Sets*

A.   Search the following items and circle every 1, 2, and 3 that you see. Measure the number of seconds it takes you to complete the task.

6064199
8461358
9846137
5159534
7967306
2795458
6583162
5179532
5904580
1576980
3679681
4863095
8289439

B.   Now search the following items and circle every 1, 4, and 7 that you see. Again measure the number of seconds it takes you to complete the task.

8431556
2759860
4819751
9568286
7078965
4667416
9515902
2086478
9593305
6388934
0869551
4351314
1697539

How many *f*'s did you find in Exercise B? In fact, there are 16 *f*'s in this selection. Schindler (1978) found that when people searched a prose passage, they were highly accurate in detecting letters in the content words—that is, the important nouns and verbs. However, they made many errors in detecting letters in the function words such as *of, on,* and *an.* Schindler considers several different explanations for these findings. One possibility is that when people learn to read sentences, they learn to direct very little of their visual attention to function words. Consequently, they fail to notice the individual

letters in the words. Did you notice all the *f*'s in the *of*'s? (There are 8.)

In summary, we have seen that performance on a search task can be influenced by physical characteristics. Two other factors —whether the targets form a natural set and context—also influence search performance. Let's see how these factors are relevant in everyday search tasks, such as the situation we described at the beginning of the chapter: the search for a particular friend at a party.

We said that search is faster when the irrelevant shapes are very different from the

---

Demonstration 12-5

Context and Search

A.   Read the passage below and count the number of *t*'s in the entire paragraph. Perform the task visually, without marking in the book.

All in all, thought Cynthia Farnsworth, the evening had been an enormous success. Most of the guests seemed to be quite impressed by the hors d'oeuvres, which were made out of artichokes and crabmeat. The soup had been a particular hit, especially since it was served in a bowl made out of a hollowed-out pumpkin. For the main course, she had decided on one of Julia Child's cold buffet recipes, *Foies de volaille en aspic*. The vegetable was one of John's favorites, cold *ratatouille*. All of them even took second helpings on the dessert, a *clafouti* made out of fresh blueberries that one of the neighborhood children had picked.

B.   Now reread the passage and count the number of times you see the letter *f* in the entire paragraph. Again, do not mark in the book. Then read the text for the answers.

---

target. If your friend is unusually tall or unusually overweight, this friend will be easier to spot than if the "irrelevant" people are similarly shaped. Notice that this point is related to two other factors influencing search speed: (1) targets are located more readily if there is great figure-ground contrast, and (2) targets are located more readily if they are larger than the irrelevant shapes. We also discussed the importance of color in search; your search for your friend will be easier if you know the color of his or her clothes.

We mentioned that search speed is also influenced by the extent to which the targets form a natural set. Suppose that you must search for three friends rather than one. The information about natural sets suggests that you will find them more easily if they are often seen together. Thus you will find three friends who always sit with you in perception class more readily than you will find Joe who works with you, Pat from your hometown, and your sister's friend Chris, because these three presumably form an unnatural set. Context is also important in searching for friends at the party. Have you ever failed to recognize someone because it seems unlikely that he or she would belong in a certain context?

Practice

In the section on divided attention we saw that practice improves our ability to perform two tasks simultaneously. Similarly, practice improves performance on search tasks. Neisser (1964) reported that search time decreases drastically when the task is practiced constantly. For example, a beginning searcher might initially require more than a second to process one line of a display such as the one in Demonstration 12-4. After two weeks of practice, however, the same person might require less than one tenth of a second to process a line. Neisser suggests that as people practice scanning, they discover the perceptual operations that help them scan efficiently. For instance, some people might initially search one line at a time, fixating each item separately and successively. After extensive practice they may be able to examine several lines at the same time.

Even more impressive is Neisser's report that practiced subjects can search for up to ten targets in the same amount of time they require for a single target. Neisser asked subjects to scan mixed lists of letters and numbers, looking for the symbols *A, F, K, U, 9, H, M, P, Z,* and *4*. At first they required almost three times as long to search for ten targets as they required to search for one target. After two weeks of practice, search speeds were identical for the one-target and the ten-target groups. Notice, then, that people with sufficient practice can pay attention to ten targets as readily as they pay attention to one target, just as we saw in the auditory attention studies.

Neisser's results suggest that search can be a parallel process, instead of a serial process. A **serial process** is one that requires the targets to be processed one at a time. For example, suppose your targets are *A, F, K,* and *U.* If you conduct a serial search on a line from the stimulus array—say *Q, Y, E,* and *U*—you would first inspect this line to see if it contains an *A,* then inspect it for *F,* and then for *K,* and then for *U.* If people require much longer to search for four targets than to search for one target, we suspect that the search process is serial.

On the other hand, a **parallel process** is one that allows all the targets to be processed at the same time. If you conduct a parallel search on a line from the stimulus array, you inspect that line only once, searching for all four targets at the same time. If people take about the same amount of time to search for four or more targets as to search for one target, we suspect that the search process is parallel. Neisser's results make us suspect that the search process is primarily serial at the beginning of practice and primarily parallel after two weeks of practice, because at that time the search speeds for the one-target and the ten-target groups were equivalent. (Incidentally, you can remember the word "serial" because a serial on television is a series that runs one episode at a time. The word "parallel" can be remembered because parallel lines are lines that go in the same direction simultaneously.)

Surprising as Neisser's results are for the ten-target group, it is important to note that the ten-target condition may not exhaust the limits of human capacity for multiple searching. Neisser points out that in some professions, even more astounding searches are demanded. For example, consider the people who work in a newspaper-clipping agency. This agency may have hundreds of clients who want clippings of any newspaper articles in which they—or their company—are mentioned. Furthermore, many clients may want relevant articles on a number of topics. For example, a peace group might ask for every article about disarmament, arms control, and nuclear weapons. Neisser remarks that it takes at least a year to train a reader to search newspapers at the rate of more than 1000 words a minute, simultaneously looking for dozens of different key words.

Neisser claimed that the search speed of practiced searchers does not depend upon the number of targets. However, before you decide to spend the next two weeks practicing on search tasks, consider some less optimistic information. Rabbitt (1978) points out, for example, that people scan for ten targets as quickly as for one target only when the targets are relatively rare. When the targets appear frequently in a display, then a ten-target search does take longer than a one-target search.

Furthermore, Rabbitt notes that the error rates reported for Neisser's subjects were very high, often more than 20%. Rabbitt relates this error rate to a concept called the speed-accuracy trade-off. According to the **speed-accuracy trade-off**, faster speeds produce lower accuracy. You have probably noticed this if you have ever proofread a paper. The faster you proofread, the more misspellings and typographical errors you miss. The speed-accuracy trade-off holds true for other search tasks, too. Careful, accurate search requires more time.

Rabbitt describes studies in which subjects were instructed either to search quickly (and presumably make many errors) or to search accurately (and presumably work slowly). These studies showed that Neisser's results held true when subjects searched *quickly.* In other words, when they were fast and sloppy, the number of targets did not influence search speed. However, when subjects searched *accurately,* search time increased markedly as the number of targets increased. If people want to search accurately, they must look for all the items in the target set, and they must examine every item in the stimulus array. However, if they want to search quickly, they can omit some of the target items from the search, and their examination of the stimulus array may be incomplete. Thus their search for ten items may be impressively rapid because it is really just a partial search.

Other research by Schneider and Shiffrin (1977) demonstrated that search speed depends on the number of targets on some tasks, but not on other tasks. Some of their tasks were *consistent* tasks; in these tasks the target items and the nontarget items never overlapped. For instance, the target items might be letters of the alphabet, and the nontarget items might be numbers. After several hours of practice on consistent tasks, four targets could be processed just as quickly as one target. On *varied* tasks, however, the target items and the nontarget items varied. A target item on Trial 1 might appear as a nontarget item on Trial 2. Even after extensive practice on varied tasks, people required more time to search for four targets than to search for one target.

We have seen that practice improves search speed. Furthermore, in some conditions—when targets are rare, when error rates are high, and when tasks are consistent—practiced subjects can search for many targets as quickly as they can search for a single target. In other words, practiced subjects can do several things at once. Does this sound familiar? Recall the studies on divided attention that showed that practiced subjects could read and take dictation at the same time or type and recite prose at the same time. When tasks are repeated so often that they are performed automatically, our ability to do several things at once is impressive!

Application: Reading X-Rays

It is likely that you have had an X-ray taken at some point in your life. A radiologist then looked at the X-ray to determine whether there were any abnormal structures in the film, a process called **film reading**. (Kundel & Nodine, 1978). Film reading involves search and recognition. The radiologist must decide whether any usual structures differ from the accepted limits for size, shape, and position (for example, an enlarged heart) or whether any new structures are present that are not normally part of the film (for example, a lung tumor).

Kundel and Nodine decided to investigate how radiologists searched for a particular kind of lung abnormality, a faint, round structure called a nodule. This kind of nodule might be found in the early stages of lung cancer. Their study is particularly important because earlier research had shown that errors in film reading are surprisingly high for detecting small lung cancers. One estimate, for example, showed that radiologists missed about 30% of small lung cancers and mistakenly reported small lung cancers—when none existed—about 5% of the time (Guiss & Kuenstler, 1960).

Kundel and Nodine recorded the eye movements of radiologists as they examined an X-ray. Sometimes the X-ray was normal. Other times, the researchers altered the X-ray so that it contained a small nodule. Try Demonstration 12-6 to understand your own search techniques. The results showed several tendencies in search techniques. First of all, radiologists typically either detected the nodule in the first 10 seconds of search or else missed it completely. Second, scanning patterns were neither very systematic nor very complete. Third, radiologists often began by giving the entire film a preliminary survey, moving their eyes in a wide circle.

Thomas (1976) provides some additional information about reading X-rays. He points out that highly experienced radiologists really have little understanding of their own search techniques. They instruct their students to proceed in an orderly fashion through the X-ray, inspecting the film rib by rib. In fact the "masters" do not really search in this systematic fashion—they just *think* they do. (Incidentally, the nodule in Demonstration 12-6 is located below the fifth rib on the left side of the X-ray, in the patient's right lung.)

Summary: Search

- Search involves looking for a specific target that is relatively hard to find.
- The useful field of view is the area around the fixation point from which information can be processed; its size is determined by the density of irrelevant items.
- Search speed is influenced by the similarity between the target and the background items, figure-ground contrast, relative size,

Demonstration 12-6

Searching an X-Ray

Search the X-ray below, to see whether or not there is a nodule in one of the lungs. The answer appears at the end of this section.

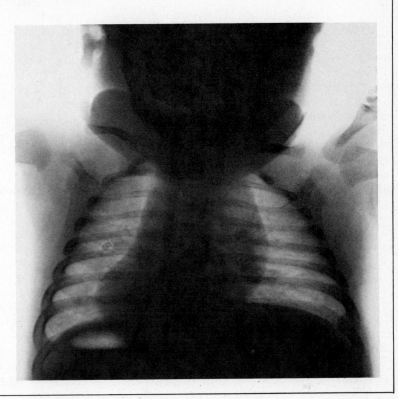

color contrast, the extent to which targets form a natural set, and context.

- With extensive practice on a task in which targets are rare, error rates are high, or tasks are consistent, people can search for ten targets as quickly as they can search for one target; thus search can be parallel instead of serial.
- On tasks in which targets are frequent, error rates are low, or tasks are inconsistent, a search for many targets requires much more time than a search for a single target, even with extensive practice.
- When radiologists search for abnormalities in an X-ray, they usually either locate it within 10 seconds or miss it completely; furthermore, their search patterns are not systematic or complete.

Viewing Pictures

The section on search involved tasks in which people examined a visual stimulus in order to determine whether it contained a specified target. When people view pictures, they are not looking for specified targets. Instead, they make spontaneous eye movements in order to determine the content of the picture. Their eye movements can be recorded so that we have a record of their visual attention.

Do you remember why eye movements are necessary when you look at a picture? As we discussed in the early chapters of this book, the fovea is the tiny central region of the retina in which acuity is greatest. We must therefore move our eyes so that the fovea registers the particular region of the picture that we want to see.

In Chapter 3 we examined eye movements in reading. Are the eye movements you use in viewing pictures similar to the eye movements you use when you read a paragraph? Rayner (1978) argues that there are important differences in the two processes. First of all, picture viewing is a more exploratory process than reading. When you look at a picture, you must first explore it because it is typically unclear where the information is located in an unfamiliar picture. When you read a paragraph, the text is presented in horizontal lines, so you know beforehand where you should fixate.

A second difference between picture viewing and reading is that the information in a picture is more directly visual, whereas the information in reading involves meaning and language structures. A third difference is that the fixation durations are generally longer in picture viewing. In picture viewing, people pause at a particular location for an average of about 300–350 milliseconds. In contrast, good readers pause for an average of about 200 milliseconds.

What do we look at in a picture? Look at a picture in this book. Notice that your attention is not evenly divided among all the regions of the picture. Instead, you look frequently at some regions and ignore others. In this section we will discuss the features of a picture that we attend to. Incidentally, we will mention this topic again in Chapter 13 in connection with the relationship between perceptual qualities of a stimulus and how much people like the stimulus. Liking is measured either in terms of a like-dislike rating scale or in terms of viewing time, and we will see in Chapter 13 that these two measures are not equivalent. In this current chapter we will see that what we look at is influenced by several factors: informativeness, familiarity, and instructions.

Informativeness

The title of a classic article in picture viewing reveals the importance of informativeness in picture viewing: ''The Gaze Selects Informative Details Within Pictures'' (Mackworth & Morandi, 1967). Mackworth and Morandi asked people to look at two pictures, instructing them to choose which picture they preferred. Actually, Mackworth and Morandi were not really interested in preference, but they used these instructions so that the subjects would not suspect the real purpose of the study. A special camera recorded the subjects' visual fixations on each picture. A different group of people performed a separate task. Each of the pictures was divided into 64 tiny squares, and people rated each individual square as to whether it was informative or uninformative. **Informativeness** was defined in terms of recognizability, or the ease with which a square could be recognized at another location.

Mackworth and Morandi found that the group that had viewed the pictures did not distribute their attention randomly. Instead, attention was consistently concentrated in certain regions. For example, when they looked at a picture of eyes peering through a crimson mask, they tended to spend most time looking at the eyes. Furthermore, there was a strong correlation between viewing patterns and the informativeness ratings. The parts of the picture that were most frequently examined were those that the separate group of subjects had rated as being most informative. For example, that group had rated the eyes as being highly informative. Mackworth and Morandi believe that peripheral vision is important in visual attention. It is peripheral attention that edits out the uninformative, boring parts of the picture.

Try Demonstration 12-7. Which part of the picture did you fixate on most frequently? This demonstration resembles a study by Loftus and Mackworth (1978), which was an extension of the Mackworth and Morandi study. In the Loftus and Mackworth study, people looked at pictures containing either an informative or an uninformative critical object. In Demonstration 12-7 the turtle was an informative object because it could not be predicted from the rest of the scene. However, if the turtle had appeared in a swamp scene, it would be uninformative —and an object such as a toaster would be informative. Loftus and Mackworth showed four pictures: (1) a farm scene with a tractor, (2) a farm scene with an octopus, (3) an underwa-

Demonstration 12-7   Look at the picture below for about one minute. Then read the text.

Informativeness and Picture Viewing

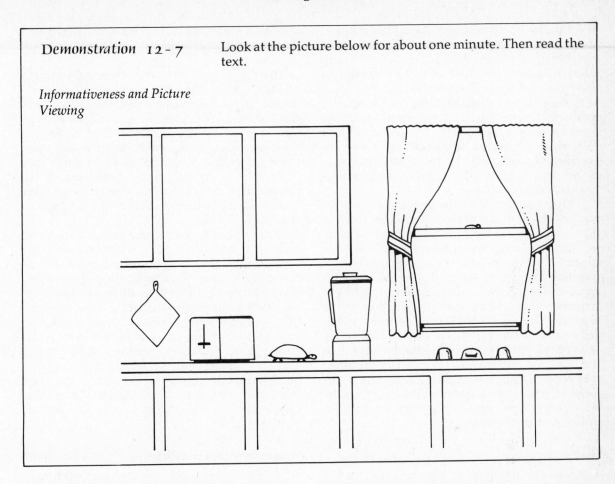

ter scene with an octopus, and (4) an underwater scene with a tractor. Thus two pictures contained an informative critical object, and two contained an uninformative critical object. In all cases a special camera recorded eye movements.

Loftus and Mackworth drew several conclusions about informative objects. First of all, informative objects are found faster. For example, people immediately looked at the octopus when it was part of the farm scene. They were much less likely to look at the octopus first when it was part of the underwater scene. Furthermore, informative objects are looked at more often. Not only did the octopus in the farm scene attract the first fixation, but people also repeatedly returned to examine the octopus. Finally, informative objects are looked at for longer durations. In summary, informative objects are looked at first, frequently, and for a

long time. Loftus and Mackworth argue that in the early stages of picture viewing, people first make a quick determination of the gist of a scene. Next they conduct partial pattern recognition on the objects in the periphery. Then they figure out the likelihood of a given object in view of the gist of the scene. Eye fixations are then directed to objects that are unlikely to appear in the scene.

Familiarity

If you have seen something before, will your viewing patterns be different on the second viewing? This question has a practical application; how do children view a television program the second time they see it? As Flagg (1978) notes, 96% of American homes have television sets, and the average child watches television for more hours than he or she spends in school.

Still, there is surprisingly little information about the moment-to-moment visual activity of watching television. Flagg decided to study what children watched when they viewed episodes of *Sesame Street*. In her study, four- and six-year-old children viewed three segments of *Sesame Street*. These three segments were initially unfamiliar to the children, and they were presented among other, irrelevant portions of *Sesame Street*. One of the three segments was repeated five times, another four times, and another twice.

Flagg found that as the segments were repeated, children tended to have longer fixation durations. For example, one segment had average fixation durations of about 430 milliseconds the first time it was viewed and average fixation durations of about 460 milliseconds the fifth time it was viewed. She also found a slight tendency to fixate on a smaller portion of the television screen during later repetitions of the segments. Thus repetitions of a previously viewed television program had some impact on the attention patterns of children, but the effect was rather small. It would be interesting to see if the effects of familiarity on viewing would be stronger for other children's programs that are not educationally oriented.

Instructions

Try Demonstration 12-8, which illustrates the effects of instructions on picture viewing. This demonstration is based on a study by Yarbus (1967), a Russian who began his studies on visual attention in the 1950s. Yarbus asked people to look at a picture in order to obtain several different kinds of information, and he recorded their eye movements. When there were no specific instructions, people's faces in a picture received far more than their share of attention, and certain areas of the picture received no attention whatsoever. In other words, people's spontaneous attention patterns are *not* random.

Yarbus found that the viewing patterns changed with different instructions. For example, when observers viewed the picture with the instructions to give the ages of the people, almost all of the attention was directed toward the faces. In contrast, their attention was more evenly distributed around the room when they were told to remember the positions of the people and the objects in the picture. Were your viewing patterns similar for "American Gothic"?

Let's return to the picture that you might be looking at during the party we described at the beginning of the chapter. As we have seen in this section, your attention would not be evenly divided among all regions of the picture, because you would look most at the most informative, least predictable part. If you returned to look at the picture several times during the party, your fixation patterns might change slightly. Finally, your viewing patterns would be different if someone suggested that you notice a particular aspect of the painting, rather than allowing you to scan the picture spontaneously.

Summary: Viewing Pictures

- When we view pictures, we move our eyes so that the fovea registers the part of the picture that we want to see.
- Viewing pictures differs from reading because picture viewing is more exploratory, rather than systematically horizontal, because the information is directly visual, and because the fixation durations are longer.
- People concentrate their visual attention on the most informative part of the picture; informative objects are found faster, looked at

---

Demonstration 12-8

The Influence of Instructions on Eye Movements in Picture Viewing

Turn back to Figure 5–8, Grant Wood's familiar "American Gothic." Spend about a minute examining it. Now examine it for one minute with the following instructions: "Guess the ages of the people." Now examine it for one minute with the following instructions: "Remember the positions of the people and the objects in the picture."

more often, and looked at for longer durations.

- When children watch a television program that they have previously seen, they have somewhat longer fixation durations and

fixate on a somewhat smaller portion of the television screen; however, the influence of familiarity on fixation patterns is small.
- Instructions can influence the pattern of picture viewing.

Review

1. Go back to the five different interpretations of attention discussed in the beginning of the chapter: selective attention, search, vigilance, mental concentration, and activation. Think of an occasion in the last few days to illustrate each of the different interpretations.

2. Imagine that you are supposed to be listening to a lecture, but you are really concentrating on a nearby whispered conversation in the classroom. What features of the lecture might you notice (at least some of the time), and what features would you not notice?

3. What is divided attention, how do people perform on divided attention tasks, and how can performance on these tasks be improved?

4. As a college student, you are now a skilled reader. Contrast your reading with that of a five-year-old, stressing the attention aspects that LaBerge and Samuels describe.

5. Contrast the various models of attention, emphasizing the nature of the limits on attention. How do Norman and Bobrow explain practice effects, and how could the other theories be modified to explain practice effects?

6. Imagine that you were asked to search for a particular book, located somewhere in your room. Describe how the useful field of view would be relevant. Describe how physical characteristics would influence search speed in this example.

7. We discussed in some detail the influence of practice on search. Under what conditions does practice improve search speed, and under what conditions does it have little influence?

8. Your sister-in-law is an intern in radiology. Describe to her what you know about radiologists' search patterns, and include some advice that might improve her accuracy.

9. Right now you are reading a sentence of text. How do your eye movements differ from the movements you would use if you were looking at one of the pictures in this book?

10. Look at a picture somewhere in your room (or else look at one of the pictures in this book). Discuss how informativeness and instructions could influence your pattern of examination.

New Terms

selective attention
vigilance
mental concentration
activation
attention
shadowing technique
dichotic listening

semantic
automatic
prequestions
attenuation model
resources
resource-limited task
data-limited task

search
useful field of view
serial process
parallel process
speed-accuracy trade-off
film reading
informativeness

chapter 13

MOTIVATION AND PERCEPTION

Outline   The Effect of Motivation on Perception
  Adjustment of the Eyes
  Recognition of Stimuli
  Responses to Ambiguous Stimuli
  Quantitative Judgments
The Effect of Perception on Motivation
  What Is Esthetics?
  Perceptual Characteristics and Esthetic Judgments
  Cross-Cultural Studies of Esthetics

Preview

Motivation involves our desires and needs, and it is related to perception in two ways. First of all, our desires and needs can influence many different perceptual responses. Second, perceptual characteristics can influence our desires. This chapter is therefore divided into two parts: (1) the effect of motivation on perception and (2) the effect of perception on motivation.

In the first part of the chapter we will see how pleasantness and desirability influence a variety of perceptual responses. It is obvious, for example, that we can simply shut our eyes when we see something unpleasant. Less obviously, however, our pupils may grow smaller when we see unpleasant things, and they grow larger when we see pleasant things. We can also fail to recognize certain unpleasant words, even though we would recognize pleasant words presented for the same length of time. Furthermore, physiological and psychological needs can influence these recognition thresholds. Motivational factors also affect our interpretation of ambiguous figures. Finally, people believe that pleasant stimuli are more frequent, more probable, heavier, and larger than other stimuli.

In the second half of the chapter most of the research about the effect of perception on motivation is in an area called esthetics, or the study of beauty. Perceptual qualities of objects clearly influence our preferences. We will see, for example, that people prefer certain colors and certain shapes. Many studies have examined another perceptual characteristic, complexity. In general, people give the most positive ratings to pictures that are intermediate in complexity—not too simple and not too complex.

In this chapter on motivation and perception we will see that perception can sometimes be influenced by factors other than the physical qualities of the stimuli and the nature of the perceptual systems. Specifically, the motivational state of the perceiver can influence perception.

Motivation is a difficult term to describe. According to Lefton (1979), **motivation** is "a general condition within an organism which produces goal-directed behavior. It is an inferred condition initiated by drives, needs, or desires" (p. 563). Thus motivation is concerned with issues such as the influence of our needs and desires on behavior as well as factors that determine these needs and desires.

Motivation is related to perception in two ways. First, our needs and desires can influence the way we perceive. In the first half of the chapter, we will discuss the effect of motivation on perception, because motivational factors can influence eye adjustment, stimulus recognition, perception of ambiguous stimuli, and quantitative judgments. However, please keep in mind in this part of the chapter that motivation may influence perception, but it certainly does not rule it completely. As Klein (1970) stresses, the fact that we generally perceive effectively is evidence that perception is attuned to the environment. At the same time, however, the fact that people differ in what they see is evidence that motivation can influence perception in important ways.

The second way in which motivation is related to perception is that perception has an effect on motivation; we will discuss this in the second half of this chapter. Our primary interest here will be the influence of perceptual qualities on desires, preferences, and evaluations. What influence do color, shape, and complexity have on people's esthetic judgments, or judgments about how much they enjoy looking at various objects?

The Effect of Motivation on Perception

In the section on signal detection in the first chapter of this book we talked about one aspect of motivation's influence on perception. Remember that one criticism of the standard psychophysical techniques is that they do not take into account the observer's criterion in the calculation of thresholds. For example, one person may be particularly anxious to say "Yes, I hear it" to a possible signal because he wants to impress the experimenter with his fine hearing ability. Another person may be very cautious about saying "Yes, I hear it" because a nickel is subtracted from her payment for every time she says "Yes, I hear it" when no signal has been presented. Thus one way that motivation influences perception is that motivational factors influence an observer's readiness to report signals.

In this part of the chapter we will discuss four other areas in which motivation influences perception: (1) adjustments of the eyes, (2) recognition of stimuli, (3) responses to ambiguous stimuli, and (4) quantitative judgments about stimuli. We will see that the attractiveness, desirability, and usefulness of various stimuli have an important influence on these four kinds of perceptual responses. All of these topics are covered more thoroughly in a book called *The Pollyanna Principle* (Matlin & Stang, 1978). We use the term **Pollyanna Principle** to refer to the general tendency for pleasant items to be processed more efficiently and more accurately than less pleasant items. This tendency is also true in language, memory, and thought, but our concern here is with perceptual processing.

Adjustment of the Eyes

We can avoid unpleasant visual stimuli very easily and very effectively by simply closing our eyes or looking in a different direction. Erdelyi (pronounced "*Air*-day-yih") wrote an article in 1974 that we will discuss frequently in this chapter. In this article he noted that mechanisms of selectivity such as eye-closing and eye-averting are so obvious and commonplace that there is a temptation to dismiss them as trivial. Nonetheless, we frequently use these methods, as when we look away from the movie screen at the most gruesome part of a horror movie.

Luborsky, Blinder, and Mackworth (1963) selected several "threatening" pictures, such as a picture of a fist thrust toward a face. Then they established that the pictures were indeed threatening by measuring the galvanic skin response to each picture. (The **galvanic skin response** is the change in the electrical responsiveness of the skin as sweat is produced.)

These authors found that people avoided looking at the threatening pictures. They showed two clear-cut ways of avoiding those pictures that were most threatening. First of all, they spent less time fixating on the picture. Second, they spent more time examining the "ground," or background, and less time examining the "figure." Naturally, you need sophisticated equipment to measure these examination patterns. Some people in a horror movie may seem to be looking at the picture, but they are really examining the wallpaper in the background rather than the knife descending upon our hero's throat!

Try Demonstration 13-1 before you read any further. Hess (1975) wrote a book called *The Tell-Tale Eye: How Your Eyes Reveal Hidden Thoughts and Emotions*, which describes another way that our eyes can adjust to various stimuli. In particular, the pupils of our eyes dilate when something is interesting or appealing. Hess, who is known for his work on animal behavior, first noticed the phenomenon one night in bed when he was looking at a book of unusually beautiful animal photographs. His wife glanced over at him and remarked that the light must be bad because his pupils were extremely large. However, the reading light was perfectly normal. Being a true scientist, he rushed to the laboratory the next morning to try the first of a series of experiments on pupil dilation to pleasant stimuli. Now look at the size of the pupils

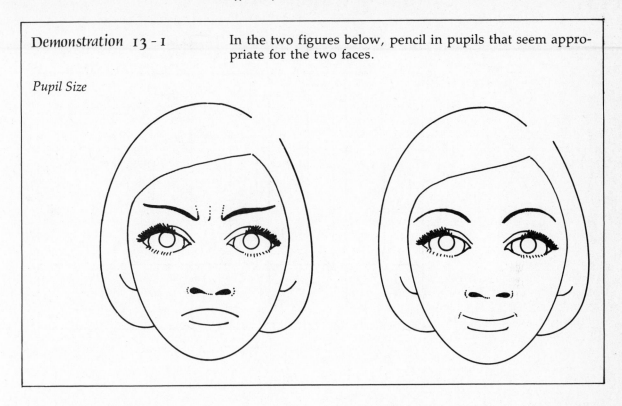

Demonstration 13 - 1   In the two figures below, pencil in pupils that seem appropriate for the two faces.

Pupil Size

you have drawn in Demonstration 13-1. Are the pupils larger in the friendly face than in the angry face?

Let's discuss one of Hess's studies. Women and men looked at five different kinds of photographs: a baby, a mother with a baby, a nude male, a nude female, and a landscape of a rural scene. Figure 13-1 shows the changes in pupil size for each sex for each kind of picture. Notice that the sex differences are impressive and quite consistent with stereotypes. Women's pupils grow larger for pictures of babies, mothers and babies, and nude males. Males' pupils do not respond at all to babies, but they grow larger for pictures of nude females.

In later research, Hess found that when people looked at something they found to be boring, distasteful, or negative, their pupils grew smaller. However, this is consistently true only for mildly negative pictures, such as a photograph of a cross-eyed child. Strongly negative pictures, such as a picture of a mutilated soldier lying on a battlefield, produced results ranging from good constriction to a

fairly high dilation. To some people, a bloody scene is fascinating!

Pupillometrics, or the measurement of pupil size, has an application in advertising. For example, here is how magazine advertisements for *Encyclopaedia Britannica* were tested (Hess, 1975). A large number of observers looked at two different advertisements for the encyclopedia. One was the standard ad showing a family and the other was a new ad showing boys in a pool. A verbal questionnaire for this new ad had shown that the ad was very appealing. However, the observers' pupils did not dilate at all for the new ad, whereas they had dilated substantially for the standard ad. The two ads were included in different copies of a magazine, together with a reply postcard that had been coded according to the version of the ad with which it appeared. The return rate for the postcards was much higher for the standard ad than for the new ad. Thus pupillometrics predicted the public's response better than the questionnaire did. Hess feels that this area of research has not been appropriately developed by advertising agencies.

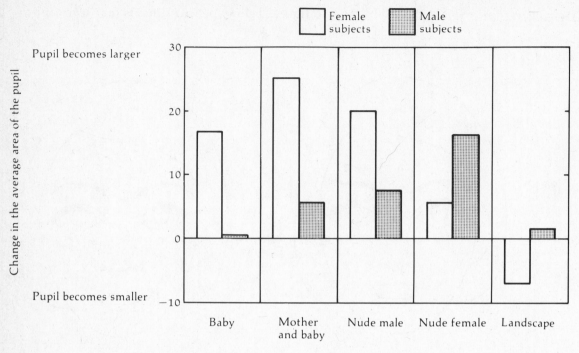

Figure 13-1 Change in pupil size for different pictures.

Other researchers have questioned some of Hess's conclusions. For example, Janisse (1977), in his book *Pupillometry: The Psychology of the Pupillary Response,* argues that Hess's conclusions are only half correct. Janisse concludes that the pupil dilates to interesting stimuli, but it does not constrict to unpleasant stimuli. Thus Janisse believes that measurements of pupil size are not an ideal tool for marketing research.

Recognition of Stimuli

In this section we will talk about stimuli that are presented for very short exposure periods. There are three areas of relevant research: perceptual defense, physiological and psychological need, and subliminal perception. Perceptual defense research is concerned with finding thresholds for the recognition of threatening or unpleasant stimuli. The second topic focuses on the change in thresholds for stimuli representing physiological or psychological needs. Subliminal perception research examines whether messages at below-threshold level can

influence behavior. We will discuss these areas separately.

Perceptual Defense and Vigilance

Perceptual defense means a relative elevation of recognition thresholds to threatening, emotional, or unpleasant stimuli (Postman, Bruner, & McGinnies, 1948). Thus an exposure time that would allow an observer to recognize a neutral stimulus would not be long enough to permit recognition of a threatening stimulus. Presumably, perceptual defense would occur because people *defend* themselves against threatening things.

Perceptual vigilance, on the other hand, means a relative lowering of recognition thresholds to these threatening stimuli. An observer could therefore recognize a threatening stimulus that is presented for a shorter exposure period than the period necessary for recognition of a neutral stimulus. Presumably, perceptual vigilance would occur because people are *vigilant* or watchful for threatening stimuli.

Both of these phenomena, perceptual defense and perceptual vigilance, were suggested in the 1940s by a group of people who argued for a New Look in psychology. The **New Look** view argued that the perception of external stimuli is influenced by internal events, such as attitudes, values, needs, expectancies, and defenses. This area of research attempted to coordinate the two very different fields of psychodynamics and psychophysics.

You may be wondering, at this point, why the New Look psychologists proposed both perceptual defense and perceptual vigilance. How could both of these phenomena be true, since they are exactly the opposite of each other? As Erdelyi (1974) explains, researchers proposed and found evidence for individual differences in reactions to threatening stimuli. You remember that Hess found that some observers' pupils constricted to threatening pictures, a reaction similar to perceptual defense, whereas other observers' pupils dilated to threatening pictures, a reaction similar to perceptual vigilance. In general, however, more studies have reported perceptual defense than perceptual vigilance, and so this area of research is often known by the general term "perceptual defense."

In one of the classic studies, McGinnies (1949) presented words that were neutral in affect, such as *dance* and *broom*, and "taboo" words that were presumably threatening, such as *bitch* and *raped*. On the first trial, each word was shown only very briefly. The exposure duration was gradually increased on subsequent trials until the word was recognized. The thresholds were substantially higher for the taboo words than for the neutral words, demonstrating perceptual defense.

People who were skeptical about the concept of perceptual defense proposed an explanation involving word frequency. According to Howes and Solomon (1950), taboo words were low in frequency in the English language, particularly in comparison to the neutral words used in perceptual defense studies. Thus people may fail to recognize a taboo word because infrequent words are difficult to recognize, not because of their threatening nature.

However, there is good evidence that the word frequency explanation cannot entirely account for the results (Erdelyi, 1974). Other psychologists suggested that response suppression could explain the results of perceptual defense experiments. According to the **response suppression** argument, people can perceive a taboo word such as *bitch*, but they resist reporting the word until they are absolutely convinced that they have perceived the word correctly. Thus response biases rather than perceptual mechanisms would account for the phenomenon. However, Erdelyi cites several studies in which perceptual defense was demonstrated even though there was no possibility of response suppression. Furthermore, there are several studies using signal detection methods in which the emotional nature of the words influenced the perceptual aspects of detection (d'), rather than the criterion aspects (β) (Dixon, 1971).

Here is one example of a study in which different kinds of words yielded different thresholds, and neither word frequency nor response suppression could explain the differences. Johnson, Frincke, and Martin (1961) presented pleasant words, such as *prosper*, *jewel*, and *income*, and unpleasant words, such as *dismal*, *hunger*, and *typhoon*. The lists of pleasant and unpleasant words were matched in terms of word frequency and other verbal characteristics. The words were presented, one at a time, on a **tachistoscope** (pronounced "tah-*kiss*-toe-scope"), an instrument that projects visual stimuli for very brief durations. They used a modified method of limits, presenting each word for 1/50 of a second, then 1/25, 1/10, 1/2, and 1 second, until the word was recognized. The average threshold for the pleasant words was found to be .06 second, in comparison to an average threshold of .09 for unpleasant words.

Since you probably do not have a tachistoscope in your bedroom, we will have to demonstrate perceptual defense with more primitive equipment—a typewriter and carbon paper. Try Demonstration 13-2 to see if people recognize pleasant words more readily than unpleasant words.

Erdelyi estimated that more than a thousand studies examined perceptual defense

---

Demonstration 1 3 - 2

Perceptual Defense

Take eight sheets of white typing paper and seven sheets of carbon paper. Assemble the typing paper with carbon paper in between. Type the list of words below, leaving sufficient space between the words so that you can cut them out later. Remove the pieces of carbon paper, leaving the typing paper sheets in order. The words should be dark and legible on the first few sheets, but increasingly blurry on the later sheets. Cut through the sheets, taking care to leave the sheets in the correct order. You should end up with 16 piles, each pile containing eight copies of one word. Turn the piles over, so that the blurry copy is on the top.

Find a willing friend to whom you can show the words. Take one word pile, selected at random, and present the blurriest version of the word. Allow your friend approximately one second to identify the word. If he or she cannot identify it, present the next stimulus in the series. Continue this process until the word has been correctly identified. Record the number of the trial on which the word was identified. Repeat the process for the other 15 words. Compute the average score for the unpleasant words (first eight) and for the pleasant words (second eight). Is this average smaller for the pleasant words, as perceptual defense would predict?

empty	beggar	honey	silver
filth	ant	circus	smile
hostage	frown	cherry	friend
morgue	battle	doe	dawn

---

prior to his article in 1974. Some experiments in this area produced negative results, and some produced ambiguous results. Many, however, produced positive results, showing evidence for perceptual defense. In a recent article, for example, Blum and Barbour (1979) demonstrated in three well-controlled experiments that there was an inhibitory delay for anxiety-linked stimuli. Motivational factors clearly can influence perceptual thresholds.

How can we explain perceptual defense? An information-processing approach to the issue proposed by Erdelyi (1974) has been well received. Erdelyi suggests that stimuli in a perceptual defense experiment pass through many different stages of storage and transformation. He proposes that there are certain control processes in long-term memory that influence what material is selected to be passed on for further processing and what material is to be

forgotten. Furthermore, these control processes operate at every stage in the processing of the stimuli—they are not limited to just one or two aspects of perception. Thus the control mechanisms impose selectivity in the very first stages of perception. As we discussed in the section on adjustment of the eyes, people can avoid fixating on threatening stimuli, and their pupils can narrow as well.

These control processes operate at the sensory memory stage as well. **Sensory memory** is the name that information-processing psychologists have given to the first recording of information about a stimulus. For example, a person may begin to analyze the information in sensory memory, but stop analyzing it before the process is complete. That is similar to the way you turn your eyes away from an unpleasant picture before you have thoroughly explored it. Since there are so many sensory impressions in sensory memory, any information that has not been completely analyzed will not be passed along to the next stage in information processing, short-term memory. Erdelyi argues that the control processes also select against threatening stimuli in long-term memory and in the production of the response. Thus people fail to respond to a threatening stimulus because control processes are "protecting" us at many different points in the information-processing sequence.

Zajonc (1980) has outlined a theory about the relationship between feeling and thinking that supplements Erdelyi's model. Zajonc (pronounced "*zie*-unce" to rhyme with "science") argues that we can like something or be afraid of something before we know exactly what it is—possibly even without knowing at all what it is. Affective reactions, such as likes and dislikes, are very basic, inescapable, and difficult to change. Furthermore, they are automatic and quickly aroused. Zajonc proposes that we can have an affective reaction before we have finished the perceptual task of feature discrimination or the cognitive task of recognizing whether something is familiar or unfamiliar. Thus we know whether something is good or bad very quickly—so quickly that this knowledge can influence further identification. If the stimulus is threatening enough, further processing of the stimulus grinds to a halt.

The idea that a stimulus can produce an affective reaction before perceptual processing is complete is extremely important, because it resolves a paradox, or puzzle. Here is the apparent paradox about perceptual defense. How can observers defend themselves against a threatening stimulus before they have even identified it? On the other hand, once they have identified the stimulus enough to know that it is threatening, then they should be able to report what it is! Notice that this paradox is based on the idea that we first complete perception and recognition, and then the affective reaction follows. Zajonc says that the affective reaction is independent of perception and recognition, however, and it actually comes first. According to Zajonc's theory, then, there is no paradox.

Physiological and Psychological Needs

The literature in this area of threshold determi-

nation is not as extensive as the perceptual defense literature, and no current theorists have rekindled interest in this area the way Erdelyi and Zajonc revived the topic of perceptual defense. Nonetheless, this topic represents another important way in which motivation influences perception.

Wispé and Drambarean (1953) performed a classic study about the influence of food and water deprivation on perception. The people in their study were randomly assigned to one of three groups. The control group ate a normal lunch. Another group ate and drank nothing during the 10 hours prior to the experiment. A third group was deprived for 24 hours prior to the experiment. During the experiment, thresholds were determined for both neutral words, such as *serenade* and *hunch*, and "need" words such as *lemonade* and *munch*. In each category of words there were some common words and some uncommon words.

Figure 13-2 shows the results. Notice that common words have lower thresholds than uncommon words, which should not surprise you. Notice also that the thresholds for the "need" words are much lower for the two deprived groups than for the control group. However, the thresholds for the neutral words are almost identical for the deprived and the control groups.

One likely explanation for these findings is that deprivation influences response tendencies such as the criterion for responding, rather than perceptual activities. Remember that a similar argument, response suppression, was proposed as an explanation for perceptual defense. It may be that people who have gone without food and water are more likely to respond with food- and drink-related words when the tachistoscope presents a word so quickly that its identity is ambiguous. For example, a food-deprived person might respond "munch" when this word is presented very rapidly, because he or she has a very lenient criterion for supplying food-related words. A person who was not food-deprived might wait several more trials until he or she is convinced that the word is "munch"; this person has a very stringent criterion for supplying food-related words.

Wispé and Drambarean looked at the kinds of words people supplied before they gave the

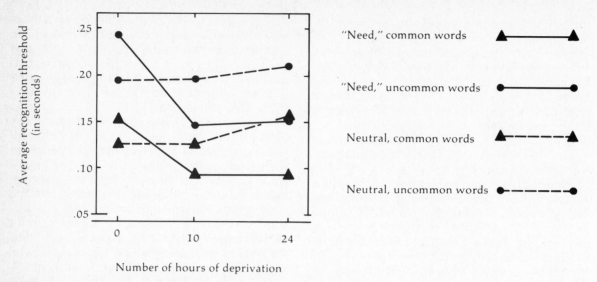

Figure 13-2   Recognition threshold, as a function of type of word.

correct responses, and they found that the subjects in the two deprived groups gave more words concerning food and liquid. This explanation is not perfect, but it does make sense. I recall a day when I was dieting, and food responses abounded. I typed *peace* as *peach*, I read *streak* as *steak*, and I said *food* instead of *foot*.

Other studies have shown lower thresholds for words representing psychological needs and values. Postman, Bruner, and McGinnies (1948) gave people a test called the Allport-Vernon scale of values. This test provides scores for six value areas in which people can seek gratification of certain hypothetical needs: esthetic, economic, political, religious, social, and theoretical. For example, someone may receive a high score in the social area, a low score in the religious area, and average scores in other areas.

Postman and his colleagues used a tachistoscope to present words related to the six value areas. In general, they found that people had lower recognition thresholds for words that were related to their highly valued areas. For example, a person with a high social score and a low religious score would recognize words related to social activity, such as *friendly* and *helpful* more readily than words related to religious activity, such as *prayer* and *sacred*. Thus psychological motivation as well as physiological motivation can influence perceptual thresholds.

Subliminal Perception

Subliminal literally means "below the limen, or threshold." **Subliminal perception** means that people can respond to or perceive a stimulus that is below the threshold for conscious detection. A shortened form of subliminal perception is **subception**. There is evidence for subliminal perception in certain studies (for example, Dixon, 1971), but we will concentrate on the area of subliminal perception that has received the most publicity: subliminal perception in advertising.

In the 1950s a commercial firm claimed that very brief presentations of the words "Eat Popcorn" and "Drink Coca-Cola" boosted the sales of popcorn and Coca-Cola among motion picture audiences. This claim was accepted uncritically by many people and has become "common knowledge" among people who know very little about other areas of perception. The problem is that there was very little evidence for these claims.

Detailed reports of this notorious "experiment" have not been available in any published form, but summaries can be found in a *Life* magazine article (Brean, 1958) and in an excellent review of subliminal perception by McConnell, Cutler, and McNeil (1958). Apparently, more than 45,000 unsuspecting movie viewers saw filmed messages presented at speeds that were claimed to be 1/3000 of a second in length. In contrast, remember that the study by Johnson and his colleagues discussed earlier in the chapter used maximum speeds of 1/50 of a second. McConnell and his colleagues point out the likelihood of technical defects at a speed of 1/3000 of a second—if, indeed, such a speed could ever be achieved. At any rate, these messages were presented every 5 seconds.

The firm claimed that popcorn sales rose more than 50% and Coca-Cola sales rose more than 18%, in comparison to some unspecified previous period. Keep in mind that there were no reports of even the most elementary scientific precautions. There were no adequate controls and no provisions for replication, for example. Thus experimental psychologists do not have enough information to judge the validity of this ''study.''

Furthermore, as McConnell and his colleagues point out, it is unclear how subliminal stimulation could actually produce increased popcorn sales among people who had seen the ''Eat Popcorn'' message. Did the ads simply raise an already existing but weak need for popcorn? Did they create a need that had not previously existed? Did people in the audience rise like automatons during the movie, missing part of the feature in order to satisfy a sudden craving, or did they buy it on the way home?

In summary, McConnell and other critics argue that we cannot trust the claims of subliminal perception enthusiasts. People will probably not stampede the refreshment counters to buy Coca-Cola if they have seen ''Drink Coke'' briefly flashed across the screen. Some more modest subliminal perception effects are possible, however. Hawkins (1970) found that people who received a ''Drink Coke'' or a ''Coke'' subliminal message rated themselves as being thirstier than people who received a nonsense syllable subliminal message. However, we do not know from these findings whether the people who received the ''Coke'' message would actually be more likely to leave their seats in search of a drink. We also do not know whether they would be more likely to buy a Coca-Cola than some other drink. Thus Hawkins's findings show some evidence of subliminal perception. However, they are nowhere nearly as impressive as the earlier claims that subliminal perception could make us into robots in search of whatever product a scheming advertiser wanted to promote.

Responses to Ambiguous Stimuli

There are some pictures and scenes that are ambiguous because they allow more than one perceptual interpretation. For example, you can see the cube in Figure 13-3a in either of two ways. Sometimes the square surface on the left seems to be near to you, and sometimes it seems to be farther away. Many studies have shown that motivational factors can influence which version of a figure is perceived.

For example, Solley and Santos (1958) modified the cube in Figure 13-3a by emphasizing either the left square surface (as in Figure 13-3b) or the right square surface (as in Figure 13-3c). Observers in their study saw 101 exposures of 13-3b, 101 exposures of 13-3c, and 54 exposures of the standard cube, 13-3a. During each exposure, people had to report which version of the cube they saw. Solley and Santos systematically reinforced one interpretation of

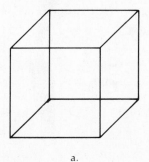
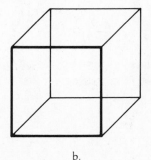
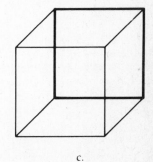

a.   b.   c.

Figure 13-3   (*a*) An ambiguous cube and (*b* and *c*) two variants.

the cube more often than the other interpretation. For example, they might say, "Good, you're doing fine," on 70% of the 13-3b trials but on only 30% of the 13-3c trials.

Toward the end of the session the observers showed a definite preference for reporting the interpretation of the standard cube that had been reinforced more often. For example, people who had been reinforced more often for 13-3b trials tended to report the standard cube as having the left surface nearer. Reinforcement, in the form of verbal rewards, had a clear-cut influence on what was reported. Unfortunately, however, we do not know whether people reported what they saw or whether they reported what they thought the experimenter wanted them to report.

Under some conditions, motivational factors can influence the interpretation of pictures in which it is unclear which surface is the figure and which is the ground. In general, the pictures used in these studies were similar to the vase-faces ambiguous picture in Figure 5-9. These studies are controversial, however, be-

cause some showed a reinforcement effect and some did not (Solley & Murphy, 1960).

Do you remember the stereoscope, which we discussed in Chapter 6? This instrument allows an experimenter to present a different picture to each eye. It is typically used in depth perception studies, but it also provides information about motivation and perception. J. Ross (1976) mentions that the blending of features that one sees in a binocular combination is typically more attractive than either the picture presented to the left eye or the picture presented to the right eye. Try Demonstration 13-3, which illustrates binocular combination. Your left eye looks at a face that is too narrow, and your right eye looks at a face that is too wide. What you actually "see," however, is an attractive blend of the two. As Ross says, "The selective blending of features that occurs in binocular combination indicates that the visual system apparently has the ability to accept or to reject information on aesthetic grounds" (p. 80).

The stereoscope has also been used to reveal

Demonstration 13 - 3

Binocular Combination

Take a piece of plain white or gray cardboard, approximately 20 cm wide, and line it up along the dotted line in the figure below. Rest your nose on the cardboard edge that is closest to you. Each eye should look at just the one figure on the appropriate side of the cardboard. Try to fuse the two separate images into a single, unified image.

some interesting information about racial prejudice. Pettigrew, Allport, and Barnett (1958) showed stereoscopic photographs to people of four different racial groups in South Africa. In some cases, people saw a white person on one side and a black person on the other side. If these two pictures are viewed as a single, fused picture, it would look racially mixed. People who were from three racial groups—black, Indian, and racially mixed—tended to report seeing a picture of a racially mixed person. However, people who were white tended to see this picture as being either all-black or all-white. White people in South Africa in the 1950s were very concerned about racial relations, according to Pettigrew and his colleagues, and so they could not tolerate ambiguity. Racially apprehensive people apparently need to give a definite response. People are either black or white, and in-between responses are not acceptable.

We have discussed stimuli that are ambiguous because it is unclear which surface is nearer, which surface is figure and which is ground, and which eye's input should be favored. Other stimuli are ambiguous because the forms are unclear or unstructured. Do you remember the conversation that Hamlet had with Polonius?

Hamlet:	Do you see yonder cloud that's almost in the shape of a camel?
Polonius:	By the Mass, and 'tis like a camel indeed.
Hamlet:	Methinks it is like a weasel.
Polonius:	It is backed like a weasel.
Hamlet:	Or like a whale?
Polonius:	Very like a whale. (*Hamlet,* Act III, Scene II)

A cloud can be a camel, a weasel, or a whale. Similarly, projective tests used by clinicians allow many alternative interpretations. A **projective test** is a test in which a person responds to a relatively unstructured or ambiguous stimulus; the responses are considered to be projections, or the throwing forth, of unconscious attitudes, needs, or fears that might not

be expressed by a more direct test (Wilkening, 1973).

The Thematic Apperception Test is one of the more structured projective tests. The **Thematic Apperception Test (TAT)**, developed by Murray (1936), is a series of pictures for which people make up stories. The stories are scored according to the amount of emphasis they place on certain motives. For example, one TAT card shows a man sitting at his desk. One respondent may focus upon the picture on the man's desk and stress affiliative motives. Another respondent may focus upon the paper the man is writing upon and stress achievement motives.

Other tests are less structured than the TAT. For example, the **Rorschach inkblot test** is a projective test with inkblotlike designs; people's responses on this test are interpreted as projections of their own fantasies. Demonstration 13-4 has a figure similar to a Rorschach inkblot.

Some of the Rorschach cards are colored. Typically, people's responses to the dimension of color are interpreted as reflecting their emotional life. However, Frank (1976) seriously questions this practice, because factors that influence response to color on the Rorschach, such as saturation and amount of area covered, vary from one card to the next. Thus it is impossible to draw conclusions using the current set of Rorschach cards. Frank feels that the test should be revised. In summary, people may reveal something about themselves from their responses to ambiguous stimuli, but the current version of the Rorschach test is inadequate.

Quantitative Judgments

Think about the number of formal and informal quantitative judgments you make every day: How tall is she? How many people were at the party? How big was the cake? How much does the roast weigh? Quantitative judgments such as these are influenced by the pleasantness and the value of the stimulus that is being judged. Matlin and Stang (1978) reviewed studies that showed that pleasant stimuli are sometimes (but not always) judged to occur more frequently than neutral or unpleasant stimuli, even when their objective frequencies are iden-

Demonstration 13-4

Responding to Ambiguous Figures

Ask five friends to tell you what they think the figure below represents. Assure them that you do not plan to draw any clinical implications and that you simply want to see the variety of responses that an ambiguous figure suggests.

tical. Pleasant stimuli and events are also judged to be probable.

Try Demonstration 13-5 to see if your friends think that more valuable paper money *weighs* more, as MacDougall (1906) reported in one of the earliest studies on the relationship between motivation and perception. Dukes and Bevan (1952) found, similarly, that children judged jars filled with candy to be heavier than jars filled with the identical weight of sand and sawdust. A pound of jelly beans "weighs" more than a pound of an unattractive mixture.

Most of the quantitative judgment studies are concerned with estimates of size. Some early studies indicated, for example, that the estimated size of coins was related to their

value. Baker, Rierdan, and Wapner (1974) conducted a more recent version of these studies. People judged the size of coins, which could be considered pleasant and valuable, as well as plain metal disks, which had no monetary value. People looked at each stimulus, felt it with a blindfold on, and then felt disks in a comparison series. The study used the method of limits, and the stimuli were compared with comparison disks that ranged from 50% to 150% of the size of the stimuli.

Baker and his colleagues found that people judged the coins to be larger than the plain metal disks. Furthermore, more valuable coins showed greater overestimation. For example, the overestimates for half-dollars were greater

Demonstration 13-5

Quantitative Judgments

Ask five friends to guess how many one-dollar bills it would take to equal one pound. Then ask five other friends to guess how many ten-dollar bills it would take to equal one pound. If your subjects are like MacDougall's, their estimate will be about 50% greater for the one-dollar bills. One-dollar bills seem to weigh less, and so it seems to take more of them to equal one pound.

than the overestimates for quarters, presumably because the difference in value between half-dollars and metal disks is greater than the contrast in value between quarters and metal disks.

In a second experiment, Baker and his colleagues (1974) found that people drew larger representations for chocolate bars than for unpainted pieces of wood. See if you find the same results in Demonstration 13-6.

Beginning in the late 1950s, some researchers started to examine children's representations of symbols connected with various holidays. The value of a holiday was assumed to be strongest on the day of the holiday and less strong before or after the holiday. If value is related to size, then we should expect to find drawings of Santa Claus to be largest right near Christmas. In fact, Solley and Murphy (1960) found that children's drawings were substantially larger several days prior to Christmas than they were in early December or a week after Christmas.

On the other hand, drawings of witches decrease in size on Halloween (Craddick, 1963). Perhaps the children want to make these frightening creatures go farther away from themselves. They may give the witches a "perceptual shove," because smaller retinal size is equated with greater distance from the witch (Solley, 1966). If you see a small child often, you

may want to repeat one of these holiday studies.

Adults show a similar distortion when they estimate the size of people. People with more status or value are judged to be taller. For example, Kassarjian (1963) questioned California residents prior to the 1960 presidential election about their voting intentions. They also asked which of the two major candidates, Kennedy or Nixon, was taller. Kennedy was in fact a half-inch taller than Nixon. However, Nixon supporters were undecided about who was taller, but Kennedy supporters overwhelmingly believed that Kennedy was taller.

In summary, motivational factors influence quantitative judgments. Pleasant and valuable stimuli are judged to be more frequent, more probable, heavier, and larger than less pleasant and less valuable stimuli. These findings demonstrate an extension of the Pollyanna Principle that we discussed at the beginning of the chapter. We process pleasant items more efficiently and more accurately than other items, and we also tend to overestimate the abundance and size of pleasant items.

Summary: The Effect of Motivation on Perception

- Motivation is a condition that produces goal-directed behavior. One way it is related

---

Demonstration 13-6

Size Judgments

For this demonstration you will need a small, flat chocolate bar. Cut out pieces of cardboard that are the same size and paste them together until they are equivalent in thickness to the chocolate bar. If possible, paste brown paper on top or paint the surface brown.

Now take four pieces of blank white paper, and find a willing friend to act as the subject. Show the friend the cardboard figure, holding it about one yard away, and ask your friend to draw its shape on the first piece of paper. Now hide the figure and ask your friend to draw it from memory. Repeat the process with the chocolate bar. Then compare the sizes for the four figures. Are the chocolate bars drawn larger than the cardboard figures? Some researchers have found that the discrepancy between the size of the valued object and the neutral object is greater when the objects are not physically present. Did you find this?

to perception is that motivational factors can influence perceptual responses. The influence of motivation on perception is part of the Pollyanna Principle, which states that pleasant items are processed more efficiently and more accurately than less pleasant items.

- We often avoid unpleasant items by avoiding looking at them. Also, the pupils of the eyes sometimes grow wider for pleasant pictures and smaller for boring or mildly negative pictures.
- Perceptual defense means a rise in the recognition thresholds for unpleasant stimuli, whereas perceptual vigilance means a lowering in the thresholds for unpleasant stimuli. Both of these effects have been found, though perceptual defense is more common.
- Erdelyi suggests that perceptual defense operates because control processes show selectivity at many different stages in information processing.
- Zajonc proposes that we have affective reactions before we have completely perceived stimuli. Thus we know that something is unpleasant very quickly, and we halt the identification process before it is complete.

- Physiological and psychological needs can influence the recognition thresholds of relevant words.
- Subliminal perception means that people can respond to a stimulus that is below the threshold for conscious detection. There is some modest evidence for subliminal perception, but there is no trustworthy evidence that subliminal presentation of specific products leads to increased purchasing of those products.
- After they have been reinforced for a particular interpretation of an ambiguous figure, people are more likely to report that interpretation.
- Motivational factors influence people's interpretations of stereoscopic pictures, in which a different picture is presented to each eye.
- Many projective tests, such as the Thematic Apperception Test, use ambiguous stimuli. People's motivations and attitudes are assumed to influence their interpretations of these stimuli.
- People believe that pleasant or valuable stimuli are more frequent, more probable, heavier, and larger than other stimuli.

The Effect of Perception on Motivation

In the first part of this chapter we explored a number of ways in which motivation influences perception. Our attitude toward something determines how we perceive it. If we like or need something, we open our eyes, widen our pupils, recognize it more easily, choose to see it in an ambiguous picture, and think that it is quantitatively greater. In these studies, motivation is the **independent variable**, or the variable that the experimenters manipulate, whereas perception is the **dependent variable**, the measure describing the subjects' behavior.

However, in other studies, perception influences motivation. In these studies, perception is the independent variable, and motivation is the dependent variable. Experimenters doing research in this area manipulate the perceptual qualities of objects, by varying shape or color, for example. Then they measure motivation either by asking people to judge the objects in terms of preference, beauty, or interest level or by recording the amount of time people spend looking at the objects. They frequently find a systematic relationship between perceptual qualities and judgments.

What Is Esthetics?

In this discussion of perception's influence on motivation, we are primarily concerned with an area called esthetics. **Esthetics** (pronounced "ess-*thet*-icks") is the study of beauty. Notice that this word is treated as if it were singular, so we say "esthetics is . . ." Also, you may have seen an alternate spelling, "aesthetics." I will stick with the simpler spelling, however, because it looks more esthetically pleasing to me.

Child (1978) proposes that the central question of esthetic theory is: "Why do people enjoy or seem to enjoy perceptual experience itself?" (p. 111). We often perform perceptual activities because we need to reach certain goals. For example, you read a textbook because the material in it will be included in a test. You listen to see if a train is coming before you cross the railroad tracks. You touch the bathwater to see if it will scald you. However, Child stresses that there are always some perceptual experiences that seem to be enjoyed for their own sake. Hochberg (1978b) points out, too, that esthetics involves *disinterested* evaluation of stimuli. The word "disinterested" is important because it emphasizes that esthetic judgments are not concerned with the goals that stimuli can accomplish for us. When we say that an object is beautiful, for example, we do not care whether it can also make us healthy, wealthy, and wise.

Berlyne (1980) says that esthetic behavior includes activities "that figure in the creation, performance, and appreciation of painting, sculpture, music, poetry, story-telling, dance, and drama" (p. 328). Notice that this list involves visual and auditory experiences; touch, smell, and taste are missing. This neglect of touch, smell, and taste in esthetics also applies in informal usage of the term "esthetics." When we think of a person with esthetic interests, we imagine someone who attends symphonies or wanders through art galleries. We do not picture someone sitting down to a dinner and appreciating the subtleties of the foods' texture, odor, and taste. Our discussion of esthetics therefore is limited to visual and auditory experiences.

The field of esthetics can be divided into two parts, **speculative esthetics**, which includes art theory and art criticism, and **scientific esthetics**, which applies the scientific method to the study of beauty (Berlyne, 1980). Since this is a psychology textbook, we will look only at scientific esthetics. This area of research was founded in 1876 by Gustav Fechner, who was also the founder of psychophysics (Hochberg, 1978b).

How can we measure esthetic reactions scientifically? In other words, what dependent variables can we use to assess people's reactions to various objects? According to Berlyne, verbal judgments have been the major dependent variables. For example, people **rate** an object by indicating a point along a scale that corresponds to their judgment of that object. Alternatively, people **rank** an object by placing it in order, together with other objects, according to the amount of some quality that it possesses. Other kinds of dependent variables include measures of exploration and attention. For example, we might measure the number of seconds a person spends exploring various pictures. Finally, dependent variables may include physiological recordings, such as measures of arousal.

Perceptual Characteristics and Esthetic Judgments

A major effort in scientific esthetics has been to identify the perceptual characteristics that are important in esthetic judgments. Three kinds of characteristics have received the most attention: color, shape, and complexity.

Color

In Chapter 4, I mentioned that an important question when I was a child was, "What's your favorite color?" Well, what *is* your favorite color? Most people in Western cultures say that their favorite color is blue (Berlyne, 1980).

According to Berlyne, the early researchers in scientific esthetics were particularly interested in the color variable. However, this topic has been generally ignored in more recent years. One exception is an elaborate study by Helson and Lansford (1970), which involved 156,250 ratings of object colors! They asked people to rate 125 different colors. Most of the 25 colors that were best liked were blue, purplish-blue, green, or bluish-green. On the other hand, most of the 25 colors that were least liked were yellow or had a yellow tint.

Helson and Lansford also found sex differences in color preferences. Women liked warm colors, such as red, orange, and yellow, better than men did. Men liked cool colors, such as blue, purplish-blue, and purple, better than women did.

Finally, Helson and Lansford asked people to rate various color combinations. It was difficult to make many generalizations about preferences for color combinations. For example, there were no consistent contrasts in either hue or saturation that were most preferred. However, there was one generalization that could be made about contrasts in lightness. Specifically, people tended to prefer color combinations in which there was a large difference in brightness between the object and the background. Thus people liked color combinations in which one sample was light and one was dark, and they did not like color combinations in which the two samples were similar in lightness.

Intriguingly, color preference depends upon the temperature of the room. Kearney (1966) asked people to make color judgments in a room that was hot (about 40°C), cool (about 16°C), or cold (about −2°C). When the room was hot, people tended to prefer hues from the cooler end of the spectrum, such as blue. How-

ever, when the room was cold, they preferred hues from the warmer end of the spectrum, such as red. So, if you are planning on selling refrigerators to Eskimos, be sure to paint them red!

Shape

Which of the rectangles in Demonstration 13-7 appears to be the most esthetically pleasing to you? Many experimenters, beginning with Fechner, have demonstrated that people in Western cultures tend to prefer rectangles that have certain specified proportions. In particular, they prefer rectangles in which the shorter side is about two-thirds (actually, .618) the length of the longer side. In Demonstration 13-7, Figure *c* would be selected most fre-

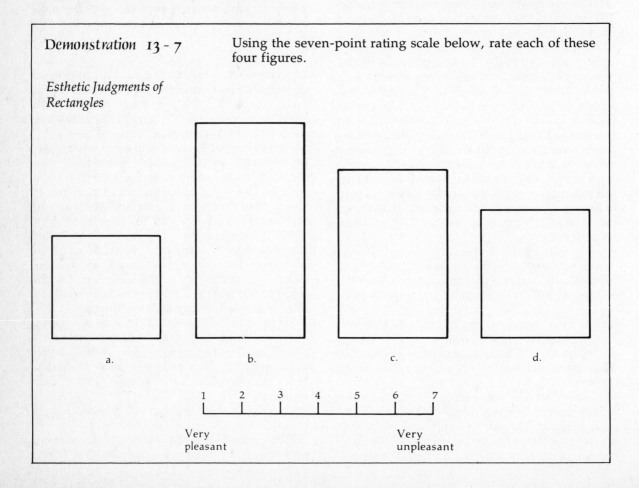

Demonstration 13 - 7   Using the seven-point rating scale below, rate each of these four figures.

Esthetic Judgments of Rectangles

a.   b.   c.   d.

1   2   3   4   5   6   7

Very pleasant   Very unpleasant

quently as the most esthetically pleasing rectangle.

Hochberg (1978b) discusses several possible explanations. For example, some theorists have suggested that if figures are too easily seen as a unit, they are not interesting enough. On the other hand, if figures are seen as a unit only with great difficulty, the esthetic effect is lost. Presumably, the proportions of this ideal rectangle are "just right"—challenging, but not too challenging.

Complexity

Although we have some information about color and shape, by far the most research has been conducted on a third perceptual characteristic: complexity. Studies on the relationship between complexity and preference have examined pictures, architecture, cinema, and music.

Daniel Berlyne (pronounced "Burr-*line*") conducted many studies on complexity in pictures. He found, for example, that babies preferred to look at a checkerboard of 16 black-and-white squares, rather than simpler pictures, such as a card that was half black and half white (Berlyne, 1958).

Berlyne's later research showed that the relationship between complexity and preference is not a simple one (for example, Berlyne, 1974). The relationship may depend, for example, on the dependent variable that is selected to measure preference. Demonstration 13-8 shows a very simple version of his study. Some pictures showed only one kind of item, such as Figure *a* in Demonstration 13-8. However, there were also pictures showing greater variety, with the highest level of variety represented in Figure *d*.

Some people rated the pictures on various evaluative scales such as UGLY–BEAUTIFUL, DISPLEASING–PLEASING, and DISLIKE–LIKE. Their ratings showed that they preferred pictures with intermediate levels of complexity. Thus Figures *b* and *c* would be most likely to receive ratings of "beautiful," "pleasing," and "like." Figure *a*, which is very simple, and Figure *d*, which is very complex, were not as well liked. Thus when verbal rating scales are used to measure preference, people prefer intermediate levels of complexity.

Berlyne also measured how long another

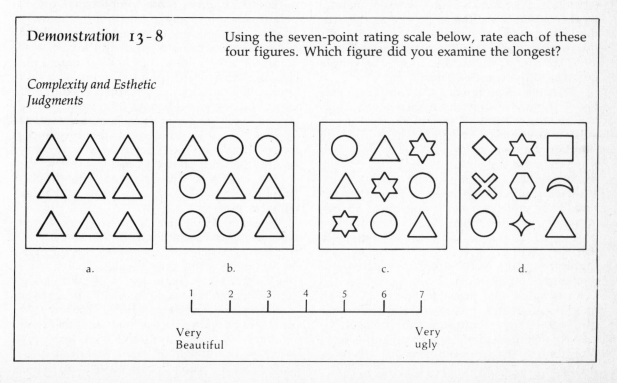

Demonstration 13-8   Using the seven-point rating scale below, rate each of these four figures. Which figure did you examine the longest?

Complexity and Esthetic Judgments

a.   b.   c.   d.

1   2   3   4   5   6   7

Very Beautiful   Very ugly

group of people looked at each picture. He found that people looked longer at the more complex pictures. Thus if we were to measure preference in terms of looking time, Figure *d*—the most complex—would win. Finally, Berlyne showed a third group of people some pairs of pictures and asked them to choose which one of each pair they wanted to see again. He found that there was no relationship between complexity and choice patterns.

According to Berlyne's study, then, we cannot make any general conclusions about the influence of complexity on preference. If we measure preference on a verbal rating scale, moderately complex pictures are preferred to simple or very complex pictures. If we measure preference in terms of looking time, very complex pictures win. If we measure preference in terms of choices for reinspection, there is no consistent pattern in the choices. Berlyne's study clearly illustrates the importance of the dependent variable in research on esthetics.

A study by Francès (1976) demonstrates that there are differences in preference for simple versus complex pictures, as a function of educational level. Francès tested one group of university students in Paris and one group of manual workers, who were the same age as the students. In general, the students tended to prefer the complex pictures to the simple ones. However, the workers tended to prefer the simple pictures to the complex ones.

Research on preference and complexity has been extended into environmental psychology. In one study, students saw pictures of urban and rural scenes that differed in complexity (Kaplan, Kaplan, & Wendt, 1972), and they rated them on verbal preference scales. People preferred the rural scenes to the urban scenes. However, within each category, complex pictures were preferred over simple ones. The researchers note that different results might have been obtained if they had included extremely complex pictures; their study eliminated such highly complex possibilities as junkyards and city slums, for example. If these pictures had been included, they probably would have been liked less than other pictures. The study probably would have replicated Berlyne's (1974) finding that moderately complex pictures were liked more than simple or very complex pictures.

Hooper (1978) discusses this study by Kaplan and his colleagues and other relevant research in relation to architecture. She feels that people like to avoid monotonous environments. Current architectural theories are reacting against the formality and starkness shown in many earlier architectural structures. Those structures were too simple; some novelty and variety are preferable.

A book by Prak (1977) called *The Visual Perception of the Built Environment* explores this issue further. Prak argues that architects achieve complexity by going against the Gestalt laws, such as similarity, continuation and nearness. For example, an architect might disrupt a tendency to group elements on the basis of similarity by using different building materials, such as concrete, brick, wood, and steel. Prak suggests that architects usually try to strike a balance between coherence, which can be obtained by clinging to the Gestalt principles, and contrast, which can be obtained by disrupting the Gestalt principles. Again moderate complexity seems to be preferred.

Hochberg and Brooks (1978) discuss complexity and esthetics in motion pictures. Some motion pictures are more complex than others because they frequently cut from one view to another. Sometimes in a movie you will be aware that the camera dwells on a particular scene for a very long time. Other times, the camera quickly shifts from a close-up, to a shot from a medium distance, and then to a different view. Hochberg and Brooks found that people looked much longer at more complex movies. Specifically, they looked at film sequences longer if the sequence showed one view every second than if it showed one view every four seconds. This is similar to Berlyne's (1974) finding that looking time is greater for more complex pictures.

Deutsch (1978) reviews some studies on complexity and esthetics in music. In general, the results parallel Berlyne's findings for preference using verbal rating scales. That is, people prefer intermediate levels of complexity, somewhere in between simplicity and chaos.

Steck and Machotka (1975) showed that complexity preferences are relative, rather than absolute. They manipulated complexity by varying the number of tones that were presented in a 10-second musical segment. Thus the simplest selection (with a complexity level of 1) had only five tones, but the most complex selection (with a complexity level of 16) had 120 tones. Subjects heard eight selections, which were chosen from different regions of the complexity range. Thus one person might hear selections in which the complexity levels ranged from 1 to 8. Another person, however, might hear selections ranging from 9 to 16. Steck and Machotka found that people preferred selections that were intermediate in complexity with respect to the selections they had heard. Thus people who heard levels 1 to 8 preferred level 3. Those who heard levels 9 to 16 preferred level 11.

In other words, there does not seem to be one single level of complexity that we like best. Instead, our preferences depend on what else we have heard. It would be interesting to see if this same tendency holds true in everyday life when people attend concerts. If we hear a concert of five complex modern selections, we should prefer the piece that is intermediate in complexity for that concert—even though it might be considered extremely complex in comparison to selections at another concert.

Sometimes your emotional state can influence the relationship between complexity and preference for musical selections. Konečni, Crozier, and Doob (1976) compared the preferences of three groups of people. One group of people were angered by one of the experimenters' helpers, and then they were allowed to think they were shocking this person (though the shock was not really received). A second group were angered, but they could not retaliate. A third group received no treatment. Then everyone listened to musical selections differing in complexity. The people in the angry/no retaliation group preferred simpler selections than the other two groups, who did not differ from each other. The next time you are angry and have not been able to vent your wrath, see whether you prefer to listen to simple music!

Cross-Cultural Studies of Esthetics

We would not expect to find many important differences between the anatomy of your eye and the anatomy of the eye for someone living in a different culture. The structure of the eye is about the same, whether you live in Uganda, the United States, or India. However, we might expect to find some cross-cultural differences in esthetic preferences.

There are two extreme positions on the existence of cross-cultural differences. According to the **nativist position**, there is a common thread running through all the human species, so there is little variability in the preference for art forms. According to the **empiricist position**, perception depends upon the culture we experience. Mere repeated exposure to the art forms in our culture, combined with the reinforcement values of these forms, leads to large variability in esthetic preferences from one culture to the next (Lonner & Triandis, 1980). (Remember from the discussion in earlier chapters that the empiricist position argues that learning is extremely important in perception; similarly, the empiricist position argues that we learn various esthetic preferences.)

Which is correct, the nativist position or the empiricist position? The truth is certainly somewhere in between these two extreme positions. However, in a chapter on cross-cultural esthetics, Berlyne (1980) argues that the truth lies somewhat closer to the nativist position. Berlyne writes:

> Evidence is accumulating for the existence of principles of esthetic reaction that are valid for the human race as a whole. Even when intercultural differences have been discovered, the same independent variables are often found to govern aesthetic behavior [p. 35].

A representative study in cross-cultural esthetics was conducted by Berlyne, Robbins, and Thompson (1974), who studied people in Uganda, a country in eastern Africa. Their subjects were 100 urban people, 100 rural people, and 100 people from a community located in between the urban and rural regions. The patterns that people judged were 16 pairs of stimuli that differed in complexity or regularity. Some sample pairs appear in Figure 13-4. The observers rated each stimulus on seven scales, such as pleasant–unpleasant (or, in the Luganda language, *kisanyusa–sikisanyusa*). Also, the experimenters noted the looking time for each stimulus. Similar procedures were

Figure 13-4 Figures rated in Berlyne, Robbins, and Thompson's (1974) study.

used for a sample of Canadian students, to allow cross-cultural comparisons.

Naturally, there were some differences between the Ugandan and the Canadian subjects. However, the similarities were greater than the differences. This tendency was particularly true for the verbal rating measures. There were also impressive similarities between the ways in which the various judgments were related to each other. For example, the same three rating scales were correlated with looking time for both Ugandans and Canadians.

The looking time data showed an interesting trend. Canadians preferred to look at the more complex member of each pair; they looked at more complex pictures an average of 3.7 seconds and at less complex pictures an average of 2.6 seconds. When the data for all Ugandans were combined, there was no difference in looking time for the two kinds of pictures. However, a closer inspection of the data showed that rural people preferred to look at the less complex pictures, intermediate people showed no preference, and urban people preferred to look at the more complex pictures. Thus preference for complexity, measured in terms of looking time, increased with the degree of Westernization of the three Ugandan populations.

Summary: The Effect of Perception on Motivation

- The perceptual qualities of objects determine motivations. Most of the research on the influence of perception on motivation is in the area of esthetics, or the study of beauty.
- Scientific esthetics measures esthetic reactions in terms of ratings, exploration, attention, and physiological reactions.
- In general, people prefer blue shades and dislike yellow shades. Sex differences, color combinations, and temperature can influence judgments.
- People have preferences for particular shapes. For example, rectangles are judged most pleasant if the shorter side is about two-thirds the length of the longer side.
- The relationship between complexity and preference depends upon the measure used. If the measure of preference is a rating on a scale such as DISLIKE–LIKE, intermediate levels of complexity are preferred. If the measure of preference is the amount of time spent looking, high levels of complexity are preferred.
- Studies in architecture and music also show that people judge intermediate levels of complexity to be most pleasant.
- The preferred level of complexity may depend upon the nature of the other items to be judged and upon emotional state.
- Although there are some cross-cultural differences in esthetic preferences, the similarities are often greater than the differences.

Review

1. The first half of the chapter examines the influence of needs and desires on perception. However, your needs and desires might be very different from another person's. How are individual differences relevant in the studies on pupil size changes and perceptual defense?

2. Erdelyi's (1974) article concludes: "Selectivity . . . starts at the beginning and ends only at the very end of information processing." Identify the stages in which selectivity can operate, resulting in perceptual defense. Begin with the adjustment of the eyes and end with the formation of the response.

3. Have you ever said something like, "I

can't even remember what he looked like, but I know I didn't like him"? How is this related to Zajonc's work on thinking and feeling? How does Zajonc's work answer a potential paradox about perceptual defense?

4. We discussed the influence of physiological and psychological needs on thresholds. Suppose you deprived people of food or water and then showed them ambiguous pictures, which had no clear-cut shapes. From what you know about motivation and perception, what results would you expect to find?

5. It is very likely that you will hear someone discussing subliminal perception and advertising as if it were a well-established "fact." How would you summarize the current status of subliminal perception as an advertising tool?

6. Imagine that you are a counselor and you have asked a 10-year-old boy to draw a picture of himself. The picture is extremely small. What other findings is this related to (name as many as possible), and what would you be tempted to conclude about the child?

7. What is esthetics, and what two areas compose this field of study? How can esthetic reactions be measured?

8. Imagine that you are working for an advertising agency. What ideas about color preference would be relevant for you? Mention sex differences, the influence of temperature, and the findings on color combinations.

9. Suppose that you are a teacher and you are responsible for decorating a bulletin board at your school. What facts about complexity and preference would be relevant for you? Keep in mind that different measures of preference produce different results.

10. In our culture we tend to value height, and valued people (for example, presidential candidates) are seen as being taller than less valued people. Suppose that we find another culture where short stature is valued. In this culture, valued people are seen as shorter. Would this finding support a nativist position or an empiricist position? Summarize each position as part of your answer.

New Terms

motivation
Pollyanna Principle
galvanic skin response
pupillometrics
perceptual defense
perceptual vigilance
New Look
response suppression
tachistoscope

sensory memory
subliminal
subliminal perception
subception
projective test
Thematic Apperception Test
(TAT)
Rorschach inkblot test
independent variable

dependent variable
esthetics
speculative esthetics
rate
rank
nativist position
empiricist position

chapter 14

THE DEVELOPMENT OF PERCEPTION

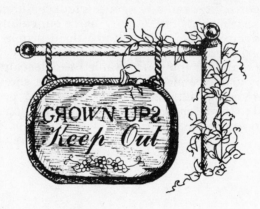

Outline   Infancy
     Vision in Infancy
     The Other Senses in Infancy
   Childhood
     Shape Perception in Childhood
     Constancy and Illusions in Childhood
     Attention in Childhood
   Late Adulthood and Old Age
     Vision in Adulthood and Old Age
     The Other Senses in Adulthood and Old Age

Preview

Most research discussed in the previous 13 chapters employed college-age subjects. In this chapter we examine perception in three other age categories: infancy, childhood, and late adulthood and old age.

Research with infants is hampered because of their limited abilities in communicating their perceptual skills to researchers. However, several research techniques have been developed, revealing that infants are more perceptually mature than we once thought. For example, at a young age, babies can see colors, and they can distinguish their mothers' voices from the voices of strangers. Also, they respond differently to sweet, bitter, and sour substances shortly after birth. However, the acuity, eye coordination, and constancy skills of young infants are quite different from the skills of adults.

Research with children is difficult because they may not understand the task instructions, and they have limited motor skills. As children grow older, they change in their responses to constancy and illusion tasks, their attention to parts of a design, and their ability to pay attention to desirable information and to ignore irrelevant information.

Research that compares older adults with college-age students frequently fails to equate the two groups in regard to factors such as education level and health. Some visual impairments are more common among elderly people. Color perception and various acuity measures may also change during the aging process. As they grow older, people experience a hearing loss for certain tones, which may affect speech perception. However, elderly people may not differ from younger people in their senses of touch, smell, and taste.

A 6-month-old infant, a 7-year-old, a 20-year-old, and a 70-year-old are four of the people who are gathered together at a family reunion. They are all now looking at Uncle Amos, who has just entered the front door with an enormous yellow chrysanthemum. They all hear the shouts of amazement that little Cousin Emily has grown so tall. They all feel the gust of cold wind that blows through the open door. They all smell the distinctive burnt smell of the roasted chestnuts that exploded in the oven. They all will soon taste Aunt Susan's special nonalcoholic eggnog. In other words, these four people all encounter the same sights, sounds, touch sensations, smells, and tastes. However, are their perceptions equivalent? Alternatively, do the perceptual processes change

so substantially as we grow older that they all perceive the world quite differently?

In the first 13 chapters of this book we concentrated almost exclusively upon perception in young adults. As you can imagine, most perception research uses college students, who typically take part in an experiment as part of their course in introductory psychology. In this chapter we will examine how perception changes as a function of development. What kinds of perceptual abilities does a young infant have? How does perception develop during childhood? Furthermore, how do the perceptual abilities of older adults differ from the abilities of young adults?

In this chapter you will see that our perceptual systems continue to develop from the moment of birth through late adulthood and even old age. The infant comes into the world with remarkably good perceptual systems. These perceptual systems continue to develop and mature. Many aspects of perception remain strong throughout old age, but other aspects show some deterioration and loss as we grow older.

We will examine three different age categories in this chapter: (1) infancy, (2) childhood, and (3) late adulthood and old age. As we will note, each age category presents methodological problems in research. Infant subjects cannot supply verbal responses, and so researchers must devise other methods of assessing their perceptual abilities. Children can provide verbal responses, but researchers must still be concerned that performance deficits might be due to motor inability or failure to understand the instructions. In the case of elderly subjects, any performance deficits might be due to poor health and other factors, rather than to a decline in perceptual abilities.

Infancy

Research in infant perception is flourishing. L. B. Cohen (1979) remarks that research on many areas of infancy—such as social, language, and cognitive development—progressed rapidly in recent years. He proposes that infant perception has perhaps been the leading area in this advancement. Cohen speculates that psychologists learned more about infant perception in the last 15 to 20 years than in all previous years. Nonetheless, we will see that our knowledge in some areas is still far from complete.

In the last 100 years, psychologists drastically revised their ideas about what infants perceive. William James, the 19th century American psychologist, proclaimed that the world of a newborn is a "great blooming, buzzing confusion" (James, 1890, p. 488). Thus newborn infants opened their eyes and saw an unstructured, unpatterned chaos. However, we now have evidence that the newborn has remarkably good perceptual systems—much better than we had ever thought.

It is difficult to assess infants' perceptual abilities because their motor and verbal skills are so limited that they cannot inform us about their perceptual capacities. After all, an infant cannot say, "The left-hand figure is farther away." In animal research, psychologists have had to devise special techniques to gather information from pigeons and rats. Similarly, psychologists have been forced to invent clever methods for discovering infants' perceptual capacities. The results obtained with these methods are a major reason for our altered assessment of infant perception in recent years.

Most of the methods are variations of one of three basic methods: preference, habituation, and conditioning. We will be examining each of these methods in this chapter. It seems, then, that infants are not severely handicapped with respect to their perceptual capacities, but they are handicapped in terms of informing us about what they can perceive.

Vision in Infancy

Our discussion of infant vision will include five topics: (1) visual abilities, (2) color perception, (3) shape perception, (4) distance perception, and (5) constancy. For an excellent overview of other aspects of infant vision, read a chapter by L. B. Cohen, DeLoache, and Strauss (1979). A two-volume book entitled *Infant Perception: From Sensation to Cognition* (L. B. Cohen & Salapatek, 1975) includes chapters on more specialized topics.

Visual Abilities

How does the visual equipment of a newborn compare with the visual equipment we have as adults? Actually, our knowledge on this topic is limited. Anatomical studies of the infant's visual system are rare, and the few studies that have been done are questionable for methodological reasons. In particular, researchers disagree about whether the retina is mature at birth. Some believe that the fovea is partially blocked at birth and that foveal vision is not mature until about the fourth month, but others argue that infants' foveas are well developed at birth. In general, considering the entire visual system, the visual pathways mature in the same order in which information is processed. That is, the baby's retina matures first, then the lateral geniculate nucleus, and then the cortex (L. B. Cohen, DeLoache, & Strauss, 1979).

When ophthalmologists measure your acuity, they may ask you to name the letters in each row of the Snellen eye chart. Think for a moment how you might try to measure acuity for a newborn. As you can imagine, early researchers had difficulty devising a measurement technique.

Robert Fantz was responsible for a major breakthrough in measuring acuity in infancy, using the preference method. The **preference method** is based on the idea that if the infant spends consistently longer looking at one figure, in preference to another figure, then the infant must be able to discriminate between the two figures. Researchers using the preference method try to discover the smallest width of a striped pattern that a baby will prefer to a uniform gray pattern that is equivalent in brightness.

Fantz (1961) placed the infants in a small crib inside a special "looking chamber." He attached pairs of test objects—slightly separated from each other—onto the ceiling of the chamber. The researcher could look through a peephole to see the infants' eyes. Mirrored in the center of the eye, just over the pupil, would be the tiny image of the test object that the infant was looking at, for example, a striped patch or a gray patch. The amount of time the infant spent looking at the striped patch and the amount of time spent looking at the gray patch were both recorded. For example, a particular infant might look at the striped patch 65% of the time and the gray patch 35% of the time. The testing sessions were carefully controlled, so that the striped patch would appear on the left half of the time and on the right half of the time, to ensure that any effects of position preference did not confound the study.

What does the information about looking times tell us? Well, if the infants were *unable* to tell the difference between the two objects, then the two looking times should be roughly equivalent. For example, the baby might look at one figure 48% of the time and at the other figure 52% of the time. However, if the baby looks at one figure for a consistently longer time (such as 65% for a striped patch and 35% for a gray patch), then we can conclude that the baby can tell the difference between the two figures. That is, the baby's acuity is good enough that the narrow stripes are distinguishable from the gray patch.

Fantz found that infants under 1 month of age could distinguish between a gray patch and stripes 1/8 inch wide when both patches were placed 10 inches from the infants' eyes. By the time they reached the age of 6 months, infants could distinguish between the gray patch and stripes 1/64 inch wide. Now try Demonstration 14-1 to illustrate the preference method for measuring infant acuity.

Naturally, different methods yield somewhat different acuity measures. With a single line, rather than black-and-white stripes, infant acuity measures are more impressive. In any event, all measures show a rapid improvement during the first year until infant acuity is comparable to adult acuity at the age of about 1 year (L. B. Cohen, DeLoache, & Strauss, 1979). Thus as we noted earlier, skills such as acuity are quite impressive in the newborn, but they also improve as the infant matures.

Fantz presented his striped and solid patterns at a 10-inch (or 25-cm) distance. Psychologists believed for a long time that infants had maximum acuity for objects at a 19-cm (roughly 8-inch) distance, and objects either nearer or farther were quite blurry. It was argued that infants had very poor accommodation abilities and that their lenses were relatively fixed at a particular thickness; the lens could not become thick enough to see closer objects or thin enough to see more distant objects.

However, Salapatek, Bechtold, and Bushnell (1976) determined that infants' acuity is quite good for more distant objects, as well as for objects 19 cm away. They used the preference method to test 1- to 2-month-old infants at viewing distances from 30 to 150 cm (roughly 1 foot to 5 feet). These researchers found that infants showed the same acuity at all distances.

Demonstration 14-1

The Preference Method for Measuring Acuity

Prop up your textbook and walk backward until the narrow-striped patch on the right is indistinguishable from the uniform gray patch in the middle. If 1-month-old babies saw these two patches at a distance of 10 inches, they would look at them equally; they would appear to be the same. However, if the striped patch on the left looked as different from the uniform gray patch as it does to you now, babies might look at the striped patch more than at the uniform gray patch; they would appear to be different. Incidentally, when all stimuli are presented at a distance of 10 inches from babies, 1-month-olds can distinguish the left-hand striped patch from the uniform gray patch; 6-month-olds can distinguish the right-hand striped patch from the uniform gray patch.

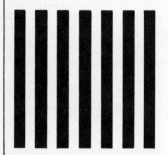  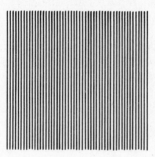

Furthermore, Atkinson and Braddick (1981) found that even newborns showed excellent accommodation for objects at a distance of 75 cm (roughly 2 1/2 feet).

Thus babies' accommodation skills are better than we had previously thought. For some years, articles in popular magazines urged parents to position themselves about 8 inches away from their babies if they really wanted to be seen, but it now seems that this advice was incorrect.

If you have had the opportunity to watch a newborn baby, you might have noticed something unusual about the baby's eye movements. In particular, the eyes occasionally move in different directions from each other. The eye muscles are not well enough developed at birth to keep both eyes on the same target. Thus newborn babies must often receive information from only one eye and ignore information from the other eye. Like other visual abilities, however, eye coordination improves rapidly during the first few months of life.

Color Perception

Can babies see color? In general, the evidence shows that infants are trichromats by the time they are 3 months old, though some researchers have argued that the evidence is not firm (e.g., Werner & Wooten, 1979). One of the primary researchers in infant color vision is Marc Bornstein (1976). Much of his research demonstrated that infants can tell the difference among certain hues in the spectrum. However, he also showed that infants seem to sort colors into separate color categories in much the same way that adults sort colors.

Adults typically divide the spectrum into a small number of basic color names. For example, consider the spectrum in Color Plate 1. If we ask English speakers to name the color represented by a light of 450 nm, almost everyone would reply "blue." If we ask them to name the color represented by a light of 480 nm, they would still respond "blue." However, a light of 510 nm would produce the answer "green."

Notice that 480 nm is equally distant *physically* from 450 nm and 510 nm (that is, 30 nm from each). However, 480 nm is closer *psychologically* to 450 nm than it is to 510 nm; after all, people respond "blue" both to 450 nm and to 480 nm, but they have a different psychological response, "green," to 510 nm.

Bornstein, Kessen, and Weiskopf (1976) wondered whether infants divide the spectrum in the same fashion. Unfortunately, you cannot point to a light of 480 nm and expect an infant to produce a color label. Instead, Bornstein and his colleagues used the habituation method. The **habituation method** is based on the observation that a baby will look less and less at something that is presented repeatedly. For example, if we present a 480-nm light repeatedly, an infant would show habituation and pay less attention to it after several exposures. If we then present a 680-nm light, the baby will probably show **dishabituation,** or an increase in looking time. Apparently, the 680-nm light looks different from the previous 480-nm light, and so the baby will pay attention to it.

As we said earlier, adults think that a 510-nm light looks quite different from a 480-nm light, but a 450-nm light looks much the same as a 480-nm light. Using the habituation method, Bornstein and his colleagues showed that 4-month-olds agree with adults.

Specifically, they habituated infants to a 480-nm light. Then when they presented a 450-nm light, the infants ignored the light, indicating that they perceived that it was the same color as the earlier 480-nm light. However, when infants who had been habituated to a 480-nm light were shown a 510-nm light, they showed dishabituation; they looked at the new light. This dishabituation indicates that they perceived that it was a different color from the earlier 480-nm light. Combining this information with data from other wavelengths, Bornstein and his colleagues concluded that infants' and adults' color worlds are organized quite similarly. Incidentally, more information on color vision can be found in a review article by Bornstein (1978).

Shape Perception

Most of the work on shape perception has ex-

amined the issue of what forms infants prefer to look at. For example, Fantz (1961) demonstrated that infants are more interested in looking at patterns than at bright colors. Fantz presented 2- to 3-month-olds with six test objects that were flat disks six inches in diameter. Three of these objects had patterns—a cartoonlike face, a patch of printed words, and a bull's-eye. The other three were plain—red, fluorescent yellow, and white. The disks were presented one at a time, and Fantz measured how long the infants looked at each object the first time it was presented. The cartoonlike face was the clear winner, followed by the newsprint and the bull's-eye. Try Demonstration 14-2 to see if your results are similar.

Many of you will experience difficulty in locating infants and children to test with the demonstrations in this chapter. Demonstrations 14-2 and 14-4 may be tested with an adult, if necessary. If you do locate a child of the appropriate age, you must be sure to obtain permission from the child's parents before proceeding. Tell the parents that you will not be testing the child's abilities. Instead, you simply want to observe a normal child's perceptual reactions, as part of a course assignment. Be sure to show the material to the parents before you begin.

The human face is probably the shape that has been investigated most thoroughly. Psychologists used to think that babies were born with an unlearned preference for the human face. However, more recent research suggests that babies prefer to look at faces because faces have a high degree of contour and because they move. Other objects that have the same amount of contour and movement capture babies' attention just as much as faces do (Flavell, 1977).

Other researchers have investigated what parts of the human face babies prefer to look at. In general, 1-month-olds scan the outside borders of the face, such as the border between the hair and the skin and the border between the chin and the clothing. By the time infants are 2 months old, however, they pay attention to internal features of the face, particularly the eyes (Haith & Campos, 1977). Other aspects of infants' scanning behavior are found in a book by Haith (1980).

Demonstration 14 - 2

Infants' Preferences for Shape

This demonstration requires you to locate a 2- to 6-month-old infant. You will also need to make six test objects, each a circle 6″ in diameter. Cut three circles out of plain white paper. Leave one of them white. On the other two, draw a cartoon-like face and a bull's eye, using a black marker; use the designs below. Cut a fourth circle out of newspaper. The fifth and sixth circles should be cut from bright yellow and red paper. Using a watch with a second hand, present one test object at a time. Measure the number of seconds the baby looks at each object before glancing away. Incidentally, if you cannot find an infant, try the demonstration on an older child or adult to see if the results are comparable to Fantz's results with young infants.

According to Fantz, Fagan, and Miranda (1975), infants over the age of 2 months prefer to look at curved lines, rather than straight lines, a preference that might have a physiological basis. Furthermore, as infants mature, they prefer to look at designs with many small elements, rather than a few large elements, and designs that are three-dimensional, rather than flat. Finally, infants with Down's Syndrome, a common form of mental retardation, show different kinds of preferences than normal infants. Other determinants of shape preference, such as novelty and complexity, are also discussed by Haith and Campos (1977).

Distance Perception

A 10-month-old infant crawls down the hallway and pauses at the top of the stairs, looking back and forth between the step and the next step down. Can infants see depth? Are they aware which surfaces are farther away from them? These questions were investigated by E. J. Gibson and Walk (1960), who measured depth perception with a visual cliff.

As Figure 14-1 shows, a **visual cliff** is a kind of apparatus in which infants must choose between a side that looks shallow and a side that

looks deep. Babies are placed on a central board with a sheet of strong glass extending outward on both sides. On one side, a checkerboard pattern is placed directly under the glass. On the other side, the same checkerboard pattern is placed some distance beneath the glass. The apparatus is called a visual cliff because of the apparent drop-off on the "deep side" of the central board. To an adult the pattern on the upper side of Figure 14-1 looks farther away because the elements in the pattern are smaller. Gibson and Walk wondered whether infants' perceptions would be similar.

In one experiment, Gibson and Walk tested 36 babies who were between 6 and 14 months of age. They placed a baby on the central board and asked the baby's mother to call to the baby from both the shallow and the deep side. Gibson and Walk found that 27 babies moved off the central board at some time during the experiment, and all 27 crawled at least once onto the shallow side. In contrast, only 3 babies crawled onto the deep side. Thus babies who are old enough to crawl are able to discriminate between deep and shallow; their depth perception is well enough developed that they could avoid the potentially dangerous deep side.

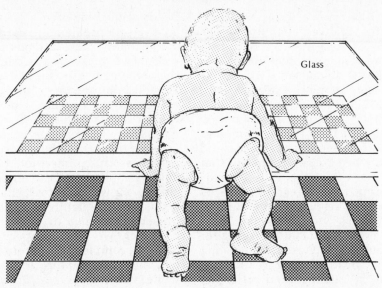

Glass

Figure 14-1   The visual cliff.

The visual cliff was originally designed to test infants who were old enough to crawl. More recently, researchers have used change in heart rate as an index of depth perception. Infants as young as 2 to 4 months of age showed a greater change in heart rate for the deep side of the visual cliff than for the shallow side (Campos, Langer, & Krowitz, 1970). Thus young infants are remarkably well equipped to perceive depth.

Campos and his colleagues have also found that there are developmental patterns in the heart-rate changes (Campos, Hiatt, Ramsay, Henderson, & Svejda, 1978). When a 5-month-old is placed on the deep side of the visual cliff, the heart rate decelerates. At this age, heart rate deceleration indicates that the infant is interested in the depth, but is not a-fraid of it. In contrast, when a 9-month-old is placed on the deep side of the visual cliff, the heart rate accelerates. Acceleration indicates that the infant is afraid. Thus the emotional response to depth changes as infants grow older. However, it is unclear whether the change is due to maturation or experience (Walk, 1979).

Constancy

In Chapter 7 we talked about the nightmare that

would result if all of our perceptual constancies were to disappear. Objects would grow and shrink, become alternately regular in shape and then irregular, and change from light to dark. Objects would also change their color, speed, location, and even their existence from moment to moment. Fortunately, we know from our own experience that adults have perceptual constancy. However, none of us can remember what objects looked like when we were infants. Are infants blessed with the constancies? Alternatively, do parents grow and then shrink as they approach and then move away? Does the shape of the baby food jar change as the infant inspects it from different angles? Unfortunately, the answers to these questions are still controversial.

Cognitive psychologists in the tradition of the Swiss psychologist Jean Piaget have extensively examined one aspect of constancy called **object permanence,** or the belief that an object still exists even though it is no longer visible. (For example, you know that a paperclip still exists, even if you completely cover it with your hand.) This research is summarized by Gratch (1979). Of the more perceptual constancies, only size constancy and shape constancy have been examined systematically. These topics are summarized by Day and McKenzie (1977).

The extent to which infants have size constancy is unclear. Let's look at a classic experiment by Bower that showed evidence of size constancy in infancy, and then we will summarize some more recent negative evidence.

So far we have discussed two major methods for assessing infants' perceptual skills: preference and habituation. Bower (1966) employed the third major method: conditioning. In the **conditioning method** the experimenter selects a response that the subject can make and delivers a reward when the subject makes that particular response. Bower selected head-turning as an appropriate response in his studies. Thus infants responded by turning their heads as little as one centimeter, a response that was neither difficult nor tiring for even young infants. Bower chose an interesting reward for these head-turning responses: peekaboo. When the infant turned his or her head, the experimenter would pop up in front of the infant, smiling and nodding, patting the infant on the stomach, and speaking cheerfully. This multimedia peekaboo game proved to be such a delightful reward for young babies that they responded for a long time in order to earn a peekaboo.

How did Bower use the conditioning method to provide information about size constancy? Bower trained infants to perform the head-turning response only when a particular white cube was present. If they turned their

heads when the cube was not present, they received no peekaboo reward.

Next Bower tested for **generalization,** or the tendency to make a learned response to stimuli that resemble the original stimulus. In the generalization phase of the experiment, Bower presented the original white cube and three other cubes, as illustrated in Figure 14-2. He measured the number of head-turning responses that each cube elicited. The number of responses can be interpreted as an index of an object's similarity to the original cube. For example, we would expect infants to turn their heads most frequently when the original cube is presented during the generalization phase. However, we would expect almost no head turns if a completely different object, such as an old tennis shoe, were to be presented. The white cubes numbered 1, 2, and 3 in Figure 14-2 should elicit an intermediate number of responses, depending upon the extent to which the infants perceive them as being similar to the original cube.

Bower was particularly interested in the number of responses provided to Stimulus 1, which was a cube the same size as the original cube, except that it was far away. A large number of responses to this cube could be interpreted as a demonstration of size constancy, or the recognition that an object stays the same size despite changes in its distance.

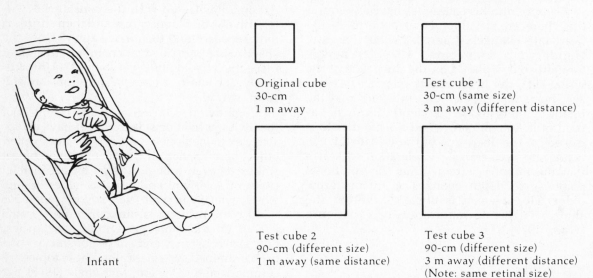

Original cube
30-cm
1 m away

Test cube 1
30-cm (same size)
3 m away (different distance)

Test cube 2
90-cm (different size)
1 m away (same distance)

Test cube 3
90-cm (different size)
3 m away (different distance)
(Note: same retinal size)

Infant

Figure 14-2   The setup for Bower's (1966) experiment.

Infants 6 to 8 weeks of age responded a total of 98 times to the original stimulus, 58 times to Stimulus 1, 54 times to Stimulus 2, and only 22 times to Stimulus 3. Because of the relatively large number of responses to Stimulus 1, Bower concluded that infants have some size constancy. Further evidence for this conclusion came from Stimulus 3, an object that occupied the same amount of space on the retina as the original stimulus. Infants recognized that this stimulus was different from the original stimulus, and so they responded less.

However, more recent evidence is more pessimistic about infants' skills on size constancy tasks. Some studies have used the habituation method, whereas others have used conditioning methods that are more similar to Bower's method. As Day and McKenzie's (1977) review of the literature concluded, these studies on 6-week-old to 4-month-old infants have provided little evidence for size constancy. Thus we must conclude that there is not strong evidence for substantial size constancy in young infants.

It is also unclear whether infants have shape constancy. Bower (1966) used the conditioning method to test infants for shape constancy in rotated figures. He concluded that infants responded as if objects kept the same shape, in spite of the angle from which they were viewed. However, a more recent replication by Caron, Caron, and Carleson (cited by L. B. Cohen, DeLoache, & Strauss, 1979) failed to find evidence for shape constancy.

In summary, it is highly unlikely that young infants have the same kind of size constancy and shape constancy that we have as adults. Learning is probably involved, to some extent, in the development of constancies. As babies interact with the environment, they see that qualities of objects remain constant when viewed in different circumstances. As we will see in the section on childhood, constancy improves as children mature. Nonetheless, infants may have moderate size constancy and shape constancy on some tasks. Cohen and his coauthors (1979) conclude a review of this literature by noting,

This area remains wide open to investigation, and we expect much more

definitive evidence on the existence of perceptual constancies in infants to be available in the near future [p. 423].

The Other Senses in Infancy

We saw in the earlier chapters of this book that perception researchers are primarily interested in vision; hearing, touch, smell, and taste are relatively neglected. The same tendency is true of the research on infant perception, so this section on the four "other senses" is shorter than the section on vision.

Hearing

The auditory system is relatively well developed at birth (Walk, 1978). However, researchers disagree about whether newborns can hear pure tones and discriminate among them. It seems, though, that newborns are sensitive to more complex noises, which are more similar to the sounds in their everyday environment (Haith & Campos, 1977).

When children hear their name called, they look in the direction of the sound. Unfortunately, it is unclear whether infants have this ability to coordinate vision with hearing. An early report was optimistic; a baby 3 *minutes* old was reported to move her eyes in the direction of a clicking sound (Wertheimer, 1961). However, there are mixed results in the research on whether infants become disturbed if their mothers' voices appear to come from a location that is different than their mothers' bodies. One study reported that even 1-month-olds were distressed by the discrepancy (Aronson & Rosenbloom, 1971), but another study reported no distress in infants as old as 7 months (McGurk & Lewis, 1974).

It is possible that infants are aware that vision and hearing should be coordinated, but only the appropriate experimental techniques can reveal this awareness. Maynard (cited by L. B. Cohen, 1979) used the preference method to reveal infants' appreciation for the coordination of vision and hearing. Maynard took two identical films of a jumping toy kangaroo and projected them side by side. The only difference between the films was that they were out of phase; one film was slightly ahead of the other. A speaker, located exactly between the two films, produced a jumping sound that matched one of the two films but was out of phase with the other. Maynard found that 4-month-olds looked significantly longer at the film in which the jumping picture matched the jumping sound. Thus babies as young as 4 months appreciate the fact that the sight of a toy landing on a surface should be matched with the sound of a toy making a slight "thud."

Infants seem to be able to distinguish their own mothers' voices from strangers' voices. However, psychologists do not know how early this ability develops. Some earlier studies proposed that babies as young as a few days could recognize their mothers' voices, but more recent research suggests that this skill does not develop until the infant is 1 to 2 months old (Horowitz, 1974; Mills & Melhuish, 1974).

The most impressive research on infant hearing involves speech perception; it seems that even young infants have a surprisingly sophisticated ability to perceive the basic sounds of language. In particular, they can make distinctions among many different speech sounds, and they categorize speech sounds at an early age. Most of this research has been conducted by Peter Eimas and his colleagues.

Here is how Eimas and his coauthors demonstrated that infants could distinguish among speech sounds, such as *bah* and *pah* (Eimas, Siqueland, Jusczyk, & Vigorito, 1971). Basically, they used the habituation method, combined with the nonnutritive sucking technique. In the **nonnutritive sucking technique,** babies suck on nipples that do not provide liquid, and their continuous sucking produces a stimulus. In this experiment, 1- to 4-month-old babies were required to suck at least two times a second in order to produce a sound. For example, babies might suck to produce the sound *bah*. At first, the babies would suck vigorously to produce the *bah* sound. However, after about five minutes, habituation occurred, and the number of sucking responses decreased. Then the researchers presented a new sound, such as *pah*. They found that the babies showed dishabituation; sucking returned to the previous vigorous level. In other words, babies indicated by their dishabituation that *pah* sounded different from *bah*. Other kinds of

speech distinctions that babies can make are discussed in a review by Eimas and Tartter (1979).

You may recall from the section on infant vision that infants divide the color spectrum into distinct categories. Similarly, Eimas demonstrated that infants divide speech sounds into distinct categories. The physical speech stimulus is really a continuum, similar to the continuum in the color spectrum. For example, in terms of the physical stimulus, there is a continuum in between the speech sounds of *bah* and *pah*, so that there are some sounds in between that resemble *bah* more than *pah*, some that are intermediate, and some that resemble *pah* more than *bah*. As adult speakers of English, however, we hear only *bah* or *pah*; all the in-between sounds are categorized as either *bah* or *pah*. *Physically*, there is a continuum; but *psychologically*, there are distinct, separate speech sound categories.

Research conducted by Eimas and his colleagues (e.g., Eimas et al., 1971; Eimas, 1975; Eimas & Tartter, 1979) demonstrated that infants, like adults, perceive speech sounds categorically. In other words, a sound that is physically closer to *bah* than to *pah* will be categorized as *bah* (even though it is a little like *pah*). To infants, as well as adults, sounds are perceived as either *bah* or *pah*, and not some intermediate sound. The discovery of categorical speech perception in young infants encouraged Eimas to propose that humans have biologically based feature detectors for speech sounds, much like the visual feature detectors we discussed in other chapters (Eimas, 1975; Eimas & Tartter, 1979). In any event, it is clear that infants are remarkably well equipped to process the language they hear around them. At a very early age they can distinguish among highly similar speech sounds.

Touch, Smell, and Taste

Haith and Campos (1977), in their review of research on human infancy, beg perception researchers to adapt the clever methods used in vision research in order to examine touch, smell, and taste. We know very little about infants' skills in these three areas.

Touch is primarily studied in connection

with reflexes. Newborn infants have many reflex responses to being touched at different spots. For example, if you touch a baby's cheek on one side of the mouth, the baby's head will turn in the direction of the touch. This particular reflex makes sense, because it allows babies to find a nipple that has slipped to the side of their mouths. Other reflexes are more puzzling, such as the reflex of curving the back in response to stroking alongside the spine. Other aspects of reflexes and touch sensitivity are discussed by Reese and Lipsitt (1970).

One-year-old infants are able to recognize the shapes of objects by touch alone, as was demonstrated by Gottfried and Rose (1980). These researchers found that babies placed in a dark room played with new objects more than familiar objects. Perhaps future research will determine whether even younger infants have tactile recognition memory.

One of the most impressive demonstrations of infant ability is related to touch. Meltzoff and Moore (1977) found that 2- and 3-week-old infants can imitate an adult's gestures. An experimenter stuck out his tongue, opened his mouth, and puckered his lips. The infants' responses were surprisingly similar to the adult's, as Figure 14-3 shows.

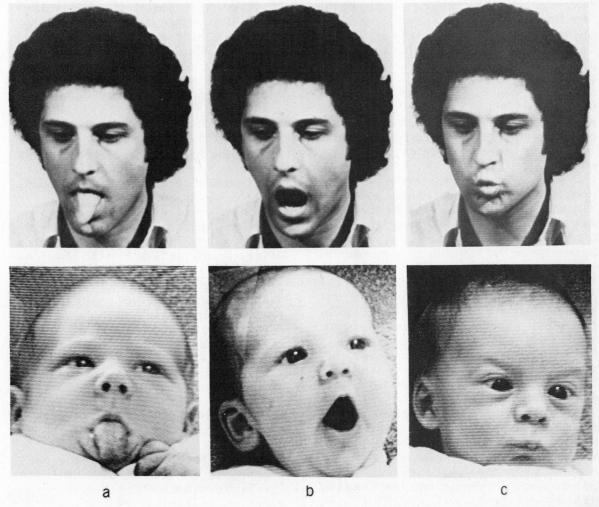

a   b   c

Figure 14-3 Sample photographs of 2- and 3-week-old infants imitating an adult (Meltzoff & Moore, 1977).

Research on smell has demonstrated that young infants are sensitive to a wide variety of odors, such as the rotten egg smell of the oriental seasoning asafoetida and the pleasant smell of lavender (e.g., Self, Horowitz, & Paden, 1972).

Several studies also tried to determine whether newborns can discriminate between the smell of their mothers and the smell of strangers. Macfarlane (1977) offered an optimistic report in a study performed with nursing mothers. He took two breastpads and placed one on each side of an infant's mouth. One of the pads had been worn for several hours by the infant's mother, and the other had been worn by another nursing mother. By the time the infants were 6 days old, they could discriminate between the two pads. That is, they turned to their own mother's pad more frequently than to the stranger's pad. However, in a similar study, Russell (1976) found no differences in sucking responses made to the mother's pad and to a stranger's pad until 6 weeks of age. Thus babies can smell the difference between mother and a stranger at a young age, but it is unclear just how early this skill is acquired.

Steiner (1979) examined the facial expressions that infants make in response to various taste stimuli. He found, for example, that when a sweet substance is placed on the tongue of a normal infant just a few hours old, the infant relaxes his or her face into an expression of enjoyment resembling a smile. A sour substance leads to a puckering of the lips, and a bitter substance causes an expression of disgust. Furthermore, Steiner even found the facial reaction to sour stimuli in premature babies and in severely retarded babies. It seems, then, that babies do not need to engage in higher mental processes in order to decide whether a taste is pleasant or unpleasant; the response is inborn and reflexlike.

Several chapters in a book called *Taste and Development* (Weiffenbach, 1977) are devoted to the origins of the preference for sweet substances. This is a topic with enormous practical implications because of the relationship between sugar consumption and heart disease, diabetes, and obesity. As Lipsitt (1977) notes, most studies use sucking or facial expression as an indication that the infant tastes a particular

substance; however, sweet substances also affect the heart rate of newborns.

Desor, Maller, and Greene (1977) report that infants drank more water when it had been sweetened. For example, 1- to 3-day-old infants drank more than twice as much of a very sweet solution as they drank of plain water. Furthermore, newborns even preferred the sweet solution to regular infant formula. Finally, Desor and his coauthors demonstrate that newborns' sweet preference is quite similar to the preference shown by older infants and by adults. Thus the preference for sweets is not learned, and it is not modified by experience with other foods.

In summary, we see that infants have demonstrated competence in touching, smelling, and tasting. Clearly, each of these perceptual processes develops further as the infant matures, but some skills are present shortly after birth.

Summary: Infancy

- Each of the age categories examined in this chapter—infancy, childhood, and late adulthood/old age—presents methodological problems in research.
- Psychologists are more optimistic about infants' perceptual abilities than they used to be, primarily because of the development of three research methods that can reveal infants' skills: preference, habituation, and conditioning.
- It is unclear whether the fovea is primitive or well-developed at birth.
- The preference method can be used to measure acuity, by finding the narrowest stripes that will be looked at for a greater amount of time than a gray patch.
- Infants show good accommodation for objects 5 feet away, as well as for nearby objects.
- Babies' eyes occasionally move in separate directions.
- Babies seem to be trichromats by the age of 3 months, and they also sort the colors of the spectrum into distinct color categories in the same way adults do.
- Babies prefer to look at patterns and objects with contour and movement, which ex-

plains their interest in the human face; they also prefer curved designs, designs with many small elements, and 3-D designs.

- Studies using the visual cliff show that infants as young as 2 to 4 months perceive depth; their emotional reaction to depth changes as they grow older.

- A study by Bower using the conditioning method showed evidence of size and shape constancy in young infants, but other studies have failed to support these results; thus infants' constancy abilities are not known.

- Some studies show that infants realize that sounds and sights must be coordinated, but at least one study showed that infants were insensitive to discrepancies.

- Infants can distinguish their mothers' voices from strangers' voices.
- Infants can distinguish among speech sounds, such as *bah* and *pah*, and they divide the speech sound continuum into distinct categories.
- When babies are touched on various parts of their bodies, different reflexes are elicited.
- Babies as young as 2 to 3 weeks can imitate an adult's facial gestures.
- Infants can smell the difference between their mother and a stranger when they are 6 weeks old, or perhaps earlier.
- Babies make different facial expressions in reaction to different taste substances; from birth they prefer sweetened water to plain water.

Childhood

Ironically, we seem to know less about children's perceptual abilities than about infants' perceptual abilities. The nonvisual senses have been particularly ignored, so we will confine our discussion of childhood perception to vision.

Fortunately, it is somewhat easier to perform research on children than on infants. A 5-year-old can point to show the direction that the letter E is facing, for example. However, a 3-year-old might not understand the task instructions. Furthermore, children's motor skills are still somewhat limited. For example, if we ask 5-year-olds to copy a figure and their figures are quite different from the original, the difference might very likely be due to their limited motor coordination in handling a pencil, rather than to distorted perception.

Let's look at three topics in our discussion of children's vision: (1) shape, (2) constancy and illusions, and (3) attention. Other topics are covered in a book called *The Development of Cognitive Processes* (Hamilton & Vernon, 1976).

Shape Perception in Childhood

Try Demonstration 14-3, which illustrates children's ability to copy and match shapes. Several studies, summarized by Vernon (1976), showed that young children are highly inaccu-

rate in copying geometric figures. It might be tempting to conclude that young children have poor shape perception. However, as you probably discovered in doing Demonstration 14-3, children can discriminate between different shapes, even if they cannot copy them correctly. As Vernon points out, the motor skills of young children may be inadequate for drawing shape characteristics with precision. In contrast, children are reasonably accurate in arranging matchsticks into a series of shapes, a task that presumably requires less motor skill than drawing.

Incidentally, these studies suggest that it may be unwise to teach children to print letters at an early age. There seems to be a rapid improvement in copying shapes when children are between 5 and 6 years of age. This is the approximate age at which our schools teach children to print, so educators have planned a curriculum appropriate to a developmental level.

As children grow older, there is a substantial change in their perception of the relationship between the parts and the whole in a shape. Try Demonstration 14-4 to determine how children respond to a whole figure made up of identifiable parts. In a classic experiment, Elkind, Koegler, & Go (1964) asked children to describe figures similar to those in the dem-

Demonstration 14-3

*Copying and Matching
Shapes*

For this demonstration you will need to locate a child between 3 and 5 years of age. Draw neatly two identical circles, squares, triangles, and two identical more complex figures. Show the child one of each figure and ask him or her to copy it as carefully as possible.

Now present two identical figures plus one different figure, as illustrated below. Ask the child to point to the two figures that are the same of the three. Repeat this matching test with each of the other three kinds of figures.

Demonstration 14-4

*Children's Whole-Part
Perception*

For this demonstration, you will need to locate a child between the ages of 3 and 11 years of age. Ask the child to describe each of the figures below.

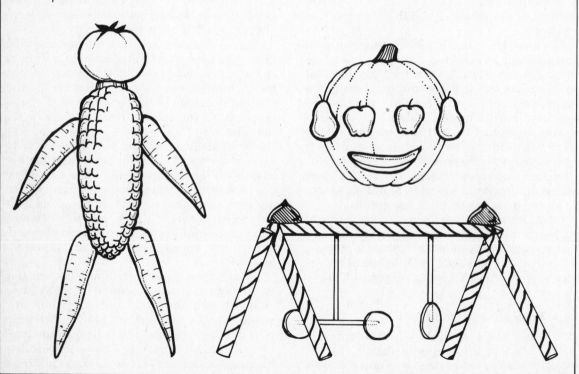

onstration. Children who were 4 and 5 years of age focused upon the parts in each figure. A typical description of the top right figure, for example, might be "a banana and some other fruit." In contrast, 7-year-olds often reported both the parts and the whole in each figure, for example, "fruits and a face." Still older children, 8 or 9 years of age, almost always responded in terms of both the parts and the whole, pointing out the relationship between the two, such as "a face made out of fruit."

Children are less sensitive than adults to the orientation of a figure. For example, children under the age of 10 can remember a picture of a face equally well upright and upside down, whereas adults have difficulty with upside-down faces (Carey & Diamond, 1977). Think about how children's printing is represented by adults. For example, an adult cartoonist might show a boy's clubhouse with a sloppily lettered sign, "GIRLS ƘEEP OUT." In fact, children really do make many letter reversals in their printing. In other words, young children cannot discriminate letter orientation as accurately as adults can. Very young children have difficulty discriminating an upright figure from the same figure turned upside down, but their accuracy on these tasks increases rapidly as they grow older. However, reversals from left to right are a much more frequent cause of difficulty (Vernon, 1976). Thus even a 6-year-old will have difficulty telling a *b* from a *d*.

Most children outgrow their difficulties with letter orientation during the early school years. However, children with **dyslexia** (pronounced "diss-*lehks*-ee-ah") continue to confuse letters of similar shapes but different orientations. A dyslexic child typically has a good vocabulary, knows what the words mean, and can use the words in conversation (Smith, 1978). However, he or she is unable to read. Often the difficulty extends beyond merely confusing similar letters to confusing similar words, such as "bat" and "bit." It is relatively simple to identify a child who has dyslexia. However, there is disagreement about the kind of remedial training that should be used to correct it (Smith, 1978). In general, however, training involves practice in discriminating different shapes and letters. Other perceptual aspects of

dyslexia are discussed by Vellutino (1979) and by Badcock and Lovegrove (1981).

In this section on shape perception we have seen that young children have trouble copying shapes, a difficulty that is at least partially due to the motor aspects of the task. Furthermore, young children also have trouble determining the relationship between the parts and the whole in a picture, and they are also relatively insensitive to the orientation of a figure. Each of these perceptual skills improves as children mature.

Constancy and Illusions in Childhood

We saw in the last section that infants probably have little size or shape constancy in comparison to adults. Children also typically perform quite differently from adults on tasks that require them to make constancy judgments. In a typical experiment, a stick is placed at different distances from the viewer. The observer is asked to adjust the height of a comparison stick until it matches the height of the distant stick. Adults are very accurate on this task. For example, if a stick one meter high is placed 30 meters away, adults adjust the height of the comparison stick so that it is approximately one meter high. In other words, adults acknowledge that the size of the stick remains the same, even though the distance changes.

In general, children show fairly good constancy up to a distance of about three meters. When objects are moved farther away, however, children show less constancy. For example, at a distance of 30 meters, children might adjust the comparison stick so that it is only 70 cm, rather than 100 cm (one meter). To children, a distant figure seems to look smaller.

Some psychologists argue that children might not understand the instructions. Perhaps they believe that they are supposed to adjust the height of the comparison stick so that it is the same height as the distant figure *seems* to be (that is, apparent height), instead of the same height as the distant figure *really is*. As children grow older, they may be more likely to adopt the "really is," objective interpretation that the adults typically adopt. As a consequence, it may be the interpretation of instructions, rather than constancy itself, that changes as children grow older.

Furthermore, young children do not distinguish between "apparent" and "objective" instructions on a constancy task. Tronick and Hershenson (1979) found that some children between the ages of 3 and 6 were able to make distinctions on illusions tasks in terms of how big an object looked versus how big it really was. Thus these children do know the difference between apparent size and objective size on a two-dimensional illusions task. However, their size adjustments on a constancy task were nearly the same for "apparent" ("How big does it seem to be?") and for "objective" ("How big is it really?") instructions. Tronick and Hershenson also found that children—both the children who could distinguish between apparent and objective size on the illusions task and the children who could not distinguish—perceived size constancy up to a distance of about 3 meters.

Most of the common illusions become less powerful as children grow into adults. Both the Poggendorf illusion (see Demonstration 7-7) and the popular Müller-Lyer illusion (see Figure 7-7) are stronger in children than in adults. Weintraub, Tong, and Smith (1973) speculated that the decrease in the Müller-Lyer illusion with increasing age might be due to a change in sensitivity to brightness contours. That is, as children grow into adults, they become less sensitive to contours that are produced by a difference in intensity between two surfaces; perhaps this decreased sensitivity accounts for the decrease in the illusion. In their studies, Weintraub and his coauthors simulated a decline in sensitivity, but this simulation had no influence on the magnitude of the illusion. Thus the decrease in the illusion is not related to changes in sensitivity to brightness contours. Currently, then, we do not have a satisfactory explanation for why the Müller-Lyer illusion decreases with age (Davidoff, 1975).

Attention in Childhood

As children grow older, they pay attention to different aspects of an object. For example, kindergarteners pay attention to shape and color, and they ignore the number of items in a picture. Sixth graders pay relatively less attention to shape and color, and the number of items is now almost as important to them as shape and color (Odom & Guzman, 1972). Furthermore, young children base their recognition of pictures mainly on the central figure. In contrast, older children use additional peripheral details when they recognize pictures (Meyer, 1978).

As children grow older, they have increasing control over their attention processes. Flavell (1977) states:

> One thing that seems to develop, then, is the capacity for controlled selective attention to wanted information coupled with controlled selective inattention to unwanted information [p. 169].

Consequently, older children can adjust their attention to meet the demands of the task. For instance, in a study by Hale and Taweel (1974), 8-year-old children paid attention to two features of a stimulus (for example, color and shape) when this was a useful strategy. However, they paid attention to only one feature (for example, color) when the other feature (for example, shape) did not provide helpful information. In other words, 8-year-olds can be flexible about what they attend to. In contrast, 5-year-olds did not show this kind of flexible strategy of attention.

As Flavell wrote, older children also develop the ability to ignore unwanted information. For example, recall Neisser's selective looking experiment that was illustrated in Figure 12-2. Neisser (1979) tried a variant of this study with fourth and first grade children. The children were instructed to monitor a ball game by pressing a key whenever a critical event occurred in the ball game. However, Neisser included an irrelevant event in the film. For about 4 seconds, a young woman with an open umbrella sauntered across the playing area. Adults who monitored the ball game did not notice the umbrella woman, and they had no idea what Neisser was talking about when he mentioned her. When fourth graders were tested, 22% noticed the umbrella woman, but 75% of the first graders noticed her. Young children could not ignore the umbrella woman, even though she was irrelevant to the assigned task.

Furthermore, the way that children scan pictures changes as they grow older. For example, Vurpillot (1968, 1976) showed children drawings of pairs of houses and instructed them to determine whether the two houses were the same or different. She analyzed eye movement recordings and found that children under the age of 5 were incomplete and unsystematic in their scanning patterns. Often they would not compare all of the pairs of windows; they would respond "same" prematurely. Their search times were generally shorter than those of older children. Furthermore, older and younger children differed in the efficiency of their scanning. Children under the age of 5 seldom compared windows a pair at a time, as older children did. Thus older children are better able to use their attention strategically in order to accomplish their goals; attention patterns clearly change as children mature.

Summary: Childhood

- Testing perceptual abilities in children is difficult because of their limited understanding of task instructions and limited motor skills.

- Children show inaccuracy in copying geometric figures, which may be due to motor skill inadequacies rather than perceptual inadequacies.
- As children grow older, they change from describing a figure in terms of its parts to describing the figure in terms of the parts, the whole, and the relationship between parts and whole.
- Children are less sensitive than adults to the orientation of a figure; children with dyslexia do not outgrow this insensitivity to orientation.
- Children show good constancy for objects up to 3 meters away, but poorer constancy for more distant objects.
- Many illusions become less powerful as children grow into adults, but the reason for this change is not clear.
- As children grow older, they pay more attention to number of items in a design and more attention to peripheral details.
- As children grow older, they are increasingly able to pay attention to desirable information and increasingly able to ignore irrelevant information.
- As children grow older, they search pictures in a comparison task more completely and more systematically.

Late Adulthood and Old Age

Right now, try Demonstration 14-5 in order to see what young adults think about the effects of aging on sensory and perceptual processes. You may be surprised to learn in this section that some of these processes do not change much during the aging process.

Before examining the research findings, we need to discuss a potential methodological problem in studies using elderly people as subjects. It is often difficult to locate a group of young subjects who are identical to the elderly group in all the important characteristics except their age. Imagine, for example, that you want to know whether hearing sensitivity declines during the aging process. You test a group of college students, whose average age is 19, and a group of residents of a nursing home, whose

average age is 78, and you find that the college students have more sensitive hearing.

The problem is that the two groups differ with respect to age, but they also differ with respect to a number of **confounding variables**, or factors that are present to different extents in the two groups. For example, the college students are probably much healthier than the nursing home residents. Furthermore, the college students almost certainly have had more education than a general population of people in a nursing home. Many studies fail to equate the education level or intelligence of their young and elderly subjects. For example, Basowitz and Korchin (1957) used young doctors and nurses for their young group and a general nursing home population for their el-

---

Demonstration 14-5

Attitudes Toward the Perceptual Abilities of the Elderly

Ask several young adult friends what they believe about the perceptual abilities of elderly people. Here are some sample questions:

- Does color perception change as people grow older?
- Does vision for nearby objects change as people grow older?
- Do elderly people and young people respond differently to glare?
- Do elderly people and young people differ in their ability to see fine details?
- Does hearing change as people grow older? Does it change a lot if the people are tested in a quiet room?
- Does sensitivity to touch change as people grow older? Does it change for everyone?
- Does the ability to smell change as people grow older? Does it change a lot or not very much?
- Does the ability to taste change as people grow older? Does it change a lot or not very much?

---

derly group in a study on figure-ground relationships.

If you make no attempt to control for confounding variables such as health, education level, or intelligence, then any differences between your young subjects and your elderly subjects could be due to these factors rather than the critical factor, which is the changes in the perceptual processes that occur with aging. In summary, we must often be cautious about the interpretation of studies comparing young and elderly subjects, particularly when other factors might be responsible for any differences in performance.

Vision in Adulthood and Old Age

Let us examine some of the changes that occur in the structure and functioning of the visual system. More detailed information on this subject can be obtained from an article by Fozard, Wolf, Bell, McFarland, and Podolsky (1977).

First of all, elderly people are more likely to have visual impairments than young people. You may recall our discussion of glaucoma in Chapter 2; in glaucoma there is extra fluid inside the eyeball, and this extra fluid causes too much pressure. The additional pressure may damage the optic nerve, and it may cause cataracts (clouded lenses). Although the inci-

dence of glaucoma is relatively low among young people, as many as 13% of people over the age of 65 may have glaucoma (Fozard et al., 1977).

The type of glaucoma that is most often associated with old age increases gradually. Furthermore, it is not related to the kinds of problems for which people would consult an eye specialist, such as needing a new pair of glasses. Thus regular physical examinations performed on older people should include an assessment of fluid pressure in the eyeball, just as these physical examinations include an assessment of blood pressure. As a result, abnormal eyeball pressure problems could be detected before they cause damage.

The lens of the eye becomes somewhat yellow as we age. The yellow lens absorbs the wavelengths from the blue-green portion of the spectrum. Consequently, older people are less sensitive to colors such as green, blue, and violet than younger individuals are.

In addition to becoming somewhat yellow, the lens of the eye becomes less elastic. As a result, the eye muscles have difficulty changing the shape of the lens so that nearby objects can be seen. This difficulty is called **presbyopia** (pronounced "prez-bee-*owe*-pee-ah"); it is one kind of farsightedness. Incidentally, *presby* means old, and *opia* refers to eyes, so *presbyopia* means, literally, *old eyes*. A person who previously was nearsighted—seeing nearby but not distant objects—may now require bifocals. **Bifocals** are special eyeglasses that have two types of lenses, an upper lens for improving eyesight for distant objects and a lower lens to be used for reading and other close work. Older people who have presbyopia and do not use glasses find that they can see an object more clearly if they hold it some distance from their eyes.

Older people also have more difficulty with glare, in contrast to younger people (Fozard et al., 1977). The primary reason for this difficulty is the changes in the lens of the eye. Thus on a bright, sunny day they might have trouble locating a friend on a beach or noticing a stop sign when they are driving. Inside, a too bright lamp might make it difficult to read the slick surface of some magazines. Facilities that are designed for elderly people should be carefully planned in order to reduce the problem of glare.

Acuity, or the precision with which we see fine details in a scene, also decreases after the age of 40 to 50 (Corso, 1971). The decline is particularly noticeable for dynamic visual acuity, which, you may recall from Chapter 3, is the ability to perceive details on a moving object. Furthermore, Fozard and his colleagues point out that tests of acuity for stationary objects are less accurate in predicting how older people can perceive details on a moving object, in contrast to their predictive value for younger people. Thus the standard types of static acuity tests given by motor vehicle departments may not be very useful in predicting how well older people can see a moving object.

Furthermore, the standard kind of acuity tests may not predict how well an older driver can see at night. Sivak, Olson, and Pastalan (1981) conducted a study in an actual driving situation. The subjects either drove or rode in an automobile at night while watching for a small reflecting sign that had been placed along the side of the road. The sign showed the letter *E*, which faced either to the right or to the left. Sivak and his colleagues measured the distance at which people could identify which direction the *E* was facing. The observers in this study were 12 people between 18 and 24 years of age

and 12 people between 62 and 74. The groups were equivalent on measures of static acuity with a well-lit target. (However, the authors do not mention how the observers were selected or whether other kinds of potentially confounding variables were controlled.)

The results of the study showed that the older observers needed to be much closer to the sign in order to identify it, in comparison with the younger observers. Typically, a young observer identified the sign at a distance of 200 meters, and an elderly observer identified the same sign at a distance of 140 meters. An implication of this finding is that at night, older drivers—in contrast to younger drivers—have less time in which to act on the information contained in highway signs. In establishing standards for highway signs, data from older drivers in nighttime conditions should be considered.

A number of researchers have investigated whether aging influences susceptibility to various illusions. You may remember that sensitivity to many illusions decreases as children mature into adults. However, there is no clear pattern in the reaction to illusions as adults grow older (Fozard et al., 1977). In some cases, elderly people are more susceptible to illusions than younger people, but in many other cases they are less susceptible. In still other cases, age is unrelated to the magnitude of the illusion. Eisner and Schaie (1971) suggested that confounding variables might account for some of the differences.

Some theorists propose a **perceptual regression hypothesis**, whereby people become more childlike in their perceptual responses as they grow older. We noted that children are more strongly influenced by most illusions than young adults are, so the perceptual regression hypothesis would predict that elderly people would become increasingly susceptible to illusions as they age. However, the results on illusions are so varied that they offer little support for the perceptual regression hypothesis.

Finally, there is some evidence that elderly people have more difficulty in suppressing irrelevant stimuli and that they are more easily distracted by details. Layton (1975) discusses the results of several studies using the **Stroop Color-Word Test**, a reading test in which the names of colors are printed in an inappropriate ink color

Try Demonstration 14-6, which is a modification of the Stroop test. Your subject probably took longer to read the second list, in which the word *red* was printed in green, than he or she took to read the first list, in which all words were printed in black. This difference in reading times is greater for elderly people than for young people. In other words, elderly people are more distracted than young people by the irrelevant ink color. However, Layton points out an important confounding variable. People who were born in the early 1900s grew up in a less complex and less interfering environment than younger people, and they may not have had the opportunity or need to develop their perceptual capacities as fully during childhood. It is conceivable that a different kind of research approach, which tested the same group of people as they grew older, would not find a relationship between age and difficulty in suppressing irrelevant stimuli.

In this section we saw that some visual impairments are more common among elderly people. Color perception, vision for nearby objects, the response of the eye to glare, and various measures of acuity also change as people grow older. However, some more complex kinds of visual processes, such as the response to illusions, show little systematic change during aging. Finally, elderly people may have more trouble suppressing irrelevant stimuli.

The Other Senses in Adulthood and Old Age

In hearing, the most common aging problem is probably presbycusis (pronounced "pres-bee-*koo*-siss"). You know that *presby* means old, and *cusis* is similar to the word *acoustic*, so *presbycusis* literally means *old hearing*. More specifically, **presbycusis** means a progressive loss of hearing in both ears for high-frequency tones. According to some estimates, approximately 13% of Americans over the age of 65 show advanced signs of presbycusis (Corso, 1977).

Some kinds of presbycusis, such as those that involve the loss of auditory neurons, can affect speech perception. Difficulty in understanding speech presents obvious problems in communicating with other people. Also, as Whitbourne and Weinstock (1979) note, impaired speech perception influences measures of intellectual functioning. Older adults may receive low scores simply because they did not hear the question properly. In social interactions we may conclude that an older person is becoming less intellectually competent, when in fact this person has difficulty with speech perception.

A large-scale study focused upon age-

Demonstration 14-6	For this demonstration you will need to make two lists of color names. Write the first list with a black marker; it consists of the 20 words listed below. For the second list, rewrite the same words with colored markers in inappropriate colors. For example, the word *red* should be printed in green. Ask a friend to read each list of words; measure the number of seconds required to read each list.

The Stroop Color-Word Test

red	yellow	green
green	red	yellow
yellow	green	red
blue	blue	blue
green	blue	
yellow	red	
blue	yellow	
red	green	

related decrements in hearing for speech (Bergman, Blumenfeld, Cascardo, Dash, Levitt, & Margulies, 1976). The participants in this study were 282 adults in the New York City area between the ages of 20 and 89. Some test sentences were presented normally, without any distortions or other competing noises. As Figure 14-4 shows, people of all ages performed reasonably well on these normal sentences. For example, people in the oldest age group (80 to 89) made only about 15% more errors than people in the youngest age group (20 to 29).

However, the pattern was quite different when the speech was distorted in several different ways. For example, when the sentences were presented in a reverberation pattern—which resembled listening to echoing speech in a hall with poor acoustics—the elderly group made close to 60% more errors than the youngest age group. In many of these speech-distorted conditions, even people in the 40 to 49 age group made substantially more

errors than people in the youngest age group. In summary, most elderly people can understand speech quite well in an ideal, quiet environment. However, in a noisy environment that distorts speech, middle-aged and elderly people have more difficulty than young people in understanding speech.

Think about the implications of this study. If you want to speak to an elderly person, do not leave the record player on at full volume in the background. Furthermore, an elderly person will have more difficulty than a young person in hearing you if a faulty telephone connection distorts your voice. Finally, an echo from a microphone system in a large auditorium will also create more problems for an elderly person than for a young person.

Corso (1977) discusses other issues related to hearing in the elderly. One important question is whether decrements in hearing in the elderly are due to deterioration in the auditory system or to a change in the decision-making processes. Some studies using the signal detection method (see Chapter 1 or Chapter 15) have demonstrated that young and old adults did not differ in their sensitivity to tones. Thus both groups were equally able to detect a pure tone against a noisy background; their d' measures were similar. However, young and old adults did differ in their decision criteria (β). Specifically, older people used more conservative criteria. They needed to be quite certain that they really heard the tone before responding, "Yes, I hear it." In summary, sensory factors may contribute to the difference between elderly people's hearing and young people's hearing. However, higher-level, cognitive factors are also important.

Let us now consider age changes in touch. Kenshalo (1977) reviews this literature and cautions us that changes in touch sensitivity may not be a direct consequence of changes due to aging, per se. Instead, these changes may be the result of injury or disease conditions that affect the skin, the receptors, and the nervous system. Elderly people are more likely than young people to have these health problems, as we mentioned in the discussion of confounding variables.

Kenshalo concludes that some people lose their skin sensitivity during the aging process.

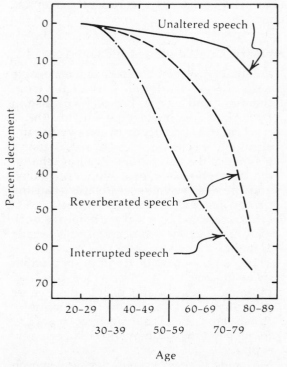

Figure 14-4   Relative decrease in intelligibility for speech (after Bergman, Blumenfeld, Cascardo, Dash, Levitt, & Margulies, 1976).

However, it would be a mistake to believe that most elderly people have deficiencies. For example, one study showed that only 5% of an elderly sample showed a loss of sensitivity to vibrations in the upper extremities; 40% showed a loss of sensitivity in the lower extremities. Thus a substantial number of people—but not the majority—may lose some of their sensitivity to vibrations in their feet. However, only a small number lose sensitivity in their arms.

Many studies have been conducted on pain sensitivity during the aging process, but the results are mixed; the instructions to the subjects seem to have an important influence on whether sensitivity increases, decreases, or stays the same. One study used a signal detection procedure in order to make separate assessments of sensitivity and decision criteria (Clark & Mehl, 1971). Older females showed some decline in their sensitivity to pain, but older males did not. However, both elderly groups adopted a much higher criterion for pain than the younger groups. That is, elderly females and males seemed to report pain only when they were positive that the stimulus was painful. In contrast, young females and males were more willing to say, "This is painful" when there was even a slight possibility of pain. In other words, elderly people seem to endure more pain before complaining about it.

We know surprisingly little about age changes in taste and smell. Engen (1977) concludes,

> Although a number of investigators have observed that taste sensitivity decreases with age, one must view this conclusion cautiously. Not all experiments have been able to verify it [p. 560].

There is some evidence that elderly people may dislike bitter tastes more than young people, but this finding is still tentative. Similarly, we cannot draw any firm conclusions about smell. However, it seems likely that smell is not affected by the aging process per se but by confounding variables associated with age. Health—rather than changes in the perceptual processes that are associated with age—may be the crucial variable.

In summary, we have seen that some perceptual processes show some decline as we grow old. However, that decline is not inevitable; in many cases, perception in the elderly is quite similar to perception in young adults.

Because of space limitations this chapter has not discussed several topics relevant to infancy, childhood, and old age. For example, we have not looked at studies that examine how early experience influences later perception. Most of this research examines the perceptual capacities of animals that were reared from birth in either an enriched or a deprived environment. Several resources you can consult on this issue include books by Aslin, Alberts, and Petersen (1981), by Walk and Pick (1978), and by Rosinski (1977), as well as research reports by Held and Hein (1963), Blakemore (1974), and Grobstein and Chow (1975). We also have not considered theories of perceptual development. Some relevant resources on this topic include E. J. Gibson (1969), Salapatek (1975), and Pick (1979) for theories of perceptual development in infancy and childhood. Corso (1971), Layton (1975), and J. E. Birren and Schaie (1977) discuss theories of perceptual aging.

Summary: Late Adulthood and Old Age

- Frequently, studies compare elderly people with college students, who differ from them not only in age, but probably also in education level, intelligence, and health.
- Several changes occur in the eye during aging: there may be extra fluid, causing glaucoma; the lens becomes yellow, changing perception of green, blue, and violet; and the eye becomes less elastic, causing presbyopia (a kind of farsightedness).
- Older people have more difficulty with glare, and acuity also decreases, especially at night.
- There is no systematic trend in susceptibility to illusions.
- In some cases, elderly people have more difficulty in suppressing irrelevant stimuli.
- Presbycusis is a hearing loss for high-frequency tones; it may affect speech perception.
- Most elderly people can understand speech well in a quiet environment, but they have more difficulty than young people in a noisy environment that distorts speech.

- In some studies, elderly and young people are similar in their hearing sensitivity, but elderly people use more conservative decision criteria.
- Many people lose their sensitivity to touch in their lower extremities as they age, but the upper extremities show little change; health problems, rather than the aging process per se, may be responsible.
- Some studies show that taste and smell become less sensitive during the aging process, but other studies show no change; again health problems may be responsible for many differences.

Review

1. To what extent is the infant's visual world close to the "great blooming, buzzing confusion" that James described? In what respects is their world orderly and somewhat similar to the visual world of the adult?

2. The section on vision introduced you to three experimental methods. Name those three methods and describe how you might use each of those methods to discover something about infants' capacities for smell.

3. In two areas in this chapter we discussed how infants' perception is in terms of distinct categories, rather than allowing responses that are in between pairs of categories. Discuss these two areas.

4. Imagine that you have been asked to design toys for infants that will attract their visual attention. What kinds of characteristics should these toys have?

5. Suppose that a good friend of yours has just had a baby. List for the friend the kinds of nonvisual perceptual skills that the baby would possess by the age of 2 to 3 months.

6. Your brother teaches elementary school. From the section on perception in childhood, what hints could you give him that might be useful in a teaching situation?

7. As Flavell (1977) said, older children develop the ability to pay attention to wanted information and to ignore unwanted information. Summarize some studies that support this statement.

8. Discuss the concept of confounding variables and point out why this concept is relevant in studies comparing young adults with elderly adults.

9. Aunt Mary, who has just had her 85th birthday, will be visiting you for the weekend. What kinds of information from the chapter would be helpful in making her visit as successful as possible?

10. Go back to the list of questions in Demonstration 14-5 and fill out the questions with the appropriate answers as to what really happens to perceptual processes during aging. You are allowed to respond "contradictory information" where appropriate.

New Terms

preference method	conditioning method	presbyopia
habituation method	generalization	bifocals
dishabituation	nonnutritive sucking technique	perceptual regression hypothesis
visual cliff	dyslexia	Stroop Color-Word Test
object permanence	confounding variables	presbycusis

chapter 15

PSYCHOPHYSICS

Outline   Measuring Responses to Low-Intensity Stimuli
        Classical Psychophysical Measurement of Detection
        The Theory of Signal Detection
    Measuring Responses to High-Intensity Stimuli
        Classical Psychophysical Measurement of Discrimination
        The Relationship Between Physical Stimuli and Psychological Reactions

Preview

Chapter 1 introduced you to psychophysics, and we have mentioned psychophysical techniques many times throughout the other chapters of the book. In this chapter we examine psychophysics in more detail. The chapter is divided into two parts: (1) measuring responses to low-intensity stimuli and (2) measuring responses to high-intensity stimuli.

Suppose that we are interested in people's responses to a low-intensity stimulus, such as a faint noise. One way to investigate this area would be to measure a detection threshold, which is the intensity required for the stimulus to be reported half of the time. This threshold could be measured by using three classical psychophysics methods: the method of limits, the method of adjustment, and the method of constant stimuli. Another way to investigate low-intensity stimuli is to use the Theory of Signal Detection. This newer approach emphasizes that people's decision-making strategies, as well as their sensitivity, determine whether people report that they perceive a stimulus.

Suppose, instead, that we are interested in people's responses to high-intensity stimuli, such as a noise that is clearly audible. One way to investigate this area would be to use classical psychophysics methods to determine whether people can tell the difference between two similar stimuli. Another important area of research with high-intensity stimuli concerns the relationship between the intensity of the physical stimuli and the magnitude of the psychological response. A typical question in this area might be whether a solution tastes twice as sweet if we double the amount of sugar it contains.

We briefly discussed psychophysics in the introductory chapter to this book. As we noted, **psychophysics** is the study of the relationship between physical stimuli and the psychological reactions to those stimuli. Our discussion of psychophysics is divided into two sections. In the first section we will describe how people respond to low-intensity stimuli that are difficult to detect. We will discuss both the classical psychophysical methods and the newer Theory of Signal Detection in this first section. In the second section, on responding to high-intensity stimuli, we will examine how people respond to stimuli that are easy to detect. We will now look at the classical psychophysical methods for measuring discrimination and at the nature of the relationship between physical intensity and psychological response.

Measuring Responses to Low-Intensity Stimuli

You are standing on the subway platform, gazing down the dark tunnel to your right. Is that a faint light that you see, signaling the arrival of your train? Do you hear a distant rumble, assuring you that the Lexington Avenue Express is on its way? These are questions involving detection. In detection studies we provide low-intensity stimuli and notice whether people report them. Let's examine two approaches to the detection problem.

Classical Psychophysical Measurement of Detection

The classical psychophysics approach to detection centers upon the measurement of detection thresholds. A **detection threshold** is the smallest amount of energy required for the stimulus to be reported 50% (.50) of the time. For example, we might want to measure a detection threshold for sound in order to determine how intense a sound must be in order for people to say "I hear it" half the time and "I don't hear it" half the time. There are three classical methods of measuring thresholds, which we will examine now. These methods were developed by Gustav Fechner (pronounced "*Feck*-nurr"), a German scientist and philosopher, in the middle 1800s.

The Methods of Limits

Try Demonstration 15-1, which is an example of how the method of limits can be used to measure a detection threshold. In the **method of limits** you begin with a stimulus that is clearly noticeable, and then you present increasingly weaker stimuli until the observer reports, "No, I *can't* detect it." On other occasions you begin with a stimulus that is clearly too weak, and then you present increasingly stronger stimuli until the observer reports, "Yes, I *can* detect it." Thus the observer is presented with a series of descending and ascending trials in which a stimulus is systematically decreased (**descending trials**) or increased (**ascending trials**) in intensity.

In Demonstration 15-1 we include only six series of trials. A formal psychophysics experiment would be more likely to have 100 series. Notice that the method of limits is an appropriate name because a series of trials stops when the observer reaches a limit and changes the response either from yes to no or from no to yes. The familiar Snellen eye chart, illustrated in Figure 3-1, is an application of the method of limits, because the tester begins with a row of large letters and presents increasingly smaller letters until the letters are too small to be recognized.

The method of limits can be modified to meet the needs of the experiment. For example, if you want to measure a threshold for the perception of a spot of light when a person has been adapted to darkness, it would be a mistake to include the series of trials that begins with a very bright light. Instead, you would use series of trials that begins with a very dim light and present increasingly brighter lights; this method is called the **ascending method of limits.**

Another variation is the **forced-choice method**, which requires the observer to choose which one of several presentations actually contains the stimulus. For example, an experimenter might ask an observer to smell four test tubes, one containing a particular substance dissolved in water and the other three containing only plain water. The observer would be asked to identify which test tube contained the odorous substance. The amount of odorous substance could be systematically increased or decreased from trial to trial.

The Method of Adjustment

In the **method of adjustment** the observer—rather than the experimenter—adjusts the intensity of the stimulus. Typically, the observer makes adjustments that are continuous—for example, by adjusting a knob—rather than discrete—for example, by tasting separate solutions containing different amounts of a substance.

This method can be used to obtain a threshold very quickly, and so it may be used to locate an approximate threshold. However, many observers tend to be sloppy when they use this method, and there is great variation from one observer to the next. Consequently, psychophysicists use it less than other methods. Notice, though, that the method of adjustment is what you use most often in everyday life, for example, when you adjust the knob on your radio so that the sound is just barely audible.

The Method of Constant Stimuli

In the **method of constant stimuli** the stimuli are presented in random order, as in Demonstration 15-2. The experimenter usually selects between five and nine stimuli, such that the weakest stimulus is clearly below threshold and the strongest stimulus is clearly above

Demonstration 15 - 1

Using the Method of Limits to Measure a Detection Threshold

In this demonstration you will use the method of limits to measure an observer's ability to detect sweetness. First, take one teaspoon of table sugar and dissolve it in one 8-ounce glass of cool tap water; stir to dissolve. Line up five empty glasses, and fill them as indicated:

| One tablespoon sugar solution + Six tablespoons tap water | Two tablespoons sugar solution + Five tablespoons tap water | Three tablespoons sugar solution + Four tablespoons tap water | Four tablespoons sugar solution + Three tablespoons tap water | Five tablespoons sugar solution + Two tablespoons tap water |

Now you may begin the trials. Blindfold your observer and present a solution (as specified below). The observer tastes a small sip and says "yes" if sweetness is detected and "no" if sweetness is not detected. Then the observer spits out the solution, rinses with tap water for about 20 seconds, and repeats the procedure with the next trial in the series. Continue a series until your observer shifts responses from "yes" to "no" or from "no" to "yes." When the shift occurs, begin the next series.

Below is a table indicating the order in which you should present the solutions. For example, begin the first series with solution 1 because this has an asterisk. Begin the second series with solution 4, follow with solution 3, etc. I have recorded my observer's responses; record your observer's responses next to mine. (Incidentally, save any remaining solution for Demonstrations 15-2 and 15-4.)

SERIES NUMBER

		1	2	3	4	5	6
not very sweet	1	*No*				*No*	
	2	No	No	*No*	No	No	No
	3	No	Yes	No	Yes	Yes	Yes
	4	Yes	*Yes*	Yes	Yes		Yes
very sweet	5				*Yes*		*Yes*
Threshold for each series		3.5 ___	2.5 ___	3.5 ___	2.5 ___	2.5 ___	2.5 ___

The overall threshold equals the average of the midpoints (thresholds) calculated for the individual series. The overall threshold for my observer was 2.8. What is the overall threshold for your observer?

threshold. (As you can imagine, these values must be chosen after pretesting with a speedy method such as the method of adjustment.)

We present each of the five solutions four times in Demonstration 15-2. In contrast, in a formal psychophysics experiment, each stimulus might be presented 100 times. As a consequence, the method of constant stimuli is extremely time-consuming. However, this method is preferred when psychophysicists want to obtain a very careful measurement of a threshold, because it eliminates some of the biases found in the other two methods. For example, when the stimuli are presented in random order, you do not know what kind of stimulus to expect on the next trial, unlike in the method of limits or the method of adjustment. Incidentally, the forced-choice option can also be used with the method of constant stimuli.

Let's review these three methods by describing how each method would be used to measure the threshold for perceiving a low-intensity tone. To use the *method of limits*, the experimenter begins by presenting the tone at an intensity that is high enough that the observer is certain to say, "Yes, I hear it." Then the experimenter presents weaker and weaker tones until the observer reports, "No, I can't hear it." On alternate trials the experimenter begins with a low-intensity tone and increases the intensity until the observer says, "Yes, I hear it."

To use the *method of adjustment*, the observer makes adjustments in the intensity of the tone by perhaps turning a knob. On half of the trials the observer begins with a high-intensity tone and turns the knob until it is inaudible. On the other half of the trials the observer begins with a low-intensity tone and turns the knob until it is audible.

To use the *method of constant stimuli*, the experimenter presents in random order a variety of tones having differing intensities. Each time a tone is presented, the experimenter reports either "No, I can't hear it" or "Yes, I can hear it."

How do experimenters decide which method to use? The method of constant stimuli provides the most reliable data, and it is relatively free of biases. However, a disadvantage is that the experimenter needs to pretest the

stimuli in order to locate stimuli that are at near-threshold levels. The method of adjustment produces errors and is typically used only for stimuli that are continuously adjustable; however, it may be useful for pretesting the stimuli that will be used with the method of constant stimuli. The method of limits requires less preplanning than the method of constant stimuli and may be the choice of an experimenter who wants fairly reliable thresholds without too much investment of time.

The Theory of Signal Detection

The **Theory of Signal Detection,** or TSD, argues that the thresholds obtained by classical psychophysics methods measure not only the observer's sensitivity but also his or her decision-making strategy, or criterion (Green & Swets, 1966). The **sensitivity measure** depends upon two factors: (1) the intensity of the stimulus and (2) the sensitivity of the observer. Thus the sensitivity measure would be high in a study on hearing when the stimulus is a very loud tone and when the observer has excellent hearing ability. The sensitivity measure would be low if the stimulus is a quiet tone or the observer has impaired hearing. The symbol d' is used to represent sensitivity; it will be discussed later.

The **criterion** (pronounced "cry-*tear*-ee-un") measures the observer's willingness to say, "I detect the stimulus" when he or she is uncertain about whether the stimulus has actually been presented. For example, suppose that you are waiting for the subway train to arrive, as we described earlier, and you know that another train just left one minute ago. Your criterion would be different from that in a situation in which you know that the last train left 20 minutes earlier. Incidentally, criterion is often symbolized by the Greek letter β (pronounced "*bay*-tuh"). Also, the plural of *criterion* is *criteria*.

The criterion that an observer selects depends upon several factors. One important factor is the probability that the stimulus will occur. For example, the stimulus "light from an approaching subway train" is more likely or

Demonstration 15-2

Using the Method of Constant Stimuli to Measure a Detection Threshold

In this demonstration you will use the method of constant stimuli to measure the ability to detect sweetness. Use the solutions from Demonstration 15-1 or else mix up more according to those instructions. Blindfold an observer. The observer will sip, report, spit, and rinse as in the previous demonstration. However, you will present the solutions in random order, as indicated below. Again record your observer's responses next to mine.

TRIAL	SOLUTION NUMBER	RESPONSE	TRIAL	(TRIALS, CONTINUED) SOLUTION NUMBER	RESPONSE
1	2	No	11	5	Yes
2	5	Yes	12	4	Yes
3	4	Yes	13	1	No
4	1	No	14	2	No
5	3	Yes	15	3	Yes
6	2	No	16	2	Yes
7	4	Yes	17	5	Yes
8	1	No	18	1	No
9	5	Yes	19	4	Yes
10	3	No	20	3	Yes

SUMMARY TABLE

SOLUTION NUMBER	NUMBER OF "YES" RESPONSES	PROPORTION OF "YES" RESPONSES
1	0	.00
2	1	.25
3	3	.75
4	4	1.00
5	4	1.00

Now plot the proportion of "Yes" responses below, as I have done. Notice where the horizontal line corresponding to .50 "Yes" responses crosses the line you make to connect the plotted proportion. This is the threshold.

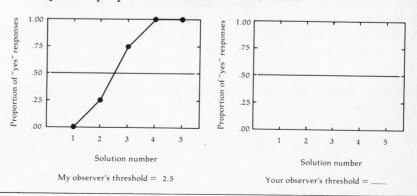

My observer's threshold = 2.5   Your observer's threshold = ____

probable if the last train left 20 minutes earlier than if it left one minute earlier. Another important factor is the **payoff**, or the rewards and punishments associated with a particular response. If I tell you that I will pay you 50¢ every time you correctly report seeing a light, you will be likely to say "I see it" if there is even the slightest chance that the light had been presented. In contrast, if I tell you that you must pay me 50¢ every time you report seeing a light when no light was actually presented, you will say "I see it" only if you are absolutely convinced that the light has been presented. Notice that the criterion is determined by our strategies in making decisions, rather than by our perceptual sensitivity.

We should mention, incidentally, that the Theory of Signal Detection is not an alternative procedure for determining thresholds. In fact, we *cannot* calculate thresholds with this method. However, TSD has contributed to our understanding of some of the problems that occur in measuring thresholds with the classical methods. For example, in some variants of the classical methods, the experimenter occasionally uses "catch trials," in which no stimulus is presented. Nonetheless, observers often report that they detect the stimulus on these trials. TSD explains that these errors occur because the observer is very willing to say, "I detect the stimulus."

Let us examine the Theory of Signal Detection in more detail. We will talk about situations involving an observer who must listen for a quiet tone, although signal detection theory can also be applied to vision, the skin senses, smell, and taste. We need to discuss the following items: (1) outcomes of a signal detection trial, (2) receiver operating characteristic curves, and (3) probability distributions.

Outcomes of a Signal Detection Trial

In a signal detection experiment the experimenter presents a tone or **signal** that is weak and difficult to detect. Thus the signal has an intensity that is close to the observer's threshold. Usually, the intensity of the signal remains constant throughout a single testing session, unlike the situation in the classical psychophysics methods. Furthermore, the experimenter presents the signal on some trials and does not present the signals on other trials. For example, the experimenter might decide to present the signal on 50% of the trials in a given session.

Examine Table 15-1. Notice that the signal can be either present or absent. Now, in the best of all possible worlds the observer says "Yes, I hear it" whenever the signal is present and "No, I don't hear it" whenever the signal is absent.

In reality, however, observers make mistakes. As Table 15-1 shows, there can be two different kinds of mistakes. Observers sometimes think that they hear a signal when the signal is absent and they sometimes think that they do not hear a signal when the signal is present. Notice that each of the four possible outcomes of a signal detection trial has a descriptive name. Spend some time memorizing these names, because we will use them in our discussion of signal detection theory. Imagine yourself trying to decide whether your doorbell just rang. Notice that your decision could represent a **hit** or a **correct rejection** (two kinds of correct decisions) or a **false alarm** or a **miss** (two kinds of mistakes).

In a typical signal detection experiment an observer listens for a tone that has a constant intensity and frequency. The experimenter pre-

Table 15-1 The four possible outcomes of a signal detection trial.

		WAS THE SIGNAL PRESENT OR ABSENT?	
		PRESENT	*ABSENT*
What Did the Observer Respond?	"Yes, I hear it"	hit (correct)	false alarm (mistake)
	"No, I don't hear it"	miss (mistake)	correct rejection (correct)

Table 15-2 Example of the percentages of hits and misses when signal was present and false alarms and correct rejections when signal was absent.

What Did the Observer Respond?	WAS THE SIGNAL PRESENT OR ABSENT?	
	PRESENT	ABSENT
"Yes, I hear it"	hit = .70	false alarm = .32
"No, I don't hear it"	miss = .30	correct rejection = .68

sents the tone on 50% of the trials and presents no tone on the other 50% of the trials. Table 15-2 shows how often each of the four possible outcomes might occur in a hypothetical experiment. Notice that when the signal is really present, the observer reports it 70% of the time. However, when the signal is absent, the observer reports it (incorrectly) 32% of the time.

Remember that we said that one factor influencing the criterion is the probability that the stimulus will occur. In Table 15-2 we discussed a situation in which the probability of the stimulus was .50. If we change the probability of the stimulus, then we can also change the observer's criterion. As a consequence, the observer will change the frequency with which he or she reports the stimulus. Table 15-3 shows some representative frequencies, as a function of stimulus probability.

Receiver Operating Characteristic Curves

The data from signal detection experiments are often depicted in a receiver operating characteristic curve. A **receiver operating characteristic curve**, or **ROC curve**, shows the relationship between the probability of a hit and the proba-

bility of a false alarm. The data in an ROC curve are obtained from many sessions in which the experimenter has manipulated the observer's criterion.

In an ROC curve, the sensitivity is constant. That is, the tone does not change in its intensity, and the observer does not change in his or her sensitivity. However, the observer's criterion changes, either because the experimenter manipulates the probability of the tone's occurrence (as we showed in Table 15-3) or because the experimenter manipulates the payoffs (for example, by varying the amount of money paid for each hit or subtracted for each false alarm). Each point along a given ROC curve represents a different criterion that the observer has adopted. Figure 15-1 shows an ROC curve that has been plotted for the data from Table 15-3.

Suppose that we repeat the signal detection experiment with a more intense tone (or else with a more sensitive observer). Again the experimenter manipulates the probability of the tone's occurrence so that the observer changes his or her criterion. In this case we would obtain an ROC curve such as Curve A in Figure 15-2. (Curve B is taken from Figure 15-1, for

Table 15-3 The probability of a hit or a false alarm, as signal probability increases from .10 to .90.

Probability of a Signal	PROBABILITY	
	HIT	FALSE ALARM
.10	.32	.08
.20	.42	.12
.30	.52	.17
.40	.62	.25
.50	.70	.32
.60	.78	.41
.70	.84	.50
.80	.90	.61
.90	.93	.73

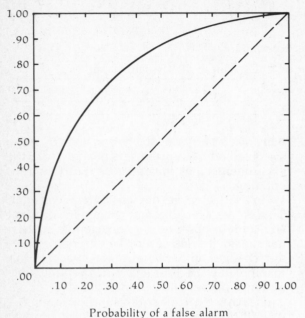

Probability of a false alarm

Figure 15-1   A receiver operating curve.

comparison's sake.) A third curve, Curve C, represents either a softer tone or else a less sensitive observer. Compare those three curves. Notice that for any given false alarm rate, the three curves differ enormously from one another with respect to the probability of a hit. For example, when the probability of a false alarm is .20, Curve A has a very high hit rate (.88), Curve B has a medium hit rate (.53), and Curve C has a low hit rate (.32).

Notice that Curves A, B, and C in Figure 15-2 are labeled $d' = 2.0$, $d' = 1.0$, and $d' = .5$, respectively. The measure d' (pronounced "dee prime") is an index of sensitivity; this measure tells us about the loudness of the tone and the sensitivity of the observer. When d' is 0, the observer is simply guessing; hits and false alarms occur equally often. A large d' (Curve A in Figure 15-2) means that the tone is loud or the observer is sensitive; with a large d' the observer has a high hit rate and a low false alarm rate.

Psychologists calculate the number of hits and false alarms obtained in an experiment, and they plot them on a graph. They then calculate d' from formulas or by comparing their ROC curves with curves published in reference books (for example, Gescheider, 1976). Now try Demonstration 15-3 to make certain that you know how to plot an ROC curve and how to interpret the curve.

Probability Distributions

So far, we have discussed two major points: (1) how a signal detection trial can produce a hit, a miss, a false alarm, or a correct rejection and (2) how the proportion of hits and false alarms can be plotted in a ROC curve. Now we need to look at detection from a more theoretical perspective. Specifically, we need to examine the probability distributions for noise and signal plus noise situations.

Imagine that you are sitting in a room, trying to decide whether you heard a car drive up. We refer to situations in which no signal occurs as **noise** trials. Thus if a car did *not* drive up, you experienced a noise trial in which the only sounds were the irrelevant background noises from the environment and the internal noises that your body makes. (Notice that we can have noise in the other perceptual systems as well; irrelevant visual stimuli, for example, constitute visual noise.) Noise refers to irrelevant stimuli that might be mistaken for the signal.

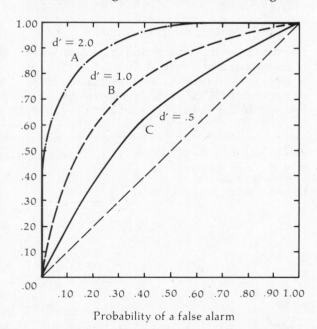

Probability of a false alarm

Figure 15-2   Three receiver operating curves.

Demonstration 15 - 3

Understanding ROC Curves

The purpose of this demonstration is to make certain that you know how to plot and interpret ROC curves. Suppose that you have gathered the data shown below at left from an observer by varying the probability of a signal's occurrence. Plot the data in the figure, and then answer the questions.

PROBABILITY OF A HIT	PROBABILITY OF A FALSE ALARM
.52	.05
.71	.15
.82	.30
.90	.42
.92	.58

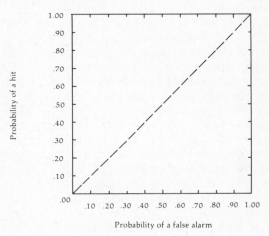

Questions about the ROC curve (answers at bottom of the demonstration):

1. Comparing your curve with the curves in Figure 15-2, what would you estimate is your d'?

2. What way, other than changing the probability of the signal, could also have been used to get your observer to change his or her criterion?

3. Notice the diagonal line in the figure. If an observer had that kind of performance, would this person be more or less sensitive than your observer?

4. Is there any point along the curve at which the false alarm rate is higher than the hit rate?

5. Does your observer's sensitivity vary from one situation to the next for the points you have plotted in the figure? If not, what does vary?

6. As the probability of a hit increases, does the probability of a false alarm increase, decrease, or stay the same?

Answers: 1. The d' is approximately 1.5. 2. You could pay money for hits and/or subtract money for false alarms. 3. Less sensitive; in fact, this person would be responding at a chance level. 4. No, the hit rate is always higher. 5. No, the sensitivity does not vary; the criterion varies. 6. The probability of a false alarm increases.

On the other hand, it is possible that the car really did drive up. We would refer to this situation as a **signal + noise** trial (pronounce the + as "plus"), because the appropriate signal (the car sound) really did occur, in addition to all the irrelevant noise.

Figure 15-3 shows a hypothetical graph of the two possible situations, *noise* and *signal + noise.* Notice that each curve is in the shape of a **probability distribution**, which shows the probability of various sound intensities. As these distributions indicate, we cannot list just a single value for the loudness of the noise or the signal + noise situations. After all, loudness varies from one moment to the next. (For example, you may hear your roommate's ticking wristwatch one moment, but it may be inaudible the next moment.) However, notice that the intensity of the noise fluctuates around a particular average level. Similarly, the intensity of the signal + noise fluctuates around another, higher average level.

In Figure 15-3 the noise and the signal + noise curves overlap to some extent. The amount of overlap corresponds to d', the measure of sensitivity we discussed earlier. Figure 15-3 shows a d' of 2.0. A d' of 1.0 would show even greater overlap, whereas a d' of 3.0 would show less overlap. In other words, as d' increases, sensitivity increases, and the noise and signal + noise situations become more and more distinguishable from one another. That is,

it becomes increasingly easy to tell whether you heard just noise or whether you heard signal + noise.

Figure 15-3 also shows a vertical line labeled *criterion.* Whenever the intensity (representing either noise or signal + noise) is above that criterion line, the observer says, "Yes, I hear it." Whenever the intensity is below that criterion line, the observer says, "No, I don't hear it." Notice in Figure 15-3 that when the observer says "I hear it," he or she can be either correct (a hit because there was signal + noise) or incorrect (a false alarm because there was only noise). Similarly, an observer who says "I don't hear it" may be either correct (a correct rejection) or incorrect (a miss). Thus the four regions of the two curves correspond to the four terms you learned in Table 15-1.

In Figure 15-3 we show a situation in which a person has set a fairly high criterion; this person says, "I hear it" only if he or she is fairly certain that the signal has occurred. Notice in this case that hits occur on only half of the trials in which the signal is presented. Furthermore, false alarms rarely occur.

Figure 15-4 shows a situation in which the d' is the same as in Figure 15-3, but the person has set a fairly low criterion; this person says, "I hear it" if there is even the slightest chance that the signal has occurred. You can see that in this case both hits and false alarms occur often. Think about situations in which you set the

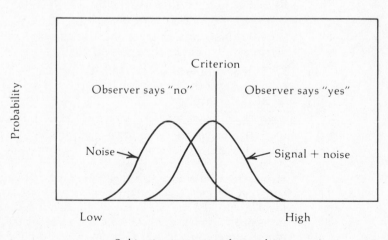

Figure 15-3   A hypothetical graph of noise and signal + noise in signal detection (fairly high criterion).

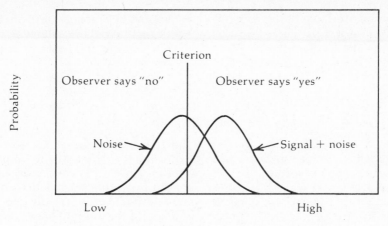

Criterion

Observer says "no"   Observer says "yes"

Probability

Noise →   ← Signal + noise

Low   High

Subjective intensity of stimulus

Figure 15-4   A hypothetical graph of noise and signal + noise in signal detection (fairly low criterion).

criterion fairly low. For example, suppose that you know that your friend should be driving by to pick you up in the next few minutes. Do you find yourself leaping up at the slightest rustle of leaves or the faintest hint of anything with four wheels?

The Theory of Signal Detection offers an improvement over classical psychophysics because it allows us to separate sensitivity from criterion. Let's consider a specific example that is discussed in detail in Chapter 14. When elderly men and young men are tested for reactions to painful stimuli, elderly men have higher thresholds. It is tempting to conclude that elderly men are simply less likely to feel the pain. However, a study by Clark and Mehl (1971) used the signal detection approach. These researchers found that elderly men and young men had similar d' values; they were equally sensitive to the pain. On the other hand, the two groups had different criteria for reporting pain (β). Elderly men reported pain only when they were positive that the stimulus was painful, whereas young men were more willing to say, "This is painful" if the pain was barely perceptible. Thus criterion—rather than sensitivity—changes as men grow older.

Summary: Measuring Responses to Low-Intensity Stimuli

- Psychophysics is the study of the relationship between physical stimuli and the psychological reactions to those stimuli.

- The classical psychophysics methods measure detection thresholds, or the smallest amount of energy required for the stimulus to be reported 50% of the time.
- The method of limits involves presenting systematically increasing or decreasing amounts of a stimulus. It provides a fairly reliable threshold without too much investment of time.
- The method of adjustment involves the observer's adjusting the intensity of the stimulus until it is barely detectable. It provides a threshold very rapidly, but errors are more likely than with the other two methods.
- The method of constant stimuli involves presenting near-threshold stimuli in random order. It provides a highly accurate threshold, but it is time-consuming because it requires pretested stimuli.
- The Theory of Signal Detection measures both sensitivity and criterion.
- Sensitivity depends upon stimulus intensity and the sensitivity of the observer.
- The criterion, which measures willingness to report the stimulus, depends upon factors such as probability of stimulus occurrence and payoff.
- The outcome of a signal detection trial can be a hit, a correct rejection, a false alarm, or a miss.
- The probability of each of these four outcomes depends upon the sensitivity measure, d', and upon the criterion measure, β.

- ROC curves can be used to plot the proportion of hits and false alarms. Each separate ROC curve represents a different *d'*.
- Signal Detection Theory can also be represented in terms of probability distributions for trials in which signal + noise occurred and for trials in which only noise occurred.

Measuring Responses to High-Intensity Stimuli

So far, we have discussed how people respond to low-intensity stimuli, such as dim lights and weak tones. In this section we will talk about the measurement of stimuli that can be readily detected. In particular, we need to discuss (1) the classical psychophysical measurement of discrimination and (2) the relationship between the physical intensity of the stimulus and the psychological reaction of the observer.

Classical Psychophysical Measurement of Discrimination

In **discrimination** studies we examine whether people can tell the difference between two stimuli. For example, a candy company may wish to determine whether consumers can discriminate between two chocolate bars and tell which one is sweeter. A dishwasher manufacturer may want to see whether consumers can determine that its product makes less noise than the competitors. In these cases, two stimuli that are clearly above threshold are being compared in order to determine whether observers think that selection A has more than, less than, or the same amount of a particular characteristic as selection B has. The experimenter's goal in a discrimination experiment is to determine the least amount that a stimulus must change in order for the observer to notice the difference.

In a discrimination experiment there is a **standard stimulus** that remains constant throughout the experiment. Another stimulus, the **comparison stimulus**, varies throughout the experiment. In general, we change the comparison stimulus according to a specified schedule and notice how much change we can make before the observer notices that the comparison stimulus is different from the standard stimulus. Psychophysicists often calculate the just noticeable difference, or jnd. The **just noticeable difference** measures how far apart the two stimuli must be from each other in order for the difference to be *just noticeable*.

Remember that we discussed three classical methods for measuring detection thresholds: the method of limits, the method of adjustment, and the method of constant stimuli. Each of these methods can also be adapted in order to measure discrimination. We will describe the method of limits and the method of adjustment briefly. We will cover the method of constant stimuli in more detail, because this method yields the most accurate measures. (For details on the other methods, consult other books, such as those by Engen, 1971a; Manning and Rosenstock, 1968; and Matlin, 1979.)

In the **method of limits for measuring discrimination** the standard stimulus remains the same, and the comparison stimulus varies from low to high on some series of trials and from high to low on other series of trials. For example, suppose that you want to examine the discrimination of pitch. Specifically, you want to determine how much change you can make in the comparison stimulus before the observer notices that it is different from a 1000-Hz standard stimulus. On some series of trials you present comparison stimuli that increase in frequency from, say, 950 Hz to 1050 Hz. On other series of trials you present comparison stimuli that decrease in frequency from 1050 Hz to 950 Hz. Your observer must reply whether the comparison stimulus is higher-pitched, lower-pitched, or the same as the standard stimulus. The calculation of the just noticeable difference involves noticing the frequency of the comparison stimulus at which the judgments change from "higher than" to "same as" and the frequency at which they change from "same as" to "lower than."

In the **method of adjustment for measuring discrimination** the observer adjusts the comparison stimulus by himself or herself until the comparison stimulus seems to match the standard stimulus. The observer repeats this adjustment task many times. Consequently, we have a large number of selections of comparison stimuli that the observer believes are equivalent to the standard stimulus. For example, suppose you want to examine discrimination for tones of different frequencies and the standard stimulus is a 1000-Hz tone. An observer might select a 995-Hz stimulus the first time, a 1003-Hz stimulus the second time, and so forth. The method of adjustment yields several measures of discrimination, but a common measure is a statistical calculation, the standard deviation.

In the **method of constant stimuli for measuring discrimination** the experimenter presents the comparison stimuli in random order and asks the observer to judge whether each comparison stimulus is greater than or less than the standard stimulus. (In some variations the observer can also say that the two stimuli are the same.) In a study on tone discrimination, for example, comparison tones of 1010, 1005, 1000, 995, and 990 Hz might each be presented 100 times for comparison with the 1000-Hz standard stimulus. Demonstration 15-4 shows how the method of constant stimuli for measuring discrimination could be used for tasting sweet solutions. Notice that the just noticeable difference is the size of the difference between the standard stimulus and the comparison stimulus that can be discriminated half the time.

The Relationship Between Physical Stimuli and Psychological Reactions

Suppose that you add 1 ml of vinegar to one glass of water and you add 2 ml of vinegar to a second glass of water. Does the second solution taste twice as sour? Similarly, does a room that has four candles seem four times as bright as a room with only one candle? In this section we will discuss the relationship between the intensity of the physical stimulus and the magnitude of the observer's reaction. For example, what is the relationship between the amount of vinegar in a solution and how sour the solution seems? Also, what is the relationship between the intensity of the light in a room and how bright the light seems? Three prominent researchers have attacked this problem, and we will briefly examine their conclusions.

Weber's Law

Ernst Weber (pronounced "*Vay*-burr"), in the early 1800s, examined the relationship between physical stimuli and psychological reactions by focusing on the just noticeable difference, a term we discussed in the discrimination section. Consider the following problem. Suppose that you can discriminate between a room in which 60 candles are lit and a room in which 61 candles are lit (surprisingly, most people can). Now suppose that 120 candles are lit in a room. Can you discriminate between that room and a room in which 121 candles are lit? After all, we have added the same one candle to make the room brighter. In fact, Weber found that the important determinant of observers' psychological reaction was not the *absolute* size of the change (for example, one candle). Instead, the important determinant was the *relative* size of the change. Specifically, we require one additional candle for *each* 60 candles if we want to notice a difference. If the standard stimulus is 60 candles, the jnd is one candle. If the standard stimulus is 120 candles, we require 122 candles in the comparison stimulus in order to notice a difference; the jnd is now two candles.

Weber's Law states that

$$\frac{\text{jnd}}{\text{S}} = k$$

Verbally, Weber's Law says that if we take the just noticeable difference (jnd) and divide it by the magnitude of the stimulus (S), we obtain a constant number (*k*). The constant, *k*, is called **Weber's fraction**. With candlelit rooms, *k* equals 1/60. Notice how you can obtain a *k* of 1/60 by dividing the jnd of 1 by an S of 60 or by dividing the jnd of 2 by an S of 120. Notice also that the jnd for 300 candles would be 5.

We have seen that Weber's fraction is 1/60 when people judge the brightness of a room. However, this fraction varies widely from one judgment task to another. For example, Weber's fraction for judging the pitch of pure tones is 1/333 (Engen, 1971a). That means that we only need to change a tone's pitch by .3% (1/333) in order for the difference to be noticeable. However, we are much less competent in noticing changes in taste and smell. For exam-

Demonstration 15-4

*Using the Method of
Constant Stimuli to Measure
Discrimination*

In this demonstration you will use the method of constant stimuli to measure an observer's ability to judge differences in sweetness. First, take two teaspoons of table sugar and dissolve it in one 8-ounce glass of cool tap water; stir to dissolve. Line up five empty glasses, and fill them as indicated:

Two tablespoons
sugar solution
+
Two tablespoons
tap water

2½ tablespoons
sugar solution
+
1½ tablespoons
tap water

3 tablespoons
sugar solution
+
1 tablespoon
tap water

3½ tablespoons
sugar solution
+
½ tablespoon
tap water

4 tablespoons
sugar solution
+
0 tablespoon
tap water

In addition, mix up a "standard stimulus" glass that has the same concentration as solution 3 by mixing 6 tablespoons sugar solution + 2 tablespoons tap water.

Now you may begin the trials. Blindfold your observer and present a solution (as specified below). The observer tastes a small sip, spits it out, rinses with tap water briefly, then tastes a small sip from a second solution, spits it out, rinses with tap water, and selects one of these two responses: (1) the first was sweeter than the second, or (2) the first was less sweet than the second. (Notice that "same as" responses are not permitted in this particular version.) You sometimes presented the standard stimulus first and sometimes presented the comparison stimulus first, and so some of the responses must be "translated" prior to recording. Record whether the comparison stimulus is sweeter or less sweet than the standard stimulus.

Below is a table indicating the order in which you should present the solutions and whether the standard stimulus or the comparison stimulus should be presented first. For example, on Trial 1 you present the standard stimulus first and the comparison stimulus, solution 4, second. I have recorded my observer's responses; record your observer's responses next to mine.

TRIAL	WHICH STIMULUS IS FIRST?	SOLUTION NUMBER OF COMPARISON STIMULUS	RESPONSE: "THE COMPARISON STIMULUS IS _____ "
1	standard	4	sweeter
2	comparison	1	less sweet
3	standard	3	sweeter
4	comparison	2	sweeter
5	standard	5	sweeter

6	comparison	1	less sweet
7	standard	4	sweeter
8	comparison	2	less sweet
9	standard	5	sweeter
10	comparison	3	less sweet
11	standard	1	less sweet
12	comparison	4	sweeter
13	standard	2	less sweet
14	comparison	5	sweeter
15	standard	3	less sweet
16	comparison	4	less sweet
17	standard	1	less sweet
18	comparison	5	sweeter
19	standard	2	less sweet
20	comparison	3	sweeter

Tabulate the number and proportion of the "sweeter" responses that are supplied for each of the five solutions. Record your observer's responses next to mine.

SOLUTION NUMBER	NUMBER OF TIMES OBSERVER SAID "SWEETER" FOR COMPARISON	PROPORTION OF THE TIME OBSERVER SAID "SWEETER" FOR COMPARISON
1	0	.00
2	1	.25
3	2	.50
4	3	.75
5	4	1.00

Now plot your values in the space on the right; mine are on the left. Record where the horizontal lines corresponding to .25 "sweeter" and .75 "sweeter" cross the curve that you make to connect the points. Notice that for my values, the lines cross at 2 and at 4. The just noticeable difference is calculated below; calculate that value for your observer as well.

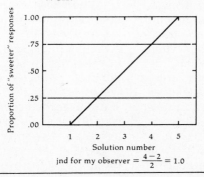

jnd for my observer = $\frac{4-2}{2}$ = 1.0

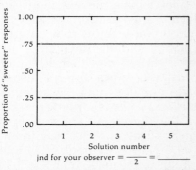

jnd for your observer = $\frac{\quad}{2}$ = _____

ple, Weber's fraction is generally about 1/5 for judging taste (McBurney, 1978), and it is generally about 1/4 for judging smells (Engen, 1971a). Thus if a particular solution contained 5 ml of vinegar, we would need to add one full milliliter to the solution in order for the change to be detectable.

In summary, Weber found that there is *not* a one-to-one correspondence between physical stimuli and psychological reactions. The very same stimulus that was sufficient to produce a noticeably brighter light in one situation (60 versus 61 candles) was not sufficient to produce a noticeably brighter light in another situation (120 versus 121 candles). Weber's Law has been found to hold true for a wide variety of psychophysical judgments, though it is more successful in the middle ranges than it is in predicting jnd's for very high or very low intensity stimuli.

Fechner's Law

Gustav Fechner used Weber's Law in order to derive a scale that related the size of the physical stimulus to the size of the observer's psychological reaction. The derivation of Fechner's scale is discussed elsewhere (for example, Engen, 1971b; Matlin, 1979). However, **Fechner's Law** states that

$$R = k \log S$$

Verbally, Fechner's Law says that the magnitude of the psychological reaction (R) is equal to a constant (k) multiplied by the logarithm of the intensity of the physical stimulus (S). In other words, Fechner's law states that psychological magnitude is proportional to the logarithm of stimulus intensity.

As you may recall, the **logarithm** of a number equals the exponent, or power, to which 10 must be raised to equal that number. It is important to know that a logarithmic transformation shrinks down large numbers more than it shrinks down small numbers. In other words, as S grows larger, R also grows larger; however, R does not grow as rapidly as S does. For example, let us suppose that k has a value of 1. If the intensity of the stimulus is 100 units, then R = 2 (because the logarithm of 100 is 2; 10^2 = 100). Now if we double the intensity of the stimulus to 200 units, then R = 2.3 (because the logarithm of 200 is 2.3; $10^{2.3}$ = 200).

Notice that a doubling of the intensity of the physical stimulus does *not* lead to a doubling of the psychological response. As S grows from 100 to 200, R grows only from 2 to 2.3. Once again, there is not a one-to-one correspondence between physical stimuli and psychological reactions. Incidentally, it should be mentioned that Fechner's Law is reasonably accurate in many situations, but—like Weber's law, on which it is based—it is inaccurate in other situations.

Stevens' Power Law

More recent research by S. S. Stevens (1957, 1961) provides an alternative view of the relationship between stimulus intensity and psychological reaction. Specifically, Stevens proposed the following equation, known as **Stevens' Power Law**:

$$R = kS^n$$

Verbally, Stevens' Power Law says that the magnitude of the psychological reaction (R) is equal to a constant (k) multiplied by the intensity of the stimulus, which has been raised to the nth power. As you may remember, the power to which a number is raised indicates the number of times that a number should be multiplied by itself. For example, 10^3 equals $10 \times 10 \times 10$.

S. S. Stevens (1970) examined a wide range of stimuli, and he found that the value for n varied from .33 for judgments of brightness, to 1.0 for judgments of the length of a line, to 3.5 for judgments of electric shock intensity. This means that the nature of the relationship between the physical stimulus and the psychological response depends upon the kind of stimulus we are judging.

When we are judging brightness or any other stimulus for which n is less than 1.0, a large increase in the physical stimulus produces a smaller increase in the psychological reaction (a relationship somewhat similar to the relationship predicted by Fechner's Law). When we are judging the length of a line or any other stimulus for which n is approximately 1.0, there is approximately a one-to-one correspondence between the physical stimulus and the psychological reaction. However, when we are judging how painful an electric shock seems or judging any other stimulus for which n is greater than 1.0, a small increase in the physical stimulus produces a large increase in the psychological reaction. Thus we can predict the nature of the relationship between the physical stimulus and the psychological reaction once we know whether *n* is less than 1.0, equal to 1.0, or greater than 1.0.

A technique that Stevens frequently used to obtain judgments is called magnitude estimation. In the **magnitude estimation** technique the observer is told that one particular stimulus in a series has a set value, perhaps 100; the observer's task is to assign numbers to other stimuli, relative to that value of 100. For example, suppose that we assigned Solution 3 in Demonstration 15-4 a value of 100. What values would you assign for Solutions 1, 2, 4, and 5? The magnitude estimation technique allows the observer to provide a direct estimate of the magnitude of stimuli, based on a specified reference value.

Stevens' Power Law makes different predictions (in most cases) from Fechner's Law. Which is correct? It is possible that some of the discrepancies are the result of different measurement techniques. However, different techniques cannot account for all of the discrepancies. In general, most psychophysicists support Stevens' Power Law. Gescheider (1976) says, for example, "There is little doubt that the power function represents the best description of the relationship between an observer's judgments and stimulus intensity" (p. 144).

In this section we have examined the relationship between the intensity of physical stimuli and the magnitude of psychological reactions. In some cases there is a one-to-one correspondence between these two factors. More often, however, a change in the physical stimulus is translated into either a greater change in the psychological reaction or a smaller change in the psychological reaction. Thus each perceptual system transforms physical stimuli in its own systematic fashion.

Summary: Measuring Responses to High-Intensity Stimuli

• Discrimination studies examine whether people can tell the difference between two stimuli.

• Discrimination studies ask people to compare a standard stimulus and a comparison stimulus. They typically involve calculating the just noticeable difference.

• When the method of limits is used to measure discrimination, the comparison stimulus is systematically increased or decreased.

• When the method of adjustment is used to measure discrimination, the observer adjusts the comparison stimulus.

• When the method of constant stimuli is used to measure discrimination, comparison stimuli are presented in random order.

• Three researchers—Weber, Fechner, and Stevens—have been primarily responsible for the investigation of the relationship between physical stimuli and psychological reactions.

• Ernst Weber found that we require larger changes in a stimulus in order to notice the difference if we are discriminating between intense stimuli than if we are discriminating between weak stimuli.

• Gustav Fechner proposed that as stimulus intensity increases, the magnitude of the psychological response increases, but not as dramatically. For example, we may increase stimulus intensity from 100 to 200 units, yet the magnitude of the psychological response may increase only from 2.0 to 2.3.

• Fechner's law says that the magnitude of the psychological response is related to the logarithm of the intensity of the physical stimulus.

• S. S. Stevens proposed that the magnitude of the psychological response is related to the intensity of the stimulus, raised to a certain power, *n*. The value of *n* depends upon the nature of the judgments.

• Stevens frequently used magnitude estimation to obtain judgments of the magnitude of the psychological response.

• In general, Stevens's predictions are more accurate than Fechner's.

Review

1. Describe how psychophysics might be relevant if you wanted to examine low-intensity stimuli in each of the following areas: vision, hearing, touch, temperature perception, pain, smell, and taste. In each case, briefly describe how you would use the method of limits to measure a detection threshold.

2. Why do we need both ascending trials and descending trials in the method of limits? Why don't we need to worry about the two kinds of trials in the method of constant stimuli?

3. Return to question 1 and describe how you would use the method of adjustment and the method of constant stimuli to measure detection thresholds in each of the areas listed.

4. Describe the advantages and disadvantages of each of the three classical psychophysics methods, illustrating each method with an example from vision.

5. You are standing near an electric coffee urn, waiting for the red light to turn on, indicating that the coffee is ready. Apply the Theory of Signal Detection to this situation, describing aspects of sensitivity and criterion.

6. Describe the four possible outcomes in question 5 with respect to the occurrence of the signal and your response.

7. The following questions apply to ROC curves: (a) If d' is large, is the probability of a hit larger or smaller than if d' is small? (b) What does d' measure? (c) Suppose that one observer has a d' of .5 and another has a d' of 1.5. If they have the same hit rate, which observer has the higher false alarm rate? (d) How is a particular point on a ROC curve related to the criterion line in the probability distributions in Figure 15-3?

8. Describe how psychophysics might be relevant if you wanted to examine high-intensity stimuli in each of the areas mentioned in question 1. Mention both discrimination studies and studies concerning the relationship between physical stimuli and psychological responses.

9. Describe how you could use each of the three classical psychophysical methods to measure color discrimination.

10. This chapter ends with the statement that a change in the physical stimulus is typically translated into either a greater change in the psychological reaction or a smaller change in the psychological reaction. Discuss this statement with reference to Fechner and Stevens. Also, how would the research of Weber, Fechner, and Stevens be related to judgments of how heavy an assortment of chocolate bars feel?

New Terms

psychophysics

detection threshold

method of limits

descending trials

ascending trials

ascending method of limits

forced-choice method

method of adjustment

method of constant stimuli

Theory of Signal Detection (TSD)

sensitivity measure

criterion

β

payoff

signal

hit

correct rejection

false alarm

miss

receiver operating characteristic curve (ROC curve)

d'

noise

signal + noise

probability distribution

discrimination

standard stimulus

comparison stimulus

just noticeable difference

method of limits for measuring discrimination

method of adjustment for measuring discrimination

method of constant stimuli for measuring discrimination

Weber's Law

Weber's fraction

Fechner's Law

logarithm

Stevens' Power Law

magnitude estimation

BIBLIOGRAPHY

Abramov, I., & Gordon, J. Vision. In E. C. Carterette & M. P. Friedman (Eds.), *Handbook of perception*. Vol. 3. New York: Academic Press, 1973.

Alpern, M. Effector mechanisms in vision. In J. W. Kling & L. A. Riggs (Eds.), *Woodworth & Schlosberg's experimental psychology* (3rd ed.). New York: Holt, Rinehart and Winston, Inc., 1971.

American Psychological Association. *Ethical principles in the conduct of research with human participants*. Washington, D. C.: Author, 1973.

Amoore, J. E. Current status of the steric theory of odor. *Annals of the New York Academy of Sciences*, 1964, *116*, 457–476.

Amoore, J. E. *Molecular basis of odor*. Springfield, Ill.: Thomas, 1970.

Anstis, S. M. Apparent movement. In R. Held, H. W. Leibowitz, & H. L. Teuber (Eds.), *Handbook of sensory physiology*. Vol. 8: *Perception*. Berlin: Springer-Verlag, 1978.

Arnheim, R. *Art and visual perception: A psychology of the creative eye*. Berkeley: University of California Press, 1974.

Aronson, E., & Rosenbloom, S. Space perception in early infancy: Perception within a common auditory-visual space, *Science*, 1971, *172*, 1161–1163.

Aslin, R. N., Alberts, J. R., & Petersen, M. R. (Eds.), *Development of perception*. Vol. 2. New York: Academic Press, 1981.

Atkinson, J., & Braddick, O. Acuity, contrast sensitivity, and accommodation in infancy. In R. N. Aslin, J. R. Alberts, & M. R. Peterson (Eds.), *Development of perception*. Vol. 2. New York: Academic Press, 1981.

Atkinson, R. C., & Shiffrin, R. M. Human memory: A proposed system and its control processes. In K. W. Spence & J. T. Spence (Eds.), *The psychology of learning and motivation: Advances in research and theory*. Vol. 2. New York: Academic Press, 1968.

Avant, L. L. Vision in the Ganzfeld. *Psychological Bulletin*, 1965, *64*, 246–258.

Backus, J. *The acoustical foundations of music* (2nd ed.). New York: Norton, 1977.

Badcock, D., & Lovegrove, W. The effects of contrast, stimulus duration, and spatial frequency on visible persistence in normal and specifically disabled readers. *Journal of Experimental Psychology: Human Perception and Performance*, 1981, *7*, 495–505.

Bahill, A. T., & Stark, L. The trajectories of saccadic eye movements. *Scientific American*, 1979, *240*, 108–117.

Baker, A. H., Rierdan, J., & Wapner, S. Age changes in size-value phenomena. *Child Development*, 1974, *45*, 257–268.

Barclay, C. D., Cutting, J. E., & Kozlowski, L. T. Temporal and spatial factors in gait perception that influence gender recognition. *Perception & Psychophysics*, 1978, *23*, 145–152.

Barten, S., Birns, B., & Ronch, J. Individual differences in the visual pursuit behavior of neonates. *Child Development*, 1971, *42*, 313–319.

Bartoshuk, L. M. The chemical senses: I. Taste. In J. W. Kling & L. A. Riggs (Eds.), *Woodworth & Schlosberg's experimental psychology* (3rd ed.). New York: Holt, Rinehart and Winston, 1971.

Bartoshuk, L. M. Taste illusions: Some demonstrations. *Annals of the New York Academy of Sciences*, 1974, *237*, 279–285.

Bartoshuk, L. M. History of taste research. In E. C. Carterette & M. P. Friedman (Eds.), *Handbook of perception*. Vol. 6A. New York: Academic Press, 1978.

Basowitz, H., & Korchin, S. J. Age differences in the perception of closure. *Journal of Abnormal and Social Psychology*, 1957, *54*, 93–97.

Bassili, J. N. Facial motion in the perception of faces and of emotional expression. *Journal of Experimental Psychology: Human Perception and Performance*, 1978, *4*, 373–379.

Beck, J. Dimensions of an achromatic surface color. In R. B. MacLeod & H. L. Pick (Eds.), *Perception: Essays in honor of James J. Gibson*. Ithaca, N. Y.: Cornell University, 1974.

Beecher, H. K. *Measurement of subjective responses. Quantitative effects of drugs*. New York: Oxford University Press, 1959.

Beets, M. G. J. Odor and stimulant structure. In E. C. Carterette & M. P. Friedman (Eds.), *Handbook of perception*. Vol. 6A. New York: Academic Press, 1978.

Beidler, L. M. Biophysics and chemistry of taste. In E. C. Carterette & M. P. Friedman (Eds.), *Handbook of perception*. Vol. 6A. New York: Academic Press, 1978.

Beidler, L. M., & Smallman, R. L. Renewal of cells within taste buds. *Journal of Cell Biology*, 1965, 27, 263–272.

Békésy, G. von. In E. G. Wever (Ed.), *Experiments in hearing*. New York: McGraw-Hill, 1960.

Bell, P. A., Fisher, J. D., & Loomis, R. J. *Environmental psychology*. Philadelphia: W. B. Saunders, 1978.

Belt, B. L. *Driver eye movements as a function of low alcohol concentrations*, Tech. Rep., Engineering Experiment Station, The Ohio State University, Columbus, Ohio, 1969.

Bergman, M., Blumenfeld, V. G., Cascardo, D., Dash, B., Levitt, H., & Margulies, M. K. Age-related decrement in hearing for speech: Sampling and longitudinal studies. *Journal of Gerontology*, 1976, 31, 533–538.

Berkeley, G. *An essay towards a new theory of vision*. London: Dent, 1709/1957.

Berlyne, D. E. The influence of albedo and complexity of stimuli on visual fixation in the human infant. *British Journal of Psychology*, 1958, 49, 315–318.

Berlyne, D. E. Verbal and exploratory responses to visual patterns varying in uncertainty and in redundancy. In D. E. Berlyne (Ed.), *Studies in the new experimental aesthetics: Steps toward an objective psychology of aesthetic appreciation*. Washington, D. C.: Hemisphere, 1974.

Berlyne, D. E. Psychological aesthetics. In H. C. Triandis & W. Lonner (Eds.), *Handbook of cross-cultural psychology: Basic processes*. Vol. 3. Boston: Allyn and Bacon, 1980.

Berlyne, D. E., Robbins, M. C., & Thompson, R. A cross-cultural study of exploratory and verbal responses to visual patterns varying in complexity. In D. E. Berlyne (Ed.), *Studies in the new experimental aesthetics: Steps toward an objective psychology of aesthetic appreciation*. Washington, D. C.: Hemisphere, 1974.

Beroza, M., & Knipling, E. F. Gypsy moth control with the sex attractant pheromone. *Science*, 1972, 177, 19–27.

Bershader, D. I can't hear you when the water's running. *The Stanford Magazine*, 1981, 9(1), 14–21, 70–74.

Birren, F. *Color perception in art*. New York: Van Nostrand Reinhold, 1976.

Birren, J. E., & Schaie, K. W. (Eds.) *Handbook of the psychology of aging*. New York: Van Nostrand Reinhold, 1977.

Blakemore, C. Developmental factors in the formation of feature extracting neurons. In F. O. Schmitt & F. C. Worden (Eds.), *The neurosciences: Third study program*. Cambridge, Mass.: MIT Press, 1974.

Blakemore, C. Central visual processing. In M. S. Gazzaniga & C. Blakemore (Eds.), *Handbook of psychobiology*. New York: Academic Press, 1975.

Bliss, J. C., Katcher M. H., Rogers, C. H., & Shepard, R. P. Optical to tactile image conversion for the blind. *IEEE Transactions. Man-Machine Systems*, 1970, 11, 58–65.

Bliss, J. C., & Moore, M. W. The Optacon reading system. *Education of the Visually Handicapped*, 1974, 4, 98–102.

Blum, G. S., & Barbour, J. S. Selective inattention to anxiety-linked stimuli. *Journal of Experimental Psychology: General*, 1979, 108, 182–224.

Bond, Z. S., & Garnes, S. *Misperception and production of fluent speech*. Hillsdale, N. J.: Lawrence Erlbaum Associates, 1980.

Bonica, J. J., & Albe-Fessard, D. G. *Advances in pain research and therapy*. Vol. 1. New York: Raven, 1976.

Boring, E. G. *Sensation and perception in the history of experimental psychology*. New York: Appleton-Century-Crofts, 1942.

Bornstein, M. H. Infants are trichromats. *Journal of Experimental Psychology*, 1976, 21, 425–445.

Bornstein, M. H. Chromatic vision in infancy. In H. W. Reese & L. P. Lipsitt (Eds.), *Advances in child development and behavior*. Vol. 12. New York: Academic Press, 1978.

Bornstein, M., Kessen, W., & Weiskopf, S. Color vision and hue categorization in young human infants. *Journal of Experimental Psychology: Human Perception and Performance*, 1976, 2, 115–129.

Bower, T. G. R. The visual world of infants. *Scientific American*, 1966, 215(6), 80–92.

Boynton, R. M. Color vision. In J. W. Kling & L. A. Riggs (Eds.), *Woodworth & Schlosberg's experimental psychology* (3rd ed.). New York: Holt, Rinehart and Winston, 1971.

Boynton, R. M. *Human color vision*. New York: Holt, Rinehart and Winston, 1979.

Braunstein, M. L. *Depth perception through motion*. New York: Academic Press, 1976.

Brean, H. What hidden sell is all about. *Life*, March 31, 1958, 104–114.

Breitmeyer, B. G. Unmasking visual masking: A look at the "why" behind the veil of the "how." *Psychological Review*, 1980, 87, 52–69.

Broadbent, D. E. *Perception and communication*. London: Pergamon, 1958.

Brown, T. S. General biology of sensory systems. In

B. Scharf (Ed.), *Experimental sensory psychology.* Glenview, Ill.: Scott, Foresman, 1975.(a)

Brown, T. S. Olfaction and taste. In B. Scharf (Ed.), *Experimental sensory psychology.* Glenview, Ill.: Scott, Foresman, 1975.(b)

Bryant, J. S. Feature detection process in speech perception. *Journal of Experimental Psychology: Human Perception and Performance,* 1978, *4,* 610–620.

Burg, A. Vision and driving: A report on research. *Human Factors,* 1971, *13,* 79–87.

Cain, W. S. Differential sensitivity for smell: "Noise" at the nose. *Science,* 1977, *195,* 796–798.

Cain, W. S. History of research on smell. In E. C. Carterette & M. P. Friedman (Eds.), *Handbook of perception.* Vol. 6A. New York: Academic Press, 1978.(a)

Cain, W. S. The odoriferous environment and the application of olfactory research. In E. C. Carterette & M. P. Friedman (Eds.), *Handbook of perception.* Vol. 6A. New York: Academic Press, 1978.(b)

Cain, W. S. To know with the nose: Keys to odor identification. *Science,* 1979, *203,* 467–470.

Cain, W. S., & Drexler, M. Scope and evaluation of odor counteraction and masking. *Annals of the New York Academy of Sciences,* 1974, *237,* 427–439.

Campos, J. J., Hiatt, S., Ramsay, D., Henderson, C., & Svejda, M. The emergence of fear on the visual cliff. In M. Lewis & L. A. Rosenblum (Eds.), *The development of affect.* Vol. 1. New York: Plenum, 1978.

Campos, J. J., Langer, A., & Krowitz, A. Cardiac responses on the visual cliff in prelocomotor human infants. *Science,* 1970, *170,* 196–197.

Cannon, J. T., Liebeskind, J. C., & Frenk, H. Neural and neurochemical mechanisms of pain inhibition. In R. A. Sternbach (Ed.), *The psychology of pain.* New York: Raven, 1978.

Carey, S., & Diamond, R. From piecemeal to configurational representation of faces. *Science,* 1977, *195,* 312–314.

Carlson, N. R. *Physiology of behavior* (2nd ed.). Boston: Allyn and Bacon, 1980.

Carlson, V. R. Instructions and perceptual constancy judgments. In W. Epstein (Ed.), *Stability and constancy in visual perception: Mechanisms and processes.* New York: Wiley, 1977.

Carpenter, E. If Wittgenstein had been an Eskimo. *Natural History,* February 1980, *89,* 72–77.

Carterette, E. C., & Friedman, M. P. Preface. In E. C. Carterette & M. P. Friedman (Eds.), *Handbook of perception.* Vol. 6B. New York: Academic Press, 1978.

Chapman, C. R. The hurtful world: Pathological pain and its control. In E. C. Carterette & M. P. Friedman (Eds.), *Handbook of perception.* Vol. 6B. New York: Academic Press, 1978.

Chapman, C. R., Wilson, M. E., & Gehrig, J. D. Comparative effects of acupuncture and transcutaneous stimulation on the perception of painful dental stimuli. *Pain,* 1976, *2,* 265–283.

Chaves, J. F., & Barber, T. X. Hypnotism and surgical pain. In T. X. Barber, N. P. Spanos, & J. F. Chaves (Eds.), *Hypnosis, imagination, and human potentialities.* New York: Pergamon, 1974.

Cherry, E. C. Some experiments on the recognition of speech with one and with two ears. *Journal of the Acoustical Society of America,* 1953, *25,* 975–979.

Child, I. L. Aesthetic theories. In E. C. Carterette & M. P. Friedman (Eds.) *Handbook of perception.* Vol. 10. New York: Academic Press, 1978.

Clark, W. C. Sensory-decision theory analysis of the placebo effect on the criterion pain and thermal sensitivity (*d'*). *Journal of Abnormal Psychology,* 1969, *74,* 363–371.

Clark, W. C., & Mehl, L. A sensory decision theory analysis of the effect of age and sex on *d',* various response criteria, and 50% pain threshold. *Journal of Abnormal Psychology,* 1971, *78,* 202–212.

Clark, W. C., & Yang, J. C. Acupunctural analgesia? Evaluation by signal detection theory. *Science,* 1974, *184,* 1096–1098.

Clulow, F. W. *Color: Its principles and their applications.* New York: Morgan and Morgan, 1972.

Cohen, L. B. Our developing knowledge of infant perception and cognition. *American Psychologist,* 1979, *34,* 894–899.

Cohen, L. B., DeLoache, J. S., & Strauss, M. S. Infant visual perception. In J. D. Osofsky (Ed.), *Handbook of infant development.* New York: Wiley, 1979.

Cohen, L. B., & Salapatek, P. *Infant perception: From sensation to cognition* (2 vols.). New York: Academic Press, 1975.

Cohen, S., Glass, D. C., & Phillips, S. Environment and health. In H. E. Freeman, S. Levine, & L. C. Reeder (Eds.), *Handbook of medical sociology.* Englewood Cliffs, N. J.: Prentice-Hall, 1977.

Cohen, S., Glass, D. C., & Singer, J. E. Apartment noise, auditory discrimination, and reading ability in children. *Journal of Experimental Social Psychology,* 1973, *9,* 407–422.

Cole, R. A., & Jakimik, J. A model of speech perception. In R. A. Cole (Ed.), *Perception and production of fluent speech.* Hillsdale, N. J.: Lawrence Erlbaum Associates, 1980.

Cole, R. A., & Scott, B. Toward a theory of speech perception. *Psychological Review,* 1974, *81,* 348–374.

Coleman, P. D. An analysis of cues to auditory depth perception in free space. *Psychological Bulletin,* 1963, *60,* 302–315.

Collings, V. B. Human taste response as a function of

locus of stimulation on the tongue and soft palate. *Perception & Psychophysics*, 1974, 16, 169–174.

Comfort, A. Communications may be odorous. *New Scientist and Science Journal*, 1971 (February 25), 412–414.

Coren, S. Brightness contrast as a function of figure-ground relations. *Journal of Experimental Psychology*, 1969, 80, 517–524.

Coren, S. Subjective contours and apparent depth. *Psychological Review*, 1972, 79, 359–367.

Coren, S., & Girgus, J. S. Illusion decrement in intersecting line figures. *Psychonomic Science*, 1972, 26, 108–110.

Coren, S., & Girgus, J. S. *Seeing is deceiving: The psychology of visual illusions.* Hillsdale, N. J.: Lawrence Erlbaum Associates, 1978.

Coren, S., Girgus, J. S., Erlichman, H., & Hakstean, A. R. An empirical taxonomy of visual illusions. *Perception & Psychophysics*, 1976, 20, 129–137.

Coren, S., Porac, C., & Ward, L. M. *Sensation and perception.* New York: Academic Press, 1979.

Corso, J. F. Sensory processes and age effects in normal adults. *Journal of Gerontology*, 1971, 26, 90–105.

Corso, J. F. Auditory perception and communication. In J. E. Birren & K. W. Schaie (Eds.), *Handbook of the psychology of aging.* New York: Van Nostrand Reinhold, 1977.

Craddick, R. A. Size of Halloween witch drawings prior to, on, and after Halloween. *Perceptual and Motor Skills*, 1963, 235–238.

Craig, K. D. Social modeling influences on pain. In R. A. Sternbach (Ed.), *The psychology of pain.* New York: Raven, 1978.

Cumming, G. D. Eye movements and visual perception. In E. C. Carterette & M. P. Friedman (Eds.), *Handbook of perception.* Vol. 9. New York: Academic Press, 1978.

Dallenbach, K. M. The temperature spots and end-organs. *American Journal of Psychology*, 1927, 39, 402–427.

Dallos, P. Cochlear physiology. *Annual Review of Psychology*, 1981, 32, 153–190.

Das, A. K. Tea tasting at the Tocklai Experimental Station, Assam, India. Personal communication, 1981.

Davenport, R. K., & Rogers, C. M. Perception of photographs in apes. *Behavior*, 1971, 39, 318–320.

Davidoff, J. B. *Differences in visual perception: The individual eye.* New York: Academic Press, 1975.

Day, R. H. Visual spatial illusions: A general explanation. *Science*, 1972, 175, 1335–1340.

Day, R. H. Induced visual movement as nonveridical resolution of displacement ambiguity. *Perception & Psychophysics*, 1978, 23, 205–209.

Day, R. H., & McKenzie, B. E. Constancies in the perceptual world of the infant. In W. Epstein (Ed.), *Stability and constancy in visual perception: Mechanisms and processes.* New York: Wiley, 1977.

Dearborn, G. V. N. A case of congenital general pure analgesia. *Journal of Nervous and Mental Disorders*, 1932, 75, 612–615.

Desor, J. A., & Beauchamp, G. K. The human capacity to transmit olfactory information. *Perception & Psychophysics*, 1974, 16, 551–556.

Desor, J. A., Maller, O., & Greene, L. S. Preference for sweet in humans: Infants, children and adults. In J. M. Weiffenbach (Ed.), *Taste and development: The genesis of sweet preference.* Bethesda, Md.: U. S. Department of Health, Education, and Welfare, 1977.

Dethier, V. G. The taste of salt. *American Scientist*, 1977, 65, 744–750.

Dethier, V. G. Other tastes, other worlds. *Science*, 1978, 201, 224–228.

Deutsch, D. The psychology of music. In E. C. Carterette & M. P. Friedman (Eds.), *Handbook of perception.* Vol. 10. New York: Academic Press, 1978.

Deutsch, J. A., & Deutsch, D. Attention: Some theoretical considerations. *Psychological Review*, 1963, 70, 80–90.

DeValois, R., & DeValois, K. Neural coding of color. In E. C. Carterette & M. P. Friedman (Eds.), *Handbook of perception.* Vol. 5. New York: Academic Press, 1975.

DeValois, R., & DeValois, K. Spatial vision. *Annual Review of Psychology*, 1980, 31, 309–341.

Dichgans, J., & Brandt, T. Visual-vestibular interaction: Effects on self-motion perception and postural control. In R. Held, H. W. Leibowitz, & H. L. Teuber (Eds.), *Handbook of sensory physiology. Volume 8: Perception.* Berlin: Springer-Verlag, 1978.

Dirks, D. D. Effects of hearing impairment on the auditory system. In E. C. Carterette & M. P. Friedman (Eds.), *Handbook of perception,* Vol. 4. New York: Academic Press, 1978.

Ditchburn, R. W. *Eye-movements and perception.* Oxford: Clarendon Press, 1973.

Dixon, N. F. *Subliminal perception: The nature of a controversy.* London: McGraw-Hill, 1971.

Dobelle, W. H., Mladejovsky, M. G., & Girvin, J. P. Artificial vision for the blind: Electrical stimulation of visual cortex offers hope for a functional prosthesis. *Science*, 1974, 183, 440–444.

Dodd, D. H., & White, R. M. *Cognition.* Boston: Allyn and Bacon, 1980.

Dowling, J. E., & Boycott, B. B. Organization of the primate retina: Electron microscopy. *Proceedings of the Royal Society* (London), Series B, 1966, *166*, 80–111.

Dukes, W. F., & Bevan, W., Accentuation and response variability in the perception of relevant objects. *Journal of Personality*, 1952, *20*, 457–465.

Dunn-Rankin, P. The visual characteristics of words. *Scientific American*, 1978, *238*, 122–130.

Durlach, N. I., & Colburn, H. S. Binaural phenomena. In E. C. Carterette & M. P. Friedman (Eds.), *Handbook of perception*. Vol. 4. New York: Academic Press, 1978.

Durrant, J. D., & Lovrinic, J. H. *Bases of hearing science*. Baltimore, Md.: Williams & Wilkins, 1977.

Egan, J. P. *Signal detection theory and ROC-analysis.* New York: Academic Press, 1975.

Egeth, H. E., Marcus, N., & Bevan, W. Target-set and response-set interaction: Implications for the study of human information processing. *Science*, 1972, *176*, 1447–1448.

Eimas, P. D. Speech perception in early infancy. In L. B. Cohen & P. Salapatek (Eds.), *Infant perception: From sensation to cognition*. Vol. 2. New York: Academic Press, 1975.

Eimas, P. D., & Corbit, J. D. Selective adaptation of linguistic feature detectors. *Cognitive Psychology*, 1973, *4*, 99–109.

Eimas, P. D., Siqueland, E. R., Jusczyk, R., & Vigorito, J. Speech perception in infants. *Science*, 1971, *171*, 303–306.

Eimas, P. D., & Tartter, V. C. On the development of speech perception: Mechanisms and analogies. In H. W. Reese & L. P. Lipsitt (Eds.), *Advances in child development and behavior*. Vol. 13. New York: Academic Press, 1979.

Eisner, D. A., & Schaie, K. W. Age change in response to visual illusions from middle to old age. *Journal of Gerontology*, 1971, *26*, 146–150.

Elkind, D., Koegler, R., & Go, E. Studies in perceptual development: II. Part-whole perception. *Child Development*, 1964, *35*, 81–90.

Engen, T. Cross adaptation to aliphatic alcohols. *American Journal of Psychology*, 1963, *76*, 96–102.

Engen, T. Psychophysics: I. Discrimination and detection. In J. W. Kling & L. A. Riggs (Eds.), *Woodworth & Schlosberg's experimental psychology* (3rd ed.). New York: Holt, Rinehart and Winston, 1971. (a)

Engen, T. Psychophysics: II. Scaling methods. In J. W. Kling & L. A. Riggs (Eds.), *Woodworth & Schlosberg's experimental psychology* (3rd ed.). New York: Holt, Rinehart and Winston, 1971. (b)

Engen, T. Taste and smell. In J. E. Birren & K. W. Schaie (Eds.), *Handbook of the psychology of aging.* New York: Van Nostrand Reinhold, 1977.

Engen, T., Kuisma, J. E., & Eimas, P. D. Short-term memory of odors. *Journal of Experimental Psychology*, 1973, *99*, 222–225.

Engen, T., & Ross, B. M. Long-term memory of odors with and without verbal descriptions. *Journal of Experimental Psychology*, 1973, *100*, 221–227.

Epstein, W., & Franklin, S. Some conditions of the effect of relative size on perceived relative distance. *American Journal of Psychology*, 1965, *78*, 466–470.

Erdelyi, M. H. A new look at the New Look: Perceptual defense and vigilance. *Psychological Review*, 1974, *81*, 1–25.

Eriksen, C. W., & Schultz, D. W. Information processing in visual search: A continuous flow conception and experimental results. *Perception & Psychophysics*, 1979, *25*, 249–263.

Escher, M. C. *The graphic work of M. C. Escher.* New York: Ballantine, 1971.

Evans, F. J. The placebo response in pain reduction. In J. J. Bonica (Ed.), *Advances in neurology*. Vol. 4. New York: Raven, 1974.

Fantz, R. E. The origin of form perception. *Scientific American*, 1961, *204*(5), 66–72.

Fantz, R. L., Fagan, J. F., III, & Miranda, S. B. Early visual selectivity. In L. B. Cohen & P. Salapatek (Eds.), *Infant perception: From sensation to cognition*. Vol. 1. New York: Academic Press, 1975.

Favreau, O. E., & Corballis, M. C. Negative aftereffects in visual perception. *Scientific American*, 1976, *235*, 42–48.

Feather, B. W., Chapman, C. R., & Fisher, S. B. The effect of a placebo on the perception of painful radiant heat stimuli. *Psychosomatic Medicine*, 1972, *34*, 290.

Festinger, L., Allyn, M. R., & White, C. W. The perception of color with achromatic stimulation. *Vision Research*, 1971, *11*, 591–612.

Flagg, B. N. Children and television: Effects of stimulus repetition on eye activity. In J. W. Senders, D. F. Fisher, & R. A. Monty (Eds.), *Eye movements and the higher psychological functions*. Hillsdale, N. J.: Lawrence Erlbaum Associates, 1978.

Flavell, J. H. *Cognitive development.* Englewood Cliffs, N. J.: Prentice-Hall, 1977.

Fletcher, H. Loudness, pitch and timbre of musical tones and their relation to the intensity, the frequency, and the overtone structure. *Journal of the Acoustical Society of America*, 1934, *6*, 59–69.

Forbes, T. W. Visibility and legibility of highway signs. In T. W. Forbes (Ed.), *Human factors in highway traffic safety research*. New York: Wiley, 1972.

Fordyce, W. E. Learning processes in pain. In R. A. Sternbach (Ed.), *The psychology of pain.* New York: Raven, 1978.

Fozard, J. L., Wolf, E., Bell, B., McFarland, R. A., & Podolsky, S. *Handbook of the psychology of aging.* New York: Van Nostrand Reinhold, 1977.

Francès, R. Comparative effects of six collative variables on interest and preference in adults of different educational levels. *Journal of Personality and Social Psychology,* 1976, *33,* 62–79.

Frank, G. On the validity of hypotheses derived from the Rorschach: I. The relationship between color and affect. *Perceptual and Motor Skills,* 1976, *43,* 411–427.

Franks, J. J., & Bransford, J. D. Abstraction of visual patterns. *Journal of Experimental Psychology,* 1971, *90,* 65–74.

Fraser, A. B., & Mach, W. H. Mirages. *Scientific American,* 1976, *234,* 102–111.

Friedman, S. L., & Stevenson, M. B. Perception of movement in pictures. In M. A. Hagen (Ed.), *The perception of pictures,* Vol. 1. New York: Academic Press, 1980.

Frisby, J. P. *Seeing.* Oxford: Oxford University Press, 1980.

Gelb, A. Die ''Farbenkonstanz'' der Sehding. *Handbuch der normalen und pathologischen Physiologie,* 1929, *12,* 594–678.

Gescheider, G. A. *Psychophysics: Method and theory.* Hillsdale, N. J.: Lawrence Erlbaum Associates, 1976.

Gesteland, R. C. The neural code: Integrative neural mechanisms. In E. C. Carterette & M. P. Friedman (Eds.), *Handbook of perception.* Vol. 6A. New York: Academic Press, 1978.

Gibson, E. J. *Principles of perceptual learning and development.* Englewood Cliffs, N. J.: Prentice-Hall, 1969.

Gibson, E. J., & Levin, H. *The psychology of reading.* Cambridge, Mass.: MIT Press, 1975.

Gibson, E. J., Schapiro, F., & Yonas, A. Confusion matrices for graphic patterns obtained with a latency measure. In *The analysis of reading skill: A program of basic and applied research.* Final Report, Project No. 5-1213, Cornell University and U. S. Office of Education, 1968. Pp. 76–96.

Gibson, E. J., & Walk, R. D. The ''visual cliff.'' *Scientific American,* 1960, *202* (4), 64–71.

Gibson, J. J. *The perception of the visual world.* Boston, Mass.: Houghton Mifflin, 1950.

Gibson, J. J. Perception as a function of stimulation. In S. Koch (Ed.), *Psychology a study of a science.* Vol. 1. New York: McGraw-Hill, 1959.

Gibson, J. J. Observations on active touch. *Psychological Review,* 1962, *69,* 477–491.

Gibson, J. J. *The senses considered as perceptual systems.* Boston, Mass.: Houghton Mifflin, 1966.

Gibson, J. J. *The ecological approach to visual perception.* Boston, Mass.: Houghton Mifflin, 1979.

Gilchrist, A. L. Perceived lightness depends on perceived spatial arrangement. *Science,* 1977, *195,* 185–187.

Gillam, B. Geometrical illusions. *Scientific American,* 1980, *242,* 102–111.

Glass, D. C., & Singer, J. E. *Urban stress.* New York: Academic Press, 1972.

Glass, D. C., Singer, J. E., & Friedman, L. N. Psychic cost of adaptation to an environmental stressor. *Journal of Personality and Social Psychology,* 1969, *12,* 200–210.

Gogel, W. C. An indirect method of measuring perceived distance from familiar size. *Perception & Psychophysics,* 1976, *20,* 419–429.

Gogel, W. C. The metric of visual space. In W. Epstein (Ed.), *Stability and constancy in visual perception: Mechanisms and processes.* New York: Wiley, 1977.

Gogel, W. C. The adjacency principle in visual perception. *Scientific American,* 1978, *238,* 126–139.

Gogel, W. C., & Tietz, J. D. Adjacency and attention as determinants of perceived motion. *Vision Research,* 1976, *16,* 839–845.

Goodson, F. E., Snider, T. Q., & Swearingen, J. E. Motion parallax in the perception of movement by a moving subject. *Bulletin of the Psychonomic Society,* 1980, *16,* 87–88.

Gottfried, A. W., & Rose, S. A. Tactile recognition memory in infants. *Child Development,* 1980, *51,* 69–74.

Graham, C. H. Visual space perception. In C. H. Graham (Ed.), *Vision and visual perception.* New York: Wiley, 1965.

Graham, C. H., & Hsia, Y. Color defect and color theory. *Science,* 1958, *127,* 675–682.

Gratch, G. The development of thought and language in infancy. In J. D. Osofsky (Ed.), *Handbook of infant development.* New York: Wiley, 1979.

Gray, J. Personal communication, 1979.

Green, D. M. *An introduction to hearing.* Hillsdale, N. J.: Lawrence Erlbaum Associates, 1976.

Green, D. M., & Swets, J. A. *Signal detection theory and psychophysics.* New York: Wiley, 1966.

Gregory, R. L. *Eye and brain* (2nd ed.). New York: World University Library, 1973.

Gregory, R. L. Choosing a paradigm for perception. In E. C. Carterette & M. P. Friedman (Eds.), *Handbook of perception.* Vol. 1. New York: Academic Press, 1974.

Gregory, R. L. *Eye and brain: The psychology of seeing* (3rd ed.). New York: McGraw-Hill, 1978.

Gregory, R. L., & Gombrich, E. H. *Illusion in nature and art.* New York: Charles Scribner's Sons, 1973.

Grobstein, P., & Chow, K. L. Receptive field development and individual experience. *Science,* 1975, *190,* 352–358.

Grützner, P. Acquired color vision defects. In D. Jameson & L. M. Hurvich (Eds.), *Visual psychophysics.* Vol. III/4. Berlin: Springer-Verlag, 1972.

Guiss, L. W., & Kuenstler, P. A retrospective view of survey photofluorograms of persons with lung cancer. *Cancer,* 1960, *13,* 91–95.

Haber, R. N. Information processing. In E. C. Carterette & M. P. Friedman (Eds.), *Handbook of perception.* Vol. 1. New York: Academic Press, 1974.

Hagen, M. A. Picture perception: Toward a theoretical model. *Psychological Bulletin,* 1974, *81,* 471–497.

Hagen, M. A. (Ed.) *The perception of pictures.* Vols. 1 and 2. New York: Academic Press, 1980.

Haith, M. M. *Rules that babies look by.* Hillsdale, N. J.: Lawrence Erlbaum Associates, 1980.

Haith, M. M., & Campos, J. J. Human infancy. *Annual Review of Psychology,* 1977, *28,* 251–293.

Hale, G. A., & Taweel, S. S. Age differences in children's performance on measures of component selection and incidental learning. *Journal of Experimental Child Psychology,* 1974, *18,* 107–116.

Hall, M. J., Bartoshuk, L. M., Cain, W. S. & Stevens, J. C. PTC taste blindness and the taste of caffeine. *Nature* (London), 1975, 253, 442–443.

Halle, M., & Stevens, K. N. Speech recognition: A model and a program for research. In J. A. Fodor & J. J. Katz (Eds.), *The structure of language: Readings in the philosophy of language.* Englewood Cliffs, N. J.: Prentice-Hall, 1964.

Hamilton, V., & Vernon, M. D. *The development of cognitive processes.* London: Academic Press, 1976.

Hanig, D. P. Zur Psychophysik des Geschmackssinnes. *Philosophische Studien,* 1901, *17,* 576–623.

Hardy, J. D., Stolwijk, J. A. J., & Hoffman, D. Pain following step increase in skin temperature. In D. R. Kenshalo (Ed.), *The skin senses.* Springfield, Ill.: Thomas, 1968.

Hassett, J. Sex and smell. *Psychology Today,* March 1978, *11,* 40–45.

Hawkins, D. The effects of subliminal stimulation on drive level and brand preference. *Journal of Marketing Research,* 1970, *7,* 322–326.

Healy, A. F. Detection errors on the word *The:* Evidence for reading units larger than letters. *Journal of Experimental Psychology: Human Perception and Performance,* 1976, *2,* 235–242.

Held, R., & Hein, A. Movement-produced stimulation in the development of visually guided behavior. *Journal of Comparative and Physiological Psychology,* 1963, *56,* 872–876.

Heller, H. C., Crawshaw, L. I., & Hammel, H. T.

The thermostat of vertebrate animals. *Scientific American,* 1978, *239,* 102–113.

Helmholtz, H. von. *Handbuch der physiolgischen Optik.* Hamburg & Leipzig: Voss, 1866.

Helson, H., & Lansford, T. The role of spectral energy of source and background color in pleasantness of object colors. *Applied Optics,* 1970, *9,* 1513–1562.

Henderson, D. C. The relationships among time, distance, and intensity as determinants of motion discrimination. *Perception & Psychophysics,* 1971, *10,* 313–320.

Henning, G. J., Brouwer, J. N., Van der Wel, H., & Francke, A. Miraculin, the sweet-inducing principle from miracle fruit. In C. Pfaffman (Ed.), *Olfaction and taste.* New York: Rockefeller University Press, 1969.

Henning, H. Die Qualitatsreibe des Geschmacks. *Zeitschrift für Psychologie,* 1916, *74,* 203–219.

Henning, H. Psychologische Studien am Geschmacksinn. In E. Abderhalden (Ed.), *Handbuch der biologischen Arbeitsmethoden.* Berlin: Urban & Schwarzenberg, 1927.

Hess, E. H. *The tell-tale eye: How your eyes reveal hidden thoughts and emotions.* New York: Van Nostrand Reinhold, 1975.

Hilgard, E. R. A neodissociation interpretation of pain reduction in hypnosis. *Psychological Review,* 1973, *80,* 396–411.

Hilgard, E. R. Hypnosis and pain. In R. A. Sternbach (Ed.), *The psychology of pain.* New York: Raven, 1978.

Hochberg, J. Perception: I. Color and shape. In J. W. Kling & L. A. Riggs (Eds.), *Woodworth & Schlosberg's experimental psychology* (3rd ed.). New York: Holt, Rinehart and Winston, 1971. (a)

Hochberg, J. Perception: II. Space and movement. In J. W. Kling & L. A. Riggs (Eds.), *Woodworth & Schlosberg's experimental psychology* (3rd ed.). New York: Holt, Rinehart and Winston, 1971. (b)

Hochberg, J. Higher-order stimuli and inter-response coupling in the perception of the visual world. In R. B. MacLeod & H. L. Pick, Jr. (Eds.), *Perception: Essays in honor of James J. Gibson.* Ithaca, N. Y.: Cornell University Press, 1974.

Hochberg, J. *Perception* (2nd ed.). Englewood Cliffs, N. J.: Prentice-Hall, 1978. (a)

Hochberg, J. Art and perception. In E. C. Carterette & M. P. Friedman (Eds.), *Handbook of perception.* Vol. 10. New York: Academic Press, 1978. (b)

Hochberg, J. Sensation and perception. In E. Hearst (Ed.), *The first century of experimental psychology.* Hillsdale, N. J.: Lawrence Erlbaum Associates, 1979.

Hochberg, J., & Brooks, V. The psychophysics of form: Reversible-perspective drawings of spatial objects. *American Journal of Psychology,* 1960, *73,* 337–354.

Hochberg, J., & Brooks, V. Pictorial recognition as an unlearned ability: A study of one child's performance. *American Journal of Psychology,* 1962, *75,* 624–628.

Hochberg, J., & Brooks, V. The perception of motion pictures. In E. C. Carterette & M. P. Friedman (Eds.), *Handbook of perception.* Vol. 10. New York: Academic Press, 1978.

Hochberg, J., & McAlister, E. A quantitative approach to figural "goodness." *Journal of Experimental Psychology,* 1953, *46,* 361–364.

Holway, A. F., & Boring, E. G. The moon illusion and the angle of regard. *American Journal of Psychology,* 1940, *52,* 509–516.

Holway, A. F., & Boring, E. G. Determinants of apparent visual size with distance variant. *American Journal of Psychology,* 1941, *54,* 21–37.

Hooper, K. Perceptual aspects of architecture. In E. C. Carterette & M. P. Friedman (Eds.), *Handbook of perception.* Vol. 10. New York: Academic Press, 1978.

Horowitz, F. D. (Ed.) Visual attention, auditory stimulation, and language discrimination in young infants. *Monographs of the Society for Research in Child Development,* 1974, *39* (5, Serial No. 158).

Howes, D., & Solomon, R. L. A note on McGinnies' "Emotionality and perceptual defense." *Psychological Review,* 1950, *57,* 229–234.

Hubel, D. H., & Wiesel, T. N. Receptive fields of single neurons in the cat's striate cortex. *Journal of Physiology* (London), 1959, *148,* 574–591.

Hubel, D. H., & Wiesel, T. N. Receptive fields and functional architecture in two nonstriate visual areas (18 and 19) of the cat. *Journal of Neurophysiology,* 1965, *28,* 229–289.

Hubel, D. H., & Wiesel, T. N. Brain mechanisms and vision. *Scientific American,* 1979, 241(3), 150–162.

Hurvich, L. M. *Color vision.* Sunderland, Mass.: Sinauer Associates, 1981.

Hurvich, L. M., & Jameson, D. An opponent-process theory of color vision. *Psychological Review,* 1957, *64,* 384–404.

Hurvich, L. M., & Jameson, D. *The perception of brightness and darkness.* Boston: Allyn and Bacon, 1966.

Ittelson, W. H., & Kilpatrick, F. P. Experiments in perception. *Scientific American,* 1951, *185*(2), 50–55.

Jaeger, W. Genetics of congenital colour deficiencies. In D. Jameson & L. M. Hurvich (Eds.), *Visual psychophysics.* Vol. VII/4. Berlin: Springer-Verlag, 1972.

James, W. *The principles of psychology.* New York: Henry Holt, 1890.

James, W. *Psychology: Briefer course.* New York: Holt, 1892.

Jameson, D. Theoretical issues of color vision. In D. Jameson & L. M. Hurvich (Eds.), *Visual psychophysics.* Vol. VII/4. Berlin: Springer-Verlag, 1972.

Janisse, M. P. *Pupillometry: The psychology of the pupillary response.* Washington, D. C.: Hemisphere, 1977.

Jesteadt, W., Luce, R. D., & Green, D. M. Sequential effects in judgments of loudness. *Journal of Experimental Psychology: Human Perception and Performance,* 1977, *3,* 92–104.

Johansson, G. Visual perception of biological motion and a model for its analysis. *Perception & Psychophysics,* 1973, *14,* 201–211.

Johansson, G. Projective transformations as determining visual space perception. In R. B. MacLeod & H. L. Pick, Jr. (Eds.), *Perception: Essays in honor of James J. Gibson.* Ithaca, N. Y.: Cornell University Press, 1974.

Johansson, G. Visual motion perception. *Scientific American,* 1975, *232,* 76–88.

Johansson, G. Spatial constancy and motion in visual perception. In W. Epstein (Ed.), *Stability and constancy in visual perception: Mechanisms and processes.* New York: Wiley, 1977.

Johansson, G., von Hofsten, C., & Jansson, G. Event perception. *Annual Review of Psychology,* 1980, *31,* 27–63.

Johnson, H. *The world atlas of wine.* New York: Simon and Schuster, 1971.

Johnson, R. C., Frincke, G., & Martin, L. Meaningfulness, frequency, and affective character of words as related to visual duration threshold. *Canadian Journal of Psychology,* 1961, *15,* 199–204.

Judd, D. B., & Wyszecki, G. *Color in business, science, and industry.* New York: Wiley, 1975.

Juola, J. F. Pattern recognition. In R. Lachman, J. L. Lachman, & E. C. Butterfield (Eds.), *Cognitive psychology and information processing: An introduction.* Hillsdale, N. J.: Lawrence Erlbaum Associates, 1979.

Kahneman, D. Method, findings, and theory in studies of visual masking. *Psychological Bulletin,* 1968, *70,* 404–425.

Kahneman, D. *Attention and effort.* Englewood Cliffs, N. J.: Prentice-Hall, 1973.

Kallir, O. (Ed.) *Grandma Moses: My life's history.* Harper, 1946.

Kanizsa, G. Subjective contours. *Scientific American,* 1976, *234*(4), 48–52.

Kaplan, S., Kaplan, R., & Wendt, J. S. Rated preference and complexity for natural and urban visual material. *Perception & Psychophysics,* 1972, *12,* 354–356.

Kare, M. R., & Ficken, M. S. Comparative studies

on the sense of taste. In Y. Zotterman (Ed.), *Olfaction and taste.* New York: Macmillan, 1963.

Kassarjian, H. H. Voting intentions and political perceptions. *Journal of Psychology,* 1963, *56,* 85–88.

Kaufman, L., & Rock, I. The moon illusion. I. *Science,* 1962, *136,* 953–961.

Kearney, G. E. Hue preference as a function of ambient temperatures. *Australian Journal of Psychology,* 1966, *18,* 271–275.

Kennedy, J. M. *A psychology of picture perception.* San Francisco: Jossey-Bass, 1974.

Kenshalo, D. R. The cutaneous senses. In J. W. Kling & L. A. Riggs (Eds.), *Woodworth & Schlosberg's experimental psychology* (3rd ed.). New York: Holt, Rinehart and Winston, 1971.

Kenshalo, D. R. Age changes in touch, vibration, temperature, kinesthesis, and pain sensitivity. In J. E. Birren & K. W. Schaie (Eds.), *Handbook of the psychology of aging.* New York: Van Nostrand Reinhold, 1977.

Kenshalo, D. R. Biophysics and psychophysics of feeling. In E. C. Carterette & M. P. Friedman (Eds.), *Handbook of perception.* Vol. 6B. New York: Academic Press, 1978.

Kenshalo, D. R., Holmes, C. E., & Wood, P. B. Warm and cool thresholds as a function of rate of stimulus temperature change. *Perception & Psychophysics,* 1968, *3,* 81–84.

Klatzky, R. L. *Human memory: Structures and processes* (2nd ed.). San Francisco: W. H. Freeman, 1980.

Klein, G. S. *Perception, motives, and personality.* New York: Knopf, 1970.

Koelega, H. S., & Köster, E. P. Some experiments on sex differences in odor perception. *Annals of the New York Academy of Sciences,* 1974, *237,* 234–246.

Konečni, V. J., Crozier, J. B., & Doob, A. N. Anger and expression of aggression: Effects on aesthetic preference. *Scientific Aesthetics,* 1976, *1,* 47–55.

Kovi, P. The sweet truth about wine. *Cuisine,* September 1980, *9,* 12–14.

Kroeze, J. H. A. Functional equivalence of the two sides of the human tongue. *Perception & Psychophysics,* 1979, *25,* 115–118.

Kruger, L. M. David Katz: Der Aufbau Der Tastwelt (The world of touch): A synopsis. *Perception & Psychophysics,* 1970, *7,* 337–341.

Kundel, H. L., & Nodine, C. F. Studies of eye movements and visual search in radiology. In J. W. Senders, D. F. Fisher, & R. A. Monty (Eds.), *Eye movements and the higher psychological functions.* Hillsdale, N. J.: Lawrence Erlbaum Associates, 1978.

Kupchella, C. *Sights and sounds.* Indianapolis: Bobbs-Merrill, 1976.

Kuznicki, J. T., & McCutcheon, N. B. Cross-enhancement of the sour taste on a single human

taste papilla. *Journal of Experimental Psychology: General,* 1979, *108,* 68–89.

LaBerge, D., & Samuels, S. J. Toward a theory of automatic information processing in reading. *Cognitive Psychology,* 1974, *6,* 293–323.

LaFrance, M., & Mayo, C. *Moving bodies: Nonverbal communication in social relationships.* Monterey, Calif.: Brooks/Cole, 1978.

Lakowski, R., Aspinall, P. A., & Kinnear, P. R. Association between color vision losses and diabetes mellitus. *Ophthalmic Research,* 1972, *4,* 145–159.

Lang, G. The best seafood in the world (naturally, a report from Hong Kong). *Food & Wine,* July 1979, *2,* 59–67.

Lappin, J. S., & Preble, L. D. A demonstration of shape constancy. *Perception & Psychophysics,* 1975, *17,* 439–444.

Lawless, H. T., & Skinner, E. F. The duration and perceived intensity of sucrose taste. *Perception & Psychophysics,* 1979, *25,* 180–184.

Layton, B. Perceptual noise and aging. *Psychological Bulletin,* 1975, *82,* 875–883.

Lefton, L. A. Metacontrast: A review. *Perception & Psychophysics,* 1973, *13,* 161–171.

Lefton, L. A. Eye movements in reading disabled children. In J. W. Senders, D. F. Fisher, & R. A. Monty (Eds.), *Eye movements and the higher psychological functions.* Hillsdale, N. J.: Lawrence Erlbaum Associates, 1978.

Lefton, L. A. *Psychology* (1st ed.). Boston: Allyn and Bacon, 1979.

Leibowitz, H. W. Sensory, learned, and cognitive mechanisms of size perception. *Annals of the New York Academy of Sciences,* 1971, *188,* 47–62.

Leibowitz, H. W., Shiina, K., & Hennessy, R. T. Oculomotor adjustments and size constancy. *Perception & Psychophysics,* 1972, *12,* 497–500.

Leshowitz, B. Measurement of the auditory stimulus. In E. C. Carterette & M. P. Friedman (Eds.), *Handbook of perception.* Vol. 4. New York: Academic Press, 1978.

Levine, J. D., Gordon, N. C., & Fields, H. L. The role of endorphins in placebo analgesia. In J. J. Bonica, J. C. Liebeskind, & D. Albe-Fessard (Eds.), *Advances in pain research and therapy.* Vol. 3. New York: Raven Press, 1979.

Liebeskind, J. C., & Paul, L. A. Psychological and physiological mechanisms of pain. *Annual Review of Psychology,* 1977, *28,* 41–60.

Lindsay, P. H., & Norman, D. A. *Human information processing: An introduction to psychology* (2nd ed.). New York: Academic Press, 1977.

Lippman, C. W. Certain hallucinations peculiar to migraine. *Journal of Nervous and Mental Diseases,* 1952, *116,* 346–351.

Lipsitt, L. P. Taste in human neonates: Its effect on

sucking and heart rate. In J. M. Weiffenbach (Ed.), *Taste and development: The genesis of sweet preference.* Bethesda, Md.: U. S. Department of Health, Education, and Welfare, 1977.

Loftus, G. R., & Mackworth, N. H. Cognitive determinants of fixation location during picture viewing. *Journal of Experimental Psychology: Human Perception and Performance,* 1978, *4,* 565–572.

Lonner, W. J., & Triandis, H. C. Introduction to basic processes. In H. C. Triandis & W. Lonner (Eds.), *Handbook of cross-cultural psychology: Basic processes.* Vol. 3. Boston: Allyn and Bacon, 1980.

Loudon, D. L., & Della Bitta, A. J. *Consumer behavior: Concepts and applications.* New York: McGraw-Hill, 1979.

Luborsky, L., Blinder, B., & Mackworth, N. Eye fixation and recall of pictures as a function of GSR responsivity. *Perceptual and Motor Skills,* 1963, *16,* 169–183.

Ludel, J. *Introduction to sensory processes.* San Francisco: W. H. Freeman, 1978.

MacDonald, W. A., & Hoffman, E. R. The recognition of road pavement messages. *Journal of Applied Psychology,* 1973, *57,* 314–319.

MacDougall, R. On secondary bias in objective judgment. *Psychological Review,* 1906, *13,* 97–120.

Mace, W. M. James J. Gibson's strategy for perceiving: Ask not what's inside your head, but what your head's inside of. In R. Shaw & J. Bransford (Eds.), *Perceiving, acting, and knowing: Toward an ecological psychology.* Hillsdale, N. J.: Lawrence Erlbaum Associates, 1977.

Macfarlane, A. *The psychology of childbirth.* Cambridge, Mass.: Harvard University Press, 1977.

Mackay, D. G. Aspects of the theory of comprehension, memory, and attention. *Quarterly Journal of Experimental Psychology,* 1973, *25,* 22–40.

Mackworth, N. H. Stimulus density limits the useful field of view. In R. A. Monty & J. W. Senders (Eds.), *Eye movements and psychological processes.* Hillsdale, N. J.: Lawrence Erlbaum Associates, 1976.

Mackworth, N. H., & Kaplan, I. T. Visual acuity when eyes are pursuing moving targets. *Science,* 1962, *136,* 387–388.

Mackworth, N. H., & Morandi, A. J. The gaze selects informative details within pictures. *Perception & Psychophysics,* 1967, *2,* 547–552.

Maga, J. A. The influence of color on taste thresholds. *Chemical senses and flavor,* 1974, *1,* 115–120.

Mandler, J. M., & Johnson, N. S. Some of the thousand words a picture is worth. *Journal of Experimental Psychology: Human Learning and Memory,* 1976, *2,* 529–540.

Manning, S. A., & Rosenstock, E. H. *Classical psychophysics and scaling.* New York: McGraw-Hill, 1968.

Marks, L. E. A theory of loudness and loudness judgments. *Psychological Review,* 1979, *86,* 256–285.

Marks, W. B., Dobelle, W. H., & MacNichol, E. F. Visual pigments of single primate cones. *Science,* 1964, *143,* 1181–1183.

Mastai, M. L. d'O. *Illusion in art.* New York: Abaris, 1975.

Matlin, M. W. *Human experimental psychology.* Monterey, Calif.: Brooks/Cole, 1979.

Matlin, M. W. *Cognition.* New York: Holt, Rinehart and Winston, 1983.

Matlin, M. W., & Stang, D. J. *The Pollyanna Principle: Selectivity in language, memory, and thought.* Cambridge, Mass.: Schenkman, 1978.

Maugh, T. H., II. Malodor counteractants: The nose no longer knows. *Science,* 1975, *190,* 870, 919.

McBurney, D. H. Psychological dimensions and perceptual analysis of taste. In E. C. Carterette & M. P. Friedman (Eds.), *Handbook of perception.* Vol. 6A. New York: Academic Press, 1978.

McBurney, D. H., & Gent, J. F. On the nature of taste qualities, *Psychological Bulletin,* 1979, *86,* 151–167.

McBurney, D. H., & Moskat, L. J. Taste thresholds in college-age smokers and nonsmokers. *Perception & Psychophysics,* 1975, *18,* 71–73.

McBurney, D. H., & Shick, T. R. Taste and water taste of twenty-six compounds for man. *Perception & Psychophysics,* 1971, *10,* 249–252.

McClelland, J. L. Perception and masking of wholes and parts. *Journal of Experimental Psychology: Human Perception and Performance,* 1978, *4,* 210–223.

McClintock, M. K. Menstrual synchrony and suppression. *Nature,* 1971, *229,* 244–245.

McConnell, J. V., Cutler, R. L., & McNeil, E. B. Subliminal stimulation: An overview. *American Psychologist,* 1958, *13,* 230–242.

McDowell, E. D., & Rockwell, T. H. An exploratory investigation of the stochastic nature of the drivers' eye movements and their relationship to the roadway geometry. In J. W. Senders, D. F. Fisher, & R. A. Monty (Eds.), *Eye movements and the higher psychological functions.* Hillsdale, N. J.: Lawrence Erlbaum Associates, 1978.

McGinnies, E. Emotionality and perceptual defense. *Psychological Review,* 1949, *56,* 244–251.

McGurk, H., & Lewis, M. Space perception in early infancy: Perception within a common auditory-visual space? *Science,* 1974, *186,* 649–650.

Meltzer, P. How to taste and remember wines like a pro. *Food & Wine,* Summer 1980, *3*(2).

Meltzoff, A. N., & Moore, M. K. Imitation of facial

and manual gestures by human neonates. *Science*, 1977, *198*, 75–78.

Melzack, R. *The puzzle of pain.* London: Penguin, 1973.

Melzack, R., & Casey, K. L. In D. Kenshalo (Ed.), *The skin senses.* Springfield, Ill.: Thomas, 1968.

Melzack, R., & Dennis, S. G. Neurophysiological foundations of pain. In R. A. Sternbach (Ed.), *The psychology of pain.* New York: Raven, 1978.

Melzack, R., & Wall, P. D. On the nature of cutaneous sensory mechanisms. *Brain*, 1962, *85*, 331–352.

Melzack, R., & Wall, P. D. Pain mechanisms: A new theory. *Science*, 1965, *150*, 971–979.

Meyer, J. S. Visual and verbal processes involved in the development of picture-recognition skills. *Child Development*, 1978, *49*, 178–187.

Miller, J. D. Effects of noise on people. In E. C. Carterette & M. P. Friedman (Eds.), *Handbook of perception.* Vol. 4. New York: Academic Press, 1978.

Mills, M., & Melhuish, E. Recognition of mother's voice in early infancy. *Nature*, 1974, *252*, 123–124.

Moncrieff, R. W. *Odour preferences.* New York: Wiley, 1966.

Moore, B. C. J. *Introduction to the psychology of hearing.* Baltimore, Md.: University Park Press, 1977.

Moore, M. E., Linker, E., & Purcell, M. Taste sensitivity after eating: A signal detection approach. *American Journal of Psychology*, 1965, *78*, 107–111.

Moray, N. Attention in dichotic listening: Affective cues and the influence of instructions. *Quarterly Journal of Experimental Psychology*, 1959, *11*, 59–60.

Moray, N. *Attention: Selective processes in vision and hearing.* London: Hutchinson, 1969.

Moreland, J. D. Peripheral colour vision. In D. Jameson & L. M. Hurvich (Eds.), *Visual psychophysics.* Vol. VII/4. Berlin: Springer-Verlag, 1972.

Moskowitz, H. R. Odors in the environment: Hedonics, perfumery, and odor abatement. In E. C. Carterette & M. P. Friedman (Eds.), *Handbook of perception.* Vol. 10. New York: Academic Press, 1978. (a)

Moskowitz, H. R. Food and food technology: Food habits, gastronomy, flavors, and sensory evaluation. In E. C. Carterette & M. P. Friedman (Eds.), *Handbook of perception.* Vol. 10. New York: Academic Press, 1978. (b)

Mozell, M. M. Olfaction. In J. W. Kling & L. A. Riggs (Eds.), *Woodworth & Schlosberg's experimental psychology* (3rd ed.). New York: Holt, Rinehart and Winston, 1971.

Murray, H. A. Techniques for a systematic investigation of fantasy. *Journal of Psychology*, 1936, *3*, 115–143.

Naus, M. J., & Shillman, R. J. Why a Y is not a V: A new look at the distinctive features of letters.

Journal of Experimental Psychology: Human Perception and Performance, 1976, *2*, 394–400.

Neisser, U. Visual search. *Scientific American*, 1964, *210*, 94–102.

Neisser, U. The control of information pickup in selective looking. In A. D. Pick (Ed.), *Perception and its development: A tribute to Eleanor J. Gibson.* Hillsdale, N. J.: Lawrence Erlbaum Associates, 1979.

Neisser, U., & Becklen, R. Selective looking: Attending to visually significant events. *Cognitive Psychology*, 1975, *7*, 480–494.

Newman, C. V. The influence of texture density gradients on judgments of length. *Psychonomic Science*, 1970, *20*, 333–334.

Newman, C. V., Whinham, E. A., & MacRae, A. W. The influence of texture on judgment of slant and relative distance in a picture with suggested depth. *Perception & Psychophysics*, 1973, *14*, 280–284.

New York Times. Doctors' scrawl. March 23, 1980.

Nordmark, J. O. Frequency and periodicity analysis. In E. C. Carterette & M. P. Friedman (Eds.), *Handbook of perception.* Vol. 4. New York: Academic Press, 1978.

Norgren, R. On the anatomical substrate for flavor. In D. Muller-Schwarze & M. M. Mozell (Eds.), *Chemical signals in vertebrates.* New York: Plenum, 1977.

Norman, D. A., & Bobrow, D. G. On data-limited and resource-limited processes. *Cognitive Psychology*, 1975, *7*, 44–64.

Odom, R. D., & Guzman, R. D. Development of hierarchies of dimensional salience. *Developmental Psychology*, 1972, *6*, 271–287.

Paap, K. R., & Ogden, W. C. Letter encoding is an obligatory but capacity-demanding operation. *Journal of Experimental Psychology: Human Perception and Performance*, 1981, *7*, 518–527.

Palmer, S. E. Visual perception and world knowledge: Notes on a model of sensory-cognitive interaction. In D. A. Norman & D. E. Rumelhart (Eds.), *Explorations in cognition.* San Francisco: Freeman, 1975. (a)

Palmer, S. E. The effects of contextual scenes on the identification of objects. *Memory & Cognition*, 1975, *3*, 519–526. (b)

Parkes, A. S., & Bruce, H. M. Olfactory stimuli in mammalian reproduction. *Science*, 1961, *134*, 1049–1054.

Patterson, R. D., & Green, D. M. Auditory masking. In E. C. Carterette & M. P. Friedman (Eds.), *Handbook of perception.* Vol. 4. New York: Academic Press, 1978.

Penfield, W., & Rasmussen, T. *The cerebral cortex of man.* New York: Macmillan, 1950.

Pettigrew, T. F., Allport, G. W., & Barnett, E. D.

Binocular resolution and perception of race in South Africa. *British Journal of Psychology*, 1958, *49*, 265–278.

Pfaffmann, C. The vertebrate phylogeny, neural code, and integrative processes of taste. In E. C. Carterette & M. P. Friedman (Eds.), *Handbook of perception*. Vol. 6A. New York: Academic Press, 1978.

Pfaffmann, C., Frank, M., & Norgren, R. Neural mechanisms and behavioral aspects of taste. *Annual Review of Psychology*, 1979, *30*, 283–325.

Piaget, J. *The construction of reality in the child*. New York: Basic Books, 1954.

Pick, A. D. (Ed.). *Perception and its development: A tribute to Eleanor J. Gibson*. Hillsdale, N. J.: Lawrence Erlbaum Associates, 1979.

Pirenne, M. H. Vision and art. In E. C. Carterette & M. P. Friedman (Eds.), *Handbook of perception*. Vol. 5. New York: Academic Press, 1975.

Plomp, R. *Aspects of tone sensation*. New York: Academic Press, 1976.

Pola, J., & Matin, L. Eye movements following autokinesis. *Bulletin of the Psychonomic Society*, 1977, *10*, 397–398.

Pollack, I., & Pickett, J. M. The intelligibility of excerpts from conversational speech. *Language and Speech*, 1964, *6*, 165–171.

Posner, M. I., Goldsmith, R., & Welton, K. E., Jr. Perceived distance and the classification of distorted patterns. *Journal of Experimental Psychology*, 1967, *73*, 28–38.

Postman, L., Bruner, J. S., & McGinnies, E. Personal values as selective factors in perception. *Journal of Abnormal and Social Psychology*, 1948, *43*, 142–154.

Poulton, E. C. Skimming lists of food ingredients printed in different sizes. *Journal of Applied Psychology*, 1969, *53*, 55–58.

Poulton, E. C. *Environment and human efficiency*. Springfield, Ill.: Thomas, 1970.

Poulton, E. C. *The environment at work*. Springfield, Ill.: Thomas, 1979.

Prak, N. L. *The visual perception of the built environment*. Delft: Delft University Press, 1977.

Rabbitt, P. Sorting, categorization and visual search. In E. C. Carterette & M. P. Friedman (Eds.), *Handbook of perception*. Vol. 9. New York: Academic Press, 1978.

Ratliff, F. *Mach bands: Quantitative studies on neural networks in the retina*. San Francisco: Holden-Day, 1965.

Rayner, K. Eye movements in reading and information processing. *Psychological Bulletin*, 1978, *85*, 618–660.

Rayner, K., & McConkie, G. Perceptual processes in reading: The perceptual spans. In A. S. Reber & D. L. Scarborough (Eds.), *Toward a psychology of reading*. Hillsdale, N. J.: Lawrence Erlbaum Associates, 1977.

Rechtschaffen, A., & Mednick, S. A. The autokinetic word technique. *Journal of Abnormal and Social Psychology*, 1955, *51*, 346.

Reese, H. W., & Lipsitt, L. P. *Experimental child psychology*. New York: Academic Press, 1970.

Regan, D., Beverley, K., & Cynader, M. The visual perception of motion in depth. *Scientific American*, 1979, *241*(1), 136–151.

Remez, R. E. Adaptation of the category boundary between speech and nonspeech: A case against feature detectors. *Cognitive Psychology*, 1979, *11*, 38–57.

Restle, F. Moon illusion explained on the basis of relative size. *Science*, 1970, *167*, 1092–1096.

Richards, W. Visual space perception. In E. C. Carterette & M. P. Friedman (Eds.), *Handbook of perception*. Vol. 5. New York: Academic Press, 1975.

Richards, W. Selective stereoblindness. In H. Spekreijse & L. H. van der Tweel (Eds.), *Spatial contrast*. Amsterdam: North Holland, 1977.

Riggs, L. A. Vision. In J. W. Kling & L. A. Riggs (Eds.), *Woodworth & Schlosberg's experimental psychology* (3rd ed.). New York: Holt, Rinehart and Winston, 1971.

Risset, J. C. Musical acoustics. In E. C. Carterette & M. P. Friedman (Eds.), *Handbook of perception*. Vol. 4. New York: Academic Press, 1978.

Ritter, M. Effect of disparity and viewing distance in perceived depth. *Perception & Psychophysics*, 1977, *22*, 400–407.

Robinson, J. O. *The psychology of visual illusion*. London: Hutchinson, 1972.

Rock, I. *An introduction to perception*. New York: Macmillan, 1975.

Rock, I. In defense of unconscious inference. In W. Epstein (Ed.), *Stability and constancy in visual perception: Mechanisms and processes*. New York: Wiley, 1977.

Rock, I., & Brogsole, L. Grouping based on phenomenal proximity. *Journal of Experimental Psychology*, 1964, *67*, 531–538.

Rock, I., & Ebenholtz, S. The relational determination of perceived size. *Psychological Review*, 1959, *66*, 387–401.

Rockwell, T. Skills, judgment, and information acquisition in driving. In T. W. Forbes (Ed.), *Human factors in highway traffic safety research*. New York: Wiley, 1972.

Roederer, J. G. *Introduction to the physics and psychophysics of music* (2nd ed.). New York: Springer-Verlag, 1975.

Rosinski, R. R. *The development of visual perception*. Santa Monica, California: Goodyear, 1977.

Ross, H. E., & Ross, G. M. Did Ptolemy understand the moon illusion? *Perception*, 1976, *5*, 377–385.

Ross, J. The resources of binocular perception. *Scientific American*, 1976, *234*(3), 80–86.

Rubin, E. *Synsoplevede Figurer*. Copenhagen: Cyldendalske, 1915. Abridged translation by M. Wertheimer: Figure and ground. In D. C. Beardslee & M. Wertheimer (Eds.), *Readings in perception*. Princeton, N. J.: Van Nostrand, 1958.

Rushton, W. A. Kinetics of cone pigments measured objectively in the living human fovea. *Annals of the New York Academy of Science*, 1958, *74*, 291–304.

Rushton, W. A. H. Visual pigments and color blindness. *Scientific American*, 1975, *232*, 64–74.

Russell, M. J. Human olfactory communication. *Nature* (London), 1976, *260*, 520–522.

Safire, W. "Mondegreens: I led the pigeons to the flag." *The New York Times Magazine*, May 27, 1979, 9–10.

Salapatek, P. Pattern perception in early infancy. In L. B. Cohen & P. Salapatek (Eds.), *Infant perception: From sensation to cognition*. New York: Academic Press, 1975.

Salapatek, P., Bechtold, A. G., & Bushnell, E. W. Infant visual acuity as a function of viewing distance. *Child Development*, 1976, 860–863.

Scharf, B. Loudness. In E. C. Carterette & M. P. Friedman (Eds.), *Handbook of perception*. Vol. 4. New York: Academic Press, 1978.

Schiffman, S. S. Physiochemical correlates of olfactory quality. *Science*, 1974, *185*, 112–117.

Schiffman, S. S., & Dackis, C. Taste of nutrients: Amino acids, vitamins, and fatty acids. *Perception & Psychophysics*, 1975, *17*, 140–146.

Schindler, R. M. The effect of prose context on visual search for letters. *Memory & Cognition*, 1978, *6*, 124–130.

Schmidt, F., & Tiffin, J. Distortion of drivers' estimates of automobile speed as a function of speed adaptation. *Journal of Applied Psychology*, 1969, *53*, 536–539.

Schneider, R. A. New insights into the role and modifications of olfaction in man through clinical studies. *Annals of the New York Academy of Sciences*, 1974, *237*, 217–223.

Schneider, W., & Shiffrin, R. M. Controlled and automatic human information processing: I. Detection, search, and attention. *Psychological Review*, 1977, *84*, 1–66.

Segall, M., Campbell, D. T., & Herskovits, M. J. *The influence of culture on visual perception*. Indianapolis: Bobbs-Merrill, 1966.

Sekuler, R. Visual motion perception. In E. C. Carterette & M. P. Friedman (Eds.), *Handbook of perception*. Vol. 5. New York: Academic Press, 1975.

Sekuler, R., Pantle, A., & Levinson, E. Physiological basis of motion perception. In R. Held, H. W. Leibowitz, & H. L. Teuber (Eds.), *Handbook of sensory physiology*. Vol. 8: *Perception*. Berlin: Springer-Verlag, 1978.

Self, P. A., Horowitz, F. D., & Paden, L. Y. Olfaction in newborn infants. *Developmental Psychology*, 1972, *7*, 349–363.

Shaffer, L. H. Multiple attention in continuous verbal tasks. In P. M. Rabbitt & S. Dornic (Eds.), *Attention and performance*. Vol. 5. London: Academic Press, 1975.

Sharma, S., & Moskowitz, H. Effect of marihuana on the visual autokinetic phenomenon. *Perceptual and Motor Skills*, 1972, *35*, 891.

Shepard, R. N. Recognition memory for words, sentences, and pictures. *Journal of Verbal Learning and Verbal Behavior*, 1967, *6*, 156–163.

Shlaer, S. The relation between visual acuity and illumination. *Journal of General Physiology*, 1937, *21*, 165–188.

Sivak, M., Olson, P. L., & Pastalan, L. A. Effect of driver's age on nighttime legibility of highway signs. *Human Factors*, 1981, *23*, 59–64.

Sivian, L. S., & White, S. D. On minimum audible sound fields. *Journal of the Acoustical Society of America*, 1933, *4*, 288–321.

Smith, M. D. *Educational psychology and its classroom applications* (2nd ed.). Boston: Allyn and Bacon, 1978.

Solley, C. M. Affective processes in perceptual development. In A. H. Kidd & J. L. Rivoire (Eds.), *Perceptual development in children*. New York: International University Press, 1966.

Solley, C. M., & Murphy, G. *Development of the perceptual world*. New York: Basic Books, 1960.

Solley, C. M., & Santos, J. Perceptual learning with partial verbal reinforcement. *Perceptual and Motor Skills*, 1958, *8*, 183–193.

Spelke, H. W., Hirst, W., & Neisser, U. Skills of divided attention. *Cognition*, 1976, *4*, 215–230.

Standing, L. Learning 10,000 pictures. *Quarterly Journal of Experimental Psychology*, 1973, *25*, 207–222.

Standing, L., Conezio, J., & Haber, R. N. Perception and memory for pictures: Single-trial learning of 2560 visual stimuli. *Psychonomic Science*, 1970, *19*, 73–74.

Steck, L., & Machotka, P. Preference for musical complexity: Effects of context. *Journal of Experimental Psychology: Human Perception and Performance*, 1975, *104*, 170–174.

Steinberg, R. *The cooking of Japan*. New York: Time-Life Books, 1969.

Steiner, J. E. Human facial expressions in response to taste and smell stimulation. In H. W. Reese & L. P. Lipsitt (Eds.), *Advances in child development and behavior.* Vol. 13. New York: Academic Press, 1979.

Sternbach, R. A. *Pain: A psychophysiological analysis.* New York: Academic Press, 1968.

Sternbach, R. A. Psychological dimensions and perceptual analyses, including pathologies of pain. In E. C. Carterette & M. P. Friedman (Eds.), *Handbook of perception.* Vol. 6B. New York: Academic Press, 1978.

Sternbach, R. A., & Tursky, B. Ethnic differences among housewives in psychophysical and skin potential responses to electric shock. *Psychophysiology,* 1965, *1,* 241–246.

Stevens, J. C., & Green, B. G. History of research on feeling. In E. C. Carterette & M. P. Friedman (Eds.), *Handbook of perception.* Vol. 6B. New York: Academic Press, 1978.

Stevens, J. C., Marks, L. E., & Simonson, D. C. Regional sensitivity and spatial summation in the warmth sense. *Physiology and Behavior,* 1974, *13,* 825–836.

Stevens, S. S. The measurement of loudness. *Journal of the Acoustical Society of America,* 1955, *27,* 815–829.

Stevens, S. S. On the psychophysical law. *Psychological Review,* 1957, *64,* 153–181.

Stevens, S. S. To honor Fechner and repeal his law. *Science,* 1961, *133,* 80–86.

Stevens, S. S. Neural events and the psychophysical law. *Science,* 1970, *170,* 1043–1050.

Stevens, S. S., Volkman, J., & Newman, E, B. A scale for the measurement of the psychological magnitude of pitch. *Journal of the Acoustical Society of America,* 1937, *8,* 185–190.

Stromeyer, C. F. Form-color aftereffects in human vision. In R. Held, H. W. Leibowitz, & H. L. Teuber (Eds.), *Handbook of sensory physiology.* Vol. 8: *Perception.* Berlin: Springer-Verlag, 1978.

Sumner, D. On testing the sense of smell. *The Lancet,* 1962, *II,* 895.

Takagi, S. F. Biophysics of smell. In E. C. Carterette & M. P. Friedman (Eds.), *Handbook of perception.* Vol. 6A. Academic Press, 1978.

Taus, R. H., Stevens, J. C., & Marks, L. E. Spatial location of warmth. *Perception & Psychophysics,* 1975, *17,* 194–196.

Taylor, W., Pearson, J., Mair, A., & Burns, W. Study of noise and hearing in jute weaving. *Journal of the Acoustical Society of America,* 1965, *38,* 113–120.

Teghtsoonian, R., Teghtsoonian, M., Berglund, B., & Berglund, U. Invariance of odor strength with sniff vigor: An olfactory analogue to size constancy. *Journal of Experimental Psychology: Human Perception and Performance,* 1978, *4,* 144–152.

Thomas, E. L. Advice to the searcher or what do we tell them? In R. A. Monty & J. W. Senders (Eds.),

Eye movements and psychological processes. Hillsdale, N. J.: Lawrence Erlbaum Associates, 1976.

Thurlow, W. R. Audition. In J. W. Kling & L. A. Riggs (Eds.), *Woodworth and Schlosberg's experimental psychology* (3rd ed.). New York: Holt, Rinehart and Winston, 1971.

Treisman, A. M. Contextual cues in selective listening. *Quarterly Journal of Experimental Psychology,* 1960, *12,* 242–248.

Treisman, A. M. Monitoring and storage of irrelevant messages and selective attention. *Journal of Verbal Learning and Verbal Behavior,* 1964, *3,* 449–459.

Treisman, A. M., Squire, R., & Green, J. Semantic processing in dichotic listening: A replication. *Memory & Cognition,* 1974, *2,* 641–646.

Tronick, E., & Hershenson, M. Size-distance perception in preschool children. *Journal of Experimental Child Psychology,* 1979, *27,* 166–184.

Van Dyke, D. Personal communication, 1980.

Van Heyningen, R. What happens to the human lens in cataract. *Scientific American,* 1975(6), *233,* 70–81.

Vaughan, D., & Asbury, T. *General ophthalmology* (8th ed.). Los Altos, Calif.: Lange Medical Publications, 1977.

Vellutino, F. R. *Dyslexia: Theory and research.* Cambridge, Mass.: MIT Press, 1979.

Verillo, R. T. Cutaneous sensation. In B. Scharf (Ed.), *Experimental sensory psychology.* Glenview, Ill.: Scott, Foresman, 1975.

Vernon, M. D. Development of perception of form. In V. Hamilton & M. D. Vernon (Eds.), *The development of cognitive processes.* London: Academic Press, 1976.

Vierling, J. S., & Rock, J. Variations of olfactory sensitivity to Exaltolide during the menstrual cycle. *Journal of Applied Psychology,* 1967, *22,* 311–315.

Vogel, J. M., & Teghtsoonian, M. The effects of perspective alterations on apparent size and distance scales. *Perception & Psychophysics,* 1972, *11,* 294–298.

Volkmann, F. C., Schick, A. M. L., & Riggs, L. A. Time course of visual inhibition during voluntary saccades. *Journal of the Optical Society of America,* 1968, *58,* 362–369.

Vurpillot, E. The development of scanning strategies and their relation to visual differentiation. *Journal of Experimental Child Psychology,* 1968, *6,* 632–650.

Vurpillot, E. *The visual world of the child.* New York: International Universities Press, 1976.

Walk, R. D. Perceptual learning. In E. C. Carterette & M. P. Friedman (Eds.), *Handbook of perception.* Vol. 9. New York: Academic Press, 1978.

Walk, R. D. Depth perception and a laughing

heaven. In A. D. Pick (Ed.), *Perception and its development: A tribute to Eleanor J. Gibson.* Hillsdale, N. J.: Lawrence Erlbaum Associates, 1979.

Walk, R. D., & Pick, H. L., Jr. *Perception and experience.* New York: Plenum, 1978.

Wallach, H., & O'Connell, D. N. The kinetic depth effect. *Journal of Experimental Psychology,* 1953, *45,* 205–217.

Wallach, H., & O'Leary, A. Adaptation in distance perception with head-movement parallax serving as the veridical cue. *Perception & Psychophysics,* 1979, *25,* 42–46.

Walsh, J. W. T. *Photometry.* New York: Dover Publications, 1958.

Ward, L. M., Porac, C., Coren, S., & Girgus, J. S. The case for misapplied constancy scaling: Depth association elicited by illusion configurations. *American Journal of Psychology,* 1977, *90,* 609–620.

Warren, R. M., & Warren, R. P. Auditory illusions and confusions. *Scientific American,* 1970, *223,* 30–36.

Wasserman, G. S. *Color vision: An historical introduction.* New York: Wiley, 1978.

Weiffenbach, J. M. (Ed.) *Taste and development: The genesis of sweet preference.* Bethesda, Md.: U. S. Department of Health, Education, and Welfare, 1977.

Weinstein, S. Intensive and extensive aspects of tactile sensitivity as a function of body part, sex, and laterality. In D. R. Kenshalo (Ed.), *The skin senses.* Springfield, Ill.: Thomas, 1968.

Weintraub, D. J., Tong, L., & Smith, A. J. Müller-Lyer versus size/reflectance-contrast illusion: Is the age related decrement caused by a declining sensitivity to brightness contours? *Developmental Psychology,* 1973, *8,* 6–15.

Weisenberg, M. Pain and pain control. *Psychological Bulletin,* 1977, *84,* 1008–1044.

Weisstein, N. Tutorial: The joy of Fourier analysis. In C. S. Harris (Ed.), *Visual coding and adaptability.* Hillsdale, N. J.: Lawrence Erlbaum Associates, 1980.

Wenger, M. A., Jones, F. N., & Jones, M. H. *Physiological psychology.* New York: Holt, Rinehart and Winston, 1956.

Werner, H. Studies on contour. *American Journal of Psychology,* 1935, *37,* 40–64.

Werner, J. S., & Wooten, B. R. Human infant color vision and color perception. *Infant Behavior and Development,* 1979, *2,* 241–274.

Wertheimer, M. Untersuchungen zur Lehre von der Gestalt: II. *Psychologische Forschung,* 1923, *4,* 301–350. Abridged translation by M. Wertheimer: Principles of perceptual organization. In D. C. Beardslee & M. Wertheimer (Eds.), *Readings in perception.* Princeton, N. J.: Van Nostrand, 1958.

Wertheimer, M. Psychometer coordination of auditory and visual space at birth. *Science,* 1961, *134,* 1692.

Wertheimer, M. The problem of perceptual structure. In E. C. Carterette & M. P. Friedman (Eds.), *Handbook of perception.* Vol. 1. New York: Academic Press, 1974.

Westheimer, G. Visual acuity and spatial modulation thresholds. In D. Jameson & L. M. Hurvich (Eds.) *The handbook of sensory physiology.* Vol. III/4. *Sensory psychophysics.* Berlin: Springer-Verlag, 1972.

Wever, E. G. *Theory of hearing.* Reprint (originally published in 1949). New York: Wiley, 1970.

Whitbourne, S. K., & Weinstock, C. S. *Adult development: The differentiation of experience.* New York: Holt, Rinehart & Winston, 1979.

White, B. W., Saunders, F. A., Scadden, L., Bach-y-Rita, P., & Collins, C. C. Seeing with the skin. *Perception & Psychophysics,* 1970, *7,* 23–27.

Wilkening, H. E. *The psychology almanac: A handbook for students.* Monterey, Calif.: Brooks/Cole, 1973.

Wispé, L. G., & Drambarean, N. C. Physiological need, word frequency, and visual duration threshold. *Journal of Experimental Psychology,* 1953, *46,* 25–31.

Wittrock, M. C., & Lumsdaine, A. A. Instructional psychology. *Annual Review of Psychology,* 1977, *28,* 417–459.

Wolfert, P. *Couscous and other good food from Morocco.* New York: Harper & Row, 1973.

Woodrow, K. M., Friedman, G. D., Siegelaub, A. B., & Collen, M. F. Pain tolerance: Differences according to age, sex and race. *Psychosomatic Medicine,* 1972, *34,* 548–556.

Wright, W. D. Colour mixture. In D. Jameson & L. M. Hurvich (Eds.), *Visual psychophysics.* Vol. III/4. Berlin: Springer-Verlag, 1972.

Yarbus, A. L. *Eye movements and vision.* New York: Plenum, 1967.

Yost, W. A., & Nielsen, D. W. *Fundamentals of hearing: An introduction.* New York: Holt, Rinehart and Winston, 1977.

Zajonc, R. B. Feeling and thinking: Preferences need no inferences. *American Psychologist,* 1980, *35,* 151–175.

Zakia, R. *Perception and photography.* Englewood Cliffs, N. J.: Prentice-Hall, 1975.

Zakia, R., & Todd, H. *101 experiments in photography.* Dobbs Ferry, N. Y.: Morgan & Morgan, 1969.

Zwislocki, J. J. Masking: Experimental and theoretical aspects of simultaneous, forward, backward, and central masking. In E. C. Carterette & M. P. Friedman (Eds.), *Handbook of perception.* Vol. 4. New York: Academic Press, 1978.

NAME INDEX

A

Abramov, I., 26, 27
Albe-Fessard, D. G., 220
Alberts, J. R., 330
Allport, G. W., 297
Allyn, M. R., 78
Alpern, M., 48, 49, 52, 53
Amoore, J. E., 228, 230
Anstis, S. M., 140
Aristotle, 201, 227, 247
Arnheim, R., 127
Aronson, E., 317
Asbury, T., 30, 31, 32, 124
Aslin, R. N., 330
Aspinall, P. A., 71
Atkinson, J., 312
Atkinson, R. C., 8
Avant, L. L., 85

B

Bach-y-rita, P., 210, 211
Backus, J., 184, 192
Badcock, D., 323
Bahill, A. T., 48
Baker, A. H., 298, 299
Barber, T. X., 220
Barbour, J. S., 292
Barclay, C. D., 134
Barnett, E. D., 297
Barten, S., 131
Bartoshuk, L. M., 245, 247, 249, 255, 256,
        257, 258
Basowitz, H., 325
Bassili, J. N., 134
Beauchamp, G. K., 236

Bechtold, A. G., 311
Beck, J., 155
Becklen, R., 269, 274
Beecher, H. K., 216, 218
Beets, M. G. J., 228, 234, 236
Beidler, L. M., 248, 249
Békésy, G. von, 178, 179, 181
Bell, B., 326, 327
Bell, P. A., 193, 194
Belt, B. L., 51
Berglund, B., 233, 234
Berglund, U., 233, 234
Bergman, M., 328, 329
Berkeley, G., 6, 7, 8, 125, 126, 130, 151
Berlyne, D. E., 301, 303, 304, 305, 306
Beroza, M., 240
Bershader, D., 194
Bevan, W., 298
Beverley, K., 137, 138
Birns, B., 131
Birren, F., 77, 78
Birren, J. E., 330
Blakemore, C., 20, 330
Blinder, B., 288
Bliss, J. C., 210
Blum, G. S., 292
Blumenfeld, V. G., 328, 329
Bobrow, D. G., 271, 273, 274
Bond, Z. S., 189
Bonica, J. J., 220
Boring, E. G., 6, 149, 165
Bornstein, M., 75, 312, 313
Bower, T. G. R., 316, 317, 321
Boycott, B. B., 21
Boynton, R. M., 62, 67, 71, 74, 78, 79
Braddick, O., 312
Braille, L., 210

Brandt, T., 135
Bransford, J. D., 105
Braunstein, M. L., 120, 121, 122
Brean, H., 294
Breitmeyer, B. G., 88, 89
Broadbent, D. E., 272, 273, 274
Brosgole, L., 101
Brouwer, J. N., 258
Brown, T. S., 202, 203, 230
Bruce, H. M., 240
Bruner, J. S., 290, 294
Bryant, J. S., 188
Burg, A., 51
Burns, W., 192
Bushnell, E. W., 311

C

Cain, W. S., 226, 227, 228, 231, 232, 233, 235, 236, 237, 238, 239, 241, 255
Campbell, D. T., 111
Campos, J. J., 313, 314, 315, 317, 318
Cannon, J. T., 220
Carey, S., 323
Carlson, N. R., 23, 28, 203
Carlson, V. R., 152
Carpenter, E., 97
Carroll, L., 32
Cascardo, D., 328, 329
Casey, K. L., 217
Carterette, E. C., 214
Chapman, C. R., 218, 219, 220, 221
Charpentier, C. M., 128
Chaves, J. F., 220
Cherry, E. C., 266, 267
Child, I. L., 300, 301
Chow, K. L., 330
Chulow, F. W., 67
Clark, W. C., 218, 219, 330, 343
Cohen, L. B., 310, 311, 317, 318
Cohen, S., 193, 194
Colburn, H. S., 184
Cole, R. A., 187, 189, 190, 191, 192
Coleman, P. D., 185
Collen, M. F., 215
Collings, V. B., 250
Collins, C. C., 210, 211
Comfort, A., 241
Conezio, J., 110
Corballis, M. C., 141
Corbit, J. D., 188
Coren, S., 85, 90, 96, 97, 146, 158, 159, 160, 163, 166, 167
Corso, J. F., 327, 328, 329, 330

Craddick, R. A., 299
Craig, K. D., 221
Crawshaw, L. I., 211
Crozier, J. B., 305
Cumming, G. D., 47, 48
Cutler, R. L., 294, 295
Cutting, J. E., 134
Cynader, M., 137, 138

D

Dackis, C., 247, 248
Dallenbach, K. M., 211
Dalos, P., 177
Das, A. K., 262
Dash, B., 328, 329
Davenport, R. K., 111
Davidoff, J. B., 71, 324
da Vinci, L., 127
Day, R. H., 140, 162, 163, 315, 317
Dearborn, G. V. N., 215
Della Bitta, A. J., 62, 93
DeLoache, J. S., 310, 311, 317
Dennis, S. G., 217
Desor, J. A., 236, 320
Dethier, V. G., 247, 248
Deutsch, D., 192, 272, 304
Deutsch, J. A., 272
DeValois, K., 72, 73, 74, 76, 77, 123
DeValois, R., 72, 73, 74, 76, 77, 123
Diamond, R., 323
Dichgans, J., 135
Dirks, D. D., 195
Ditchburn, R. W., 48
Dixon, N. F., 291, 294
Dobelle, W. H., 28, 72, 73
Doob, A. N., 305
Dowling, J. E., 21
Drambarean, N. C., 293, 294
Drexler, M., 239
Dukes, W. F., 298
Dunn-Rankin, P., 102
Durlach, N. I., 184
Durrant, J. D., 173

E

Ebenholtz, S., 151, 156
Edington, B., 10
Egan, J. P., 11
Egeth, H. E., 276
Eimas, P. D., 188, 237, 318
Eisner, D. A., 327
Elkind, D., 321, 322, 323

Engen, T., 233, 235, 236, 237, 330, 344, 345, 348
Epstein, W., 116
Erdelyi, M. H., 288, 291, 292, 293, 300
Eriksen, C. W., 275
Erlichman, H., 159
Escher, M. C., 97, 98
Evans, F. J., 218

F

Fagan, J. F., III, 314
Fantz, R. L., 311, 313, 314
Favreau, O. E., 141
Feather, B. W., 218
Fechner, G., 301, 302, 334, 348, 349
Festinger, L., 78
Ficken, M. S., 249
Fields, H. L., 218
Fisher, J. D., 193, 194
Fisher, S. B., 218
Flagg, B. N., 283, 284
Flavell, J. H., 313, 324
Fletcher, H., 181
Forbes, T. W., 42, 46
Fordyce, W. E., 220, 221
Fozard, J. L., 326, 327
Frances, R., 304
Francke, A., 258
Frank, G., 297
Frank, M., 252
Franklin, S., 116
Franks, J. J., 105
Fraser, A. B., 158
Frenk, H., 220
Friedman, G. D., 215
Friedman, L. N., 194
Friedman, M. P., 214
Friedman, S. L., 138
Frincke, G., 291
Frisby, J. P., 124

G

Garnes, S., 189
Gehrig, J. D., 219, 220
Gelb, A., 155, 156
Gent, J. F., 248, 257
Gescheider, G. A., 11, 340, 349
Gesteland, R. C., 226, 230
Gibson, E. J., 48, 50, 102, 103, 314, 330
Gibson, J. J., 7, 8, 9, 116, 121, 126, 130, 131, 136, 137, 151, 153, 154, 158, 169, 209, 210, 246
Gilchrist, A. L., 156

Gillam, B., 158, 166, 167
Girgus, J. S., 146, 158, 159, 160, 163, 166, 167
Girvin, J. P., 28
Glass, D. C., 193, 194
Go, E., 321, 322, 323
Gogel, W. C., 116, 140, 151
Goldsmith, R., 104, 105
Gombrich, E. H., 169
Goodson, F. E., 137, 138
Gordon, J., 26, 27
Gordon, N. C., 218
Gottfried, A. W., 319
Graham, C. H., 70, 124
Gratch, G., 315
Gray, J., 46
Green, B. G., 201
Green, D. M., 11, 173, 175, 176, 177, 183, 187, 193, 195, 196, 336
Green, J., 268
Greene, L. S., 320
Gregory, R. L., 2, 136, 163, 169
Grobstein, P., 330
Grützner, P., 71
Guiss, L. W., 280
Guzman, R. D., 324

H

Haber, R. N., 8, 110
Hagen, M. A., 110, 111, 127
Haith, M. M., 313, 314, 317, 318
Hakstean, A. R., 159
Hale, G. A., 324
Hall, M. J., 255
Halle, M., 190, 191
Hamilton, V., 321
Hammel, H. T., 211
Hanig, D. P., 249
Hardy, J. D., 216
Hassett, J., 241
Hawkins, D., 295
Healy, A. F., 276
Hein, A., 330
Held, R., 330
Heller, H. C., 211
Helmholtz, H. von, 7, 8, 72, 76, 125, 150, 151, 155, 156, 158, 178
Helson, H., 301, 302
Henderson, C., 315
Henderson, D. C., 132
Hennessy, R. T., 151
Henning, G. J., 258
Henning, H., 227, 228, 230, 247
Hering, E., 74, 76

Hershenson, M., 324
Herskovits, M. J., 111
Hertz, H., 174
Hess, E. H., 288, 290, 291
Hiatt, S., 315
Hilgard, E. R., 220
Hirst, W., 269, 270
Hochberg, J., 6, 8, 40, 87, 88, 98, 100, 110,
        115, 123, 125, 126, 127, 129, 132, 139,
        140, 301, 303, 304
Hoffman, D., 216
Hoffman, E. R., 169
Holmes, C. E., 212
Holway, A. F., 149, 165
Hooper, K., 304
Horowitz, F. D., 318, 320
Howes, D., 291
Hsia, Y., 70
Hubel, D. H., 27, 28, 29, 30
Hurvich, L. M., 62, 74, 75, 154

I

Ittelson, W. H., 116

J

Jackson, W. H., 94
Jaeger, W., 69, 71
Jakimik, J., 187, 189, 190, 191, 192
James, W., 236, 310
Jameson, D., 74, 75, 78, 154
Janisse, M. P., 290
Jansson, G., 131
Jesteadt, W., 183
Johansson, G., 120, 125, 131, 133, 134, 157
Johnson, H., 261
Johnson, N. S., 108, 109, 110
Johnson, R. C., 291
Jones, F. N., 231
Jones, M. H., 231
Judd, D. B., 62
Juola, J. F., 101, 102
Jusczyk, R., 318

K

Kahneman, D., 87, 88, 275
Kallir, O., 127
Kanizsa, G., 90
Kaplan, I. T., 52
Kaplan, R., 304
Kaplan, S., 304
Kare, M. R., 249

Kassarjian, H. H., 299
Katcher, M. H., 210
Kaufman, L., 164, 165, 166
Kearney, G. E., 302
Kennedy, J. F., 299
Kennedy, J. M., 101, 110
Kenshalo, D. R., 201, 202, 204, 207, 212, 213,
        216, 329, 330
Kessen, W., 75, 313
Kilpatrick, F. P., 116
Kinnear, P. R., 71
Klatzky, R. L., 268
Klein, G. S., 287
Knipling, E. F., 240
Koegler, R., 321, 322, 323
Koelega, H. S., 232
Konečni, V. J., 305
Korchin, S. J., 325
Köster, E. P., 232
Kovi, P., 254
Kozlowski, L. T., 134
Kroeze, J. H. A., 250
Krowitz, A., 315
Kruger, L. M., 209, 210
Kuenstler, P., 280
Kuisma, J. E., 237
Kundel, H. L., 280
Kupchella, C., 62
Kuznicki, J. T., 257

L

LaBerge, D., 270, 271
LaFrance, M., 134
Lakowski, R., 71
Lang, G., 259
Langer, A., 315
Lansford, T., 301, 302
Lappin, J. S., 152, 153
Lawless, H. T., 256
Layton, B., 327, 328, 330
Lefton, L. A., 49, 50, 89, 287
Leibowitz, H. W., 147, 150, 151, 162
Leshowitz, B., 175, 176
Levin, H., 48, 50, 102
Levinson, E., 135
Levitt, H., 328, 329
Lewis, M., 317
Liebeskind, J. C., 215, 219, 220
Lindsay, P. H., 175
Linker, E., 253
Lippman, C. W., 32
Lipsitt, L. P., 320
Locke, J., 213

Loftus, G. R., 282, 283
Lonner, W. J., 305
Loomis, R. J., 193, 194
Loudon, D. L., 62, 93
Lovegrove, W., 323
Lovrinic, J. J., 173
Luborsky, L., 288
Luce, R. D., 183
Ludel, J., 192
Lumsdaine, A. A., 271

M

MacDonald, W. A., 169
MacDougall, R., 298
Mace, W. M., 8
Macfarlane, A., 320
Mach, E., 85
Mach, W. H., 158
Machotka, P., 304, 305
Mackay, D. G., 267, 268
Mackworth, N. H., 52, 275, 282, 283, 288
MacNichol, E. F., 72, 73
MacRae, A. W., 117
Maga, J. A., 254
Mair, A., 192
Maller, O., 320
Mandler, J. M., 108, 109, 110
Manning, S. A., 344
Marceau, M., 93
Margulies, M. K., 328, 329
Marks, L. E., 176, 212, 213
Marks, W. B., 72, 73
Martin, L., 291
Mastai, M. L. d'O., 169
Matin, L., 139
Matlin, M. W., 215, 288, 297, 298, 344, 348
Maugh, T. H., II, 239
Maxwell, J. C., 72
Mayo, C., 134
McBurney, D. H., 245, 248, 249, 253, 254, 257, 348
McClelland, James L., 87, 88
McClintock, M. K., 241
McConkie, G., 50
McConnell, J. V., 294, 295
McCutcheon, N. B., 257
McDowell, E. D., 51
McFarland, R. A., 326, 327
McGinnies, E., 290, 291, 294
McGurk, H., 317
McKenzie, B. E., 315, 317
McNeil, E. B., 294, 295
Mednick, S. A., 139

Mehl, L., 330, 343
Melhuish, E., 318
Meltzer, P., 261
Meltzoff, A. N., 319
Melzack, R., 203, 204, 217, 218, 219, 220, 221
Meyer, J. S., 324
Miller, J. D., 193, 194
Mills, M., 318
Miranda, S. B., 314
Mladejovsky, M. G., 28
Moncrieff, R. W., 236
Moore, B. C. J., 175, 176, 183, 184, 187, 192, 195, 196
Moore, M. E., 253
Moore, M. K., 319
Moore, M. W., 210
Morandi, A. J., 282
Moray, N., 266, 267
Moreland, J. D., 78, 79
Moses, Grandma, 127
Moskat, L. J., 253, 254
Moskowitz, H. R., 139, 238, 239, 258, 260
Mozell, M. M., 231, 232, 233
Murphy, G., 296, 299
Murray, H. A., 297

N

Naus, M. J., 103, 104
Neisser, U., 269, 270, 274, 275, 278, 279, 324
Newman, C. V., 117
Newman, E. B., 181
Newton, I., 62, 72
Nielsen, D. W., 179, 183, 184
Nixon, R., 299
Nodine, C. F., 280
Nordmark, J. O., 184, 186
Norgren, R., 252
Norman, D. A., 175, 271, 273, 274

O

O'Connell, D. N., 122
Odom, R. D., 324
Ogden, W. C., 271
O'Leary, A., 120
Olson, P. L., 327

P

Paap, K. R., 271
Paden, L. Y., 320
Palmer, S. E., 107, 108
Pantle, A., 135

Parkes, A. S., 240
Pastalan, L. A., 327
Patterson, R. D., 187
Paul, L. A., 215, 219
Pearson, J., 192
Penfield, W., 203, 204, 205
Petersen, M. R., 330
Pettigrew, T. F., 297
Pfaffmann, C., 249, 252
Phillips, S., 193
Piaget, J., 157, 315
Pick, A. D., 330
Pick, H. L., 330
Pickett, J. M., 190
Pirenne, M. H., 120, 121, 127
Plomp, R., 186
Podolsky, S., 326, 327
Pola, J., 139
Pollack, I., 190
Porac, C., 85, 163
Posner, M. I., 104, 105
Postman, L., 290, 294
Poulton, E. C., 42, 62, 211
Prak, N. L., 112, 304
Preble, L. D., 152, 153
Purcell, M., 253

R

Rabbitt, P., 279, 280
Ramsay, D., 315
Rasmussen, T., 203, 204, 205
Ratliff, F., 85
Rayner, K., 50, 275, 276, 282
Rechtschaffen, A., 139
Reese, H. W., 319
Regan, D., 137, 138
Remez, R. E., 188
Restle, F., 165, 166
Richards, W., 116, 118, 124, 135, 136
Rierdan, J., 298, 299
Riggs, L. A., 17, 22, 37, 38, 39, 40, 41, 45, 46, 48
Riley, B., 80
Risset, J. C., 186, 192
Ritter, M., 124
Robbins, M. C., 305, 306
Robinson, J. O., 158
Rock, I., 100, 101, 151, 156, 164, 165, 166
Rock, J., 241
Rockwell, T., 50, 51
Roederer, J. G., 192
Rogers, C. H., 210
Rogers, C. M., 111

Ronch, J., 131
Rose, S. A., 319
Rosenbloom, S., 317
Rosenstock, E. H., 344
Rosinski, R. R., 330
Ross, B. M., 237
Ross, G. M., 164
Ross, H. E., 164
Ross, J., 123, 296
Rubin, E., 96, 97
Rushton, W. A., 70, 72
Russell, M. J., 237, 320

S

Safire, W., 189
Salapatek, P., 310, 311, 330
Samuels, S. J., 270, 271
Santos, J., 295, 296
Saunders, F. A., 210, 211
Scadden, L., 210, 211
Schaie, K. W., 327, 330
Schapiro, F., 102
Scharf, B., 182, 193
Schick, A. M. L., 48
Schiffman, S. S., 228, 247, 248
Schindler, R. M., 277
Schmidt, F., 135
Schneider, R. A., 225, 241
Schneider, W., 280
Schultz, D. W., 275
Scott, B., 191
Segall, M., 111
Sekuler, R., 131, 132, 135, 138, 141
Self, P. A., 320
Seurat, G., 66
Shaffer, L. H., 270
Sharma, S., 139
Shepard, R. N., 110
Shepard, R. P., 210
Shick, T. R., 254
Shiffrin, R. M., 8, 280
Shiina, K., 151
Shillman, R. J., 103, 104
Shlaer, S., 39
Siegelaub, A. B., 215
Simonson, D. C., 212
Singer, J. E., 194
Siqueland, E. R., 318
Sivak, M., 327
Sivian, L. S., 174
Skinner, E. F., 256
Smallman, R. L., 249
Smith, A. J., 324

Smith, M. D., 323
Snider, T. Q. 137, 138
Solley, C. M., 295, 296, 299
Solomon, R. L., 291
Spelke, H. W., 269, 270
Squire, R., 268
Standing, L., 110
Stang, D. J., 288, 297, 298
Stark, L., 48
Steck, L., 304, 305
Steinberg, R., 259
Steiner, J. E., 320
Sternbach, R. A., 215
Stevens, J. C., 201, 212, 213, 255
Stevens, K. N., 190, 191
Stevens, S. S., 181, 182, 348, 349
Stevenson, M. B., 138
Stolwijk, J. A. J., 216
Strauss, M. S., 310, 311, 317
Stravinsky, I. F., 187
Stromeyer, C. F., 77
Sumner, D., 236
Svejda, M., 315
Swearingen, J. E., 137, 138
Swets, J. A., 11, 336

T

Takagi, S. F., 230
Tartter, V. C., 318
Taus, R. H., 212, 213
Taweel, S. S., 324
Taylor, W., 192
Teghtsoonian, M., 151, 233, 234
Teghtsoonian, R., 233, 234
Thomas, E. L., 280
Thompson, R., 305, 306
Thurlow, W. R., 181, 184, 185
Tietz, J. D., 140
Tiffin, J., 135
Todd, H., 138
Tong, L., 324
Treisman, A. M., 267, 268, 272
Triandis, H. C., 305
Tronick, E., 324
Tursky, B., 215

V

Van der Wel, H., 258
Van Dyke, D., 32
Van Heyningen, R., 31
Vaughan, D., 30, 31, 32, 124
Vellutino, F. R., 323

Verillo, R. T., 207, 209, 214, 216, 217
Vernon, M. D., 321, 323
Vierling, J. S., 241
Vigorito, J., 318
Vogel, J. M., 151
Volkman, J., 181
Volkmann, F. C., 48
von Frey, M., 203
von Hofsten, C., 131
Vurpillot, E., 325

W

Walk, R. D., 314, 315, 317, 330
Wall, P. D., 203, 204, 217, 218, 221
Wallach, H., 120, 122
Walsh, J. W. T., 16
Wapner, S., 298, 299
Ward, L. M., 85, 163
Warren, R. M., 190
Warren, R. P., 190
Wasserman, G. S., 62, 66, 72, 74, 79
Weber, E., 345, 348, 349
Weiffenbach, J. M., 320
Weinstein, S., 205, 206, 207
Weinstock, C. S., 328
Weintraub, D. J., 324
Weisenberg, M., 215, 217
Weiskopf, S., 75, 313
Weisstein, M., 183
Welton, K. E., Jr., 104, 105
Wendt, J. S., 304
Wenger, M. A., 231
Werner, H., 86, 87
Werner, J. S., 75, 312
Wertheimer, M., 6, 91, 317
Westheimer, G., 41, 42
Wever, E. G., 178, 179, 181
Wheatstone, C., 123
Whinham, E. A., 117
Whitbourne, S. K., 328
White, B. W., 210, 211
White, C. W., 78
White, S. D., 174
Wiesel, T. N., 27, 28, 29, 30
Wilkening, H. E., 297
Wilson, M. E., 219, 220
Wispé, L. G., 293, 294
Wittrock, M. C., 271
Wolf, E., 326, 327
Wolfert, P., 245
Wood, G., 93, 95, 284
Wood, P. B., 212
Woodrow, K. M., 215

Wooten, B. R., 75, 312
Wright, W. D., 64, 66
Wyszecki, G., 62

Y

Yang, J. C., 219
Yarbus, A. L., 284
Yonas, A., 102

Yost, W. A., 179, 183, 184
Young, T., 72

Z

Zajonc, R. B., 293, 300
Zakia, R., 93, 98, 138
Zwislocki, J. J., 187

SUBJECT INDEX*

A

Accommodation, 54–58, 115–116, 125, 127, 151, 311–312
Achromatic (vision), 44
Activation, 266
Active touch, 204, 209–211
Acuity, 23, 36–43
  development of, 310–311, 327
  factors influencing, 39–42
  touch discrimination, 203, 206–207
  types of, 36–39
Acupuncture, 217, 218–220
Adaptation
  auditory, 193
  dark adaptation, 43–46
  light adaptation, 43, 45–46
  pain, 216
  smell, 234–236
  taste, 255–256
  temperature, 213–214, 216
  touch, 207–208
Additive mixtures, 64–67
Adjustment, method of, 334, 336, 344–345
Adulthood, 325–330
Advertising, 93, 238, 289
Aesthetics, 300–306
Affective tests (taste), 260
Aftereffects, 77, 141
Age, 308–331
Albedo, 154–155
Alcohol, effects of, 51
Alkaline taste, 248
Allport-Vernon scale of values, 294
Amacrine cells, 20, 21
Ambiguity, 189–191

Ambiguous figure-ground relationships, 97–98, 296
Ambiguous figures, 295–297
Ambiguous sentences, 268
Amblyopia, 31, 124
Amblyoscope, 124
Amplitude
  hearing, 175–176, 181–183
  vision, 15, 62–63
Anaglyph, 123–124
Analgesia, 220
Analgesic (pain control), 218
Analysis-by-synthesis, 191
Anomalous trichromat, 70
Anvil, 177
Apparent-distance theory, 164–165
Apparent movement, 138–141
  autokinesis, 139
  induced movement, 140
  movement aftereffects, 140
  movement in pictures, 138
  stroboscopic movement, 140
Architecture, 166, 304
Area illusions, 164–166
Areas, 17, 18, and 19, 28–29
Arousal, 181, 182
Art, 93, 115, 127, 138, 169
Articulation, 187–188
Ascending method of limits, 334
Ascending trials, 334
Aspirin, 195, 218
Astigmatism, 58
Atmospheric perspective, 117–118, 127
Attention, 264–285
  development of, 313–314, 324–325
  divided attention, 268–270

* Note: This index includes all boldfaced terms.

Attention (cont'd.)
  esthetics and, 300–306
  reading and, 270–271
  search, 274–281
  selective attention, 266–271
  theories of, 271
  viewing pictures, 281–284
Attenuation model, 272
Audiometry, 195–196
Audition, 172–197
Auditory adaptation, 193
Auditory cortex, 179–180
Auditory fatigue, 193
Auditory nerve, 177, 179–180, 196
Auditory stimulus, 173–176
Auditory system, 176–179
  inner ear, 177
  middle ear, 177
  outer ear, 176–177
Autokinesis, 139–140
Automatic (activity), 270, 280

B

Backward masking, 86–89
Ballistic movements, 48
Basilar membrane, 177–178
Beats (music), 186
Behaviorism, 8
Behavior therapy, 220–221
Bending and constancy, 157
Benham's top, 78–79
Beta (β), 10, 218, 219–220, 291, 293, 329–330,
  336–343
Bifocals, 327
Binaural (cues), 184
Binocular parallax, 123–125, 126
Binocular rivalry, 296–297
Binocular vision, 26, 27, 47, 52–53, 122–125,
  138, 149, 296–297, 312
Biological motion, 133–134
Bipolar cells, 20, 21
Blend, 239
Blindness, 31–32, 37–38, 210–211
  See also Color deficiencies
Blind spot
  retina, 20, 40
  tongue, 250
Blowfly, 248
Body odor, discrimination of, 237
Body temperature, 211
Border contrast, 85–86
Bottleneck theories, 271–273

Bottom-up processing, 105–108, 188–191
Boundaries of words, 189–191
Boundary errors, 189
Braille, 210
Brightness, 15–16, 62–63, 75, 96–97, 154–156
Brightness constancy, 154–156

C

Caffeine, 255
Candelas per meter square, 16
Case of the missing fundamental, 181
Cataracts, 31–32, 326
Catch trials, 338
Catfish, 249
Cerebral cortex, 27–29, 32, 74, 123, 135, 179,
  203, 206–207, 230, 252
Chemical senses, 224–263
  smell, 224–241
  taste, 245–263
Chickens, 249
Childhood, 321–325
  attention, 324–325
  constancy, 324–325
  illusions, 324
  shape perception, 321–323
Choroid, 19, 20
Chromatographs, 233
Cilia, 230
Ciliary muscles, 18, 54
Cinerama, 138
Classical psychophysical methods, 10, 11,
  334–336, 344–345
Closure, law of, 91–92
Cochlea, 177–178, 180, 196
Cochlear nucleus, 179–180
Coding
  color, 72–76
  odors, 226–228
  skin senses, 202–203
  sound, 177–179
  taste, 250–252
Codeine, 218
Cognition
  noise pollution and, 194
  See also Attention, Reading
Cold, perception of, 211–213
Cold spots, 211–212
Color, 20, 22, 60–81, 297, 301–302
  attention and, 275–276
  development of color vision, 312–313, 326
  factors affecting, 78–79
  importance of, 61–62
  mixing, 64–68

names, 75
nature of, 62–69
phenomena, 76–81
taste and, 254
vision deficiencies, 69–71
vision theory, 72–76
Color blindness, 69–71, 75–76
Color constancy, 156
Color contrast, 76–77
Color deficiencies, 69–71, 75–76
Color mixing, 64–67
   additive mixtures, 64–67
   subtractive mixtures, 64, 67
Color solid, 62–64
Color wheel, 62–63
Color vision deficiencies, 69–71, 75–76
Combined tones, 186–187
Communication
   smell, 240–241
   speech, 187–191
Comparison stimulus, 344
Complementary hues, 64, 75, 77–78
Complex cell, 29, 135
Complexity
   auditory, 183
   visual, 303–306
Complex tones, 174, 181, 183
Concentration, 266
Conceptually driven processing, 105–110,
   188–191
Conditioning method, 316–317
Conduction deafness, 195
Cones, 20–23, 44, 72–74
Confounding variables, 325–326, 328
Conjunctiva, 18, 30–31
Conjunctivitis, 30–31
Consonance, 186–187
Consonants, 188
Constancy, 7, 145–157
   under bending, 157
   brightness, 154–157
   color, 156
   development of, 315–317, 323–324
   existence, 157
   explanations for, 150–151, 153–155
   illusions and, 155–156, 161–163
   misapplied, 161–163, 166–167
   motion, 156–157
   odor, 233–234
   position, 157
   shape, 151–154
   size, 7, 147–151, 165
Constant stimuli, method of, 334, 336, 345
Constriction, 17, 40–41, 288

Consumer psychology, 62, 93, 238, 289
Context
   speech perception and, 189
   visual pattern recognition and, 105–110
Continuation, law of, 91–93, 304
Contour, 84–91
   subjective, 89–90
Contrast, 85–86
Contrast theory, 155–156
Control processes, 292–293
Convergence, 52–53, 122–123, 125, 127, 151
Cornea, 17–18, 30, 58
Corneal abrasion, 30
Corollary discharge theory, 135–136
Corrective lenses, 57–58
Correct rejection, 338–343
Cortex, 27–29, 32, 74, 135, 179, 203, 206–207,
   230, 252
Cortical maps, 28, 179, 203–205, 206–207
Counterirritants, 218
Criterion (β), 10, 87–88, 218, 219–220, 288,
   291, 293, 329–330, 336–343
Cross-adaptation, 235–236, 256–257
Cross-cultural studies, 97, 111, 162, 215, 221,
   259–260, 305–306
Cross-enhancement, 256–257
Crossovers in visual system, 24–26
Cue (distance), 115–118
Cutaneous perception, 200–222

D

d', 10, 218, 219–220, 291, 329–330, 336–343
Dark adaptation, 43–46
Dark adaptation curve, 43–44
Data-driven processing, 105–108, 188–191
Data-limited task, 273
Deafness, 177, 193, 194–196
Decibels (dB), 175–176
Deficiencies in color vision, 69–71, 75–76
Dependent variable, 88, 300–301, 303–304
Depth cues, 100–101
Depth perception, 6–7, 90, 114–130, 314–315
   See also Distance perception
Dermis, 201
Descending trials, 334
Descriptive tests (taste), 260
Detached retina, 31
Detection (threshold), 9–10, 38, 174, 182, 193,
   205, 207–208, 212–213, 215, 231–233,
   251–255, 334–336
   See also Threshold
Deuteranope, 70
Development of perception, 308–331

Development of perception (cont'd.)
  in childhood, 321–325
  in infancy, 310–320
  in old age, 325–330
Diabetes, 31, 71
Dichotic listening, 266–268
Dichromat, 70
Difference threshold, 231–234, 253, 344–345
Dilation, 17, 40–41, 44, 288
Direction (sound), 184–185
Direction illusions, 166–169
Discrimination, 11, 174, 205–207, 344–345
Discrimination tests (taste), 260
Dishabituation, 313
Disocclusion, 136
Disorders
  auditory, 194–196
  visual, 30–32
Disparlure, 240
Dissonance, 186–187
Distal stimulus, 145–146
Distance cues, 115–125, 147–150
Distance perception, 6–7, 114–130
  auditory, 184–185
  factors affecting, 115–125
  infancy, 314–315
  movies and, 127–130
  painting and, 127–130
  theories of, 125–127
Distinctive features (hearing), 188
Distinctive features theory, 102–103
Divergence, 52–53
Doctrine of specific nerve energies, 203
Double-blind study, 219
Double pain, 217
Down's Syndrome, 314
Driving, 46, 50–51, 135
Dynamics, 182–183
Dynamic visual acuity, 51
Dyslexia, 323

E

Ear
  inner, 177
  middle, 177
  outer, 176–177
Eardrum, 173, 177
Ear infection, 195–196
Echoes, 184
Ecological validity, 152
Education, 49–50, 89, 102, 270–271, 304, 323
Egocentric distance, 115
Elderly people, 325–330

Electrodes, 28–29
Elevation cues, 118, 126
Emotion
  depth and, 315
  music and, 305
  perception of, 134
Empiricism, 6–7, 125–126, 305–306
Encapsulated endings, 202
End note (perfume), 238
Environmental psychology, 193–194, 304
Epidermis, 201
Epithelium, olfactory, 229–230, 231
Esthetics, 300–306
Ethnic differences, 215, 221
Eustachian tubes, 177
Evolution, 131
Existence constancy, 157, 315
Expectancy and perception, 126
External auditory canal, 176–177
Eye chart, 37–38
Eye-elevation hypothesis, 165
Eye Movement Monitor, 50
Eye movements, 47–53
  convergence, 52–53
  divergence, 52–53
  miniature eye movements, 52
  motion perception, 135–136, 139, 141
  picture viewing, 281–284, 325
  pursuit movements, 51
  saccadic movement, 48–51
  vergence movement, 47, 52–53
  version movement, 47–52
Eye-movement theory, 163

F

Face, perception of, 313, 323
Facial emotion, 134
False alarm, 338–343
Familiarity and picture viewing, 284–285
Familiar size, 116
Farsightedness, 58
Fate, law of, 91–92
Fatigue, auditory, 193
Fatty taste, 242
Feature detectors, 29, 102–103, 188
Features, distinctive, 102–103, 188
Fechner's Law, 348–349
Feedback, 135–136
Figural goodness, 98–100
Figure, 93–98
Figure-ground relationship, 93–98, 275
Film, 127–130, 138, 304
Film reading, 280

Fixation, 48–51, 281–284
Fixation pause, 48, 51, 89
Flavor, 245–247, 259–263
Flow, retinal, 131
Focusing, 39, 52–58
Focusing problems, 57–58
Forced-choice method, 110, 334
Foreign body, 30
Formants, 188
Form perception, 84–111
    See also Shape perception
Forward masking, 86–87
Fourier analysis, 183
Fovea, 19, 22, 23, 39–41, 50–51, 78–79, 89,
    132–133, 275–276, 282, 310–311
Fragrance library, 238
Free nerve endings, 202
Frequency (sound), 174–175, 177–179, 181
Frequency
    fundamental, 174, 181
    word, 291
Frequency theory, 178–179

G

Galvanic skin response, 288
Ganglion cells, 20–24, 74
Ganzfeld, 85
Gate-control theory, 217–218, 220
Gateway Arch (illusion), 160–161
Gender differences, 232, 241, 301
Generalization, 316–317
Gestalt, 7
Gestalt approach, 7, 304
    problems with, 100–101
    shape perception and, 91–101
Gibsonian approach, 7–8, 126, 136–137, 209–
    210, 245–246
Glabrous skin, 201
Glare, 327
Glaucoma, 32, 326
Good continuation, law of, 91–93, 304
Goodness, figural, 98–100
Ground, 94–98, 275
Ground theory, 126
Grouping, laws of, 91–93
Gustatory sense, 245–263
    See also Taste
Gymnema sylvestre, 258
Gypsy moth, 240

H

Habituation method, 313
Hair cells (ear), 177–178, 196

Hairy skin, 201–202
Hammer, 177
Handwriting, perception of, 105
Haptic perception, 210, 319
Harmonics, 174–175
Hearing, 172–197, 209
    applications of, 192–196
    auditory system, 176–179
    development of, 317–318, 328–329
    impairments of, 194–196
    localization, 184–185
    loudness, 182–183
    pitch, 181–182
    sensory aspects, 173–179
    sound, nature of, 173–176
    speech, 187–191
    theories of, 177–179
    timbre, 183–184
Hearing aid, 195–196
Heart rate, 315
Heat, perception of, 211–213
Height cues, 118, 127
Hertz (Hz), 174
History of perception, 6–9
Hit, 338–343
Horizontal cells, 20, 21
Horizontal-vertical illusion, 159–160
Hormones, 240–241
Hue, 15, 62–63, 75, 82
Hypercomplex cell, 29
Hypermetropic (hypermetropia), 58
Hypnosis, 220

I

Illusions, 76–81, 138–141, 145–146, 158–167
    area, 164–166
    auditory, 190
    classification of, 158–159
    color, 76–81
    development of, 324, 327
    direction, 166–169
    explanations for, 162–166
    horizontal-vertical, 159–160
    line-length, 159–164
    moon, 164–166
    motion, 135, 138–141
    Müller-Lyer, 145, 159, 163, 190
    Poggendorf, 166–167
    Ponzo, 161–162, 167
    Sander parallelogram, 159
    shape, 166–169
    size, 159–166
    twisted cord, 167–168

Illusory movement, 138–141
Imitation, 221, 319
Impairments
    auditory, 194–196
    visual, 30–32
Incorrect comparison theory, 163
Incus, 177
Independent variable, 88, 300
Individual differences
    in color vision, 69–71
    in esthetics, 300–306
    in perceptual defense and vigilance, 290–291
    in pupil dilation, 288–289
    in smell, 232
    in taste, 255
Induced movement, 140
Infancy, 310–320
    hearing in, 317–318
    smell in, 320
    taste in, 320
    touch in, 318–319
    vision in, 311–317
Inferior colliculus, 179–180
Information-processing approach, 8, 292–293
    See also Attention
Informativeness, 282–283
Inhibition, lateral, 86, 89, 167
Instructions
    illusions, 323–324
    picture viewing, 284
Instruments, musical, 183–184
Intensity judgment, 256
Interposition, 118, 127
Invariant features, 191
Iris, 17, 30
Iritis, 30
Irrelevant stimuli, 327–328
Ishihara Test, 71

J

Just noticeable difference (jnd), 344

K

Kinesthesis, 201
Kinesthetic information, 125–126
Kinetic depth effect, 121–122, 127, 129

L

Lamaze method, 220
Language, 187–191

Large fibers (pain), 203, 217–218
Latency, 102
Lateral geniculate nucleus, 26–27
Lateral inhibition, 86, 89, 167
Law of closure, 91–93
Law of common fate, 91–93
Law of good continuation, 91–93, 304
Law of Prägnanz, 98–100
Law of similarity, 91–93, 304
Laws of grouping, 91–93, 304
Laws of nearness, 91–93, 304
Left visual field, 25
Lemniscal system, 203, 217–218
Lens, 18, 31, 57–58, 115, 311, 326, 327
Light, 15, 62–64
Light adaptation, 43, 45–46
Limits, method of, 334–336, 344
Linear perspective, 116–118, 127, 162
Line-length illusions, 159–164
Localization
    acuity task, 39
    auditory, 179, 184–185
    temperature, 212–213
    touch, 212–213
Logarithm, 348
Logarithmic scale, 175
Long-term memory, 8, 237–238, 292–293
Loudness, 182–183, 195–196
Luminance, 41, 132

M

Mach bands, 85–86
Magnitude estimation technique, 181, 233–234, 349
Malleus, 177
Marihuana, 139
Masking
    auditory, 187
    odors, 238
    visual, 86–89, 193
Medial geniculate nucleus, 179–180
Medication, 218
Medicine, 218–220
Mel scale, 181–182
Memory, 8, 101–111, 236–237
Menstruation, 241
Mental concentration, 266
Mental illness and noise pollution, 193
Metacontrast, 89
Method of adjustment, 334, 336
    for measuring discrimination, 344–345
Method of constant stimuli, 334, 336
    for measuring discrimination, 345

Method of limits, 334–336
  for measuring discrimination, 344
Mice, 240
Microvilli, 249
Middle note (perfume), 238
Migraine headaches, 32, 220
Millimicron, 15
Miniature eye movements, 52, 139
Miracle fruit, 258
Mirages, 158
Misapplied constancy theory, 161–163, 166–
  167
Miss, 338–343
Missing fundamental, 181
Mnemonic devices, 6
Modeling theory, 221
Molecular structure, 228
Molecular weight, 226–227
Monochromat, 70
Monochromatic (colors), 63, 82
Monocular perception, 115–122, 125, 136–138
Monosodium glutamate (MSG), 257–258
Mood and noise pollution, 194
Moon illusion, 164–166
Morphine, 218, 220
Moth, gypsy, 240
Motion constancy, 156–157
Motion-detecting neurons, 135
Motion parallax, 120–121, 127, 129, 137
Motion perception, 131–141
  apparent movement, 138–141
  explanations for, 135–138
  observer motion, 134–135
  real movement, 131–138
Motion perspective, 121, 126, 137–138
Motivation, 286–307
  ambiguous stimuli and, 295–297
  color and, 301–302
  complexity and, 303–306
  effect on perception of, 287–300
  esthetics, 300–306
  needs and, 293–295
  perception's effect on, 287, 300–307
  perceptual defense and vigilance, 290–293
  shape, 302–303
  signal detection theory and, 288
  subliminal perception, 294–295
Movement aftereffects, 141
Movement cues (depth perception), 118–122
Movement perception, 131–141
  See also Motion perception
Movies, 127–130, 138, 304
MSG, 257–258
Mucus, 230

Müller-Lyer illusion, 145, 159, 163, 190, 324
Multidimensional scaling, 247–248
Multiple sclerosis, 32
Music, 183–184, 186–187, 192, 304–305
Musical instruments, 183–184
Myopic (myopia), 57–58

N

Nanometer, 15
Nasal area, 229–230
Nasal cavity, 229
Nativist position, 305–306
Nearness, law of, 91–92, 304
Nearsightedness, 57–58
Needs and perception, 293–294
Negative afterimage, 77
Nerve deafness, 196
Neurons, 19, 135
New Look psychology, 290–291
Nighttime vision, 23
Noise (auditory), 192–194
Noise (in TSD), 340–343
Noise pollution, 192–194
Nonnutritive sucking technique, 318
Nontasters, 255
Nonverbal communication, 134
Normal trichromat, 69–70
Note (perfume), 238

O

Object permanence, 157, 315
Occlusion, 136
Octave, 181, 186
Odor, 224–242
  See also Smell
Odor constancy, 233–234
Odor mixture, 239
Odor pollution, 238–240
Old age, 325–330
Olfaction, 224–241
Olfactometer, 231
Olfactory bulb, 229–230
Olfactory epithelium, 229–230, 231
Op Art, 78, 80
Ophthalmologists, 17
Ophthalmology, 30–32
Ophthalmoscope, 17
Opponent-process theory, 72–76
Optacon, 210
Optic chiasm, 24
Optic nerve, 24, 32
Optic tract, 26

Organization, Gestalt laws of, 91–101
Organ of Corti, 177–178, 196
Orientation, 323
Orientation detectors, 29, 102–103, 188
Overconstancy, 149
Overtones, 175, 184

P

Pain, 214–221
　adaptation to, 216
　control of, 218–221
　elderly people and, 330
　theories of, 216–218
Pain threshold, 215–216, 343
Painting, 93, 115, 127, 138, 169
Pain tolerance, 215
Palate, 250
Papillae, 248–250, 251
Paradoxical cold, 212
Parallax, 120
Parallel process, 279
Parsing paradox, 107
Passive touch, 204–209
Pattern recognition, 101–111
　attention and, 270–271
　context and, 105–110
　picture recognition, 110–111
　theories of, 102–105
Pattern theory, 203
　of pain perception, 216–217
Payoff, 10, 338
Perception
　definition of, 2
　history of, 6–9
　measurement of, 9–11, 332–350
Perceptual defense, 290–293
Perceptual regression hypothesis, 327
Perceptual span, 50
Perceptual vigilance, 290–293
Perfumes, 235, 238
Peripheral vision, 39–40, 50–51, 78–79, 130–
　133, 277
Permanent threshold shift, 193
Personality and autokinesis, 139–140
Phantom limb pain, 216
Phenylthiocarbamide (PTC), 255
Pheromones, 240–241
Phoneme, 187, 189
Phonemic restoration effect, 190
Photograph recognition, 111
Photographs, 93, 111, 138, 149–150
Physiological zero, 213

Pictorial cues, 115–118, 127
Picture recognition, 110–111
Pictures
　movement in, 138
　recognition of, 110–111, 324
　viewing of, 281–284
　See also Art, Photographs
Pigments, 17
Pinkeye, 30–31
Pinna, 176–177
Pitch, 181–182, 195–196
Placebo, 218, 219–220
Place theory, 178–179
Poggendorf illusion, 166–167, 324
Pointillism, 66
Pollution
　noise, 192–194
　odor, 238–240
Pollyanna Principle, 288–299
Ponzo illusion, 161–162, 167–168
Position constancy, 157
Positive-negative space, 93–98
Power Law, 348–349
Practice
　attention and, 269–270
　recognizing smells and, 236
　search and, 278–280
Prägnanz, law of, 98–100
Preference method, 311, 317–318
Prequestions, 271
Presbycusis, 328–329
Presbyopia, 326–327
Prism, 62
　smell, 227–228
Probability distribution, 342–343
Projective test, 297
Proprioception, 201
Protanope, 70
Prototype, 103–105
Prototype-matching theory, 103–105
Proximal stimulus, 145–146
Psychophysics, 9–11, 332–350
　classical measurement of detection in, 334–
　336
　classical measurement of discrimination in,
　344–347
　relationship between stimuli and responses
　in, 348–349
　theory of signal detection, 336–343
PTC, 255
Pupil, 17, 40–41, 44, 288–289
Pupillometrics, 289
Pure tone, 174, 181–182

Purity, 15, 62–63, 82
Pursuit movements, 51–52

Q

Quantitative judgments, 297–298

R

Race differences, 215, 221
Radiologists, 280
Ranking, 301
Rating, 301
Reading, 49–50, 89, 102, 270–271, 282, 323, 327
Reading disabilities, 49–50, 323
Real movement, 131–138
Receiver operating characteristic (ROC) curve, 339–341
Receptive field, 29
Receptor cells
    hearing, 177–179
    skin senses, 201–203, 216–218
    smell, 230
    taste, 248–250
    vision, 20–23, 44, 72–74
Recognition
    acuity measure, 37
    patterns and, 101–111
    pictures and, 110–111, 324
    smells and, 236–238
Recognition threshold, 253, 290–291
Recruitment, 196
Reflexes, 319
Relative distance, 115
Regression movements, 49–50
Relative size, 116
Relative-size explanation, 151, 165–166
Resolution, 39–40
Resolve (acuity), 39–40
Resource-limited task, 273
Resources, 273
Response suppression, 291
Retina, 19–23, 31
Retinal disparity, 123–124
Retinal flow, 131
Retinal size, 147
Retinotopic arrangement, 28
Reverberations, 185
Rhodopsin, 44–45
Right visual field, 25
ROC curve, 339–341

Rods, 20–23, 44
Rorschach inkblot test, 297

S

Saccade, 48–51, 89, 281–284
Saccadic movement, 48–51, 89, 281–284
Saccharin, 248, 258
Saliva, 247, 256
Sander parallelogram, 159
Saturation, 15, 62–63, 75
Scaling, 301, 345, 348–349
Scanning, 281–284, 312–313, 324–325
Scientific esthetics, 301
Sclera, 16
Scotoma (scotomata), 32
Search, 265, 274–281
Selective attention, 265–271
Self-motion illusion, 134–135
Semantic (information), 267
Sensation, definition of, 8
Sensitivity measure (psychophysics), 10, 218, 219–220, 291, 329–330, 336–343
Sensory memory, 8, 292–293
Sensory storage, 8, 292–293
Serial process, 279
Sex differences, 232, 241, 301
Sexuality, 225–226, 240–241
Shading, 118, 127
Shadowing technique, 266–268
Shape constancy, 151–154, 317
Shape illusions, 166–169
Shape perception, 84–111
    attention and, 275–276
    contour, 84–91
    esthetic judgments and, 302–303
    in infancy, 313–314
    organization, 91–101
    pattern recognition, 101–111
Shape-slant invariance hypothesis, 153
Short-term memory, 8, 237–238, 293
Signal, 338–343
Signal detection theory, 10–11, 218, 219–220, 253, 288, 291, 329–330, 336–343
Signal + noise, 342–343
Similarity, law of, 91–93, 304
Simple cell, 29
Simultaneous color contrast, 76–77
Sine-wave motion, 173, 183
Size and pleasantness, 298–299
Size constancy, 7, 147–151, 315–317, 323–324
Size cue, 116–118, 127, 137

Size-distance invariance hypothesis, 150–151, 164–165
Size illusions, 159–166
Skin senses, 200–222
  background on, 201–204
  development of, 318–319, 329–330
  food and, 245–246
  pain, 214–221
  skin structure and, 201–204
  temperature, 211–213
  theories about, 202–203
  touch, 204–211, 213
  vibration, 208
Small fibers (pain), 203, 217–218
Smell, 224–242
  adaptation, 235–236
  applications, 238–242
  classification, 227–228, 235–236
  development of, 320, 330
  olfactory processes, 231–237
  olfactory system, 229–230
  recognizing, 236–237
  sensory aspects of, 226–230
  stimulus for, 226–228
  thresholds, 231–234
Smell prism, 227–228
Smoking and taste, 253–254
Snellen eye chart, 37–38
Soft palate, 250
Somatosensory cortex, 203, 206–207
Sone scale, 182–183
Sounds, 173–176
  See also Hearing
Sound shadow, 185
Sound spectrogram, 188
Sound waves, 195–196
Specificity theory, 203
  of pain perception, 216–217
Spectral sensitivity, 73
Spectrum, 62–63, 312–313
Speculative esthetics, 301
Speech perception, 187–191
  development of, 318, 329
  speech stimulus, 187–188
  theories of, 190–191
Speech spectrogram, 188
Speed-accuracy trade-off, 279–280
Speed-reading, 50
Spinothalamic system, 203, 217–218
Stabilized retinal image techniques, 52
Standard stimulus, 344
Stapes, 177
Static visual acuity, 51
Stereochemical theory, 228

Stereoscope, 123
Stereoscopic picture, 123–124, 296–297
Stevens' Power Law, 348–349
Stimulation-produced analgesia, 220
Stirrup, 177
Strabismus, 31
Stroboscopic movement, 140–141
Stroop Color-Word Test, 327–328
Subception, 290, 294–295
Subcutaneous tissue, 201
Subjective colors, 77–78
Subjective contour figures, 89–90
Subliminal perception, 290, 294–295
Subtractive mixtures, 64, 67
Successive color contrast, 77–78
Sulfurous taste, 248
Superior colliculus, 26
Superior olive, 179–180, 185
Suppression of vision, 48
Surface characteristics and touch, 210
Surrealism, 127
Sweet preferences, 320

T

Taboo words, 291
Tachistoscope, 291–294
Taste, 245–263
  adaptation, 255–256
  coding, 250–252
  cross-adaptation, 256–257
  cross-enhancement, 256–257
  development of, 320, 330
  food tasting, 259–260
  modifiers, 257–258
  receptors, 248–249
  stimulus, 247–248
  tea tasting, 261–263
  thresholds, 252–255
  tongue regions, 249–251
  wine tasting, 261
Taste blindness, 255
Taste bud, 248–250
Taste modifiers, 257–258
Taste pore, 249
Taste-test laboratories, 260
Taste tetrahedron, 247–248
Tea tasting, 261–263
Tectorial membrane, 177–178
Television, 283–284
Temperature, 211–213
  adaptation, 213–214, 216
  body temperature, 211
  influence on color preference of, 302

influence on taste of, 254
thresholds, 212–213
warm and cold spots, 211–212
Template-matching theory, 104
Temporal lobe, 230
Temporary threshold shift, 193
Texture explanation, 151, 153–154
Texture gradient, 116–118, 126, 127
Texture of food, 246
Thematic Apperception Test (TAT), 297
Theory of misapplied constancy, 161–163
Theory of Signal Detection (TSD), 10–11, 218, 219–220, 253, 288, 291, 329–330, 336–343
Therapy for pain, 220–222
Thermal adaptation, 213–214, 216
Three-dimensional perception, 98–100
Threshold, 9–11, 334–336
    audition, 174, 182, 193
    light detection, 43–44
    motion perception, 132–133
    pain, 215–216
    smell, 231–234
    taste, 251–255
    temperature, 212–213
    touch, 205–209
Threshold shifts, 193
Timbre, 183–184
Tinnitus, 194–196
Tolerance of pain, 215
Tone combinations, 186–187
Tongue movement, 256
Tongue regions and taste, 249–251
Top-down processing, 105–110, 188–191
Top note (perfume), 238
Touch, 200–211, 213
    active, 204, 209–211
    adaptation, 207–208
    development of, 318–319, 329–330
    passive, 204–209
    thresholds, 206–208
    vibration, 208–209, 330
Tracking shot, 129–130
Trichromat
    anomalous, 70
    normal, 69–70
Trichromatic theory, 72–73
Tritanope, 70
Tumors in visual system, 32
Tuning fork, 173
Turbinate bones, 229

Two-point discrimination threshold, 205–207
Tympanic membrane, 173, 177

U
Underconstancy, 149
Urea, 257
Useful field of view, 275

V
Velocity threshold, 132–133
Vergence movement, 47, 52–53
Version movement, 47–52
Vestibular sensation, 201
Vibration, 208–209, 330
Vigilance, 265–266
Vision substitution system, 210–211
Visual acuity, 36–43
    See also Acuity
Visual angle, 36–37, 147
Visual cliff, 314–315
Visual cortex, 27–29, 32
    color vision in, 74
    depth perception and, 123
    motion detection in, 135
    neurons in, 28–29, 102–103
    spatial arrangement in, 28
Visual field, 25
Vocal cords, 187
Volatile (substances), 226
Volley principle, 179
Vowels, 187–188

W
Warm spots, 211–212
Warmth, perception of, 211–213
Water taste, 257
Wavelength, 15–16, 62–63
Weber's fraction, 345, 348
Weber's Law, 345, 348
Weights, 233, 298
White light, 62, 187
White noise, 187
Wine, 254, 261
Word boundaries, 189–191
W, X, and Y ganglion cells, 20

X
X-rays, 280